UNCIVIL WAR

When Operation Banner was launched in 1969, civil war threatened to break out in Northern Ireland and spread across the Irish Sea. *Uncivil War* reveals the full story of how the British army acted to save Great Britain from disaster during the most violent phase of the Troubles but, in doing so, condemned the people of Northern Ireland to protracted, grinding conflict. Huw Bennett shows how the army's inability to repress loyalist violence undermined the prospects for peace and heightened Catholic distrust in the state. British strategy consistently under-estimated community defence as a reason for people joining or supporting the IRA, whilst senior commanders allowed the army to turn in on itself, hardening soldiers to the suffering of ordinary people. By 1975 military strategists considered the conflict unresolvable: the army could not convince Catholics or Protestants that it was there to protect them and settled instead for an unending war.

Huw Bennett teaches International Relations at Cardiff University. He is the author of *Fighting the Mau Mau: The British Army and Counter-Insurgency in the Kenya Emergency* (2012).

Cambridge Military Histories

Edited by

HEW STRACHAN, Professor of International Relations, University of St Andrews and Emeritus Fellow of All Souls College, Oxford

GEOFFREY WAWRO, Professor of Military History, and Director of the Military History Center, University of North Texas

The aim of this series is to publish outstanding works of research on warfare throughout the ages and throughout the world. Books in the series take a broad approach to military history, examining war in all its military, strategic, political and economic aspects. The series complements *Studies in the Social and Cultural History of Modern Warfare* by focusing on the 'hard' military history of armies, tactics, strategy and warfare. Books in the series consist mainly of single author works – academically rigorous and groundbreaking – which are accessible to both academics and the interested general reader.

A full list of titles in the series can be found at:
www.cambridge.org/militaryhistories

UNCIVIL WAR

The British Army and the Troubles, 1966–1975

Huw Bennett

CAMBRIDGE
UNIVERSITY PRESS

Shaftesbury Road, Cambridge CB2 8EA, United Kingdom

One Liberty Plaza, 20th Floor, New York, NY 10006, USA

477 Williamstown Road, Port Melbourne, VIC 3207, Australia

314–321, 3rd Floor, Plot 3, Splendor Forum, Jasola District Centre,
New Delhi – 110025, India

103 Penang Road, #05–06/07, Visioncrest Commercial, Singapore 238467

Cambridge University Press is part of Cambridge University Press & Assessment,
a department of the University of Cambridge.

We share the University's mission to contribute to society through the pursuit of
education, learning and research at the highest international levels of excellence.

www.cambridge.org
Information on this title: www.cambridge.org/9781107136380

DOI: 10.1017/9781316479841

First published 2024

Printed in the United Kingdom by TJ Books Limited, Padstow Cornwall

A catalogue record for this publication is available from the British Library.

A Cataloging-in-Publication data record for this book is available from the Library of Congress

ISBN 978-1-107-13638-0 Hardback

For Claudia, Lina and Orla, with love

Contents

Figures

Maps

Tables

Illustrations

Abbreviations

ACC	Assistant Chief Constable
ACDS(Ops)	Assistant Chief of the Defence Staff (Operations)
AG	Adjutant General
APS	Assistant Private Secretary
AUS(GS)	Assistant Under-Secretary (General Staff)
BAOR	British Army of the Rhine
BBC	British Broadcasting Corporation
BGS(Int)	Brigadier General Staff (Intelligence)
C2(AD)	Central Department 2 (Army Department)
CCDC	Central Citizens' Defence Committee
CDC	Citizens' Defence Committee
CDS	Chief of the Defence Staff
CGS	Chief of the General Staff
CLF	Commander Land Forces
Col GS	Colonel, General Staff
COS	Chief of Staff/Chiefs of Staff
CPR	Chief of Public Relations
CSA	Chief Scientific Adviser
CS gas	2-chlorobenzalmalononitrile gas (tear gas)
DASD	Director of Army Staff Duties
DCDA	Derry Citizens' Defence Association
DCDS(I)	Deputy Chief of the Defence Staff (Intelligence)
DCS(A)	Deputy Chief Scientist (Army)
DGI	Director-General of Intelligence
DMO	Director of Military Operations
D of DOP	Director of Defence Operational Plans
DOpsINTCOM	Director of Operations Intelligence Committee Northern Ireland
DPP	Director of Public Prosecutions
DPR(A)	Director of Public Relations (Army)
DS	Directing Staff

DS6	Defence Secretariat 6
DS10	Defence Secretariat 10
DUP	Democratic Unionist Party
DUS(Army)	Deputy Under-Secretary (Army)
DYH	Derry Young Hooligans
EEC	European Economic Community
EOD	Explosive Ordnance Disposal
EOKA	Ethniki Organosis Kyprion Agoniston (National Organisation of Cypriot Fighters)
FCO	Foreign and Commonwealth Office
FOI	Freedom of Information
GOC	General Officer Commanding
GSO 1	General Staff Officer, Grade 1
GSO 2	General Staff Officer, Grade 2
HMG	Her Majesty's Government
HQNI	Headquarters Northern Ireland
INLA	Irish National Liberation Army
INTSUM	Intelligence Summary
IRA	Irish Republican Army
IS	Internal Security
ITV	Independent Television
IWMSA	Imperial War Museum Sound Archive
JIC	Joint Intelligence Committee
JSCSC	Joint Services Command and Staff College
KOSB	King's Own Scottish Borderers
LAW	Loyalist Association of Workers
LHASC	Labour History Archive and Study Centre
LHCMA	Liddell Hart Centre for Military Archives
LSE	London School of Economics and Political Science
MA	Military Assistant
MI5	Military Intelligence, Section 5 (The Security Service)
MI6	Military Intelligence, Section 6 (The Secret Intelligence Service)
MO3	Military Operations, Branch 3
MO4	Military Operations, Branch 4
MOD	Ministry of Defence
MP	Member of Parliament
MRF	Military Reaction Force
NATO	North Atlantic Treaty Organisation
NCO	Non-commissioned Officer

NEC	National Executive Committee
NICRA	Northern Ireland Civil Rights Association
NIO	Northern Ireland Office
NITAT	Northern Ireland Training and Advisory Team
OC	Officer Commanding
OIRA	Official Irish Republican Army
OP	Observation Post
PIRA	Provisional Irish Republican Army
PRONI	Public Records Office of Northern Ireland
PS	Parliamentary Secretary/Private Secretary
PSO	Personal Staff Officer
PS2(Army)	Personal Services, Branch 2 (Army)
PS4(A)	Personal Services, Branch 4 (Army)
PUS	Permanent Under-Secretary
PUSD	Permanent Under-Secretary's Department (Foreign and Commonwealth Office)
RA	Royal Artillery
RAF	Royal Air Force
RARDE	Royal Armament Research and Development Establishment
RCT	Royal Corps of Transport
RGJ	Royal Green Jackets
RM	Royal Marines
RMP	Royal Military Police
RNAS	Royal Naval Air Station
RPG	Rocket-Propelled Grenade
RSRM	Royal Scots Regimental Museum
RTÉ	Raidió Teilifís Éireann (Radio and Television of Ireland)
RUC	Royal Ulster Constabulary
SACEUR	Supreme Allied Commander Europe
SAS	Special Air Service
SCDS	Staff of the Chief of the Defence Staff
SDLP	Social Democratic and Labour Party
SoS	Secretary of State
SPG	Special Patrol Group
TNA	The National Archives
UDA	Ulster Defence Association
UDR	Ulster Defence Regiment
UFF	Ulster Freedom Fighters

UKLF	United Kingdom Land Forces
UKREP	United Kingdom Representative
UPV	Ulster Protestant Volunteers
USA	United States of America
USC	Ulster Special Constabulary
UVF	Ulster Volunteer Force
UWC	Ulster Workers' Council
VAG	Vice Adjutant General
VCDS	Vice Chief of the Defence Staff
VCGS	Vice Chief of the General Staff

INTRODUCTION

Perceptions about the British Army in Northern Ireland became fixed in a little over ten minutes on Sunday 30 January 1972. The conflict's most iconic image doesn't feature any soldiers. A hunched-over priest waves a bloody handkerchief as 17-year-old Jackie Duddy is carried away. He was one of thirteen people killed by paratroopers on Bloody Sunday, an event central to how Britain's actions in Northern Ireland are judged. The legacy of that day, like many others marked by grief, is still felt in Northern Ireland's present. What happened, why, and how the past might inform the future, are questions regularly and publicly discussed. More than 250,000 soldiers served in Northern Ireland between 1969 and 2006.[1] (See Map 1.) Yet the campaign is treated in Britain with nervous silence. There is no official history; only passing references are to be seen at the Imperial War Museum and the National Army Museum.[2] In British memories the violence in the 1970s melds into despondency about a decade rife with 'industrial conflict, inflation and unemployment'.[3]

The 1998 Good Friday Agreement ended the conflict, more or less, and to general relief. This book helps explain why peace came so late. In the early 1970s the British government feared a civil war with the potential to spread across all Northern Ireland, south through the Republic and over the Irish Sea into cities containing the diaspora population – to London, Manchester, Birmingham, Liverpool, Glasgow and beyond. In seeking to prevent that catastrophe the army held violence at a level acceptable to the majority of British people – those living in England, Scotland and Wales – without doing enough to make a political settlement viable. British military strategy saved Great Britain from disaster by condemning the people of Northern Ireland to protracted, grinding conflict for decades. Strategic decisions flowed from beliefs about the violent relationships between the British state, republicans aiming to unify Ireland, and loyalists determined to keep their place in the United Kingdom. By 1975 military strategists considered the conflict fundamentally unresolvable. Whether the Troubles qualified as a civil war is debatable. For historians the question is how 'civil war' acquired meaning

1

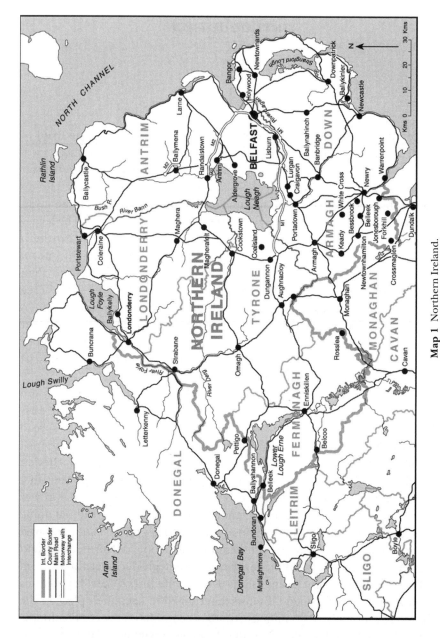

Map 1 Northern Ireland.

© Peter Wood, from *Operation BANNER* by Nick van de Bijl, Pen & Sword Books.

for those making strategy.[4] British strategists saw civil war as something looming on the horizon, to be kept at bay, and at times a reason for invoking strategic change.

Soldiers at the sharp end shared the belief in their indispensable presence without always seeing how this might contribute to perpetuating the conflict. Marine Goulds arrived in the town of Newry, astride Counties Armagh and Down, six months after completing commando training:

> To say the least I was a bit apprehensive about going over to Ulster. I didn't know what to expect one way or the other and when you get down to facts it is the unknown that induces fear ... there have been bombings, shootings, arms finds, and two Marines have been killed. Now I believe that Newry is not a normal British town, but a town where the majority of people wish it to be so, but are prevented from leading a normal peaceful existence by a minority of die hard terrorists. It is now my opinion that we have to be here, that if we withdraw all the British forces from Ulster the people of this country would suffer far greater than they have done in the past five years. Because of this we have to stay whether we, or any minority, like it or not.[5]

Historical knowledge about the Troubles has been extracted for various purposes. American officers in Iraq after the 2003 invasion wearied of their British counterparts lecturing them on Northern Ireland – not least because these lessons came from the campaign's endgame.[6] History deserves more careful handling. Controversies surrounding the conflict are perpetuated by a criminal justice approach occupying a space that might better be dealt with by a move towards truth and reconciliation. Despite allegations about veterans being persecuted, since 2011 the Director of Public Prosecutions (DPP) for Northern Ireland has brought cases against six military veterans for conflict legacy offences, compared to twenty-one against ex-paramilitaries.[7] In May 2021 criminal proceedings against two former paratroopers for shooting dead Joe McCann in 1972 collapsed, owing to problems with the prosecution's evidence.[8] In February 2023 David Holden became the first ex-soldier to be convicted of a Troubles-related killing since the 1998 Good Friday Agreement. A judge imposed a three-year suspended sentence for the manslaughter of Aidan McAnespie, who was shot at a check-point in County Tyrone in 1988. The judge criticised Holden for giving 'a dishonest explanation to the police and then to the court'.[9] The prospects for securing convictions in other historical cases are uncertain even as the victims' quest for justice is unimpeachable. Though the conflict is largely over, the major participants continue to fight a 'battle for the historical record'.[10] Anxieties over potential prosecutions mean veterans are reluctant to talk, government departments drag out freedom of information requests inordinately and doors are slammed shut by regimental museums who see their primary purpose as upholding reputations rather than facilitating research.[11]

Looking backwards from the Good Friday Agreement age can obscure earlier contexts. Peace at any price was not a universally shared aim during the early 1970s. In December 1971 Reginald Maudling, the home secretary, told reporters that Irish Republican Army (IRA) activities could be reduced to an 'acceptable level'.[12] By the end of 1975, 1,502 people had died in the conflict.[13] The government's toleration of suffering on such a scale, even though responsibility must be shared between the belligerents, is perplexing. When mindless killing, like Bloody Sunday or other atrocities, is so prominent, we assume strategy must have been absent.[14] Writings on the Troubles have sometimes deformed our understanding of the violence by reducing it to two basic types: primitive regression (in atavistic, savage terms), or cultural solidarity (referring to cultural collision, or ethnic conflict). Instead, the war should be treated as a political dispute about sovereignty over territory, where each party claimed to hold a democratic right to prevail.[15] There is an alternative to atavistic or cultural interpretations of the violence – strategy, 'the central political art ... the art of creating power'.[16] *Uncivil War* asks: how was British military strategy towards Northern Ireland made and what were its implications? Military strategy is 'the process by which armed force is translated into intended political effects'.[17]

The British Army's operations in Northern Ireland have received less scholarly attention than one might expect. The IRA has been subjected to more sustained analysis.[18] *Uncivil War* addresses the imbalance, without suggesting the army played a more decisive role than other actors in the conflict. Military strategy is often understood in relation to grand strategy, the longer-term orchestration of all elements of state power towards achieving political objectives.[19] The British government's endeavours to coordinate multiple departments of state over thirty years is a topic already ably dissected.[20] Looking closely at the army over a shorter time span brings new insights to the fore. There was no shortage of opinions at the time, as Lieutenant Davies noted in 1972:

> Wherever you go in Belfast in uniform, people will always come up to you and put you right on your facts. If it's a Protestant speaking he will tell you of the doings of the 'Fenian Bastards' and if it's a Catholic speaking you can hear him talk of the 'Orange Bastards'. And if your luck is really out, he will also tell you what he thinks of the Army and of how the 'Green Howards' would have done it.[21]

4

Military strategy is addressed by existing studies in three ways: as repressive, reactive or missing. Three totemic events make repression the dominant perspective. When a mass curfew was imposed on the densely inhabited Falls Road area in Belfast in July 1970, people saw ordinary streets drenched in tear gas, soldiers kicking down doors and houses trashed in the search for arms. (See Map 2.) In August 1971 the army pulled hundreds of men from their beds to be interned without trial, amidst chaotic street violence and, it soon transpired, brutal interrogation for an unfortunate few. The Bloody Sunday shootings in Derry and the state's failure to hold anyone to account tarnished the army's reputation, perhaps abroad more than in Britain. (See Map 3.) These events appear in popular and academic accounts with a predictable regularity; they are defining moments in the conflict's history. Collectively they are seen to symbolise the British Army's bid to crush rebellion with harsh methods lifted from experiences in the empire, defining a 'colonial strategy' until the police assumed control.[22] By implication these harsh tactics meant an essential continuity between 1969 and 1975.

Alternatively, authors cast the army as a victim of wicked republicanism, emphasising strategy's reactive nature. By this logic soldiers were on the back foot against terrorists who pursued their goals in a ruthless, cunning manner. The prime suspects are of course the Provisional Irish Republican Army (PIRA).[23] Horrific acts committed by republicans are remembered, such as the Abercorn restaurant bombing in March 1972, when 2 people died and 130 were injured. The sub-field of terrorism studies reifies groups such as the IRA when explaining political violence, with a particular interest in how people become terrorists and how these groups are organised.[24] Some scholars argue that the British government's refusal to abandon reform as the central response to the crisis in Northern Ireland and crack down on the IRA allowed the organisation space to grow.[25] Others claim rivalries within the republican movement promoted violence as groups used attacks on the security forces to attract popular backing.[26] In this genre the British Army is pitied for falling into traps set by devious terrorists.[27]

The third commonplace reading of military strategy in Northern Ireland claims the army signally lacked one. Sophisticated policy analyses have ignored military records.[28] The government is blamed for failing to give the army any strategic direction in the early years.[29] Senior generals have perpetuated this belief. David Richards, who ended his career as Chief of the Defence Staff (CDS), records in his memoirs being asked in 1993 to write the first campaign plan for operations in Northern Ireland, suggesting a prior omission.[30] More generally, unpicking British military strategy in the Cold War years is complicated by the need to align national priorities with

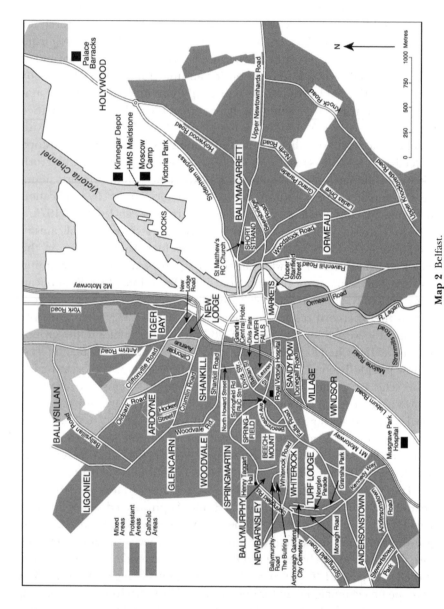

Map 2 Belfast.

© Peter Wood, from *Operation BANNER* by Nick van de Bijl, Pen & Sword Books.

those emanating from the United States and the North Atlantic Treaty Organisation (NATO).[31] Whereas the repression motif places blame for suffering in the early years squarely on the military's shoulders, studies framed around reaction to IRA violence or a strategy vacuum end up removing responsibility from the armed forces.

These accounts need to be questioned. By 1971 mid-ranking officers were taught: 'the Army is faced with a situation unlike that previously met elsewhere. . . . The Army's previous experience, training and techniques do not fully cover this situation.'[32] The coercive measures applied in the 1970s never reached the intensity seen in the colonies. Forced population movement, executions and collective punishments never entered the army's tactical repertoire in Northern Ireland.[33] The colonial continuity narrative also assumes the army stumbled blindly from one setting into another without any reflection. In reality, officers observed changes to the strategic environment during the end of empire, afterwards, and throughout the Northern Ireland conflict. The repression template cannot account for variation during the conflict, either in time or place. Military tactics in January 1970 were markedly different from those in September 1971; practices in the countryside diverged from those in the major urban centres. Blaming republicanism is equally misleading. It is true that the PIRA leadership launched an offensive against Britain in January 1970, before the Falls curfew, internment and Bloody Sunday. Yet focusing solely on the IRA's part in starting the Troubles ignores how republicans made choices in relation to their own communities and their opponents, not in isolation, as their strategy changed over the years.[34]

Uncivil War uncovers the running discussions between ministers, officials and officers rather than looking for a single plan agreed by politicians and then followed slavishly by soldiers.[35] A Ministry of Defence (MOD) civil servant called the process 'Defence by Discussion'.[36] These debates could be protracted and fractious.[37] Such disputation is normal in armed forces.[38] Yet in the British case a reputation for anti-intellectualism means such debates are sometimes sidelined.[39] Studies specifically about civil–military relations in Northern Ireland remain fixated on a few set-piece turning-points.[40] By exploring strategy in a more dynamic, continual sense this book illuminates the historical contingencies in which strategists made choices, downplaying the sense of inevitability so common to accounts of the conflict.[41]

Moving beyond a handful of decisions by senior leaders brings two further benefits. Firstly, the significance of seemingly mundane events becomes more apparent. Some 250,000 houses were searched in mainly

Catholic areas between 1971 and 1976, sometimes accepted by household-ers with little more than a shrug of the shoulders, at other times met with vitriol as soldiers ripped up floorboards or caused other damage. Each search in isolation made only a small mark on the social fabric. Over years the rancour accumulated.[42] Secondly, because strategy comprises a continual dialogue between the political and military domains, goals are adjusted as implementation on the ground shows what is feasible.[43] *Uncivil War* accounts for the military's ability to push politics from the ground up.[44] Unlike most existing works on the British Army in Northern Ireland, the analysis avoids refracting events through a counter-insurgency lens. Counter-insurgency often falls into an obsession with military technique.[45] By focusing on strategy this book keeps military thought and action within the political parameters of the time.

Uncivil War assesses continuity and change in military strategy between 1966, when serious disorder became a possibility, and 1975, when the government decided to begin handing over primary responsibility for secur-ity to the police. PIRA, intent on killing service personnel, was clearly the main threat for the British government.[46] However, British strategic equa-tions about how to use force always accounted for the expected impact on loyalism. The government believed republican and loyalist violence could mix and combust unpredictably, and so aimed to prevent a spiral down-wards into catastrophic civil war. Military strategy produced a level of vio-lence acceptable to the United Kingdom's majority, without reaching a political settlement, thus consigning Northern Ireland to protracted conflict. By 1975 strategists settled for an unending war for three reasons. Firstly, the refusal to repress loyalist violence undermined the prospects for peace and heightened Catholic distrust in the state as a protector. Secondly, military strategists knew a great deal about the IRA but erred in perceiving the organisation as solely offensive.[47] British strategy consistently under-estimated community defence as a reason for people joining or supporting the IRA. Thirdly, in seeking protection from the conflict's divisive politics, senior commanders turned the army in on itself, hardening soldiers to the suffering of ordinary people in Northern Ireland. The British Army became increasingly hostile towards the Irish in general and dismissed complaints about the security forces' conduct as propaganda. Consequently the army could not convince Catholics or Protestants that it was there to protect them.

Where did the fear of civil war come from? The army's experience in the English civil war, 1642–51, is widely regarded as the birthplace for a deep aversion to politics. Events at the Curragh in March 1914, when over

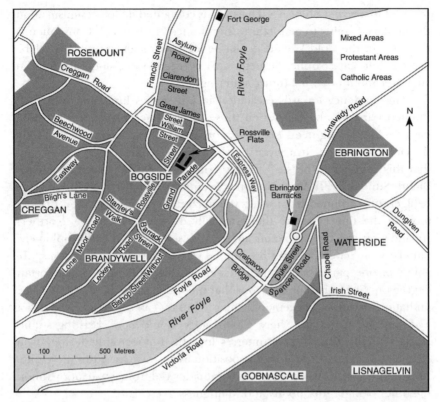

Map 3 Derry/Londonderry.
© Peter Wood, from *Operation BANNER* by Nick van de Bijl, Pen & Sword Books.

a hundred officers threatened to resign if ordered to suppress Ulster loyalism, further entrenched the lesson.[48] Anxieties about civil war were tied together with a distaste for politics. Most professional soldiers prefer to concentrate their efforts on tactics and avoid the messy political world.[49] By the 1970s the defence community was absorbed by several decades of thinking about a horrendous 'imaginary war'.[50] The British Army's primary occupation, affecting about 60,000 personnel, was preparing for war in Germany after a Soviet invasion. The distinction between armour and artillery units devoted to German defence, and infantry formations liable to be pulled out for global emergencies, engendered different 'mental worlds' in the army.[51] Yet ideas from the Cold War seeped across into the perceived dangers in Northern Ireland. By the early 1950s both civilian and military strategists expected any nuclear exchange to rapidly escalate into a global disaster. 'Pure deterrence' was preferred over the alternative – a graduated reaction to a Soviet offensive. These ideas contained deep pessimism about the military's ability to maintain restraint once war began.[52] Consequently, the army in the Cold War held to a belief in war's almost uncontrollable descent into catastrophe. Strategy-makers reached decisions shrouded in anxieties about potential future suffering.

The tendency towards escalation in war makes limitation difficult.[53] Limited wars only happen when those involved accept the need to hold back.[54] As 21 Engineer Regiment observed after their tour in 1971: 'Discipline must be firm, even harsh, and the soldiers must understand that this is going to be so.'[55] Apart from a few major atrocities, such as Bloody Sunday or PIRA's explosion of twenty-four bombs on 21 July 1972, all belligerents refrained from using the maximum violence at their disposal most of the time. Despite their radically different visions for Northern Ireland's future, the key actors shared a desire to avoid catastrophic civil war. Thomas Schelling describes limited wars as bargaining situations: 'the ability of one participant to gain his ends is dependent to an important degree on the choices or decisions that the other participant will make'. If limitation requires agreement, then conflict can be conceived of as a struggle to negotiate where those limits should be.[56] Existing studies argue that the British government's impetus for restraint derived from Northern Ireland's constitutional position as a province within the United Kingdom.[57] *Uncivil War* suggests limitation derived from expectations about the other belligerents' ability and willingness to escalate.

The army certainly faced greater legal constraints than in the colonies. However, the constitutional position does not account for the government's reluctance to expend greater resources on the conflict. In the summer of 1972 massive troop deployments into contested areas significantly reduced violence.[58] The government abstained from such operations earlier, or for longer, due to higher-priority national interests. Preparations for Britain's accession to the European Communities in January 1973 and the subsequent referendum in 1975 consumed a vast amount of the government's policy-making capacity, and Prime Minister Edward Heath's time.[59] Maintaining the troop levels promised to NATO placed serious restrictions on how many soldiers might be sent to Northern Ireland, and how often. In other words, though limitations to the rules of engagement applied because Northern Ireland was within the United Kingdom, resource constraints, intellectual and material, pushed the British government to pursue limited strategic objectives. The goal of preventing a catastrophic civil war was achieved by 1975 largely at the expense of ordinary Catholics, who were forced to endure an 'open-ended militarization of everyday life'.[60]

Loyalist groups, most prominently the Ulster Volunteer Force (UVF) and the Ulster Defence Association (UDA), needed the British government's help to remain British. They could not risk antagonising the government to the extent that military forces were permanently withdrawn; hence the low number of loyalist attacks on British Army personnel. One battalion described their 'love–hate relationship' with the local UDA.[61] Loyalist violence towards Catholics increased between 1972 and 1974: to punish them for attacks by the IRA, and to warn of the bloodbath to come if the British withdrew.[62] When a large-scale strike brought down the devolved Executive in May 1974, loyalists had succeeded in more than blocking a united Ireland. Even power-sharing with constitutional nationalists was off the table for the foreseeable future. Militant loyalists defined their actions as defensive, simply responding to a republican threat. From 1972 they pursued individual murders as their primary tactic, as the security forces effectively prevented the mass incursions into Catholic areas seen in earlier times.[63] Though the British Army came to believe eliminating republican violence would automatically make loyalist aggression disappear, the evidence presented in this book shows that at several junctures a decrease in republican activity brought about an upsurge in loyalist violence, representing an intention to finish off the IRA for good.

Republican strategy aimed to coerce the British into leaving and loyalists into joining a united Ireland. By 1975 PIRA had managed to persuade the British government to abolish the Stormont parliament that effectively locked Irish nationalists and republicans out of power. They succeeded in bringing the British to the negotiating table and saw the Sunningdale Agreement, designed to achieve peace without their participation, fall to pieces. These achievements led them to believe a final push for ultimate victory was viable.[64] It was not. PIRA strategy assumed that inflicting punishment on the British, through economic damage and in soldiers' and police officers' lives, must cause their enemy to be defeated. They under-estimated the United Kingdom's willingness to absorb punishment. As Secretary of State (SoS) for Northern Ireland Merlyn Rees said a few days after PIRA bombed pubs in Birmingham, killing 21 and injuring 182: 'These fellows have got to be beaten. And if they're not beaten by us they will be beaten by the Protestants.'[65] Insurgent movements are only likely to win on home soil when they achieve majority popular support (whether voluntary or coerced), and escalate their military campaign to decisively defeat the incumbent state's forces in battle.[66] Neither of these conditions ever applied for PIRA. As a movement with appeal to a minority in Northern Ireland the prospects for mass mobilisation were poor; after 1972 it became obvious that creating an all-Ireland uprising was impossible. PIRA's capacity for remarkable tactical and organisational innovation cannot outweigh its ultimate strategic myopia.[67]

Addressing the British Army's place in the conflict is uncomfortable for a society still immersed in nostalgic visions of heroism in the Second World War. Operation Banner, as it came to be known, was an unwanted war and one without simple morality tales about good and evil for the nation to unify around. The Northern Ireland conflict should not be written off any longer as something that happened over there, distantly 'across the water'. While prone to caricatures when thinking about Irish people, military analysts could also recognise how:

> the people have been in the middle of a civil war – complete with shooting, intimidation and murder. This has an enormous effect on their lives and reactions – especially when dealing with soldiers. There would be some surprising changes in the people of Knightsbridge or Cardiff if they had had similar troubles.[68]

This is a war with complex legacies for Britain, comprising moments of service and self-sacrifice as well as error, misunderstanding and intended brutality. *Uncivil War* aims to advance our historical understanding about the military dimensions.

1

BAGGAGE

> When a soldier gets off the ferry from England, Belfast looks the same as any other large city, he may breathe a sigh of relief.... It really looks quite like England except that the people's accents are different, but then they vary all over England. He smiles as he thinks of somebody from Kent trying to understand a Geordie. But then he starts to realise that all is not the same as his home in England. You wouldn't find barbed wire barricades outside Woolworth's, would you?[1]
>
> Royal Regiment of Fusiliers, 1972

After August 1969 the ferries kept coming with their camouflaged passengers for thirty years. The ideas brought by soldiers influenced their conduct as the conflict expanded, as did the plans made in the years and months when a military deployment came to seem more likely.[2] Historians of Ireland and writers on the British Army agree colonialism played a decisive part in the Troubles. The consensus holds that the colonial legacy loomed large in the army's tactical repertoire on arrival in Northern Ireland. There are two problems here: soldiers did not carry their intellectual baggage unthinkingly from the colonies into Northern Ireland. And what might be considered colonial tactics were notably absent between August 1969 and May 1970. The colonial imprint on the conflict cannot be entirely rejected. The whole period up to 1998, when power-sharing came about, might even be described as a decolonisation process.[3] Military thought prior to 1969 disavowed that the army could behave in a colonial fashion in the United Kingdom. Once the army was on active operations, this belief contributed to a defensiveness about the army's intentions. Ideas about the army's benign purpose reduced the space for critical questioning about how soldiers treated civilians.

Debates within the army must be set alongside political developments in Northern Ireland at the same time. The rapid pace of change in the late 1960s is an essential context for appreciating how soldiers experienced events, and for remembering that 'history is made by people who do not know what is going to happen next'.[4] Sectarian tensions had reached dangerous levels by 1968. Violence along the lines of previous decades could be predicted. But the disorder's transformation in 1970–1 into a rebellion against the state, contiguous with ongoing communal violence, was far from inevitable. For strategists, higher national priorities prevailed over concerns for what might happen in Northern Ireland. Involvement in politics there was seen as dangerous for the army, yet senior officers recognised their duty to assist the civil authorities in an emergency. Soldiers found it difficult to reconcile their views of Northern Ireland as basically British, and therefore deserving help, with a sense that politics functioned there in an alien fashion. Senior officers worried about the implications for Irishmen in the British Army if they got stuck in a civil war, in case enmity spread within the army itself. Troops finally marched into Derry city on 14 August 1969, then Belfast the next day, too late to prevent eight people being killed.[5] These events destroyed the legitimacy of the Royal Ulster Constabulary (RUC) in Catholic areas, and created a perceived need for community defence by the IRA from future Protestant invasion. By their hesitancy, strategists contributed to a problem to beset the British Army for decades to come.

THINKING ABOUT REBELLION AT THE EMPIRE'S END

The British Army's colonial heritage is obvious and irrefutable.[6] For some the army was: 'a colonial army, experienced in colonial campaigns. It was therefore inclined to treat the situation as a colonial one.'[7] The prior experience of senior officers is a case in point. General Sir Ian Freeland (General Officer Commanding (GOC), 1969–71) served in Cyprus; his successor from 1971 to 1973, General Sir Harry Tuzo, commanded a brigade in Borneo. Brigadier Frank Kitson, who commanded 39th Brigade in Belfast, 1970–2, fought in Kenya and Malaya.[8] The robotic application of colonial methods is seen as a marker of the army's failure as a 'learning institution', a weak spot diagnosed in twenty-first-century wars too.[9] Blinkered repetition apparently stemmed from an innate anti-intellectualism.[10] In fact the army was more curious than is normally assumed.

Military embodiments of colonialism in the 1960s cannot be separated from the deeper, contested relationships between Britain and Ireland. For some writers any policy pursued by the British government other than withdrawal constituted colonialism.[11] Colonialism can be read into the modern Troubles in various guises: in an unbroken chain from the sixteenth-century plantations to the present day, as partially defeated by the Irish Republic's emergence in 1921, as present still in softer, cultural forms, or kept alive by Ulster unionists who defy a British wish to disengage. In the 1960s Irish republicans reanimated colonial rhetoric in the mould of Third World anti-imperialism to forge international solidarity and justify their resistance to the state.[12]

Military theorising about how to respond to rebellion, most often discussed in terms of counter-insurgency, originated from colonial soldier–scholars such as Hubert Lyautey, Joseph Gallieni and Charles Callwell.[13] In this sense, all counter-insurgency is colonial. Military doctrine and education preserved lessons from the colonies. Doctrine manuals stressed the need to use the minimum force necessary, to gain the support of the population, and to build an efficient intelligence machine. Senior commanders wrote after-action reports for the conflicts in Palestine, Malaya, Kenya, Egypt, Cyprus and Oman.[14] The doctrine released just as the army deployed to Northern Ireland, *Counter Revolutionary Operations*, is criticised for being tainted by Aden, for ignoring lessons from Aden due to a fixation on Malaya and for excessively concentrating on rural settings.[15] Elements from earlier doctrine survived: securing popular backing for the government, civil–military co-ordination, minimum force and sound intelligence, for example.[16] *Counter Revolutionary Operations* illustrated common tactical problems with images from Aden.[17]

A fuller picture of military thought can be painted by looking to the teaching at the Staff College at Camberley, the 'Brain of the Army'.[18] Camberley educated those officers selected for future promotion to high command. The curriculum for 1966 contained a lecture on internal security, an instructional film, a presentation on psychological operations, plus a discussion period.[19] The 1967 course added films about Borneo and Aden. Colonial policemen gave talks.[20] In 1969 renowned expert Robert Thompson spoke on revolutionary warfare, before Lieutenant-General Walter Walker lectured on his direction of the Borneo campaign.[21] Thompson's *Defeating Communist Insurgency* and Julian Paget's *Counter Insurgency Campaigning* were key readings which drew on British colonial experience.[22]

Military and imperial history often elevate national perspectives at the expense of international connections.[23] An internationalised professional military culture emerged in the nineteenth century. The concept of the concentration camp, for example, was widely disseminated, so that camps appeared between 1896 and 1907 in Cuba, South Africa and the Philippines.[24] In the 1950s Western armed forces were influenced by the French debate over the Indochina war as inferior forces defeated a modern army, aided by popular support.[25] Counter-revolutionary warfare theory denied rebellions stemmed from genuine grievances, emphasising instead indoctrination by external actors. After the Second World War Britain, France and the United States collaborated to suppress rebellions. French, Vietnamese, American and Philippine troops trained at British facilities in Malaya. By the mid 1960s Western militaries shared a similar approach to counter-insurgency.[26] *Quelling Insurgency*, a doctrine publication from 1965, went into depth about the wars in Algeria, Vietnam and Cuba.[27] 1969's *Counter Revolutionary Operations* opened with a section on Vietnam.[28] The doctrine stated:

> the outbreak of insurrection, however deep the groundswell of disaffection, is never spontaneous. . . . Any insurrection therefore must have its roots in conspiracy, by definition the work initially of a close knit gang and it is at this conspiratorial stage of development that it is most easily checked, either by measures of political concession or by counter subversive action.[29]

Here doctrine conflated disorder with insurrection, encouraging officers to find an existential threat to society. Any terrorist attacks – whether sabotage or assassination – could signify intensifying local violence, 'or could be part of the first phase of revolutionary war'.[30] By deciding violent incidents constituted an insurgency, the army therefore judged a violent reaction to be justified. This was not a uniquely British conclusion. However, as the intelligence assessments about the IRA from 1966 to 1969 described below prove, officials disregarded doctrine's more alarmist tendencies in refraining from seeing a revolutionary threat where none existed.

Abandoning certain colonial-era techniques, such as intelligence organisation, would have seemed perverse. Ideas on riot control held their currency too. Teaching notes advised troops were best deployed as a deterrent 'before trouble starts', and giving crowds time and space to disperse.[31] *Counter Revolutionary Operations* related the appropriate degree of force to the political climate. Soldiers were to adhere to the minimum force principle 'most conscientiously' when confronted with civil disturbances not amounting to rebellion. When facing 'violent threats with serious political undertones', commanders were allowed 'some latitude'. Armed rebellion justified soldiers using violence to 'show firmness of purpose to dissident elements'. Soldiers could only fire on rioters if they were armed and 'in a position to inflict grievous injury'.[32]

Besides searching for inspiration from other militaries, British thinkers pondered the changing global order. European colonialism was transformed between 1945 and 1967: 'a world hospitable to empires became more hostile to them'.[33] Scholars are divided on when changes in the human rights regime began to impinge upon military operations. One position holds that repression provoked a backlash once Northern Ireland operations started.[34] Another interpretation depicts the Aden insurgency (1962–7) as the turning-point, with media coverage accorded a major part in heightening public awareness about rights violations.[35] Archival studies show human rights intruded earlier on.[36] Liberation movements in Indochina and Algeria were adept at mobilising international support through the United Nations General Assembly.[37] International Committee of the Red Cross monitors in Kenya criticised cruelty in detention camps, though they failed to expose the systematic torture taking place.[38] From April 1955 British forces fighting the EOKA movement on Cyprus came under criticism in the courts on the island, in the United Nations and in diplomatic exchanges with Greece.[39] However, officials in Cyprus, Aden and Northern Ireland practised 'cooperative manipulation', appearing to cooperate with critics while continuing with brutal methods in secret.[40] Staff College teaching notes from 1967 reflected on the recent controversy surrounding interrogation:

> Some students may argue that the means justifies the end, and where the end involves human lives the means can be severe. In other words, torture = information = destruction of terrorists = saving innocent lives. However by denying the individual the basic human rights of justice and a free trial, we destroy the very principles which we are fighting to uphold or restore. It is interesting to see how the efforts of Amnesty International in Aden have resulted in an almost total abandonment of interrogation as a means of acquiring information.[41]

During one training exercise Directing Staff (DS) claimed collective punishments like curfews, fines and evictions 'punish simple people who have acted wrongly under threat of torture or death'. Officers were advised to avoid them as they alienated people, resulting in a diminished flow of intelligence. Brutal interrogation, rough searching and stealing from the population were counterproductive, though 'We have been guilty of all on occasions in the past.'[42] Writing in a leading military journal, Major Peter de la Billière argued Aden set a precedent for future wars, where the National Liberation Front's skilful propaganda condemned British repression before a global audience.[43]

The army's ability to approach the colonial past with a certain analytical acuity must be recognised if the decisions taken in Northern Ireland are to be accurately contextualised. Rather than importing old ideas wholesale, some elements in counter-insurgency were judged to have enduring value, and others repudiated as politically intolerable. Having considered these questions the army fell into a complacency trap, dismissing external critics who often invoked colonial comparisons when castigating the army. How could such allegations be valid? After all, officers had diligently weighed up what should stay and what should go. The ideas that remained were validated by counterparts in the United States, France and elsewhere sharing them. This certainly does not imply that the army overturned cultural assumptions about race. Only in December 1968 did the MOD abolish a 3 per cent limit on the enlistment of black people into the army and a total ban on black soldiers in the Foot Guards, Household Cavalry, Highland and Lowland regiments, the military police, the military prison service, the Army Education Corps, the Physical Training Corps and the Intelligence Corps.[44] In December 2019 the Service Complaints Ombudsman found: 'incidents of racism are occurring with increasing and depressing frequency'.[45] Addressing Britain's colonial military legacy in tactical terms alone has clear limitations.

THE GROWING RUPTURE IN NORTHERN IRISH POLITICS

As the British Army came to terms, more or less, with the need to adjust after empire, politics in Northern Ireland saw a number of crucial developments. The Unionist Party had been in power continuously since the statelet's formation in 1921 without a Catholic ever occupying ministerial office.[46] Catholics were persistently ignored in policy-making, despite constituting 34.9 per cent of the population in the 1961 census.[47] Captain Terence O'Neill, Northern Ireland Prime Minister from March 1963 until May 1969, believed in the need for change. Educated in England, working in London and Australia and wartime service in the Irish Guards may have informed his liberal outlook. O'Neill sought to develop a political culture where Catholics accepted the constitution.[48] Assimilating the minority into the mainstream promised to remove the border as a central issue in Northern Irish politics: this was to be achieved by improved socio-economic conditions.[49] Elements within unionist politics accepted his ambitions in a context where the United Kingdom's expanding welfare state, matched with a modernising ethos, emphasised the benefits that the union bestowed on all citizens.[50] O'Neill appealed to those who believed in an 'Ulster British ideology'. His supporters identified primarily with Great Britain and wanted a liberal, democratic Northern Ireland.[51] To observers in Britain this all appeared rather tame, if worthy. In Northern Ireland such notions smacked of bold radicalism.

The hope that economic progress might neutralise political grievances proved to be naïve. Instead, incremental reforms opened up an acrimonious debate about whether they should happen at all, and if so, how quickly. But at the beginning the focus on economics got results. Public expenditure per head rose from 88 per cent of the English level in 1959–60 to 118 per cent in 1969–70, due to O'Neill lobbying the Treasury in London. Between 1958 and 1970 the Northern Ireland economy grew on average 4.9 per cent each year, compared to 3.6 per cent in the United Kingdom as a whole. A political thaw complemented these achievements. Sectarian tensions eased during the 'Orange–Green' talks between nationalist and Orange Order leaders in 1962–3.[52] In 1965 the Nationalist Party accepted the role of Official Opposition in the Northern Ireland House of Commons, breaking their abstentionist tradition. Catholic politicians were finally involved in formal political life.[53] Opinion polls, always worth reading cautiously, suggested in the late 1960s that only a minority of Catholics (34 per cent) were dissatisfied with the constitution. Only 14 per cent wanted a united Ireland.[54] Attitudes held before widespread violence occurred did not determine what happened later.

Liberal unionist reforms coalesced with demands from the nascent civil rights movement, born in May 1963 at the formation of the Homeless Citizens' League in Dungannon.[55] Further campaigning organisations followed: most notably the Campaign for Social Justice in 1964, and the Northern Ireland Civil Rights Association (NICRA) in 1967. NICRA set out six core demands: one man one vote in local elections; a halt to gerrymandering of electoral wards to create false unionist majorities; banning discrimination in government jobs; stopping discrimination in housing allocation; repealing the Special Powers Act; and for the B Specials police reserve to be abolished. People joining the movement often found inspiration in civil rights activism in the United States. Dissatisfaction with housing attracted particular concern. Although house building was substantial after the Second World War, the new stock was allocated on a sectarian basis.[56] Discontent with political repression formed another major grievance. Stormont used the Civil Authorities (Special Powers) Act to exclude Catholics from political life. Initially designed to reimpose order after partition, justification for employing the Act shifted by the 1930s to silencing those who advocated union with the south. Regulations were issued banning meetings, processions, flying the tricolour, wearing the Easter Lily, circulating newspapers and singing republican songs.[57] The Act remained in force until 1973, seriously diminishing O'Neill's credibility as a reformer with civil rights advocates.

The extent of disadvantage faced by Catholics has always been contested. NICRA's lack of interest in discrimination by nationalist-dominated councils certainly undermined its credibility with Protestants.[58] A property qualification for voting in local elections affected everyone, with 28 per cent of Catholics and 18.5 per cent of Protestants disenfranchised in Belfast.[59] However, Catholics were disadvantaged to a greater degree than Protestants. According to one calculation, Catholics were underrepresented by 12.1 per cent across the Province. The gerrymander was most famous in Derry, where despite there being 14,429 Catholic to 8,781 Protestant voters, the latter controlled the council.[60] Catholics fared less well in employment: they were more likely to work in lower-status jobs, and suffered twice as much from unemployment.[61] By 1968 disillusionment with constitutional routes to solving these iniquities was setting in. Radicals in the civil rights movement wanted assertive action: street demonstrations would gain attention in Britain and abroad, forcing Stormont to buckle under external pressure. Some moderates then began to adopt more confrontational tactics for fear of losing influence in the movement.[62] In June 1968 Austin Currie, a Stormont Member of Parliament (MP), started squatting a house in Caledon in County Tyrone to protest against the property being allocated by the council to a single Protestant woman over Catholic families with children. On 24 August NICRA mounted its first civil rights march, from Coalisland to Dungannon.[63]

Conservative unionists disbelieved the claims made by civil rights activists. In an opinion survey in 1968, 74 per cent of Protestants denied that discrimination against Catholics existed.[64] Any acknowledged difficulties faced by Catholics were blamed on character deficiencies, such as poor self-discipline.[65] A conflict within unionism, between secular modernisers and religious traditionalists, pre-dated the clashes brought about by civil rights.[66] Ulster loyalist ideology, probably the most widely supported set of beliefs amongst Protestants, viewed itself in an existential struggle with evil forces, embodied in the Catholic church and Irish nationalists. Any concessions to those seeking to modify Protestant dominance would lead to loyalist defeat and destruction. Constant vigilance against opponents, including enemies within like liberal unionists, required a firm stance.[67] Fundamentalist Protestant denominations, such as the Free Presbyterian Church led by the Reverend Ian Paisley, claimed unique insight into God's will. Catholicism represented everything wrong in the world. Rome's hand was detected behind republicanism and its puppets in the civil rights movement.[68] Prime Minister O'Neill lacked strong enough support to defeat these ideas.[69] According to his harsher critics, he did not bother to sell reform as an imperative to his own party.[70]

The UVF, originally formed in 1912 to fight Home Rule, was reinvented in 1966 amidst concerns about O'Neill's reforms.[71] On 27 May 1966 the UVF went looking for known republican Leo Martin. Failing to find him, they shot John Scullion, a labourer who was singing republican songs. He died from his wounds. The next month four Catholic barmen were shot leaving a pub in Belfast.[72] O'Neill banned the UVF in June. RUC intelligence assessed the threat to law and order from extreme Protestants to be 'equal or even greater' to that posed by republicans.[73] Although the UVF invoked Paisley's rhetoric, he publicly denounced those who turned to force. Paisley himself was imprisoned for refusing to be bound over to keep the peace after participating in an illegal protest. The attendant publicity only increased Protestant support for his opposition to reconciliation with Catholics.[74] O'Neill's intention to improve living conditions for Catholics annoyed poor Protestants, who felt ignored.[75] Meanwhile, civil rights marches through predominantly Protestant areas were viewed as deliberately provocative.[76]

The Northern Ireland cabinet was divided between those who believed the civil rights movement imperilled the state, and those who thought that concessions should be made.[77] Minister of Home Affairs William Craig argued republican involvement in NICRA meant they were a front for the IRA.[78] Republicans certainly attended NICRA's first meeting and constituted part of its membership, but did not control the group.[79] Under Cathal Goulding's tenure as Chief of Staff the IRA was heavily informed by Marxist ideology, seeking to forge a class alliance with unionist workers. Described as 'light-hearted and gregarious', Goulding's standing derived in part from his family's long association to republicanism. His grandfather belonged to the 'Invincibles' group responsible for killing Lord Cavendish, the British chief secretary in Dublin in 1882.[80] Yet many in the republican movement were sceptical about Marxism. Keeping military activity on the boil kept traditionalists happy.[81] The Irish police discovered twelve IRA training camps in 1965 and eleven in 1966. In November 1965 the RUC warned that the IRA was planning an offensive, and five men were arrested near the senior British Army commander's house for plotting to kidnap him. However, police reports in July 1967 and January 1968 discounted an IRA offensive. A November 1968 assessment portrayed the civil rights movement as distinct from the IRA, posing no threat to the constitution.[82]

Volatile situations arose when politics moved increasingly to the streets. Protests by civil rights campaigners drew loyalist counter-demonstrations.

A march in Derry on 5 October 1968 brought worldwide television coverage when the police batoned protesters, marking a turn to a more violent phase. Radical activists sought to challenge unionist power in the city, from the outset assembling the marchers in the Protestant Waterside district. Activist Eamonn McCann wanted to provoke the RUC in order to unveil the state's repressive character. The police drove the marchers from the city centre and into the Bogside, in what appeared to be an assault on the Catholic area, triggering a counter-attack from local people set on defending their community.[83] Minister for Home Affairs William Craig's decision to ban the march had only served to cause resentment and increase the numbers of those who participated. Police behaviour on the day was later described by Lord Cameron's official inquiry as involving 'unnecessary and ill controlled force' against demonstrators, only a minority of whom were disorderly.[84] In all, 11 policemen and 77 civilians sustained injuries.[85]

Dramatic events such as these undermined attempts by liberal unionists to address discontent. By the end of 1968 concessions had been made at London's insistence. Derry's council was replaced by a Development Commission, an ombudsman was appointed to investigate complaints about public bodies, housing was to be allocated more fairly, and multiple votes for business owners were abolished. Crucially, though, rigged local elections lived on. These measures split the civil rights movement. They convinced moderates of the government's good intentions, but were insufficient to pacify the more ambitious.[86] The People's Democracy, formed at Queen's University Belfast, argued for pressure on Stormont to be ramped up. The group arranged a march in early January 1969 from Belfast to Derry, defying Terence O'Neill's plea for a temporary hiatus, which NICRA agreed to.[87] The marchers met demonstrations by loyalists at frequent intervals. At Burntollet a loyalist mob viciously attacked them as the police looked on. The mob included off-duty members of the B Specials police reserve. There was later rioting in Derry, where the police assaulted innocent bystanders.[88] Greater numbers of Protestants wondered whether conciliation with a seemingly unreasonable minority was wise, and Catholics asked if peaceful protests were getting them anywhere.[89]

ACCEPTED PERCEPTIONS OF IRELAND

Those in the MOD's Main Building spent much of the late 1960s absorbed in a major defence review. Defence Secretary Denis Healey announced on 22 February 1966 cuts to equipment programmes, including the CVA-01 aircraft carrier, plus a permanent departure from Aden.[90] Over the next two years, driven by a weak economy and military overstretch, the government pursued further retrenchment, leading to the decision in January 1968 to withdraw all forces from east of Suez. Healey planned to cut the army from 211,000 enlisted personnel in 1968 to 173,000 in 1973.[91] When the troops left Aden in November 1967, the ambitious officer might have been advised to switch his attention from rebellions to tanks. The directive for forces based in Northern Ireland listed their prime duty as preparing to reinforce an overseas garrison. Readiness for internal security was given as the second priority – a remote contingency not to interfere with training for war.[92]

The MOD was no different from the British political firmament as a whole. Between 1921 and 1968 the House of Commons spent on average two hours discussing Northern Ireland annually.[93] Before the 1964 general election Harold Wilson promised his future administration would support civil rights. The election gave him a slim majority, empowering the unionists to frustrate his legislative programme.[94] Compelled to pay attention to Northern Ireland, but to avoid antagonising the Unionist Party, Labour hoped economic and social modernisation would promote harmony. (See Illustration 1.1.) MP Paul Rose, who founded the Campaign for Democracy in Ulster in 1965, struggled to overcome ignorance about Northern Ireland in the House.[95] When Home Secretary Frank Soskice visited Ulster in April 1965, the Northern Ireland Labour Party warned him O'Neill's reforms were superficial gestures.[96] A fact-finding mission by the Campaign for Democracy in Ulster in April 1967 reported widespread discrimination

Illustration 1.1 Captain Terence O'Neill and Harold Wilson at 10 Downing Street, 5 November 1968.
(Courtesy of Keystone/Hulton Archive/Getty Images.)

against Catholics. Wilson's Cabinet ignored both calls to action.[97] The pressure in the Commons for intervention had diminished since the 1966 general election gave Labour a 100-seat majority. Though sympathetic, Labour leaders thought civil rights activists exaggerated their case.[98]

When they thought about Northern Ireland at all, soldiers liked to dwell on the Province's bucolic charms, a leitmotif in recollections of service there. Cecil Blacker went to Lisburn in 1962 to command 39th Infantry Brigade. A horse fanatic, he enjoyed participating in riding events north and south of the border.[99] Another officer at the headquarters relished the 'pleasantly relaxed' atmosphere, taking up hockey, tennis and dinghy sailing on Loch Neagh.[100] Arriving at Palace Barracks for a two-year tour in June 1968, 2nd Queen's Regiment reflected: 'it is hard to imagine that we can do anything else but thoroughly enjoy our stay here'.[101] Later, in July 1970, 1st King's Own Scottish Borderers found replenishment in the Antrim countryside 'an agreeable change from the streets of Belfast'.[102] Even during their difficult 1971 tour in Derry, 2nd Royal Green Jackets appreciated the 'exceptionally comfortable' Shackleton Barracks. As a residential battalion, many families came with the soldiers – the schools in Ballykelly and Limavady were deemed far better than those attended by army children in Germany.[103] Officers wrote these accounts. A sergeant arriving in Omagh with the 4th/7th Royal Dragoon Guards in September 1966 recalled the unit's wives' horror: 'they had never seen married quarters like them. We didn't have fridges or anything.'[104]

Stephen Robson, based at Ballykinler from October 1968, went on rural patrols to prevent anticipated IRA sabotage on the electricity network. The battalion played darts and football against local teams, without noticing any animosity. Sectarian tensions were invisible to him.[105] Charles Millman, an officer with experience in Berlin, Kenya, Borneo and the MOD, and a Staff College education, observed the July marching season in Belfast in 1965. Yet 'the real depth of this divide did not truly reach me – then or throughout the year I was at Lisburn'.[106] Military testimonies refrain from mentioning Northern Ireland's constitutional status prior to the army's active deployment in 1969; the topic probably did not seem relevant. Sentiments expressed in the early years may have reflected deeper beliefs. Jim Parker, in Belfast from mid August 1969, placed Belfast in the same league as Manchester, Dundee and Liverpool.[107] Brigadier James Cowan went to command 8th Brigade in Derry in January 1970: 'one was operating in the United Kingdom. We were at home; these were allegedly our people, and I think it made a difference to the way people approached their jobs.'[108] Another officer, in Northern Ireland from April to August 1971, shared Cowan's qualified sense of affinity: 'you were dealing with, ostensibly, your own people'.[109] A National Defence College thesis from 1973, by an MOD civil servant, concluded a more ruthless campaign against the IRA was impossible because 'the people who are involved are themselves British'.[110]

Having tackled rioting on Belfast's Shankill Road in October 1969, the Parachute Regiment saw the city 'as British as Glasgow, Newcastle, Leeds or Hull', yet beset by an 'inborn bigotry' simply 'beyond the comprehension of anyone who is not Irish'.[111] Most benignly, though patronisingly nonetheless, soldiers could view the Province's divisions as sadly unresolvable.[112] In this respect military attitudes mirrored those found in wider British society.[113] Some struggled to believe their presence might be part of the problem. As late as October 1970, Paul Garman, a subaltern during 2nd Royal Anglian's tour in Belfast, admitted it took 'a little while to sink in' that some people refused to identify as British, and 'hated you intensely'.[114] Others approached the Northern Irish with distaste. The second in command of 1st Light Infantry, the resident battalion at Abercorn Barracks in Ballykinler from August 1968 until April 1970, suggested:

> to the average British soldier, they were no different to the Chinese in Hong Kong, or the Arabs in Aden, or the Malays in Singapore. They were wogs, they were not British people. British people didn't behave like that, and they couldn't relate this lot, who were manning barricades and throwing petrol bombs and so on, they couldn't relate, they were not the same as people in our street at home.[115]

Attitudes throughout the army towards Northern Irish people hardened as the violence intensified.[116] However, traces of sympathy never entirely disappeared. At some stage in the early 1970s the MOD began compiling a narrative of events, to inform battalions preparing to go on tour. The Irish in general were apparently obsessed with distant historical events (presumably in a manner more deleterious than the tradition-saturated regimental cultures within the British Army). Over the years to come, according to the ministry's narrative, the 'nature of the Irish' came to shock British soldiers in two ways:

> firstly, the irrational and subjective approach to events by the Irish. A brutal murder would be a saintly act if committed for the 'right' side, and a shot in self-defence by a soldier at an IRA sniper would as certainly be a 'brutal murder'. It was not so much that the Irish had a total disregard for the truth as that it was regarded solely as an alternative method of communication; and perjury as a necessary technique. The second aspect was the appalling capacity for hate, and lust for violence, which the British Army found within Northern Ireland.[117]

25

Before and after August 1969 the army and the MOD were torn between contempt for the Irish and a strong sense of obligation to them. In 1970 the Army Staff College syllabus covered military aid to the civil power within the United Kingdom for the first time. The whole subject occupied one afternoon, including film extracts showing riots in London and Northern Ireland. Instructing staff were clearly told that Northern Ireland 'is a very special case with special factors which do not apply in this country'. Yet lessons from experience there might be applied in England in the future.[118] The ambiguity about Northern Ireland's filial connections was tangible. These sentiments appeared in government policy discussions prior to August 1969 – and not only within the armed forces.

The MOD started taking a closer interest in Northern Ireland in 1966 when intelligence predicted an IRA offensive to mark the 1916 Easter Rising.[119] Any relevant knowledge from the IRA's 1956–62 border campaign failed to register.[120] The Chiefs of Staff have been criticised for recommending that intelligence-gathering be left to the police rather than MI5.[121] In fact, the decision emanated from MI5. The Security Service effectively pressed for the police to retain primacy, as 'IRA activities constituted a "law and order" problem and were not a security one'.[122] The organisation responsible for tackling subversion within the United Kingdom refused to do its job in Northern Ireland. By giving so much power to the RUC, a police force known to have little interest in addressing loyalism, MI5 made it difficult for the government to understand the danger from loyalism. Lieutenant-General Sir Geoffrey Baker, the Vice Chief of the General Staff (VCGS), visited Northern Ireland in late March. His intelligence briefing from the RUC expected the IRA to be planning a long-term campaign. Baker found these conclusions to be 'formed on a basis of reliable information'.[123] The most likely time for trouble was expected to be 16–17 April, so the army despatched an extra battalion between 15 and 20 April, under the cover of a training exercise.[124] Not much happened over Easter 1966. In November the MOD decided to downgrade the Northern Ireland command to just District status.[125]

After the disastrous events in Derry on 5 October 1968, Denis Healey told the home secretary that soldiers lacked training in riot control in the United Kingdom, and he did not wish them to acquire it.[126] The GOC Northern Ireland, Lieutenant-General Sir Ian Harris, thought major violence in Derry and Belfast simultaneously was likely to force the police to ask for assistance. Harris expected military involvement to make matters worse.[127] The MOD instructed Harris to await orders before committing troops.[128] Prime Minister Wilson sought clarification about the legal position.[129] The Treasury solicitor doubted whether British law on the army's role applied in Northern Ireland, whereas Home Office lawyers were certain it did.[130] General Baker, now Chief of the General Staff (CGS), believed the army was obliged to assist the civil authorities.[131] Nevertheless, his Director of Military Operations (DMO), Major-General Read, visited Northern Ireland in December to underline the army's reluctance to get involved. Harris agreed to avoid using troops until absolutely essential and made sure all troops were trained in internal security tactics. The RUC Deputy Inspector General 'could not see the Army being called upon until the guns were out'.[132] The CDS, Marshal of the Royal Air Force (RAF) Sir Charles Elworthy, argued the *Manual of Military Law* expressed the common-law 'duty of every person to come to the assistance of the civil authorities to maintain law and order if called upon to do so'. The MOD's insistence on granting permission beforehand had no basis in law. Elworthy informed Healey:

> It is probably the most unpopular and thankless duty a serviceman has and commanders would certainly be most loath to undertake this duty unless it was absolutely essential. However, they are also conscious of the most unpleasant consequences, political and social, as well as the loss of life which could ensue if there were a delay in taking action when the situation demanded it.[133]

The attorney general backed up Elworthy. So the GOC was now to refer to the ministry 'if humanly possible'.[134] Healey railed against the common-law obligation, rather prioritising 'the requirements of political prudence which necessitate prior consultation between Ministers before troops are committed'.[135] According to Cecil Blacker, who served in the MOD in the late 1960s, Healey had a tendency to bully the service chiefs.[136] Though Elworthy only took a third in his Cambridge law degree, he was sure enough of his ground to insist that 'it remains illegal under the Common Law for a military commander to refuse to assist on his own responsibility and irrespective of what "instructions" he may be given by MOD'.[137] His view reflected an emerging consensus in Whitehall.[138] It has been argued that the army disliked the legal requirement to respond to the civil power's call for help, so ignored it.[139] However, on 4 January 1969 the minister for home affairs asked the GOC to put a company of troops on standby in response to intelligence about an impending IRA attack. Northern Ireland Command agreed without informing the MOD.[140] In the event nothing happened. But the principle of officers in Northern Ireland taking action without prior reference to London had been firmly established as legally necessary.

Debates about the Heath government's policy from June 1970 have missed this crucial factor. Military officers did not simply respond to events because Labour or Conservative administrations adopted radically different security policies. They did so because the common law empowered them to take the initiative, and as violence became worse the alternative, waiting for a reply from London, would have been extremely dangerous.

Whitehall now began seriously thinking about intervention. The Home Office and MI5 could not imagine troops having to be used in the United Kingdom.[141] Recognising the deficit in soldiers' knowledge about assisting police operations, the army began writing new doctrine.[142] The MOD thought for the first time about the large numbers from Ireland, north and south, serving in the armed forces. Involving them in anything more than minor, short-term support to Stormont risked 'very considerable repercussions'.[143] The precise danger here remains obscure, as the military intelligence and Security Service records on political activity or affiliations within the army are beyond public examination. However, various other sources suggest that fears over soldiers becoming politicised had realistic foundations. If not igniting a civil war within the army, strife in Ireland might at least cause serious disciplinary problems. Irish regiments had not been stationed in Northern Ireland, with short exceptions for training or ceremonial purposes, since 1933. In July 1972 the CGS called for the policy to be upheld to protect Irish regiments from 'tensions and bitterness'. If sent on operations, soldiers might end up confronting friends or neighbours. Their families might be intimidated by militants. Individual military policemen from Ireland were no longer deployed, after experience showed them 'to be insufficiently impartial'.[144]

As the army went onto the streets in August 1969, Headquarters Northern Ireland (HQNI) itself relied upon several officers from Irish regiments serving in key staff positions. The assistant adjutant and quarter-master-general, Lieutenant-Colonel P. J. C. Trousdell, and his deputy, Major A. J. French, both came from the Royal Irish Rangers. General Freeland's aide-de-camp, Captain P. A. H. Dawson, and senior staff officer Lieutenant-Colonel K. Neely came from the same regiment.[145] Only from spring 1974 were there no staff officers at HQNI from Irish regiments.[146] Most papers created by the headquarters are still retained by the MOD, so assessing whether these officers displayed particular types of attitudes is impossible. However, people in Northern Ireland did attempt to manipulate national identities within the army. Within a week of 1st Queen's Regiment entering Derry, Corporal Rundle was implored to follow his Irish roots and defect to the Bogsiders – with his gun and ammunition.[147] Terence Hubble, in Belfast with the Black Watch during June and July 1970, remembered the difficult position facing an Irish sergeant-major in the battalion, whose father and other relations took part in marches that summer.[148] By 1974 a National Defence College study noted the IRA's repeated attempts to incite Irishmen in the army to desert to Sweden, to 'accidentally' lose their weapons and ammunition at arranged places, and to deliberately fire wide in gun-battles. When soldiers ignored these entreaties the IRA turned to threatening their families, or worse. As a result Irish soldiers were banned from spending their leave at home in Ireland.[149]

Despite the official silence on politicisation in the armed forces, a few traces survive which suggest a hidden history yet to be fully revealed. Even before August 1969 battalions were aware of the potential for dissension within their ranks, though perhaps prone to treat the matter lightly: 2nd Queen's Regiment's Corporal Mahon, from 'South of the Border', was mocked for empathising with the civil rights protesters, and his alleged tendency to break into renditions of 'We shall overcome'.[150] During 3rd Light Infantry's 1971 tour in Belfast a Catholic soldier from Northern Ireland in the battalion was discovered to be 'pro-IRA'. The battalion sent him back to barracks in Minden, West Germany. Several fights broke out between soldiers 'who had tendencies to the IRA or to the loyalists'.[151] In the same period the Guards Independent Parachute Company returned a southern Irish sergeant to England. Months earlier an officer whose parents owned property in Ireland was kept off operations in case the IRA burned the property down.[152] While based in Celle, West Germany from May 1970 to September 1974, 1st Royal Green Jackets went to Belfast on three occasions. In early 1972 Kenneth Ambrose was promoted to command a platoon:

> The reason I got that job was because at the time the Officer Commanding 6 Platoon was not able to resolve his conscience as far as the British Army's operations in Northern Ireland, that's the real reason why . . . he felt that, if push came to shove, he was on the verge of becoming a conscientious objector, actually. He was very political. He had been to university for a number of years and I think he'd probably let that, the attitudes which came out of university came with him into the Army, which of course should never have happened.[153]

PLANNING FOR THE WORST

Early catastrophic thinking about Northern Ireland lingered in the strategic imagination for years to come. The fear of organised Protestant resistance to London was of particular importance, a fear based not on an intelligence failure, as some scholars have contended, but on a direct threat from the Northern Ireland government itself. By January 1969 Sir Philip Allen, Permanent Under-Secretary (PUS) at the Home Office, thought the future held possibilities ranging from serious rioting to suspension of Stormont and rule by the governor. He opposed direct rule from London as impracticable.[154] Major-General Read cautioned that in a full-scale British intervention the Northern Ireland authorities might refuse to stand aside. Soldiers could find themselves fighting loyalist organisations, the B Specials or even the wider population.[155] The MOD and the Home Office conducted a detailed joint assessment. They imagined five scenarios.[156] The first envisaged sporadic or minor disturbances by civil rights activists or counter-demonstrators, with little need for army back-up. Any military involvement was expected to come after approval from London and to last for a short time. Under scenario two, serious but isolated rioting took place. Public buildings and police stations might be attacked. The violence was likely to be spontaneous, and the police would need help to restore order. As in scenario one, the GOC would liaise with London and deploy for as short a period as possible. Scenario three posited widespread riots, simultaneously in at least half a dozen places, with firearms being used. Troops may have to protect military bases and vulnerable points (such as essential services and police stations), and confront rioters. The military's actions would probably provoke further violence. Political intervention by the British government was inevitable. The police would remain loyal, though they might be less effective, and the B Specials could join in the rioting. The IRA was 'without doubt' going to incite violence, possibly attacking police stations and military bases. Public support for the security forces was expected to be buoyant.

Scenario four predicted a 'Breakdown of law and order'. The scenario involved intercommunal violence, with guns, property destruction, looting, disruption to essential services, and attacks by the IRA and loyalists. The army would have to restore law and order and maintain essential services, and possibly close the border with the Republic, in the worst case to repel an incursion by Irish government forces. Military courts and preventative detention might be needed. Of the B Specials, 'very considerable numbers ... would actively be supporting the extremists and militants of their community, violence aimed primarily at the other community, and secondly at HMG [Her Majesty's Government] and even at her forces'. The IRA would attack Protestants and government forces. An extra army division would be required to handle the disorder. Scenario five imagined the British forcibly taking control when Stormont refused to hand over power.

Therefore the army's first task would be to depose the Northern Ireland regime, before handling the law-and-order situation. The B Specials were expected to overwhelmingly back an illegal government, and some regular police and civil servants would resign. The IRA was likely to fight both the British government and the Northern Ireland authorities, and try to provoke civil war. Loyalist militants would support the illegal government. Most of the population would side with their co-religionists. Even in this most catastrophic outcome, the review tellingly expected 'the bulk of the populace' to 'secretly hope HMG successfully establishes law and order'.[157] Officials dreaded provoking civil war, yet harboured suspicions that the Northern Irish, deep down, really wanted British leadership.

Sending these scenarios to the prime minister, Denis Healey insisted 'military intervention might well exacerbate the difficulties that it was designed to resolve'. His staff only intended to write plans for scenarios one to three; scenarios four and five were too alarming to contemplate.[158] Healey later suggested these scenarios might necessitate two whole army divisions being sent – a vast commitment.[159] When ministers discussed intervention they wondered whether ejecting Northern Ireland from the United Kingdom might be preferable.[160] Home Office civil servants argued withdrawal was bound to be construed as the government having 'betrayed the minority and run away from our proper responsibilities'.[161] The cabinet secretary claimed independence was not in the United Kingdom's interest, for political, economic and military reasons. Withdrawal would produce an illiberal regime, or one unable to impose order, leading to domestic and international calls for the United Kingdom to intervene.[162] The prime minister, home secretary, chancellor, foreign secretary and defence secretary all individually believed a united Ireland to be the only viable long-term solution.[163] But collectively in the Cabinet Northern Ireland Committee they agreed to send troops if lives were endangered, and that independence or an associated status for Northern Ireland were impossible. Only direct rule from London was a practicable alternative to governance by Stormont.[164] Despite regular discussion in government over withdrawal, the basic position decided upon in April 1969 remained in force for decades: a British presence was necessary to prevent civil war.

The MOD wished to stay in Northern Ireland for slightly different reasons. The navy's facilities could comfortably be removed, apart from the valuable aircraft yard at Sydenham and an armament depot in Antrim. For the army, recruitment in Ireland was bound to be adversely affected. More seriously, a withdrawal was likely to encourage the IRA to go on the offensive. Shutting RAF facilities risked weakening the United Kingdom's radar, air traffic control, air defence, maritime strike and reconnaissance capabilities.[165] Overall, each of the COS believed withdrawal was 'unrealistic', due to the 'serious repercussions on our military operational capability and credibility'. It would be deeply embarrassing for Britain.[166] These considerations affected Healey's scepticism about intervention. Reporting to the cabinet, he now argued 'we cannot wash our hands of Northern Ireland's affairs ... our responsibility for the integrity of the Province as part of the United Kingdom includes some responsibility for law and order'. Healey deplored withdrawal as a 'cumbersome and embarrassing operation'. Britain would be perceived at home and abroad to have shirked her responsibilities – an 'incalculably damaging' charge.[167]

Rioting broke out in Derry on Saturday 19 April 1969 after the police banned a civil rights procession for fear that loyalists might shoot at it. Intense fighting took place between the police and rioters in the Bogside: 181 policemen and 79 civilians were injured. Later that night, bombs exploded at an electricity pylon in County Armagh and a reservoir in County Down. Water supplies to Belfast were reduced, so the army gave some technical assistance.[168] The army also agreed to guard other vulnerable points, such as water and electricity facilities, against sabotage, from 21 April;[169] 104 RAF personnel arrived as well to guard air force installations.[170] A mains water pipeline was damaged in another bombing on 24 April. London agreed to Terence O'Neill's request for more guards, sending 1st Prince of Wales' Own Regiment and a Royal Engineers troop.[171] However, a much more consequential appeal was denied. The rioting and sabotage prompted the Northern Ireland government to consider a huge shift in their position on reform. O'Neill's cabinet secretary asked the Home Office if London would deploy troops in exchange for universal suffrage in local elections. London replied: 'It is not possible for Her Majesty's Government in the United Kingdom to give any secret pledges of military assistance.'[172] This key civil rights demand only came into force in November 1969 – too late to halt the political violence. The British government had missed an unprecedented opportunity to defuse the conflict, being so fixated on keeping the army out.

For the Unionist Party the bombings symbolised O'Neill's weakness. He resigned on 28 April, having lost the party's confidence. His replacement as prime minister was Major James Chichester-Clark. A well-placed civil servant described him thus: 'In gentler times his good nature and honest hard work would probably have seen him through a successful political career. He was not on the intellectual wing of the party.'[173] While the police blamed the IRA for the attacks, the MOD held Protestant extremists responsible, which proved to be correct.[174] More sabotage followed, including at the guarded electrical installation in Tandragee. The assailants escaped after a chase by police tracker dogs.[175] Despite the change in leadership Stormont continued to call for more military support. On 7 May they asked for soldiers to protect Belfast harbour and television transmitters.[176] The MOD refused because there was no evidence of a threat.[177] When the CGS made a trip to Northern Ireland in mid May he urged the new prime minister not to call troops onto the streets.[178] At a meeting on 21 May at 10 Downing Street, Chichester-Clark was pressed to release the army from guarding vulnerable points. Wilson and Callaghan threatened constitutional implications if the army came to support Stormont.[179]

The threats worked. By 6 June the army only retained responsibility for fifteen vulnerable points.[180] The chief of staff at HQNI, Brigadier Dyball, lobbied Stormont to end the guard duties altogether. There was 'no intelligence to indicate that anything is likely to happen'. By the start of July the police agreed to take over most remaining guard duties.[181] As a further buffer the MOD proposed giving the police CS gas, to 'provide an additional rung in the escalatory ladder short of opening fire or calling in the military'.[182] The Cabinet Northern Ireland Committee gave approval a week later.[183] Lieutenant-General Sir Ian Freeland assumed command of HQNI on 9 July. Awarded the Distinguished Service Order in Normandy, he came with political experience as deputy chief of the general staff in the MOD. Within his headquarters, fellow officers came to know him as '"Smiling Death", because if they do not meet up to his professional excellence, they are given the "chop"'.[184] Soldiers remained prepared if truly needed. After serious rioting on the weekend of 12 July, a company of 2nd Queen's Regiment moved to Derry as a precaution.[185]

On 1 August London rejected a request from Stormont for helicopters to transport the police and assist them in surveillance missions.[186] After Chichester-Clark's cabinet verged on calling for military support to control rioting on 3 August, Callaghan asked them to do everything in their power to avoid doing so, threatening direct rule if the troops were called out.[187] In response, Harold Black, the secretary to the Northern Ireland cabinet, went to meet Callaghan's officials on 5 August. He said direct rule was bound to provoke 'a frightening reaction by the Protestant community which could make anything that had happened up until now seem like child's play'. A provisional unionist government might attempt to exercise control and 'wholesale sectarian strife would break out'.[188] The Northern Ireland government understood very well London's trepidations and effectively threatened organised insurrection against the crown to stay in power.

This pivotal moment – where London backed down – raises the question of how far an intelligence deficit on unionist and loyalist politics contributed to the British government's decision-making. Eunan O'Halpin argues that the Joint Intelligence Committee (JIC), responsible for providing the cabinet with integrated assessments, paid limited attention to Northern Ireland until 1970, thus distorting policy. Though conceding that much intelligence paperwork is still kept secret, he criticises the JIC for ignoring loyalist threats.[189] However, the discussion above shows that fears about loyalist rebellion in response to a British intervention loomed large in official thinking about the future. It is extremely unlikely, given all the interdepartmental planning taking place in 1969, that no intelligence assessment on loyalism was conducted at all. O'Halpin correctly suggests loyalist terrorism was a central element in Whitehall thinking, neglected in many studies. But his wider reasoning on the early Troubles applies here too: British problems derived from political judgements rather than flawed intelligence.[190] Northern Ireland's most senior civil servant blackmailed the Home Office with a Stormont-sponsored uprising. Subtle intelligence analyses based on secret sources were hardly necessary.

However, the British government's failure to effectively grip the intelligence apparatus in Northern Ireland caused serious problems. At HQNI the staff officer, grade 2 for operations also looked after intelligence. He was supported by a counter-intelligence detachment under a Captain Brown. These officers liaised daily with the RUC Special Branch, who shared their information, and from December 1968 sent weekly assessments to the MOD.[191] In April 1969 a military liaison officer and a security liaison officer (the latter from MI5) were attached to Special Branch headquarters to improve co-ordination.[192] General Baker regarded Special Branch in May as being 'sadly inefficient'. Indeed, 'speculation and guesswork largely replace intelligence'.[193] Freeland complained to London about the RUC's inability to produce intelligence.[194] In late July the security liaison officer and the military intelligence liaison officer moved out from RUC headquarters following 'a modest amount of friction' due to the advisers trying to drive the police to change their ways too quickly. Sir Martin Furnivall-Jones, MI5 director-general, rather incredulously claimed intelligence continued to flow despite the row.[195]

James Chichester-Clark mixed moral indignation with threats to amplify the direct rule warning. Writing to the home secretary, he complained that press reports about 'British troops' falsely presented Northern Ireland as a foreign country: 'The British Army is our Army too. I and many other Ulstermen have been proud to serve in it.' Stormont ministers accepted a military deployment would be accompanied by close supervision by London. Yet he and his colleagues were 'appalled – I must not understate our reaction' – by the prospect of direct rule. Chichester-Clark claimed his administration had done everything possible to adopt the reforms advocated by Wilson.[196] He and his minister of home affairs, Robert Porter, met Callaghan on 8 August. The Northern Ireland prime minister predicted the reaction to direct rule would be 'very violent indeed'. Callaghan disagreed, labelling the assessment 'entirely unrealistic'. In his view British public opinion expected ministers in London to have control over policies which might affect soldiers. Chichester-Clark hoped Stormont could remain in existence while the UK government directly controlled law-and-order matters. In Callaghan's terms, such an arrangement meant the Northern Ireland government acting as 'agents of the United Kingdom Government over a very wide field'.[197] Defence Minister Roy Hattersley, delegated to deal with Northern Ireland by Healey, feared it would be difficult to withdraw troops once committed. Substantial resources were likely to be needed, with consequences for the country's overall defence commitments.[198] National priorities dominated thinking about a local problem.

When the annual Apprentice Boys march went past the Bogside on 12 August, intense rioting broke out, lasting all night and into the next day. The Bogside was described by Hattersley as 'under a state of siege'. Police officers used CS gas on a large scale and committed almost all their reserves.[199] On 14 August Harold Wilson broke his holiday in the Isle of Man to meet the home secretary at RAF St Mawgan in Cornwall. Callaghan reported that Chichester-Clark expected violence that night. In Callaghan's opinion, when the request came it must be met, but he wanted troops committed in a limited area, not the whole province. Wilson agreed. During the meeting, Callaghan spoke on the phone to Lord Stonham in the Home Office, who told him that Belfast had called to say the police were losing control in Derry and were likely to request military assistance soon. Wilson and Callaghan decided to send a police liaison officer and a Home Office civil servant to advise the GOC, and two police consultants to advise the Northern Ireland government.[200] This was a late stage indeed for independent information channels to the cabinet to be established.

At 4.35pm on 14 August Harold Black, the secretary to the Northern Ireland cabinet, phoned the Home Office to say the inspector general was about to formally ask the GOC for troops.[201] All B Specials police reservists had already been mobilised, and still the police were unable to control the situation. When troops deployed in Derry the atmosphere calmed, while Belfast experienced further violence, including shootings. Amongst those killed was Hugh McCabe, a Queen's Royal Irish Hussar on leave in Belfast, shot with an RUC bullet. Later that night Roy Hattersley authorised the sending of another infantry battalion to Northern Ireland. A company of 1st Royal Regiment of Wales and two troops of 17th/21st Lancers moved to Derry.[202] At a COS meeting in London, the Acting CGS, General FitzGeorge-Balfour, recommended Northern Ireland be reinforced with a full brigade. He thought substantial forces on the ground would deter the IRA from trying to exploit the prevailing chaos. At this meeting the chiefs expected the IRA to become active soon.[203] Clearly influenced by RUC intelligence that disproportionately emphasised the republican threat, the military's senior leadership sent their troops to aid the civil power, expecting an IRA offensive. Direct threats from Northern Ireland's elected representatives to contest British interference by force did not get a mention.

CONCLUSION

The British government approached the growing trouble in Northern Ireland as a government of Great Britain, not that of the United Kingdom. Perhaps Westminster's traditional orientation towards compromise was the ultimate flaw. Sending in the troops, but too late to stop trust in the authorities being shattered; pushing reforms insufficient to satisfy civil rights campaigners but strong enough to antagonise conservative unionists; worrying about an IRA offensive but ignoring loyalist violence. Decisive action on all these fronts was notably absent. What drove thinking in this period was an overwhelming focus on other business. For most British politicians most of the time Northern Ireland simply did not register. The MOD consistently thought about wider strategic priorities, to the point where the defence secretary advocated ignoring the legal duty to aid the regime in Belfast.

Even once the cabinet collectively accepted their obligation to the people of Northern Ireland they attempted to hold off an intervention for as long as possible. In so doing they missed an opportunity to secure a major victory for the civil rights movement and thus potentially defuse the expanding protest movement that incited such an infuriated response from conservative unionists. Until early 1969 London could perhaps be forgiven for struggling to keep pace with a complex, fast-moving political scene. After the Burntollet march the battle lines appeared more starkly drawn. Acquiescing in the RUC dominating intelligence reporting even after plans concluded they could offer armed resistance to the crown in the worst-case scenario was a major misjudgement. Strategists needed a firmer evidence base to make decisions about the likelihood of a Protestant rebellion.

When the mass arrests, brutal interrogations, controversial shootings, curfews and internment without trial in the early 1970s are described, comparisons with earlier events in Palestine, Malaya, Kenya, Cyprus and Aden become almost automatic. The colonial model is seductive precisely because of its simplicity. The tactical repertoire displayed in Northern Ireland did replicate some methods witnessed in the colonies. Whether these practices would have been applied in mainland Britain is open to question. Conduct in Northern Ireland replicated methods applied in Algeria, Vietnam, Afghanistan, Iraq and other insurgencies. Those mainstays of counter-insurgency – co-ordinated civil–military command arrangements, intensive intelligence-gathering, trying to win popular support and so on – are generic military principles. They offer only limited insight into the actual conduct of war. The military mind was not put into hibernation when the troops left Aden, only to be rebooted in August 1969 with the old colonial ideas perfectly preserved, ready for application. Instead, officers took forward those principles which seemed to have validity, such as ideas about riot control. At the same time, officers were aware that many colonial techniques were now unacceptable. When they thought about Northern Ireland, soldiers often romanticised the place and the people. Hostile attitudes towards the civil population amidst rising violence existed alongside many friendships and romantic relationships. Even before August 1969 the army's leaders understood Northern Ireland's politics could divide the army in terms of identity. What was the right response to political violence in a country many took to be British? The army knew in advance that going into action in Northern Ireland risked deepening the conflict; but was legally bound to assist a civil power whose fundamental legitimacy never secured universal consensus.

2

THE ARMY'S SHORT-LIVED ULSTER HONEYMOON

The 2nd Battalion is now in the unhappy land of Ulster with the unenviable job of helping to prevent civil war.[1]

Pegasus: Journal of the Parachute Regiment
and Airborne Forces, 1970

On 18 August 1969 a police informer asserted the 'Honeymoon with Army is over'.[2] In his first press interview General Freeland echoed the gloomy sentiment, predicting soldiers could come under attack without rapid political progress.[3] Informer and general alike were too pessimistic, for the honeymoon lasted longer than they expected. But all honeymoons must end. The army's task in Northern Ireland was to prevent violence between Protestants and Catholics, while the British government's reform programme addressed the conflict's underlying causes. Though the existence of a peace-keeping phase is widely agreed upon, the manner and timing of its demise are disputed. In essence two explanations exist for the honeymoon turning into sustained political violence. The first account blames the IRA: for failing to protect Catholics in August 1969, and then for being supplanted by a new, Provisional movement that went on the offensive from January 1970.[4] This argument is correct, but does not account for PIRA's ability to recruit ever more members.

A second explanation assigns responsibility for the descent into violence to the British government. The Wilson administration's decision to rehabilitate Stormont by imposing reforms is seen as a fatal error. Unionists successfully resisted some reforms, undermining Catholic confidence in the process. By October 1969 London capitulated to Stormont for fear that pushing too hard would result in total non-co-operation, and thus direct rule. Effectively the British government ended impartiality by taking sides.[5] That decision owed as much to street violence in Protestant areas as it did to intergovernmental summits and memoranda.[6] Drawn into a conflict 'they little understood' the army made matters worse.[7] Military repression towards Catholics followed amidst tolerance of Protestant militancy.[8]

Repression is sometimes linked to intelligence failure. Insufficient intelligence on republicans is identified as the reason for indiscriminate measures, such as house searches, being adopted.[9] In another view, intelligence officers missed PIRA's emergence, and under-estimated the dangers of Protestant violence.[10] Indeed, the loyalists 'seem seldom to have registered in Whitehall's collective consciousness as a fundamental problem'.[11]

The honeymoon phase entrenched in British strategic thinking divergent ideas about nationalist and unionist violence. Rather than being important only for ending, what happened during the honeymoon phase mattered. Contrary to expectations, the army partially repaired trust between Catholics and the British state. This change to the status quo proved highly destabilising. The renewed peacefulness encouraged strategists to believe they could control Catholic violence through negotiation. Consequently they under-estimated the anger remaining from August 1969 and exaggerated their ability to be regarded as community defenders. Conversely, strategists feared Protestant violence, a reasonable concern given that the initial clashes with soldiers came from Protestants.[12] The army's movement into Catholic areas in October 1969 is rightly deemed 'momentous'.[13] However, a critical decision was taken in anticipation of Protestant violence, in an extension of the British state's reaction to Stormont's threats before the army arrived. On 31 August Brigadier Hudson, commanding forces in Belfast, handed over responsibility for the Shankill area to the RUC. From here began the trend, to which there were exceptions, where the army dealt with Catholic areas and the police the Protestants. The army made itself partisan: Catholics only saw soldiers repressing them, and the army relied upon the mainly Protestant police to impartially tackle loyalist militants, which they did not.[14] The posture stemmed from fears of Protestants, and the government's refusal to send additional police or military manpower from Britain. Only from late 1972 did the army acquire the knowledge and capacity to confront loyalist violence.

REPAIRING TRUST IN NO-GO LAND

Just before 5pm on 14 August 1969, 1st Prince of Wales' Own Regiment moved to Derry, under strict orders: 'No shooting unless absolutely nec [sic] because of retaliatory action.' Local politicians like Eddie McAteer agreed to help calm rioting in exchange for the army taking over barriers in the city from the police.[15] Derry fell quiet, but in Belfast the violence worsened.[16] A child was shot in Dover Street and a civilian shot dead in Divis Street. By 3.30am HQNI recorded 121 casualties, including 4 dead.[17] Trouble flared again at 8.30 that morning. There was rioting, shooting, arson and 'voluntary evacuation'. At 6.25pm 39 Brigade deployed 17th/21st Lancers, 2nd Queens and 1st Royal Regiment of Wales onto Belfast's streets.[18] The Queen's Regiment recorded being 'well met by terrified civilians'.[19] (See Illustration 2.1.) General Freeland warned his troops to expect 'an operation which might be one of the trickiest that you have ever experienced'. He instructed soldiers to be impartial and adhere to the principle of minimum force.[20] Soldiers were not universally welcomed: that night a soldier received a minor gunshot wound near Cupar Street. Soldiers used CS gas against petrol bombers in Waterville Street and Northumberland Street.[21]

The IRA in Belfast, perhaps thirty- to forty-strong, mobilised on 14 August with an arsenal of two submachine guns, a rifle and six handguns. Between then and 16 August at least seventy Protestants in the city suffered gunshot wounds. There is little doubt the IRA were shooting people as the army moved onto the streets. Though the organisation's actions in the city might be seen as largely defensive, an attack on Crossmaglen police station on 17 August was certainly offensive. IRA leaders decided against further attacks after the raid, but this was not known by the security authorities.[22]

Illustration 2.1 Members of the Queen's Regiment disembark from the troop carrier *Sir Tristram*, 28 August 1969.
(Courtesy of Mirrorpix via Getty Images.)

Any potential for alarm in HQNI was soon doused, when an intermediary for the IRA approached to promise 'no further trouble' in Belfast if the army replaced the RUC in certain areas.[23] William Philbin, the Catholic bishop of Down and Connor (the diocese for Belfast), said troops could expect a 'good reception'.[24] The army and police agreed to patrol together, working from police barracks.[25] Soldiers quickly provided some reassurance – people in Etna Drive handed in 15 gallons of petrol intended for molotov cocktails.[26] The army's reception in Belfast was such that a submachine gun stolen from a Royal Hampshires check-point was returned to them by the IRA.[27]

A Joint Security Committee was set up by Prime Minister Chichester-Clark to co-ordinate the response to the emergency. Chaired by the minister of home affairs, the army, police, Special Branch and MI5 attended. At its meeting on 16 August concern was expressed about IRA incursions from the Republic, so the army was authorised to spike small roads on the border.[28] Despite the Crossmaglen raid HQNI refrained from blaming the IRA, as they lacked intelligence to prove responsibility.[29] In London the JIC put the violence in Derry down to sectarianism, and held 'strong suspicions' of IRA involvement.[30] Derek Faulkner, a Home Office civil adviser sent to support General Freeland, thought the IRA more active in Belfast than Derry, but also blamed the unrest on socialists, civil rights activists and, above all, hooligans. Faulkner was accompanied by J. A. McKay as the police liaison officer. Their real function was to inform the home secretary about goings-on at HQNI.[31] Freeland needed help in any case. His headquarters staff only comprised a brigadier as his COS, three staff officers for operations and six staff officers for administration.[32] With 39 Brigade running operations in Belfast and Counties Antrim, Down and Armagh, 24 Brigade was activated on 18 August to command forces in Counties Londonderry, Tyrone and Fermanagh.[33]

At a meeting between the British and Northern Irish cabinets on 19 August reforms intended to stabilise the situation were agreed. Some scholars claim the army struggled in the early months because they lacked an accompanying political programme, and answered to too many masters.[34] These claims are mistaken. The Downing Street Declaration set out policies designed to win back Catholic confidence while reassuring Protestants. All citizens were guaranteed 'the same equality of treatment and freedom from discrimination as obtains in the rest of the United Kingdom', a clear promise to the civil rights movement. The governments announced an arms amnesty to reduce the amount of weaponry in circulation and set up an inquiry into the August violence. To reassure unionists, London pledged to uphold Northern Ireland's constitutional position in the United Kingdom, unless the people and parliament in Northern Ireland wished a change. Diplomat Oliver Wright was sent to Stormont as the British government's representative – a post that came to be known as the United Kingdom Representative, or UKREP. The agreement gave General Freeland overall responsibility for security operations, including the deployment of the police for security tasks. They remained under their inspector-general for normal policing. Freeland reported to the MOD, not the Northern Ireland government. The B Specials, also under Freeland's control, were to be withdrawn from riot control duties.[35] The army could, and did, refuse Stormont's preferences.

Repairing trust took more than formal pronouncements from Downing Street. Though we have known for some time about the street negotiations between local figures and army commanders, most writings emphasise the top-level talks between the British and Northern Ireland cabinets.[36] Niall Ó Dochartaigh's rich study of negotiation during the conflict observes how dialogue between the army, police and defence associations acted to prevent violent escalation.[37] An immediate question facing the army was what to do about the hundreds of barricades erected throughout Belfast, Derry and some smaller towns in the mid-August clashes. Barricades were a reminder that normal law and order had broken down. For many unionists they represented an affront to the state's right to rule. To many soldiers they seemed untidy. To people who lived amongst them, feelings were mixed – barricades could offer protection, but also inconvenience the daily routine. Even after the violence had died down, new barricades went up, such as those in Andersonstown in Belfast.[38] The territory behind the barricades became known as the 'no-go' areas. General Freeland understood why people rejected the police's presence and believed the only way to force compliance upon them, by martial law, was 'unthinkable in the UK'.[39]

The street committees which controlled the barricades aimed to protect residents from expected attacks. The St Columbs Wells Protection Association, chaired by republican Seán Keenan, was created in Derry in January 1969 after the Burntollet incident. A Citizens Defence Committee appeared in Newry in June. The Derry Citizens' Defence Association (DCDA) formed on 20 July 1969, with a mixed political membership, though also chaired by Keenan. In early August the Unity Flats Defence Association came into being in Belfast. Each street in the barricaded Catholic areas sent a representative to the Central Citizens' Defence Committee (CCDC), created in Belfast on 16 August, under republican Jim Sullivan's chairmanship.[40] Paddy Devlin held the Stormont parliamentary seat of Belfast Falls for the Northern Ireland Labour Party. He served as secretary to the CCDC, alongside figures such as Paddy Kennedy (Republican Labour Stormont MP for Belfast Central), Canon Pádraig Murphy and fruit importer Tom Conaty. The committee assisted residents by liaising with the army, city hall, the housing authorities and social services.[41]

Battalion commanders developed close contacts with local politicians, citizens groups and clergymen. On 19 August, 2nd Queens met Paddy Devlin and Gerry Fitt, Republican Labour MP at both Stormont and Westminster. Brigadier Dyball, the COS, toured the Catholic areas in Belfast with three priests. The priests confirmed there were armed men in the area and predicted a 'Battle Royal' if the police attempted to pass the barricades. Brigadier Hudson, commanding 39 Brigade, persuaded the police to abandon their plan to enter the no-go areas that night. The army had to choose its interlocutors carefully, and initially did so on the basis of ignorance. A two-man patrol into Albert Street, accompanied by Father Murphy, beat a hasty retreat when agitated residents declared the priest 'did not dictate policy in this area'.[42] Ian Paisley accused 3rd Light Infantry and 1st Hampshires of discriminating against Protestants by only stopping and searching them, and not Catholics. The Brigade protested: 'Not true of course!'[43] John McKeague, of the Shankill Defence Force (later the Shankill Defence Association), phoned HQNI, asserting the army unfairly searched cars in Protestant but not in Catholic areas. Protestant vigilantes were prevented from guarding the streets while their Catholic equivalents were left alone.[44] In Belfast the army was to come under constant pressure from unionists to clamp down on the Catholic no-go areas.

In Derry, Lieutenant-Colonel Charles Millman, commanding 1st Queens, got a 'good reception' from people behind the barricades on his first encounter, despite exchanging fractious banter with renowned activist Bernadette Devlin.[45] His second in command, Major Mike Reynolds, claims to have been used as the main interlocutor with the Bogsiders due to his Catholic faith. Reynolds emphasised his distance from Derry people, suggesting neither he nor Millman, 'being Englishmen, really understood the "Irish problem"'.[46] In a three-hour meeting on 23 August, Paddy Doherty from the DCDA justified the barricades as a protest symbol against Stormont's misrule.[47] Millman believed Bogsiders only heard 'a filtered version of govt and Army statements'.[48] He suggested the barricades come down now his troops were able to offer protection. He proposed six incentives to the DCDA. Firstly, no male RUC officer was to enter the Bogside. Secondly, the army would man barriers to stop attacks on the area. Thirdly, soldiers would allow people to pass through the barriers to go about their everyday lives. Fourthly, Royal Engineers could clear the barricades. Fifthly, military patrols would provide extra security. Sixthly, Millman would recommend to his superiors that the B Specials be disarmed. The DCDA promised to put the offer to their full committee.[49]

HQNI was not impressed: 'No firm undertakings are to be entered upon or guarantees given by local commanders without reference to this HQ.' Freeland insisted 'common policies must obtain throughout the province'.[50] This insensitivity to political geography was to be repeated with greater ramifications later on. A barricade on Springmartin Road in Belfast came down after talks between the Royal Hampshires and Protestant residents. Freeland approved such 'purely local military' actions.[51] But a meeting between the Hampshires and the CCDC underscored Freeland's naïvety in conceiving of high politics as separable from street politics. The CCDC called for the police to be disarmed and replaced by an impartial force, for recently arrested men to be released, an amnesty for rioters, civil rights reforms and a weapons amnesty.[52] Brigadier Hudson understood people 'think that their lives and property are threatened'. He was alert to potential threats, warning 'militant parties' might provoke soldiers into opening fire, as an excuse to escalate street violence.[53] It has been argued that little was being gathered by the 'intelligence agencies' in the honeymoon phase, a flawed claim if military intelligence is taken into account.[54] Contacts with community leaders fostered optimism in 39 Brigade: 'Very few hard-line vigilante groups exist. The majority seem to genuinely want peace.' The estimated forty IRA activists in the city were thought to pose no serious danger.[55]

Colonel Millman appreciated the need for patience as he kept building relationships in Derry, including with Protestant groups like the Middle Liberties Unionist Association. Quite often meetings did not seem to achieve anything tangible.[56] Political requests also seemed hard to separate from military operations in both cities. Brigadier Leng, commanding 24 Brigade, met nationalist former members of the Derry Corporation. They said unemployment, poor housing and unfair political representation in the city had to be addressed for peace to return. Immediate demands included disarming the police and an amnesty for rioters, and for English policemen to patrol the Bogside and the Creggan.[57] Leng reflected upon the situation:

> nowhere else in the World could so many bigotted [sic] and inflexible people be gathered into one community. In simple terms it appears that the Protestants/Unionists have given over the years not an inch to the Catholics. Now that concessions are beginning naturally they flow towards the Catholics who bay for more; while the Unionists are bitter about losing

so much so quickly. The control of the 'B' Specials is causing great resentment and has to be handled with extreme care. . . . Intelligence is non existant [sic]. We have not yet even had <u>one</u> INTSUM [intelligence summary] from HQ N.I.[58]

Millman's efforts began to yield results in late August. The Creggan Tenants Association suggested the military police carry out traffic control and minor criminal investigations, and the DCDA asked for school bus services to resume.[59] Brigadier Leng followed up these ideas in a meeting with the DCDA leadership on 31 August in the Ardoen Hotel. Leng called for the RUC to be allowed back into the Bogside – a gambit which was immediately rejected. The DCDA were open to the idea of military police entering the area with some RUC support. Seán Keenan and his associates pressed for the Special Powers Act to be repealed, viewing it as inextricably connected to repression. From the DCDA's perspective the army were discredited by having used the act to conduct a cordon and search on 20 August (which found nothing). Keenan wanted to know whether such operations were carried out in Protestant areas. Brigadier Leng said information on illegal arms would be followed up, irrespective of location. He promised to enquire about the chances of an amnesty for rioters being granted by Stormont. The meeting ended with Keenan pledging to remove a barricade in William Street and Leng undertaking not to dismantle barricades before the Hunt Report, announced by Chichester-Clark on 26 August to consider options for future policing, came out.[60]

When the Hunt Commission visited Derry, Millman suggested British policemen be sent to the Bogside and, in the longer term, the creation of a separate police force for the city.[61] Brigadier Leng asked for the Royal Military Police (RMP) to operate in the Bogside. As the Special Powers Act could not easily be rescinded he suggested the army and police declare they would only invoke it in exceptional circumstances.[62] HQNI and the MOD saw the Special Powers Act as essential for the army's operations.[63] An offer from the Northern Ireland attorney general to abolish the Act was rejected by London in January 1970.[64] The DCDA removed the first barricades on 1 September. Seeing this progress, HQNI approved the RMP entering the Bogside. The DCDA did not immediately agree. However, James Doherty from the Tenants Associations, claiming to speak for more people than the DCDA, argued people wanted the barricades gone;[65] 24 Brigade concluded 'the united front presented by the Bogsiders is definitely beginning to crack'.[66] A power struggle was underway between 'left-wing extremists, civil rights, students and the DCDA'.[67] The talks provoked Protestant indignation. Soldiers found posters reading 'CHANGE YOUR REGT'S NAME FROM QUEENS OWN TO POPES OWN REGT. TRATIORS [sic]'.[68]

In Belfast, violence broke out in the early hours of 30 August. When a police car drove into a Catholic area, a hostile crowd attacked it with stones and bottles. A Protestant mob then gathered to support the police. The Royal Regiment of Wales got in between the crowds and persuaded them to leave by threatening to use CS gas.[69] Barricades soon went up in Tennent Street and the Shankill Road in protest at the army's refusal to enter the Catholic no-go zones. These events induced Brigadier Hudson to hand over responsibility for the Shankill to the RUC.[70] This was the beginning of the pattern whereby the army dealt with Catholic unrest, and the police trouble from Protestant quarters, a decision taken for short-term practical reasons with major long-term effects. From this point onwards military strategy was more likely to emphasise the danger from republicanism, and was less interested in loyalist groups.

As in Derry, the army's association with Catholic defence groups upset some Protestants. Mr Quinn complained to his Stormont MP after he was stopped and his car searched in Belfast by 'soldiers under the command of vigilantes'.[71] Soldiers stopped and searched Stormont MP John McQuade, an Ulster Unionist, prompting a formal complaint.[72] These petty aggravations were sufficient to cause serious violence. Where Mr Quinn turned to his elected representative, others settled matters themselves. On 2 September Ian Paisley phoned 39 Brigade to say Protestants intended building their own barricades if the Catholic ones stayed up. Barricades duly appeared around Ravenhill Road and Woodstock Road. Another new Protestant barricade was found by soldiers to be 'surrounded by drunken Irishmen and too Large [sic] to move'.[73] The police persuaded people in Sandy Row to remove their barricade.[74] RUC liaison officers told 39 Brigade they expected Protestant barricades to go up across Belfast. Indeed, a barricade was constructed in Bann Street 'In protest to Falls road barricades'. A 600-strong Protestant crowd gathered at 11.50am on 4 September in Northumberland Street to demand the army dismantle the Catholic barricades.[75]

General Freeland appealed to the Catholic church to break the deadlock. Cardinal Conway and Bishop Philbin agreed to bring their influence to bear.[76] In the morning of 6 September, Freeland talked to Paddy Devlin, representing the defence group in Albert Street, and by 11.44 the street was open.[77] Devlin had to temper his personal desire for the barricades to be removed with the necessity of appearing a tough negotiator, to maintain political credibility.[78] Progress was too slow. On Sunday 7 September Protestant and Catholic crowds confronted each other in Percy Street.

The Hampshires fired three CS grenades and sixteen cartridges at the Protestant crowd, and one cartridge at the Catholic crowd. The Catholic group dispersed, but the Protestants were only angered and hung around.[79] An army board of inquiry found the use of CS gas to be justified, as the officer in charge 'repeatedly warned the crowds of his intentions'.[80] The next morning 'Defenders' shot at Protestant youths attempting to petrol-bomb Catholic houses, killing Jack Todd.[81] General Baker in London worried relations between the army and Protestants were damaged by press reports about an alleged army agreement with the IRA.[82] The army was moving too slowly to placate Protestant sentiment in Belfast, and providing insufficient protection for Catholics to feel safe.

EXASPERATING DIPLOMACY

Less than a month after arriving, the army adjusted its approach in order to placate Protestant outrage. A night-time vehicle control system would operate in central Belfast. Barricades were going to start coming down as the army guaranteed security, and a peace-line was to be built separating the Falls and Shankill areas, initially from coiled wire, later high walls.[83] Chichester-Clark announced the measures in a television broadcast on 9 September 1969.[84] Minister of Home Affairs Robert Porter felt sufficiently optimistic to shoot down a proposal to criminalise barricade erection.[85] These initiatives caused problems in Derry. Colonel Millman rang 24 Brigade 'very perturbed', having received no advance warning and fearing for relations with the DCDA.[86] Brigadier Leng reacted with 'some dismay'. People in Derry phoned his headquarters with 'garbled stories which, in general terms, indicated that the Barriers were to be removed by force'. The broadcast came just as the military police were about to be granted access to the Bogside.[87] Now the DCDA declined to let them in.[88] In Belfast the announcement was well received by many Protestants, who began dismantling their barricades.[89]

Sensing an opportunity to jolly things along, Jim Callaghan flew to Northern Ireland. Meeting Catholic representatives in Belfast, he argued the six battalions present in the city, shortly to be supplemented by another, were able to guarantee security, rendering the barricades redundant. He promised military commanders must ask those behind the barricades if they felt safe before any dismantling happened.[90] Protestant barricades continued to fall.[91] Yet soldiers and policemen were needed to hold apart Catholic and Protestant crowds in the New Lodge Road–Halliday Road area.[92] In Derry, the DCDA consented to Lieutenant-Colonel Millman's troops manning barriers around the city.[93] Independent nationalist Stormont MPs John Hume and Ivan Cooper conceded the army were able to provide security in the Bogside; Millman cautioned that if the barricades came down in Belfast, he was likely to receive orders to remove those in Derry.[94] Conflicting information arrived about how such a change in policy might be received. A man from the Creggan said Bogsiders were ready to admit the RMP; yet Fathers Mulvey, Daly and Rooney stated people wanted the barricades to stay.[95]

Callaghan's visit had reassured few Protestants. At 2am on 14 September shots were fired at an off-duty soldier going to a chip shop in Belfast. Freeland regarded the incident 'as the most serious event of the emergency so far'.[96] Barricades went back up. By the evening of 15 September, 161 barricades stood in Belfast, about 120 in the Falls.[97] Though optimistic about the negotiations in 'no go land', Freeland realised time was running out.[98] He thought the army's 'image as an impartial force' had been eroded by defending Catholics from Protestant attacks.[99] Brigadier Hudson reassured Paddy Devlin, Jim Sullivan, Father Murphy and others that the RUC remained banned from the no-go areas. A schedule was agreed to remove the barricades the next day.[100] (See Illustration 2.2.) By 6.10pm on 17 September all

Illustration 2.2 Major-General Tony Dyball and Father Murphy inspect a barricade in the Falls Road area of Belfast, 16 September 1969.
(Courtesy of Bettmann via Getty Images.)

barricades in Turf Lodge, Ballymurphy, Whiterock and Gransha were gone.[101] Despite complaints about police patrols in Ardoyne and 'provocative visits by Unionist Ministers to the Falls Road', only eleven remained in the Falls.[102] Having closely watched events in Belfast, the DCDA announced the dismantling of the barricades in Derry. In return the military police could pass into the no-go areas, if invited.[103] The last barricades came down in Derry on 23 September.[104] The CCDC were satisfied with the protection afforded by the army to Catholic areas.[105]

Denis Healey commended soldiers for 'acting not only as policemen, but also as diplomatists'.[106] Not everyone welcomed the softly-softly approach. In Derry the commander of 1st Grenadier Guards violated the agreement with the DCDA and drove two vehicles into the Bogside. Millman skilfully 'laughed off' the misdemeanour with the DCDA.[107] Lieutenant-Colonel May, commanding the Hampshires, resented having to place soldiers at former barricade sites to guarantee security: 'it made no military sense to disperse one's battalion in pairs of soldiers like that'.[108] In Northern Ireland in 1969 the epitome of military sense should have been protecting people who might otherwise seek security from paramilitaries. A Royal Marines officer complained about:

> negotiation; time consuming and often exasperating argument and persuasion aimed at restoring some semblance of normality. The situation required everyone, at every level, to be adept in diplomacy. The Marine on the street corner in his dealings with passers by, some drunk, some sober, and the Colonel who grudgingly curbed his tongue in uncharacteristic fashion in discussions with self appointed committeemen claiming to represent all shades of local opinion.[109]

The major advances in repairing trust between the British state and Northern Ireland's Catholic communities also depended upon consent from those not directly involved in the negotiations. According to an intelligence appreciation, the IRA leadership in Dublin instructed volunteers in Belfast to avoid disputes with the army over the barricades. Apparently the decision was reached after the Irish government promised not to crack down on the IRA if they restricted themselves to a defensive posture in the north.[110] However, changes were afoot. Christopher Herbert served as director of intelligence at HQNI, an MI5 officer with extensive colonial, counter-subversion and technical operational experience. He warned Denis Healey that the IRA in the north now numbered about 100–200, and traditionalist members wanted action. Considering themselves the rightful protectors of Catholics, they 'now see the hated British Army doing this role', so could try to restore their former status.[111] Herbert was right to be worried. At last the army had succeeded in making Catholics feel safe. Rather than British Army repression proving the crucial spur to republican aggression, the army's successful offer of protection from 17 September gave republicans a simple choice. They could admit their own redundance and disappear, or make a fighting comeback.

At the same time, the British Army's continuing ability to protect Catholics depended upon at least tacit acquiescence from most Protestants, which was threatened by those who instead sought for Catholics to be punished. Within the army's first week on the streets thoughts turned towards 'right-wing Protestant extremist elements'. General Freeland asked the police to provide more intelligence on the threat, which was being ignored.[112] By early September Freeland thought the UVF represented the 'most dangerous' threat facing him.[113] The director of intelligence deemed Protestant extremists 'one of the biggest threats'. A month after Freeland's demand for more intelligence on them, HQNI still struggled to persuade RUC Special Branch to move away from their 'sole concentration on the IRA to the other targets and in particular to the Extreme [sic] Protestant threat'. Unfortunately, 'There was a natural reluctance to do this.'[114] In formal terms, the police came under Freeland's command for security operations. In practice, the police's most important security unit refused to comply with his direction to provide intelligence on the chief threat facing Northern Ireland. There is no evidence to suggest Lisburn called on London to intervene on their behalf with the RUC or their Stormont masters.

A chance event in Derry destabilised the fragile political equilibrium. Although the incident was instigated by rioters, the army was held responsible for letting violence get out of control. If the British government really wished to see peace enforced on the streets in Northern Ireland, then sufficient manpower was essential to protect all elements of the population. In this sense, the long-running reluctance to intervene in Ireland continued to affect what happened. On 24 September a riot broke out between Protestant and Catholic youths in Derry. A Catholic mob gave a severe beating to William King, who later died in hospital. As a result the barricades in Derry went back up again; 1st Queens' regimental history noted how 'within hours the work of months had been rendered of no account'.[115] Commander Albert Anderson, Stormont Unionist MP for Derry, berated Brigadier Leng the next day. He intended going on television to say 'rather nasty things against the Army'.[116] King's death strengthened the hand of unionist politicians who had been calling for soldiers to repress Catholics ever since they arrived. Up until now General Freeland had brushed off these demands. It was only at this point that the Joint Security Committee learned the full details about the negotiations concerning the no-go areas. Robert Porter was 'disturbed' to hear about the deal to keep the police out. General Freeland downplayed the agreements as mere 'verbal assurances'.[117]

HQNI buckled. Major-General Toler, the recently appointed deputy army commander, directed 24 Brigade to adopt a 'tougher line'. Brigadier Leng decided to seal the barriers around the Bogside and the Creggan to prevent anyone leaving from 8pm that night. Millman was to inform the DCDA this was in response to the 'bad behaviour' of 'young hooligans from Bogside'.[118] Leng intended to maintain his 'barbed-wire siege' until 3 October, apart from one temporary exit.[119] This was serious collective punishment, a radical shift from the previously sensitive attitude towards Derry Catholics. Nothing was done to identify and arrest those who killed King. Trouble spread to Belfast in the early hours of 28 September, when Protestants petrol-bombed Catholic houses in Coates Street. Soldiers and policemen struggled to keep crowds apart in Louisa Street, and Hastings Street police station was set alight.[120] Someone in the Unity Flats shot at petrol-bomb-wielding Protestants. Brigadier Hudson directed 2nd Light Infantry to 'convince these people that if RCs open fire on us we will return fire'. Mr Largy, thought to be a leading figure in the flats, 'took well the point'. There were no more shots.[121] Following the disorder, fifty barricades went back up in Belfast.[122]

The army's inability to prevent King's death in Derry and the violence in Belfast precipitated a shift in tactics. Brian Faulkner went on the offensive at the Joint Security Committee. Though his call for a crackdown was rebuffed, Freeland approved more aggressive riot control tactics, no longer just keeping the factions apart, but making multiple arrests.[123] One or two platoons in each battalion would chase and arrest rioters, as snatch squads.[124] On 30 September soldiers received instructions on when to open fire (a move wrongly dated in existing studies to July 1970).[125] Copying practice in Aden, cards were produced for soldiers to carry at all times. They stressed fire could only be opened if a soldier or someone he was protecting came under attack, to the extent that death or serious injury were likely. The rules permitted the shooting of someone attacking property, if there was no other way to stop them. Soldiers were prohibited from shooting someone who ran away when challenged, or at vehicles which failed to halt.[126] Freeland also expanded the use of CS gas, to assist in making arrests, and against those throwing petrol bombs 'and similar lethal missiles'. Less drastic tactics and clear warnings had to be tried first.[127] The Joint Security Committee settled on three further measures: strengthening the peace-line, warning the CCDC that the no-go zones must be occupied by the army, and for Freeland to make a public statement about action against petrol bombers.[128]

Battalions had been improvising their own responses to riots since August: 2nd Light Infantry's Lieutenant-Colonel Sibbald believed poor housing, unemployment, fear of the other community and heavy drinking contributed to riots breaking out. He perceived the Irish in stereotyped terms, talking of their 'Love of rumour, tragedy and drama'. As the situation was unlike previous conflicts, senior officers accepted existing doctrine was not entirely appropriate.[129] Some knew this before arriving: Brigadier Cowan read widely on Northern Ireland's history and politics before taking over 8 Brigade in early 1970;[130] 1st Royal Horse Artillery followed the daily situation reports issued by 39 Brigade while preparing in England for their departure to Belfast.[131] In Derry, Millman's soldiers adapted their riot-control tactics soon after arriving, based on three steps. First, soldiers got up on the rooftops when trouble seemed imminent. Second, a rioting crowd was sealed off to stop others joining. Third, troops moved in quickly to separate rival factions.[132] Michael Gray, commanding 1st Parachute Regiment, relied upon 'the library in Belfast, looking up riot, insurrection, and the best guide I found was from the old Turkey, the way the Turks handled riots'. He trained his men in Aikido, so that they could make arrests without having to hit people hard.[133] John Marsham, a 3rd Light Infantry officer, recalled the pleasure derived by some soldiers from riots:

> Soldiers love having a proper job and the riots were the best thing, you know, since sliced bread, they really enjoyed it. We had our, the Rugby 15 were formed into the pack, I think; the scrum were formed into a snatch squad. Under a chap called Corporal Power, who was an absolute brute of a man and armed with pick handles they we were [sic] just grabbing ring leaders out of the mob whichever one it happened to be.[134]

The defence secretary was angered to learn about the new tactics on the television news.[135] Reporters had filmed 3rd Light Infantry practising with the new snatch squads. Ever adept at finding a scapegoat, senior officers sacked 39 Brigade's public relations officer.[136] Healey accepted the sterner line, but 'was not happy that the responsibility for deciding how the policy to snatch ring leaders from mobs was to be carried out should be delegated to Unit level'. He preferred a single technique for all soldiers and policemen.[137] Freeland insisted the 'method must be left to the

Commander on the spot'.[138] Healey backed down.[139] Serious disturbances broke out in east Belfast on the night of 4 October. The police and army responded with CS gas and snatch squads after petrol bombs, stones and bottles were thrown at them. One soldier suffered a fractured skull and another a gunshot wound.[140] Healey adopted the army's logic to rebut a unionist MP's complaints: 'the judgement of the experienced and responsible officer on the spot must be conclusive'.[141] Even the most domineering defence secretary in the MOD's history allowed HQNI substantial tactical autonomy: a pattern established under the Wilson administration and to continue under Edward Heath.

General Freeland also exercised autonomy in his control over the B Specials police reserve. The force's deserved reputation for brutality meant disbandment was essential to soothe Catholic fears. On 20 August 1969 the cabinet instructed Freeland to begin collecting their weapons and withdrawing them from operations as far as possible.[142] The arms did not all end up at their intended destination. An NCO in 2nd Light Infantry recalled 'the weapons went from over the big raincoats, to under the raincoats'.[143] Loyalist paramilitaries certainly got their weapons from somewhere. At a press conference on 22 August, Freeland announced that only 500 B Specials were on duty, mostly in rural areas. They were removed from any involvement in riot control duties. Instead, they guarded vulnerable points and manned vehicle check-points.[144] In early October Denis Healey learned the GOC had extended the deployment of fifty B Specials in the Shankill, when he had only approved their short-term use. Healey chastised the CGS for the step being taken without ministerial authorisation.[145] The CGS defended Freeland, claiming the B Specials were only armed with truncheons and had a stabilising effect.[146] Talking over the problem at the Labour Party conference in Brighton, Healey and Callaghan agreed to let Freeland continue employing the B Specials on the Shankill.[147]

The future of the B Specials fell within the purview of Lord Hunt's review. His report intended to rebuild public trust in the RUC and to increase its capabilities so that the army could be withdrawn. Hunt advised the police be expanded, receive better training and equipment, have fuller links with forces in Britain, and recruit more Catholics. Most controversially, he proposed the police be disarmed, an independent prosecutor be created, and the B Specials be replaced by a police reserve, and a local military unit under the GOC's command. Chichester-Clark's cabinet nearly resigned over the disbandment of the B Specials.[148] Some in HQNI objected too. Major George Styles, deputy assistant director of ordnance services, believed in using the B Specials as a 'weapon' to crush the 'terrorists'.[149] Callaghan visited Belfast to secure agreement to the Hunt report, announcing the new measures with Chichester-Clark on 10 October. In addition, the RUC inspector-general was to be replaced by Sir Arthur Young, commissioner of the City of London Police, and investments worth over £5 million a year injected into the economy.[150]

REFORM AND ITS DISCONTENTS

The report was received by some Protestants as an unjustified attack on their police force. Violence erupted on the Shankill within hours of its being published, and was even worse the next night (11 October). Under Lieutenant-Colonel Ballenden, 3rd Light Infantry deployed to assist the police at 11pm. According to Ballenden, his troops came under 'a heavy hail of rocks and bottles' until 11.25pm, when he warned the crowd that CS gas would be used. Soldiers fired three CS cartridges two minutes later. After snatch squads ran forward to make arrests, about six shots were fired at the soldiers, followed by petrol bombs and then further shots. Ballenden refrained from shooting back as his marksmen could not identify the shooters. At 12.30am troops advancing up the Shankill behind armoured vehicles were forced to halt by the heavy fire directed at them. Ballenden reckoned on four or five automatic weapons, 'and a large number of shotguns, .22 weapons and pistols' being fired from the crowd, side streets and rooftops. At about 1am he gave three warnings through a loudhailer that soldiers were authorised to shoot gunmen and petrol bombers. Marksmen opened fire at 1.16am, about an hour and forty minutes after soldiers were first shot at. They believed they hit four petrol bombers and two gunmen. Troops made about twenty baton charges, arresting sixty-odd people. Ballenden estimated at least 1,000 rounds were fired at soldiers that night. In return they fired 66 rounds, 82 CS grenades and 396 CS cartridges.[151] General Freeland was seriously worried by:

> the effect on the morale and discipline of our soldiers after firearms have been used against them by their own countrymen. A soldier will normally accept the hazard of becoming a casualty in Wartime and even on IS operations outside his own homeland, but when wounded by his own people or seeing his friends wounded or killed, he is liable to become very angry indeed. You will have seen the Daily Mirror article which reported an interview with wounded soldiers who threatened revenge. This article has caused us a lot of trouble and not improved our image with the Protestants. We shall have to watch discipline carefully because there have already been signs of deep resentment and rough handling of suspects.[152]

Jim Callaghan informed the House of Commons the events represented 'a most serious turning point'. Police constable Victor Arbuckle and two civilians were killed, and fifty-seven people injured.[153] The MOD suspected Arbuckle's death outraged Protestants, increasing support for the army and police. By contrast, Catholics may have sought IRA protection amidst an evidently dangerous Protestant threat.[154] Oliver Wright concurred, arguing quiet now prevailed because the army had shot rioters on the Shankill – 'proof that the British regulars meant business'.[155] Chichester-Clark pressed again for the RUC to enter the Bogside and Falls Road. Holding back might incite Protestant violence 'on a scale far in excess of anything which had occurred to date'. The ministers of home affairs, development and education threatened to resign if there was any delay. Freeland agreed to introduce joint army–police patrols from 17 October.[156] There was no need for the haste. In Derry, all the Catholic barricades had been down since 7 October, and a military police detachment entered the Bogside the next day.[157] Also on 8 October the military police entered the no-go areas in Belfast.[158] Within a day of Chichester-Clark's histrionics, deals were reached with the defence committees for joint army–police patrols in the Falls Road, the Bogside and the Creggan.[159]

Military appreciations of loyalist militancy after the Shankill episode fluctuated. A day after arriving on the Shankill on 14 October, 1st Parachute Regiment received a demand for a meeting from the Workers Committee for the Defence of the Constitution. Expecting a demand to leave, the Paras were surprised to learn the committee wanted them to stay. Within a week 'local residents who had previously been anti-military ... had changed their attitude and were producing tea and cakes for soldiers'.[160] For 3rd Light Infantry, also in Belfast, 'the Protestants were much more the aggressors than the Catholics'.[161] In Derry, 24 Brigade identified the Ulster Protestant Volunteers (UPV) as a particular risk, due to their anger at the Hunt report and 'general dislike of the military'. Intelligence suggested the UPV planned an attack on 1st Queens, whom they blamed for King's death in September.[162] Brigade intelligence officers had been watching the UPV since August, knew the group was led by William Porter and put their numbers at somewhere around 170.[163] Discontent manifested itself in less dramatic form on 18 October when Protestants held a sit-down protest on Craigavon Bridge.[164] Further loyalist sit-down protests happened in Enniskillen and Portadown, as well as Derry.[165] Though resentment amongst B Special men persevered, by late October 24 Brigade thought most were 'loyal sensible citizens', willing to accept the reforms.[166]

Leading unionists warned Lieutenant-Colonel Millman about a 'serious danger of "Loyalist Terrorism" as the reforms progress and this could escalate into more widespread insurrection'.[167] Special Branch in Bessbrook detected 'Extremist Protestants' using a tunnel for storing weapons, and conducting training.[168] In mid December, 24 Brigade received information from 'a reliable source' that 'Protestant extremists' intended to mount arson attacks in Dungiven.[169] Military intelligence in Belfast noted money was being collected on the Shankill to buy weapons.[170] Yet police intelligence set the threat from loyalist groups as low.[171] HQNI's intelligence committee described late 1969 as 'merely a lull'. Over three years since O'Neill proscribed the group, the UVF mystified the security forces. They knew a split existed in the UVF, but doubted the group even existed. This was a strange claim, given the recent conviction of UVF members for sabotage bombings. Special Branch deemed them unprepared to launch any offensive operations.[172]

General Freeland under-estimated his troops' ability and willingness to confront loyalism and thereby safeguard the army's reputation for impartiality. He was in a position to take decisive action against loyalists because the danger from republicanism was limited. Intelligence stated the IRA leadership continued to favour non-violent social change, and predicted only 'unco-ordinated splinter group activity by Northern Ireland Commanders', especially bank robberies to raise funds.[173] Police intelligence regarded the IRA as unready to launch large-scale attacks.[174] The authorities were not aware that in September Billy McMillen, IRA commander in Belfast, was confronted by traditionalist republicans demanding his resignation over the movement's inaction.[175] The dissension in the movement was, however, noticed. Military intelligence discerned an impaired position for those who negotiated with the army. Jim Sullivan's absence from a meeting between the chief of staff and the Belfast Command followed 'unfavourable comment he has roused in IRA and circles in Eire over his close association with British Army officers and the Inspector General of the RUC'.[176] Having expanded in Belfast, the IRA now comprised about 450 activists, with about 1,200 auxiliaries, holding 500 weapons.[177] Intelligence officers expected the dispute between the leadership and traditionalists pushing for armed struggle to culminate at the Sinn Féin conference on 10–11 January 1970. Traditionalists in the Falls Road were lobbying for 'militant action' against British soldiers. The leadership preferred to wait for the Hunt reforms to weaken the police before attacking the army, as conflict could then be justified as resistance against 'an Army of Occupation'.[178] Intelligence assessments doubted whether Catholics backed the IRA. They might well accept IRA protection in times of danger, or hide guns for them. But army intelligence decided 'there is no real affection for the IRA'.[179]

This judgement rested on a belief that nobody could reasonably support the IRA. Indeed, 8 December marked seven weeks without serious unrest. Most of the civil rights movement's demands were being tackled; for HQNI, 'minority opinion should therefore be satisfied'.[180] Good relations with many residents naturally promoted such optimistic sentiments. Brigadier Leng ordered his troops to be 'helpful and polite' to civilians, but 'hold themselves aloof' and avoid expressing political or religious opinions. Soldiers were advised that 'becoming involved with local girls' might cause problems.[181] This sort of injunction was, predictably, flouted. Three privates apparently left behind 'many broken hearts' when 1st Queen's Regiment departed Derry in December 1969.[182] After another battalion returned to England from Belfast, 'Many riflemen returned to Ireland during their leave to renew acquaintances ... some to marry Irish girls.'[183] In May 1970, 1st Royal Scots received endless invitations to have dinner at the homes of residents in Mayo Street, off the Shankill.[184]

Commanders attempted to reinforce the peace, and keep soldiers busy, through community relations schemes. For example, 1st Royal Hampshires played sports against local teams and visited youth clubs. Soldiers went to the seaside town of Bangor for three-day leave breaks.[185] 1st Parachute Regiment opened a boxing club on the Shankill, built a playground, and ran canteens.[186] The 'Paradise Club', catering to all communities, held four functions a week, with its own resident disc-jockey. B Company gave swimming lessons and a Christmas party for a school for the disabled, and took great pride in receiving thank-you letters and paintings from the children.[187] 1st Royal Horse Artillery started a community centre, held carol services and distributed toys.[188] All this served an instrumental purpose too: 1st Royal Scots noted most vital intelligence 'comes from four old Protestant women who always appear at the sentry posts about two in the morning'.[189] HQNI funded entertainment events where soldiers could chat people up for useful information.[190] These convivial encounters may have lulled the army into a false sense of security, leading the MOD to decide against introducing psychological operations (military propaganda).[191] By mid 1971 this would be seen as a major mistake, as the army lacked the resources to explain its position to the population.

Behind the scenes the army's relations with the police also cast a cloud over the future. Since November Freeland had been pressing London for the police to take over from the army, if necessary by British policemen reinforcing the RUC in large numbers.[192] The army found Chief Constable Young difficult, despite his experience in working alongside soldiers in Malaya and Kenya. Chichester-Clark later summed up the Stormont view: 'He was a good policeman, but I think Young just never clearly understood Northern Ireland. . ... He was a little bit too quick to criticize every institution that there was here.'[193] In December Young wrote to Freeland, proposing the police take responsibility for 'purely passive measures', leaving the army to handle serious violence, including riots, under police direction. The MOD was alarmed, because far higher military force levels would be needed.[194] Freeland agreed the army should only be available for riot control where the police could not cope:

> In Northern Ireland, as we all know to our cost, the rioters are a tough lot and are not going to become angels just because the RUC act more gently. . ... When the Army is called in because the Police cannot deal with a situation, the accepted principle is that the senior Army Officer assumes command and it is his decision and his alone as to how to deal with the situation confronting him. He will of course consult with the senior Police Officer present, so that the Police can be warned of intended action and can cooperate if necessary, but the latter will not have any power of veto. This clear definition of responsibility between Military and Police Commanders has stood for many years – ever since I have been a soldier – and I am sure it cannot be changed.[195]

Freeland instead proposed the RUC form anti-riot squads.[196] The CGS had already reassured him that he would block any move to place soldiers under police command.[197] Poor relations between Freeland and Young did not always poison army–police interactions elsewhere. Brigadier James Cowan got on famously with Frank Lagan, police chief in Derry.[198] Although Young did not endear himself to the army high command, his appointment contributed to changing public attitudes to the police. On the Falls Road, people called on the CCDC to allow full police access, so that life might get back to normal.[199] This had been unimaginable only a few months earlier. General Freeland agreed a plan for joint policing in Belfast with the deputy inspector-general, securing the consent of the CCDC and nationalist MPs Gerry Fitt and Paddy Devlin. It entailed an unarmed RUC presence throughout the entire city, day and night, with support from the military police where necessary. Police re-entered the Falls Road shortly afterwards.[200]

This dramatic change in the policing of Catholic areas failed to satisfy Protestant opinion. For three nights from 25 January 1970 the Parachute

Regiment faced hostile crowds on the Shankill, apparently 'organised by an outside faction'.[201] Robert Porter and James Chichester-Clark talked to clergy and laymen from the area to find out what was going on. Remarkably, the discontent rested upon perceived slow progress towards policing in Catholic areas. The same sentiment also pervaded the parliamentary Unionist Party. Clearly frustrated, Freeland and Young wondered what else they could do: 'The alternative to diplomatic progress was shooting and bloodshed.' Freeland pointed out these gripes distracted from the fact that violence was taking place on the loyalist Shankill, not in the republican Falls Road.[202] By mid February military intelligence considered the 'main threat to political stability in the Province has now become the extreme wing of the Protestants'. Since the new year six bombs had been detonated, including at an army base, a Catholic church and at Crumlin Road prison. The army classified these as 'isolated acts of violence by Protestant extremists', at the same time as calling them a 'pattern'. The explosions apparently happened without any 'controlling organisation'.[203] Apart from embarrassing the authorities, the ongoing bombings 'had a disquieting effect, particularly on the minority community'.[204] The interpretation of the Protestant extremist threat as disorganised contrasted with how the army saw republican violence as deeply conspiratorial.

'IT MUST SUIT THE CATHOLICS TO BE CLOBBERED BY US'

The December 1969 IRA Army Convention adopted two controversial measures: dropping parliamentary abstentionism, and forming a national liberation front with radical left organisations. These moves, combined with anger at the leadership's lack of offensive action, prompted a breakaway faction to meet on 18 December. The new group, the Provisional IRA (PIRA), elected an executive and army council. Sinn Féin split along the same lines at the convention on 10–11 January 1970. The experiences of nationalists in Northern Ireland were decisive in shaping the Provisionals. Much of the fighting to come would be concentrated in Belfast.[205] PIRA's Belfast commanders thus exercised considerable autonomy. The army council consisted of Ruairí Ó Brádaigh, Seán MacStíofáin, Dáithi Ó Conaill, Paddy Mulcahy, Sean Tracey, Joe Cahill and Leo Martin. Ó Brádaigh, president of Provisional Sinn Féin, was a former IRA chief of staff, and MacStíofáin, the new CoS, a former director of intelligence. Cahill and Martin came from Belfast; all the others lived in the south. They were a middle-aged group, Ó Conaill the youngest, at 31, and a teacher by profession, like Ó Brádaigh.[206]

HQNI knew about PIRA's formation by 7 January, though they identified Rory Brady, as the British called Ó Brádaigh, as CoS. Most Belfast units were understood to have gone over to PIRA.[207] Intelligence suggested the Official IRA (OIRA) kept nearly all the money and weapons.[208] Though unknown to the British, the strategy set out by Mac Stíofáin at the army council meeting in January was far from difficult to anticipate, echoing closely the revolutionary warfare theory so familiar to army officers. Phase one entailed defending Catholics in Belfast. In phase two ongoing defence was to be mixed with retaliation against loyalists, to deter further attacks. The third phase envisioned an offensive against the United Kingdom to force a negotiated withdrawal from Northern Ireland and thence Irish reunification.[209] The Provisional's decision to wage war came before the British Army adopted repressive measures or committed atrocities such as Bloody Sunday.[210]

Leading figures in PIRA drew on their long experience, including the 1956–62 campaign, to conceptualise and execute their strategy. Some members, such as former paratrooper Phil O'Donnell in Derry, used knowledge gained in the British military to train recruits.[211] But what about the ordinary rank-and-file volunteers – why did increasing numbers join PIRA?[212] Scholars of republicanism avoid singular explanations for their motivation, though the global atmosphere of rebellion in the late 1960s is a commonly emphasised theme. Perceptions of an unjust society could matter more than personal experiences of discrimination. Some witnessed police brutality or felt their communities to be under threat from loyalists. A wish for a united Ireland was not necessarily the priority at the outset, though this could become a deeply held ambition over time.[213] Between 1969 and 1976 the average age of recruits was 22, and about 95 per cent were males, perhaps making members more willing to take risks.[214] In certain cases, like that of Gerry Adams, protracted family involvement in republican politics provided an environment where activism seemed a natural choice. As recruitment accelerated from 1970 to 1972, encounters with police and army violence became a central motivation for many, seeking to strike back at state brutality.[215]

Interpretive caution is essential here. Studies based on interviews with former PIRA members, often decades after recruitment occurred, cannot validate whether the stated reasons for joining were those paramount at the time. The republican narrative of the conflict's outbreak, driven by British repression, is confirmed by these interviews. They do not explain why people joined the IRA before British military tactics became more repressive from mid 1970. Hundreds had already joined for other reasons. British strategists unwittingly assisted the PIRA recruiting sergeants in early 1970 without radically changing tactics. Within weeks of the army being deployed, decision-makers questioned whether the impartial stance was sustainable. UKREP Oliver Wright predicted the future trajectory of relations between the army, Catholics and Protestants in a report to the home secretary on 13 September 1969:

> The re-establishment of law and order is the essential pre-requisite to the establishment of justice. Justice is a Catholic interest; the involvement of H.M.G. in the U.K. is their best guarantee of obtaining it. Ideally, this process should be gradual enough and accompanied by enough military protection to reassure the Catholic moderates, but swift enough to take the wind out of the sails of the Protestant extremists.... In the last resort, it must suit the Catholics to be clobbered by us if that is the only way we can get justice for them.... The danger comes from the extremists on both sides; the main danger from the Protestant extremists, since they can exploit majority opinion and have no interest in the success of the reform programme.... This may entail the use of force against the Catholics. Obviously H.M.G. would wish to avoid having to make so repugnant a decision. But it would be the only way of ensuring that Catholic grievances were eventually redressed. H.M.G. might have to be cruel to be kind. And it would be better than the use of force against the Protestant extremists, however repulsive their attitudes and behaviour, since they are the majority community.[216]

At Easter time 1970 the army's shift away from neutrality became more obvious. In the first instance, the new Ulster Defence Regiment (UDR) became operational on 1 April. As early as October the director of army staff duties (DASD) in the MOD warned that the new unit might be distrusted by Catholics. Recruiting in Northern Ireland risked implicating 'the Army in local politics and squabbles' as soldiers' reliability was suspect. Instead, a civilian paramilitary force controlled by Stormont was advocated.[217] There could hardly have been a more clueless suggestion. Denis Healey insisted upon the local army unit.[218] When Major-General Dyball met senior B Special officers to discuss the new regiment, they claimed admitting 'Roman Catholics with Nationalist sympathies' would prompt mass Protestant resignations. Dyball refused the demand to exclude all Catholics.[219] The Home Office wanted to ignore Lord Hunt's advice to have 'Northern Ireland' in the regiment's title, fearing it would be seen by Protestants as pandering to Catholics and the Irish Republic. Officials in the MOD agreed: the B Special commanders should be placated to ensure sufficient recruitment.[220] This decision has rightly been criticised for poleaxing the regiment's reputation for inclusivity.[221]

The office of the adjutant general (AG) cautioned that 'the hasty formation of this politically inspired force will end as a military failure'.[222] Overall, the army department wanted rapid progress, so that UDR units reduced the need for withdrawals from the British Army of the Rhine (BAOR) to go to Northern Ireland.[223] Denis Healey accepted large numbers of former B Specials to get the regiment operational quickly.[224] Intelligence assessments warned vetting recruits was going to 'be a major issue' due to gaps in Special Branch records on Protestants.[225] Though the regiment was banned from riot control duties, the 2,440 men enlisted by vesting day included 1,423 ex-B Specials. The Northern Ireland government had encouraged them to sign up, causing public outrage.[226] All seven battalions were commanded by former B Special county commandants.[227] The security forces also proved biased in less public fora. Over the first weekend of April several bombs went off in Belfast. Special Branch believed these to be the work of ten to fifteen known Protestant extremists. HQNI rejected a proposal to detain and interrogate them as politically impossible.[228] Fear pervaded such decisions. Military intelligence noted former B Specials in Fermanagh were hostile to the army and intended to 'keep in existence an organisation in case they are needed again to defend the Province'.[229]

Major clashes between Catholics and the army during Easter 1970 seemed to confirm the army's abandonment of neutrality.[230] Stormont lifted the ban on processions on 5 February, taking a 'calculated risk' to restore normality.[231] On Easter Sunday a group in the republican parade in Derry attacked the Victoria Police Barracks, attempting to remove its Union Jack flag. Rioting broke out again later in the Bogside.[232] On Easter Monday a Catholic march clashed with a Protestant mob, developing into 'a major riot situation in the Ballymurphy area'.[233] The next day 1st Royal Scots confronted crowds around Springfield Road from 6pm, responding to stones and bottles with repeated baton charges. Only the arrival of Saracen armoured personnel carriers persuaded the crowd to disperse. During the evening of Wednesday 1 April more intensive rioting happened in Ballymurphy. Soldiers fought the inhabitants and tried to prevent nearby Protestant residents from attacking the area. Petrol bombs were greeted with large quantities of CS gas.[234] The trouble had been foreseen by the Ballymurphy Tenants' Association, who asked 1st Royal Scots to prevent an Orange march from skirting the area. An attempt by the Scots to reach a compromise by persuading the Orangemen to refrain from playing music near Ballymurphy was ineffective. Though the Scots have been blamed for allowing the march, the real responsibility lay with the Northern Irish government and General Freeland for optimistically hoping all would be well.[235]

The MOD later identified the Ballymurphy riots as a turning-point in souring relations with Catholics.[236] Some scholars argue PIRA's strength only became evident in June; or that the government dismissed the Easter violence as driven merely by boredom and drunkenness.[237] However, intelligence officers concluded the escalation was orchestrated by PIRA, for four reasons. Firstly, Catholic squatters were apparently inserted into empty houses in the Protestant New Barnsley estate, to provoke a reaction. Secondly, the security forces discovered a large, prepared stock of petrol bombs. Thirdly, soldiers captured several known republicans. Fourthly, a source disclosed a 'Brady type Republican meeting' took place at a school 'where anti-Army and anti-Protestant tactics were discussed'. Overall, the Provisionals were thought to have intended to 'destroy the image of the Army as the protector of the Roman Catholics'. PIRA was also becoming more militant to win support away from the Official IRA.[238] PIRA blamed the trouble on 'Orange provocation', and claimed they actively sought to restrain rioters who wished to vent 'their anger and frustrations brought on by generations of living in squalor and constant provocation'.[239] However, the incentives for PIRA to provoke anti-army feeling after the successful peace moves negotiated between the British and the CCDC were real enough. The CCDC itself recognised support from Catholics in Belfast for conciliation was waning.[240]

The Easter violence, the worst since the October confrontation on the Shankill, alarmed the army. By 2 April, twenty-eight soldiers had sustained injuries in Ballymurphy. A petrol bomber's accidental self-immolation illustrated how high the stakes were becoming.[241] Possessing or using petrol bombs had been made a criminal offence on 3 December 1969.[242] Freeland now decided to communicate directly with the public: on 3 April he announced petrol bombers were liable to be shot after due warning. Intelligence sources, perhaps seeking to confirm policy, believed this was 'welcomed by the great majority on both sides who are totally fed up with continued violence'. Both the Official and Provisional IRAs threatened to kill British troops in retaliation for any petrol bomber shot dead.[243] Freeland's statement has been criticised as an overreaction, as petrol bombs were 'hardly provocative or even as dangerous as throwing stones'.[244] Troops did not share the sentiment. Terence Friend, a gunner in Belfast from June 1970, recalled: 'The thing that I really feared was to be caught by a petrol bomb. What a horrendous and painful way to die. And if you didn't die, what agony to suffer and be horribly maimed for life.'[245]

Freeland's next public address got him into hot water. Speaking to the BBC *Panorama* television programme on 6 April, he said the army should avoid an indefinite commitment to 'policing jobs', when they had 'many other jobs to do, proper soldiering jobs'. These remarks caused a political storm. Harold Wilson faced questions in the Commons, and pledged to keep troops in place until their task was complete.[246] Chichester-Clark flew to London for discussions, surprisingly asking for Freeland to stay on.[247] The CGS mildly rebuked Freeland on 17 April. General Baker accepted Freeland had acted in good faith, and believed the petrol-bomber remark produced 'a dramatically good effect on the soldiers, whose morale had been a bit shaken by recent events'. Nevertheless, the CGS set out restrictive guidelines for media relations in the future, requiring interviews by all senior officers to be cleared with the ministry beforehand. Baker sent him on three weeks' leave from 7 May.[248] Before going, Freeland wrote to London setting out his reflections on recent events. He identified a lingering 'undercurrent of bitterness and antagonism', especially towards the police in the Unity Flats in Belfast, and the Bogside and the Creggan in Derry. Social conditions such as slum housing, high unemployment, ingrained 'politico/religious feelings' and excessive drinking meant rioting was likely to be common for the foreseeable future. Freeland again proposed other police forces send men to support the RUC in building its capacity.[249] He clearly remained deeply pessimistic about the army's ability to control civil unrest, despite the reprimand.

CONCLUSION

After a promising few months keeping the peace in Northern Ireland, strategists soon returned to the pre-deployment negativity about the army's presence. Whether in Oliver Wright's sentiment about 'clobbering the Catholics' for their own good, or Freeland's desire to have his soldiers replaced by policemen, nothing good was expected to come from the army being on the streets. This was quite remarkable, given the significant successes achieved in low-level negotiations by battalion commanders and others. Time after time they had managed to keep rioting mobs away from each other, or to defuse clashes before they reached the streets at all. Not all officers relished their job as diplomats, and some appeared almost deliberately to jeopardise the fragile quiet with their unauthorised patrols into no-go land. The hostility towards keeping soldiers in a policing role appears to have derived from three sources. Firstly, many servicemen, including General Freeland, objected in principle to undertaking such tasks as fundamentally unmilitary and therefore inappropriate. This resentment would probably have arisen in any geographical context. Secondly, at times those with higher defence policy on their minds wished to reduce the military footprint in Northern Ireland so as to preserve manpower for other commitments, most notably the British contribution to NATO in Germany. Thirdly, and most importantly of all, strategists feared coming into direct conflict with the large, majority population, who appeared to be well-organised, aggressive and capable. Though the Shankill violence in October 1969 was interpreted in some quarters as showing the army's ability and willingness to confront anyone who challenged law and order, the consensus amongst strategists was that these events meant Protestants must not be provoked.

Loyalist violence was difficult for strategists to comprehend, not because there was no intelligence on the threat, but because the evidence was contradictory. At certain times army units got on well with Protestant communities and assessed the risk from militants accurately. At other junctures the precise evidence needed from Special Branch was lacking. But intelligence certainly cannot be held entirely responsible for the decision to placate loyalist hardliners: HQNI's determination not to have known bombers arrested and interrogated is a case in point. These conclusions demonstrate the importance of understanding the thinking behind policy decisions, and the perceptions of those who implemented them. Large-scale data projects, which abstract masses of separate incidents from these contexts, are misleading. One output from the Northern Ireland Research Initiative, for instance, argues the British Army unilaterally ended the peace-keeping phase by moving to repression.[250] As has been shown, the evidence indicates British tactics changed in response to both loyalist and republican violence. PIRA was formed with an offensive intent, recruited several hundred members, and organised sustained anti-army rioting at Ballymurphy by Easter 1970, before the army began using CS gas on a large scale, arresting hundreds of people, searching houses systematically, or using deadly force on a regular basis. The British Army's basic error in early 1970 was not one of escalating to offensive tactics, but rather of failing to reassure that they remained impartial and able to protect ordinary Catholics from loyalist militancy, as the permitted Orange march near Ballymurphy appeared to prove.

3

ESCALATION AND THE EROSION OF IMPARTIALITY

The Protestant Unionist Party seeks to preserve its power and avoid the absorption of Ulster into a 32 county Republic. This policy has relegated the Catholic minority in Northern Ireland to second class citizenship with some genuine grievances against its treatment by the Stormont Government, in spite of recent reforms. Added to this are militant opportunists, thugs and certain individuals with a vested interest in perpetuating unrest to maintain their own positions. . ... The Army is playing its classic role of containing the violence generated by this situation, buying time for the politicians. The Army's IS [internal security] operations are in the preparatory or 'pre-insurgency' phase, with prevention rather than repression the guiding principle.[1]

Army Staff Course, 1971

During the summer of 1970 the British Army's tactics in Northern Ireland unmistakably shifted into a more aggressive gear. Responsibility is frequently pinned upon Edward Heath's administration, elected in June, and particularly Reginald Maudling, the new home secretary, for his indolence, for letting the army have their head, and for referring to the Province as a 'bloody awful country'.[2] Backbench Conservative MPs pushed the government towards coercion rather than reform, and Heath's slim majority made Unionist Party voices more resonant than before the election.[3] Politicians representing mainly Catholic constituencies certainly perceived a marked deterioration. Paddy Devlin claimed soldiers started to 'knock young people about' within days of the vote.[4] An eyewitness situated at a quite different vantage point drew the opposite conclusion, however. Robert Ramsay, Brian Faulkner's private secretary (PS), was a man with every incentive to accentuate Unionist influence on British conduct. He stated the Heath government talked a much more pro-unionist game, but practised 'foot-dragging' on cracking down on the IRA.[5]

Continuities across the June 1970 electoral divide remained prominent aspects of government policy. Heath maintained the reform agenda demarcated by Wilson and Callaghan.[6] Conservative and Labour politicians aimed to avoid direct rule from London at almost any cost.[7] What deserves much closer scrutiny are the ways in which loyalist power influenced British strategy. To claim, as some scholars have, that they 'played no central part' in British strategy is a serious error.[8] Prior to the general election, three important tendencies had already taken root. Firstly, fear of loyalist rebellion deterred strategists from impartially addressing violence from wherever it came. Secondly, the decision to leave mainly Protestant areas to the police compounded the intelligence deficit on loyalism caused by Special Branch's refusal to gather information on these targets. Thirdly, successes in negotiating in Catholic areas bred confidence. Fear of loyalism fused with overconfidence about the army's ability to attack and suppress republicanism. From May 1970 – before the Conservative electoral victory – the British Army launched a preventative assault on republicans, to ward off the danger of civil war by eliminating the only belligerent deemed defeatable.

HALTING THE MARCH TO CIVIL WAR

In the weeks following the Easter violence intelligence officers puzzled over the absence of rioting. Giving themselves the benefit of the doubt, they credited increased army patrolling in interface areas with the calm.[9] Ongoing liaison with local committees also gave the feeling of a situation more or less under control. Committee members tended to encourage a positive image of their position. Battalions could still rely on the CCDC, which condemned violent individuals for their 'betrayal of the Catholic community'.[10]

Even when riots returned, over the weekend of 9–10 May, military confidence remained high. Intercommunal clashes in the Tiger's Bay and New Lodge areas in Belfast turned into a Catholic riot against the army. The army believed PIRA organised events in New Lodge to provoke soldiers into 'strong-arm methods'. Gerry Fitt and an (unnamed) priest agreed. Several soldiers were wounded by pub darts, but the expected overreaction was avoided.[11] Scholars partly attribute the violence in 1970 to competition between the Official and Provisional IRAs for members, impressed by their audacity. The rivalry's outbreak is dated to June or November.[12] Military intelligence detected the phenomenon earlier. During riots in Ardoyne and New Lodge on 17 and 18 May three PIRA members were arrested. The motive was thought to be to win supporters away from the Officials and discredit the British Army. Sources suggested PIRA's Ardoyne Company planned shootings of soldiers, policemen and Protestants.

The army and police responded by mounting searches, finding hand grenades and gelignite. HQNI's belief that people deplored violence was reinforced by priests and the CCDC publicly condemning it.[13] House searches became more frequent. The army knew the annoyance and damage involved caused 'friction and resentment'. But being 'inactive' was judged 'much worse'.[14] Special Branch sources indicated the Provisional leadership had no intention of taking offensive action during the marches. However, in reacting to Protestant violence the senior command might prove incapable of controlling their men. Both IRA wings were recruiting new members with a 'genuine fear' that Catholics were soon to be attacked.[15]

The risks posed by the marching season were palpable. On 2 June, 250 Orange marchers in Belfast, angered at being re-routed, rioted, the first Protestant violence against the security forces for months.[16] The previous November James Callaghan had promised police officers in Britain they would not be seconded to the RUC until normality was restored. This poleaxed Freeland and Young's wish for 1,500 British policemen to reinforce them.[17] The largest Orange parade might attract 35,000 marchers and 60,000 spectators – 'sizeable minorities' relished the opportunity for a bust-up. Yet the Northern Ireland government wanted the parades to proceed. General Freeland agreed, because banning them might provoke unmanageable disorder. If the marching season went badly, General Baker foresaw the Chichester-Clark government collapsing and London having to take direct control. Banning the marches threatened 'to set off disorders worse than those of last August'.[18] An extremely volatile period was approaching. The most obvious solution, to cancel the marching season, was ruled out by the army's fear of loyalist militancy. The only remaining alternative was to go after the IRA: a position reached through several key decisions from April to June 1970, under the Labour government's tenure. Having won the general election on 18 June, the Conservatives reinforced HQNI with five units, to add to the nine already present.[19] General Freeland now possessed the resources to attack the IRA pre-emptively.

Before the weekend of 26–8 June the CCDC implored army and police commanders to cancel an Orange march in north Belfast, in vain. Catholics rioted on the Friday, incensed by the Orangemen.[20] Lieutenant Huskissen from 2nd Queens was hospitalised with a flying brick to the face. Soldiers responded with a 'considerable quantity of gas'.[21] In Derry Bernadette Devlin was arrested on her way to make a speech. The 1,200 people awaiting her spontaneously attacked the army; the violence continued throughout the weekend, with looting and arson.[22] The next day violence flared throughout Belfast. The RUC station in New Barnsley came under attack and British-owned department stores in the city were firebombed.[23] In a confrontation between Catholics and Protestants in Ballymacarrett, east Belfast, about 1,500 shots were fired by the two sides. The violence centred around St Matthew's Catholic church, where PIRA fought a gun-battle against a loyalist mob, without any soldiers in sight. The army presented the events at the church as tragically resulting from overstretch in the city.[24] However, 2nd Queens were available, but remained in their armoured vehicles to avoid further casualties.[25]

PIRA presented themselves as heroically defending the church from a blood-crazed loyalist mob. Belfast commander Billy McKee was wounded, and volunteer Henry McIlhone died.[26] The PIRA gunmen killed two Protestants near the church, and three others after an Orange march near Springfield Road turned violent.[27] The siege at St Matthew's was a totemic event in establishing the Provisionals' reputation as community defenders.[28] Brigadier Frank Kitson, who commanded 39 Brigade from September 1970, later argued that permitting the Orange marches to proceed played directly into PIRA's hands, allowing them to emphasise their relevance as protectors against loyalists.[29] Sectarian rage in east Belfast rose 'to fever pitch'.[30] On the evening of 28 June the army success-fully defended St Matthew's from a 1,000-strong Protestant mob.[31] Nobody noticed this belated redemptive act.

Over the weekend 6 civilians died and 150 were injured; 164 soldiers were injured.[32] HQNI saw 'a deliberate escalation', to shooting and arson. Intelligence stated 'Brady units' aimed to discredit the security forces, and achieved 'a considerable measure of success'. Unionists abhorred the army's weakness.[33] London agreed to expedite the planned reinforcements, while HQNI intensified searches for arms.[34] The Joint Security Committee author-ised General Freeland to publicly warn that civilians carrying or using fire-arms were 'liable to be shot without warning'.[35] Freeland directed that the principles of aimed single shots and minimum force still applied. Fire could be opened against gunmen who were shooting, against anyone carrying a weapon in an area where there had been firing, or against anyone carrying a weapon who refused to halt. Petrol bombs were classed as lethal weapons. Petrol bombers could be shot after a warning was given in the area.[36] For the army, the more aggressive stance came in reaction to PIRA's offensive. Stormont ministers craved more, pushing Freeland to cancel his deal with the Bogsiders to minimise army patrols to keep tensions low. He refused.[37]

In London, the Treasury solicitor agreed the rise in shootings justified adjusting the rules of engagement. However, allowing soldiers to shoot those carrying arms where no firing was taking place went too far.[38]

Modified instructions were issued on 30 June by the CGS.[39] The revised instructions allowed shooting in three circumstances. Firstly, shots could be fired at gunmen who were themselves shooting. Secondly, soldiers could shoot anyone carrying a weapon in an area in which firing was taking place, or had taken place very recently. Thirdly, fire could be opened on anyone carrying a weapon who refused to halt when called to do so, if there was 'a reasonable supposition that he is about to use his weapon for offensive purposes'. Petrol bombs were still to be treated as lethal weapons; efforts short of lethal force should be made to deal with them. If these failed to stop petrol bombs being thrown, soldiers could open fire after giving a warning in the area, and then treat any petrol bomber in the vicinity as a sniper.[40] Close supervision was clearly exercised by London – even by the Conservatives. In Belfast, journalists demanded more force, not less. At a press briefing Major-General Dyball was asked why soldiers had not shot any petrol bombers.[41] HQNI therefore thought the press supported a move to a tougher stance.

Pursuing the search policy agreed before the election, on Friday 3 July 1st Royal Scots discovered rifles and ammunition at 24 Balkan Street, in the Falls Road area, after receiving a tip-off from Special Branch.[42] Outside a rumour spread that during the search a dead girl was moved from her coffin.[43] A crowd in a 'vicious mood' gathered as the search party departed. As 2nd Queens, who deployed to support the Royal Scots, noted: 'this was no normal riot'. Gelignite bombs, grenades and firearms were used against troops. Fighting quickly spread through the surrounding streets. At 7.30pm the brigade commander ordered 2nd Queens to clear and secure Leeson Street, thought to be a republican stronghold. They occupied Leeson Street, taking fire from snipers in side streets. Four soldiers were shot. In return the soldiers shot one sniper. At the same time, 2nd Queens and 1st Royal Scots cleared Albert Street. Two soldiers suffered gunshot wounds.[44] The army issued 'curfew orders' for the area at 10pm.[45] Besides officers with loudhailers, a helicopter flew overhead, announcing the curfew over a loudspeaker to the area's 8,000 inhabitants.[46] By 4am on 4 July the Falls Road area was occupied. (See Illustration 3.1.) A major search operation then began.[47]

General Freeland briefed the Joint Security Committee on Saturday that five battalions took part in the operation. He claimed 'a lot of shooting throughout the night' justified imposing the curfew on residents 'for their own safety'. Ammunition was still being found, and 287 arrests had been made. Freeland intended to maintain the 'tight clamp down on the area' for the whole weekend. Exceptions would be made to permit bread and milk

Illustration 3.1 Fighting in the Falls Road area of Belfast, 4 July 1970.
(Courtesy of Keystone/Hulton Archive/Getty Images.)

deliveries and for people to attend church on Sunday. The GOC advised the detention of known extremists be considered: his first statement in favour of internment. The committee discussed whether to legalise the curfew by an Order under the Special Powers Act. A decision was deferred, but the committee did ban all processions in Belfast, Armagh and Derry for the next three days.[48] A later opinion by the Treasury solicitor concluded the GOC 'had no statutory power to impose these restrictions'.[49] Prime Minister Heath was informed about the curfew on the Saturday, and the army's view that the operation was 'very successful in administering a shock to the extremists and in boosting morale among the troops and the moderates'. Heath knew of Freeland's plan to maintain the curfew.[50] The intelligence assessment for the period argued that OIRA, dominant in the area, were determined to 'resist Army pressure and thus emulate the Brady performance in Ardoyne and Ballymacarrett the previous weekend'.[51] The Officials also wanted to safeguard the weaponry they had recently stored in the area.[52]

THE FALLOUT FROM THE FALLS ROAD CURFEW

The long-dominant impression that the curfew was plotted with malice aforethought by ministers in Stormont or Westminster has been meticulously overturned.[53] However, the operation's controversy was obvious by the time Prime Minister Heath learned what was going on, and he allowed the curfew to persist. As the Borderers recorded, after intensive gun-fights, the 'firing had died down' by 2am on 4 July, allowing the soldiers to break for tea and sandwiches.[54] Yet the curfew lasted until 9am the next day. Attempts by a priest to have the curfew called off, or for soldiers to stop using so much CS gas, were brushed aside by HQNI. The CCDC estimated about 1,000 houses were searched, accompanied by much brutality and property destruction. They recorded eighty-four cases of looting by soldiers.[55] It is suggested that Scottish regiments, such as the Black Watch, were especially brutal during the searches, smashing Catholic items in a sectarian rage.[56] The CCDC claimed this was not the case – they received as many complaints about English battalions as Scottish.[57]

Defence Minister Lord Balniel received Gerry Fitt, Frank McManus and Paddy Devlin in the House of Commons. Fitt described the situation as 'very dangerous', with public faith in the army demolished. Fitt complained about damage to property and of two girls being molested. Balniel suggested complaints be reported to two centres opened to receive them, to facilitate investigations. Fitt doubted anyone would go to these places run by the army and police.[58] Expecting complaints to surge, HQNI supplied London with briefing points. Firstly, the operation 'was not an elaborately preplanned cordon/curfew/search exercise. It was a battle.' Troops conducting a search came under attack. Secondly, any 'hardships' suffered were blamed on the 'gunmen and their hooligan accomplices'. The hardships incurred were anyway deemed trivial. Thirdly, Lisburn denied that soldiers were abusive or damaged property. Fourthly, and illogically given the previous claim, complaints 'giving prima facie grounds' for investigation would be followed up by the civilian and military police.[59] The army knew some complaints were entirely genuine. Some units checked the kit of soldiers involved in searches for 'loot'.[60] A court martial on 9 July reduced a Royal Scots corporal to the ranks, another corporal to lance-corporal, and gave a private fifty-six days in detention. A further court martial on 24 July gave a private fifty-six days in detention, and a lance-corporal was reduced to the ranks and given eighty-four days in detention. The nature of the charges is unknown.[61]

The Royal Marines applauded the arms search and derided any complaints: 'the most severe curfew has been imposed on the troops themselves. Men from 45 Commando have not had any leave for 14 days.'[62] General Freeland's civil adviser sought to deflect criticism in the curfew's aftermath by adopting a new public relations policy. As far as A. P. Cumming-Bruce was concerned, the normal press releases and conferences failed to deal with the 'unjust comments' coming the army's way. In future, HQNI had arranged for 'two of the most photogenic Ministers' (Brian Faulkner and Roy Bradford) to take turns at giving television interviews to 'deal with current slanders'. Army spokesmen would still do their job, but Lisburn aimed to use 'Stormont as our mouth-piece'. Hearing the defence in a Northern Irish accent would be more persuasive.[63] Cumming-Bruce did not consider the drawback: the army's critics could portray soldiers as unionist puppets. The MOD, however, did notice, advising Cumming-Bruce to use the ministers sparingly.[64]

The Royal Scots despaired: 'this extraordinary mass hysteria which grasped the Irish minds and bodies. They stood, they screamed, they threw. We could see this intense and fanatical hatred of goodness-knows-what being turned upon the troops.'[65] HQNI recognised the 'distress' caused to Catholics. Yet finding weapons mattered more. Chichester-Clark was triumphant, military and police morale sky-high, and ninety-three fire-arms were in the bag.[66] Freeland insisted the operation was 'anti-arms, not anti-catholic'. He declared an ambition to find arms without prejudice, but apparently lacked 'firm information about protestant arms'.[67] However, intelligence reports admitted the existence of 'as many weapons in the Shankill as there were in the Lower Falls'. The 'highly charged atmosphere', with the 12 July celebrations imminent, ruled out searching there.[68] Taoiseach Jack Lynch rightly described the British position as 'unilateral disarming'.[69] Freeland knew the main threat came from loyalism. Fear propelled him to confront republicanism instead. Reginald Maudling confirmed Belfast's decision to allow further Orange parades.[70]

Chichester-Clark expected a 'very different' line on security from the Conservatives.[71] Now he sought to capitalise on it. Writing to Maudling, he argued Labour's toleration of the no-go areas was foolish, and denigrated the defence committees, 'whose members were of very doubtful origins'. Revelling in the acclaim on Stormont's backbenches brought forth by the curfew, he dismissed all the brutality allegations as propaganda and called for more hard medicine for the rebellious. Direct rule was alluded to if London failed to proscribe the medicine so ardently desired.[72] The Cabinet Northern Ireland Committee rejected the demands as too provocative. No searches in Catholic areas were to be conducted without approval from London ministers.[73] Maudling refused to prohibit negotiations with the defence committees.[74] Chichester-Clark made no headway in a meeting in Downing Street either. Maudling felt Catholics perceived themselves to be 'taking all the punishment'. Heath asked why arms searches against Protestant extremists could not be carried out. Chichester-Clark asserted it was 'difficult to see what could be done'.[75] The problem was partly about intelligence tasking from the top: the assessment for 8–20 July contained nothing about Protestant extremists.[76] Nobody was looking for inconvenient evidence.

Freeland and Young found a way forward short of the crackdown desired by unionists: a ban on marches for six months, and regaining control over the Falls and Bogside.[77] Seven policemen went into the Bogside on 23 July, then more over the next few days.[78] Despite these careful steps, riots broke out on 31 July in New Lodge Road in Belfast. Crowds threw bottles, stones and petrol bombs.[79] For the first time, troops shot dead a man with a petrol bomb: 1st King's Own Scottish Borderers shot Daniel O'Hagan at 4.35am on the corner of Shandon Street and New Lodge Road, after warnings had been given and after petrol bombs had set vehicles alight. The army believed O'Hagan to be an IRA member, a claim denied by his family. Local witnesses said O'Hagan had not been throwing anything when soldiers shot him.[80] Riots hit Belfast for the next four nights. Trying to get a vantage point, soldiers from 2nd Queens secured observation posts (OPs) atop the Artillery Flats, and had objects thrown at them as they ascended: a javelin, a telephone and 'literally the kitchen sink'.[81] The riots, also the first time the army used rubber baton rounds, were taken to be a reaction to O'Hagan's death. Such localised, independent action made future predictions difficult.[82] PIRA retaliated on 11 August by booby-trapping a car in Crossmaglen, killing Constables Samuel Donaldson and Robert Millar, the first policemen killed by the IRA in the modern Troubles.[83]

As the riots diminished in Belfast, they flared up in Derry. For four nights from 5 August the Bogsiders erected barricades and fought the army. The ban on processions was ignored several times on 12 August, the date for the Apprentice Boys' march, prompting the army to fire CS gas at a group trying to enter the old city. Several bomb explosions and arson attempts over the previous fortnight were ascribed to Protestants intent on 'stirring things up'. Yet no action was taken against them. HQNI was more interested in the Bogside, where four groups appeared to be at play. Firstly, the 'hooligan element', non-political and looking for a fight, consisted of about seventy people. Secondly, the 'general body of householders' wanted a return to law and order, but would protect their children if they indulged in hooliganism. Thirdly, an 'intellectual element', including British and European students, anarchists and Maoists, mostly favoured restraint, with a few advocating violence, notably 'two German anarchists from Köln'. Fourthly, Republicans. OIRA and the Derry Labour Party attempted to calm the situation. Based over the border in County Donegal, the Provisionals encouraged hooliganism. Intelligence officers believed the warning that petrol bombers would be shot succeeded as a deterrent in the city.[84]

Surveying the Province on 11 August, HQNI argued Catholics blamed the Conservatives for a harsher policy since the election, though there appeared to be limited support for an IRA offensive. Large numbers of loyalists objected to the ban on parades and were willing to forcibly oppose the security forces. Security policy was hampered by the courts dealing with prosecutions somewhat lethargically. Of the 423 people arrested since 1 July, only 72 had been dealt with. Lisburn advocated 'special courts' as the solution. The government information services were poorly co-ordinated between Westminster and Stormont. Even more seriously, obstacles remained in co-ordinating the intelligence agencies. The army suggested a resident minister from London to impose coherence and 'take the political load off the GOC and Chief Constable'.[85] This was a short step from direct rule – so gained no traction. Westminster's reserves of political vision were sadly depleted. Newspaper magnate Cecil King, fond of Lord Carrington ('the nicest man, and very shrewd in a quiet way'), lamented how 'on Ireland there are no bright ideas'.[86] On his counterpart, Reginald Maudling, the judgement is invariably harsh. His lacklustre efforts to bring the constitutional parties together so as to undercut any popular support for violence proved totally inadequate.[87]

With the army's reputation amongst Catholics crumbling, General Freeland ordered a renewed impetus on community relations, co-ordinated by a new cell at Lisburn. The army derived two benefits: fostering the goodwill of the local population, and to 'encourage the two main factions in the Community into at least accepting each other ... to lay firm foundations for peace and stability'. This ambitious agenda showed an intention to address the conflict's causes. Community relations activities included running youth clubs, dances, sporting events and adventure training weekends.[88] By the end of September, soldiers were busy on multiple projects. For example, 16 Light Air Defence Regiment built an adventure playground; 2nd Coldstream Guards helped flooded residents in west Belfast by sandbagging houses, providing food, and cleaning streets and houses; the Royal Anglians in Derry taught weekly judo and gymnastics classes to teenage boys.[89] Overturning the judgement made in October 1969, the MOD advised Lisburn to appoint a staff officer for psychological operations with his own committee. The information research department of the Foreign and Commonwealth Office (FCO) agreed to support the initiative.[90] These efforts to woo public opinion sat uneasily alongside the complaints still coming into the two centres established after the Falls curfew.[91] A complaints centre was also set up on the Shankill. By 1 October ninety complaints had been received there, including eight for wrongful arrest and twenty-one for assault.[92]

Confidence in the security forces depended upon them being seen to adhere to the law. In early September ministers caught up with the controversy surrounding Daniel O'Hagan's shooting. Ian Gilmour, a junior defence minister, thought the report by HQNI raised troubling questions. It stated shots were fired at O'Hagan as the officer finished giving a second warning. Other accounts 'gave a different impression'. Evidence was missing that all means short of shooting had been tried, as the rules of engagement demanded. Gilmour did nothing about his misgivings. An early opportunity to hold the army to account for a lethal shooting was missed. Gilmour did query the recently revised 'yellow card'. Were the rules too loose – should soldiers only open fire on orders from an officer, if present?[93] On instructions from the CGS, HQNI drew up a new version of the yellow card.[94] This was the third version: the original was issued in September 1969, the second in July 1970, and the third was approved in December 1970. The latest version addressed the concern about control remaining with the commander on the spot.[95] Since the Falls curfew, investigations into civilian deaths involving the military had been conducted solely by the RUC.[96]

Another weakness in the bid to win Catholic support was the glaring inability to get on top of loyalist violence. Fear of a confrontation with Protestants continued to be deeply felt. When the Director of Defence Operational Plans (D of DOP) visited Northern Ireland in late August, he was told direct rule from London might well be needed. He called this outcome 'disastrous for the Army'. HQNI estimated seventeen units would be required to handle direct rule. The visiting director thought this too optimistic. He urged London to 'do our utmost to see that direct rule is avoided'.[97] Trepidation about loyalism was grounded in experience. When 1st Parachute Regiment moved onto the majority-Protestant Shankill in September their commander ordered patrols to revive friendships made on an earlier tour. Within hours soldiers were firing CS gas at a 1,000-strong rioting crowd.[98] The Unionist Stormont MP for the area, Desmond Boal, demanded an inquiry. When Chichester-Clark refused, Boal recruited a queen's counsel to conduct his own inquiry. The barrister criticised the army for weighing into the crowd, 'waving batons'. Soldiers arrested people 'indiscriminately', including those out shopping.[99] Though Stormont and the army ignored the inquiry, the paratroopers' inability to revive friendships amongst Protestants strengthened the case for limiting the army's commitment in Northern Ireland.

HOW MUCH TOUGHNESS WAS ENOUGH?

Strategists reflected on the Falls curfew and refused Stormont's call for escalation. With the autumn closing in, the path to confrontation with republicans was taken, as violence imposed a political cost for inaction, alternative policy avenues were shut down, and victory over the Provisionals appeared feasible. By 22 September, 26 people had died since the army's deployment, with another 841 injured. There had been 126 bombings. The expense to the taxpayer of the emergency was over £14 million (nearly £170 million in today's money).[100] To abolish Stormont, confront loyalism and restore the army's fading neutrality would have been a bold political move, achievable only with support across parliament. At their conference in October, Labour voted down a motion favouring direct rule.[101] Harold Wilson's administration left other legacies. Firstly, the decision to shy away from a showdown with loyalism persisted for many years, with ramifications for violence levels. Secondly, Callaghan's promise to Britain's police officers that they would not have to serve in Northern Ireland left only the army to prop up law and order. Thirdly, cuts made by Denis Healey put the MOD on the defensive, worrying about stretched resources. Together these factors led strategists incrementally towards a war against republicans, a tantalisingly defeatable enemy. The connections between Labour and Conservative administrations are forgotten by scholars who accept Callaghan's book on Northern Ireland as factually accurate, instead of a partisan example of blame-shifting.[102]

A review by the Home Office and MOD backed Freeland's wish for police involvement in riot control.[103] Summoning Freeland and Young to the Home Office, Maudling made clear his desire for the police to eventually take over fully from the army. Young agreed in principle. In practice, with only 3,500 policemen to hand, the prospects did not look good.[104] Emboldened by Maudling's support, Freeland confronted Young at a study day. Young left halfway through – it is not difficult to imagine why. The GOC argued those in the police who avoided riot control – including the chief constable – were swimming against the political tide. Soldiers were willing to assist the police and would work closely with the Special Patrol Group (SPG), the RUC's public order specialists. Freeland intended to withdraw from 'areas of no risk' and concentrate more on public relations and training.[105] Young responded in writing. He proposed expanding the

SPG in Belfast from four to six units (around 200 policemen), and tentatively agreed to 'positive duties in riotous situations', subject to manpower availability. However, Young insisted the police command joint riot squads, and hoped the army would bear the brunt of the violence.[106] Sir Arthur's intransigence kept the army on the front line. One potential escape route from a military clash with the IRA had been blocked off.

Wider defence policy also propelled decision-makers towards victory. Within a few weeks of assuming office, Lord Carrington realised Northern Ireland brought 'serious repercussions in Germany'.[107] A former regular guards officer, Carrington had served as parliamentary secretary (PS) to three ministers of defence, then as the first lord of the admiralty. His knowledge of defence and 'down-to-earth commonsense' made a favourable impression.[108] General Baker cautioned against taking the sympathy of NATO allies for granted. Force reductions in Europe by the USA, Canada, Belgium and the Netherlands made British withdrawals a sensitive topic.[109] Sending four battalions to Northern Ireland reduced the efficiency of two BAOR brigades.[110] The COS collectively warned that non-infantry units were ill-suited to internal security, so could only manage short tours. Keeping eight units in Northern Ireland was a strain. More than ten created 'severe penalties', especially on training. Diplomatic problems loomed. NATO's secretary-general proposed referring the matter to the defence planning committee if Britain kept withdrawing so many units. Responding to a crisis outside Europe might now be impossible. Retaining a large presence in Northern Ireland threatened the army's morale and recruiting. Soldiers disliked leaving their wives and girlfriends behind (there was accommodation for only three accompanied battalions). Infantry soldiers could look forward to returning to Northern Ireland every eighteen months. A drop in recruitment was likely to necessitate 'drastic measures to maintain the required strength of our armed forces'.[111]

The army exaggerated the grand strategic drawbacks to Northern Ireland. General Goodpaster, the Supreme Allied Commander Europe (SACEUR), judged Britain's withdrawals 'were being handled with considerable skill'.[112] His annual report for 1970 lamented shortcomings in the alliance's readiness to repel a Soviet offensive. A 'downward trend' in NATO's conventional capabilities had been in evidence for years and was likely to continue. Strong in armour, anti-tank weaponry, engineers and highly trained personnel, 1st British Corps' deficiencies lay in medical units, air defence and land-based nuclear weapons. Northern Ireland was only referred to fleetingly: 'to a limited extent this has interrupted mechanized training'. Goodpaster rated the United Kingdom's ability to meet its mission as 'moderate', equal to Germany, and better than the Netherlands and Italy.[113] This was an improvement from the 'limited' rating of 1969. The 1969 report commended an increased war authorised strength from 76 per cent to 80 per cent between December 1968 and December 1969.[114] Despite the greater emphasis on conventional forces in NATO's 'flexible response' strategy, adopted in 1967, the alliance still relied overwhelmingly on vast nuclear stockpiles to deter Soviet aggression.[115] Western security was hardly liable to disintegrate because battalions were being sent to Ireland, a point omitted by the COS in their advice to ministers. NATO was a fig leaf for a distaste for getting drawn deeper into an unpleasant civil conflagration.

The MOD successfully used these anxieties to deny HQNI the higher force level necessary for tackling political violence from both communities. In mid October the CGS predicted tension over the winter, as NICRA debated returning to street protests. PIRA were expected to mount an 'aggressive defence of entrenched areas and continuing harassment by terrorist activities'. Freeland thus estimated he needed ten battalions until November, then nine until Easter. Even so, the CGS disagreed, arguing for a reduction to eight battalions in November.[116] Carrington was mindful of the 'very considerable strain' on the army. He informed the prime minister that reducing the forces in Germany was having a serious political and military impact. He endorsed the CGS's advice and opted for eight battalions in Northern Ireland over the next six months, rather than Freeland's figure, which would have meant taking more men from NATO. Heath approved.[117] A comparatively benign situation in Derry made Belfast look like a problem that could be cracked. Brigadier Cowan reported that the security forces had isolated the 'hooligan element' from the public. Cowan confessed 'it would be unrealistic to expect the British Army to be "loved" by this intensely Nationalist (and sometimes Republican) community' in the Bogside and the Creggan.[118]

The next wave of violence hit Belfast on 29 October, in Ardoyne. A crowd was dispersed with water cannon and CS gas at about 3.30am on 30 October. The following night severe rioting in Ardoyne and Crumlin Road saw soldiers stoned, petrol-bombed and shot at with automatic weapons. Thirty-three soldiers incurred injuries. Four IRA members, one armed with a pistol, were arrested.[119] Here was a pre-packaged enemy awaiting a response. The man to give it was the recently appointed Commander Land Forces (CLF), the GOC's deputy for day-to-day operations. As a former defence fellow at Oxford, and army director of public relations, Major-General Anthony Farrar-Hockley understood the political dimensions of his role. 'Farrar the Para' was tough. He had fought in the Second World

War, Palestine, Korea, Cyprus, Aden and Borneo, earning a Military Cross and the Distinguished Service Order (twice).[120] Farrar-Hockley was remembered by a fellow officer as 'not the easiest of men to get on with'.[121] Brigadier Cowan recalled: 'I think he reckoned that he was God's greatest gift to the intelligence world, etcetera, he knew exactly what was going to happen and what the IRA were going to be up to.'[122]

Farrar-Hockley adjusted military strategy in response to the Ardoyne disturbances. He expected IRA attacks on the border and in the countryside, with hooliganism in Belfast, Derry and other towns. The threat demanded 'tougher measures to combat disorder and violence'. In the countryside this meant snap road checks, searches for arms, cordon and searches in training areas, ambushes in response to intelligence, and night patrols. In the cities and towns he ordered 'more effective use' of baton rounds and water cannon, snatch squads, and the reconnaissance of likely rioting areas to 'prepare ambushes'. As in the countryside, searches for arms, ammunition and explosives would be carried out.[123] In accordance with his approach, HQNI reviewed its policy towards the defence committees. Contact with the CCDC in Belfast broke off after the Falls curfew. The army rebuffed several attempts by the CCDC to resume contact. The Joint Security Committee pushed for liaison committees to replace the 'CCDC and the vigilante organisations'. Behind this lay Stormont's opposition to the existing committees in Catholic areas, and their suspected infiltration by OIRA. Brigadier Bayley argued that the replacement committees should assist the army in understanding public opinion, giving advance warning of changes in the security situation. They could also be a forum for explaining the goals behind security policy. Bayley advocated the committees include 'as wide a range of opinion as carries weight locally'.[124]

As the year ended, the mood amongst policymakers was optimistic. The UKREP confidently proclaimed a 'great improvement in the law and order situation'. The bombings then happening were 'trifling affairs', conducted by the IRA and, in fewer cases, Protestant extremists. Three battalions had been moved out of Belfast into the countryside, restoring a more normal feel to much of the city.[125] Farrar-Hockley's tougher measures appeared to be working. A review on future marches by John Taylor, minister of state for home affairs at Stormont, advised they be permitted. He argued marching was integral to Ulster's political culture; trying to ban them altogether would create immense problems. Taylor conceded the overall number might be reduced.[126] On a visit to Northern Ireland in early January 1971 General Baker noted the much calmer atmosphere, especially in Derry.[127] It was no wonder the Falls curfew impressed so few leading figures in the British firmament at the time as a decisive turning-point. General Freeland, however, struck a more downbeat note. He believed the Northern Ireland commitment to be deeply damaging to the army:

> We are a political football to be reviled by either side of the sectarian barrier as it suits them. There are few thanks and little real appreciation of what this rotten job is going to mean for the Army if we are committed to it for too long. The total involvement of the Army also acts as a disincentive for this divided community to get a move on and try and solve their problems; it is very convenient to have the British Army to shelter behind and to blame for their own short-comings! ... the Army has been committed to a job where there appears to be little hope of a political initiative. The danger facing us immediately ahead is that the Regimental Officers and even their soldiers are beginning to wonder where this job is leading.[128]

The calm is normally believed to have evaporated in February 1971. Responsibility is placed either on PIRA, for killing the first British soldier, or on the British Army, for provoking PIRA by searching for arms.[129] In fact, the storm broke on the afternoon of 11 January. Soldiers came under bombardment with stones and petrol bombs on the nationalist Ballymurphy estate in Belfast. People from the area demanded the army leave. Far from doing so, on 14 January a joint army–police search operation was mounted, which 'provoked violent local reaction'. The rioting that evening witnessed multiple arrests, baton rounds, and soldiers having automatic gunfire and gelignite bombs aimed at them.[130] Discussing these events at the Joint Security Committee, the GOC believed the Provisionals were trying to get men out to attack soldiers, though they had limited success. Searches for weapons located a Thompson submachine gun, ammunition and rockets. It was questionable whether these finds were worth the resulting bother – the GOC admitted the searches 'heightened tension in the area'. But Chichester-Clark wanted more. Freeland put up some resistance: blanket search operations would only be permitted after shootings, and with approval from ministers in London.[131]

When Northern Ireland ministers felt fobbed off by the generals, they appealed above their heads. On 18 January James Chichester-Clark, Senator Jack Andrews and Brian Faulkner travelled to London to complain about the army. Freeland's softness accounted for the Ballymurphy rioting. Stormont proposed troops go 'to the very heart of the trouble spots', to stamp down on unrest. Searches should be stepped up. Lord Carrington pointed out that more frequent large searches would require at least two extra battalions in Northern Ireland. Faulkner disputed Carrington's opinion that the Falls curfew showed large searches were a bad idea. He highlighted the absence of serious riots in the Falls since then. Maudling cautioned against alienating moderate Catholic opinion. Carrington concurred: indiscriminate searching 'would do more harm than good'.[132] Chichester-Clark maintained that violence in Catholic areas was organised by PIRA. He advocated making life 'more unpleasant for the inhabitants of these areas', so they pushed the IRA out.[133] Ten days later Chichester-Clark repeated his frustration at riots, though recognising the security forces faced a dilemma. Excessive severity could provoke more trouble, whereas lenience incensed Protestants. The army must stop negotiating with vigilantes and start 'suppressing them'. Stormont detected 'the beginning of a massive IRA campaign'. Carrington described the army's task as 'distasteful', 'not its proper role' and 'detrimental to military commitments elsewhere'. Stronger measures would be counterproductive.[134] General Freeland's orders issued on 3 February attempted to balance Stormont's wishes with sufficient restraint:

> Our first and overriding priority must be to seek out and bring to trial the ring leaders of the subversive elements. Our second priority must be the capture of arms, explosives and other devices. Our third priority, which may at times have to come second, must be to stamp out as quickly as possible any riots or disturbances, making the maximum number of arrests. Our fourth priority will be a continuation of protective and deterrent operations throughout the Province.[135]

His plan came alive at first light on 3 February. An intelligence-based operation was mounted to capture incendiary devices being manufactured in Clonard, off the Falls Road. One source of the intelligence, John Kavanagh, was the first informer to be killed by the IRA, on 27 January. HQNI told London 'a mass reaction was not anticipated' to the searching of eight houses, yet assembled a 'strong force', including reserves from Derry.[136] Experience showed quite clearly that searches caused aggravation. Indeed, the search was initiated by Farrar-Hockley against the advice of the intelligence staff at HQNI.[137] The reaction initially came from women and children, later joined by men. A few arrests quietened things temporarily, before crowds gathered in Clonard and the Falls in the afternoon. Petrol bombs were thrown. At 8pm unrest spread to Ballymurphy and Ardoyne, then to New Lodge. Seven soldiers were wounded, one very seriously. According to one report the army 'fired back 4 times and inflicted casualties'.[138] Another source claimed soldiers fired six times, and also used baton rounds and water cannon. They arrested fifty-four people. Three times soldiers came under machine-gun fire.[139]

HQNI attributed the violence to PIRA's 1st and 2nd Battalions, based in Clonard. At first light on 4 February soldiers cordoned off Ardoyne and Clonard, then searched 'houses known to harbour IRA members or sympathisers'. People were allowed to enter and exit the areas only by submitting to a search.[140] The army decided to counter claims that the searches occurred without proper cause. Major-General Farrar-Hockley named Frank Card, Billy McKee, Leo Martin, and Liam and Kevin Hannaway as PIRA leaders in a televised press conference, to 'unsettle the local IRA leadership' and 'discredit them'.[141] In effect, the army obeyed the Northern Ireland government's injunction to stop negotiations, ignoring Carrington and Maudling's more cautious line. For a fortnight the PIRA leaders had been talking covertly to the army – Farrar-Hockley's comments enraged them.[142] The inhabitants of Ardoyne 'fiercely opposed' soldiers, with such severity that search teams were withdrawn at 11.45am, until reinforcements arrived.[143] Could such widespread opposition have been entirely the IRA's doing? No weapons were found in Ardoyne or Clonard. Troops poured into west Belfast. Small crowds in New Lodge, Ardoyne and the Falls threw petrol and gelignite bombs at soldiers, who made sixty arrests.[144]

Violence resumed the next evening, Friday 5 February; 94th Locating Regiment, Royal Artillery deployed under command of 3rd Queens. At 12.45am on 6 February H and I Troops met fierce resistance from a crowd about seventy-five to a hundred-strong at New Lodge Road and Lepper Street, throwing rocks, milk bottles, gelignite bombs, nail bombs and petrol bombs. At 12.50am the battery commander ordered I Troop to snatch a man who appeared to be directing the riot. Three baton rounds were fired, one of which hit the man, but the squad failed to catch him. Gelignite and petrol bombs were thrown, and automatic fire hit a soldier in the foot. Further baton rounds were fired. H and I Troops moved back down Lepper Street as the crowd followed closely on. At 1.15am a gelignite bomb and about fifteen rounds of automatic fire hit five soldiers. Gunner Robert Curtis died instantly.[145] Elsewhere in Belfast an armoured truck driven by 1st Parachute Regiment was set on fire. The Paras shot dead one person and injured others. In the nationalist Bone district in north Belfast, 3rd Queens shot dead a man who was firing a pistol from within a crowd. The man killed by the Paras, Bernard Watt, was alleged to be about to throw a bomb. His inquest found the evidence inconclusive. James Saunders, the man killed in the Bone, was an officer in PIRA's 3rd Battalion. Gunner Curtis had joined the army against his parents' wishes. He was the first soldier killed on operations in Northern Ireland. That morning Chichester-Clark publicly declared his government to be at war with PIRA.[146] Niall Ó Dochartaigh argues this violence escalated 'beyond the intentions or expectations of those in charge on both sides'.[147] The argument presented here is that the escalation was entirely intentional.

A SHOOTING WAR WITH THE IRA

The MOD was split on what to make of these events. Julian Thompson, an assistant secretary to the Chiefs of Staff, noted with delicacy: 'there was not a great deal of, how shall I put it, unanimity as to how it [Northern Ireland] should be dealt with'.[148] The Director-General of Intelligence (DGI) argued the casualties inflicted on PIRA might have damaged the movement's morale, but the 'hard core' were unlikely to be discouraged. As intelligence suggested the IRA lacked popular support, Lord Carrington urged the army not to antagonise the population. He criticised Farrar-Hockley for publicly naming IRA leaders without approval from London.[149] Ian Gilmour, a junior defence minister, shared the scepticism about the operations against PIRA. Between 16 January and 11 February 1971 the army had searched thirty-three houses, finding a rifle, two pistols and ammunition in Ballymurphy, ammunition in Andersonstown, training publications in Clonard, and one rifle, two shotguns and four shotgun cartridges in Springfield – a 'scarcely overwhelming' haul.[150] They suggest Farrar-Hockley's intention was to provoke PIRA into gun-battles.

Gilmour and Richard Sharples, the Home Office minister, attempted to mend the damage in a meeting with nationalist politicians on 12 February. Formed in August 1970, the Social Democratic and Labour Party (SDLP) aimed to achieve Irish unification and civil rights through constitutional means.[151] The party's creation promised to galvanise the nationalist cause in a fashion with which Stormont and London could transact. Gerry Fitt and Austin Currie pressed for a political initiative. Fitt believed the army acted 'on misleading information to make searches in volatile areas, and were being used deliberately by extremists to cause trouble'. Paddy Devlin accused the army of singing to Stormont's tune. John Hume decried the breakdown in dialogue. His regular contacts with officers in Derry had come to an unexplained end. Given recent events, Gilmour's retort was unconvincing: 'there had been no shift of policy towards over-reaction'.[152] A Home Office briefing told Edward Heath the most recent violence started in mid January 1971 when the IRA tried to win Catholic support by attacking the security forces. Apart from rioting on the Shankill on 23–4 January, trouble had been concentrated in Catholic areas. There was a growing number of bombings, the majority carried out by PIRA. The worst violence broke out after the army searched for arms in Clonard on 3 February. The Home Office portrayed this operation as essential to pre-empt an impending offensive by PIRA: 'The Brady group were known to have been planning a major campaign of violence for some time.' Despite the most volatile days in Belfast since August 1969, the Home Office noted 'less discouraging aspects', namely:

> The Army has had an identifiable enemy for almost the first time. Its prompt reaction has done much to prevent the Protestant population from taking the situation into its own hands. Such a development is still possible, and is made more likely when, as has happened, the IRA publicly buries its dead or innocent Protestant children are shot at.... Equally encouraging has been the inactivity of the Goulding group of the IRA, which has not apparently come to any reconciliation with the Brady group, and the inability of the latter group to get any large measure of public support.... Finally, it is encouraging that, through all this, disturbances in Londonderry have been only sporadic and on a small scale.[153]

An offensive against PIRA, evaluated at an early stage, thus appeared winnable. This view came to dominate government thinking, despite reservations amongst leading Northern Irish nationalist politicians and some in the MOD. The British Army did not have a monopoly on overconfidence: they and the PIRA leadership thought their opponent lacked the resolve to fight on.[154] When Lieutenant-General Vernon Erskine-Crum took over as GOC different choices might have been made. In his first address to the press, he stated: 'This is not a "campaign" in which to compare casualties, nor a "war" to be "won".'[155] He suffered a heart attack the next day and died a month later. As in 1969, the worst-case loomed in strategic thinking. A paper by the COS underscored the dangers of direct rule. Guerrilla warfare, intercommunal violence fuelled by access to 70,000 legally held firearms and attacks on the security forces could be expected. 'Considerably greater military resources' would be needed, particularly as the UDR's reliability might falter.[156] The director of intelligence at HQNI argued that under direct rule most RUC officers would carry on with their jobs. However, 'some elements of the RUC would be less than ardent in their duties, others would actively connive against the administration, and the security of the Special Branch would be in question'.[157] The authorities relied overwhelmingly on Special Branch for intelligence. The government thus wished to avoid confronting Protestants not only because of the prospective violence, but because a core element in the state's security apparatus might turn against its masters.

Gunner Curtis' death propelled the British government towards war. Beforehand, the evidence supported Chichester-Clark's assessment that Edward Heath regarded Northern Ireland with little interest, even 'as a bad smell'.[158] Now Heath intervened decisively. At Chequers on 13 February he argued 'the time had perhaps come to reconsider the strategy for the security forces'. Public opinion in Britain 'would not indefinitely tolerate the situation in which British soldiers were being killed in Belfast'. The dynamic had changed from intercommunal rioting to 'outright shooting between the British Army and the IRA'. Strategists should ask 'how the tactical advantage could be transferred to the security forces'. Ministers authorised an operation on 15 February to detain known republicans.[159] A war between the IRA and the British Army was underway. Heath reiterated to Carrington his desire to 'transfer the confrontation to ground and times of our choosing'. He asked the defence secretary to examine whether more effort should be made to stop IRA movement across the border with the Republic.[160] Although the border suggestion marked a change in emphasis, Heath's wish for the army to take the initiative had effectively already happened with Farrar-Hockley's searches at the beginning of the month. Echoing senior military sentiments, Lord Carrington argued the focus should remain on PIRA's 'urban bases in the Catholic areas'.[161]

Street violence between Catholics and Protestants, and against the security forces, continued over the following weeks. On 26 February crowds clashed in the Markets area in Belfast. The unrest got worse in the evening, with petrol bombs and nail bombs being thrown.[162] Two police officers were killed and four injured by gunfire at Oldpark Road. As a result the chief constable decided to re-arm all foot patrols in Belfast. The Northern Ireland minister of education pressed for republican areas to be sealed off and searched. Major-General Thomas Acton, chief of staff at HQNI and Acting GOC since Erskine-Crum's death, preferred to keep the security forces in 'suspect areas' rather than closing them off and permitting the IRA to dominate them.[163] Acton now stood against a whirlwind of demands from Stormont for harsher repression. He 'explained that top Army priority was to eliminate the Bradyite leaders by isolating them from the Roman Catholic community. Some had already been eliminated by shooting or detention and more would be.' He accepted 'community alienation' as an inevitable by-product.[164] A bid for another curfew in the Falls was resisted following shootings there. Chichester-Clark exclaimed 'the sensible element of the Roman Catholic population would welcome stern measures against the IRA and, anyway, the time was past for allowing people's feelings to dictate tactics'.[165] Stymied, Chichester-Clark tried to circumvent Lisburn, appealing to the home secretary for 'vigorous' action and threatened to resign unless security policy changed. Maudling defended the army's policy to only search areas where firearms were used, but agreed to consult with the defence secretary about possible changes.[166]

Major-General Acton advised London to reject Chichester-Clark's ultimatum. Allowing Stormont to dictate tactical decisions would undermine the army's freedom of action. Acton argued there had been no change in the situation drastic enough to warrant the measures being demanded.[167] Maudling met with Northern Ireland ministers on 4 March. They tried another tack this time, emphasising the economic costs imposed by the ongoing turmoil. Maudling again delayed by stating the need to consult with Carrington.[168] Some Northern Ireland ministers clearly viewed all Catholics 'as an enemy population ... one member of the Northern Ireland Cabinet told Mr. Maudling that he would not mind seeing the Army mow down a crowd among whom a gunman had taken refuge'.[169] Further trouble tended to support the Stormont case. The security forces searched a bar in the Falls area on the afternoon of 5 March, after learning that three Protestants who were storing arms for OIRA had been kidnapped by the Provisionals. Though the hostages were released later elsewhere in the city and the security forces recovered nearly 6,000 rounds of ammunition, the search provoked rioting. By night-time barricades were being erected, and petrol and nail bombs being thrown. Soldiers from 3rd Parachute Regiment opened fire around midnight, injuring one man and killing another. Ballymurphy, Ardoyne and New Lodge also experienced petrol bombings and shootings.[170]

When the cabinet met on 10 March, the home secretary noted with relief the recent decline in intercommunal violence. Unfortunately, though, that meant popular rage fixed ever more on the security forces. Maudling registered Chichester-Clark's threat to resign as genuine. An impending meeting of the Ulster Unionist Council might bring about his downfall, leaving the field clear for a hardliner such as William Craig. Craig's advocacy of re-arming the RUC, reviving the B Specials, introducing internment and keeping the army present in strength alarmed the British government. Maudling would rather impose direct rule than see such a man in power. His cabinet colleagues agreed.[171] Maudling's gravest shortcoming was his lack of imagination. He left the army waiting for a political solution while doing nothing to search for one. His only strong feelings about Northern Ireland were that withdrawing the army must cause civil war – 'the abdication of responsibility' – and that Protestant power should be respected.[172] The MOD regarded its prime objective as 'to bring about a situation in which the Army need no longer be deployed in massive strength'.[173] Though the government kept the tough-speaking William Craig from high office, in effect someone who spoke in softer tones came to apply a very similar, repressive agenda.

The calls on Chichester-Clark for drastic steps amplified radically when three off-duty soldiers were murdered on 10 March. The young Royal Highland Fusiliers were lured from a pub and shot by the IRA, their bodies dumped on a hillside road. Their deaths hardened attitudes in the army. Raymond Hall, 3rd Light Infantry's sergeant-major, recalled, 'We became more determined then to stamp out the IRA ... we were now, not on the Protestant side, but we were now being attacked by the Catholics.'[174] The Parachute Regiment deduced:

> it is not the Shankill loyalist and our many ex-Servicemen friends with whom we shall do battle; it is the provisional groups of the IRA now recognisably active ... as soldiers' lives are in danger shooting may be the only solution to the sniper, nail bomber and arsonist.[175]

Paratroopers arrived in force on the lower Falls the next morning, ready for vengeance. They threw a cordon around the house of a PIRA officer killed a few days earlier to prevent a military funeral. The grieving family 'did not take the CO's words kindly' when he tried to justify this highly confrontational intervention. Though the Paras stopped a PIRA honour guard firing shots over the coffin, the move antagonised the community.[176] On 12 March thousands of shipyard workers marched to demand internment for the IRA. That afternoon Chichester-Clark and his ministers met shop stewards from Harland and Wolff, and International Computers. The leading shop steward, loyalist Billy Hull, said the marchers were protesting not only at the soldiers' murder, but also the government's failure in 'overcoming the subversive elements'.[177] Amidst these events Lieutenant-General Harry Tuzo, a gunner who earned a Military Cross in Normandy, arrived as the new GOC. A senior civil servant described Tuzo as 'a handsome, engaging and energetic man, a thinker and a diplomat as well as a man of action'.[178] The briefing given to him on arrival listed riot control as the most prominent military practice, adding 'Also elimination of IRA gunmen'.[179]

Tuzo's first major encounter with Stormont ministers thus came as the familiar pro-repression refrain hit an especially feverish pitch.

Chichester-Clark urged intensified military operations. The ministers of agriculture and commerce foretold a dreadful Protestant backlash unless the army did something drastic. Tuzo made the right sympathetic noises and promised to examine how tactics might be modified.[180] Tuzo thought Protestant public opinion craved 'ostentatiously firm measures', preferably for consumption on television. He refused to change his policy or the rules of engagement, divining 'no magic formula'. In his opinion Stormont's wishes were justified only by their political logic and had no value in security terms.[181] The UKREP tipped off the Home Office that Chichester-Clark was heading for a row with Maudling. Chichester-Clark planned to demand massive army reinforcements, a 'third force' under Stormont control (in other words, the B Specials reborn) and a junior MOD minister based in Northern Ireland to ensure the army obeyed Stormont. Chichester-Clark was prepared to publicly announce these measures had been rejected if he did not get his way. Sir Harold Black, his cabinet secretary, confessed this amounted to blackmail.[182] Maudling wondered whether army reinforcements alone might do the trick. Heath objected to reinforcements exceeding those already planned for the Easter period.[183] There were limits to his willingness to save Chichester-Clark's administration.

The showdown between London and Stormont took place on 16 March. As expected, Chichester-Clark requested the occupation of Catholic areas, generous use of cordons and curfews, and further military support for the police. Without 'drastic measures' people might 'take the law into their own hands', leading to a 'general uprising'. Heath argued relations between Protestants and Catholics were improving. General Tuzo offered cordons and curfews in limited areas for short periods. The CGS said permanently locating troops in Catholic areas might upset moderate opinion and leave soldiers vulnerable to attack. Heath promised only a 'more active policy on patrolling, cordons and curfews' should be adopted. Chichester-Clark desired four or five more battalions. Tuzo countered that even such a reinforcement was unlikely to make much difference in the campaign against the IRA, where lack of intelligence constituted the main weakness. Heath was blunt: 'it was unrealistic to suppose that if the communities in Northern Ireland were really bent on civil war, this could be effectively prevented by the provision of more British troops'.[184] When the Cabinet Northern Ireland Committee convened the next day, they agreed to send two battalions to bolster Chichester-Clark's standing, and to authorise Tuzo to conduct 'a more effective demonstration of preventive activity'.[185]

Minor concessions such as these only appeased Stormont for a few days. The police appreciated the closer support now coming from the army. General Tuzo counselled against 'dancing to the enemy's tune'. Chichester-Clark and his ministers were not pleased. He adjourned the meeting to speak to Edward Heath on the telephone.[186] Chichester-Clark said he intended to resign that evening. The further forces sent by London were insufficient, and the army's approach was still too soft for his liking. Chichester-Clark pressed for 'a confrontation', to 'either kill or capture I.R.A.'. Heath decided to send the CGS and Lord Carrington to Belfast for further discussion.[187] Before he went, Carrington received a report from Acton, Farrar-Hockley and Burroughs. The UKREP and the generals firmly opposed a harder line because it would only increase Catholic support for PIRA. They understood Chichester-Clark's problems with unionist opinion, but considered the existing security policy to be working. Acton and Burroughs made the important point that the recent violence, though very dramatic and upsetting, had been confined to a small part of Belfast. They criticised Northern Ireland ministers for 'flapping'.[188]

When Lord Carrington and General Baker arrived in Belfast, James Chichester-Clark lambasted the security forces for condoning the no-go areas, leading to 'a massive loss of confidence throughout the country'. Carrington and the CGS repeated old promises: quicker reaction to IRA attacks, examining whether to base army posts in 'difficult areas' and using the UDR. The only new measure was public relations work to 'counter ill-informed criticism'.[189] London's record of the meeting gives a fuller sense of the British reasons for preventing Stormont from dictating military strategy. Politicians in Northern Ireland under-estimated the British public's 'disgust' with events, which could be expected to result in people questioning whether the Province should remain in the United Kingdom. Showing remarkable ignorance about the army's aggressive search tactics over the preceding weeks, Carrington argued against antagonising 'certain sections of the population'. Chichester-Clark called for precisely such a 'rough house in the troublesome areas'. London's resistance prompted him to resign as prime minister, as he had threatened he would.[190] Many in the Conservative Party sympathised with the outgoing Northern Irish prime minister. At a meeting of the home affairs committee on 22 March, attended by over 160 backbenchers, Maudling and Carrington came under severe criticism for refraining from tougher action.[191] Chichester-Clark's replacement, Brian Faulkner, knew London was bound to give him a freer rein in the deepening war.

CONCLUSION

Only in presentational terms did Brian Faulkner differ from William Craig, or other rabble-rousers like Ian Paisley. Widely credited as the most accomplished politician on the Northern Ireland scene, Faulkner's indirect approach to repression enabled the British government to pretend, to the public and themselves, that the utmost restraint prevailed over military strategy at all times. Even his political opponents saw green shoots, welcoming the appointment of Northern Ireland Labour Party politician David Bleakley as minister for community relations in late March.[192] The self-deception at the heart of British military strategy in Northern Ireland also stemmed from the incremental nature of the escalation. Each gradual change in tactics, whether the expansion in house searching or the adoption of rubber bullets, seemed reasonable and carefully considered to those who gave approval. Certainly, on occasion the step towards innovation was initiated by the soldiers in Northern Ireland without waiting for permission from London. Such tactical responsiveness happened under Labour control too and was, in truth, unavoidable unless the military were to be denied any freedom of action whatsoever.

The move towards war against the IRA began prior to the 1970 general election and must be understood in terms of the army's place in British democracy, and relations with friends as much as enemies. Labour and Conservative governments agreed on fundamental questions about the conflict: that the ghost of militant loyalism should not be awakened, that the British police be kept out of it and that wider defence commitments must not be sacrificed for Northern Ireland's sake. The cabinet-sanctioned strategy of war against the IRA only came into play from March 1971 because the Labour Party presented no opposition. Reluctance to tackle loyalism head-on, to search the Shankill for weapons and to arrest UVF members derived from British democracy too, rather than pragmatic considerations about manpower availability alone. Indeed, the NATO argument seems to have been made most emphatically by British commanders hesitant to condemn their men to endless, thankless tours in Northern Ireland. Entreaties from foreign embassies to restore the battalions back to West Germany are notable by their absence from the archives.

Though cabinet ministers and soldiers alike held Northern Ireland's populist unionists in nothing less than contempt, they recognised their fundamental political identity as the majority in a democratic system. Turning down the more outrageous demands for repression blinded military strategists to the slow slide towards war they had embarked upon. How could anyone reasonably object to house searches? Catholics in Northern Ireland were not privy to the conversations where British ministers and generals refused to machine-gun them in the street. What they could see was their doors being kicked down at all hours, their floorboards being ripped up, while Protestant neighbours in streets close by went on with their lives, unmolested. The Falls Road curfew might have incurred less ire if the Shankill had been searched soon after. Meanwhile PIRA only needed to mobilise a small number to shoot and bomb, to kill one British soldier, then to murder brutally three more, before the long sought-after provocative logic kicked in. How keenly Catholics empathised with the IRA's growing aggression the army did not know. They had already stopped listening.

4

EDWARD HEATH'S BID FOR VICTORY

The GOC said that while the situation remained serious the events of last night during which the IRA and associates suffered a fair casualty rate had been to Army advantage. Street crowds were substantially reduced and the position was resolving itself into a proper military war against the terrorists. If this state of affairs could be maintained it would increasingly favour Army operations.[1]

Joint Security Committee, August 1971

The introduction of internment in August 1971 is regarded as a watershed moment. Breaking ancient prohibitions against detention without trial and forcible confessions, Britain's democratic leaders incited a fervent reaction across Northern Ireland. Classified as 'a political and security catastrophe', internment is widely believed to have rested upon 'poor intelligence', hence the arrest of hundreds of innocent people, and no loyalists.[2] In a broader sense, the growing violence in the months surrounding August is still written off as a time when 'a decision was never made at any political level to defeat the IRA militarily'.[3] The suggestion that British strategy lacked purpose, or stumbled into repression by mistake, deserves to be challenged. What if we begin from a more troubling starting-point, borne out by comparative studies on war, that liberal democracies are willing to attack the innocent for perceived strategic gains?[4] Rather than viewing internment as a single event, the implications of Prime Minister Heath granting the army permission to wage war against the IRA are examined over a longer time span. Though dissent from this line always existed, only from November 1971 did the strategic consensus begin to decisively turn away from a belief that the IRA could, and should, be defeated.

The wartime mindset began to take hold because the initial operations in the spring and early summer of 1971 appeared to be successful. Even as PIRA escalated their violence in May, to include more bombings, shootings and assassination attempts, soldiers retained some sympathy for the Catholic population, and thought of their own approach as reasonably

93

discriminate. An arms amnesty, searches and arrests provided plentiful statistical evidence to feed the optimistic mood. Improvements to the military intelligence system gave credence to General Tuzo's wish for a gradual, low-key attrition of the IRA, especially targeting the Provisional leadership. Scholars generally attribute the demise of these last vestiges of restraint, embodied in the decision by London to permit internment, to a fear of Faulkner losing power and thus triggering direct rule.[5] Faulkner's hand was forced by unionist outrage at the accelerating PIRA bombings.[6] Yet the turn towards repression began building months before internment, and derived as much from the nature of British common law, Britain's global commitments and London's calculations about blame politics as it did from fears of a loyalist backlash. The escalation in the war against the IRA took place gradually. Strategists pondered whether to continue, or whether to listen to voices calling for restraint, and then fought on. The growing hurt done to those adjacent to the targets of the military failed to register as meaningful enough to force any major rethink in strategy.

'RAPID AND AGGRESSIVE ACTION' – WITHIN LIMITS

The British Army's shift towards an offensive against the IRA is often believed to have coincided, more or less, with internment.[7] The change can be detected earlier on, and derived from pressures unrelated to London's desire to avoid direct rule. General Tuzo's orders on 24 March for 'rapid and aggressive action' satisfied the new Northern Ireland prime minister, Brian Faulkner.[8] However, the MOD had earlier told Lisburn in no uncertain terms to resist calls for internment.[9] General Tuzo understood as well as his predecessor the intention to avoid what internment represented – indiscriminate repression. Brigadier Frank Kitson, commanding 39 Brigade in Belfast, described his approach as 'de-escalation and attrition'. He aimed to keep Catholics on-side whilst wearing down the IRA.[10] Stormont ministers kept up their traditional insistence on crackdowns. Tuzo, like Freeland, often declined. Minister of Agriculture Harry West's call for a search in the Bogside in July met a brick wall. Tuzo argued it 'would only create a disorderly situation which was the objective of the IRA'.[11] Those further down the command chain shared the sentiment. A 1st Parachute Regiment major noted the IRA trying to 'goad troops into hasty action which will bring troops into disrepute'.[12]

Faulkner went to Downing Street on 1 April with General Sir Michael Carver and Howard Smith, the incoming CGS and UKREP. Faulkner planned to declare a weapons amnesty, and to review all licences to hold revolvers.[13] Within a fortnight 2 machine guns, 852 rifles, 670 handguns,

244 shotguns, 67 grenades and 110,769 rounds of ammunition had been handed in. The check on firearms certificates produced 2,421 weapons.[14] Adding to the rosy vista, Easter 1971 passed off more peacefully than many feared.[15] On 13 April parading Junior Orangemen approached Catholic houses in Ballymacarrett, prompting shots to be fired to defend the area. Nine companies of troops were drafted in as 2,000 Protestants tried to attack St Matthew's church. The next day eighty-two houses nearby were searched. That evening soldiers held a mob back from St Matthew's. Meanwhile, PIRA leaders Francis Card, William McKee and Brian Burns were arrested in Ardoyne for possessing explosives.[16] These events possessed the raw ingredients for a public relations bonanza. Catholics had been saved from a loyalist mob. Well-known Provisionals sat in police custody. Without a psychological operations team at HQNI, no mark was made on public perceptions of the army's ability to protect the population impartially.

The VCGS, Cecil Blacker, believed 'the IRA have had a considerable sorting out in Belfast and haven't liked it'.[17] Outside Belfast quiet mostly prevailed until late April.[18] In Derry 1st Royal Anglians appreciated 'only a handful of miscontents indulge in the jolly sport' of rioting. Policemen patrolled the Bogside and the Creggan. Soldiers courted local girls.[19] More people expressed their opinions peacefully than by enlisting in the IRA. In the afternoon on 6 April a hundred residents gathered outside the Taggart Hall to protest against army operations in Ballymurphy. A crowd convened again in the evening: the few stones thrown bothered nobody.[20] Similar demonstrations cropped up throughout the spring. In New Lodge in late May 400 people listened to anti-army speeches. The police remarked: 'No incidents.'[21] Amidst such a lull the Parachute Regiment briefed their men that Catholics 'tend towards conciliation' and must be given 'the same rights' as other citizens in the United Kingdom.[22] Kenneth Ambrose, a Royal Green Jacket, found Belfast in May 'very British ... I'd grown up in streets like this'. Ambrose felt 'a great deal of sympathy for the Catholics, because I'd read in the newspapers, as everybody else had, about how they were the underdog'. His affinity vanished as the shootings began.[23]

Military strategists concentrated on PIRA as the main threat, especially in Belfast, where the organisation was strongest and conducted the most operations. PIRA controlled eighteen companies there. Brigadier Kitson characterised the volunteers as 'basic working class people' with an 'emotional longing for the unity of Northern Ireland with the Republic ... most of their motivation comes from a desire for prestige amongst their neighbours'. Provisional company commanders exercised considerable autonomy from higher command.[24] The PIRA offensive in spring 1971 took several forms. John Kavanagh was shot in late January, the first person killed on suspicion of being an informer. Detective Inspector Cecil Patterson, a Special Branch officer, was shot dead in February, causing 'jubilation in IRA circles since he was known to be one of their best informed officers on IRA activities'.[25] A bombing campaign launched in late April was intended to inflict economic damage that the British government would end up paying for.[26] In the first week of May bombs exploded at public buildings, bars and homes, including those of two Special Branch officers.[27]

The following week an IRA team mounted a landmine and machine-gun attack on a Royal Engineers patrol near Cullaville.[28] Private Larter became the first military gunshot casualty in Derry for months, shot in the hand accompanying his fiancé. Off-duty troops were henceforth banned in the Bogside and the Creggan.[29] Breaking off social contacts made antagonism between civilians and soldiers likelier. On 15 May the Royal Highland Fusiliers in Belfast stopped three men in a car, who opened fire with a submachine gun. The soldiers shot dead PIRA volunteer William Reid.[30] A week later a car on the M1 motorway opened fire on an army Landrover.[31] The bombing of Springfield Road police station on 25 May killed Sergeant Michael Willets, who won the George Cross for shielding a mother and her children from the blast.[32] By 11 June, 1st Parachute Regiment possessed 'Positive int[elligence] beginning of main IRA offensive'.[33] During May and June explosions struck such targets as a reservoir in Derry, the police station in Lurgan and a hotel in County Antrim.[34]

The security forces responded with searches and arrests. Between 1 January and 6 July 1971 they arrested 817 people, of whom 420 were subsequently convicted in court.[35] Remarkably, the security forces even waylaid Ruairí Ó Brádaigh, president of Provisional Sinn Féin and such an important figure that the Provisionals were often referred to as the 'Brady IRA'. Stopped in the street, he was sent on his way because 'nothing was found'.[36] Finds made during house searches built up over time, giving the impression of progress. During the first four months of 1971, 4 machine guns, 21 shotguns, 38 rifles, 105 handguns, 38 grenades, 280lbs of gelignite and 13,875 rounds of ammunition were discovered.[37] A single search operation in the Newtownards Road in Belfast on 26 June recovered a grenade, two nail bombs, thirty-three rounds of ammunition, radio receivers, two small-arms training manuals and three bloodstained field dressings.[38] A soldier reflected on house searches:

> There was nothing new in this task, we had done it so many times before.
> Brief simple orders, stressing the importance of thoroughness, politeness

and of all the precautions we have devised against allegations (sometimes malicious allegations) of search parties stealing or wantonly damaging property, and then the teams were away. House after house; each a bright centre of family life belying the drab darkness of the street outside, and yet as we entered the door into a little world of light and warmth, so at once another barrier was closed against us, a barrier of sullen distrust and antipathy.[39]

HQNI set great store on intelligence to identify the enemy. The notion that there 'was very little actionable intelligence before internment' is widespread.[40] Yet military intelligence improved before internment. From at least March 1970 army units ran undercover agents.[41] In January 1971 a General Staff Officer, Grade 1 (GSO 1) was posted to Lisburn with responsibility for intelligence, and with three other officers and several clerks to support him.[42] By late April the number of military intelligence officers had doubled since the start of the year.[43] Soldiers from 3rd Light Infantry patrolled in 'black face' camouflage at night with infra-red imaging devices, and put surveillance teams in derelict houses and sheds;[44] 3rd Parachute Regiment placed IRA leaders in their area under continuous surveillance, causing 'considerable anxiety' to those watched. The battalion chaplain liaised with local priests, building a better sense of attitudes in Catholic communities.[45] The headquarters of 16 Brigade, based in Lurgan, created a card index of personalities, groups and organisations. A map demarcated the Catholic and Protestant populations, and the strengths of republican and loyalist groups. Pins were placed in another map to denote security incidents. Intelligence summaries were regularly compiled, and an order of battle maintained for PIRA and OIRA – with a photographic library of members.[46] After June 1971, 19 Brigade formed a 'Bomb Squad' with the police to disrupt the IRA's bombing campaign.[47] Tuzo's preference for gradual attrition might have worked if given time.

General Tuzo's bid for limited attrition suffered from self-inflicted difficulties – in addition to PIRA's desire to provoke British overreaction. Intelligence-gathering was affected by the army's organisational needs. Only a few battalions were based in permanent barracks for two-year, residential tours. They had the time to get to know their area and the people better than the majority of battalions, on roulement tours of four months, or emergency tours lasting only a few weeks.[48] The numbers of wanted men arrested often fell when new units arrived. A battalion normally took a month to reach operational effectiveness.[49] Few battalions, like 1st Royal Green Jackets, believed a six-month tour, with a break in the middle, would be better, without adversely affecting morale.[50] On their tour 42 Commando struggled to build effective relations with the police and UDR, but argued the long hours and intense tempo of operations militated against anything longer than four months.[51] The intelligence shortcomings imposed by roulement and emergency tours were accepted because the alternative threatened to damage the army.

The 1971 Staff College teaching notes on Northern Ireland observed 'there is a limit to the provocation that units should have to take'.[52] After their four-month tour in County Londonderry, 1st Coldstream Guards reported eighteen soldiers applied for discharge from the army. They expected a higher rate if tours increased to six months.[53] In June 1970 the DASD in London opposed longer tours because commanding officers found the strains imposed during four months already made it 'difficult to maintain the requisite standards of discipline, alertness and efficiency'. As a result, artillery, engineer, marine and air-force units retrained to make up for the shortfall in infantry. The morale rationale also overrode concerns in NATO. Rotating units from their bases in Germany caused turmoil and annoyed the SACEUR.[54] His displeasure was worth tolerating. The MOD blocked an attempt by HQNI to extend to six-month tours in October 1973 as likely to put an unacceptable burden on military families and undermine retention rates.[55] Intelligence suffered, and military operations were consequently less accurate in affecting only militants, because the army prioritised organisational well-being over Northern Ireland. The need to be wary of over-stretch existed due to Britain's global defence commitments. Indirectly then, military intelligence suffered as a consequence of something very British – the desire to be a world power.

Britishness pervaded another self-inflicted problem: the law on lethal force. Deciding how to manoeuvre within legal bounds presented strategists with grave difficulties.[56] Existing accounts pay insufficient attention to the different position concerning lethal force, compared to detention and inter- rogation. One view holds the army behaved as though martial law existed, rendering the civilian courts irrelevant.[57] This is a misinterpretation. Violence by soldiers escalated in 1971 with permission from the civil courts, not despite them. As will be shown, the courts did exercise jurisdiction over the army and examined closely the circumstances under which soldiers applied violence. Very rarely did judges and juries rule against soldiers in lethal-force cases – the first instance was in 1974. Colonial attitudes apparently encouraged soldiers to act with impunity.[58] In another telling, 'Traditional English liberties did not apply to Northern Ireland after 1969', as the British treated it as 'a place apart'.[59] In fact the law on lethal force was utterly English.

Scholars sympathetic to the army lament the negative effects of legal constraints on military effectiveness.[60] Extensive scrutiny by journalists is believed to have imposed extra restraints.[61] Even a classic study on terrorism is fundamentally flawed on this count: acting within the law is believed to have proved efficacious for the security forces, and occasions when the army broke this principle, such as on Bloody Sunday, were an 'aberration'.[62] These claims ignore the structural effect of the common law in enabling soldiers to open fire on civilians on numerous occasions. The law cannot impose a meaningful restraint when it permits soldiers to shoot whenever they subjectively feel in mortal danger, regardless of the objective reality. The culture of the local legal profession in this period embodied a politics of silence regarding rights violations by the state.[63]

The army attempted to circumscribe lethal violence by issuing rules of engagement. These rules, carried as a 'yellow card', never had legal force. The ability of soldiers to use force derived from the common-law right of a citizen to defend themselves or others from immediate danger. Only a court could determine whether the degree of force applied in an incident had been proportionate and the minimum necessary to achieve the object.[64] In late March 1971 the DMO in the MOD proposed altering the 'yellow card', anticipating 'a clamour in Westminster for tougher action'.[65] The ministry's legal experts advised that the common law allowed what he intended without any need for fresh legislation.[66] The implication is important and often missed: lethally violent actions by the army were governed by the courts, implementing the common law as elsewhere. As an adviser to the Northern Ireland attorney general stated: 'we in Northern Ireland do not want to be treated, and should not be treated, any differently from any other part of the United Kingdom'.[67] Criticising the army for producing unsatisfactory versions of the 'yellow card' is therefore beside the point.[68] Ministers in London first questioned whether the rules of engagement were being followed in September 1970, in response to Daniel O'Hagan's shooting. Some soldiers resented the 'yellow card'. In June 1970 Terence Friend was manning a sangar at a base in Belfast. At 4.30am a patrol returned from tackling a riot. The officer coming in addressed him:

> 'All looters to be shot on sight, no warning, no yellow card, no fuck all, just take the bastards out, got it?' 'Yes Sir!' I got it alright, it was the best news I'd heard in a long time, and the transformation in me was almost miraculous. I became instantly wide awake. I viewed the corner shop fifty yards away with fresh interest. Come on you little bastards, I thought to myself, help yourselves. I was keyed up and raring to go, two days and nights watching this insanity with a sense of overwhelming helplessness and frustration. Now it was payback time.[69]

Friend did not get his revenge. A crucial court judgement in March 1971 clarified the army's powers to kill. On 29 October 1970 youths had attacked police and marines in Ardoyne. After bottles and bricks were thrown, the marines opened fire.[70] The use of firearms without the marines having first come under fire breached the rules of engagement. At the time General Freeland commented that although petrol bombs were thrown, they were 'not thrown lethally. There was therefore no justification for firing to kill.'[71] In late March 1971 Marine Norbert Bek came before the Belfast City Commission for wounding three men with a single shot on that day. Bek felt his life had been in danger. The jury took 23 minutes to find Bek not guilty.[72] His commanding officer backed Bek in breaching the 'yellow card', describing the trial as a 'test case'.[73] Soldiers then in Northern Ireland would have paid close attention. They faced situations like that confronted by Bek every day. The acquittal signalled that Northern Ireland juries would treat soldiers sympathetically, even where they admitted violating the rules of engagement. A war against the IRA where civilian deaths caused by the army came to be seen as inevitable developed with permission from the judicial system. Controversial shootings by soldiers in Derry in July 1971, in Ballymurphy in August 1971 and in Derry in January 1972 were possible because soldiers understood the chances of the criminal courts sending them to prison were low. Marine Bek was acquitted by his peers according to British legal standards. HQNI lacked the legal authority to stop soldiers shooting.

THE MAKING OF 'A PROPER MILITARY WAR'

Whether soldiers in Derry knew about the Bek case is unclear. Gunmen began firing at soldiers in the city from 4 July, with sporadic shootings over the next few days, in a 'deliberate escalation of the Provisional IRA offensive in Derry'.[74] Shortly before midnight on 7 July a patrol confronted twenty-five youths; a shot was fired at a petrol bomber. Just after midnight a shot was fired 'at a man in a hostile crowd who was carrying a rifle. He was seen to fall and was understood to have been taken to a hospital in Letterkenny', over the border.[75] The man hit, Seamus Cusack, died from his wounds. According to the MOD, the shot was fired after a warning, at someone aiming a rifle at soldiers. The 1st Royal Anglians who shot him went into action knowing a Landrover had recently been attacked with petrol and explosive bombs.[76] The next afternoon Desmond Beattie was shot dead as riots continued in the city. A platoon commanded by Lieutenant 'A' were facing down Lecky Road, where a lorry was drawn up across the street as a barricade, with about fifty people behind it. Around 3pm three explosions 'created a considerable cloud of dust'. Shortly afterwards the lieutenant noticed a man clutching an 'object which was the size of a 2 oz tobacco tin'. The man appeared to be about to throw a bomb. Lieutenant 'A' decided 'action had to be taken to prevent either death or serious injury amongst my troops'. He dropped to one knee, aimed at the man's chest and fired a shot. A soldier fired independently at the same time.[77]

Britain's common law empowered soldiers to shoot Cusack and Beattie. The government's reaction, however, cannot be attributed to such a deeply embedded structural factor. These shootings prompted outrage in Derry, and elsewhere in Northern Ireland. Military strategists had the opportunity to attempt to calm the febrile mood, and to de-escalate. They did not do so. They made no effort to empathise with Catholics, who felt the shootings proved the army was now out to get them. The army's reaction to the Cusack and Beattie deaths underscored the human cost of Heath's war against the IRA. The government refused calls for a public inquiry to investigate eyewitness claims that Cusack and Beattie were both unarmed when shot. Defence Minister Lord Balniel added to the outrage by saying in the House of Commons that rioters 'are simply asking for trouble'.[78] General Tuzo's Civil Adviser believed those calling for a public inquiry simply wanted to 'have at' the army.[79]

An alternative inquiry was set up under barrister and Labour peer Lord Gifford. The army declined to participate, feeding the sense that there was something to hide. The final report, described by the MOD as 'relatively moderate', concluded neither man was armed. Eleven eyewitnesses saw Cusack unarmed just prior to being shot; eighteen eyewitnesses to the shooting said the soldier did not give a warning before firing. Gifford believed he was shot to deter others from rioting. Beattie appeared on a 'strong possibility' to have been shot unarmed, running away from soldiers. Gifford drew attention to official lack of interest in whether the army followed the law. None of the civilian witnesses examined by him had been approached by the police.[80] On 16 July the SDLP withdrew from Stormont in protest at the government's refusal to hold an inquiry.[81] Faulkner had just made an important concession to the SDLP in offering them the chairmanship of several Stormont committees. Without a voice in Northern Ireland's political institutions, PIRA drew increasing Catholic support as the sole group able to drive the pace of events.[82] Republicans in Derry felt sufficiently confident to hold an open meeting on 10 July. About 500 people gathered to hear Seán Keenan and Ruairí Ó Brádaigh speak.[83]

The fallout from the Beattie and Cusack shootings prompted a change in HQNI's approach. In early July intelligence depicted a 'promising' future.[84] On 19 July General Tuzo went to London to secure approval for new operations because 'the IRA were getting more efficient'. He aimed to 'shake their morale' by harassing IRA leaders, searching their homes and arresting them on suspicion so they could be questioned by the police for forty-eight hours. Tuzo judged the likely reaction – to 'raise the temperature with the Catholic community' – as a price worth paying. Carrington agreed, though he insisted the army's actions be timed to respond to IRA attacks.[85] Heath approved, and two more battalions were sent to assist.[86] Operation Linklater began at first light on 23 July. Some 100 properties were targeted in Belfast and south-eastern Northern Ireland.[87] Soldiers found berets, literature and an order of battle, but no weapons.[88] Three leaders were arrested: William McMillen, the OIRA commander in Northern Ireland, and the PIRA commanders for Lurgan and Armagh.[89] The home secretary publicly acclaimed 'a new phase in the battle against the IRA'.[90] Maudling's statement took Tuzo by surprise, who wished to avoid raising Protestant expectations. He preferred slow, 'steady attrition'. Maudling's interference strengthened those in the Northern Ireland cabinet lobbying for internment.[91] Tuzo and the UKREP believed internment could only suc-ceed if introduced simultaneously in the Republic.[92]

As predicted, the searches provoked an angry reaction. In Edward Street, Lurgan, on the night of 23 July, 150 people gathered to begin a protest, which later descended into petrol-bombing, an attempt to attack Protestant houses and a bus being destroyed by fire.[93] Not all protests turned violent. A civil rights meeting in Cookstown on 31 July, attracting about 400 people, was addressed by Bernadette Devlin, Michael Farrell, Austin Currie and others.[94] A second round of Linklater searches on 26 July, in Belfast, led to one arrest. On 27 July, a third round targeted houses belonging to the Andersonstown Provisionals.[95] The army aimed to demonstrate they knew the identities of leading PIRA figures. Searches of fifteen buildings uncovered two guns, some ammunition, a crossbow, a beret with combat jacket, and a map showing the location of police stations. Six men were arrested.[96] General Tuzo lamented achieving only 'some success' with Linklater. Operations in several rural districts had been cancelled because senior RUC officers opposed upsetting 'an apparently tranquil situation'. The police resisted holding those arrested for the full forty-eight hours permitted by the Special Powers Act, and central to Tuzo's plan.[97] As a next step, the MOD proposed sending reinforcements, deploy-ing the UDR more extensively, further searches, or 'stiffening' the rules of engagement. Tuzo dismissed these ideas as 'non-starters or of little value'.[98] He advocated improved surveillance, which had led to several bomb attacks being thwarted, and concentrating on republican leaders, perhaps by requiring compulsory daily reporting to police stations.[99]

Continuing violence propelled the strategic debate away from further investment in Linklater operations. On 6 August gunmen drove a stolen bus past an army post on Springfield Road in Belfast, firing automatic weapons. With tensions high, a sentry at the post thought he heard shots at 7.44 the next morning. After calling a van to stop he fired one shot. The driver, father-of-six Henry Thornton, died from the shot. The noise the sentry heard was Thornton's van backfiring. During the evening several hundred people bombarded the police station with stones, and shots were fired. Soldiers came under machine-gun fire in Ardoyne.[100] In the early hours of Sunday 8 August, 1st Green Howards deployed to the junction of Butler Street and Crumlin Road in Belfast to separate Catholic and Protestant mobs. After firing rubber bullets the Green Howards were bombarded with bricks, then fired at by gunmen. They responded with rifle fire, CS gas and rubber bullets. Calm was restored by 8am.[101] In the evening of 8 August a soldier from 2nd Parachute Regiment on duty at Springfield Road received a bullet wound fired from Clonard. Half an hour later a Royal Green Jackets soldier was hit in a drive-by shooting in Mulhouse Street. Shootings took place in other areas of Belfast throughout the night. Private Hatton from the Green Howards died after being shot in Ardoyne.[102]

The decisions to introduce internment and deep interrogation should be understood as important elements within the wider offensive against the IRA. That offensive had been gathering pace since February. Planning for both internment and deep interrogation began in March.[103] These measures owed much to colonial precedent. Stormont had previously invoked internment under the Special Powers Act in 1921–4, 1938–46 and 1956–62.[104] Great emphasis is often put on the British government reluctantly accepting Stormont's wish for internment, as the last bulwark against having to take direct control of Northern Ireland.[105] Stressing London's reluctance naturally tends to shift blame to Stormont for what most consider to be an unmitigated disaster. Internment aimed to placate unionists, gather intelligence on the IRA and intimidate the Catholic population as a whole.[106] The internment decision should be interpreted as a deliberate military escalation – and not a mistake based on ignorance. The fallout was expected. A joint Home Office–MOD memorandum written in March predicted internment was bound to 'do more harm than good', having little effect in deterring people from terrorism.[107] Just before mounting the arrests – Operation Demetrius – HQNI predicted that both IRA factions, the civil rights organisation and

People's Democracy would react energetically, with (variously) demonstrations, kidnappings and violent attacks.[108]

The 342 arrests made during Demetrius are often assumed to have rested on inaccurate intelligence. Many obviously innocent people, without connection to the IRA, found themselves in detention. Special Branch are blamed for drawing up the arrest lists, and the exclusion of Protestants is cited as evidence for the intelligence being outdated.[109] Three separate Special Branch reports, written between May and August 1970, had listed 62 loyalists and 15 anarchists for detention besides 145 republicans.[110] In mid March 1971 the cabinet secretary informed Ted Heath that about 400 people had been proposed as candidates for internment – 'not only IRA men but also extreme Protestants'.[111] Army officers participated in finalising the lists before the arrest teams began knocking at doors. At Special Branch headquarters officers noticed inaccuracies in the names and addresses, and the inclusion of people 'in no respect a threat to peace', whose only offence was to oppose unionism. Only a very few Protestants had made the list. Brigade and battalion headquarters possessed enough intelligence of their own to correct the lists to a certain extent. Brigadier Kitson dragged his Special Branch adviser from a pub so they could agree amendments.[112] Brigadier Cowan had the list for 8 Brigade's area changed too.[113] The Home Office only examined the identities of the internees afterwards. The internment orders, signed by Faulkner, contained hardly any information about the reasons for detention and no supporting evidence. Some simply accused the suspect of stirring up 'anti-Northern Ireland Government feeling'.[114] An MOD official would 'guess that 1/3 of those interned have very shaky dossiers'.[115]

The army has been commended for behaving constitutionally in implementing a policy decided upon by the government against the advice of the GOC Northern Ireland and the CGS.[116] The lack of constitutional protections for the generals to invoke when making their case might more appropriately arouse discomfort. Something else of significance to civil–military relations is noteworthy here too. At a meeting in Downing Street on 5 August the prime minister, home secretary, defence secretary and foreign secretary approved Brian Faulkner's request for internment. Heath stated: 'It would be essential that the policy should be seen to be impartial in its application; and it would presumably be desirable for this purpose that those interned should include a certain number of Protestants.'[117] Only two Protestants were detained in the August sweep: one an anarchist and the other an OIRA member.[118] Somewhere between Downing Street and Belfast the injunction to arrest Protestants either got lost, was ignored, or was selectively interpreted in a manner obviously contrary to the prime minister's intent.

Interrogation in depth could only happen amidst the chaos created by internment, and be practised on people picked up for internment. A subsequent inquiry suggested ministers never knew in advance what the interrogations involved.[119] Senior figures certainly perpetuated this belief. Faulkner claimed he authorised the interrogations, Operation Calaba, on the basis that London had already agreed.[120] The CGS, General Carver, asserted he knew deep interrogation was going to be used without understanding the precise methods.[121] Interrogation in depth entailed five techniques designed to wear down the subject prior to questioning: a restricted diet, sleep deprivation, stress positions, exposure to white noise, and hooding. In April 1971 the Joint Services Interrogation Wing trained the Special Branch in the techniques. The home secretary and defence secretary discussed interrogation on 9 and 10 August. Carrington received a briefing note summarising the safeguards in the army's interrogation doctrine, explaining it would be conducted by the RUC with military support, and describing the role of isolation, fatigue, white sound, and deprivation of a sense of place and time. The director of intelligence at HQNI spent an hour explaining the techniques to Faulkner on 11 August. The MOD anticipated controversy. Brigadier Lewis, the senior army intelligence officer in Whitehall, expected complaints from Amnesty International.[122] Lewis noted the advantage in having the RUC handle 'an exceptionally sensitive subject and one which has caused severe political embarrassment in the past'.[123] Precisely what ministers learned in their briefings is unknown. The brutality inherent in the process was possibly skirted over. Perhaps the ministers drifted off. Maybe they remembered the controversy over the methods, applied in Aden, only five years earlier, but shared Brigadier Lewis' hope that Special Branch would take the blame.

Ted Heath called Brian Faulkner to London on 5 August, and announced that if Stormont wished to invoke internment, the British government approved. In return, London expected all marches to be banned indefinitely, rifle clubs to be shut, and 'a certain number of Protestants' to be interned, for the sake of balance. Faulkner argued against banning rifle clubs and marches, but gave way on the marches when Heath insisted. Interning Protestants and the prohibition on rifle clubs were ignored. The prime minister hoped internment and the ban on marches could 'provide an opportunity for fresh initiatives to promote political reconciliation'.[124] Given the SDLP's absence from formal politics this statement is staggering. Heath's biographer rightly concludes: 'he totally failed to grasp the realities of Ulster politics'.[125] An attempt by the Foreign Office to secure the Irish government's agreement for parallel internment, north and south, failed. With the British government seemingly bent on repression, Taoiseach Jack Lynch calculated public opinion in Ireland would not accept such a move.[126] Brigadier Kitson expected PIRA leaders, whom his troops were covertly monitoring, to disappear once internment began.[127] Ted Heath and General Carver chose to be away on leave when the arrests started.[128] Though most probably a coincidence, a more apt symbol of London's urge to shift ownership of the coming carnage is hard to imagine.

STIRRING UP THE HORNETS' NEST

The arrests began on 9 August 1971. Tom Largey remembered:

> I was lying in bed with my wife when the Brits came in. It was about 4.00 am and they just came smashing through the front door. My wife got up, still in her nightdress, and was the first one down the stairs. The Brits just pushed past her. I was still getting dressed when they came into the bedroom and forced me down the stairs. I remember my wife calling out that I had not even had anything to eat but they just pushed me through the door. I didn't even have on a pair of shoes.[129]

Soldiers questioned the morality of what they were asked to do. Royal Green Jacket Kenneth Ambrose recalled:

> you knock on the door once, and then you knock the door down. So, I mean, you've got, you feel like a Nazi to be absolutely honest, because it's the sort of thing that you imagine went on in the Second World War. The sort of things that you see when you go through a door, and you've got a cocked weapon in your hand and you don't really know what to expect. But what you see on the other side is a little five-year-old girl crying, and you think to yourself, this can't be right, there's something wrong here.[130]

Violence spread throughout Northern Ireland in an unprecedented way. PIRA recruited new members and mounted operations in previously quiet places, like Lurgan, Newry, Dungannon and Enniskillen.[131] By one reckoning, in the four months before Operation Demetrius eight people died due to the Troubles; in the next four months the number killed stood at 114.[132] In Belfast, 2nd Parachute Regiment was at the centre of the fighting. Their commanding officer described the reaction to internment as 'like the stirring up of a hornets' nest'. In Ballymurphy the army believed most shooting came from Catholics, though Protestant and Catholic gunmen also shot at each other. Some barricades were booby-trapped and 'defended from properly sited fire positions'. Extensive fighting took place around the paratrooper bases in the Henry Taggart Memorial Hall and the Vere Foster School. The battalion estimated they shot up to twenty people.[133] Protestants gathered in Mayo Street at 11am on 9 August to force Catholics from their homes. Later Protestants in Farringdon Gardens were ejected from their homes. During a battle in Albert Street at 4.50pm around seventy people attacked an army post. In the following hour soldiers shot into the crowd, and two Royal Green Jackets received gunshot wounds. Gunfire was reported at 6pm in Leeson Street, Slate Street, Cyprus Street and Farringdon Gardens. Between 10 and 11pm 700 people attended a protest meeting in Coalisland. Afterwards the crowd attacked the police station, burned vehicles, broke windows and petrol-bombed the army. In Clady, Winston Donnell, a UDR soldier, was killed in a drive-by shooting.[134]

At 2.40am on 10 August, 1st Parachute Regiment launched Operation Moonbeam to seize control over Ardoyne, encountering 'a great deal of opposition in the form of barricades, sniping, bombing and missile throwing'.[135] Later in the morning two Royal Green Jackets on Albert Street Mill were shot, and in the afternoon a soldier was shot in the Falls area.[136] (See Illustration 4.1.) A large number of barricades also went up

Illustration 4.1 Soldiers patrol the streets of Belfast, 10 August 1971.
(Courtesy of Sygma via Getty Images.)

during the morning in Derry; at 1.55pm shots fired in Bligh's Lane hit Bombardier Paul Challener, who died in hospital. Intensive gun-battles continued throughout the night.[137] In the early hours of 11 August, 1st Parachute Regiment moved into the Turf Lodge, Ballymurphy and Whiterock, leading to 'a lot of shooting'.[138] At 4.45am the army shot dead someone they claimed to be a sniper in the Whiterock Road, and, attempting to capture Inglis's Bakery from gunmen an hour later, shot dead another two. In Armagh earlier in the night, 200 people 'went on rampage', turning cars and lorries into barricades, throwing petrol bombs and rioting.[139] In the early hours on 12 August, 1st Parachute Regiment assaulted the Beachmount and Falls areas.[140]

Between 9 and 11 August ten people died during the shootings in Ballymurphy. An inquest began in November 2018, investigating five separate incidents over those three days.[141] Helping to evacuate children from the area on 9 August, Eilish Meehan heard about Father Hugh Mullan's death: 'There was panic ... you don't shoot a priest, we thought we were going to be overrun, massacred.'[142] Father Mullan was shot dead by paratroopers near Springfield Park on 9 August as he knelt down to assist a wounded man. He and Francis Quinn, killed in the same incident, were unarmed and posing no threat to soldiers when shot. The coroner was meticulously even-handed in assessing the army's actions. Though soldiers were justified in shooting at gunmen in the Moyard flats, there were no gunmen near to Mullan and Quinn.[143] Witness C4, a Royal Signaller visiting family in Belfast prior to discharge from the army, described what he saw on 9 August as 'murder. Shooting civilians who weren't involved in any terrorist action.'[144]

Near the Henry Taggart Hall that same day paratroopers shot Joan Connolly, Daniel Teggart, Noel Phillips and Joseph Murphy. Again, the coroner established the context: 'The events of the evening occurred after a day in which people were gathered, shouting, throwing stones and other missiles; there may have been some sporadic gunfire and those in the Hall would viably think they were under attack by the community.' The four killed in this second incident also were unarmed and posed no threat. In a third incident, the next day, Edward Doherty died when a Royal Engineer fired into a crowd with his Sterling submachine gun in an attempt to protect himself from a petrol bomber. No warning was issued beforehand. Doherty was walking home from visiting family and presented no danger to the soldier. On the Whiterock Road on 11 August paratroopers shot Joseph Corr and John Laverty in their backs as they crouched or lay on the ground. Soldiers who went to give medical aid found no weapons on or near them.

Outside Corpus Christi Church the same day John McKerr died from a single bullet shot to the head. The coroner could not establish who killed the 'entirely innocent man'. Neither the police nor the army at the time tried to find out.[145]

Geoffrey Howlett, commanding 2nd Parachute Regiment, called the events a 'full-blown battle'. At the time the battalion believed those shot to have been in the IRA. With hindsight Howlett accepted this view to be mistaken. No soldiers were investigated, disciplined or prosecuted for the ten deaths.[146] One document suggests senior officers recognised the damage done. On 16 August, 1st Parachute Regiment company commanders received orders to: 'Get on with the Cats [Catholics]. Modify behaviour ... Behaviour – yellow card – no arbitrary shooting.'[147] Despite the lack of disciplinary action, these comments reflected the acknowledgement that soldiers had gone too far. The paratroopers' conduct might be compared with other regiments in mortal danger. The archives contain many instances where soldiers appear to have exercised greater control in similar, though of course not identical, scenarios. On 23 August Private George Crozier from the Green Howards was fatally wounded by a sniper in Flax Street, Belfast. Fire was not returned by soldiers, as they could not see the sniper. On 29 August soldiers from the Light Infantry came under fire near the M1 motorway. They refrained from shooting at an uncertain target.[148]

General Tuzo felt positive. The situation was 'resolving itself into a proper military war'.[149] Some battalions shared the sentiment: 2nd Parachute Regiment celebrated inflicting casualties in Ballymurphy after the IRA's 'stupidly suicidal attacks'.[150] Reginald Maudling avoided Catholic outrage until 11 August, when he met Gerry Fitt and John Hume. Fitt said Catholics were incensed at the army wrecking houses during searches and asked for compensation for the families of those killed. Hume argued for power-sharing at Stormont. He accepted such a change must be balanced by a promise to keep Northern Ireland in the United Kingdom until a majority voted otherwise. Hume promised to meet further repression with 'a campaign of passive resistance and civil disobedience'.[151] Carrington saw little need for compromise, concluding that internment 'achieved a large measure of success', capturing half of PIRA's leadership in Belfast.[152] According to newspaper magnate Cecil King, who socialised with leading politicians, Carrington privately believed the army exaggerated internment's effectiveness.[153] Farrar-Hockley claimed the arrests only netted six PIRA leaders, as the major blow struck OIRA.[154] The concern for OIRA made sense. Between July 1970 and September 1971 the group expanded from seven to eleven companies in Belfast and went on the offensive against the army in June 1971.[155]

Deep interrogation proceeded at Ballykelly from 11 to 17 August. Twenty Special Branch interrogators, backed up by twelve military intelligence advisers, practised the five techniques on James Auld, Joseph Clarke, Michael Donnelly, Kevin Hannaway, Patrick McClean, Francis McGuigan, Sean McKenna, Gerald McKerr, Patrick McNally, Michael Montgomery, Patrick Shivers and Brian Turley. Forced to stand in stress positions against a wall for up to six hours at a time, guards forced the men back to their feet when they collapsed. In total Turley and Donnelly spent nine hours at the wall – for Auld the number was forty-three. The men received only bread and water until 15 August.[156] In his report on Operation Calaba, Lieutenant-Colonel Nicholson, the senior military officer involved, suggested the techniques worked. Calaba revealed ten subjects were connected with the IRA, while the other two should never have been arrested. Interrogation produced six summaries detailing IRA plans, arms caches, safe houses and supply routes; over forty sheets outlining the IRA order of battle; personality cards on around 500 people for future use; and information on forty unsolved incidents.[157] These results came at a high moral price. They brought lasting shame on the army and the British government. Patrick Shivers' wife, Betty, recounted how 'This took over his mind and his life, what happened to him . . . and you could see the fear in his eyes, and the horror of it, and that's how Pat lived his life.' Patrick Shivers was selected for interrogation by mistake.[158]

Alongside the lasting psychological harm being inflicted at Ballykelly, by 13 August the Home Office estimated the violence caused by internment had cost twenty-five civilians and three soldiers their lives.[159] About 10,000 people fled their homes in the month after internment, due to intimidation.[160] Edward Gunn, a Catholic living in a largely Protestant part of Belfast, decided to emigrate to New Zealand after his home came under repeated attack by stone-throwing gangs: 'The boys, whoever they are, they've scared the wits out of me, and out of my family.'[161] On 15 August the SDLP declared a civil disobedience campaign to oppose internment, calling for a rent and rates strike. John Hume explained: 'the action of withdrawal of consent from the present system of government in Northern Ireland is not the action of a few agitators, but is representative of a whole people'.[162] A civil rights meeting in Newry the next evening attracted 1,000 people, with similar meetings held in Omagh, Dungiven and Coalisland.[163] Hume and Fitt gave Maudling four days to talk them out of this significant political act.

After a week of death and destruction Ted Heath met Douglas-Home and Carrington after cabinet on 16 August to consider how to proceed. Maudling was on holiday in Majorca, despite mounting pressure from Labour to recall Parliament to debate internment.[164] Here was the opportunity for reflection, perhaps to pull the army back. Instead, the troika approved a plan by Tuzo to provoke the 'hooligan element' in Derry onto the streets, encircle them, arrest as many as possible and take down the city's barricades. When Carrington reported that Special Branch had paused questioning at Ballykelly to analyse the results, Heath instructed deep interrogation be resumed immediately.[165] Launched in Derry on 18 August, Operation Huntsman provoked shooting between the IRA and the army that left volunteer Eamon Lafferty dead. An attempt to clear barricades in the Creggan provoked a 200-strong sit-down protest, led by John Hume and Ivan Cooper. As rioting commenced, and soldiers used blue-dyed water cannon and baton rounds, Hume, Cooper and three others were arrested.[166] General Tuzo believed the deterioration in Derry since internment to be outweighed by the damage done to the IRA leadership in Belfast.[167]

The UKREP, Howard Smith, disagreed. Internment's political consequences were far graver than expected, making direct rule highly probable. People expected a political breakthrough from London.[168] The burgeoning civil disobedience campaign certainly validated his analysis. In the afternoon on 23 August around 350 people held an anti-internment protest at the courthouse in Omagh. On 26 August, 130 women and children staged a protest in Upper Springfield Road, Belfast.[169] The vast majority of the civil disobedience protests passed off peacefully. In September loyalist protests became more common. On 2 September 200 employees held a lunchtime meeting outside the AEI electrical-engineering factory in Larne, calling for a 'third force' to protect the Province.[170] Ian Paisley, William Craig and trade unionists addressed 20,000 workers in Victoria Park, Sydenham, on 6 September, telling them of the urgent need for such a 'third force'. The same day anti-internment protests took place in Beragh, Sixmilecross, Fintona, Fivemiletown, Clogher, Ballygawley, Aughnacloy, Castlederg, Newtownstewart, Gortin and Dromore.[171]

As soon as internment began, family members of those arrested made allegations to the press of military brutality. Some units found the complaints amusing: 'Brutality? They were only hurried along by three 17-stone RMP and an Alsatian war dog that hadn't been fed for a week! What could be more humane?'[172] Heath understood the political imperative to rebut the claims. He felt an internal investigation by the army must lack credibility.[173] For presentational reasons, an inquiry was to be painted as General Tuzo's idea.[174] Tuzo realised 'the other side has already scored a major propaganda victory'. He and the chief constable defended interrogation as 'vital to the conduct of future operations'.[175] Interrogation in depth was now only to take place with approval from London.[176] On 31 August the government announced an inquiry headed by Sir Edmund Compton, a former civil servant and parliamentary commissioner for administration. It was to be held in private, without complainants able to confront the witnesses, and without legal representation. Compton's remit was to investigate allegations of physical brutality.[177] The MOD agreed to exempt Special Branch officers from questioning, as they threatened to refuse to conduct further interrogations otherwise.[178] Military personnel testifying before the inquiry were assured their evidence could not be used in any disciplinary proceedings against them.[179] The government effectively gave legal immunity to the participants in deep interrogation.

The perception that the security forces were losing the propaganda battle prompted Stormont to create a unit for 'psychological warfare with the terrorists with the aim of persuading more people to help the Security Forces'.[180] London granted HQNI greater latitude in deciding when to hold press conferences or briefings. Television interviews were permitted if army officers avoided politics.[181] Clifford Hill, an information research department officer sent to review public relations, recommended the UKREP possess his own staff to co-ordinate all information work and 'plan a systematic campaign of counter-propaganda'. At HQNI, he found the public relations staff hard pressed, without time for 'positive and offensive' work. Hill advised extra financial resources be made available for cultivating journalists, including spending in restaurants.[182] Downing Street appointed Hill as press liaison officer on the UKREP's staff.[183] Sir Dick White, intelligence co-ordinator in the cabinet office, collected intelligence material that could be used for propaganda.[184]

A bullish mood prevailed at HQNI and amongst the ministers leading policy-making. Whitehall officials, however, responded to internment with pessimism. Heath's think-tank in the cabinet office, the central policy review staff, argued defeating the IRA 'masks a hopeless desire to return to the status quo ante'. A bargain had to be struck with the Irish government.[185] The Home Office regarded reconciliation as a remote prospect. Though street violence was down by late August, bomb attacks proceeded at the same pace, if not higher.[186] Dramatic events showed everyone PIRA's resilience. On 29 August gunmen ambushed two army vehicles near Crossmaglen, killing one soldier and wounding another. Bizarrely, given

Illustration 4.2 Rioting in Derry, 14 September 1971.
(Courtesy of Mirrorpix via Getty Images.)

all the efforts to destroy his organisation, British authorities refused Ruairí
Ó Brádaigh entry to England on 28 August, returning him to Ireland.[187] Sir
Burke Trend deplored 'the absence of any realistic prospect of making
progress'. (See Illustration 4.2.) The IRA fought on, civil disobedience was
inflicting serious social and economic damage, and Labour's backing of the
ruling Conservatives in parliament could no longer be taken for granted.
Sooner or later 'the elastic must snap'. Granting Northern Ireland independence struck Trend as too radical; shared control with Dublin seemed
more realistic.[188]

ACCEPTING THE POLITICAL PENALTIES

The British government's war against the IRA as a strategy is normally
believed to have disintegrated in reaction to Bloody Sunday. The decay set
in earlier and the idea decomposed gradually. Ted Heath ruminated on
Burke Trend's advice for a week before making the first tentative steps away
from the quest for victory. He telephoned Faulkner to propose talks between
themselves and the taoiseach. The Northern Ireland premier demanded the
taoiseach crack down on the IRA first. Heath rebuked him: 'public opinion

isn't going to have 17 battalions over there and just have people refusing to talk'.[189] Heath's changing attitude coincided with violence returning to the streets. General Tuzo's upbeat reading – there were no more gunmen than before; those out there were simply active over a wider area – must have seemed far-fetched.[190] At Chequers on 26 September Heath again posited a tripartite meeting. Opinion in Westminster expected efforts to be made in this direction. The civil disobedience campaign's popularity indicated political re-engagement must be attempted. Faulkner followed the pattern set by all those holding his office since August 1969: to demand more troops and more repression. He refused to countenance letting 'any minority representative into the Government'. Heath 'could not accept this'.[191] Tuzo continued to reassure Faulkner he aimed to destroy the IRA prior to any political settlement coming forward.[192]

After internment the Irish government called for power-sharing, and assisted the SDLP in their bid to create an alternative assembly. At first Heath paid little attention. On 27 September Lynch made it absolutely clear that there would be no security co-operation from his government unless the British did something serious about Stormont.[193] Ireland's assistance would grow more critical as PIRA operations became dependent on cross-border movement. Faced with Faulkner's intransigence, Heath looked for fresh ideas. A MOD assessment written at his behest described existing policy as 'maximum vigour in the elimination and apprehension of identifiable terrorists, tempered by a scrupulous care to avoid actions which are, or may be represented as being, indiscriminate as between the terrorists and the general body of the minority community'. Options for escalation included looser restrictions on firearms, using undercover 'Q squads' to target the IRA, more restrictions on movement (such as identity cards, curfews, and cordon and searches) and free-fire zones on the border. Republican violence had expanded dramatically throughout 1971, from 36 bombings in January to 175 in September. The IRA carried out attacks on police stations with automatic weapons (and occasionally rockets), sniper and hit-and-run shootings, raids and ambushes across the border, intimidation against Catholics, and 'cunning and effective propaganda'. These tactics granted the IRA the initiative despite their small numbers. Absent any political initiative to terminate the conflict, the offensive was likely to continue or intensify. This appreciation of the situation provided three options for the future:

a. Option One. To maintain operations at low intensity in the hope of thus assisting progress in the political field. The danger of this option lies in mounting Protestant pressure which might find practical expression in the formation of a third force and which might make the imposition of Direct Rule inevitable. b. Option Two. To abandon all hope of political progress with the minority communities, and adopt a 'tough policy'. . ... This option might have short-term benefits, but is unlikely to eliminate terrorism in the long term. c. Option Three. To continue our present policy, but to remove those restraints on the operations GOC Northern Ireland wishes to carry out, which are motivated by·a desire not to disturb the current 'political initiatives'. This option would certainly include intensification of border operations, including humping and cratering of roads, and an operation in Londonderry. . ... Option Three represents for the time being the best reconciliation of all the factors which have to be taken into account.[194]

Option Three appears to have been chosen, as Tuzo recommended a major operation in Derry before 20 October. He believed occupying the Bogside and the Creggan would win over the population's support for the government.[195] The UKREP foresaw action in Derry having implications elsewhere. The IRA would intensify operations in Belfast to draw the security forces away from Derry. Overall, the UKREP advised any operation in Derry be matched by a serious political initiative.[196] However, General Carver effectively argued for any such initiative to be limited in scope, as the threat of a Protestant backlash, should direct rule be imposed, was now greater than ever. Carver recommended more operations on the border and 'a more uninhibited use of the security forces in Londonderry and Belfast'. Another three battalions were going to be needed, bringing the total to sixteen.[197] Heath accepted the plan to escalate the offensive against the IRA. He decided that 'the first priority should be the defeat of the gunmen using military means and that in achieving this we should have to accept whatever political penalties were inevitable'.[198]

The government's strategy remained defeating the IRA, with major political reform afterwards. London's leverage over Stormont was consequently circumscribed. When Heath brought Faulkner to Downing Street on 7 October he opened by warning: 'the British public was losing patience. The Westminster Government could not continue to support Stormont unless public opinion at home was behind it.' Faulkner argued the SDLP's refusal to engage until internment came to an end prevented progress. Maudling suggested giving the SDLP ministerial positions to bring them onside. Faulkner refused to serve alongside 'Republicans, whether or not they eschewed the use of violence'. The London ministers backed down, then crumbled, agreeing to send another three battalions and to start a road-cratering programme on the border. Carrington knew this to be ineffective in stopping IRA movements. Placating unionism mattered more than alien-ating communities who traversed the border daily in their farming, business and cultural lives. Though Heath recoiled from Faulkner's request for the army to formally liaise with loyalist paramilitaries, Carrington believed vigilantes 'contributed to the safety of some areas'. The ministers granted army commanders discretion in deciding how to deal with them.[199] Loyalist militancy was brewing. Faulkner's officials recognised that 'It might be necessary to detain some Protestants for security reasons.'[200] Conciliation remained the favoured choice. The police regarded Shankill vigilantes as 'well organised' and 'responsible'.[201] Major-General Ford instructed units to keep in close touch with vigilantes, but to stop them carrying arms or indulging in 'other illegalities'.[202] Protests from the CCDC about the army's closeness to loyalists fell on deaf ears.[203]

Despite the government's anxiety about public opinion, another phase of deep interrogation went ahead from 9 October. Defence Minister Lord Balniel had approved a second wave a month earlier.[204] Though a degree of uncertainty hovers over what ministers knew before the initial interrogations, this time they knew what they were letting people in for. At some point in September Lord Balniel observed the five techniques being implemented on troops undergoing resistance to interrogation training.[205] Tuzo assured Special Branch that they 'will be completely protected from any repercussions . . . assuming that there is no improper conduct on their part'.[206] The second-round subjects were William Shannon and Liam Rogers, arrested on 9 and 11 October respect-ively. After *The Sunday Times* published allegations of brainwashing during interrogation, Harold Wilson and Jim Callaghan asked to meet Heath, Maudling and Carrington on 18 October, on privy-counsellor terms. Heath accepted Wilson's proposal for the latest allegations to be scrutin-ised by the Compton inquiry.[207] Heath banned further deep interroga-tion unless authorised by himself, Maudling and Carrington, and tasked the cabinet's intelligence co-ordinator, Sir Dick White, to conduct an internal review into the methods.[208]

The MOD braced itself for 'a substantial political rumpus'. The CDS and General Carver cautioned against blaming Special Branch, and thereby destroying their morale.[209] How to present deep interrogation to the out-side world split opinion. The secretary of the JIC, Brian Stewart, recom-mended wall-standing, hooding and white noise be described as for 'protective and defensive purposes' – to prevent prisoners attacking or identifying anyone.[210] Air Marshal Sir Harold Maguire, Director-General of Intelligence in the MOD, who survived Japanese captivity during the

Second World War, preferred to be honest. He acknowledged the offensive use of the three methods, intended to 'lead to the breakdown of a detainee's morale'.[211] Carrington, Balniel and Sir Ned Dunnett, the PUS at the MOD, agreed: they were for 'interrogation', not 'handling' purposes. Ted Heath sided with Stewart and Burke Trend.[212] The intention behind the treatment meted out to people mattered a great deal. Sir Philip Allen, PUS at the Home Office, informed ministers that it 'would be held legally to constitute an assault' if the matter came before the courts.[213]

HQNI seemed impervious to the rising media and parliamentary opposition to attrition. General Tuzo believed arrests imposed 'a radical effect on the effectiveness, and hence the morale' of the IRA.[214] Criticism of the security forces was dismissed as an IRA smear campaign, directed particularly at the most effective battalions.[215] The MOD's Northern Ireland Policy Committee agreed that 'operations to defeat the IRA were entering a crucial stage'. The meeting endorsed the GOC's focus on reducing bombing and shooting in Belfast before turning to Derry.[216] The IRA adapted to British tactics. Seventeen shootings took place in Catholic areas in Belfast on 26–7 October, suggesting 'a systematic campaign of retaliation against members of the security forces and their families'. Two soldiers were wounded, ten houses belonging to RUC families were attacked and three women hospitalised.[217] On 27 October two soldiers died from a bomb explosion in Derry, a sniper shot dead a policeman in Toome and a soldier was killed with a Claymore mine near Enniskillen. Even in dark times intelligence assessments sought out the light. IRA morale was 'beginning to crack slightly', thanks to seventy-six arrests in a week.[218] Noting that fifty-five terrorists had been shot dead or wounded in October, compared to twenty-four in September, Major-General Ford lauded the 'toll which if maintained would have telling effect'.[219]

External criticism was also deplored for the potential effect on military morale. In Newry on 23 October soldiers shot dead Sean Ruddy, Thomas McLaughlin and Robert Anderson in the act of robbing men depositing money into a bank night safe. The soldiers believed them to be armed and attempting to bomb the bank – neither was true. Lord Balniel asked if they had breached the 'yellow-card' rules.[220] The VCGS thought so. He protested against a possible manslaughter charge:

> VCGS said it would be disastrous to Army morale if a charge were brought in. … Lord Balniel said that he very much appreciated VCGS's views and indeed would do all he could to publicly support the men concerned. … VCGS repeated that he thought that if the matter was brought before the

Courts it would severely affect the role of the Army in aiding the civil power in keeping law and order. The <u>Minister</u> agreed.[221]

Eight solicitors in Newry complained to the lord chancellor about the shootings.[222] The CLF shared the worry about the implications for morale from any prosecution. He intervened to ensure the military police's report included background information about the number of armed robberies in the preceding six weeks, and that intelligence from Special Branch told the soldiers' company commander to expect three men to rob the bank on one of five nights.[223] The Treasury solicitor considered the soldiers who had opened fire in Newry, and the officer commanding them, 'at risk in law'.[224] None of the soldiers concerned ultimately faced a criminal charge.[225] The road to Bloody Sunday had several waypoints where ministers and senior generals paused to consider whether to keep on going. They chose to do so in the knowledge that unarmed people were being shot.

A paper written by Colonel Maurice Tugwell, in charge of information policy at HQNI, sheds light on the attitudes developing in some quarters by November. A paratrooper who fought in Europe during the war, and Malaya and Cyprus afterwards, Tugwell completed a doctorate on revolutionary propaganda in 1979. The paper contained reasonable propositions: the IRA intended to convince the British public that Northern Ireland was ungovernable, and was thus to be abandoned. Provoking soldiers into opening fire indiscriminately and publicising the harshness of interrogation were designed to discredit the army and justify resistance. However, wide experience, staff college training and evident academic competence did not prevent Tugwell from proceeding to offer a stunningly simplistic analysis. Restrictions on military activity became a cunning ploy by the IRA, rather than legal and moral imperatives. He discerned a 'bogus concern over the position of soldiers with the law. This is part of the campaign to harness the law to its own destruction.' Tugwell ignored the propagandist's professional duty to differentiate between multiple audiences. All of the following were labelled as IRA mouthpieces: the Association of Legal Justice, the (Official Sinn Féin) republican clubs, the CCDC, the *Irish News*, the Catholic Ex-Serviceman's Association, NICRA, the SDLP, the People's Democracy, university groups and teachers, Raidió Teilifís Éireann (RTÉ), and 'A number of RC priests'. Hostility towards the IRA from Catholics received scant attention. Instead, racist assertions abounded about 'The indigenous Irish', with their 'breath-taking ability to lie with absolute conviction'.[226]

Many soldiers would have been disgusted by these sentiments. An article in the Green Howards' journal read: 'The population of the Ardoyne is by no means all bad. They live in fear, and are terrorised by the gunmen in their midst. Although all the people are Catholics, not all are I.R.A.'[227] Doubts about attrition existed in HQNI. Intelligence officers struggled to judge whether arrests were being offset by IRA recruitment.[228] On 8 November even the normally ebullient Major-General Ford questioned whether the IRA would crack after all. Reinforcements kept coming over the border, and only small numbers might sustain a bombing campaign for a long time.[229] Ministers had misgivings too, as criticism in parliament made the strategy of defeating the IRA before launching a political initiative less appealing. Fears that changing tack would result in direct rule, and even incite 'widespread non-co-operation by the RUC', again proved decisive.[230] Brian Faulkner's tokenistic move to embrace reform by appointing a Catholic, Dr G. B. Newe, as minister of state in his department failed to impress. Heath secretly instructed the civil service to examine how best to appoint an SoS for Northern Ireland.[231] Heath knew direct rule and the abandonment of military victory must come. Every day he prevaricated meant more human suffering.

General Carver received a detailed briefing at HQNI on 10 November. Amidst a rise in violence over the preceding two months, IRA tactical sophistication stood out. A quarter of shooting incidents now involved automatic fire. Several times a week bomb disposal teams confronted complex devices with multiple anti-handling mechanisms – they could take twelve hours to neutralise. For a three-week period the IRA's bombing of the electricity system nearly brought the Province to a standstill. They abandoned the tactic without realising their proximity to success. Despite all this, Major-General Ford claimed 'the military battle of attrition was going well'. He explicitly intended to 'kill and wound as many as possible'. With about 100 IRA members being shot, interned or fleeing to Ireland each month, Ford hoped Belfast might be secured by March. He described the city as the 'pivot' for the IRA. The Bogside and the Creggan in Derry continued to be 'completely dominated by the IRA'. Straying into politics, Ford stressed:

> there is no requirement more urgent than the maintenance of determination in Britain to see this problem through. If the IRA believe they are winning, and right now I think a lot of them do, this is not because they have killed a number of soldiers or because they have created havoc in parts of Belfast, but because they detect an air of war-weariness in Britain. The Labour initiative, criticism of internment, talk of direct rule and a negotiated settlement – all these are the straws in the wind of IRA victory. They must know that if once they can end internment, our ability

to crush them is virtually ended. And if a sizeable proportion of the UK public turns against the war (and subsequently against the Army), our morale and standing will be in grave danger.[232]

Ford's emotive reference to a stab in the back from a home population lacking the stomach for the fight in Northern Ireland dredged up lingering resentment, in some military quarters at least, at Britain's ignominious scuttle from Aden in 1967, a humiliation imposed by the Labour government. On 8 September 1971 Harold Wilson announced a '12 point plan' for Northern Ireland, ultimately leading to reunification. By early November press speculation predicted the imminent demise of the bipartisan consensus on Northern Ireland at Westminster.[233] For Major-General Ford, betrayal seemed to be in the air, just when victory was in sight. HQNI signally missed PIRA's political declaration only three days beforehand. PIRA's five-point plan set out prerequisites to a ceasefire: a halt in British Army operations, abolition of Stormont, elections for a nine-county Ulster parliament, the release of detainees and compensation for those injured by the army.[234] The reasonableness of these conditions may certainly be questioned. HQNI's failure to even notice them indicates the firm attachment to a military victory.

CONCLUSION

When generals invoke war-weariness amongst the general public as a reason for their strategy facing difficulties, something is often wrong with the strategy itself, not the public. The British Army's opposition to internment before the fact cannot obscure the extent to which senior commanders wished for it to be retained afterwards. Military strategy after March 1971 escalated by many little steps. A single directive from the prime minister telling the army to wage war against all Catholics in Northern Ireland never existed. Yet, by 6 October, when Heath stated his willingness to accept the political penalties associated with destroying the IRA, that is almost exactly what transpired. Certainly, some battalions interpreted their orders to give greater licence to use force than others. The Parachute Regiment in Ballymurphy in the days surrounding internment opened fire on anyone in sight. The Green Howards, at roughly the same time in the same city, refrained from shooting even when taking casualties. Commanders and policymakers had a limited ability to minimise shootings because the common law empowered individual soldiers to decide for themselves whether to pull the trigger. Soldiers breached the rules of engagement and opened fire when not in direct danger even though the police and the courts scrutinised their actions. The law did not prevent escalation, the law allowed it. At several junctures ministers and senior officers paused to consider the implications of the attritional strategy. The rise in fatalities inflicted by the army did not happen without anyone noticing. Doubts were expressed, then pushed aside so the offensive might continue.

The adoption and survival of attrition as a strategy rested upon information confirming its effectiveness. The abundance of such positive information partly explains why ministers and senior generals decided to carry on as they were, even after late August 1971, when several leading officials strongly advised the opposite. Those who favoured turning to a political compromise understood the deep human and moral costs building up the longer the war mentality prevailed. However the government chose to present interrogation in depth to the world, voices in the strategic community wanted to be honest about the deliberate brutality involved. Though we cannot be certain about precisely what ministers knew before authorising deep interrogation, the likelihood is that they understood well enough, given the scandal over the same issue in Aden only a few years earlier. We can be sure that a defence minister knew what was being inflicted on the final two men subjected to deep interrogation because he watched those methods in a training exercise. All these moral choices were made in the belief that defeating the IRA justified them. But defeating the IRA was further away than the advocates of military victory appreciated. PIRA proved remarkably adept at adjusting itself to the British Army's tactics, by devising more complex bombs, by targeting intelligence officers, by using the border to their advantage. Crushing the IRA required co-operation from Catholic moderates, primarily the SDLP, and the Irish government. The British government's warlike approach so alienated those two crucial partners as to undermine its own plausibility.

5

THE ROAD TO BLOODY SUNDAY

The Secretary of State thought that the choice rested between some
initiative of the sort CGS envisaged, aimed at moving towards the
Roman Catholic demands while not losing Protestant support, and
continuing the present policy of waiting and hoping that the interparty talks might produce a likely solution.[1]

Lord Carrington, December 1971

On 23 March 1972 the British cabinet stopped waiting and hoping. They
suspended Stormont, scaled down military operations, and prepared to
negotiate with nationalists and republicans. The military offensive against
the IRA now proceeded alongside a political attempt to deprive republicans
of their support base, rather than being a pre-condition to constitutional
reform. Why did Heath's government take so long to strategically adapt, and
what effects did the delay result in? Scholars have long understood that the
deteriorating situation during late 1971 to early 1972 persuaded the government to impose direct rule from London.[2] A straight causal line is often
drawn between internment, Bloody Sunday and direct rule. Bloody Sunday,
when the Parachute Regiment shot dead thirteen unarmed protesters during
an anti-internment march on 30 January, is considered to have happened in
the context of a policy vacuum, or amidst frenetic efforts to secure peace. The
army apparently lacked direction due to 'no readily available political solution' short of total withdrawal (which was impossible).[3] Edward Heath
claimed to have known for years only enforced power-sharing between
unionists and nationalists could solve Northern Ireland's problems.[4] Lord
Saville's inquiry absolved the British government of responsibility for Bloody
Sunday, finding 'genuine and serious attempts were being made at the
highest level to work towards a peaceful political settlement'. He judged the
British Army institutionally innocent on the basis that no evidence for
a culture of impunity towards lethal force could be found.[5]

Saville's report numbers 5,088 pages; 385 cover the pre-march period.
The inquiry sought advice from two distinguished political historians, but

no experts on military affairs. Lord Saville ignored previous army shootings because he could not hope to delve into them in any depth. As a consequence, the inquiry paid little attention to the interactive nature of military strategy. However, the persistence of an offensive strategy intended to defeat the IRA and force nationalists to accept minor constitutional reforms contributed to Bloody Sunday. The direct-rule decision is frequently attributed to the fallout from Bloody Sunday.[6] Accounts centred on the policy-making process assume the massacre prompted an immediate change in official attitudes, which then had to be worked out into concrete proposals.[7] But the thinking and planning necessary for strategic adaptation had already taken place. The offensive strategy endured for weeks longer because ministers decided to delay direct rule. In the meantime, other important developments changed their calculations, underscoring the imperative to avoid reifying any single event with turning-point status.[8] The massacre certainly propelled large numbers to join the IRA, a recruitment glut essential for the expansion in violence seen during 1972.[9] Those new recruits proved effective because IRA strategy and tactics changed prior to Bloody Sunday.

The timing and nature of the direct-rule decision in March 1972 can only be explained by bringing together violence in Northern Ireland, parliamentary politics at Westminster and strategic debate. To an extent these connections have been noticed, in the wrangling between soldiers and policemen over security policy prior to Bloody Sunday and in Heath's preoccupation with the European Communities Act over these same months.[10] By weaving violence, parliament and bureaucracy together with new archival information we can see how often adaptation nearly happened. These near-misses illuminate civil–military relations in Britain's democracy. The factors interacted in different ways during the five months under consideration here and are assessed in five sequential phases. As is common for governments waging limited wars such as counter-insurgencies, military logic was subordinated to higher political interests.[11]

The first phase, around November 1971, witnessed bargaining within government and with the Labour opposition over modifications to interrogation. Labour succeeded in forcing the government to abandon in-depth interrogation. But the party became sidetracked on to this single issue, thereby deflecting attention from wider strategy. In the second phase, civil servants and military leaders attempted to capitalise on the destabilisation brought about by Wilson to force through a major strategic shift. They failed because the evidence necessary to support a radical change was too ambiguous. Though things were clearly going wrong in Northern Ireland, defeat was not imminent. As the offensive strategy survived this bureaucratic assault, commanders in Northern Ireland, with consent from London, decided to increase the pressure on nationalists and republicans, in the third phase. Operation Forecast, the mission to arrest rioters in Derry during the protest march on 30 January, followed a logic already present in Belfast. Sending the Parachute Regiment to Derry to conduct an arrest operation was foolhardy. The reaction to Bloody Sunday by the army, the cabinet and the Labour opposition facilitated, in phase four, a cover-up that destroyed Catholic faith in British intentions. Parliament was too busy with Europe, and afraid to offend the army, to enforce accountability for a massacre on UK soil. With the crucial vote on Europe completed, in the fifth phase direct rule loomed. As the Official and Provisional IRAs combined their offensive into a more dangerous configuration, loyalists began to mobilise, rendering a Protestant backlash likely even without Stormont's suspension. Wilson not only signalled parliamentary support to Heath for imposing direct rule, he provided a secret channel to the Official and Provisional IRAs, both of whose leaderships indicated a willingness to negotiate and end violence.

EXTIRPATING THE GUNMEN: A BIPARTISAN CONSENSUS

The first step towards strategic adaptation is for a leader at the centre of power to put change on the agenda.[12] Ideas about cross-community government involving unionists and nationalists had been circulating in Ireland and Britain since at least August 1969.[13] On 11 November 1971 Reginald Maudling changed his mind about delaying a political initiative. Maudling has been widely lambasted for his indolence in office.[14] These charges are justified prior to November 1971. From then onwards he repeatedly argued for a shift in strategy. Northern Ireland affairs before direct rule came to be dominated by the prime minister, the home secretary and the defence secretary. Other senior ministers, such as the chancellor and the foreign secretary, attended the Cabinet Northern Ireland Committee, but they spoke less than the three core ministers, who made the major decisions. Heath chose yes-men for the cabinet in June 1970.[15]

Maudling's failure to achieve strategic adaptation, as Heath and Carrington blocked him, seems to bear this out. A former party leadership contender, Maudling consistently deferred to the prime minister. Lord Carrington did not speak at the meeting on 11 November. He avoided drastic change whilst at the helm of the MOD. At times he recognised the limits to a military offensive, noting, for example, the IRA's ability to bring off spectacular bombings even when under the cosh.[16] Yet Carrington understood the republican campaign simply: 'criminality masquerading as nationalist struggle'.[17] His service as a regular army officer, and the IRA assassination threat against his family, may have influenced his thinking. Carrington backed Heath instinctively, as a loyal supporter without his own substantial political base in the Conservative Party or the country.[18] (See Illustration 5.1.) The leadership dynamic around the prime minister affected the propensity for strategic adaptation.

When making his case on 11 November, the home secretary said the present system meant permanent Catholic exclusion from government. He proposed a 'government of national defence and reconstruction' in which Protestants and Catholics would serve together. Labour's likely support for the idea loomed large in his thinking. The ministers decided to sound out Labour before approaching Faulkner.[19] Over the next few weeks the government and opposition negotiated how far strategy should change. In one view, Heath's desire to maintain bipartisan consensus and prevent Northern Ireland from affecting Westminster politics gave Labour 'significant influence'.[20] What is clear from the archival evidence, however, is Labour's reluctance to insist on change beyond adjustments to interrogation. Harold Wilson began openly criticising the government on Northern Ireland in mid September, in response to disquiet amongst Labour members over internment and interrogation. He may have feared being

Illustration 5.1 Edward Heath and Peter Carrington at the Conservative Party annual conference in Blackpool, 10 October 1973.
(Courtesy of Evening Standard/Hulton Archive/Getty Images.)

outmanoeuvred by James Callaghan, a potential leadership rival, and splits developing in a party already divided over Europe.[21]

While Maudling, Carrington and Heath met in Whitehall, a delegation from Labour's National Executive Committee (NEC) went to Belfast. The party's research department briefed them beforehand, arguing 'The military campaign against the I.R.A. must be intensified' and that 'Internment must stay until the political situation permits its removal.' The research department suggested the escalating violence be checked by combined political and military measures, to remove Catholic support for PIRA.[22] The NEC delegates heard from the SDLP about the 'almost total alienation' of Catholics, 26,000 of whom were on rent strike in protest at government policy. They called for Stormont to be suspended, and for talks between unionists, nationalists, the British and the Republic. The SDLP and the Northern Ireland Labour Party agreed that internment was the most objectionable policy.[23] Jim Callaghan hoped these two parties, the Irish Labour Party and his own party, could agree on a political programme to put before the British, Irish and Northern Irish governments. The prospects for agreement were hardly helped by his publicly proclaimed belief in retaining internment.[24] By contrast, Tony Benn, who chaired the talks, deduced the concerns over internment should be addressed by transferring control over all security policy to London.[25] With a united left-wing opposition to the government's general strategy elusive, back in Westminster the Labour Party focused on interrogation instead.

An inquiry led by Edmund Compton was a classic in the whitewashing genre – held in secret, limited in scope, lacking judicial powers and comprising only British officials.[26] Maudling presented the findings to parliament on 16 November. Compton was sympathetic to the security forces, performing 'semantic gymnastics', in Labour MP George Cunningham's phrase, to find some ill-treatment but no 'physical brutality'. To cool the parliamentary heat over the issue, Maudling announced another inquiry, into future interrogation.[27] HQNI were relieved at the 'generally satisfactory' press reaction to Compton.[28] The shadow cabinet agreed to resist pressure from a minority of MPs for a division against the government in the Commons on Northern Ireland, endorsing the more limited emphasis upon interrogation.[29] Even here, Labour soft-pedalled. After the parliamentary debate, former minister Roy Hattersley telephoned the MOD to find out whether the five techniques had been used in Aden, on Labour's watch. The answer was yes – and during the Confrontation in Indonesia. Denis Healey, now shadow defence secretary, inspected the ministry's papers on interrogation under his tenure.[30] Ivor Richard, then a junior defence minister, observed resistance to interrogation training in May 1970, which included the five techniques.[31] Labour held back in order to cast a veil over their own past choices.

Wilson now went to Northern Ireland for the first time since becoming party leader, holding twenty-two meetings over three days.[32] His press secretary, Joe Haines, proved racism towards the Irish existed in left-wing quarters as much as on the right, when he recalled the meetings: 'The greatest progress made was in the emptying of the Irish whiskey bottle. They spoke, and they spoke. They argued, disputed, debated, discussed, contested, and controverted.'[33] General Tuzo struck an upbeat note. A high proportion of IRA leaders had been captured, and the rank and file lacked training. Internment worked at a time when intimidation prevented people from supplying information to the security forces. The IRA's ability to sustain a high level of attacks was not necessarily significant, a strange claim for a general intent on reducing the IRA's operations. Tuzo warned Wilson off making security a 'plaything of party politics at Westminster'. He expected direct rule or withdrawing the army to provoke Protestant violence. Wilson accepted the army should be kept in place and believed violence had to end before a political initiative.[34] He reassured the Northern Ireland cabinet of his opposition to direct rule unless absolutely necessary, and to withdrawing the army. His position on reform differed slightly from what Tuzo heard: though violence must end before major political changes came into effect, talks should begin at once, to give Catholics hope. He advocated a coalition government that included constitutional nationalists. Faulkner blamed the SDLP for absenting themselves from politics and objected to a coalition.[35]

Cardinal William Conway, leader of the Catholic church in Ireland, thought along the same lines, urging a power-sharing government to mend Catholic 'despair' only 'when the IRA were beginning to crack'.[36] Canon Murphy and Tom Conaty, from the CCDC, disagreed. Aiming to defeat terrorism without a political solution was a mistake. Their efforts to sustain good relations between the army and Catholics in Belfast had been destroyed by repression. Maudling shunned attempts by Murphy and Conaty to discuss these points in person.[37] Gerry Fitt, Ivan Cooper, Austin Currie, Paddy Devlin, John Hume and Paddy O'Hanlon met Wilson on 17 November. The SDLP advocated suspending Stormont for a year to allow for wide-ranging consultations. They foresaw a less cataclysmic Protestant reaction than the government. The SDLP's supporters would only allow them to meet Maudling if internment had been abolished.[38] Maudling and Heath blamed the SDLP's intransigence for the political stagnation. However, the party curbed its demands by late September, no longer asking for Stormont to be abolished, an interim governing commission, or a guaranteed constitutional summit.[39] On returning to London, Wilson met Heath, Maudling and Carrington. Though explaining that the SDLP's demand on internment expressed legitimate Catholic sentiment, he chose to align with the Conservative government rather than his Irish social-democratic comrades. Wilson shared General Tuzo's 'qualified optimism' and concurred with Heath: 'there could be no solution until the gunmen had been extirpated'.[40]

Three days later Wilson proposed a fifteen-point plan for Northern Ireland in the House of Commons. Though suggesting Britain slowly move towards leaving Northern Ireland, the plan stuck to the principle that violent resistance must be crushed before any political solution came into effect.[41] Wilson's position on Northern Ireland never really deviated from three core beliefs: in a reformed government where power-sharing became the norm; in closer co-operation between north and south; and a reluctance to impose Irish unification against unionists' wishes.[42] Tony Benn regarded Wilson's speech as 'a remarkable success'. In a meeting of the parliamentary party later that night, discontent was expressed from the left over Wilson's failure to condemn internment outright.[43] In the shadow cabinet Michael Foot pressed for an end to bipartisanship and clear opposition to internment. Wilson deflected the discussion away from security, winning support for his aim to hold interparty talks at Westminster before anything else.[44]

Wilson and Callaghan took the proposal to Heath in Downing Street on 15 December. He agreed to hold Conservative–Labour talks in London first, and then bring in the Northern Ireland parties in early January.[45] Two days later Callaghan changed tack, asking Maudling to move straight to talks between London and Belfast without Labour and the Conservatives first reaching a common position. Nothing should be off the table. Callaghan thought the Democratic Unionist Party (DUP) and the SDLP might reach a compromise. Maudling favoured power-sharing, with the border issue kicked into the long grass.[46] By Tony Benn's reckoning, Callaghan's stance was motivated partly by a desire to prevent Northern Ireland affairs from drifting into the hands of Labour's NEC, and thus away from his own direct influence. In strict policy terms Callaghan shared the government's anxiety about provoking a Protestant rebellion by aligning too closely with the SDLP. Stark warnings from the SDLP's Paddy Devlin that military operations were driving people towards PIRA went unheeded.[47]

Unbeknown to Labour, the government started to realise that the controversy around interrogation might not be over. Heath deplored Lord Parker's willingness to listen to 'those who held the extreme view that interrogation was totally unacceptable', such as the 'disreputable' Amnesty International.[48] The Northern Ireland attorney general, Basil Kelly, doubted whether the five techniques were legal. Despite this, he was 'glad that he had not been asked to initiate any public prosecution of the members of the security forces involved'.[49] Accountability was avoided by the police investigating and prosecuting themselves. The MOD received a tip-off that Lord Gardiner, a member of Parker's inquiry and lord chancellor in Wilson's government, intended to condemn the five techniques as illegal.[50] The UK attorney general, Sir Peter Rawlinson, knew Gardiner personally, having worked in his chambers after wartime service in the Irish Guards. The only Catholic in the cabinet, Rawlinson sought to convey the 'mood of the Province and the Republic of which relations and friends wrote and spoke'.[51] He tried to persuade Parker to avoid references to international law. The Geneva Conventions did not apply in Northern Ireland, and reference to them or the European Convention on Human Rights threatened the government's international reputation. Parker, for his part, noticed the military interrogation doctrine cited the Geneva Conventions. Rawlinson believed that if the incidents described by Compton had happened in England, they would have been unlawful.[52]

The concession may have emboldened Gardiner in damning deep interrogation. Rawlinson made no endeavour to extend his verdict on interrogation to the repressive measures more widely at issue. Once Lord Carrington understood deep interrogation must be permanently abandoned, he encouraged Special Branch to 'do everything possible and legal short of it'.[53] Thomas Hennessey argues deep interrogation proved remarkably successful in degrading the IRA by taking men and weapons out of circulation.[54] Yet IRA attacks continued. The guns and fresh volunteers never dried up. Samantha Newbery's judgement is persuasive: the political costs outweighed the short-term tactical advantages. She notes the damaging effect on Anglo-Irish relations, as the Irish government referred British conduct to the European Commission of Human Rights. In 1978 the European Court of Human Rights ruled the five techniques constituted 'inhuman and degrading treatment'. Heath announced their proscription in the Commons on 2 March 1972.[55] Deep interrogation's relative value diminished over time as high-volume routine questioning became more fruitful.

Most regular interrogation happened under Special Branch auspices at three regional holding centres (later renamed police holding centres).[56] In late November 1971 mass arrests and questioning constituted the 'principal remaining source of intelligence'. Fear of being sent for deep interrogation prompted many people to talk freely under normal police questioning.[57] During December the security forces arrested 496 people.[58] About half were released within forty-eight hours. The rest ended up in internment.[59] These figures do not include people who were stopped and questioned in the street. An officer on the PIRA Belfast Brigade staff arrested in mid January 1972 also 'divulged information' to his interrogators.[60] The situation differed in the countryside. Arriving in October 1971, 5 Brigade were 'disturbed at the weakness of the intelligence network'. Between October and April the interrogation centre in the Brigade's area, in Armagh, dealt with 121 suspects, producing 'Very little hard information'.[61]

DETECTING STRATEGIC SUCCESS OR FAILURE

The offensive against the IRA remained the dominant strategy with the Labour leadership's acquiescence. Forcing reform to interrogation practices enabled Wilson and Callaghan to placate left-wing critics in the party. At heart they both believed Heath's priorities to be correct. The impetus for strategic adaptation would have to come from elsewhere. As early as May the MOD's PUS, Sir James Dunnett, told his counterpart in the Home Office that a united, federal Ireland seemed the only long-term solution.[62] Dunnett and others who favoured negotiation failed to convince the prime minister and defence secretary to stop offensive operations. Why? On conventional battlefields progress is relatively obvious: the front line is advancing, retreating or static. Irregular conflicts lack such clarity. In the United States Army in Vietnam, commanders struggled to understand the conflict. Few officers possessed experience in waging unconventional wars or knew much about Vietnam. The army hobbled itself with an overabundance of different metrics. Measuring success or failure became so complicated that the most important factors could not be identified.[63] Though the officer corps in Northern Ireland possessed plenty of relevant experience, they also faced a mass of conflicting data. Scott Gartner's concept of 'dominant indicators' is helpful here. Gartner argues that modern armed forces produce too much information for any individual or organisation to fully assess. Consequently, they 'reduce the available information to specific indicators'. Dominant indicators are those relied upon by leaders to evaluate their strategies.

Leaders are unlikely to change strategy when their dominant indicator is moving in a positive direction.[64]

The information available to strategists increased in late 1971. From late October ministers met to discuss the Province twice a week, and the PUS at the MOD convened a daily meeting with other top Whitehall officials.[65] The Brigadier General Staff (Intelligence) (BGS(Int)) was tasked to bring intelligence with serious consequences to the notice of the ministry's leadership.[66] From November the Directorate of Military Operations produced a monthly report for those in the ministry, units liable for deployment and 10 Downing Street.[67] From December HQNI produced a weekly summary for the same reason.[68] Ministers received briefings from the CGS, whilst the MOD and the Home Office regularly corresponded with their representatives in Belfast. In Northern Ireland there were three leading categories of indicators. Firstly, casualty data. The main metrics were the numbers killed and wounded. Secondly, data on operations by the security forces, including searches, arms and ammunition finds, and arrests. Thirdly, data on terrorist operations, such as shootings and bombings. Reports also made qualitative assessments of progress by the security forces, IRA operations, significant events and future prospects.

The statistics should not be taken as perfectly accurate.[69] They do, however, show the information decision makers relied upon at the time. (See Figure 5.1.) Reports showed modest fluctuations in casualties, only indicating a radically higher cost in human suffering in the two weeks preceding the direct-rule decision. The imperative to abandon the existing

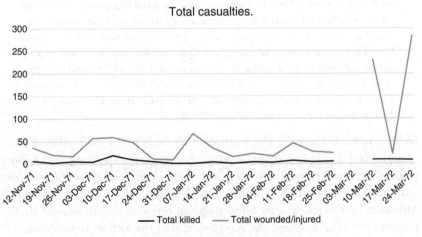

Figure 5.1 Total casualties, November 1971–March 1972.

strategy came late. Rare events like the McGurk's Bar bombing, which killed fifteen people and injured twenty-one others in Belfast on 4 December, made little mark. It was written off as an accidental detonation by the IRA (in fact the UVF were responsible).[70]

HQNI's weekly summaries consistently supported the offensive strategy against the IRA. Like many professional armies, the British valued operations above intelligence, action before analysis.[71] Successful arrests, and arms and ammunition finds constituted the dominant indicators, registering more than casualty numbers. The report for the week ending 17 December noted: 'Arrests of wanted men have continued at a high rate.' Even though the number had declined from the week before, those taken into custody included 'a number of key IRA personalities'.[72] Early January saw the IRA 'facing considerable difficulties' as the security forces recovered 'a large quantity of arms and ammunition'.[73] On 21 January Major-General Ford observed 'the IRA are having difficulty in finding members of the right calibre to assume officer appointments and in some areas of Belfast are losing the support of more moderate Catholics'.[74] The monthly reports followed the same line. Captured documents revealed PIRA felt itself under 'an unacceptable degree of pressure' by late November. Arrests and casualties were expected to produce a further drop in IRA attacks.[75] The report for December opened by claiming:

> the effects of the Security Forces operations against the IRA are biting. In Belfast the 1st and 2nd Battalions of the Brady IRA have been forced to reorganise. At best three companies have been so hard hit by arrests that they have become ineffective, and battalions have been forced to form small Active Service Units of remaining men from all companies. In the 3rd Battalion (BRADY) three companies are believed to have merged. In addition, vigorous attempts are being made to improve security; arms have been withdrawn from company QMs [quartermasters] and placed under battalion control, and arms dumps are rapidly moved after the arrest of important members. ... The Goulding IRA in Belfast has also suffered and it is estimated that two companies of the 1st Battalion and one of the 2nd Battalion are now virtually non-effective.[76]

Daily reports reinforced the positive outlook. On 14 November Belfast experienced the first twenty-four-hour period without shooting or bombing since internment came into force.[77] A day later police questioning led to 54 guns and 11,000 rounds of ammunition being seized in County Antrim.[78] Attempts by republicans to open negotiations – swiftly dismissed by the government – heightened the impression that the IRA were weakening.[79]

British Army battalions in Belfast saw progress: 1st Royal Scots thought their arms and ammunition finds and arrests were 'wearing the enemy down'.[80]

Bottom-up change within armies can improve operational performance. Militaries adapt by refining existing tactics, techniques and/or technologies, or by exploring new operational means. Adaptation is prompted by the fear of defeat and enabled by poor organisational memory (avoiding being stuck in old habits), decentralisation that allows junior leaders to be creative, and personnel turnover (so new arrivals bring fresh ideas).[81] The British Army's regimental system and disdain for formal doctrine have always been conducive to learning; the rotation of units through Northern Ireland on short tours promoted fresh ideas at the tactical level. Learning became systematically embedded after direct rule. In late 1971 and early 1972 the army adapted in two key areas: bomb disposal and, to a greater extent, intelligence-gathering.

Innovation in bomb disposal cannot be fully assessed as the most sensitive information, on radio-controlled bombs and electronic countermeasures, is still classified. Nevertheless, the Royal Army Ordnance Corps teams certainly adapted to new devices developed by the IRA. In 1970, 321 Explosive Ordnance Disposal (EOD) Unit deployed to reinforce the limited capacity in Northern Ireland, with sections for Belfast, Derry and Lurgan. Each section comprised an officer and two to five non-commissioned officers (NCOs) to act as operators, defusing bombs. The senior ammunition technical officer at HQNI produced bulletins to guide operators on the latest devices and how to tackle them. At first operators were instructed to dismantle bombs rather than letting them go off, both to collect evidence on their construction and to protect property. After several operator deaths commanders imposed a more strict adherence to a stipulated 'soak time', leaving devices for a waiting period before approaching them.[82] From 27 September 1971 the army, police and forensic science service operated a data reference centre to analyse explosive devices, bullets and weapons to provide useable intelligence on techniques and particular incidents.[83] On 18 November EOD officers deployed 'Pigstick', a miniature cannon which fired water and gas into a device to disrupt it.[84] The capacity for adaptation was limited by the shortage of bomb disposal officers as the IRA campaign accelerated in these months.[85] The data on bombs placed (almost entirely by the IRA) and those defused by EOD operators suggests the army normally lacked the capacity to match the bombers. (See Figure 5.2.) Successive attempts by Stormont to restrict access to bomb-making materials proved ineffective. The Explosives Act (Northern Ireland) of May 1970, for

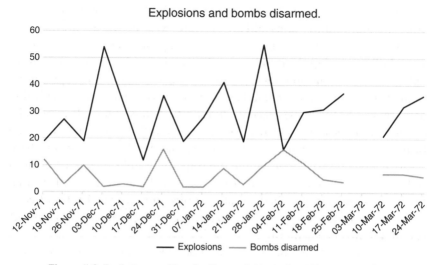

Figure 5.2 Explosions and bombs disarmed, November 1971–March 1972.

example, empowered the police to control the manufacturing, sale and use of explosives.[86]

Battalion performance at intelligence-gathering had been improving since at least Easter time 1971, a trend that continued throughout the year and into 1972. An intelligence team from 2nd Royal Regiment of Fusiliers was sent to Belfast for an extended handover five weeks before the battalion's main body arrived.[87] Much information came from basic patrolling. Gunners from 25 Light Regiment Royal Artillery counted the milk bottles outside houses thought to be used by IRA leaders, to judge when they might be present.[88] A young boy informed a Glosters patrol on 22 December about a .38 pistol he found on waste ground. A few weeks later the battalion's senior officers met local policemen to agree how to share information. Photo boards were placed in the canteen showing IRA suspects, to help soldiers remember faces. It seemed to work. The adjutant of E Company, 2nd PIRA Battalion was picked up in Osman Street, Belfast the next day.[89] Around November 1971, 39 Brigade began using about half a dozen 'turned' IRA members, called 'Freds', to gather intelligence. Safely anonymous in armoured cars, they would be driven around Belfast to identify IRA volunteers for arrest and interrogation.[90] In Belfast, and probably elsewhere, signals intelligence-gathering took place.[91]

Improvements in intelligence-gathering could only achieve so much. Soldiers normally searched vehicles without precise intelligence, to catch

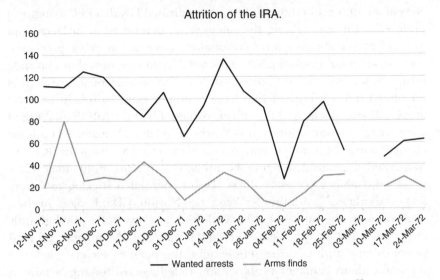

Figure 5.3 Attrition of the IRA, November 1971–March 1972.[92]

wanted terrorists and interdict their supply routes: 42 Commando searched nearly 1,000 vehicles each week. Their newsletter noted 'only a very unlucky or stupid terrorist is caught'.[93] HQNI and brigade headquarters often detached companies from their battalions, placing them temporarily under another unit for specific operations. The practice damaged soldiers' knowledge about their own patch.[94] RUC Special Branch, the lead intelligence organisation, resisted suggestions the whole system be computerised. The army routed intelligence through computers at Blandford in Dorset, home to the Royal Signals.[95] There were also political limits on military innovation. Prime Minister Heath personally authorised amendments to the 'yellow card' in November 1971, permitting automatic weapons to be used, officers to allow soldiers to keep their weapons cocked and ready to fire, and vehicles to be shot at.[96] Heath and Carrington resisted change to the most controversial tactic of all, internment without trial. Overall, incremental tactical adaptation produced episodic success against the IRA, rather than a consistent upward trend. (See Figure 5.3.) Offensive action endured because the security forces staved off any catastrophic defeats.

Tactical and operational adaptation is meaningless if higher-level commanders, or political leaders, block change.[97] Edward Heath's private secretary, Douglas Hurd, observed the prime minister hungered for new ideas from others, despite not being an innovator himself.[98] Throughout

November 1971 senior officials broadly confirmed Heath and Carrington's preference for maintaining the offensive. A deterioration in Derry mid month featured almost as an afterthought to General Carver's appreciation for 'encouraging' results in Belfast. General Tuzo's caution about possible future IRA attacks on soft targets (such as the families of security forces members) did not prevent him from planning extra patrols in Catholic areas.[99] Frank Steele, an MI6 officer working for the UKREP, established a wide range of connections across Northern Ireland. He expected Catholic alienation from Stormont to endure even if the army wiped out the IRA, and so advised a political initiative be prepared.[100] More influential voices prevailed. Cabinet Secretary Burke Trend counselled sticking to victory first – talks later.[101] Admiral Sir Peter Hill-Norton, CDS, hedged his bets in recommending internment be abolished 'at some point', though only after 'careful study'.[102] When Carrington's PUS spoke up for enforced power-sharing and a border referendum, the defence secretary ignored the point about Faulkner's cabinet and railed against forcing 'a million Ulster Protestants into a United Ireland against their will'.[103]

In mid December two simultaneous reassessments presented the opportunity for strategic adaptation. Harold Wilson's fifteen-point plan prompted a growing realisation that direct rule might be on the cards.[104] Kenneth Bloomfield, the highly regarded deputy secretary to the Northern Ireland cabinet, secretly met the UKREP, Howard Smith, in Belfast on 17 December. Smith's account of the meeting was read by Heath.[105] Bloomfield thought Stormont incapable of devising political reforms acceptable to Catholics. Faulkner's expectation that Catholics would co-operate after the IRA were defeated was 'quite unrealistic'. Bloomfield believed only full power-sharing would be enough, yet the unionists were unwilling to make such an offer, and Catholics were reluctant to accept it from them. Only intervention by London to impose power-sharing could break the impasse. Since August 1969 British governments had avoided such action for fear of a violent Protestant reaction. In Smith's words, a man of 'such high ability, who has been at the centre of things for so long' in Stormont, judged the risk worth taking. Even those who opposed power-sharing 'would accept it if it was imposed on them'. Smith implored ministers to heed the advice.[106] This was a momentous occasion. For the first time someone at the centre of the Northern Ireland government suggested that major constitutional change, the key to re-engaging moderate nationalists such as the SDLP, was possible.

On the same day as Bloomfield's meeting, General Carver concluded a tour to Northern Ireland by deciding that the time was coming 'very soon' for a political initiative. (See Illustration 5.2.) He confirmed Bloomfield's judgement: 'There are now a number of responsible and senior RUC officers, who are not only prepared to accept but even advocate that Westminster should become responsible for law and order.' He perceived the IRA in Belfast to be 'under very considerable pressure' from arrests, internment, shootings by the army, arms and ammunition finds, and intelligence-gathering. Carver advised London to intervene before mid February, when terrorism would be sufficiently under control and Protestant opinion not firmly against a change. His proposal contained three elements:

> a. Law and order become the responsibility of Westminster. Until terrorism is finally eliminated, and in order to hasten its elimination, the GOC resumes full responsibility for the direction of all security operations, Army and Police, designed to restore normal processes of law and order. b. As many as possible of those areas of public administration, in which inter-sectarian problems loom large, should be made the responsibility of public boards on which minority communities are fully represented. These boards would themselves be responsible to the Government of Northern Ireland. c. The method of representation and election to the Parliament of Northern Ireland would be revised by a further commission in the light of a. and b.

Illustration 5.2 General Sir Michael Carver, Chief of the General Staff, 8 April 1971. (Courtesy of Keystone/Hulton Archive/Getty Images.)

The preference for reforms short of power-sharing attested to Carver's acute grasp of Carrington's reservations. He made operational recommendations too, such as appointing a new deputy to assist the GOC on policing, and replacing the chief constable with someone more dynamic. The suppression of the IRA in certain areas, such as Ballymacarrett in Belfast, proved military gains needed to be quickly followed by social improvements. Repairs to properties and access to social security benefits stood out as priorities. Without state assistance people looked to the paramilitaries. Carver advised against upsetting the political balance by mounting any major operations in Derry.[107] Lord Carrington reacted with apprehension to the idea about London assuming responsibility for law and order.[108] He seemed unable to appreciate the distinctions between direct rule, power-sharing, responsibility for law and order, and Irish reunification. Writing to a fellow Guards officer from the war Carrington said: 'unless and until the Northern Ireland people as a whole have expressed a clear wish to join the South, Northern Ireland remains a part of the United Kingdom'. The onus lay with Dublin, to amend their constitution to make unification palatable for unionists. He believed the IRA must be defeated 'as an essential preliminary. . .. There can be no question of negotiating with them.'[109]

In the MOD on 22 December, General Carver reiterated the lessons from his trip to Belfast. Carrington proved anxious to avoid destabilising Brian Faulkner. Hill-Norton backed Carver, arguing people in Northern Ireland were sufficiently fed up to accept direct rule. In discussion there was even consideration of redrawing the international border along the River Foyle, to hand the Catholic areas of Derry to the Republic. Any attempt to seize control over Derry would be dangerous, given Catholic support for the IRA, based on 'generally good administration'.[110] The CGS, the CDS and the PUS all favoured a radical change in Northern Ireland, a position already held by the cabinet secretary and the home secretary. Lord Carrington blocked them then and in subsequent meetings on 7 and 18 January 1972. On the latter occasion he invoked loyalist rage as a reason to maintain the existing policy.[111] Lord Saville's contention that the government attempted to reach a peaceful solution before Bloody Sunday is untenable. Carrington and Heath prevented anything greater than gradual tactical adaptation in the war against the IRA because they believed the slow squeeze to be pushing nationalists into accepting the status quo.

'FREE TO PURSUE THE WAR AGAINST THE TERRORISTS': THE STRATEGIC LOGIC FOR CONFRONTATION IN DERRY

General Carver's championing of an imminent strategic adjustment proved influential. In the weeks before Bloody Sunday, debate over when and how to change course intensified. The decision to mount an arrest operation during the civil rights march on 30 January 'represented a direct and deliberate' rejection of the existing non-confrontational approach in Derry.[112] Divisions in the military have been seen as crucial in explaining Bloody Sunday. Major-General Ford pushed for harsher repression, supported by such officers as Lieutenant-Colonel Wilford, commanding 1st Parachute Regiment. The Saville inquiry has been criticised for assigning responsibility for Bloody Sunday to those at the bottom of the chain of command rather than emphasising Major-General Ford's role.[113] Ford and Wilford's attitudes matter for understanding how the arrest operation on 30 January turned into a massacre. But the decision to confront the anti-internment marchers derived from the government's ongoing strategy of squashing nationalist resistance before a dramatic political intervention. Carver wanted an initiative once the IRA came under control in Belfast. That opportunity existed for the first two weeks of January 1972. While Heath and Carrington prevaricated, the IRA adapted their campaign across the whole province. As the IRA escalated from mid January 1972, and protest marches increased in number, the window for a political settlement based on republican and nationalist submission began to close.

General Tuzo aligned himself to the emerging strategy in his Christmas public message. Though confident about the campaign against the IRA, he regretted the army's tendency to 'collide' with Catholics.[114] Tuzo reached out to Cardinal Conway on 11 January, going to talk to him in Armagh. Initially finding the cardinal 'rigid and unreceptive', the men slowly warmed to each other. Conway had often condemned IRA violence and might soon openly condemn the army. Many Catholics believed HQNI condoned soldiers beating people up. Conway argued a political initiative should be timed to balance '(1) The IRA being groggy, but (2) The right-wing Unionists not being aware of the extent of this'.[115] Two Catholic Conservative MPs visiting Northern Ireland thought the time had come. Norman St John-Stevas, MP for Chelmsford, recalled a province 'politically virtually paralysed'. Though the troops appeared to be in fine spirits, the constant searches and patrols made them 'very unpopular' in Catholic areas. St John-Stevas doubted the army's claim to be on the verge of victory.

He understood that a guerrilla campaign could be pursued by the IRA almost indefinitely. A political settlement must now be proposed.[116] David James, MP for North Dorset, labelled British policy 'disastrously wrong'. An urgent initiative was essential as 'almost the whole [Catholic] community' tacitly supported the IRA.[117]

While senior officials in the MOD accepted 'a limit in the extent to which terrorism could be reduced by military means alone', fears about a loyalist backlash persisted at HQNI.[118] The JIC judged any violent resistance to direct rule to 'be of manageable proportions'. Most civil servants, judges and police officers would accept the new regime. Once London acted, major changes must come quickly, before Catholics lost heart and looked to republicanism for answers.[119] The JIC secretary reported that the IRA faced real difficulties in maintaining their offensive in Belfast. Arrests and arms finds had plateaued, suggesting further progress was unlikely.[120] Informed by the intelligence assessments, General Carver pushed for a move away from attrition at the next Cabinet Northern Ireland Committee meeting. The minutes are vague – someone suggested IRA violence might be as low as it was going to get in Belfast, and the time thus ripe for grasping the moment politically. Maudling wished for lengthy consultations with Labour before acting. He bridled at the SDLP's insistence on ending internment before talks commenced.[121]

Republicans refused to accept the British Army's efforts to politically marginalise them through attrition. Decentralisation certainly aided the IRA's ability to adapt and survive the British onslaught in the months after internment, with individual companies and battalions able to exercise considerable autonomy from the Dublin leadership.[122] Understanding the adaptive dynamics within republican units is difficult on the available evidence. The claim that violence escalated 'beyond the intentions or expectations of those in charge' is an exaggeration.[123] Centralised direction occurred alongside more spontaneous, bottom-up innovation. The volunteers who flooded in after 30 January joined groups already undergoing organisational, technological and tactical change. Army intelligence officers detected the alterations and passed the information to senior leaders, essential prerequisites for strategic adaptation.[124]

In December the Provisional and Official IRAs rebuilt their units in Ardoyne with new members.[125] Local commanders began to exercise greater autonomy, making it harder to generate intelligence on them by arresting those from other units.[126] PIRA attempted to counteract interrogation. A house search in Belfast recovered a PIRA intelligence officer's notes from the debriefings of volunteers arrested, plus a list of Special Branch officers, with photographs.[127] The Fianna Éireann, the IRA youth organisation, grew and became more prominent.[128] By 11 January the army knew of sixty-two Fianna members. One 16-year-old engineer officer was trained in bomb-making and had taken part in an arson attack.[129] Counteracting the Fianna pulled the security forces into a carefully laid trap. On 3 December 1971 a Belfast magistrate heard about eleven boys, aged 13 to 16, being arrested in the early hours for Special Branch interrogation. Suspected Fianna members, the boys were held without their parents' consent or presence, and threatened with borstal, before being released twelve hours later.[130] The effect on local opinion can readily be imagined.

The Provisionals generated their most intensive innovations in bomb-making before 1977; the Belfast and Armagh brigades proved the most creative.[131] Some bomb-makers were thought to be Royal Engineers veterans. The campaign expanded in 1971 with a ten-fold rise in both incidents and explosive quantities.[132] Trooper John Warnock became the first soldier to die from a roadside bomb, after an attack at Derrybeg on 6 September. Captain David Stewardson was the first bomb disposal officer to be killed, when a bomb with an anti-handling device exploded at Castlerobin on 9 September. In late October PIRA modified these 'Castlerobin' models to run off a timer.[133] The winter of 1971 illustrated the constraints on PIRA, as they could not access more than about a ton of explosives a month. This was probably because the Irish government tightened controls on gelignite from October, moving all supplies to central depots under military guard after a series of large-scale thefts.[134] As a result, quartermasters sourced ammonium nitrate fertilizer, readily available for agricultural purposes. PIRA also started on another compound, 'Co-op Mix', made from sodium chlorate and nitrobenzine.[135] Bomb disposal officers defused the first radio-controlled bomb in Aughnacloy on 19 January. Two days later Private Charles Stentiford, from 1st Devon and Dorset Regiment, was killed at Derrynoose by a landmine detonated electrically from over the border.[136]

The British Army noticed a change in IRA tactics in early November 1971. Ramps were built outside army posts and police stations to protect against drive-by shootings, and the police were armed to defend them. The IRA adapted by attacking 'soft' targets, conducting assassinations and detonating larger bombs.[137] According to Chief of Staff Seán MacStiofáin, from August 1971 the Provisionals embarked upon 'a wide-spread bombing campaign against pre-listed economic targets'.[138] The expansion to mass-casualty bombings came on 29 September, when a bomb detonated at the Four Step Inn on the Shankill Road. The attack cannot be explained by a military rationale: the intention was to terrorise.

These bombings sometimes involved warnings so that people could be evacuated from the area. A plan to shut central Belfast to Christmas shoppers saw fifteen devices planted in the city on 20 December, then another twenty-five real and hoax bombs before Christmas Day.[139] Policemen and UDR soldiers on duty were deemed legitimate targets by PIRA from internment onwards.[140] In December, attacks began on them when off-duty. For many, these seemed nothing more than callous sectarian murders.[141] The IRA shot dead Sean Russell whilst he was watching television at home with his family. He was the first Catholic UDR soldier to be killed. On 10 December, off-duty UDR sergeant Kenneth Smyth and former member Daniel McCormick were killed at Clady. On 12 December, OIRA committed the first political assassination in the conflict, shooting Senator Jack Barnhill. Two days later, gunmen attacked five magistrates at their homes in Belfast. At the month's end OIRA burnt down the house of Ivan Neill, speaker of the Northern Ireland House of Commons.[142]

As 1972 began, the preference for 'soft' targets continued: on 3 January a bomb injured at least thirty-two people in Belfast's central shopping district.[143] Activity also increased in the countryside and on the border.[144] By mid January the majority of bombings occurred in these areas, striking security forces' patrols, hotels, shops, electricity installations, government buildings and a fuel depot. Attacks on locally recruited soldiers and policemen continued. IRA gunmen sought out and shot dead Raymond Denham, a police reservist, in his workplace in the Falls Road area. The next day the IRA killed off-duty UDR member Maynard Crawford on his way home from work in Newtownabbey.[145] Bombs went off at pubs, schools and premises belonging to contractors working for the army.[146] British intelligence reported a staff meeting in Cavan, in Ireland, on 17 January of the PIRA leadership; whether this constituted the army council or another grouping is unclear. The attendees decided to intensify operations in the countryside and on the border, and to further target Special Branch and UDR personnel. Enhanced recruitment of volunteers in the Republic was to be a priority.[147] During that week more than half of bombings again occurred in the countryside.[148] Between 18 and 29 January PIRA conducted twelve attacks on policemen, killing three and wounding five.[149]

These changes in IRA organisation, technology and tactics penetrated British strategic thinking. General Carver informed the Cabinet Northern Ireland Committee on 20 January about PIRA's Cavan meeting, but drew no drastic inferences, counterposing the news with information about arrests. Reginald Maudling understood the implications of the IRA moving their offensive beyond Belfast. He 'did not believe, however excellent the performance of the Army, that military action alone could produce a complete solution to the problems of Northern Ireland'. Fellow ministers worried about a backbench rebellion in the Conservative Party, and Harold Wilson gave Heath his support for holding off from direct rule.[150] Heath had already shrugged off the Irish ambassador's warning about IRA reorganisation and revival, while denying Catholic alienation from the army.[151] The taoiseach encountered equal stubbornness at a Brussels meeting. He asked for co-operation, even suggesting modifying Ireland's constitution to make reunification palatable to unionists. Heath paid no attention, simply demanding the SDLP drop their objection to internment.[152] When Faulkner came to Downing Street on 27 January Heath proposed a package comprising the IRA's defeat in Belfast, some reduction in internment, and constitutional reform talks. Ministers accepted Faulkner's outright hostility without a fight.[153] With senior officials and ministers split over whether to stop the offensive and alter Northern Ireland's governing system, only a higher authority could decide whether to act.[154] Prime Minister Heath knew operations against the IRA in Belfast had plateaued and the Provisionals were pivoting towards a sustainable campaign. Party politics trumped strategic logic as he let the war roll on.

Meanwhile in Belfast, on 13 January, the Joint Security Committee renewed the ban on marches. Lord Saville judged the ban 'not unreasonable'; protests undermined law and order.[155] Yet marches represented one of the few avenues left for peaceful political expression for Catholics estranged from Stormont. The ban and subsequent decision to arrest the marchers are better understood as deriving from the wartime mindset. Indeed, the Joint Security Committee hoped proscribing marches should leave the army and police 'free to pursue the war against the terrorists'.[156] General Carver recalled 'something needed to be done' about rioters in Derry. The march on 30 January presented an opportunity to arrest 'hooligans' – an idea he ascribed to General Tuzo.[157] The Director of Operations Committee, chaired by Tuzo, issued instructions for all marches to be stopped and for arrests to be made.[158] Checking the power of NICRA appeared desirable because the army believed it had become a front for OIRA, labelled 'the long-term political threat', more organised, more ideologically coherent than the Provisionals.[159] Major-General Ford's reports bracketed civil rights movement and OIRA activities together: that for the first week in January referred to 'NICRA/Goulding IRA tactics'. A week later Ford described OIRA's likely move to 'a more militant campaign, particularly in Londonderry'. On 21 January he wrote

of 'NICRA and other Republican organisations'. A revived civil disobedience campaign seemed to present a threat to government authority not
seen since August 1971.[160]

Though Belfast, home to PIRA, preoccupied military minds, Derry was
not forgotten. Since early 1970 senior officers in the city, such as Brigadier
Cowan, lamented: 'I don't think that the Belfast military side wholly understood the difference between Belfast and Londonderry.'[161] General Tuzo had
favoured dominating Derry, particularly the republican-controlled Bogside
and Creggan, since early October 1971. Major-General Ford's paper on
'Future Military Policy for Londonderry', of 14 December, regarded occupying the Bogside and the Creggan as 'the correct military solution'. He
accepted 'political drawbacks' (mass resistance) precluded such action 'in
the present circumstances'.[162] The senior police officer in the city, Chief
Superintendent Lagan, and his army counterpart, Brigadier MacLellan,
wished to retain the non-confrontational stance.[163] General Carver shared
Tuzo's desire to pacify Derry at the right time. Attention shifted to Derry in
mid January as progress against the IRA in Belfast stalled.[164] In the second
half of the month Derry witnessed a great deal of violence. The security forces
came under fire on sixty-one occasions and had fifty-two nail bombs thrown at
them. IRA gunmen opened fire several times from behind civilians.[165] On
10 January Ford wrote to Tuzo, floating the idea of restoring order by 'shoot-
[ing] selected ring leaders amongst the DYH [Derry Young Hooligans], after
clear warnings have been issued'. Ford acknowledged he would proceed no
further without direct instructions, and never ordered anyone to be shot.
General Tuzo never corrected Ford's thinking.[166]

Over the weekend of 22–3 January NICRA organised four anti-
internment marches, including one near the new internment camp at
Magilligan, near Derry. Soldiers from 1st Parachute Regiment, brought in
specially from Belfast, manhandled and beat marchers in full view of the
press and television cameras. The adjutant of 2nd Royal Green Jackets, the
resident battalion in Derry, felt compelled to constrain one paratrooper
from assaulting a civilian by thumping him. The 2nd Royal Green Jackets'
commanding officer told his brigadier he never wanted the Paras anywhere
near him again, calling them 'hooligans in uniform'.[167] General Tuzo, quite
content to see a board of inquiry investigate the adjutant's conduct, decreed
the Paras acted 'reasonably'.[168] The Bloody Sunday inquiry examined
Major-General Ford's decision to employ 1 Para for the arrest operation
during the 30 January civil rights march in Derry. Lord Saville argued that
although the events at Magilligan raised concerns about the paratroopers'
propensity for using excessive force on rioters, nothing suggested 1 Para

might present a 'risk of death or serious injury to civilians by reason of unjustified gunfire'.[169] He reached this conclusion without investigating 1 Para's previous conduct in Northern Ireland.

1 Para had been used for the most aggressive operations in Belfast from the internment arrests in August 1971 onwards. Four paratroopers detained for armed robbery expressed 1 Para's ethos: 'We are storm-troopers.... Aggression is what we are taught in no uncertain manner until it is shown in our everyday nature. We now find ourselves in a situation where our pent up aggression, frustration and restlessness has led us to total disaster.'[170] Much depended upon discipline within battalions. Steve Corbett, a gunner in Belfast from November 1971 to March 1972, felt quite content to fire rubber bullets at rioters. He held back from firing his rifle: 'I was just frightened to death of making a grave error.'[171] Some commanding officers kept a close eye on their soldiers' shooting. At 3am on 16 December 1971, two platoons from 1st Gloucestershire Regiment were ambushed near Ross Street in Belfast, and two step-brothers in the unit were shot (one died later from his wounds). The soldiers fired 259 rounds whilst withdrawing. The commanding officer deemed fire discipline 'not tight enough' and issued orders on 'effective fire control'. When someone threw a gelignite bomb at a platoon that night, no shots were fired back. The next day, troops at a roadblock refrained from returning fire when someone fired a single shot at them, because children from a nearby primary school were in the way.[172] The orders were clearly obeyed. 1 Para's records for the months before Bloody Sunday are missing from the National Archives.

General Tuzo and the chief constable planned to handle anti-internment marches in Dungannon on 29 January and Derry the next day in a similar fashion to Magilligan: by stopping the participants reaching their intended destination, and making arrests. Derry was expected to be challenging: 'The operation might well develop into rioting and even a shooting war.'[173] Ministers in London knew about the plan to stop the march and make arrests. Lord Carrington learned about 1 Para's involvement only after the event.[174] His indifference to the details following the furore over the Magilligan march is conspicuous. Brigadier MacLellan drew up the army's Operation Forecast plan for dealing with the march in the city. The paratroopers were to be available as an arrest force, to be sent in only on MacLellan's orders. The army disagreed with Chief Superintendent Lagan's advice to allow the march to proceed without attempting to arrest large numbers.[175] An intelligence report regarded the week beforehand as 'reliable and detailed' said the IRA planned to attack the security forces during the march.[176] Given these known risks, the intention to conduct an arrest operation with paratroopers was foolhardy. The company sergeant-major of Support Company in 1 Para later said his men were briefed to expect snipers during the march: 'Sniper fire is very, very accurate, very pinpointed. It's feared by soldiers ... none of the people in my Company wanted to be killed by a sniper.'[177]

'IT WAS JUST MASS MURDER, AND THERE CANNOT BE ANY EXCUSE FOR IT' – JOHN HUME

John Hume's judgement has stood the test of time.[178] The anti-internment march began in the Creggan at about 3pm on 30 January, with people joining the crowd as it made its way down towards the intended destination, the city centre. Around 15,000 people participated. The army put up barriers to divert people towards Free Derry Corner in the Bogside. These attempts to frustrate the marchers in going along their chosen route provoked some to riot, at army barriers 12, 13 and 14. At barrier 14, in William Street, 2nd Royal Green Jackets soldiers used baton rounds and water cannon to hold people back. Just after 3.55pm Lieutenant-Colonel Wilford, commanding 1 Para, asked 8 Brigade for permission to send a company through barrier 14 to arrest rioters. No reply was received. At about the same time two paratroopers from Support Company fired five shots, wounding Damien Donaghey and John Johnston. Shortly afterwards an OIRA man in the area fired a rifle, missing soldiers and hitting a drainpipe. At 4.07pm Brigadier MacLellan gave 1 Para orders over the radio to mount an arrest operation by sending one company through barrier 14. He directly ordered them 'not to conduct a running battle' down Rossville Street. Lieutenant-Colonel Wilford now disobeyed his superior officer. In addition to sending a company through barrier 14, he sent Support Company in vehicles through barrier 12, in Little James Street. The paratroopers chased people down Rossville Street. It was impossible for peaceful marchers and those who had been rioting to be distinguished.[179] Wilford later told journalist Peter Taylor: 'When we moved on the streets we moved as if we in fact were moving against a well-armed, well-trained army.'[180]

After the vehicles went through barrier 12 the soldiers inside them disembarked in Eden Place and the car park of the Rossville Flats. (See Illustration 5.3.) People in these areas began to run away as the paratroopers arrived. Soon after, Lieutenant 'N' fired three rifle shots over the heads of people in an alleyway near Chamberlain Street, hitting buildings. Lieutenant 'N' told the Bloody Sunday inquiry that he fired to prevent the crowd from attacking him. This was against the rules of engagement. Saville rejected his claim, arguing he fired to frighten people and make them move. Lieutenant 'N''s shots may have confused soldiers, leading them to believe they were under fire from the IRA. Soon after, soldiers from Mortar Platoon opened fire in the Rossville Flats car park, killing Jackie Duddy, and wounding several others. Whilst these events were taking place in the car park, the Anti-Tank Platoon reached the southern end of Kells Walk, on the western side of Rossville Street, and opened fire. One shot hit and mortally wounded Michael Kelly. Five more people were soon shot and mortally wounded nearby: Hugh Gilmour, William Nash, John Young, Michael McDaid and Kevin McElhinney. Alexander Nash was hit and injured when he went to aid his son, William.[181]

Four soldiers from the Anti-Tank Platoon went to Glenfada Park North where they shot and mortally wounded William McKinney and Jim Wray. They shot and injured Joe Friel, Michael Quinn, Joe Mahon and Patrick O'Donnell. Jim Wray was shot twice, the second time probably as he lay on the ground dying. One paratrooper went into Abbey Park, firing a shot that killed Gerard McKinney, passing through him to mortally wound Gerald Donaghey.[182] Before being shot Gerard McKinney shouted out 'No, no' with his hands up in the air.[183] Paratroopers in the south-eastern corner of Glenfada Park North shot across Rossville Street, killing Bernard McGuigan and mortally wounding Patrick Doherty. Patrick Campbell and Daniel

Illustration 5.3 A victim's blood on the pavement near Rossville Flats, Derry, 30 January 1972. (Courtesy of William L. Rukeyser/Getty Images.)

McGowan received gunshot wounds. Only ten minutes elapsed between the paratroopers entering the Bogside and the last person being shot. No paratrooper was injured by gunfire. None of those shot was armed with a firearm or bomb, except for Gerald Donaghey, who (according to the Saville inquiry report) may have possessed nail bombs in his pockets. None posed a threat of death or injury to anyone. In no instance did the paratroopers issue a warning before opening fire. Consequently, the Bloody Sunday inquiry concluded that the soldiers fired without any justification.[184]

Brian Rainey, a teacher marching that day, saw the paratroopers come into Rossville Street: 'I could not believe my eyes. I had never seen anyone shot before. I remember the way they fell was most unusual, they just dropped together in a lifeless way, not forwards or backwards, just sideways in a heap on top of one another.'[185] Maura Duffy went to Altnagelvin Hospital in the evening with neighbours to look for her brother, John Young, who hadn't come home. 'I couldn't believe that John was dead. We then drove home and not a word was spoken in the car that I can remember. I just remember thinking how am I going to tell my mammy and daddy.' Maura was 20, John 17. 'His past-times were music, clothes and girls. He adored music and loved the Beatles.'[186]

The British government found excuses for thirty-eight years before accepting John Hume's verdict on the greatest loss of life caused by the army at home since Peterloo in 1819.[187] Many British people still struggle to believe their soldiers killed innocent civilians. David Charters argues the government responded skilfully to the massacre in avoiding a crisis in civil–military relations.[188] The absence of anything resembling a civil–military crisis in the weeks after Bloody Sunday is striking indeed, but to be regretted rather than celebrated. As Scott Gartner explains, 'Something must happen for a decision maker to determine that the implemented strategy is failing and needs to be replaced.'[189] Bloody Sunday made no such imprint on the consciousness or consciences of Heath, Carrington, Maudling, Carver or Tuzo. After Bloody Sunday the government denigrated the victims and instigated a whitewash inquiry. Eamonn McCann suggests the widespread despair at British policy in Northern Ireland in 1972, which fed republican and loyalist paramilitary recruitment, might have been avoided if the government had reacted differently to Bloody Sunday.[190]

The lies began early. At the end of the operation Ford and Wilford said to television reporters that the army came under fire first. Other officers told the press some of those shot were on a wanted list – a claim never backed up by evidence. Major Loden, commanding Support Company, wrote a list detailing the circumstances in which each victim was shot as a gunman or bomber. The adjutant, Captain Mike Jackson (later CGS), helped edit the list. Lord Saville concluded that soldiers made false statements to justify their shooting. He neither investigated nor condemned officers for passing on the lies.[191] HQNI blamed the casualties on the IRA, and provided talking points for defending the army's reputation. Soldiers fired at identified targets to defend themselves or others from injury. Soldiers never fired 'into a peaceful crowd', and 'those hit were men of "military age", which would have been remarkable had we fired into a crowd'.[192] General Carver received a phone call at home on the Sunday evening: 'My first reaction was to heave a sigh of relief that so few had been killed.' He assumed people died in a gun-battle between the army and the IRA.[193] Taoiseach Jack Lynch told Heath the paratroopers acted 'beyond what a disciplined force might be expected to [do]' and called for direct rule immediately. Heath became angry, blaming first the march organisers for putting people in harm's way, then the IRA for 'trying to take over the country', then Lynch himself for failing to deal with the IRA in the Republic. Despite all the coverage on the television and radio, Heath refused 'to prejudge the Army'.[194]

When the Cabinet Northern Ireland Committee met on the Monday, General Carver claimed the paratroopers came under fire from the Rossville Flats, leading to a gun-battle. He stated: 'At no time had fire been directed against NICRA marchers', though civilians may have been hit in the cross-fire. Some committee members questioned these facts; an inquiry was essential.[195] Later that day Lord Chief Justice Widgery agreed to lead the inquiry. The prime minister reminded Widgery 'we were in Northern Ireland fighting not only a military war but a propaganda war'. In 2003 Heath denied these words implied he pressurised Widgery to exonerate the army.[196] In the Commons, Reginald Maudling stated, 'The Army returned the fire directed at them with aimed shots and inflicted a number of casualties on those who were attacking them with firearms and with bombs.' He announced an inquiry would be held. Merlyn Rees, for the Labour Party, asked for the inquiry to consider policy as well as events, particularly the question of who authorised the arrests. Harold Wilson called for the interparty talks to provide a political settlement to be accelerated. The speaker of the house prevented Bernadette Devlin, the only person in the Commons who witnessed the events in Derry first-hand, from speaking. She physically assaulted Maudling after calling him 'a murdering hypocrite'.[197] On 1 February Rees and Wilson again pressed the government to convene political negotiations.[198] The Cabinet Northern Ireland Committee decided on 9 February 'the moment for a political initiative had arrived'. The civil disobedience campaign and international hostility to the government weighed heavily in the discussion. For the first time the committee accepted some internees must be released. Yet nothing changed.[199] At the same time, and again a week later, the shadow cabinet agreed to hold back and see what the government came up with.[200]

Chip Chapman, who commanded 2 Para from 1999 to 2001, notes the tendency for commanders to regard their men with a 'messianic devotion'. He counsels officers remember that soldiers have 'a great propensity to lie and cheat to preserve their own ass'.[201] As the commanding officer, Derek Wilford bore responsibility for establishing whether his men told the truth, and for instituting disciplinary procedures against those who broke the law. He did neither. Carver waited until the Saturday before travelling to address 1st Parachute Regiment, promising to support them provided they told the truth.[202] As a brigadier in the Second World War, he had removed four commanding officers, all older and more experienced than himself, because they were unfit to continue in their posts.[203] Carver served as deputy and then chief of staff at East Africa Command during the Kenya Emergency, at a time when the commander-in-chief, General Erskine, was grappling with a series of scandals over murders, rapes and tortures committed by soldiers.[204] General Carver knew from personal experience how to deal with poor leadership and military crime. After Bloody Sunday he left 1 Para and HQNI alone.

Deflecting blame onto victims is a 'strategy of denial consistently used by states complicit in human rights violations'. In Britain, where the army is generally considered a force for good, the state manages criticism by techniques such as 'denying the victim' and 'condemning the condemners'.[205] Paranoia about anti-British sentiment had been building throughout 1971. Heath's 'propaganda war' remark to Widgery reflected an already implanted belief in allegations against the army coming from enemies who fabricated victimhood. A paper by junior defence minister Geoffrey Johnson-Smith credited the IRA with holding the propaganda initiative. The media appeared to play into republican hands by sensationalising any controversies. Johnson-Smith advocated aiding the media only when it 'benefit[s] our aims'. British soldiers should be portrayed as fair, self-disciplined and efficient, in contrast to the 'evil' IRA. Above all, the army must react quickly to allegations.[206] The besieged mindset proliferated. One regiment decried 'the terrorists' tactics in attempting to destroy the will of the people of Britain to fight a campaign they can and must win'.[207] The senior military police officer in Northern Ireland saw a 'propaganda and legal campaign against the Army', even though the government settled many lawsuits because they were legitimate.[208] HQNI wrote off criticism over Bloody Sunday: 'few people are concerned any more with the truth, only with enjoying an orgy of self righteous condemnation'.[209]

Reactions to the massacre in the military varied and are hard to locate through a pervasive silence. The Parachute Regiment's journal deplored press criticism, adding 'Further comment is unnecessary.'[210] The Royal Anglians regretted the difficulties faced by army wives in Derry afterwards as shopkeepers refused to serve them;[211] 5 Brigade, based in Armagh, lamented the army's 'tardiness at coping with adverse propaganda', rather than the killings.[212] In early March the army's monthly report on Northern Ireland encapsulated the single lesson from Bloody Sunday – without directly mentioning it. Entitled 'Maintaining High Standards', a section on training noted the 'relentless pressures which are applied by hostile elements in order to discredit the army'. The only way to counter propaganda was to pay attention to bearing and turnout, observing traffic laws, good manners and avoiding foul language.[213] Some officers formed a more realistic appraisal of the reasons for hostility to the army. Lieutenant-Colonel Riddle, commanding 1st King's Own Scottish Borderers, wrote how 'the Catholic population have not exactly welcomed us with open arms. The Army is understandably unpopular because of what we have to do – "lifting", house searching, vehicle searches and the like.'[214] Riddle's humanity fell by the wayside as the British government defamed Bloody Sunday's victims. Jim Wray's brother, Liam, recounted the damage done by the lies:

> I was a target of a lot of abuse in the workplace. Their attitude of the 'other tradition' especially was that my brother was an IRA man. That was it there was no question of it. So you're caught in a situation where your brother has been murdered and you're treated as if he deserved what he got, and that you somehow were in league with that.[215]

Major-General Ford soon 'went on with other things'.[216] His briefing to Sir James Dunnett on 3 February barely acknowledged Bloody Sunday's importance, aside from bringing a temporary rise in violence. Wearing down the IRA in Belfast whilst containing them elsewhere remained the main theme. General Tuzo possessed more finely tuned political antennae. He knew Bloody Sunday turned Catholic opinion from despair into fury, and was willing to consider scaling down internment or search operations. Even so, he clung to the offensive mindset, describing internment as 'an effective weapon' and attributing the army's difficulties to 'one of the most virulent propaganda campaigns ever'.[217] The days following Bloody Sunday witnessed multiple street demonstrations, strikes and closures, and violence in Belfast in particular, with the IRA most active in the west and south-west of the city. The assassination attempts on police and UDR members continued, as did sniping and ambushes.[218] Journalists flocked to Derry. Only on 2 February did unrest return, with some petrol-bombing.[219] NICRA intended to hold a march on 6 February in Newry. A large attendance was expected. Tuzo and Shillington put the police in the lead with the army only coming in if serious rioting arose.[220] In the event 10–12,000 people marched peacefully.[221]

RE-CONFIGURING THE WAR AGAINST THE IRA

The decision to suspend Stormont has attracted detailed scrutiny from scholars who believe that upholding the existing constitutional order was the British government's primary objective.[222] For Labour and Conservative governments the institutional arrangements in Northern Ireland only mattered insofar as they prevented catastrophic civil war, and kept the Province's affairs away from regular parliamentary life. Some writers claim the suspension owed much to the Labour Party, and that Edward Heath pushed through direct rule 'to a large extent independent of events in the region'.[223] Parliament's concentration on Europe certainly explains why direct rule did not come weeks earlier. But the logic for suspending Stormont revolved around political violence's existing and projected course. Labour's leader, Harold Wilson, functioned not as an external force on military strategy, but to decipher republican intentions in a rapidly changing situation. In early 1972 the IRA blew up more people than ever before, in the process mobilising thousands of loyalists expecting civil war. The British government suspended Stormont to forge a more productive alliance with the Irish government, to undercut support for republicanism by conceding to nationalist demands and to see whether the IRA might be split by negotiation.

It is worth setting out the essential continuities. Firstly, the main political parties in Northern Ireland stuck to their existing positions. On 16 February Brian Faulkner implored Heath to carry on fighting the IRA, refusing a place for Catholics in his cabinet.[224] A fortnight later, after press speculation about direct rule, he proposed additional members in the Stormont Commons and Senate, to increase Catholic representation, and more interparty committees.[225] Heath recognised these concessions as meaningless.[226] John Hume told the taoiseach the SDLP 'had not changed their demands' – for Stormont to go, a commission to administer the north, constitutional talks and an end to internment.[227] Secondly, military logic dictated a political settlement. The army has been criticised for thinking the IRA 'defeated'.[228] In fact, military appreciations differentiated republican operations in Belfast from those elsewhere, and the army recognised divisions between the Officials and Provisionals. Certainly, Major-General Ford expected a break in republican morale to induce surrender.[229] But Ford was not in charge of military strategy. The MOD believed: 'No dramatic improvement in the security situation can be expected from military measures alone. At best, they will merely stabilise violence.'[230] General Carver reported violence levels on 28 February to be similar to a month before. More significantly, the Officials appeared to be growing in strength relative to the Provisionals, and becoming more militant.[231] With the IRA checked in Belfast, the government needed the Irish government and the SDLP to combat violence in Derry, on the border and in the countryside. These potential partners expected something in return – the end of unionist hegemony as embodied by Stormont.

Three near-simultaneous developments in the week of Wednesday 16 to Wednesday 23 February made a drastic overhaul an attractive proposition. Parliamentary politics, Anglo-Irish relations and republican escalation beyond Belfast came together to provide a logic for abandoning the existing strategy. On 16 February Harold Wilson spoke confidentially to Heath and Maudling, completely reversing his position of 20 January. He now promised to back Heath if he suspended Stormont.[232] Given the rancorous debates after Bloody Sunday, this represented a move to reconstruct bipartisanship and neutralise Northern Ireland in Westminster. Bitter rivals over many years, Wilson and Heath shared the very recent experience of trying to hold their parties together over the European Economic Community (EEC). Heath signed the Treaty of Accession on 22 January in Brussels alongside Ireland, Denmark and Norway. The government's main problem came from about sixty Conservative MPs opposed to EEC membership.[233] Bringing Britain into Europe was Edward Heath's ultimate political ambition. He could not afford to complicate the parliamentary arithmetic by antagonising allies over Northern Ireland. Prior to the crucial second reading of the European Communities Bill on 17 February, he announced the government would resign if the vote was lost. He won by 309 votes to 301.[234] Resolving the EEC vote freed Heath for the challenges of Ireland and made available the skills of a consummate political fixer, heretofore devoted to steering through the Bill: Willie Whitelaw, Leader of the House of Commons.

Heath had allowed relations with the Irish Republic to atrophy as an accepted price to pay for the military offensive. A fellow EEC member could not be so easily ignored. British indifference to Irish protests about internment, interrogation, Bloody Sunday and other elements of security policy partly derived from the Irish government's inability to counteract republicanism. The inflamed conversation between Lynch and Heath on 30 January epitomised a longer-running disgruntlement. Lynch lacked a majority in the Dáil and so relied on support from members against co-operation with the Northern Ireland regime. Henry Patterson notes Lynch welcomed direct rule amidst a worsening security situation.[235] Whilst true, the taoiseach also did something to precipitate it. Republican activity in Ireland in late 1971 and into 1972, including arms raids, bank robberies and murders, was destabilising Lynch's position. After Bloody Sunday a mob of at least 20,000 burned down the British embassy in Dublin.[236] On 18 February London instructed the British ambassador to tell Lynch an initiative was on the way.[237] At the Fianna Fáil annual conference on Saturday 19 February Lynch called for a new governing framework in Northern Ireland to bring both communities together.[238] The next day Justice Minister Desmond O'Malley signalled a tougher line by announcing IRA men released by district judges would be re-tried.[239]

At the same time republican violence outside Belfast demonstrated what might be gained by forging closer Anglo-Irish co-operation. The nature of the violence mattered. On 13 February 1972, gunmen shot dead Thomas McCann, an off-duty Royal Army Ordnance Corps soldier visiting his sick mother in Dublin, dumping his hooded and gagged body on the border near Newtownbutler. On 16 February the IRA abducted UDR member Thomas Callaghan from the bus he was driving for his regular job in the Creggan, then murdered him. The next day bomb disposal operatives tackled a 40lb gelignite bomb on the Belfast to Heysham ferry, the first ever found on a passenger ship. 39 Brigade observed an 'influx' of explosives into the city.[240] Explosives supply lines could only be shut down with better liaison between the British and Irish security forces. On 22 February OIRA bombed the Parachute Regiment barracks in Aldershot in retaliation for Bloody Sunday, attracting widespread condemnation in Britain and Ireland for killing six civilians and a Catholic padre.[241] The outrage spurred action by Lynch and radical thinking in London. Irish Special Branch officers arrested Cathal Goulding, chief of staff, and seven other Officials in Dublin.[242] Nine more were arrested on 24 February as the deputy taoiseach, Erskine Childers, publicly condemned the IRA's 'ghastly performance' at Aldershot.[243] Undeterred by Lynch's crackdown, the Officials attempted to assassinate John Taylor, a Stormont minister, shooting him five times as he sat in his car in Armagh.[244]

If more help from the Republic required an end to Stormont, then the final outcome, after many years, might be a united Ireland. The CDS's study on the implications of a united Ireland is likely to have been calculated to reassure Lord Carrington that moving against Brian Faulkner was a worthwhile risk. The study judged unification tolerable if Ireland remained neutral. If a united Ireland became hostile, or gave basing rights to an enemy power, the threat to the United Kingdom would be significant. Removing the military commitment to Northern Ireland promised a welcome relief, probably producing a net gain to the army's order of battle. The loss of defence facilities 'would not be serious'.[245] General Carver advocated a condominium, where everyone might choose for themselves whether to adopt British or Irish citizenship. The two countries would then run the six counties jointly. A most attractive feature of the scheme would be better north–south co-operation against the IRA.[246] Heath favoured a more incremental approach based on scaling down internment. Tuzo was willing to release about a quarter of the least dangerous internees, allegedly all IRA men. He firmly opposed a ban on new internments because intelligence gained from interrogating internees was especially needed outside Belfast.[247] Despite calls from Special Branch for a 'harder attitude', Tuzo intended to release 150 internees in batches of 50 at 10-day intervals, after an improvement in the security situation, ideally in late March.[248] Carver quashed Tuzo's bold proposal for judges from neutral countries to adjudicate over internee releases, as the judges might release dangerous people.[249]

At the end of February Reginald Maudling presented the cabinet with his fullest argument yet for direct rule. His eagerness to pass on responsibility for the Northern Irish people, 'possessed of a death wish', is palpable. Direct rule was a gamble. The primary danger came from a violent reaction: 'The potential Protestant backlash is not a myth.' Nevertheless, Maudling believed Stormont's days were over. Only power-sharing and running down internment stood any chance of restoring Catholic confidence and holding on to Labour's backing. Even though Belfast seemed calmer, the situation elsewhere was much worse. The war-fighting stance put a growing number in detention without trial, stretched the army, inflamed cross-community animosities and damaged Britain's reputation abroad.[250] On 4 March PIRA bombed the Abercorn restaurant in Belfast, killing 2 and injuring 130. HQNI believed Catholics in Belfast to be increasingly 'fed up' with the IRA and unwilling to help them.[251] The MOD interpreted this bombing as the start of an attempt to provoke a Protestant backlash. A bomb detonated outside the offices of the *Belfast Newsletter*, a leading unionist paper, on

20 March, killing 6 and injuring 150, seemed to follow the pattern.[252] Though the number of explosions in March remained broadly on a par with previous months, their explosive power went up dramatically, from 1,080lbs of explosive in February to 2,516lbs from 1 to 24 March. Casualties increased too, from 130 people wounded or injured in February to 535 from 1 to 24 March.[253] This horrendous suffering became the new 'dominant indicator'. Many casualties were caused by PIRA's deployment of ammonium nitrate explosives, in development since late 1971, into car bombs.[254] OIRA attacks on off-duty UDR members continued. In one instance, gunmen abducted Marcus McCausland on his way home from visiting friends in Donegal, placed a hood over his head, then executed him, on 4 March. His murder reportedly 'increased fear in the rural areas'.[255]

Whether republican leaders intended to outrage loyalists into mobilising is impossible to resolve, as civilian casualties or sectarian targeting were always defined as accidental. Reliance upon the more deadly ammonium nitrate stemmed, at least in part, from the inaccessibility of gelignite. Without doubt, the bombing and assassination offensives mounted by PIRA and OIRA respectively, with their roots well back in the autumn of 1971, had an impact. The British government discussed direct rule before the rise in civilian suffering and loyalist militancy. Ministers only acted after these two phenomena arose and when they saw a way to head them off. William Craig, former minister of home affairs, launched the Ulster Vanguard movement to oppose direct rule. At the first public meeting, in Lisburn on 13 February, he asked those 1,500 present 'to take what action they consider best to preserve majority rule'.[256] HQNI saw nothing to worry about. Vanguard meetings in Ballymena and Coleraine on 5 March, attracting 1,600 and 2,350 attendees respectively, appeared 'well-disciplined' and 'comparatively moderate'.[257]

At 3pm on 11 March Craig addressed 10,000 people at a Vanguard rally in Portadown, 2,000 of whom lined up in ranks, military-style. Craig advocated the use of violence to defend Ulster's place in the union.[258] The next week the IRA exploited fears about a 'Vanguard backlash' to push for new recruits, especially in Ardoyne.[259] With the British Army unable to protect Catholics, people looked elsewhere for security. Howard Smith met Sir Robert Porter, another former minister for home affairs, on 13 March. Porter warned that the Ulster Vanguard movement was rapidly gaining momentum and numbered 'Men of violence'. Weapons were being smuggled into the country via the Antrim coast.[260] Yet the head of Special Branch detected 'no indications of armed intent on the part of the Vanguard movement nor generally of armed Protestant "backlash" activity'.[261]

His remarks said more about Special Branch's political sympathies than the emerging reality. On 18 March Vanguard mustered 50–60,000 people at Ormeau Park in Belfast.[262] Over a loudspeaker system Craig threatened to 'liquidate the enemy'.[263]

If PIRA intended to coerce the British government by whipping up Protestant fury, then they had to communicate their ability to either suspend operations and save the situation from descending into civil war, or to escalate. The day before Bloody Sunday PIRA leaders tried to open covert negotiations via retired general Sir John Hackett in Dublin, a move rebuffed by the British government.[264] Harold Wilson's secret meeting with the Provisionals on 13 March is generally seen as indecisive.[265] This is a mistake. Wilson did not meet the PIRA leaders only once, he met them three times – in addition to OIRA. After the first contact he kept the prime minister informed. The first meeting happened on 5 March; no notes have survived, but the timing suggests a mutual desire to step back after the Abercorn bombing of the day before.[266] Wilson met privately with Heath on 9 March, presenting him with a document from PIRA which stated their intention to start a three-day truce at midnight on 10 March. They set three conditions for permanent peace: a declaration by the British government of their intention to withdraw all forces from Northern Ireland, the abolition of Stormont, and the release of all political prisoners. Wilson had already informed PIRA neither a Conservative nor a Labour government could accept such terms.[267]

When Heath discussed the secret negotiations with Wilson he avoided putting any comment on the record. There is no reference to the talks in the cabinet papers. No democratic politician wishes to admit bending to terrorist overtures. Heath faced a republican offensive that seemed to be precipitating civil war, where the British Army's proclaimed grip on Belfast proved irrelevant to the IRA's capacity for mass-casualty bombings, cross-border raids and the killing of off-duty local security force personnel. The Official and Provisional IRAs now offered to stop killing and to enter into an extended dialogue in exchange for Stormont being suspended. New evidence shows Heath understood this position. Wilson met Provisional Sinn Féin President Ruairí Ó Brádaigh and PIRA Chief of Staff Seán MacStíofáin on 11 March, with their seventy-two-hour truce in full swing. They refused to extend the truce, though accepted Wilson's point that their offensive made a political deal more difficult to broker. MacStíofáin asserted civilian deaths caused by his organisation were never intentional. Shortages of firearms and experienced bombers played a part in the greater recent reliance on car bombs. Wilson thought Ó Brádaigh more inclined towards negotiation. He suggested internment might be eased as a concession by the British government. The PIRA leaders agreed to further talks only after the British announced a political initiative.[268]

Harold Wilson brought Merlyn Rees to meet other senior Provisionals in Dublin on 13 March. Dáithí Ó Conaill, the adjutant general, Joe Cahill, the Belfast Brigade commander, and John Kelly from the general headquarters staff were present. Wilson repeated his belief in a cessation in violence being an essential precursor for political progress. Dáithí Ó Conaill argued the republican movement only adopted a military strategy in response to unionist aggression. Joe Cahill reiterated the demands made two days earlier. Wilson's suggestion that PIRA be represented at talks by the SDLP was rejected outright. John Kelly asked to speak directly with Heath. Wilson suggested the British government might be willing to return the army to a peace-keeping stance, to impose power-sharing and to release prisoners after a settlement had been reached. Ó Conaill, effectively speaking to Heath through Wilson, wanted the British to understand the potential for disaster if compromise was not forthcoming:

> Until the British Government faces up to the Unionist Government and the continuing blackmailing threat of the backlash nothing can be done. It is their responsibility. We cannot be fobbed off forever by the British Government. The Vanguard movement was created with the connivance of Brian Faulkner. It is growing and growing. There are 121,000 guns in the North (in the hands of Protestants). Four hundred of those are heavy calibre machine guns. Since June 1970 it had been the policy of the British Government to harass the Catholics and it is part of their deliberate policy to hide this fact.

To be absolutely clear, Ó Conaill threatened: 'we are going to be forced into a bigger conflict'.[269] The next day in Derry a patrol in the Bogside came under fire from a seven-strong gun team shooting rifles and Thompson submachine guns. Over 400 rounds were exchanged. PIRA numbers in the city were on the rise and their shooting was of 'improved quality'.[270] In the evening Edward Heath and Harold Wilson sat amongst 1,500 congregants in Westminster Cathedral, the largest Catholic church in the United Kingdom. At the joint service between Catholics, Anglicans and nonconformists, unparalleled in church history, the archbishop of Canterbury called on those in government to feel 'wisdom beyond their wisdom, courage beyond their courage' in striving for reconciliation.[271] After the service, at Cardinal Heenan's house, Wilson brought Heath up to speed on his covert talks. Wilson argued that the Provisionals wished for serious negotiations because they recognised their own inability to defend their people from the coming loyalist assault. He believed they would be willing to compromise on the three demands made during the ceasefire and promised to help Heath without seeking party political advantage.[272]

Manoeuvring the Provisionals into an advantageous position during extended negotiations might, of course, be a great deal easier if the Officials could be brought into play at the same time. Generals Carver and Tuzo contemplated whether to 'wean the Provisional IRA away from the Officials with the aim of concentrating the efforts of all, including the Republic, against the Officials. If they could be politically discredited, isolated, disarmed, it might then be possible in slower time to discredit the Provisionals.'[273] Harold Wilson did the government another service in finding out what the Officials thought. On 18 March Tomás Mac Giolla, president of Official Sinn Féin, told him things had got out of hand. He worried about a Protestant backlash and, according to Wilson, 'Seemed most anxious to find a way out; a face-saving withdrawal from the conflict'. Both men hoped for a breakthrough before loyalist militancy gathered greater momentum. They exchanged telephone numbers as the meeting closed.[274] Though no record exists, it seems improbable that Heath was not informed about the discussion. As promised, the IRA expanded their attacks. At Belleek on 17 March gunmen assaulted the police station, engaging the army guard for nearly an hour. In the Andersonstown area in Belfast on 21 March a ninety-minute gun-battle showed 'a greater capacity for command and control within the Provisionals'. In Derry a company of soldiers came under sustained fire from forty gunmen in the Creggan. The week up to 24 March saw explosions and shootings near the border nearly double on the week before.[275]

Having proffered cross-party harmony on Northern Ireland, Wilson reminded Heath what the alternative would be, leading an excoriating rebuke for the government's inaction in a lengthy Commons debate on 20 March.[276] When General Tuzo addressed the Cabinet Northern Ireland Committee the next day, he admitted the bomb attacks could not be stopped. The security forces lacked intelligence on the supply lines running into the north. Derry 'gave cause for considerable concern' too. Tuzo backed an initiative to regain Catholic support and isolate the IRA. At long last the prime minister announced his intentions to hold a referendum on the border, appoint a secretary of state for Northern Ireland, transfer law-and-order powers to London, modify internment and give economic aid. Heath expected Faulkner to resist law-and-order powers being removed from Stormont, but could hardly resist the final chance to land him with the blame for London's policy.[277] On 23 March the cabinet finally approved direct rule. Faulkner refused to play along, granting Heath his pretext.[278] At some point prior to 23 March, the cabinet received fresh intelligence that probably swayed their thinking. For the first time, both the Provisional and Official IRAs intended to conduct bombings in mainland Britain. The MOD believed that 'whilst no specific intelligence is at hand to suggest that a campaign here is imminent, the current situation is such that the possibility must now be considered to have increased'.[279] The JIC records necessary to supplement our understanding of this threat are closed. Heath only suspended Stormont once IRA violence had dramatically expanded, after the PIRA leadership had threatened a further intensification, amidst rising loyalist militancy, and when bombings in Britain had appeared possible. Direct rule was the right decision to open up space for dialogue. 'Waiting and hoping' until republicans had the upper hand signalled that the British government only responded to violence.

CONCLUSION

The months surrounding Bloody Sunday, and the terrible events on the day itself, cannot be viewed as anything other than a disaster. Interpreting this period inevitably comes down to a question of responsibility. As the discussion of organisation, bombing technology and tactics made clear, the republican movement deliberately used violence to coerce and intimidate the British into leaving Ireland, or at least doing away with the Stormont regime. In the latter objective they succeeded. Republicanism forced a final shift in British policy only by adopting the tactics of mass-casualty bombing, the murder of off-duty security force personnel and political assassination. Killing British soldiers and police officers failed to achieve their goals. This escalation in late 1971 and 1972 was seen coming. For a long time the British government had benefited from the belief in 'the abdication of responsibilities and the "outsourcing" of important security decisions'.[280] Lord Saville conformed to this deeply held notion about the relationship between London and Stormont. Perhaps the idea is so enduringly attractive for assigning all ownership of political violence to the Irish, of whatever political or religious affiliation. The evidence shows the extent to which ministers in London knew full well what was going on in Northern Ireland, regularly discussed what to do and intervened in quite tactical matters. An offensive against the IRA, whatever the human consequences might be, rolled on over these months on the direct authority of the prime minister, who resisted many calls for a change of course.

Reginald Maudling put change on the agenda on 11 November. His ideas for forcing a constitutional adjustment on Stormont faltered because the Labour Party, potentially his most powerful allies in such an endeavour, chose to focus on the more limited issue of interrogation practices. James Callaghan, who presented himself as a visionary on Northern Ireland, blocked more radical voices in the shadow cabinet, as he agreed with Heath and Carrington that internment without trial should be retained. Wilson dared not move without Callaghan's support, or at least acquiescence, a feat he achieved later by supplanting him with the more pliant Merlyn Rees. Wilson's ambitious pronouncements about Irish unity made more of an impact on officials and officers within the government than on ministers. Influential figures such as PUS James Dunnett could not persuade Lord Carrington to abandon the offensive against the IRA. They lacked compelling data to prove a requirement to do so. While security operations such as arrests and arms finds showed, at best, episodic success for the existing strategy, the IRA could not impose a catastrophic defeat on the British Army or the police. Even striking new information – Bloomfield's declaration that direct rule would bring no mass unionist resistance, or PIRA's redeployment away from Belfast – fell on deaf ears. In the weeks before Bloody Sunday Lord Carrington declined all the requests from his officials for strategic adaptation.

General Carver predicted a short window for the government to impose far-reaching changes on Stormont when the IRA were at a low ebb and unionists unprepared to resist. His timing was about a month off: rather than mid February, the IRA began to recover and reorganise from December, and to fight harder from mid January. By imposing a ban on marches Stormont, the army and the British government effectively aimed to extend the offensive against the IRA to all nationalists who opposed the existing regime. They were trying to force the SDLP to come to the negotiating table, abandon their demand for internment to cease first and accept minor reforms from Faulkner. The ban on the civil rights march in Derry on 30 January 1972 cannot be viewed as a technical 'law-and-order' question. Without doubt, 1st Parachute Regiment disobeyed orders in charging into the Bogside and shot indiscriminately at unarmed, innocent civilians. Putting the toughest battalion in the British Army in such a position was reckless. Major-General Ford urged the Paras in, heard the shooting, then walked away from the scene. The lies and denial about Bloody Sunday had their roots in the thinking about invented anti-army propaganda circulating for months before. The problem was that it was not all untrue. In the wake of the biggest massacre in the United Kingdom for over 150 years no crisis in civil–military relations arose. Nobody resigned. No one was sacked. Still, fifty years later, nobody has been convicted of murder. The MOD's in-house history of the conflict found Chief Superintendent Lagan's objection to the arrest operation the 'most unpleasant element' of the day.[281] Lord Carrington called 1 Para's conduct 'a pretty restrained effort'.[282]

We would like to think Bloody Sunday brought about direct rule, a keystone on the way to the Sunningdale Agreement and, years later, peace. We wish to believe thirteen murders and dozens more lives ruined achieved something, however late, in shocking politicians into action. The historical record shows no shock (or remorse) from the cabinet. Direct rule came when Westminster finished with a more pressing matter: membership of the EEC. Strategic adaptation arose when the IRA's more deadly bombing campaign and border operations might only be countered by closer co-operation with the Irish government. Heath conceded when republicans offered him a choice between negotiation or mass-casualty bombings in Britain. Fear for his British compatriots' prospective suffering, not empathy for Irish misery already endured, persuaded the most stubborn of politicians to switch direction.

6

THE MOST DEADLY YEAR

To the Irish the Battle of the Boyne and the Easter Uprising of 1916 are as real as though they happened yesterday. They are almost incapable of forgetting the past and looking forward to the future.[1]

Major M. T. O. Lloyd, July 1972

The British liked to see themselves as more modern, less emotional than the Irish. Willie Whitelaw, the new secretary of state, aimed to break from the past. The December 1973 Sunningdale Agreement – Whitelaw's great accomplishment – appeared to deliver on the promise, enshrining a consensual model for Ulster politics. Respected as a 'Mr Fix-it' in the cabinet, 'a Tory in the very best sense of the term' by Labour's Merlyn Rees, Whitelaw consulted widely and exuded calm.[2] After Maudling's studied indifference, Whitelaw's patience, commitment and cheerfulness stood out, as did his regular presence in Northern Ireland. His achievements in resetting the political scene are rightly applauded.[3] The presence of deep continuities in British policy, like bipartisanship at Westminster, is well established.[4] Yet direct rule saw London adopting 'fundamentally different' constitutional and military strategies.[5] For the army, cutting back the reliance on internment marked quite a change, designed to encourage political dialogue.[6]

Government optimism about the prospects for a settlement to the conflict proved ill-founded. The year 1972 became the most deadly in the modern Troubles: 496 people died.[7] Accounts foreground the lost opportunity when Whitelaw and PIRA met on 7 July in Chelsea. Here the main protagonists came face to face, glimpsed at peace, then saw those hopes dashed. PIRA's intransigence is often held responsible, as Provisional leaders adopted an all or nothing attitude.[8] They fought with 'little real strategic reasoning'.[9] PIRA ignored the unionist majority's hostility to their political objectives.[10] An alternative stance reads the demands made by Seán MacStíofáin and colleagues as an opening bid – nobody expected them all to be met.[11] Perhaps PIRA returned to violence after the meeting to force the British back to the table.[12] Republican leaders had to tread carefully to bring rank-and-file volunteers with them. Softening the rhetoric about a united Ireland risked internal breakdown. Some, like Dáithí Ó Conaill, apparently wished for peace.[13] These perspectives are valid, but simplify the conflict into a two-way contest between the IRA and the British.

Analysing the war in these terms has allowed scholars to explain a major trend evident by late 1972: a moderation in the intensity of violence, which had steadily grown since early 1971. A poorly judged escalation by the Provisionals over the summer is deemed pivotal in stabilising the conflict for decades to come. PIRA detonated 21 bombs on 21 July 1972, killing 9 people and injuring 130. Ten days later the British Army entered no-go areas in Derry, Belfast and smaller towns to exploit popular revulsion at the bombings by reimposing law and order. In seriously reducing violence this deployment of 22,000 troops, Operation Motorman, 'permanently altered the strategic setting'.[14] Other developments are rightly set alongside Motorman. Whitelaw dented Catholic support for the IRA, and his government decided in October to recognise the Irish state's legitimate interests in Northern Ireland.[15] Rising instability across the border propelled the Irish government into a closer alignment with the British in tackling the IRA.[16]

Republican–British interactions alone cannot account for the conflict's intractability. The next great chance for peace came with the Sunningdale Agreement. The May 1974 Ulster Workers' Council (UWC) strike, a mass loyalist uprising, snuffed out Whitelaw's bright future by destroying the power-sharing executive. The Executive's demise is therefore critical for understanding the conflict's endurance into the 1990s. As a constitutional instrument, Sunningdale proved deeply destabilising. Enforced power-sharing, and a role for the Irish state, antagonised unionists from the outset.[17] The exclusion of republican and loyalist paramilitaries incentivised them to overthrow the new order.[18] The reasons for the Executive's collapse are generally ascribed to institutional politics. Military strategy only comes into focus around May 1974: scholars question why the army failed to suppress the strike.[19] Placing responsibility at then Prime Minister Harold Wilson's door is seductive.[20] A longer-term perspective on attitudes towards loyalism is more satisfactory. A major loyalist mobilisation occurred in 1972, encompassing massed marches, intimidation and sectarian killing.[21] How this interacted with republican and British strategy is hardly studied, though the British have been accused of entering into a 'de facto alliance with loyalists'.[22] Alliance infers comradeship or affinity. In the first half of the 1970s, fear was the defining affective undertone.

The low-profile approach to operations has been cast as a failure in political and security terms.[23] In fact, the tangible security gains made by Operation Motorman, and the political advances at Sunningdale, rested upon military restraint in the first half of 1972. Yet these improvements were ultimately insufficient. The inability to reckon with past harms – epitomised by the Widgery tribunal's findings on Bloody Sunday – undercut Whitelaw's fresh start. Low-level brutality continued, particularly in tough regiments, as soldiers punished those they thought supported the IRA.[24] Between Bloody Sunday and 1975 the security forces shot dead fifty-five civilians. Six prosecutions were brought against soldiers. All but one were acquitted, and this case was overturned on appeal.[25] Only from 1995 did the European Court of Human Rights constrict the army's use of lethal force.[26] Persistent violence damaged efforts to bring Catholics into a political settlement.

The origins of the Whitelaw–MacStíofáin talks warrant re-examination. Republicans and loyalists identified London's psychological centre of gravity: the fear of a catastrophic civil war. The evidence for the choice of sectarian violence by PIRA, UVF and UDA leaders as a strategy for achieving their goals is limited. People are loath to admit killing civilians on purpose. But the evidence on behaviour in the run-up to the Chelsea talks suggests that both republicans and loyalists targeted civilians to shape the negotiations which seemed to be on the horizon. Eventually senior figures within the MOD believed loyalist attacks on Catholics might encourage republicans to modify their demands. Whitelaw acknowledged the power of loyalism by meeting the UDA leadership before he sat down with PIRA. Loyalist mobilisation prior to the Chelsea talks is likely to have convinced the government not to give anything away to republicans. The army returned to war against the IRA due to the combined influences of loyalism, and the Provisional's escalation of attacks after negotiation faltered. Operation Motorman is widely regarded as successful in reducing violence for years to come. This success has served to conceal the army's emerging relationship with loyalists, which extended the conflict's duration. The summer's events, and Motorman's achievements, persuaded the army to go back on the offensive against PIRA. In doing so they committed to retaining internment, expanding interrogation and adopting a modus vivendi with loyalists. These choices allowed the force level in Northern Ireland to be brought down, as demanded by the commitment to NATO's conventional defence, and swelling discontent in the army about repeated deployments on a deeply unpleasant mission.

A LOW PROFILE DURING THE 'INITIATIVE'

General Tuzo had a week to get used to the new dispensation before Willie Whitelaw arrived. Tuzo reported to the Northern Ireland secretary, who held responsibility for law and order, but also to the defence secretary.[27] At Whitelaw's first briefings, the army appeared satisfied with the situation in Belfast, apart from Andersonstown, where PIRA held firm. IRA morale seemed fragile in the city. Derry was a disaster: the average weekly weight of explosive detonated in February was three times greater than in January. The border areas saw frequent ambushes, assassinations and intimidation. Rural Northern Ireland generally experienced little turmoil.[28] The intelligence briefing observed: 'for the first time it is Protestant acts and Catholic reactions that will be calling the tune'. The army was jittery about the 120,000-strong Orange Order. The Provisionals mustered about 220 activists in Belfast, compared with the Officials' 135. Figures for Derry were less certain – around 100 for each faction. Perhaps 430 IRA members of all types operated outside the two cities, plus 2,000 across all 26 counties in the Republic: there was 'no shortage of recruits'. Special Branch, comprising 130 men, provided 80–90 per cent of all intelligence, so the army insisted 'nothing is done to upset this extremely valuable relationship'. The Security Service collected intelligence on Protestant organisations and ran 'technical operations'.[29]

Whitelaw superintended affairs by keeping at least one minister with a senior Whitehall official on duty in Northern Ireland at all times. Lord Windlesham and Paul Channon served as the first ministers of state, and David Howell as parliamentary under-secretary.[30] Three senior Northern Ireland civil servants were retained in Whitelaw's inner circle; more junior colleagues sometimes felt that the incoming British mandarins regarded them as 'thick-headed savages'.[31] Whitelaw earned praise from Conservative colleague Bill Deedes for enduring his twenty-one months in office with only one round of golf.[32] (See Illustration 6.1.) For the *Loyalist News* he quickly became 'Outlaw Whitelaw ... the unlawful tool of Edward Heath, treacherous Tory Leader'.[33] The VCGS did not want relations to be too amicable, reminding HQNI to keep the MOD fully informed. Though accepting Whitelaw's right to decide security policy, the ministry wanted advance notice of his intentions in case Lord Carrington wished to veto them.[34]

The radical break with history ushered in by direct rule set the scene for feats of political imagination. The British cabinet described their offering to the Northern Irish people as 'the Initiative'. Details about what exactly that meant only came later. For the army there was greater clarity. The military

Illustration 6.1 William Whitelaw talking to shoppers in Derry, 20 April 1972.
(Courtesy of Mirrorpix via Getty Images.)

presence would be reduced in Catholic areas. The main priorities were to prevent intercommunal violence from ruining the optimistic mood. Troops could still fire in self-defence but only arrest 'Key Terrorists' captured in hot pursuit or on hard intelligence. A 'Key Terrorist' was an officer in the IRA, an active service unit member, or an IRA member linked to explosives or assassinations. These conditions also applied to 'members of similar standing in other extreme organisations who use violence in the achievement of their objective'. Officers were enjoined: 'Loyal acceptance required. No cynicism to be expressed.' Soldiers were told releasing internees was essential for promoting political dialogue. The MOD wished the army to protect Catholics from Protestant violence. Donning the saviour mantle should remove the necessity for the IRA and cause 'the nearest thing to a complete military victory that we can realistically hope for'.[35] This strategy assumed that the goodwill lost by internment, deep interrogation and Bloody Sunday stood to be regained.

The low profile expected soldiers to hold back from responding to provocation. It certainly strained military morale and reduced the intelligence available to mount operations.[36] But morale had been under pressure since the opening of PIRA's bombing campaign in 1970, and to a greater degree since internment. Terence Hubble, serving with the Black Watch in late 1971, despaired: 'You were trying to win over the hearts and minds of local people – it was like hitting your head against a wall, where you would talk to wives, who called you everything under the sun. Their language was vile.'[37] Opinions about the low profile varied depending on experience and temperament. Arriving in Belfast's Ardoyne, 1st Royal Regiment of Wales detected: 'There are now signs of reason prevailing among the hard-liners on both sides, and a peaceful Ulster is just on the horizon.' The writer of C Company's notes toned down the optimism: 'even the most ardent admirer of the Irish scene could hardly describe Ardoyne as the best advert for the Irish tourist industry'.[38] 1st Worcestershire and Sherwood Foresters, on their first tour in and around Derry, settled into a daily routine of 'aggro' around the Bogside, firing baton rounds at rioters 'hurling bricks, paint, or anything else readily at hand'. Support Company searched vehicles crossing the Craigavon Bridge. Their encounters during the low profile were warmly remembered: 'The soldiers on duty on the Bridge were constantly plied with chocolate, cigarettes, soft drinks, and even bottles of beer.'[39] More senior officers accepted the desirability of 'an attempt to break down the barriers of hate and distrust that exist between the soldier and the catholic citizen'.[40]

The SDLP welcomed direct rule and NICRA cancelled all marches for a month to give the government breathing space. Continuing shootings and explosions did not distract officials from discerning 'a softening in the attitude of the Catholic communities'.[41] The PIRA command in Derry declared a halt to attacks on civilian targets for four weeks – a policy denounced by spokesmen in Dublin. Seamus Twomey, the PIRA Belfast commander, opposed moderating his offensive, warning the SDLP against 'betrayal of the people'.[42] Though IRA activity initially dropped as some volunteers in Belfast called for a truce, Twomey's hard line was obeyed. Violence then escalated. Intelligence suggested PIRA aimed to provoke conflict between loyalists and the security forces.[43] On 29 March Douglas Hurd, Edward Heath's private secretary, had a phone call from John Sullivan, who worked for Ireland's national broadcaster, RTÉ. Sullivan said Ruairí Ó Brádaigh claimed the Provisionals wanted a truce, and that he and Dáithí Ó Conaill planned to take control from Seán MacStíofáin to make this possible. Ó Brádaigh and Ó Conaill believed direct rule gave them the opportunity to win over Protestant opinion to supporting a united Ireland.[44]

This communication attracted no mention in the HQNI or MOD reports; the army may have been kept in the dark about this dissension within the PIRA leadership. In Derry, the army's ability to read popular feelings suffered from an almost total dearth of contacts with those living in the Bogside and the Creggan. Sources 'reliably reported' some shops in the Creggan removing their IRA collection boxes in early April. Women in Andersonstown, Belfast organised a peace campaign to pressurise the IRA to stop fighting after mother-of-ten Martha Crawford was shot dead in a gun-battle on 29 March.[45] The following week the group held a meeting that attracted 2,000 people. PIRA responded, in what the army considered a move to 're-assert their authority', by detonating thirty-one bombs across Northern Ireland on 13–14 April. In Derry, PIRA announced plans to hold elections in the Bogside, the Creggan and Brandywell. On 11 April the Derry Citizens Central Council sent a deputation to request PIRA commanders to request a halt to offensive action.[46] The director of intelligence at HQNI expected PIRA to repair the fractures emerging in the movement. Personnel levels were stable. Skilful public relations appeared to be regaining lost ground.[47] A fortnight later Dáithí Ó Conaill went to Derry to rally commanders to the army council's line.[48] Around the same time in Belfast OIRA convened a large meeting of all the republican clubs to discuss policy, a move taken by the British to signal renewed interest in political activity as an alternative to militancy.[49]

When he visited Northern Ireland between 5 and 7 April, General Carver instructed Tuzo to prepare for introducing the RUC into Catholic areas, and to step up the army's community relations activities. Traditionally these involved support for youth clubs, sporting facilities, outreach with old age pensioners and the like. The two generals met Whitelaw to secure his backing for closer liaison between the army and local government officials to make these projects flourish. Carver felt positive about the new strategy:

the initiative has broken the log-jam; a very considerable proportion of the Catholic population wish the bombing and shooting to stop and for life to return to normal, with internees released. This view is strongly supported by the Catholic Church. There are clear signs of this everywhere, including the Bogside and Creggan. The hard-line Provisional IRA are fighting against this, particularly at the top of their organisation. They know that if both their activity and the threat of Protestant attack diminishes, their support will wither away. . . . After the initial outburst and feeling of having been let down, there has been a remarkable degree of restraint and a general attitude of resignation by Protestants of widely differing backgrounds. . . . There have been instances of hooligan intimidation of Catholics in mixed areas, but the Orange Order and Vanguard appear to be able to exercise a degree of control over the Protestant hooligan element, if they wish to.[50]

General Ford thought the low profile could only be sustained for three or four weeks if PIRA kept up their bombing campaign.[51] Undeterred by Ford's scepticism, on 7 April Whitelaw announced the release of forty-seven low-risk internees and twenty-six detainees, and the closure of HMS Maidstone as a detention facility.[52] Military operations certainly slowed down as intended, but had already started declining before the low-profile orders were issued. Searches of occupied houses began to drop off from 21 January, while arrests of wanted persons diminished after 18 February. (See Figure 6.1.)

As Reginald Maudling had made clear, the government delayed direct rule owing to fears about loyalist reaction. Ulster Vanguard launched a two-day strike, bringing industry to a standstill. More than half of shops closed, and multiple protests took place.[53] A rally at Stormont on 29 March attracted 100,000 people. Large protests at Carrickfergus and Bangor on 3–4 April passed off peacefully. HQNI believed most people seemed to be 'adopting a "wait and see" attitude'.[54] The lack of serious trouble during the Easter marches confirmed Whitelaw's confidence in the internee releases helping to lower tensions.[55] By the end of April he had released 167 internees and detainees. Only one was thought to have returned to active service in the IRA.[56] Sir John Peck, the ambassador in Dublin, argued that the low profile improved Britain's standing in the Republic and served as an essential supplement to rising demands there for action against the IRA.[57] The MOD appreciated the Gardaí's operations near the border, which had

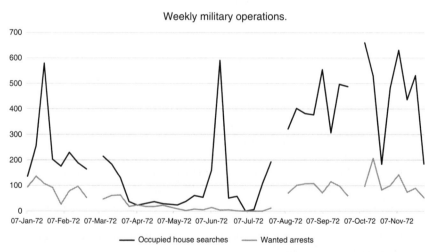

Figure 6.1 Weekly military operations, January–November 1972.[58]

THE MOST DEADLY YEAR

produced sixteen arrests by mid May.[59] On 26 May the Irish government created a special criminal court to try terrorism offences without a jury. Soon afterwards the Gardaí arrested Ruairí Ó Brádaigh and Joe Cahill, the PIRA Belfast Brigade commander.[60] Peck commended Dublin, who 'intend to do all in their power to break the Provisionals'.[61]

The atmosphere in Derry, already tiring of violence, diverged further from Belfast after OIRA murdered William Best, a soldier home on leave, on 21 May. Ranger Best, a Bogsider, had manned the barricades in Free Derry before joining the army. The OIRA commander in the city told journalists he intended 'to instil fear into the British Army'.[62] The next day, 200 people from the Creggan protested to the Officials. PIRA called on OIRA to leave Derry, resulting in fighting between the two groups.[63] At least 2,500 people turned out for Best's funeral. That afternoon, a workers' meeting held at the Essex factory 'was reported to be anti IRA'. Another meeting at Bligh's Lane roundabout attracted 500 women protesting against the IRA; and a final such protest with 200 people in attendance happened in the evening. To counter them, 200 marched in the Bogside, 'carrying tricolours and pro IRA banners'.[64] A priest from St Eugene's Cathedral told a meeting of the tenants' association: 'the people wanted an end to hostilities'.[65] Bowing to these pressures, OIRA announced an indefinite ceasefire on 29 May. Opinion in Derry was divided: the day before, 4,000 attended a peace demonstration, and 6,000 an IRA meeting.[66] Northern Ireland Office (NIO) and MOD officials contained their excitement, noting OIRA reserved the right to use force defensively, and only accounted for about 25 per cent of republican violence.[67]

Though right to be wary, the army had long regarded OIRA as the most dangerous of republicans – better organised, more ideologically coherent than the Provos, with the potential for political advancement beyond their militant campaign. An intelligence report written days before the ceasefire noted OIRA possessed agents in government departments and political parties in Northern Ireland.[68] By the end of May the MOD detected 'among the Catholic communities in BELFAST and LONDONDERRY there are growing demands for an end to violence'.[69] Yet a rift was developing between the MOD and the NIO over the proven merits of policy, and also about who called the shots. Four days before the ceasefire, General Carver alerted the Cabinet Northern Ireland Committee to the IRA's recovery whilst the army eased off. OIRA now probably numbered 800 volunteers, compared with 410 before direct rule; the Provisionals were 900-strong, as against 420 in late March. The committee opted to back Whitelaw.[70] His patience appeared to be paying off. Direct rule aimed to fragment the volatile coalition between various nationalist and republican groups formed in reaction to the government's disastrous attritional strategy. Already prone to violent disputes, the Official and Provisional IRAs now occupied incommensurable political positions that, at least in the best case, nullified OIRA as a security threat. A 'Catholic peace movement' in west Belfast collected 40,000 signatures on a petition condemning violence. And the thirty-two leading Derry public figures who withdrew from office in protest at internment decided to return. The NIO's 'cautious optimism' about all this owed something to their authorship of the emerging political dispensation.[71]

THE LOW PROFILE UNDER STRAIN

Opposition to the low profile cannot be seen as a simple response to events. Special Branch had long advocated a hard line against the IRA. Easing off felt unnatural, dangerous and contrary to the requirement for intelligence. Whitelaw appreciated the need to pay attention to Special Branch morale, yet argued that the prior habit of arresting 'relatively unimportant people' brought few benefits whilst stirring resentment. On close examination, the grounds for internment in the cases he examined appeared remarkably thin. These comments could hardly be read as anything other than a criticism of the previous offensive, a strategy strongly endorsed by Lord Carrington. Whitelaw upheld his decision to leave the republican no-go areas alone for the time being.[72] In mid April he attended a monthly Special Branch meeting to personally tackle the 'sense of depression' about the low profile. Whether his address followed an uplifting or an admonitory path is not recorded.[73] General Tuzo, spared the pep talk (or dressing-down), was also worried about the intelligence drought. Army patrols brought in about one-third of the information picked up before direct rule.[74] Though Special Branch and Lord Carrington's concerns pre-dated a turn for the worse in the security situation, Tuzo began to express doubts about the low profile as shooting incidents rose. (See Figure 6.2.)

In General Ford's estimation, the frustration amongst the troops with the low profile could be ignored 'at present' (hinting at an expiry date in the near future). He was concerned about army casualties, as twenty-five soldiers had suffered gunshot wounds in the preceding week, the highest figure ever.[75] Police holding centres produced about 60 per cent of tactical intelligence. In the month prior to direct rule, they had generated information on 165 IRA officers; in the month afterwards, 37 officers. Ford accepted the NIO's logic in holding to the low profile to drain support away from the IRA.

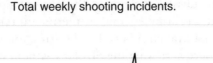

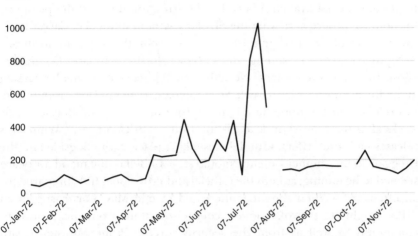

Figure 6.2 Total weekly shooting incidents, January–November 1972.[76]

But he believed a 'marked change' in Catholic attitudes had already happened; the time for a fresh offensive was now. The operational and intelligence summaries showed cracks appearing in both the PIRA and OIRA leaderships' commitment to war, and grass-roots pressures for peace. They did not, however, indicate the seismic adjustment Ford claimed. An assault on the IRA only qualified as feasible if the danger from loyalist groups remained stable. Ford explained the 'hardening of attitudes' amidst Protestants as a reasonable reaction to the government's 'one-sided concessions to [IRA] violence'.[77] HQNI's own information at this time disclosed that loyalist groups were attempting to source weapons, whilst the security forces found gelignite in Protestant areas.[78] The low-profile sceptics found an ally in Burke Trend, the cabinet secretary:

> it has recently become increasingly clear that this policy has something less than complete endorsement and backing by the security forces and, perhaps, by the MOD themselves. The Secretary of State for Defence and the CGS should therefore be given a chance to say what they really feel on this subject and to indicate whether, in their judgment, the continuation of a 'low profile' posture is likely to make unacceptable demands on the morale of the troops and the RUC. There have been several recent indications that the security forces are particularly concerned by the reduction in intelligence which has resulted from a more conciliatory policy.[79]

General Carver advised sticking to the current policy despite declining Catholic faith in the army, so long as internment remained in force, partly to placate Special Branch. Whilst Lord Carrington doubted the prospects for political progress, viewing the SDLP as without influence, Carver knew the low profile earned important credit from the Irish authorities.[80] Accepting Carver's reasoning, the Cabinet Northern Ireland Committee chose to retain internment. Nonetheless, Whitelaw continued releasing about thirty internees each week. Seán Keenan, a veteran Derry republican, was released in the hope he might improve matters in the Bogside, only weeks after the army shot dead his son Colm, a PIRA officer.[81] Whitelaw's releases had some effect, with debates taking place in the Bogside and the Creggan about whether violence should stop. In Belfast the mood for peace seemed to be waning, as both the Official and Provisional IRAs prepared for an offensive.[82] When shootings increased in mid May, Carver suggested PIRA sought 'to provoke violent counter-reactions from the Protestant community as well as from the security forces'. Prime Minister Heath wanted to nullify the provocation by upholding the low profile, with 'select-ive incursions in force into particular areas where circumstances permitted their speedy and effective execution'.[83] That day a patrol captured a Provisional company commander in Andersonstown. An arrest operation later landed the adjutant of PIRA's Belfast Brigade staff.[84]

Under direct rule, military strategy was reformulated to attempt to fracture nationalist and republican resistance by combined politico-military action, rather than by repression alone. With resistance frag-mented, the government aimed then to reconstruct a constitutional arrangement to satisfy all important constituencies, finally bringing the conflict to an end. As noted, within a month nationalist and republican politics were indeed moving in new directions. Some in the military, the police and the cabinet doubted whether the movement was going to be enough. For the time being their scepticism could be brushed aside. For Whitelaw's vision to succeed, Catholic trust in the security forces had to be rebuilt. In one view, Whitelaw faced opposition to his gentler stance from soldiers who believed in a more aggressive solution and enjoyed consider-able latitude under the army's regimental system to do as they pleased, even where this meant beating people up, or worse. The argument is valid, as is the claim that HQNI often tried to obstruct attempts to hold soldiers accountable to the law. However, the idea that political leaders, above all Whitelaw, limited the army's excesses is open to question.[85] The prime minister and defence secretary authorised and encouraged the army's offen-sive attitude before direct rule. From March 1972 the attorney general entered the fray, checking those who hankered after a return to the good old days. Whitelaw certainly favoured a subtle approach. But as the violence intensified in 1972 his willingness to tolerate military aggression softened.

Fixating on personalities obscures the underlying structural difficulties for the army. Three problems hamstrung the mission to reorient the army into a more favourable relationship with Catholic civilians. Firstly, attitudes formed in the war-fighting months from autumn 1971 could not be easily dissolved.[86] Secondly, harms done in the recent past were unforgettable for those affected. Bloody Sunday stood as only the most widely publicised tragedy seared into communal memories for years to come. Thirdly, the British common-law system proved incapable of seriously restricting the use of force by soldiers. Senior leaders and ordinary soldiers alike understood that the IRA wished to provoke the army to lash out, in the process attracting public opprobrium. Soldiers attempted to restrain themselves. For Whitelaw's strategy to succeed they failed too often. Royal Green Jacket Kenneth Ambrose described one self-defeating episode in 1972:

> You had to be careful as well, because the guys were prone to over-reaction. They had this, the locals had this habit of warning a patrol's movements by the use of dustbin lids, so they'd bang the dustbin lids if you were in their area. So one of the section commanders takes it into his head, and thinks, I know how to get out of that, I'll nick all their dustbins [laughs]. So one morning he goes round with a Pig [armoured personnel carrier] and he nicks all their dustbins, and the company commander says, 'what's all that queue at the gate then?' 'I don't know Sir, I'll go and have a look'. It turns out it's all these people want their dustbins back. Just over-reaction, you know. Just any way of trying to get back at them. We didn't do, we didn't, I felt we didn't actually make a great impression on Andersonstown in the time we were there. It was too hard. You would have needed twice as many men and probably twice as long to actually have an effect on the place, to quieten it down ... it was so ardently republican, you know, I mean, they'd got such a hate on for the army it was unbelievable.[87]

Lord Widgery presented his findings on Bloody Sunday on 18 April. The report quickly became an 'official memory', shutting down any impetus for sustained moral questioning in the British Army or the nation at large.[88] To the families of the victims it was a miscarriage of justice, an absurd insult to the community. Eileen Doherty, widow of Paddy: 'Nobody ever apologised to us. We were just ignored. I attended the Widgery Tribunal, but we were never called.'[89] Widgery argued 1 Para were sent to Derry as the only experienced unit available, without explaining why they were not asked to man barriers whilst another unit took on the arrest mission. He was at pains to defend General Ford's reputation before even describing what happened on the day. The report meekly described the decision to launch the arrest operation as of 'debatable' wisdom. Lord Widgery besmirched the reputation of four victims in suggesting they possessed weapons. Responsibility for the casualties suffered on Bloody Sunday rested ultimately with those who participated in an illegal march. 'Impressed by the demeanour of the soldiers of 1 Para', the strongest criticism he could muster focused on their 'sometimes excessive' firing, which occasionally 'bordered on the reckless'.[90]

Declan Walsh has systematically demolished the report's credibility, in research that contributed to the second public inquiry being set up. Widgery held his inquiry in Coleraine for security reasons, a Protestant-majority town requiring a seventy-mile round trip for witnesses from Derry who wished to attend. He only permitted a single legal team to represent all the deceased, even though most had no connection to each other. This placed a huge burden on the team. Lord Widgery refused to accept over 700 eyewitness statements gathered by NICRA, claiming they had been submitted late deliberately to embarrass him. In fact, the statements arrived only ten days after the proceedings opened. None of these witnesses were called to testify. In 1996 Walsh gained access to the original statements made by the soldiers involved in Bloody Sunday on the night of the massacre, plus supplementary statements taken shortly afterwards. These were concealed from the victims' legal team during the Widgery tribunal. Almost every soldier who opened fire gave contradictory accounts in these written statements and the oral testimony before Lord Widgery. In many supplementary statements the soldiers changed their accounts to make the shootings appear more justifiable. Lord Widgery knew of these contradictions and did nothing to challenge or expose them.[91] Lord Saville's inquiry declined to examine whether Widgery conducted an intentional cover-up.[92]

The MOD leaked Widgery's findings the night before publication to ensure favourable press coverage. The *Daily Telegraph*, the *Guardian*, the *Daily Mail* and the *Daily Mirror* reported Widgery as exonerating the Parachute Regiment.[93] Whitelaw and Carrington, relieved to see the army portrayed 'in a generally favourable light', decided not to begin disciplinary action against a soldier criticised in the report. They feared 'action which might look like making scapegoats'.[94] Edward Heath refrained from asking for any proceedings to be instituted, claiming he 'was not responsible'.[95] The Labour opposition declined to embarrass the government.[96]

Soldiers struggled to reconcile the official vindication of 1 Para with the hatred for the army among some civilians. Captain Dewar, in Armagh in late

1972 and early 1973, blamed 'bitterness against the Army' after Bloody Sunday on 'the innate desire for sensation of the journalist'.[97] Heath, Carrington and Whitelaw damaged the army's capacity for improvement through critical self-reflection. George Styles, the senior bomb disposal officer, though elsewhere on Bloody Sunday, believed the Paras shot the right people: 'I'm absolutely certain they did. Absolutely certain. Absolutely certain. It was no surprise.'[98] Returning for his second tour in October 1972, now as commanding officer of 2nd Queen's Regiment, Mike Reynolds objected to a brigade instruction to go easy on the population: 'After "Bloody Sunday" we will *never* win the hearts and minds of these people – they hate us. The only thing these people understand is strength.'[99]

Direct rule placed the attorney general for England and Wales in charge of the Northern Ireland legal system. Sir Peter Rawlinson began weekly visits to Belfast from 17 April. He brought a determination to uphold his office's independence from interference.[100] Rawlinson made the final decision over whether to begin proceedings against members of the security forces. He instructed the new DPP, Barry Shaw, to direct the RUC to investigate and report any criminal offences committed by the armed forces or the police.[101] Two days before Rawlinson's arrival, 1 Para set a public test for him and Shaw. OIRA commander Joe McCann was shot dead by paratroopers on Saturday 15 April in Belfast, after detectives called for assistance to arrest him.[102] HQNI's accounts prompted misgivings. The first report said McCann put his hand in his coat pocket before he was shot. A second report, by the military police, stated McCann put his hand near his pocket after being shot and did not have a weapon. The ministry concluded: 'The shooting of McCann was therefore not consistent with the terms of the Yellow Card.'[103] The VCGS reassured Lord Carrington that criminal prosecutions were rare. Although the authorities had considered about a hundred cases, no more than half a dozen proceeded to trial, none for homicide: 'in one or two such cases there was advice to prosecute which the former Attorney General of Northern Ireland turned down'.[104] A trial of two soldiers for shooting McCann collapsed in May 2021 when a judge ruled evidence central to the prosecution to be inadmissible.[105]

Charged with defending the United Kingdom's position before the European Court of Human Rights, Rawlinson needed to show that the domestic courts provided redress for those wronged by the security forces.[106] Civil-law suits presented ever greater problems in 1972.[107] By 27 March, more than sixty cases involving army and police brutality were in process. The MOD recommended settling in the county courts before cases attracted publicity in the crown courts. Claims related to the

August 1971 internment arrests were settled following a court ruling that they had been affected illegally. The ministry contested the deep interrogation cases, except that of Patrick Shivers, 'who may have been interrogated in depth in error'. Paying the others, deemed IRA supporters, was thought likely to grant the enemy a propaganda victory.[108] HQNI advocated creating a special tribunal to prevent the courts becoming overloaded (another 1,200 complaints were in the pipeline). The tribunal might comprise a former law lord, a former Irish judge and a former Australian judge, to promote an impartial image. HQNI stressed the benefits of processing complaints quickly.[109] The vice adjutant general (VAG) dismissed Tuzo's idea: the Northern Ireland courts resolved civil cases faster than those in England. A tribunal implied the courts could not cope.[110] Although Tuzo saw the political imperative for speedy justice, he seems to have been oblivious to the damage caused by soldiers breaking the law.

In late April, DS10 (the MOD branch responsible for Northern Ireland policy) raised concerns about soldiers questioning suspects for lengthy periods before handing them over to the police, violating the arrest policy.[111] An article in *The Sunday Times* alleged brutality towards prisoners on the night of 20 April, when soldiers questioned three men at the Broadway military post in Belfast for nine hours. Defence Minister Lord Balniel insisted: 'Any officer must know how sensitive is the subject of interrogation and to what extent the reputation of the Army is involved.'[112] The Irish government complained to the European Commission of Human Rights on behalf of the three men: Gerard Donnelly, Gerard Bradley and Edward Duffy. They alleged abuses by soldiers and policemen. Donnelly recounted being beaten, kicked, jumped on and electrocuted on the penis. Bradley suffered severe beatings. He was spat on, jumped on and kicked in the genitals. Duffy was put through the same abuse, his legs and arms twisted, his throat choked. A doctor's examination confirmed the allegations.[113] In March 1973 a jury found a soldier and two detectives not guilty of assault. One of the detectives agreed the men had been assaulted by someone.[114] Rawlinson noted that several High Court rulings rejected statements by people interrogated by the police because they were 'not voluntary'.[115] He and the Treasury solicitor insisted HQNI amend their orders to prevent interrogation at army posts, and for soldiers to hand over those arrested to the police as soon as possible.[116] The new arrest orders only allowed soldiers to arrest persons seen to be committing, or suspected to have committed, a breach of the peace or a serious offence, such as assault, malicious damage, theft, or possessing an offensive weapon.[117]

Tony Stephens, head of DS10, wanted the police to expedite abuse investigations: leaving them hanging 'handed [the IRA] a major propaganda advantage'. Soldiers were so blasé about mistreating civilians as to boast about it. The Home Office intercepted a letter by a soldier in Northern Ireland on its way to his brother in prison:

> We were on patrol last night, we came to a hotel and two blokes were syphoning petrol from a car, we told them to freeze and they did. When we had them in the 'pig' Armoured car one said you are a load of English bastards. I hit him in the goob [sic] but he still carried on shouting is [sic] mouth off so the lads said to me keep him quiet so I said if you don't shut your mouth I will knock your teeth so far down your throat that you will clean your teeth from your arsehole. He then started to laugh at me so with the butt of my rifle I hit him in the mouth and he lost half of his teeth down his mouth. He soon shut up after that the other bloke said he would not say anything about it to get me into trouble. I then said to him you will get the same if you don't shut it you fucking Irish bastard. We then took them back to camp and you can imagine what happened to them on the way we kicked fuck out of them.[118]

Reflecting the scale of the problem, by 23 May, 110 police officers were investigating brutality allegations.[119] General Tuzo's civil adviser found the staff of the assistant provost marshal (the senior military police officer) 'less than co-operative'. HQNI refused to share confidential military police records with the MOD. Tony Stephens argued that the CGS should be informed about cases of soldiers giving false evidence to the military police, which sometimes arose 'with the connivance or even at the prompting of SIB [Special Investigation Branch] investigators'. Military policemen were covering up criminal activity by soldiers. Stephens mentioned several troubling incidents. Anthony Friel claimed in February 1972 to have been beaten when in military custody. A military police investigation failed to cover the period when the event happened. A subsequent report could not identify the soldiers who beat him. William Wilson MP complained on behalf of a Mr McGurk on 11 August 1971. The under-SoS for the army asked for an investigation on 29 September, yet the assistant provost marshal had achieved nothing nine months later.[120] The MOD, the NIO and the attorney general faced determined resistance from soldiers, and HQNI itself, to the restraints being applied on their treatment of the civilian population.

TO THE BRINK OF CIVIL WAR

PIRA's June–July ceasefire eventually broke down during a dispute over housing allocation in the Lenadoon area of Belfast, which turned into a gunfight. Some scholars claim the army allowed the situation to spiral into a fatal ceasefire breach because the British refused to confront the loyalist UDA. The ceasefire itself is thought to have provoked loyalists who thought a London-brokered betrayal was on the horizon.[121] Other writers omit any reference to loyalism, or believe violence from that quarter swelled only in late 1972.[122] The interactions between republican and loyalist violence, and the British response to this dynamic, informed both the decisions to negotiate in July 1972 and the reasons for the ceasefire collapsing. The change in political violence from mid 1972 cannot be understood simply in relation to the Whitelaw–MacStíofáin talks. The British Army's relationship with loyalist paramilitaries mattered a great deal more in protracting the conflict. Both republicans and loyalists increasingly directed violence and intimidation at the communities believed to support their paramilitary opponents. They did so to influence the British government's position at pending negotiations, and to coerce their opponents into surrendering (in the case of loyalist violence), or accepting the requirement for a negotiated settlement (PIRA's aim for the UDA).

Defence associations sprang up in Protestant areas of Belfast in August 1969. From September 1970 they came together into the UDA.[123] At first the army observed loyalist violence as spontaneous, lacking higher direction.[124] This may have been the case, or wishful thinking by an organisation intensely focused on republicanism. Sectarian murders of Catholic civilians pre-dated direct rule, with the first attempt since the army arrived possibly arising in April 1970. The same can be said for bombings, such as the UVF attack on McGurk's Bar in December 1971. However, violence against Catholics intensified in 1972.[125] According to one estimate, in 1972 loyalists killed 121 people.[126] To read all this suffering as essentially chaotic is a mistake.[127] The UDA aimed to prevent a British withdrawal and concessions to the IRA by killing Catholics, and to protect Protestants by intimidating Catholics who lived amongst them.[128] In early April HQNI noted, in Belfast and Derry, intimidation by Tartan gangs – working-class teenage boys who sometimes co-ordinated their activities with paramilitaries. Most cases involved anonymous threats rather than physical violence.[129] The army described the Tartans as 'non-political', and loyalists in general appeared 'in disarray', despite vigilantes starting to erect chicanes in Donegal Avenue in Belfast every night. Several protests were organised against Whitelaw's internee release programme.[130] Staff officers rationalised loyalist rage as reactive. Violence in Belfast seemed a natural response to the murder of a UDR soldier on 19 April, especially as his body was booby-trapped with landmines.[131]

Without being able to attribute every incident, from 7 April 1972 HQNI noticed a growing pattern of shootings that were not directed at the security forces. (See Figure 6.3.) A surge in shootings by the IRA following Joe McCann's death seemed to provoke another swell in loyalist anger. On 22 April the police prevented a 250-strong Protestant mob from invading the largely Catholic William Street in Derry. Intelligence suggested 'extreme Protestant organisations' might be attempting to obtain firearms.[132] The suppositions about the causes of loyalist violence, and the vague references to organisations, indicate a military intelligence system confused by the shift away from a simple government-versus-republican conflict. HQNI's difficulties in adjusting perceptions do not mean no patterns existed. A week after the attempted mob incursion in Derry, Tartan gangs caused unrest in east Belfast, injuring fifteen police officers. The security forces brought the situation under control by talking to Tartan and Ulster Vanguard leaders, a move unimaginable in Catholic areas for many months.[133] The NIO treated the Tartans as reformable, wayward youths. Minister Paul Channon approved funding for community centres – 'for healthy legal and peaceful activities'; 23rd Royal Engineers helped set the facilities up.[134]

Between 7 and 10 May, sixteen bombs went off in Catholic areas of Belfast where the security forces could not have been the target. These were put down to 'intimidation', without any specific loyalist group being

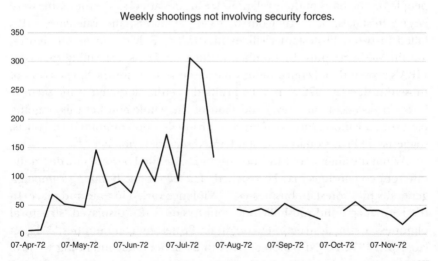

Weekly shootings not involving security forces.

Figure 6.3 Weekly shooting incidents not involving the security forces, April–November 1972.[135]

named.[136] A bombing at Kelly's Bar in Ballymurphy on the evening on 13 May prompted a major upsurge in violence. HQNI believed the explosion to be an accident on the IRA's part.[137] The bomb may have been planted by loyalists.[138] An intensive firefight broke out soon after between the army, PIRA in Ballymurphy and loyalists in the Springmartin estate. Over the next 24 hours troops expended around 900 rounds, mostly at PIRA, who fired about 1,500 shots at soldiers. Nine people were killed and eighteen wounded by gunshot; another seventy-nine received injuries from the bomb explosion. At a press conference on 14 May the UDA threatened to turn every Protestant area in Belfast into a no-go area if the barricades in the Bogside and the Creggan remained up beyond five weeks.[139]

When Maria McGuire published her memoirs of a year in PIRA, she deliberately sought to discredit Seán MacStíofáin, and to justify her own involvement in the movement. Nonetheless, the memoirs are a credible source in many respects. She began to worry about PIRA's participation in sectarian incidents when, on 17 May, the Fianna shot at Protestant workers leaving Mackie's factory in Belfast. McGuire recounts an argument about a car bomb that killed several civilians. She heard MacStíofáin saying: 'What does it matter if Protestants get killed?. . . . They're all bigots, aren't they?'[140] Ruairí Ó Brádaigh, present during the exchange, denied MacStíofáin made these sectarian remarks.[141] Weighing intentions against behaviour has bedevilled research on the Provisionals' campaign. Robert White accepted protestations from PIRA members he interviewed that they never targeted people on the basis of their religion. He argues attacks on Protestants were largely mistakes, or carried out by rogue elements, and calculates PIRA killed forty-two Protestant civilians in 1972.[142] Relying on newer figures, Martin McCleery puts the number at thirty-six. He is less willing to accept PIRA's avowal to only purposefully harm the security forces: 8.3 per cent of those murders in 1972 cannot be justified as either targeted at the security forces or as accidental. Over the span of the whole conflict this ongoing pattern, and the failure to remove individuals who committed such acts, suggests the Provisionals at least tolerated sectarian violence.[143]

When the analysis of PIRA behaviour is extended beyond murder, quite different conclusions may be reached. The economic bombing campaign generally hit Protestant businesses.[144] Violence varied in time and place. In the Fermanagh and south Tyrone countryside, PIRA displayed 'structural blindness' to the destruction wrought on Protestant communities.[145] From late April 1972 HQNI believed PIRA to be deliberately intending to 'provoke inter-sectarian clashes with the aims of bringing the Security Forces into direct confrontation with the Protestant community and the collapse of

THE MOST DEADLY YEAR

the Initiative'.[146] However, substantial evidence for this emerged around the time in May identified by Maria McGuire. A car bomb in the Protestant Sandy Row area of Belfast on 15 May injured seventeen people.[147] At 9am on 17 May the IRA abducted five Protestants in Belfast's Turf Lodge, two of whom escaped. The other three were questioned about loyalist activity, then released.[148] Other incidents led the army to see PIRA aiming 'to provoke the Protestants into violent reaction': the shootings at Mackie's factory and a bombing in Beit Street on 17 May; the shooting dead of a teenage boy in the Shankill area by a PIRA gunman on 19 May; and a bombing in Jennymount on 22 May that injured fifty-eight people.[149]

In Protestant areas of Belfast barricades sprang up in a panicked reaction to the violence. An operation to remove barricades in Willowfield on the morning of 21 May prompted an exchange of gunfire between soldiers and loyalists.[150] Whitelaw was unperturbed, dismissing the risk of a Protestant backlash.[151] The potential for loyalist aggression loomed large, however, on 27 May during a joint UDA–Vanguard rally in Woodvale Park, attended by 4,000 supporters in combat smocks, marching in ranks.[152] These developments caused the MOD to label the UDA 'a significant factor in the security situation' for the first time.[153] General Carver thought Whitelaw misunderstood the sectarian balance and underestimated Protestant opposition to a political deal with nationalists.[154] At a meeting convened by Lord Carrington, Carver argued that PIRA might be reaching the point where their attempts to stir up a civil war were about to backfire:

> There were signs of mounting Protestant frustration and it might be that the threat of direct Protestant action was now having an effect on the IRA. One possibility was that the Provisionals might step up their campaign of violence for a few weeks and then seek to call a halt in return for political recognition of the IRA. The cessation of violence would in itself create problems. The IRA might well make the exclusion of the Army and RUC from Catholic areas a condition of the truce and this would present serious difficulties. The Army could hardly be withdrawn while armed men remained at large; and an attempt might have to be made to call in arms from both sides under an amnesty. . . . In discussion, the point was made that the killing of IRA members by Protestants might be no bad thing from our point of view if it led to a cessation of violence. On the other hand, for the Government to negotiate with the IRA would be open to serious objection.[155]

The minute-taker scrupulously avoided assigning the opinion about Protestants killing the IRA to Carrington, Carver, or any of the other senior figures present. On the streets, loyalism was denied a completely free rein: 2nd Parachute Regiment deployed into Ballymacarrett and the Short Strand in Belfast several times in early June to stop attacks on the small Catholic communities in those areas.[156] On 2 and 3 June, 1st King's Own Royal Border Regiment blocked the Craigavon Bridge in Derry to stop a UDA march entering Catholic areas, firing seventy-six rubber bullets to disperse the crowd.[157] A car-bombing outside a Catholic-owned bar in Belfast's Newtownards Road, which injured forty-nine people, appeared to HQNI 'a clear attempt to provoke sectarian trouble'. That weekend loyalist barricades appeared outside the two main cities for the first time.[158] Whitelaw, Tuzo and Shillington agreed to avoid confrontations over the barricades. Whitelaw was willing to meet those putting them up to better understand their objectives.[159] Frank Steele held preliminary meetings with Billy Hull, who led the Loyalist Association of Workers (LAW).[160] Intelligence on the UDA placed its strength at 25,000. It was run by a fifteen-member inner council, with Charles Harding Smith as chairman, and a ten-member security council, and was strongest in the Shankill, Woodvale and east Belfast.[161]

Sectarian violence rose in the following week. Of the 300 recorded shootings in Belfast, roughly 60 per cent did not involve the security forces. For the first time the weekly total of explosives detonated or discovered reached over a ton (1,016 kg). On Saturday 10 June republican and loyalist gunmen exchanged shots near the UDA barricades in New Lodge and Ardoyne. During the Sunday the army were drawn into a three-way gun-battle for nearly four hours, resulting in three civilian and one military death. HQNI reluctantly conceded the UDA's participation in these shootings.[162] General Tuzo sympathised with Protestant fears of being forced into a united Ireland. He perceived the UDA as a growing threat, though less prepared for a sustained campaign than the IRA.[163] Chief Constable Shillington saw Protestant violence as fundamentally random or spontaneous.[164] Whitelaw appeared less sanguine, expecting 'very serious confrontations' with 'large numbers of Protestants'.[165] The sizeable veteran representation in the UDA worried him especially.[166]

Whitelaw's instinctive reaction was to talk himself out of a tight corner. So he met Billy Hull for LAW, and Mr Parsons and Mr Herron from the UDA, on 13 June. The delegation complained about the no-go areas in Derry and the civil disobedience campaign. Accepting that an invasion of the Bogside and the Creggan was unwise, the trio suggested the areas be blockaded, or social security benefits be suspended for those inside. First Whitelaw applied the soft-soap: he 'understood the feelings of frustration'. Then he tried reason. UDA barricades allowed PIRA to claim they were essential defenders for the Catholic people. Perhaps barricades could be temporary, and avoid the main roads? A blockade in Derry only risked worsening sectarian violence, and cuts to social security funds might be replaced by funding from sympathisers in America. Hull, Parsons and Herron threatened Whitelaw directly: 'The patience of the Protestant community was coming to an end.' If he failed to act against the IRA, they would create their own no-go areas in Belfast, thus forcing his hand.[167] The same day the Provisionals publicly invited Whitelaw to talks in Derry. (See Illustration 6.2.) His refusal probably owed a lot to his next engagement. A meeting with the UDA security council succeeded in persuading them to postpone plans to erect barricades over the coming weekend. Whitelaw promised that the British government would never permit Irish reunification against majority opinion in the north.[168] Even the temporary reprieve achieved by these meetings might mean a few lives spared.

The prospect of the Provisionals entering negotiations encouraged the SDLP to engage with Whitelaw. John Hume thought highly of Whitelaw's

Illustration 6.2 A Provisional IRA press conference in Derry, 13 June 1972. Pictured, from left, are Martin McGuinness, Dáithí Ó Conaill, Seán MacStíofáin and Seamus Twomey. (Courtesy of Corbis Historical/Getty Images.)

achievements in altering the political atmosphere. He remained convinced that any further progress hung upon the abolition of internment.[169]

Hume and Paddy Devlin met Whitelaw on 15 June, ending the boycott in place since the previous July.[170] Hume welcomed the UDA stepping away from barricade construction. The SDLP argued that the British could hardly talk with the UDA, who threatened and practised violence, whilst shunning the IRA. Whitelaw disliked the threatening tone to PIRA's invitation, or ultimatum as he preferred to call it, and questioned whether meeting them would undermine the SDLP. Hume and Devlin urged the British to bring PIRA into the political process, and to end internment, to undercut their public support.[171] NIO officials hoped to revive constitutional politics by holding council elections under proportional representation, to guarantee Catholic inclusion. Round-table political talks on Northern Ireland's future were planned to open up space for compromise. Britain's experience with rebellions showed that the IRA would have to participate.[172] Whitelaw told his cabinet colleagues: 'both sides were coming to realise that unless they exercised restraint they would find themselves on the brink of civil war'. The Cabinet Northern Ireland Committee accepted 'some understanding would have to be reached with the "Provisional" IRA; no solution seemed possible unless their point of view were represented'. Direct contact with PIRA was conscionable only after a ceasefire began.[173]

The insistence on a demonstration of good faith probably derived from the army's interpretation of the Provisionals' attitude towards sectarian violence. For the previous two months reports from Lisburn had emphasised a perceived intention by PIRA to target and thereby incite Protestants. Without doubt, the Provisionals ramped up violence in the weeks before negotiations to maximise their bargaining position. The attacks on Protestants from mid May cannot be written off simply as indiscipline by autonomous volunteers. Four hours before the truce started on 26 June republican gunmen fired into a crowd of Protestants in New Lodge.[174] PIRA probably targeted Protestants before the ceasefire for two strategic reasons: to induce fear in the British about an impending civil war; and to coerce loyalists into entering negotiations. Speaking to BBC television hours before the ceasefire began, Dáithí Ó Conaill expressed a wish to meet Protestant leaders. Interviewer Michael Charlton asked why Protestants would sit down with the Provisionals, who had brought Northern Ireland to the brink of civil war. Ó Conaill replied:

> We did come to the brink. We have not gone over the brink, and that is what matters. Now we say, instead of going over the brink, if the UDA/

Vanguard want to go over the brink, that is their decision. We say, do not go over the brink. Come and meet us. We will go and meet you, and let's get talking about the island, about problems, the problems of Ulster. It is your Ulster. It is our Ulster. Let's get talking about that here and now. Forget about going over the brink. Let's act like people who believe there's a future in this country.[175]

John Hume and Paddy Devlin brokered the British government's meeting with PIRA. Whitelaw agreed to halt arrests of IRA members and to let republican prisoners live in a separate compound, wear their own clothes and receive extra letters and visits.[176] On 20 June NIO officials Philip Woodfield and Frank Steele went to a house near the Donegal border to meet Ó Conaill and Gerry Adams, who were accompanied by solicitor P. J. McGrory. Woodfield set out the changes already implemented to prison conditions and the hiatus on arrests. Ó Conaill and Adams secured agreement to a meeting with Whitelaw ten days after fighting stopped. They requested the British release not only PIRA leader Billy McKee from prison, but also one or two Protestants, and asked for introductions to UDA leaders.[177] On 22 June the Provisionals announced a ceasefire from midnight on 26 June. Whitelaw stated that the government would reciprocate.[178] Like others, 1st Royal Regiment of Wales felt 'a mixture of relief and scepticism'.[179]

NEAR-DISASTROUS CONFRONTATIONS

The coercive measures taken by PIRA and the UDA/UVF in the run-up to the negotiations meant that British strategists came to see the avoidance of a civil war as more important than the talks themselves. This helps explain why, after the Chelsea talks debacle of 7 July, Whitelaw rejected further contacts with PIRA.[180] The attitudes and behaviour of the loyalist groups counted the most. At HQNI, General Ford certainly believed 'The desire for peace has been strengthened by the emergence of the UDA and the realisation that the Protestant community is on the verge of retaliation.'[181] This notion of loyalist military power as strategically beneficial in damaging republicanism – whether applied in violent form or implied through intimidation – persisted for many years and, arguably, had a greater influence on events than direct collusive support to loyalist paramilitaries. Operation Motorman, the army's move to retake Catholic urban areas from republican domination, succeeded in bringing down the violence levels. The operation's impact has obscured the simultaneous deeper entrenchment of the sectarian dimension to the conflict that partially explains its longevity.

The UDA in Belfast tried to derail Whitelaw's initiative, setting up barricades on Friday 30 June. The next night shootings erupted in Ardoyne and Bone. Some firing also came from the Protestant enclave west of Crumlin Road. PIRA admitted a gunman acting independently initiated the firing on 1 July. Others then joined in, believing the area to be under attack. In reply the UDA erected about 200 barricades over the weekend. On Monday 3 July a 'near-disastrous confrontation' between the security forces and UDA men occurred, when loyalists tried to extend the Woodvale no-go area into more religiously mixed streets. General Ford persuaded the UDA to back down at 11pm, after bringing in reinforcements in armoured personnel carriers.[182] Ford allowed unarmed UDA patrols, on condition they stopped intimidating Catholics (without considering that unarmed patrols could still be seen as highly threatening). Though almost all the barricades soon came down, the episode shook Catholic confidence in Belfast and Derry.[183] General Tuzo stymied Whitelaw's call for a more robust approach, due to the 'sheer weight of UDA numbers'. Whitelaw agreed force should only be used against loyalists as a last resort.[184] Violence continued to destabilise the space for a political compromise. In the week ending 5 July, ten people died in sectarian murders.[185] Intimidation proliferated in Belfast: 39 Brigade officers told Canon Montague, seeking protection for Catholics in March Street, to advise people to 'shout from his window for help'.[186] Within a week the security forces responded to 200 intimidation cases.[187]

Whitelaw hosted the Provisional leadership in Chelsea, London, on 7 July 1972. The delegation consisted of Seán MacStíofáin, Dáithí Ó Conaill, Martin McGuinness, Gerry Adams, Seamus Twomey and Ivor Bell, plus lawyer Myles Shevlin to keep notes. MacStíofáin began by reading a statement welcoming the chance to find a permanent settlement. Their vision for peace comprised three elements: a public recognition by the British that the Irish people had a right to decide their future; withdrawal of the British Army from Ireland by 1975; and an end to internment and an amnesty for offences committed before the ceasefire. Whitelaw explained the government's legal obligation to change Northern Ireland's constitutional status only with the consent of a majority in Northern Ireland. The Provisionals claimed the duty could be revoked by parliament. To prevent the meeting dissolving, it was agreed that British officials and PIRA leaders would meet on 14 July to further discuss a declaration of an intention to withdraw by the British government. PIRA threatened to resume their offensive if the declaration failed to materialise. Officials reported Whitelaw being 'depressed at the outcome of the meeting', having found

MacStíofáin 'very unpleasant'.[188] The failure to reach an agreement centred around the future position of Ulster's Protestants.

The follow-up meeting never happened. Fighting broke out in the Lenadoon estate on 9 July between PIRA gunmen and the British Army. Recent scholarship shows the British allowed the situation to escalate by blocking Catholic families from moving into houses legally allocated to them by the housing executive. They did so under pressure from the UDA, who opposed the housing decision. In public, Whitelaw blamed the IRA for the ceasefire collapsing. To his cabinet colleagues, he placed the responsibility on the UDA. Whitelaw advocated operations against PIRA to prevent the UDA going to war.[189] Heath baulked at General Tuzo's plans for a quick military victory. He emphasised the likely political costs and demanded there be 'no question of instituting an all-out military campaign against the IRA'.[190] At 9.30pm on 10 July PIRA formally terminated the ceasefire. Harold Wilson held secret talks with another PIRA delegation led by Joe Cahill in Oxfordshire on 18 July. Merlyn Rees believed Wilson cleared the meeting beforehand with Heath.[191] Wilson briefed Alastair Hetherington the next day and denied informing the prime minister in advance, relying on his police protection officer to discretely get the PIRA men into the country via Luton airport. Wilson said their demand for a referendum on reunification to be held throughout Ireland was unacceptable. He believed PIRA wished to participate in all-party constitutional talks. PIRA also sought direct negotiations with the UDA. The Provisionals appeared to seriously under-estimate loyalist willingness to fight to stay in the United Kingdom.[192] Afterwards, Wilson informed Heath about the fruitless conversation. They agreed to cut contacts with PIRA.[193]

Writing to Lord Carrington on 12 July, General Carver argued that the majority of Protestants supported the UDA (where he got his evidence from is unclear). Carver sketched out three future options, without making an explicit recommendation: firstly, only striking PIRA in retaliation for attacks by them; secondly, going on the offensive against the Provisionals by mounting 'a general invasion of the Catholic areas'; and thirdly, withdrawing from Northern Ireland entirely. The first option represented the surest way to avoid escalation. Such a policy seemed unlikely to achieve anything without a radical political programme. A new offensive was bound to remove the UDA threat to security and hearten the security forces. However, the IRA might survive, and the prospects for reconciliation with Catholics would be destroyed. Carver doubted whether an offensive could be effective whilst remaining 'within the law as it now stands'. On the third option, he thought the Protestant population would forfeit their right to support if the UDA ended up in a sustained campaign against the British Army. Perhaps the

United Nations might be invited to take over instead. He questioned whether a UN force would have the capacity to control the ensuing mayhem. British troops might find themselves stuck in any case, protecting Catholics and doing the unthinkable: 'fighting the Protestants'.[194]

After the ceasefire, the Provisionals made the army's choices much easier by radically expanding the violence directed at soldiers. In the three days following the resumption of hostilities nearly 700 shooting incidents happened. Gunmen damaged sixteen armoured personnel carriers with armour-piercing ammunition, 'disquieting' HQNI – and doubtless the soldiers inside.[195] Thursday 13 July witnessed 'an almost unprecedented level of violence in Belfast'. Gun-battles in Lenadoon, Andersonstown, Divis and Ardoyne resulted in four members of the security forces being killed and an estimated twenty-eight gunmen killed or wounded.[196] 1st Parachute Regiment entered Ballymurphy in late July fully expecting a hostile reception thanks to their reputation. After locating the middle point 'between firmness and over domination', the Paras came under repeated sniper attack. So they patrolled through gardens instead of the streets. The Paras dismissed what they regarded as fake allegations 'of intimidation, assault, indecent assault, rape, torture, pigeon murder, planting evidence, destruction of property, cutting of clothes lines ... and abusive language'.[197] As the month ended, London sent another headquarters, 24 Brigade, to share Belfast with the existing 39 Brigade.[198]

The political climate changed dramatically on Friday 21 July, when PIRA exploded more than twenty bombs in a few hours in Belfast. The bombs detonated on 'Bloody Friday', several in cars, killed 9 people and wounded 163, provoking widespread panic and anger.[199] Soldiers mounted intensive patrols throughout the weekend to prevent Protestant revenge attacks on Catholic areas. The army made 'Scores of arrests' on suspicion. The vast majority of people were released after being handed over to the police. The army believed that 'the general propaganda effect of our operations was good'.[200] HQNI, the Foreign Office, the NIO, the MOD and the Home Office had been working on several different planning documents since early July. The worst-case scenario plan, Operation Folklore, envisaged a complete breakdown in order, requiring a massive military reinforcement.[201] In the wake of the 'Bloody Friday' bombings Cabinet Secretary Burke Trend advised the prime minister to renew the offensive against the IRA. Doing so made a loyalist uprising, and thus the worst-case cataclysm, less likely.[202]

The DMO in the MOD, Major-General Coaker, suggested a simultaneous move into Belfast and Derry: Operation Motorman. The target would be the

IRA. Planners envisaged search, arrest, surveillance and interrogation operations to acquire extra intelligence.[203] Whitelaw accepted new arrests for internment to target senior PIRA leaders.[204] General Carver asked for the rules of engagement to be changed to permit soldiers to shoot anyone carrying a firearm or petrol bomb after warning them, and to open fire without warning when shooting was going on in an area. Attorney General Sir Peter Rawlinson, decorated for combat in North Africa in the war, objected. Though a soldier was unlikely to be prosecuted for firing at someone carrying a gun, the DPP would have to investigate. Rawlinson ruled out any legal immunity for soldiers.[205] Burke Trend notified the prime minister of the army's intention to ignore the UDA. He advised UDA-dominated areas be tackled 'to make it clear beyond doubt that we are not operating as allies of the UDA against the Roman Catholic enclaves'.[206] The army and police already knew themselves to be accused of 'inactivity in relation to UDA barricades and assassinations'.[207] On 27 July the cabinet authorised Motorman, to 're-occupy' areas where the IRA or the UDA 'sought to prevent the security forces operating freely'. Seven battalions plus supporting elements, such as armoured bulldozers, were to be sent.[208]

General Ford's orders clearly targeted one opponent: to 'remove the IRA from the backs of the Catholic community'. Operations were to be conducted without aggravating innocent Catholics, yet involved soldiers occupying Catholic areas. In the first phase, the 22,000 troops at Ford's disposal would establish bases in 'hard' areas, with special emphasis on the Creggan and the Bogside in Derry, and Andersonstown and Ballymurphy in Belfast. Over the following two or three days the target areas would be brought under total military control, including in Lurgan, Portadown, Armagh, Coalisland and Newry, where resources permitted. A third phase was expected to last much longer, as the army gradually built up a fuller intelligence picture and arrested IRA leaders, using interrogation, internment and covert surveillance. Ford aimed to 'effectively neutralise the Provisional IRA', returning in many senses to the pre–direct-rule attritional strategy. He avoided the same measures when it came to loyalists. Battalions were to liaise with the UDA to avoid violent clashes. 'Vigilante activity' was allowed so long as the army was not impeded. Soldiers should help loyalists remove their barricades 'because of the need to appear impartial'.[209] R. A. Custis in the MOD alerted Lord Carrington to the flagrant bias:

> This does not comply with the Cabinet directive which is clearly 'to reoccupy those areas from which either the IRA or the UDA sought to exclude the normal operation of the security forces ... it was important

that the operation should <u>be clearly seen to be directed against extremists</u> <u>of either community</u>'. Head DS10 is taking this up through DMO, with a view to amending the Directive to reflect the Cabinet's instructions more accurately.[210]

At some point that day General Carver telephoned HQNI to insist there be no 'fraternization' with the UDA. He wanted loyalist barricades down by 8am on the day of the operation. Carver also informed Tuzo that Whitelaw intended to make a public statement the night before, warning people to stay indoors, on the advice of the attorney general, to reduce the risk of casualties.[211] Ford's orders were duly amended. For example, one section was altered from setting the objective as 'to dominate the IRA', to 'dominate the IRA and Protestant extremists'.[212] General Ford witnessed Bloody Sunday without intervening, did nothing to disturb 1 Para's systematic lying about their actions, and directly ignored an instruction from the cabinet. No government minister ever moved against him.

Motorman proved to be a remarkable success. Nearly all barricades in Derry and Belfast came down on the first day, 31 July: 1st Welsh Guards moved into the Protestant Sandy Row area in Belfast, Royal Engineers dismantled loyalist barricades in Portadown, and 1st Royal Welch Fusiliers did the same in the Waterside district of Derry.[213] No security-force casualties were suffered, though car bombs in Claudy, near Derry, killed six people and injured thirty others. Most IRA members went to ground rather than fight the twenty-seven army units moving into their territory, except in Derry, where soldiers claimed to have shot six gunmen and a petrol bomber. Whitelaw had issued a public warning the night before to avoid civilian casualties. As expected, the UDA co-operated in removing their barricades (though some went up again later). The operation pushed army and police morale to a new high.[214] By 4 August joint military police–RUC patrols were back in the former no-go areas. Selective searches and arrests, including in some Protestant areas, achieved good results:[215] in the New Barnsley and Moyard areas in Belfast, 2nd Parachute Regiment noted residents 'reacted with resigned tolerance to both the military domination of the area and the head checking. . . .. Some residents are still very sullen and avoid contact, particularly in New Barnsley, but a steadily increasing number will now chat and smile.'[216]

Motorman had an enduring effect. Violence never returned to the high point of July 1972. PIRA's grip in the cities loosened, and Northern Ireland entered two decades of military stalemate.[217] The operation's success rested on the political capital built up by the army and Whitelaw in the low-profile phase. By holding back in the spring and summer, even as PIRA ramped up their offensive, the army repaired some of the self-inflicted reputational damage from the winter months.[218] However, in the early summer of 1972 – before Motorman – British strategy decisively reached an accommodation with loyalism that was to simultaneously reduce the republican threat and entrench the conflict into a lingering sectarian phase. What really shook the British were the loyalist barricades in Belfast, the 'near-disastrous' stand-off between the army and UDA on 3 July, and the sheer number of Protestants ready to fight them. As the MOD recognised, Motorman achieved 'one of the main demands of the UDA'.[219] In parliament, questions arose about why the army concentrated their efforts solely against the IRA.[220] Whitelaw explained to the Conservative Parliamentary Northern Ireland Committee: 'The U.D.A. and I.R.A. cannot be compared – U.D.A. does not kill soldiers.'[221] Ulstermen sometimes forgot the Westminster imperative to be inconspicuous. On 4 August, about 500 masked UDA men in paramilitary uniforms paraded in east Belfast. General Tuzo appreciated these 'posturings . . . made for bad publicity'.[222] Frank Steele only managed to extract from loyalist leaders a promise to consider dispensing with masks and dark glasses.[223]

Royal Marines officer David Storrie remembered a UDA march as 'quite frightening . . . this huge, disciplined, very determined group of people, our own people. It wasn't a group of Cypriots or Indians or whatever. These were people a large number of whom were ex-servicemen and it could have turned very nasty.'[224] General Ford advocated a 'conciliatory line' to assist the UDA in becoming 'more respectable'.[225] More respectable for whom? Certainly not the SDLP. Gerry Fitt pointed out the obvious imbalance in Operation Motorman: tanks in the Creggan and the Bogside, then friendly co-operation between soldiers and the UDA elsewhere. Catholics believed 'harsh military tactics would be adopted against them alone'. In a two-day meeting with Whitelaw the SDLP repeated the need to abolish internment before they could attend a constitutional conference. After several hours, the first day of the meeting broke up for the night. The next day Whitelaw made a surprising announcement: he had signed the release orders for forty-seven internees, to show his good faith. Forty-seven was not enough for the SDLP. They listed additional grievances, such as schools and community centres being occupied by the army. Drivers stopped at UDA barricades were being assaulted. On a more constructive note, the SDLP suggested legalising the republican clubs and Sinn Féin, so that the IRA might be drawn into normal politics.[226] The party's intransigence on internment, or possibly their ingratitude for his courage, blinded Whitelaw to the wisdom of their final proposition.

THE POLITICS OF FORCE LEVELS

After Motorman the British government held the highest military force level at any point throughout the conflict. To reconstruct Northern Ireland's political institutions the British had to demonstrate their impartiality, by abolishing internment (still a weapon only applied to the nationalist community) and standing up to loyalism. Despite a few successful operations against the UVF and UDA, the army stuck to a policy of appeasement. Neither the MOD nor the NIO pushed for a fundamental change. Whitelaw's department did, however, seek to end internment in order to bring the SDLP into the constitutional process. This endeavour was defeated by General Carver with backing from the SoS for defence and the prime minister. They believed internment could only be dropped if the army maintained a very high force level in Northern Ireland. Concerns about Britain's contribution to NATO, and widening cracks in the army's morale, persuaded General Carver of the need to bring the force level down. With the troop numbers dropping, internment had to stay, and the loyalist paramilitaries had to be condoned.

Frank Steele advised Whitelaw to abolish internment. The government had already committed to ending it when violence dropped; doing so would transform Catholic faith in the government. Steele admitted Protestant objections stood in the way, but thought moderate people would accept the logic. He expected few internees to leap back into armed action on release. Perhaps the biggest problem was the thirty-to-fifty 'really dangerous internees'. Overall, the security situation was good enough to take the risk.[227] The evidence in HQNI's report for the week ending 9 August supported this conclusion. Politically, the Provisionals 'have as yet failed to regain their previous support from the Catholic community'. Shooting incidents that week stood at 138, compared to 1,027 in the week ending 19 July. Bombings were down too.[228] However, in the run-up to Operation Motorman the army convinced itself that intensive interrogation was not only desirable, but in fact irresistible, and began planning accordingly. These plans relied upon internment for those going through the interrogation system. In early June Chief Constable Shillington fought to keep the police holding centres at Girdwood, Holywood, Ballykelly and Armagh open, even as the numbers passing through them for interrogation dropped off. Girdwood actually closed. Holywood, the other busiest centre, processed between 1 and 23 people each week in June instead of the 332 in January.[229]

The army planned new Special Branch–run police offices at Ballykelly, Castlereagh and Armagh for interrogation. Military personnel would record, collate and evaluate the intelligence gathered. General Carver proposed suspects undergo normal police questioning first and only be sent for interrogation if they were not going to be prosecuted.[230] General Tuzo enthusiastically agreed. He believed he could 'break the will of the IRA' within thirteen weeks. The British must get on with interrogation whilst 'closing our ears to the storms of protest'.[231] The Special Branch interrogators were not so sure. They required reassurances from the attorney general about potential prosecutions before they agreed to resume work.[232] Whitelaw wanted to consult Heath and Carrington before agreeing to anything. He also preferred to have only two offices, at Ballykelly and Castlereagh.[233] His PUS, Sir William Nield, advised rejecting the army's plan. One official accused the army of deliberate manipulation:

> The MOD continued to harass us, alleging that the secretary of state, when invited by the GOC at 5.30 in the morning on Monday 31 July whilst the operation for re-entering the no-go areas was taking place to request army cooperation in logistic and manpower support of an interrogation operation, had thereupon made that request. At a later stage the MOD maintained that there were a number of people awaiting interrogation and that it was essential to proceed forthwith to set up the interrogation centres at Castlereagh, Armagh and Ballykelly; but that the army could not play their part until they had been formally requested to do so. Meanwhile the RUC were being frustrated in the execution of their duties. At this stage the MOD had shifted over from their original position, in which they were protesting that they only wanted to be helpful if we needed their help, to a position in which they were stating what needed to be done ... the Secretary of State said ... he was not prepared to return to a Faulknerian policy of the arrest and prolonged interrogation of a large number of people.[234]

The prime minister delegated the issue to Lord Carrington, who understood the potential for controversy. Carrington sought Whitelaw's consent.[235] On 7 August Whitelaw gave permission for interrogation at two police centres.[236] General Carver argued against Steele's position at the Cabinet Northern Ireland Committee. Catholic attitudes towards the army and police had improved, resulting in more intelligence coming into the security forces. Far from contemplating ending internment, Carver requested intensive interrogation be resumed, so that the army's footprint could be reduced to eighteen units by December from the current twenty-seven. Whitelaw agreed to interrogation at special centres so long as the methods employed excluded the banned five techniques.[237] Heath and Carrington supported Carver, dismissing the proposal to end internment.

When Whitelaw informed the SDLP he tried to soften the blow by releasing another eighteen internees. John Hume lamented that 'if internment were not ended now, the SDLP would be finished'.[238] The army had effectively locked out the main nationalist party from politics. The same day the NIO discovered Ballykelly and Castlereagh had been operating since just before Operation Motorman. And on 12 August Whitelaw learned that several people a day were being interrogated 'outside the Judge's Rules' (that is, not for criminal prosecution), beyond any official policy.[239] The police and army outmanoeuvred Whitelaw to retain internment and expand interrogation.

A week later minister David Howell attempted to put the reins back on the army, denying permission for an ex-internee to be placed back in detention. NIO officials suspected the army were arresting ex-internees without evidence that they had become involved in violence.[240] Whitelaw only wanted PIRA battalion commanders or above arrested.[241] General Ford, the commanders of 24 and 39 Brigades, the head of Special Branch, the assistant chief constable for Belfast and the chief inspector at Castlereagh all complained. Frank Steele reminded the officers that internment 'tended to breed a new younger and even wilder brand of replacement IRA'.[242] HQNI admitted internment aided IRA recruitment. But prisoners only tended to talk if they knew detention might follow. The chief of staff hoped to intern another 120 IRA officers before political talks started.[243] Soldiers bridled at the restrictions, too. Lance-Corporal Kempton noted: 'The politicians are stopping us fighting back – "hearts and minds" policy. A load of shit. Our colour-sergeant is in hospital with glass in his face and eyes, and we must just stand there and take it.'[244] HQNI reprimanded units for allowing some people to be interrogated for long periods. Soldiers were only supposed to hold prisoners for up to four hours.[245] Robin Evelegh, who commanded 3rd Royal Green Jackets in Belfast between August and December 1972, noted:

> Starting with interrogation in depth, that disgraceful affair, there were continually units of the army, and places in the army, where physical violence, minor torture and brutality was used. It never did any good. Furthermore, it was entirely contrary to the orders that the army was supposed to obey, and my complaint is the weakness of the senior officers of the army, in not enforcing those orders to behave within the law, but in many cases conniving at them, winking at them, implying that if you weren't found out, it didn't matter.[246]

The Provisionals continued to inflict casualties on the security forces, thus dominating their thinking. Seven security-forces personnel were killed in the last week of August alone and twenty-six wounded.[247] General Tuzo compared the situation to Borneo and Kenya: more severe losses were being sustained but without punitive legal measures to combat the enemy. PIRA's accurate sniper fire posed a threat to military morale. Internment bothered Tuzo. Of the 341 PIRA men released since direct rule, at least 64 were thought to be active again, in addition to the 16 charged with criminal offences. Tuzo believed special courts, improved intelligence and a force level of twenty-five to thirty battalions could 'liquidate' the IRA inside six months.[248] At this meeting and afterwards Whitelaw has been credited with preventing the army from reverting to a more expansive internment policy.[249] In fact, on 1 September he compromised. Whitelaw agreed to consider detaining PIRA adjutants, quartermasters, engineer officers, intelligence officers and highly dangerous volunteers. To avoid a sudden surge in detention requests, each application should be justified by detailed intelligence on the threat posed by the individual.[250]

Internment, like the fresh offensive against PIRA in general, was expected to dampen down loyalist militancy. In August and September 1972 the army clung on to this delusory belief. On 29 August the chief constable reported that since 1 July forty-eight political or sectarian murders had occurred, of twenty-six Catholics and twenty-two Protestants. Some may have been killed by their own community. With trust in the police at a low level, investigating proved difficult.[251] The UDA blamed the murder of Catholics on the UVF, so Tuzo called for more intelligence on the latter organisation.[252] HQNI issued new orders on the UDA on 15 August. The prime aim was to avoid anything 'provocative in the eyes of public opinion' in Northern Ireland and Britain. If the UDA behaved in a 'clearly illegal' manner, or seemed liable to provoke dangerous intercommunal disorder, they should be dealt with vigorously. Illegal marchers were to be quietly spoken to, and arrested later, rather than driven off the streets. Commanders should persuade the UDA to discard masks or offensive weapons, unless doing so risked a riot. Action against the UDA was to be preceded by contact with their leaders via 39 Brigade.[253] In the second half of August at least three bombs were made by 'Protestant organisations'. UDA roadblocks caused consternation, not merely for holding up the traffic, but also when motorists were dragged from their cars and beaten up.[254]

Appeasement bred contempt. UDA men in masks and dark glasses reappeared on the streets in early September, carrying cudgels.[255] The deterioration stemmed in part from the security forces arresting UVF members thought to be linked to the recent murders. The army now realised the connections between the UVF and UDA to be rather intimate.[256] On the night of 7 September an army patrol was ambushed by around forty UDA members in Machet Street in Belfast, who threw stones at first, then opened fire. The violence spread around the Shankill. In response the army raided the UDA headquarters in Wilton Street, finding a sniperscope, three bullets, telephone-tapping equipment, bomb-making materials, walkie-talkies, batons and medical supplies.[257] A search of a farmhouse near Monkstown, north of the city, uncovered six rifles, a submachine gun, a revolver, 6,000 rounds of ammunition, forty-seven bomb detonators and two telescopic sights. The building seemed to host the Tara Brigade's County Antrim headquarters, linked to the UVF. Sixteen men were arrested and charged – three of them UDR soldiers.[258]

The LAW disrupted supply at the Belfast East and West power stations with strike action, and intimidation of Catholics continued. HQNI disparaged the 'petulant Protestants'.[259] Soldiers from 2nd Parachute Regiment on the Shankill, and in Protestant-majority estates like Springmartin and Highfield, realised that people who offered them tea were threatened. The change in mood derived from a decision by the UDA leadership of 'non cooperation' with the army and police.[260] The murder of civilians in Belfast, most Catholics, rose during September. The commander of the UDA's C Company was arrested and charged with one of these murders. Loyalists were thought to be responsible for bombing a Catholic-owned hotel in the city, killing three and injuring fifty.[261] UDA, LAW and Vanguard rallies in Belfast drew 5–6,000 people. Masked men made an appearance once more.[262] The army's ability to pacify loyalists, to split the allegedly reasonable men of the UDA from the fanatics in the tiny UVF, appeared rather tenuous. Only while the Motorman reinforcements remained in place was there any prospect of dealing with them.

General Carver understood the danger from the moment HQNI proposed a twenty-five to thirty-battalion force level in late August. General Tuzo's sudden enthusiasm for expansive troop numbers probably came as a nasty surprise. Only a few weeks earlier he and Carver had agreed to drop down to twenty-two units by 1 October, then eighteen by 1 December.[263] Planners started to get concerned about the implications of the Northern Ireland commitment for defence policy as early as October 1971. Units began to miss the training necessary for their NATO roles. Four additional battalions were added to the army's order of battle, to mitigate the 'severe strain' on the infantry.[264] A month later the CDS sounded the alarm about impending overstretch. Britain then cancelled a four-country NATO training exercise scheduled for 1972. The SACEUR expressed his 'disquiet' about the withdrawals from Germany.[265] At the NATO Military Committee in May 1972 the CDS stressed Britain's high defence spending, at 5.5 per cent of gross national product, and referred to the 'temporary problems in Northern Ireland', where troops honed their skills. All forces there would be returned to Europe in an emergency.[266] Britain's shortfall disappeared amidst the alliance's wider problems. In June the SACEUR reported severe manning deficiencies. Top-readiness forces sat at 69 per cent of the required level. Weakness in anti-tank weapons, air defence, combat service support and reserve stocks masked the Northern Ireland issue.[267]

Operation Motorman ended the charade. On 4 August 1972 NATO instituted an investigation into the withdrawals.[268] The SACEUR presented his findings to NATO's Military Committee a few weeks later. General Andrew Goodpaster noted the increase in battalions taken from BAOR for short tours, from seven and one-third battalions in July 1972, to three more by the end of the month. Leaving all the headquarters and heavy equipment in Germany made the seventy-seven-hour emergency return plans viable. However, the SACEUR was clearly alarmed by the Motorman exodus. In an emergency, such as a surprise attack, 1st British Corps in Germany would lack nearly one-third of its major combat units. Less seriously, the deployments disrupted regular training. The British annoyed Goodpaster by borrowing units from the strategic reserve in the United Kingdom that were supposed to be at his disposal, 'impacting on SACEUR's options for crisis management'. The Military Committee pressed for BAOR battalions to be returned as soon as possible, and sent Goodpaster's report to all permanent representatives on 21 September, no doubt causing the British some embarrassment.[269]

The impact of foreign policy on domestic politics often attracts insufficient scrutiny in writing on British political history.[270] Such is the case in relation to the Troubles. There are grounds for questioning whether General Goodpaster's reprimand determined force levels in Northern Ireland, and thus the army's capacity for standing up to loyalism. The Soviet invasion of Czechoslovakia in 1968 shocked NATO. Warsaw Pact armed forces appeared to be upgrading their capabilities. In December 1967 NATO formally adopted MC 14/3: a new 'flexible-response' concept aimed at meeting a non-nuclear attack symmetrically, with conventional forces, and designed to escalate gradually. So the units taken away from BAOR mattered. Still, an invasion was not expected. Furthermore, British Cold War strategy consistently prioritised nuclear over conventional deterrence, a stance favoured by many European allies.[271] Here the alliance was strong – in the 1970s the US alone maintained 7,000 nuclear weapons in Europe.[272] NATO's conventional force levels stayed fairly constant during the decade. The greatest risk of major reductions came from the United States, owing to the Vietnam war. But in December 1970 President Nixon committed to maintaining force levels.[273] The threat from the Soviets diminished during Leonid Brezhnev's tenure as general secretary of the Communist Party. Vladimir Zubok chronicles 'the rapid decline of Cold War tensions in the period from 1970 to 1972'. In May 1972 Brezhnev and President Nixon signed the Strategic Arms Limitations Talks Agreement (SALT I), and other accords, in Moscow.[274]

Such momentous embodiments of détente between East and West can hardly have escaped the MOD's attention. NATO allies' expectations conveniently supplemented the more serious rationale for holding the Northern Ireland commitment down. The defence establishment preferred to understate the other reason because careless handling might imply a lack of faith in the army's fighting prowess. HQNI's propaganda unit observed the strain on soldiers from 'seeing friends killed by snipers who might, under a different set of orders, be run to earth, and at the same time reading that IRA leaders, whose capture represented the culmination of long, skilfully conducted operations are being released from internment'.[275] The staff colonel in charge of MO4 discerned a morale problem amongst junior officers. Carrington asked Whitelaw to think carefully about the morale implications before releasing IRA bomb-makers from internment.[276] During a visit to Northern Ireland in June Carrington and Whitelaw addressed a specially convened meeting for battalion commanders. They recognised that soldiers, and some junior officers, had little faith in the low-profile posture when the shooting and bombing showed no signs of abating. This resentment caused 'real problems' for commanders. The ministers assured them the political rewards warranted the frustration.[277] Motorman temporarily boosted the army's confidence, until PIRA adapted with highly accurate sniper attacks in urban areas and roadside bombs in the countryside. In August and September the army lost 33 soldiers killed and 120 wounded.[278]

The Parachute Regiment prepared their own analysis of the morale problem. By November 1973 1st Battalion would have spent twenty-eight months in Northern Ireland; 2nd Battalion would have done five short tours by the same point, and 3rd Battalion two. Attendance at training and education courses suffered as a result, including those needed for promotion. Regimental Colonel K. C. Came noted the damaging nature of the 'non-stop Aldershot–N Ireland routine' on family life. Army families expected periodic long tours abroad to attractive places such as Cyprus – these were being cancelled. An increasing number of paratroopers were not renewing their service, or transferred out of the infantry. Many mentioned the prospect of endless operations in Northern Ireland, plus no 'overseas tours to the sun and duty free'. The commanding officers of 1st and 2nd Battalions worried about 'the cumulative effect the N Ireland life of violence may have on both the younger and older soldier. The younger a soldier, who is at a very impressionable age, is thrust into this abnormal life of search, shoot, detain, arrest and therefore must stand a very good chance of having his sense of values affected.'[279] Meanwhile, 16 Parachute Brigade's commander also warned of the effect of frequent tours on morale and training. Soldiers became 'disillusioned' when denied the chance to serve outside the United Kingdom.[280]

Exposure to the conflict certainly affected Peter McMullen, a Catholic soldier in his mid 20s from Magherafelt, County Londonderry. He transferred from the Army Catering Corps to the Parachute Regiment in 1969 and was promoted lance-corporal in January 1971.[281] Military intelligence reported McMullen went absent without leave on 27 January 1972 and was suspected of allegedly planting three bombs in Palace Barracks, Holywood, one of which exploded that night.[282] In June 1974 military investigators in Aldershot co-operating with the Hampshire police Special Branch produced a report[283] in which it was alleged that McMullen was 'strongly suspected of being responsible' for the 1972 bomb at Palace Barracks. Referring to the bombing of the officers' mess at 16 Parachute Brigade headquarters in Aldershot in February 1972, the same report noted 'fairly conclusive evidence indicates that he stole the explosive from Somerset which was used later to blow up the mess'.[284] McMullen had defected to PIRA and was also responsible for bombing an army barracks near Ripon, north Yorkshire, in March 1972. He spent several years in prison in Ireland for a firearms offence, then went to the United States. At York Crown Court in 1996 he was convicted of the bombings but set free due to time served in America whilst fighting extradition.[285] Whether the unusual case of Peter McMullen typified a wider range of subversion within the army cannot be answered until further archives on military intelligence, subversion and morale are opened up. That a soldier was willing to resort to bombing his own comrades at the least testifies to the extraordinary pressures building up on the army by early 1972.

In September General Carver pushed back against Tuzo and Whitelaw's desire to keep their existing twenty-five battalions. Without a reduction, all overseas exercises must be cancelled and training for anything other than

Northern Ireland would be severely curtailed. Troops might be unavailable for public duties. Even the Queen's Birthday parade hung in the balance. More alarmingly for the troops, the current situation necessitated cutting the interval between tours to about three months. Units were becoming 'less enthusiastic' about going back to Ireland.[286] Carver reminded Whitelaw of long-standing plans to settle at eighteen battalions by the end of 1972. Holding on to units in the hope that a political breakthrough was on the horizon seemed unrealistic. Prior experience showed force levels could safely be lowered over the winter and then raised for the Easter and summer marching periods. Carver stressed to Whitelaw and Carrington the damaging effect that the campaign was having on recruiting and on morale amongst military families subjected to repeated turbulence. Accepting these points, Whitelaw agreed to the planned reductions, so long as they were done gradually and with a promise for troops to be sent back in an emergency. Carrington reassured him accordingly.[287] By 30 September the MOD had withdrawn the 24 Brigade headquarters, 2nd Parachute Regiment, 1st Coldstream Guards, B Squadron The Blues and Royals, and two squadrons of Royal Engineers.[288]

CONCLUSION

Whitelaw's elusive political nirvana nearly happened in Darlington from 25 to 28 September 1972. The participants from the Ulster Unionist Party, the Northern Ireland Labour Party and the Alliance Party lacked the authority to make peace.[289] Tragically, HQNI's myopia on internment, permitted by Carrington and Heath, prevented the SDLP from attending the conference, scuppering the possibility of depriving PIRA of their support base. The British government's proclaimed return to a neutrality lost to public sight since the spring of 1971 fooled nobody in Northern Ireland. A teacher in Belfast wrote to Whitelaw about daily UDA intimidation: 'We Catholics are not impressed by talk of impartiality in the peace-keeping operation while this kind of situation continues.'[290] Even 2nd Parachute Regiment accepted the futility of operations without a political settlement: 'It is only possible to hold a people under by force for so long without some carrot for them to look forward to.' The Paras accepted their tactics boosted IRA recruitment.[291] By the autumn of 1972 the army knew that loyalist violence was on the rise and reinforced republicans' legitimacy as community defenders. Motorman provided the breathing space, and the troop numbers, to finally abolish internment and take decisive action against loyalists. A few operations against the UDA and the UVF showed the army possessed the intelligence to strike with great effect. At several junctures the cabinet's appetite for a stronger line against loyalists clashed sharply with the preferences of the army in London and Northern Ireland. Senior commanders feared the force-level implications of imposing security on both communities equally and used the discretion granted them over operations to push for a very cautious approach to loyalism.

Writings about this crucial year in the Troubles naturally alight on the dramatic 'what if' moment when Willie Whitelaw met the Provisional leadership. Here a case has been made for viewing another near-miss, the potential fight between the British Army and the UDA in Belfast, as equally significant. Present at that moment, 1st Royal Regiment of Wales recorded: 'It had been a close thing though, and that evening we had all taken a step nearer to Civil War.' Fortunately for them Major-General Ford talked the UDA down, as the battalion only held the Shankill with one company.[292] General Carver's decision to reduce the troop numbers in Northern Ireland was never fundamentally overturned. He deprived HQNI of the resources to tackle loyalist violence as it escalated even further into 1973. Formally, the decision derived entirely from the requirement to balance Northern Ireland with the army's commitment to defending Western Europe from the Red Army. Under the surface, senior officers recognised the strain being put on their soldiers by repeated tours where they were spat at, insulted, stoned, shot and blown up. Even the army's toughest unit, the Parachute Regiment, began to question whether Northern Ireland was morally degrading their men. Whilst Whitelaw and counterparts in the NIO laboured towards a political endgame, the army gradually became convinced that the conflict would never end. This made a lower force level, and broad appeasement of loyalism, essential components of a long-term strategy for holding the army together.

7

STRATEGY IN THE SHADOW OF LOYALIST POWER

Mr Whitelaw said he was convinced that it would be necessary to take on the militant Protestants before very long but he was anxious that we should do so at the right time.[1]

Meeting in the House of Lords, 9 November 1972

The right time never came. The strategy devised by Whitelaw and his military advisers from late 1972 aimed to solve the conflict politically by drawing moderate nationalists and unionists into the centre ground, whilst degrading PIRA militarily. Loyalism was supposed to be made irrelevant to the equation. In May 1974 the whole strategy unravelled in spectacular form when the UWC strike destroyed the power-sharing compromise. The problems encountered in cultivating peace in Northern Ireland through constitutional deal-making have been studied extensively.[2] Although the need to consider the security context is acknowledged, the contribution of violence to constitutional collapse is insufficiently understood.[3] Much changed in the decades after the Northern Ireland Executive and Assembly fell in 1974: spectacular bombings, the hunger strikes, 1985's Anglo-Irish Agreement, to name only a few waypoints. At a strategic level, however, the conflict remained intractable into the early 1990s. Civil wars often linger on, sucking all hope from a society, for a variety of reasons, ranging from inequality to economic profiteering.[4] The Northern Ireland conflict became intractable even before the 1974 UWC strike, due to the relationships between loyalism, republicanism and the British Army's own actions.

The strategic logic underpinning political progress was profoundly flawed. The British Army lacked the capacity to overcome PIRA militarily, and the decision to appease loyalism backfired. Rather than tamping down loyalism as intended, the softly-softly approach emboldened the UVF and UDA to the point where the violence they unleashed actually strengthened republicanism. The confidence to mount a province-wide strike to bring a democratically elected assembly crashing down did not appear overnight. This is important because scholars have sometimes blamed the disintegration of a political settlement solely on Harold Wilson's 1974–6 administration.[5] Wilson's responsibility does deserve to be questioned, but should be understood in the context of the longer-term factors that contributed to the impasse. At best, military strategy stabilised conflict at a lower level and hardened the army to a campaign expected to last indefinitely.

In existing studies, the influence of loyalists on the British government is either exaggerated or disregarded. British conduct towards loyalism is sometimes described as collusion, through 'commission, omission, collaboration or connivance'.[6] However, such a broad definition implies more uniformity and direction than existed.[7] Collusion certainly occurred. Between October 1970 and March 1973, for example, 222 firearms were lost or stolen from the UDR. Many ended up in loyalist hands.[8] Collusion assumes sympathy or shared objectives between the security forces and groups like the UDA and UVF. Without denying these sentiments existed in places, fear counted a lot more in British military attitudes towards loyalism. The suggestion that the government adopted an impartial stance to aggression from any quarter is flawed.[9] Downplaying loyalism replicates the justification for doing so in the 1970s: they only reacted to IRA violence.[10] Loyalism could be reactive: in the second half of 1973 the UVF bombed Catholic targets in Belfast in retaliation for attacks by the IRA.[11] Reaction never explained everything, however.[12]

Policymakers wished to isolate the 'extremist elements' within loyalism.[13] In the autumn of 1972 the NIO and HQNI disagreed about how to handle loyalist violence. Astonishingly, the army captured almost the entire UVF leadership in one go, only for their release to be ordered by the NIO (see below, page 000). The UVF and UDA effectively deterred the army from pursuing a more vigorous line against them by threatening to retaliate and throw the region into civil war. Those in the army who resented being pushed around and wanted to shut those groups down were stopped by an agreed position between the NIO, keen to proceed with political talks, and the MOD, desperate to avoid having to send more troops from Britain and Germany. Though there were ongoing operations against loyalists, these did little to dent their ability to intimidate and kill Catholics. The army persisted with the fiction that a distinction existed between the radical UVF and the moderate UDA, despite knowing better, because the thousands in the UDA's ranks were too terrifying a prospective foe.

Besides causing enormous suffering, the republican offensive exacerbated Protestant animosity towards Whitelaw's power-sharing plans.[14] The war between PIRA and the British state reached a stalemate by the time of the 1975 ceasefire.[15] The stalemate must be explained with reference to the strategic interactions between British, republican and loyalist power. Scholars have emphasised geography and organisation in accounting for PIRA's survival. In the countryside volunteers hid more easily amongst the population than in the towns. A cellular structure rolled out from 1973 proved resilient to penetration by the British. Agents and informers have been described as the security forces' 'principal intelligence option'.[16] There are two problems with this explanation for the stalemate. Firstly, the war did not relocate wholesale to the countryside. Secondly, the primacy of any form of intelligence cannot be empirically verified whilst records critical to such a determination, like the all-source assessments of the JIC, remain closed. Though PIRA's geographical and organisational changes were significant, tactical adaptation allowed for the war to proceed despite British counter-measures. Training and planning deserve emphasis, as do tactical improvements in sniping, bombing technology, bomb-attack methodology and combined-arms assaults. The crucial factor in determining the British Army's inability to stifle PIRA's offensive was not intelligence, but force levels. The army lacked enough troops to consistently impose a force concentration powerful enough to crush all republican resistance.

Tactical improvements by the British Army achieved a lower level of violence but at a political cost that jeopardised the overall mission. Systematic training promoted the effective integration of intelligence-gathering measures into a wider tactical repertoire. The army's operational approach centred around an effort to target the PIRA leadership, which did capture large numbers of officers and limit the Provisionals' full offensive potential. However, HQNI assumed that leadership decapitation would render the organisation helpless as more junior members lost direction. That did not happen. PIRA managed to replace lost leaders and reconstitute itself again and again. HQNI displayed almost no curiosity about why and how this recovery came into being. Probably around half of the people picked up on the street for questioning ended up being released within a few hours. Whether regular aggravation on a vast scale fuelled PIRA recruitment and support cannot be precisely measured. The likely effect, however, is obvious.

Senior commanders felt compelled to respond to the constant flow of criticism about soldiers. Engaging in community relations projects served to convince soldiers their presence was valued and to under-estimate the hostility directed at them as coming from a vocal minority. An obsession with propaganda also made it difficult to discern when complaints were genuine or bogus. The MOD effectively dispensed with critics by paying them off in out-of-court settlements. These reveal quite how many complaints were not vexatious at all. The army's regimental system, plus the four-month tours for many units, introduced a high degree of variation in how soldiers treated civilians. The incentives for Catholics to enact allegiance to Britain dropped every time the state's uniformed representatives disappeared, perhaps to be replaced by a regiment more inclined to knock down doors for early morning arms searches than to share a friendly cup of tea. A lack of military resources and the concern to avoid more soldiers being drawn into Northern Ireland to confront loyalists made the conflict more intractable.

'PAYING OUT ROPE': APPEASING LOYALISM

In late 1972 and early 1973 the British government sought to prevent violence from derailing progress towards a political settlement. Between 25 and 28 September 1972 William Whitelaw hosted the Ulster Unionist Party, the Northern Ireland Labour Party and the Alliance Party for talks in Darlington. They contributed to the publication, on 20 March 1973, of a White Paper, the 'Northern Ireland Constitutional Proposals'. These set the foundations for the Sunningdale Agreement on devolved power-sharing.[17] The approach taken earlier in 1972, of degrading PIRA whilst avoiding confrontation with loyalists, continued. However, over the winter months the effectiveness of this strategy unravelled. Loyalist groups expanded their operations and clashed with the security forces. The army started to question the assumption that degrading republicanism would automatically placate loyalists. A split emerged between the army, realising a more assertive posture was required, and the NIO, which wished to contain loyalism with minimal action. In part, the belief in the ability to contain the threat rested upon a distinction between a minority of extremists, and the more pliable majority. Reading the legal, mass-membership UDA's publications might have put paid to such delusions. *The Ulster Militant* stated: 'Every loyal Ulsterman has one of two choices facing him: 1. A united Ireland. 2. Removal of all RCs [Roman Catholics] from Ulster. . .. If they are not prepared to go the easy way, then it will have to be the hard way.'[18] Even more prominently, in October 1972 Ulster Vanguard leader William Craig told the Conservative Monday Club in the Commons that he and his 80,000 followers were 'prepared to come out and kill'[19] to stop power-sharing.

By the end of September HQNI began to wonder whether the dividing line between the UDA and the illegal, smaller UVF was meaningful. Three bombings in Catholic parts of Belfast injured twenty-nine people.[20] Whitelaw conceded 'a large part of the violence was now coming from the Protestant side'.[21] However, as force levels dropped the army concentrated on republicans, allowing a 'vacuum in the Protestant areas' to be filled by the UDA.[22] Despite the focus on PIRA, the army nearly removed the entire UVF leadership from the scene in one swoop. At 6pm on 10 October Major-General Ford received intelligence that the UDA planned to use Tartan gangs to target Catholics living in Belfast's predominantly Protestant areas. The UDA discovered the army knew about their plans and cancelled the attacks. Some Tartans rioted anyway. The next day HQNI heard that Gusty Spence, the UVF founder, on the run after escaping prison, would be at an address that evening with eleven others. When 1st Parachute Regiment raided the house, they found '55 to 58 UVF conferring round a table'.[23] Support Company – the men implicated in Bloody Sunday – were taken aback:

> To his horror, the mortar platoon sergeant found himself faced with not a dozen, but 63 very hard looking UVF men, the first 20 of whom advanced with bottles and glasses raised! Like Horatius at the Bridge 'those behind cried forward' and he in front unable to go back was forced to rest his pistol on the nose of the first assailant and convince him that he really did mean to blow his head off. The UVF faltered for a moment and in the next second the rest of the mortar platoon were up the stairs and surrounding the serried rows of bewildered UVF.[24]

All were sent for interrogation at Castlereagh police station. Ford informed Lord Windlesham, the duty NIO minister. Windlesham phoned the chief constable 'to express surprise at large catch and hopes that all those against whom no charges can be preferred will be released'. The UVF was an illegal terrorist organisation, known to be conducting a murder campaign against Catholics. By 9 o'clock the next morning the RUC had released all but six men, who later walked out on bail. The army believed those arrested at 'the UVF meeting involved all their Province wide leaders'.[25] On the night of the arrests the UDA and Tartans 'rampaged in the Shankill and East Belfast'. In at least eighteen incidents loyalists fired at the security forces, a pattern repeated over the following days, culminating in at least fifty shootings on 17 October.[26] The UDA only stepped down after meeting NIO minister David Howell and General Tuzo. However, sectarian attacks continued and spread to the countryside.[27] Commenting on the link between PIRA violence and loyalist rioting, the MOD recognised: 'it does not appear to have been the direct cause of the recent trouble'. In fact, PIRA engaged the security forces in a gun-battle in Ardoyne on 17 October to exploit the chaos created by loyalists.[28]

The violence unleashed in reaction to the UVF leadership arrests effectively deterred the army from taking such measures in the future. General

Tuzo told London he was 'not in a position to take firm measures against the UDA' because they outnumbered the army. The security forces lacked intelligence on the UDA and evidence for bringing prosecutions. Tuzo objected to any distraction from fighting the IRA. In any case, the UDA 'was still held in too great esteem by the general public' to be challenged. Tuzo and Whitelaw preferred a policy of 'paying out rope' to the UDA, making every effort to cultivate the Protestant population.[29] Sympathy for loyalism arose in a context where soldiers could only socialise in Protestant neighbourhoods. Former servicemen from the Province often hosted their uniformed brethren for drinks or meals.[30] At the strategic level in late 1972, the relationship is better characterised by fear than sympathy. Policy towards the UDA and the (smaller) Catholic Ex-Serviceman's Association, set out on 6 November, aimed 'to diminish their status as self-appointed protectors of sections of the community and their capacity to indulge in para-military activity'. Operations were to be targeted against 'extremist elements' whilst keeping on good terms with 'moderate law-abiding' members. Assaults into the opposing community should be stopped.[31] Whitelaw would consider granting interim custody orders, for twenty-eight days' detention, to 'Protestant terrorists' on a case-by-case basis.[32]

Putting these orders into practice in Ballymena, County Antrim, 2nd Royal Green Jackets arrested two UDA men carrying guns.[33] In Lenadoon, Belfast, 1st Green Howards persuaded the UDA to allow a few Catholic families to live on the estate. At 9.20pm on 6 November a hundred youths came onto the streets, burning three houses and damaging thirty. Troops kept Catholic and Protestant crowds apart until they dispersed. Loyalists from outside the area objected to the local agreement to accept Catholics.[34] The UDA presented themselves as community defenders. (See Illustration 7.1.) In Ardoyne they claimed the army ignored the intimidation of the small Protestant enclave, only paying attention to complaints by Catholics.[35] Whitelaw admitted the soft approach to the UDA undermined the security forces' impartiality in Catholic eyes.[36] In the MOD, General Carver argued for retaining the emphasis on neutralising the IRA and avoiding provoking Protestants before the White Paper on power-sharing came out.[37]

In private, Whitelaw's doubts deepened as the UVF murdered more Catholics. According to MOD figures, between January and November 1972 there were 105 sectarian murders, 72 of Catholics and 33 of Protestants.[38] Whitelaw suggested to his cabinet colleagues the time may have come to place more soldiers in Protestant areas. Perhaps UVF leaders should be charged with membership of an illegal organisation.[39] He maintained, nonetheless, that there could be no comparison between the UDA and

Illustration 7.1 Members of the Ulster Defence Association march along the Shankill Road in Belfast, 14 October 1972.
(Courtesy of Getty Images.)

the IRA.[40] J. T. Howe, General Tuzo's civil adviser, deemed arrests 'a critical issue'. Detaining loyalists would prove the army's impartiality.[41] On 6 December the RUC and military police created a 100-strong joint task force to tackle sectarian murders, at first in east Belfast, then in Derry.[42] Major-General Ford's orders to the army on 7 December embodied the tensions running through strategy. The top priority remained targeting the IRA. Acknowledging the growing loyalist threat, Ford argued 'attrition of the IRA will, to a large extent, cut the militant ground from under the extreme Protestants'.[43]

Only two days later General Tuzo suggested detaining UVF officers. Whitelaw only agreed to arrest Protestants on criminal charges. Intelligence on the UVF was normally too poor to reach the standard required for an interim custody order.[44] The army's concentration in Catholic areas meant relying heavily on the police for intelligence on Protestants. They 'had compiled very few dossiers on Protestant extremists' by mid December.[45] This was remarkable, given the murders going on, and the serious violence against the army in October. At the Cabinet Northern Ireland Committee, General Carver described sectarian murders as 'apparently motiveless', downplaying their political purpose. He ruled out sending reinforcements to the army–police task force. Whitelaw's request for soldiers to be sent into the predominantly Protestant areas where the killings tended to happen fell on deaf ears.[46] Carver meekly directed General Tuzo to assist the police in preventing 'inter-sectarian clashes'.[47] His insistence on a reduced force level prevented the army from protecting people effectively. Whitelaw toed the party line. Before the Conservative Parliamentary Northern Ireland Committee he talked of the 'criminal underworld' as responsible for the 'inevitable' sectarian assassinations.[48]

In Derry on 20 December two men, believed to be 'extreme Protestants', machine-gunned a bar in the largely Catholic Gobnascale estate, killing five people.[49] On 28 December the Fermanagh UVF carried out bombings over the border in Clones, Belturbet and Pettigo. Two children died in Belturbet.[50] At 2.10pm on 2 January 1973 around a hundred people held a peaceful protest on Andersonstown Road in Belfast against sectarian murder. A similar crowd gathered at Victoria police station in Derry.[51] Tuzo and Chief Constable Shillington echoed the words of Oliver Napier: loyalist killings were 'undoing the benefits of the Army's campaign against the IRA'. Whitelaw adhered to his distinction between extreme and moderate loyalists, blocking an arrest sweep on the UDA.[52] He tried to force a split by meeting Orange Order leaders. Whitelaw complained about limited co-operation with the police to solve the murders. The delegation, including Reverend Martin Smyth and James Molyneaux MP, blamed the government for letting the security situation deteriorate. Murders were 'a natural consequence'.[53] The intransigence of the Orange Order perhaps prompted Whitelaw to agree to interim custody orders for loyalists posing 'an exceptionally serious threat to security'.[54]

Despite his preference for a tougher approach, General Tuzo obeyed the CGS, turning down Shillington's request for extra manpower for the task force.[55] He only sent more army patrols into east Belfast when Whitelaw insisted.[56] HQNI judged there to be 10–15,000 'militant Protestants', mainly in Belfast, Carrickfergus, Larne, Lurgan, Portadown, Lisburn, County Londonderry and the Clogher Valley. Events in October 1972, which required five battalions to control, proved loyalists could 'create and control widespread violence'. Intelligence showed these groups to be reorganising, arming and training. The army knew some police officers deliberately shied away from confrontation. Policemen had been intimidated and physically assaulted. Some police units numbered militant loyalists in their ranks. Most importantly, HQNI feared that 'The deployment of troops into Protestant areas will inevitably lead to an armed confrontation between the Army and extremist Protestants. . ... The military implications would be more serious than anything we have yet faced in Northern Ireland.'[57] Sir Robert Mark, commissioner of the Metropolitan Police, told the *Guardian*'s editor about a conversation with Whitelaw at an Oxford college. Whitelaw, who wanted 'to let off steam', appeared worried about the RUC. Either the fourth or fifth most senior officer was believed to be close to the Vanguard movement. Whitelaw thought the leadership echelons needed a good clear-out.[58]

Intensified violence persuaded Whitelaw to adjust his course. Bearing down on PIRA alone had clearly failed. A 'spate of sectarian killings' began on 29 January 1973, when the UDA shot dead Catholic schoolboy Peter Watterson in the Falls Road and father-of-two James Trainor at the petrol station where he worked. The next day UDA member Francis Smith was shot dead, and, on the 31st, Catholic teen-agers Philip Rafferty and Gabriel Savage were abducted off the streets and executed by the UDA.[59] In the first week of February seven people died in sectarian attacks. A drive-by shooting killed one Protestant and injured four in north Belfast. A loyalist drive-by shooting on the Antrim Road killed one man and injured four. When PIRA came to defend the area, they engaged 1st Queen's Regiment in a gun-battle for over three hours. In east Belfast, rioting had been going on for the previous few nights, in protest at the police arresting seven loyalists in connection with a grenade attack on a bus carrying Catholic workers. On Saturday 3 February a 1,000-strong crowd marched on Castlereagh police station to demand that the two men being held be charged or released. They dispersed on being told their demands would be passed along – and when four companies of soldiers arrived.[60]

On the Monday Whitelaw signed interim custody orders for the men, the first for any loyalists. A widespread strike broke out on Wednesday in protest. During the afternoon a crowd assaulted the RUC station in Willowfield, east Belfast, and sacked the Catholic church next door. Gun-battles broke out in east and west Belfast.[61] Whitelaw saw the conflict entering 'a new phase, with assassinations taking place on a much greater and more indiscriminate scale'. At last the security forces possessed intelligence dossiers on loyalists.[62] Intelligence suggested that loyalist leaders decided to avoid any large-scale aggression towards the security forces. This information may have influenced the decision to arrest another seven UVF and Red Hand Commando men on 9 February, safe in the knowledge that rioting was unlikely to lead to more organised opposition.[63] Whitelaw convened a remarkable meeting at Stormont Castle the same day, with leading unionists Brian Faulkner, Phelim O'Neill, Ian Paisley and Vivian Simpson. Alarmed by recent events,

Faulkner called for 'across-the-board action to bring an early end to violence'. A recommendation for a decisive move came from a surprising quarter:

> Dr Paisley said that he wanted to make it clear that the delegation were not seeing the Secretary of State simply because Protestants had been picked up. However, as Protestants were being 'lifted' he thought it best to have large scale once-and-for-all swoops on Protestant extremists rather than a long term policy of erosion. The Secretary of State noted the point but explained there were practical difficulties. Dr Paisley said he got the impression from some Army officers that they did not have permission to pursue terrorists to the fullest extent. The Secretary of State said that no new directive had been issued which would preclude any pursuit of terrorists.[64]

The army feared that loyalist opposition to the government's White Paper 'could be more serious than anything previously encountered'.[65] By contrast, the JIC expected little prolonged unrest.[66] The MOD hoped arrests might 'avoid provoking them unnecessarily'.[67] They remained relatively infrequent. During February, 139 PIRA members were arrested, compared with 50 loyalists.[68] On 1 March the new GOC, General Sir Frank King, persuaded William Whitelaw to sign a custody order for the deputy commander of the UVF.[69] Whitelaw called in all senior police and army officers to explain his preference for criminal convictions.[70] At dawn on Friday 9 March the security forces arrested fourteen UVF suspects, with little reaction. The next day intelligence indicated that the Larne UDA intended to kill Catholics in north Belfast's Bawnmore Estate: 2nd Royal Regiment of Fusiliers intercepted and arrested about 100 men. In the week ending 14 March the security forces arrested 149 loyalists (22 in the UVF, 106 in the UDA), compared with 37 Provisionals.[71] This was the high point in arrests of loyalists: thereafter the monthly totals to June 1975 never exceeded sixty-five.[72]

The permanent decline in arrests coincided with a frank exchange between William Whitelaw and Tommy Herron, the senior UDA leader in east Belfast. Herron said the army was 'encouraging the establishment of a Protestant counterpart to the IRA'.[73] He threatened organised violence against the state if the army persisted in arresting loyalists. The peak in arrests in March 1973 depended upon the two additional British Army battalions temporarily sent to the Province to safeguard a referendum on Northern Ireland remaining in the United Kingdom (which most nationalists boycotted, and thus the status quo was retained), and for the publication of the White Paper. When the force level dropped again, the army's ability and willingness to handle loyalism decreased. In the week following the mass arrests the number of shootings remained stable, but bombings rose from twenty-six in the preceding week to thirty-one. In addition, there were at least 130 bomb hoaxes. Around a quarter of bomb incidents were attributed to loyalists, mainly targeting Catholic pubs. Arrests of loyalists during the week dropped to twenty-nine. The army resumed normal business, searching seventy-seven houses in the Falls Road area, and arresting sixty-five PIRA members.[74] The White Paper, 'Northern Ireland Constitutional Proposals', appeared on 20 March, advocating a devolved assembly with a power-sharing executive, elected by proportional representation, and a forum for all-Ireland co-operation.[75] British strategy assumed loyalist violence arose mainly in reaction to republican actions. As the new CLF, Major-General Peter Leng, reasoned in September 1973:

> Since 1 January 1973 Protestant extremists are probably responsible for more of the sectarian murders; and, in August 1973, for 8 of the 11 bombs which caused civilian casualties. . . . It is probable that the Protestant extremists would stop murdering and bombing Catholic targets if the Provisional IRA was seen to be utterly defeated. Until this happens, Protestant terrorism will probably continue. On the other hand, a cessation of Protestant activity will almost certainly not halt the Provisionals' campaign. . . . In its simplest terms, this means that Provisional IRA terrorism is the cause and Protestant terrorism is one of the effects. For this reason, the Provisional IRA continue to be the main threat to security and therefore the first priority in the Army's war of attrition.[76]

THE TACTICAL FOUNDATIONS OF PIRA'S SURVIVAL

The strategic pathway mapped out by Carver and Whitelaw in late 1972 assumed movement towards a constitutional peace on the basis of ever-eroding republican violence and a broadly static loyalist threat. As we have seen, loyalism proved far more volatile than expected, and British strategy essentially refused to adapt: the implications for the force level were too severe. Military operations did succeed in blunting PIRA's offensive, but not enough to prevent political destabilisation. Though geographical and organisational changes instituted by PIRA were important in enabling the organisation to survive, a stalemate resulted from co-adaptation by the British Army and PIRA. Co-adaptation meant both sides improved together, though in different domains, and so mutually failed to overmatch each other.

The degree to which the Provisionals pivoted from Belfast to the countryside has been exaggerated. In one view, 'the borderlands [became] the most crucial areas in the conflict for the British'.[77] Border violence affected constitutional politics: attacks caused resentment amongst unionists, deepening opposition to power-sharing.[78] PIRA did increase their operations on the border after Motorman.[79] However, incidents only reached a high level for four months. (See Figure 7.1.) Even at the peak, in November 1973, the 76 border incidents were dwarfed by the 236 shootings and 47 explosions in Belfast and Derry.[80] Following Liam Cosgrave's election as taoiseach in March 1973, co-operation between Britain and Ireland improved. Bomb disposal and intelligence officers from Lisburn and Dublin regularly shared information.[81] Although officers in Northern Ireland often craved more action, the MOD believed the border to be uncontrollable by military methods.[82] In October 1971, General Carver advised that twenty-nine battalions would be required to 'ensure compliance of strict border controls'. Even a more limited effort would involve eighteen battalions. At a maximum, the army could deploy thirty battalions to Northern Ireland. At this time – October 1971 – there were actually thirteen battalions deployed in the infantry role. Sealing the border was impossible, given the demands in the cities and, just as importantly, for the army around the world.[83]

Recent advances in scholarship on the conflict in rural areas are to be welcomed.[84] Though geographical differences mattered, PIRA maintained

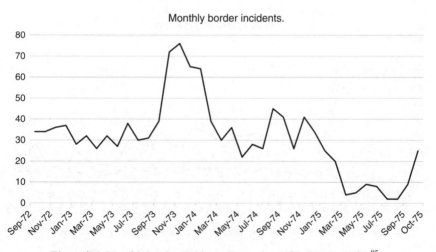

Figure 7.1 Monthly border incidents, September 1972–October 1975.[85]

the capacity to attack in towns *and* the countryside. At times the Provisionals directed additional effort to the countryside to alleviate pressure on their units in Belfast.[86] The relative scarcity of military resources in the country-side in the early 1970s may have meant that, when the army sent more troops there later on, PIRA had already prepared competent units immersed in community support networks.[87] Such an interpretation, however, implies that an earlier or more numerous deployment to the countryside might have been decisive. In reality the army never possessed sufficient troops to match the force concentration levels in the cities. As 1st Royal Hampshires, operating in Counties Armagh and Tyrone in late 1973, recognised: 'Apart from the acquisition of Intelligence, the most vital factor to success in the Border areas is force levels ... the best that can be achieved in the Dungannon and Lurgan areas is containment.'[88]

Violence did drop in Belfast. The ending of republican control over the no-go strongholds in Derry and Belfast during Operation Motorman is thought to be responsible.[89] For some, 'the British finally overwhelmed the urban insurgency mounted by the Provisional IRA'.[90] MOD statistics suggest the decrease in shootings plateaued from August 1973, and in Belfast slightly earlier. (See Figure 7.2.) A significant drop in shootings occurred after Operation Motorman ended, between March and August 1973. Figures on bombings also indicate the spread of violence across Northern Ireland. (See Figure 7.3.) Not all of these incidents were the work of republicans. For British strategy, though, that did not matter. Waging a campaign against PIRA was supposed to suppress violence as a whole. The decline achieved

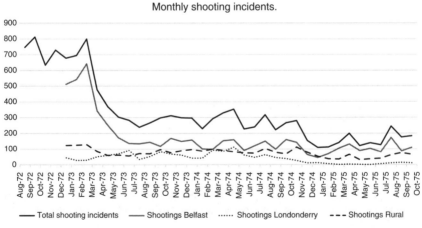

Figure 7.2 Monthly shooting incidents, September 1972–October 1975.[91]

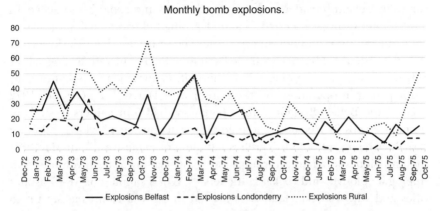

Figure 7.3 Monthly bomb explosions, January 1973–October 1975.[92]

was insufficient to promote political stability not only by reason of its volume, but also due to its capricious nature. An analysis of tactics shows PIRA sustained a capability to strike at a time and place of their choosing, instilling profound uncertainty about death and injury into everyday life.

Was PIRA's 'military power degraded considerably', as shown by a drop in the numbers of soldiers killed, owing to a 'failure to adapt tactics'?[93] No. Fatalities halved for both sides from 1972 to 1973: from 103 British soldiers killed to 58, and from 84 'IRA terrorists' to 42.[94] In his studies on the war in Afghanistan, Theo Farrell observes that opponents can end up '*co-adapting* to the war they are in'.[95] The British Army and PIRA co-adapted as they both braced for an extended war fought at a lower intensity. The Provisionals survived by adapting tactically, as well as geographically and organisation-ally. Research on learning in terrorist groups shows innovation is crucial to their survival.[96] In this sense, 'Violent nonstate actors rely on tactical diver-sity to reduce the predictability of their actions, forcing states to spread their defensive capabilities thin.' The very effectiveness of state repression makes diversification necessary.[97] PIRA co-adapted by practising a wide-ranging tactical repertoire, and by professionalising their operations through training.

The director of training oversaw a department at general headquarters in Dublin.[98] Brigades and battalions retained a training officer on their staffs. New recruits underwent weekly classes on republican ideology and basic military skills.[99] They were taught to avoid surveillance and resist interroga-tion if arrested.[100] In some cases, volunteers received a cover name, address and story with fake documents to thwart their interrogators.[101] Rural training camps in Ireland provided seclusion for firearms and explosives practice. In 1971 Kieran Conway attended a camp, learning fieldcraft, tactics for 'classic rural guerrilla war' and how to fire a rifle. The instructor, Paul Marlowe, had served in Aden and Borneo with the Parachute Regiment and the Special Air Service (SAS). As a training officer himself, Conway kept his hand in by participating in operations on the border near Derry.[102] By October 1972 each of the Belfast Brigade's three battalions had four snipers fresh from training camps in Ireland.[103] Remedial instruction was provided following casualties being suffered by careless handling of explosives.[104] In May 1973 the Provisionals opened two camps in County Galway to train volunteers in sniping, explosives and rocket launchers.[105] When supplies of AK-47 assault rifles and RPG-7 rocket launchers arrived in 1974, a camp was set up to instruct volunteers in their use.[106]

Provisional tactics adapted to the greater British force level in towns and cities. In Belfast in August 1972 PIRA began storing weapons in a larger number of smaller dumps, to limit the losses when the security forces found one. Knowledge about their location was restricted to fewer volunteers. Attacks appeared to be planned a week in advance based on careful observation of army patrolling patterns.[107] HQNI analysed the behaviour of PIRA gunmen after nine weeks of monitoring them around Ardoyne. Gunmen normally worked in groups of six to eight. A group met for a preparatory briefing somewhere beyond the security forces' eyes, then split up into ones or twos to observe the area surrounding the attack location. When the target patrol started to return to base the PIRA lookouts called for a rifle to be fetched to the firing position. A woman or man brought the gun up concealed under a coat or down a trouser leg. The gunman waited for a lookout to check it was safe to attack, quickly aimed the weapon and fired two or three rounds. This exposed him to counter-fire for only a few seconds. The team moved the weapon back to a safe area immediately afterwards.[108]

Sniper teams proved capable of operating in areas the security forces considered relatively secure. On 29 March 1973 Private Michael Marr of 1st Gordon Highlanders was shot dead by a sniper in Andersonstown. HQNI noted: 'No other soldier has been killed in this area of Belfast in similar circumstances since 23 August 1972.'[109] The Provisionals listened in to army communications, on one occasion joining a unit's radio net to order soldiers to a location. Only luck prevented them falling into an ambush.[110] Republican snipers killed three soldiers in Derry in April 1973. Extended shootings between the army and PIRA still occurred from time to time, though the 'major gunbattles' common at the beginning of the year were over.[111] By March 1974 the MOD recorded an increase in IRA sniper incidents over the preceding year, as a reaction to the effectiveness of army patrols against other shootings. Snipers depended upon their lookouts to obtain a target and normally had a well-planned escape route after firing. Deterring or counteracting snipers required sufficient troops to 'saturate an urban area'. About one infantry company (150 men) could dominate 700 terraced houses.[112] In the countryside, PIRA snipers became notoriously lethal in places like south Armagh.[113] This owed more to the British Army's inability to impose high force concentrations than it did to republican intelligence networks.

As expertise in bomb production and placement was honed, the numbers dying in 'own-goal' premature explosions diminished from thirty-one in 1973 to seventeen in 1974.[114] Most innovations happened in Belfast and Armagh, due to decentralised experimentation by bomb-makers. The improvised explosive device first appeared in Armagh in September 1972.[115] During 1974 the Derry Brigade improved bomb quality by pooling explosives officers into a group to share knowledge.[116] In January 1973 PIRA began bombing England. Explosions at Scotland Yard and the Old Bailey on 8 March caused one man to die from a heart attack, whilst 265 people were injured. The ensuing media coverage persuaded PIRA to mount further bombings in England. During the year they carried out eighty-six bombings there.[117] The British and Irish authorities sought to prevent arms and munitions reaching Northern Ireland. In March 1973 the Irish Navy intercepted the *Claudia*, carrying 5 tons of weapons, ammunition and explosives from Libya.[118] But supply problems never seriously hindered the Provisionals. Intelligence suggested that 120 tons of explosives were received by PIRA in April 1973.[119] Nearly a year later the MOD surmised the Provisionals continued to enjoy a steady flow of material.[120]

Though the technical novelty of devices mattered, for the army the methods of deployment were of equal import. In October 1972, for example, a team disguised as workmen delivered a settee to a furniture warehouse. The settee contained 250lbs of explosives. On another occasion men dressed as painters planted bombs in paint tins.[121] The Derry Provisionals prevented their explosives being found by army sniffer dogs by wrapping them in several layers of polythene; in Belfast tinfoil was used. From March 1973 PIRA increasingly planted large mines remotely detonated by wires in culverts or beside roads in the countryside. In that month five exploded close to soldiers, killing two and wounding two more. Another eight such devices failed to cause any harm. They were often planted days or weeks in advance.[122] On 7 April a command-detonated mine near Newtownhamilton killed two paratroopers. At the end of the month OIRA infiltrated a bomb into Gough Barracks in Armagh in the boot of a mechanic's car, causing one injury when it exploded.[123] In October republicans killed a soldier by infiltrating a parcel bomb into a command post in Derry. A bomb in a milk churn smuggled into another base caused severe damage to the canteen.[124]

Twelve regular soldiers died in May 1973, eleven in bomb attacks. The month marked 'a significant increase in the use of explosive ambushes, car bombs and booby traps', involving 'ingenious tactics'. A bomb hidden in a milk float evaded several check-points and two searches before exploding in Ferry Quay Street in Derry. South of Crossmaglen a 2nd Parachute Regiment patrol approached a pile of rocks on a road. The patrol leader died instantly from a command-detonated bomb. Shortly after an ammunition technical officer discovered the command wire, two soldiers crossed a nearby wall, triggering a separate pressure switch, killing them both. This was the third 'multi-phase ambush bomb' in the area. On 17 May PIRA bombed the runway at Aldergrove airport and killed four off-duty soldiers with a booby-trap bomb outside a hotel in Omagh. Another soldier hurt in the blast later died from his wounds.[125] June 1973 witnessed 110 bombings, including 31 car bombs, 2 landmines, 7 culvert bombs and 7 booby-traps. By the end of the month PIRA had mounted seventy-four separate rocket-propelled grenade (RPG) attacks.[126] Ambush bombs continued to be used regularly in the countryside. On 3 March 1974 a 'massive culvert device' struck two vehicles near Ballygawley, throwing one Landrover 30 feet. Four soldiers were wounded.[127]

Provisional bombs ranged from very large devices to book-size bombs placed in post boxes (6 of these exploded in early 1974, prompting the Post Office to fit thin, letter-only openings to 300 boxes).[128] On 21 September 1973 a bomb disposal team deactivated 'the biggest car bomb yet' outside the telephone exchange in Belfast city centre, containing around 700lbs of explosives and nine mortar bombs.[129] The 'proxy bomb' became more widespread from October 1973. A car was hijacked, a bomb loaded on board and the driver ordered to drive the car to the target location under threat of reprisal if they failed to do so. Many drivers managed to warn the security forces after abandoning their vehicle.[130] The Provisionals even hijacked a train, booby-trapping the locomotive and two nearby OPs.[131] On 28 March 1974 a tanker holding liquid gas was hijacked near the Bogside in Derry. Gunmen held the driver's mate hostage whilst the driver took the tanker with a 10lb bomb to the Odeon cinema. When the vehicle was stopped en route, the device exploded, starting a fire that completely destroyed two buildings.[132] The Provisionals expanded their use of incendiaries, planting eighty-five in April 1974, sometimes causing 'extensive and spectacular damage'.[133]

The security forces regularly searched vehicles to disrupt the movement of explosives and guns. During their August to December 1974 tour in and around Belfast, 1st Glosters searched 45,000 cars at random vehicle check-points.[134] 1st Duke of Wellington's Regiment benefited from the UDR soldiers attached to them, arresting three bombers: 'the UDR, by living amongst these terrorists, know many of them by sight'.[135] HQNI put on operations to stop PIRA bombs from disturbing public events. Before the border poll on 8 March 1973, searches by units in 39 Brigade turned up 17 firearms, 880 rounds of ammunition and 575lbs of explosives.[136] Bombings declined in April 1974 as Operation Prevent, timed to coincide with the Easter commemorations, emplaced hundreds of static, mobile and helicopter-deployed vehicle check-points.[137] Around the towns and countryside of Armagh and Tyrone, the Hampshires invented a technique for dealing with ambush bombs. When a report came in about such a device, soldiers went to investigate undercover in a civilian vehicle called a 'Q van'. They then secured a nearby landing site for a helicopter. A search team would be flown in, followed by an ammunition technical officer to disarm the device. The whole sequence could be performed at night with 'Nitesun' lights from helicopters.[138]

British Army bomb disposal went through a number of improvements from late 1972. In January the Provisionals detonated the first radio-controlled device, allowing for much more accurately timed ambushes. From October, Royal Signals personnel operated alongside bomb disposal officers with equipment capable of detecting these radio-controlled bombs.[139] First introduced in June 1972, the Mark 3 'Wheelbarrow' remotely controlled robot of November of that year represented a radical innovation. The Mark 3 was more mobile and fitted with closed-circuit television cameras, a window-breaking gun and 'Pigstick', which fired a jet of water to disrupt the explosive mechanism. New doctrine issued on 8 December placed the safety of ammunition technical officers as the priority, and required an indirect approach to be made to devices in the first instance.[140] A 'Bomb Intelligence Group' formed in 1973 brought together munitions experts and military police officers to share information on technology and tactics.[141] Bomb disposal operative David Greenaway remembered being helped by people in Strabane during his 1973 tour: 'the police went along two or three times, just couldn't find the bomb. Anyway, then they got a phone call, "right, you can't miss it now", and they'd painted an arrow pointing into a ditch, with "bomb" in the middle of the road. And that was an anti-handle device, a mercury tilt-switch.'[142] Nonetheless, prior to the 1975 ceasefire, bomb disposal officers only outsmarted PIRA's explosives teams for four short periods. (See Figure 7.4.)

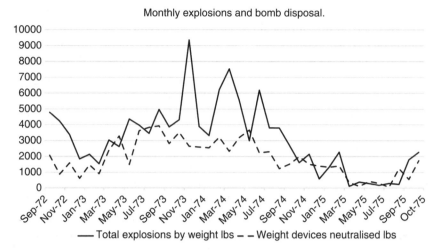

Figure 7.4 Monthly weight of explosions and devices neutralised, September 1972–October 1975.[143]

As the conflict dragged on, the Provisionals sharpened their competence at combined-arms assaults. On 28 November 1972 they mounted 10 co-ordinated attacks with Russian-made RPG-7 rocket launchers, firing 15 rockets and 1,200 rounds of supporting fire.[144] Just over a week later an RPG hit the back of a Queen's Lancashire Regiment armoured personnel carrier in Varna Street, Belfast. The projectile penetrated the armour and went out through the front, wounding 11 soldiers. Gunmen opened fire with small arms at the same time.[145] On 11 August 1973 five PIRA active service units assaulted Crossmaglen police station, firing around 600 rounds of ammunition, 17 mortars and 7 RPGs. Seven minor casualties were suffered.[146] At Forkhill RUC station on 17 September gunmen fired several hundred rounds, fifteen mortars and sixteen rockets, accurately. The occupants 'had no trouble holding off the attack, which was expected'.[147] On 15 November a ten-strong PIRA team bombed and shot up the RUC station at Keady, County Armagh, from seven different firing points, then set fire to a customs post on the way back into Ireland.[148] On 24 November a team attacked the RUC station at Belleek with RPG-7 rounds and small-arms fire.[149] When PIRA hijacked a helicopter to try to drop milk churn–filled bombs on Strabane police station, the security forces refrained from shooting 'because they could not believe that such an inept manoeuvre was in reality an attack'. The milk churns failed to detonate.[150]

During the night of 25–6 October 1973, 50 to 100 men blocked 55 rural roads. A number of obstacles contained real or fake bombs. At the same time increased operations were mounted in Belfast and Derry. Between 25 and 27 October the army's bomb disposal teams dealt with seventy-eight separate devices.[151] A similar operation a month later saw ninety roads blocked by hijacked vehicles and 'suspicious devices', attracting 'maximum publicity'.[152] In early December the Provisionals repeated the technique in Belfast. Two car bombs exploded, though sixteen more proved to be hoaxes.[153] Between February and April 1974 the Provisionals again demonstrated their capacity for simultaneous operations across the Province. Nine bombs exploded in Belfast city centre on the evening on 28 February to disrupt the UK general election then taking place. A further five bombings and seventeen shooting incidents were thought to be co-ordinated to maximise the propaganda effect.[154] On 15 March PIRA detonated fifteen bombs across Northern Ireland, planted sixty hoax bombs in Belfast, hijacked thirty vehicles in the countryside, planted bombs along the railway line and mounted shooting attacks. In general, violence seemed to be spreading more deeply across the Province.[155] Another headline-grabbing operation happened on 9 April. PIRA hijacked sixty vehicles to form roadblocks in Belfast, three containing bombs and eighteen others hoax devices. Incendiaries were planted in city centre shops.[156]

By the time of the UWC strike in May 1974, the Provisionals appeared to be on the front foot. Leadership changes worried the British Army. In January intelligence suggested Seamus Twomey, favouring an aggressive posture, was back as chief of staff, following his astonishing escape from Mountjoy prison, Dublin, in a hijacked helicopter the previous October.[157] Secret reports indicated Twomey shared the post in a 'three-man junta' with Dáithí Ó Conaill and Martin McGuinness – Twomey representing Belfast, Ó Conaill renowned for his political nous and McGuinness a master of cross-border operations. They apparently intended to build violence on the border in the spring into a wider summer offensive in the countryside and cities.[158] New cells were created in Ireland to provide weapons to the north on a more secure basis; supplies of arms were 'excellent'. Just before the UWC strike, the MOD regarded morale as high: 'it is clear that the Provisional IRA intend to continue their campaign and they may well try to escalate the level of activity'.[159]

THE BRITISH ARMY'S WAR OF ATTRITION

Restating the mission in place since Motorman, Major-General Leng specified the security forces' primary aim as 'the severe, unrelenting and continuous attrition' of PIRA. He directed 'a great effort' be made 'to eliminate their leaders'.[160] Britain's achievements in quelling republican violence are regularly attributed to intelligence, where surveillance, interrogation, and agents and informers sat centre stage.[161] Judging the relative utility of any intelligence source is currently futile. Treating intelligence as a separate component of state power is also mistaken. Intelligence in war 'maximise[s] the efficiency of the use of one's own resources'.[162] The British Army reduced Provisional capabilities by integrating intelligence into their wider tactics. From the summer of 1972 improvements in patrolling, surveillance from OPs, the use of informers and undercover operations made their mark. These gains coincided with Operation Motorman, but were not necessarily caused by it, and depended upon refinements in training. Above and beyond all other tactics, arresting suspected PIRA members was the epicentre around which everything else revolved.

Intelligence organisation affected the army's effectiveness, and the problems evident right from August 1969 never entirely disappeared. Officers from 2nd Parachute Regiment complained: 'A vast amount of concentrated effort of roulement Intelligence Sections has been totally wasted because of their inability to master the basics within a four-month span.'[163] A 1974 study discovered massive inefficiencies. About 270,000 'P cards', containing brief details about individuals, described only 100,000 people. Multiple cards on the same person sometimes contained different information.[164] In 1972 William Whitelaw had turned down a request to computerise all intelligence records.[165] An officer in the Defence Intelligence Staff found such reservations perplexing: 'the bloody pink-shirted lefties from the Home Office appeared and they put a stop, they said "it's against human rights, you can't hold this bloke's records on there"'.[166] A vehicle records computer system came into action in December 1974. This allowed mobile patrols to intercept a specific car, resulting in a more discriminate approach to searches.[167]

In September 1972 a new director and co-ordinator of intelligence was appointed in the NIO. The first incumbent, secret intelligence service officer Alan Rowley, improved information-sharing between the various agencies.[168] By that time around 500 service personnel worked on intelligence in Northern Ireland.[169] Informed by advice from pre-deployment training, 40 Commando were typical in creating small intelligence sections in each company.[170] The emphasis upon tactical intelligence-gathering only grew over time. By October 1974 a battalion might retain as many as eighty-three men on intelligence duties. Liaison intelligence NCOs and continuity NCOs provided overlap between arriving and departing units. Besides 'P cards', units and headquarters kept a fuller 'P File' on significant personalities, order-of-battle charts for paramilitary units, cards on vehicles, records connecting weapons to gunmen and incidents, incident records, aerial photographs, maps, screening proforma, electoral registers and trade directories.[171]

Mission-specific training was important because counter-insurgency doctrine only incorporated lessons from Northern Ireland in 1977.[172] Routinised training prevents soldiers from being so disoriented by combat that they cease to be effective. Collective routines impose a moral imperative to apply the skills acquired to protect comrades in danger.[173] Before 1972 units improvised. The commander of 2 Para sent his men parachuting.[174] In January 1972 the United Kingdom Land Forces (UKLF) headquarters established a Northern Ireland Training and Advisory Team (NITAT).[175] Another team was created by BAOR in May. These teams provided pre-deployment courses for all units. Instructors had served in Northern Ireland and regularly went back to refresh their knowledge. NITAT educated soldiers on the background to the conflict, the paramilitary groups and their tactics, the army's operations and the rules of engagement. A close-quarter battle range replicated conditions on the streets. NITAT ran specialist courses for small groups from each unit: the course on search techniques qualified 144 soldiers in 1972. The School of Service Intelligence operated an 'Intelligence Environmental Course (NI)', passing out 26 officers, 83 NCOs, and 104 other ranks by 23 June 1972.[176] In 1974 the army introduced additional intelligence training for commanding officers, and soldiers due to specialise in these tasks.[177]

Units combined NITAT with in-house events: 1st Royal Hampshire Regiment prepared for their deployment with a study day for officers with lectures on company operations and 'man management at Platoon level'. A ten-strong reconnaissance party were briefed at HQNI and 3 Brigade in Lurgan, before observing their predecessor battalion on operations. The whole battalion then spent a week with NITAT, a second week on battalion and company training at their barracks, followed by a study day for officers and senior NCOs with their future brigadier. Then companies ran through tactics on the NITAT range in Hythe for a week, finishing off with a full battalion exercise and television training for officers and senior NCOs.[178] Some from 1st Royal Anglian Regiment considered NITAT helpful both for inexperienced recruits, and for updating 'old sweats' on new tactics and equipment.[179] The MOD sent reading materials to units, headquarters and army libraries, including booklets about the Province for every platoon and, at a lower scale, book packs. They contained such titles as Andrew Boyd's *Holy War in Belfast*, Martin Wallace's *Drums and Guns: Revolution in Ulster* and articles from *The Economist*.[180] A pamphlet on lessons from Northern Ireland for the whole army was blocked, for reasons of security and political nervousness in Whitehall.[181]

From May 1972 the directorate of military operations issued training information in the monthly reports sent to army commands, training establishments and defence attachés. The first report recommended shooting practice to reduce 'the awful possibility of hitting an innocent man, woman or child'.[182] During 1972 units began writing fuller post-tour reports to prepare themselves and other units for the future. The commander of 2nd Parachute Regiment, in north Belfast from February to June, cautioned against battalion discotheques, a familiar hallmark in earlier tours. Discos produced 'welfare problems, including Irish marriage'. A busy social life made men 'discotheque minded', inducing them to forget their professional duties.[183] Officers in 1st Green Howards were enjoined to avoid relying too heavily on veterans as 'last year's tactics will not necessarily meet this year's conditions'. Soldiers must be prepared for common difficulties, such as 'Sluts hurling revolting abuse'.[184] British training possessed several advantages over that of PIRA. Firstly, in order to maintain security against enemy infiltration, PIRA ran a large number of camps, leading to reduced standardisation. Secondly, recruits were only permitted to fire a small number of rounds, to preserve ammunition.[185] Thirdly, PIRA volunteers trained for short periods only. From 1972 British soldiers went back to NITAT before every tour. What they learnt built upon the training given to them throughout their army career. British training was more consistent, regularised and intensive, and therefore more effective.

Exposure to a rigorous training regime helped soldiers confront the threat from PIRA gunmen. By 31 December 1974, 236 soldiers had died on operations in Northern Ireland, among them 135 from bullets and 81 from explosions. Another 567 survived gunshot wounds.[186] According to HQNI, in the year after August 1971 IRA gunmen fired at the army in 5,905 incidents. Soldiers struggled to return fire if gunmen fired only one or two shots before taking cover.[187] Improved patrolling techniques made a difference, although to what precise extent cannot be quantified. In north Belfast 2nd Parachute Regiment adopted an irregular patrolling pattern to avoid presenting predictable targets.[188] 1st Green Howards sent out night-time patrols to spot wanted men without being noticed. Movement in vehicles allowed a rapid response to incidents. A reserve section was kept at two minutes' notice.[189] 1st Gordon Highlanders favoured patrols of four men, with several groups within 150 to 200 metres of each other, so that they could support each other in case of ambush.[190] This parallel patrolling became common practice. On 28 October 1972 a Staffordshire Regiment patrol in Armagh was shot at by two men who then jumped into a car. A parallel patrol opened fire on the car. The men fled the car, leaving their weapons behind.[191]

Static OPs afforded the opportunity for surveillance and could warn of impending attacks. By late 1972 they were extensively used in Northern Ireland's towns and cities. (See Illustration 7.2.) In New Lodge in Belfast in the first half of 1973, Marines of 42 Commando manned four posts in high-rise flats, plus another eighteen overt and ten hidden posts elsewhere. By making the location of the overt OPs obvious, they aimed to divert gunmen into areas covered by the covert posts.[192] In Derry in the second half of 1973, 2nd Royal Anglians operated nineteen covert OPs. PIRA detected seven of them. The Royal Anglians put a ring of OPs around the Creggan, which 'provided good info on the gen[eral] movement and state of affairs in the estate'. Other posts were located within the estate, generally in empty buildings, though sometimes 'inserted secretly into the attic of an occupied house without the residents knowing'. Two soldiers kept watch in each OP whilst two more slept, to provide continuous surveillance. In the experience of 2nd Royal Anglians, 3–5am was the best time to change over personnel in OPs to minimise the danger of PIRA spotting them. Qualified snipers performed these tasks most effectively, though training in photography was also an advantage. Work in an OP required a patient disposition.[193]

Illustration 7.2 The view from an army observation post, overlooking the Lenadoon estate in west Belfast, 12 April 1972.
(Courtesy of Getty Images.)

Long-term urban OPs 'could detect changes in patterns of activity which patrols could not'. Soldiers relied upon photographs of wanted persons to track suspected PIRA members' movements. Night-vision equipment gave them an around-the-clock capability.[194] In the countryside static OPs played a less prominent role. The army lacked the resources to permanently observe the rural population. Through 'an efficient bush telegraph' in places where people sympathised with their aims, such as in south Armagh, PIRA could watch army patrols more consistently than the army watched them. The Green Howards employed several typical tactics in response. 'Lie Up Patrols' involved eight to twelve soldiers covering a given area for thirty-six to forty-eight hours, moving at night and lying in temporary OPs in the day. Longer patrols of thirty men or more lasted up to five days, carrying out searches, vehicle checks and 'Domination of villages and small towns'. To draw PIRA into combat, the Green Howards mounted 'come-on' ambushes. A vehicle check-point or foot patrol was repeated in the same place over several days. Covert 'killer' OPs were positioned around the ambush site to 'pre-emptively engage the enemy'. Finally, the battalion drew upon an 'Airborne Reaction Force' to fly in reinforcements by helicopter, or to rapidly move troops around.[195] Helicopters were also used to monitor the border and check whether electricity pylons had been sabotaged.[196]

Patrolling day in, day out gave soldiers knowledge of their area of responsibility, to the extent that they noticed when something was out of place. Some battalions swapped a few soldiers so that they could recognise wanted PIRA members operating outside their usual area.[197] The Gordon Highlanders believed talking to people to be 'an art that must be cultivated'. Chatty soldiers at vehicle check-points elicited a surprising amount of information from people who might never approach the army of their own volition.[198] From mid 1973 patrol leaders carried miniature tape recorders to capture information on the streets.[199] The Green Howards, like other units, debriefed patrols when they returned to base. A room with wanted photographs, aerial photographs, street plans and other informa-tion helped place the intelligence extracted from patrols into context.[200] By late 1974 in Derry, 3rd Royal Anglians had extended the technique, feeding topical information from television, radio and army briefings to soldiers before they went out, as a basis for their 'chatting up'.[201] An 'arrested terrorist' who had previously served in the British Army remarked on the striking danger posed by soldiers possessing a memory for faces.[202] The Queen's Lancashire Regiment commended Lance-Corporal Gardiner's performance in the battalion intelligence section. He came from Ireland, so 'actually understands what they are squabbling about'.[203]

Some British Army units had been running agents and informers since 1970.[204] In October 1972, 2nd Royal Fusiliers raided the Green Briar golf club and screened people with help from a 'Fred', a turned IRA member, who identified five PIRA volunteers for arrest.[205] In Derry, 40th Field Regiment Royal Artillery experienced mixed results. One informer 'gave us a lot of information of a fairly low level but never came up with anything we could tie in or act on. He made a lot of whisky out of us for his trouble.'[206] The MOD claimed 'Freds' seriously damaged PIRA in Andersonstown, and to a lesser extent in Ardoyne, Belfast.[207] Kenneth Ambrose dealt with a 'Fred' during 1st Royal Green Jackets' Belfast tour in 1973:

> I got tasked by the intelligence officer to pick this guy up, bring him back to the location, feed him, sort him out some uniform and hide his long hair, and then take him into an OP with us, where he was going to sit for four or five days. So we went through the usual procedures of, I did the recce, preparation, everything like that, and then this guy, out of the blue, in front of the other three guys who were with me, and one of them was staying behind by the way, said 'I'm not going in unless I've got a gun'. Now, in this particular case, this guy had been in the British Army. He had in fact been in the Light Infantry, and when he'd returned to Ireland having finished his time, the IRA gripped him and said, 'oh, you're the ideal bloke for us', and so common sense had prevailed and he'd become an IRA man. However, he'd soon realised that perhaps it wasn't such a good idea after all, so he'd arranged to swap sides.

Ambrose gave him a Sterling submachine gun, after surreptitiously removing the firing pin.[208] The NIO created the 'Robot phone' system in late 1972, whereby callers dialled an advertised number to give information. Phone boxes in areas hosting a strong republican presence, such as the Bogside and Andersonstown, fell victim to vandalism, as the telephone exchanges in Armagh and Dungannon did to bombings.[209] On 3–4 February 1973 information phoned in produced a pistol, six rounds of ammunition and two arrests.[210] By June the MOD considered the Robot phone to be a valuable conduit for 'the increasing willingness of people to talk'.[211] The army benefited from Special Branch informers and agents too. On 19 March 1973 the Queen's Lancashire Regiment apprehended a gunman with an Armalite rifle in a house in Abyssinia Street, Belfast, following a tip-off from Special Branch.[212] On the night of 15 August 1974 the intelligence officer of PIRA's Derry Brigade was arrested following intelligence-gathering by a helicopter, an electronic bugging device and a Special Branch agent.[213] The majority of successful operations, concluded

1st The Duke of Wellington's Regiment after their eighteen-month tour, could be attributed to 'info from SB'.[214]

The Military Reaction Force (MRF) was formed in the summer of 1971, without the head of Special Branch's knowledge, to compensate for limited police intelligence.[215] It performed covert surveillance, protection duties, counter-hijacking and arrests.[216] The unit operated by 39 Brigade in Belfast comprised a small headquarters and three sections. Each section numbered three NCOs and nine men. Sections worked in teams of four.[217] Public controversy erupted following shootings by the MRF in April 1972.[218] In 2020 the police referred seven former MRF soldiers to the public prosecution service.[219] On 2 October 1972 PIRA ambushed an MRF team in Twinbrook, Belfast, working under the cover of the 'Four Square Laundry', killing one soldier. The laundry van collected clothes from unsuspecting households, then sent them for tests to discover explosive or gunpowder traces.[220] The team's intelligence had led to the arrest of 30 per cent of PIRA officers in Andersonstown.[221] In November ministers decided to reconstitute the MRF in the 120-strong Special Reconnaissance Unit. Members were selected and trained by the SAS, before serving in Northern Ireland for a year.[222] On 19 July 1973 Special Branch and undercover soldiers arrested PIRA's brigade commander, operations officer and finance officer in Belfast. Separate operations brought in the brigade quartermaster, and the commander, operations officer and quartermaster from 3rd Battalion.[223] An operation on 17 October captured 18 PIRA members, including eight Belfast Brigade staff officers.[224] In August 1974 the army swooped on the brigade's intelligence officer after a lengthy surveillance mission against the whole brigade staff. He had been deliberately missed out until then 'to keep a line open', suggesting covert negotiations with the security forces.[225]

The army arrested large numbers to disrupt their opponents' planning and operations, to gather intelligence and to dominate the population. (See Illustration 7.3.) Internment 'produced widespread resentment and acted as a recruiting agency for the IRA'.[226] Ministers commissioned Lord Diplock to examine the legal machinery for countering terrorism. His recommendations, embodied in the Northern Ireland (Emergency Provisions) Act in July 1973, were intended to soften opposition to internment. However, the reforms proved 'only mildly less harsh', in suspending trial by jury for certain offences, relaxing the rules on evidence in court, widening powers of arrest and retaining internment.[227] William Whitelaw deflated internment by reducing the numbers interned or detained by about 350 from March 1972 to December 1973, to encourage the SDLP to participate in political dialogue. Only about 5 per cent of internees were loyalists, a fact

Illustration 7.3 Soldiers make an arrest in the Bogside, Derry, 4 September 1971.
(Courtesy of Mirrorpix via Getty Images.)

that somewhat undid Whitelaw's drive to be seen as the neutral arbiter.[228] The NIO suspected the army arrested people for internment in the full knowledge they would be released when their case came before the civil authorities, simply to remove them from circulation for a time.[229] The army kept close tabs on internee releases and regularly complained. In December 1973 the MOD criticised the release of sixty-three IRA members.[230] Meanwhile, 2nd Scots Guards, based in west Belfast, took 'a more relaxed view of the releases than some of their colleagues have at Headquarters Northern Ireland'.[231] In January the CGS told General King to stop making a fuss about releases.[232]

Far more people were arrested for a few hours than those who ended up in prolonged detention. Screening, where soldiers carried out tactical questioning, assumed a central place in military strategy. The army could detain suspects for four hours before handing them over to the police, who had to charge or release after another seventy-two hours. It has long been argued that screening 'tended to antagonise the population in Roman Catholic enclaves where it was applied and so ensured a steady flow of recruits for the IRA'.[233] Though the causal connection between screening and IRA recruitment is difficult to prove, new data on the scale of these arrests makes the claim highly plausible. HQNI firmly believed the gains outweighed any negative side-effects. Screening provided an opportunity to recruit agents and informers.[234] It also generated vast amounts of intelligence at a time when Special Branch still felt 'badly shaken' by the uproar over the five techniques and exhibited a profound reluctance to get back to interrogating, even without those now-banned methods.[235]

In September 1972 HQNI detected 'the Provisional IRA, particularly two of the Belfast battalions, are becoming increasingly isolated from Catholic support and demoralised'.[236] In May 1973 General King brimmed with confidence at the booming arrest rate: 'We are now entering the intelligence phase of the war.'[237] In the three months to the end of July 1973, arrests included fifty company commanders and above, twenty explosives officers, twenty-one adjutants, twenty-two quartermasters, eighteen intelligence officers and forty-four other officers.[238] Belfast Brigade commander Ivor Bell's capture in February 1974 brought jubilation: 'Bell's arrest will undoubtedly have a significant effect on the operations, organisation and morale of the Belfast Provisionals.'[239] Arrests provided a precise metric. The figures for paramilitary casualties were unreliable, especially as represented in the category of 'unconfirmed' killed. In their post-tour report 2nd Parachute Regiment succinctly described what screening entailed. The battalion 'set out to screen as many people as possible' to establish the identity of people living in their operational area. At first 2 Para only arrested those who had committed a crime. Soon they decided to bring in anyone who might conceivably be connected to the IRA. Within four months, questionnaires on 800 people had been completed, alongside matching photographs, allowing the intelligence section to uncover eight wanted men holding fake identity documents. The report elaborated on the nature of the questioning:

> Often they were given tea, and invariably an explanation for the questions they were being asked, these ranged, depending on the character of the person being screened, from 'I am sure that you would like to help us to arrest those who have been shooting at your friends and those who have been taking money from you' to 'We think someone who looks like you is in the IRA and we are only doing this so that you don't get arrested too often'.... Towards the end of the four month tour it was found that some people even volunteered to come in, if it was suggested that it would be in their interest.[240]

Records produced by 1st Queen's Lancashire Regiment for their deployment in late 1972 and early 1973 in Belfast shed further light on the process.

At 7pm on 14 December 1972 A Company arrested a named individual, who gave information during screening about other volunteers in the area, and PIRA's intention to use RPGs to force soldiers out of armoured personnel carriers, making them easier to shoot. He was then charged, at the Springfield Road police station, with illegally possessing weapons.[241] Following a sniper attack on a patrol on 20 January 1973, soldiers captured three men near the Divis Tower in Belfast who were believed to be close to the sniper's firing point. They were released after screening because 'Their stories agreed and it is thought unlikely that they were responsible for the shooting.'[242] A seventeen-year-old PIRA volunteer caught planting a bomb in Suffolk, Belfast, in May 1973 confessed to six other attacks and named two accomplices, who were then also arrested.[243]

At Whitelaw's direction, increasing reliance was placed upon criminal prosecution rather than internment to suppress political violence.[244] During 1973, the police charged 1,312 people with terrorism-related offences.[245] By June 1975, 1,363 people had been imprisoned for such crimes.[246] However, large numbers of arrests did not result in a criminal charge or internment. From 31 July until 27 September 1972, 808 people were arrested. Of these, 374 were released, or 46.3 per cent.[247] (See Table 7.1.) These figures are under-estimates for the proportion of people arrested by the army on spurious grounds. Unit records refer to higher numbers – if 2 Para screened 800 over four months, then the totals for all units in Northern Ireland presented in official reports can only relate to those transferred to police custody. The hundreds of thousands of 'P cards' in existence give credence to such an assessment. The HQNI weekly and MOD monthly reports do not match. For August 1973, the former cited 565 republican and loyalist arrests, and the latter 291.[248] The volume of screening was unregulated, and the political consequences barely got a mention. Even the lower, monthly statistics for arrests resulting in police custody suggest that screening functioned as a deliberate harassment tactic to dominate areas thought to sympathise with the IRA.

Table 7.1: Prosecution, internment and release of suspected IRA members.[249]

Month	Republican arrests	Republicans newly interned	Catholics charged	Release rate (%)
June 1973	274	57	59	57.66
October 1973	215	35	65	53.49
January 1974	221	15	64	64.25

By July 1973 the army's attritional campaign had weakened PIRA in Belfast by integrating intelligence into military tactics. Sending units back into the same areas they had patrolled before lessened the erosion of local knowledge brought about by every rotation. Covert surveillance and anonymous tip-offs from the population accounted, in part, for the rising volume of intelligence collected. Arrests were central to the whole endeavour: 'The intelligence cycle of arrest, leading to intelligence, leading to more arrests, is working very well.' The dragnet approach was giving way to something more discriminate. IRA leaders might be watched for weeks prior to their capture, to prepare a dossier for a detention order.[250] Other states too have practised a decapitation counter-terrorism strategy, in more recent times employing armed drones to deadly effect. Proving whether leadership-targeting works is nearly impossible.[251] Northern Ireland is no exception. The evident satisfaction among soldiers when dangerous PIRA men fell into captivity is understandable, the general trend downwards in violence unmistakable. Publishing his Defence Fellowship thesis in 1972, Lieutenant-Colonel John Baynes remarked on the closing gap between officers and men just as society at large became more egalitarian.[252] Written by a talented professional, Baynes' study is infused with his vision for what the army should become in equal measure with his analysis of what it already was. HQNI's fixation on PIRA officers and the lack of interest in their replacement smacks of institutional mirror-imaging in the assessment of leadership decapitation as a strategy.[253] The British Army remained quite rigidly structured: remove the officers, and the whole edifice crumbles. HQNI thought the Provisionals functioned the same way. Like other terrorist groups, however, PIRA withstood the onslaught, in part due to communal support.[254]

'NO REAL CONSISTENCY': THE BRITISH ARMY IN CATHOLIC COMMUNITIES

Arriving in Derry in July 1973, 2nd Royal Anglians summed up the contradiction in British strategy towards republicanism. The commanding officer directed his battalion to 'take the firmest action, without irreversibly alienating the majority of the people, to eliminate the remaining PIRA and criminal elements'.[255] Tactics like mass screening and house searches inevitably alienated people whilst also producing tangible gains against armed republicanism. Senior army figures knew this full well.[256] Short of a complete withdrawal, it is far from obvious what else the army might have done whilst the Provisionals pressed their demands by killing and maiming. Though the brutality inherent in military operations diminished after direct rule, owing to tighter supervision by the legal authorities, army leaders tolerated a certain degree of criminality in the ranks. The army rationalised the constant stream of complaints about their conduct in several ways. Firstly, community relations projects gave soldiers the impression most Catholics wanted their protection.[257] Secondly, criticism was dismissed as republican propaganda, and therefore illegitimate. Thirdly, the government created a bureaucratic procedure for handling complaints that effectively silenced victims by paying them off.

How far misdeeds by the security forces fuelled support for republicanism, compared with other considerations like Irish nationalism or socioeconomic inequality, cannot be disentangled. PIRA's survival certainly rested upon passive support by a larger group than those who took up arms.[258] The hundreds picked up in screening operations and then released might have felt aggrieved enough to join the Provisionals, or to remain fighting if already a member. When he lived in Ardoyne between September 1972 and April 1973, sociologist Frank Burton found mixed feelings towards PIRA. He placed around one-third of inhabitants as true believers. The rest fluctuated, depending upon the threat from loyalists and the British Army.[259] Around that time the community relations commission observed military conduct varied from one regiment to another. As a result 'there is no real consistency of action of the Security Forces as regards combating intimidation of families from their homes'.[260] The claim that after Motorman 'the security forces took back control of the streets permanently' is therefore misplaced, in relation to both PIRA tactical innovation and popular support.[261] The army's unit rotation policy, needed to keep force levels down, and variability in conduct due to regimental cultures imposed on Catholic communities a deeply inconsistent level of security. The Provisionals never lost all their public support, because the British Army struggled to offer a better level of protection.

Before the surge in violence in autumn 1971 soldiers quite often met civilians socially. When doing so became too dangerous, community relations projects were one of the only opportunities for contact. Whether simply reproducing the government's official line or from genuine personal conviction, military writers frequently expressed a belief in the innate goodness of most Catholics. As 40 Commando wrote, 'it is only a small minority who are the gunmen and revolutionaries ... there is still a majority of normal and law abiding citizens who have the same values as any other residents in the UK'.[262] By January 1972 every major unit was allocated £30 a month to spend on entertaining local leaders, equipment for youth clubs or community centres, materials for repairing pensioners' homes, transport for outings and consumables for Christmas parties.[263] The ministry of community relations appointed civil servants to advise units in Belfast and Derry.[264] In Unity, New Lodge, Tiger's Bay and Duncairn Gardens in Belfast, 40 Commando expected to prise 'the decent people' away from 'gunmen and terrorists' by building playgrounds and arranging baby-sitting groups;[265] 2nd Royal Green Jackets gave swimming lessons to disabled children, and put on a nativity play at Christmas. They filmed these events to put on special screenings for the parents who, coming from Ardoyne, New Lodge, Falls Road and Ballymurphy, might transmit positive opinions about the battalion into otherwise sceptical communities.[266]

The community relations officer in 2nd Royal Anglians discovered that 'Listening to people voicing their complaints and frustrations cools their temper and passions and, to some extent, their bitterness.'[267] The effort could pay off: 1st King's Own Scottish Borderers were astonished by their reception on returning to Andersonstown – 'people say "good morning" to us in the streets, cups of tea are offered discreetly and some of the girls seem quite keen on chatting up our patrols'.[268] In Ardoyne, 3rd Parachute Regiment's tour between March and July 1973 illustrates how community relations might delude officers about their own image. The battalion's civil liaison representative, E. Cadden, reinforced the notion that the Paras' efforts to liberate residents from republican oppression were appreciated. On 31 March, Father Aquinas from Holy Cross church told Cadden he had recently been reprimanded by PIRA, aggrieved at his public criticism of their actions. The Provisionals presented themselves as community defenders intent on protecting people from the paratroopers. Cadden cited statistics to prove the battalion carried out fewer house searches than their predecessors, though he conceded that soldiers 'released their tenseness in foul language'. Aquinas suspected that the Paras' fearsome reputation induced people to blow minor incidents out of proportion. Cadden could not detect any special 'hardness of attitude' on the part of paratrooper officers. Father Aquinas believed a majority of people in Ardoyne opposed PIRA but were too frightened to speak out.[269]

A few weeks later, Lieutenant-Colonel Keith Spacie noted the kindness shown to paratroopers in Ardoyne by people bringing tea and biscuits.[270] By early May intelligence indicated PIRA had suspended operations in Ardoyne due to 3 Para's presence.[271] The battalion thought their arrival heralded a mass exodus of popular support away from the Provisionals.[272] According to Cadden, 3 Para's success owed something to their Catholic chaplain's sociability, and to Spacie's grip: 'Reports of belligerence were narrowed down to individuals and these have been re-assigned to where their crass disregard for operational instructions cannot result in offence to the civil population.'[273] The stories 3 Para told themselves – apparently even the intelligence officer found a warm welcome in illegal drinking dens – jarred with those from outside the battalion.[274] Frank Burton witnessed frequent beatings meted out in the streets and was himself assaulted.[275] SDLP politician Paddy Devlin told Whitelaw the paratroopers behaved 'like a conquering army of medieval times'. He alleged they shot innocent men, hospitalised a taxi driver by beating him, shot a girl with rubber bullets and manhandled a doctor.[276] During the tour soldiers shot dead five people in contested circumstances.[277] NIO minister David Howell argued that false complaints arose precisely because the battalion was so effective.[278] By October HQNI believed the army's operations there, and in similar style across Belfast, 'beneficial to the community in the long term'.[279]

Not everyone expected thanks for the cruel-to-be-kind philosophy. Royal Army Ordnance Corps soldier Steve Kirvan occasionally volunteered for patrols with the infantry around Omagh. He learnt to politely refuse when householders offered tea and sandwiches, thought to be laced with drain cleaner and broken glass. Kirvan regretted how 'Part of the job was to get confidence, and give confidence to the local population, you had to. You couldn't trust them, after a while.'[280] As early as July 1971 the army was warned that those who openly co-operated with soldiers risked being threatened.[281] Two years later 1st Royal Hampshires attributed a distinct circumspection from Catholics in Newry to intimidation by the IRA.[282] Doubts crept in as to the advisability of community relations: 'A solider is indoctrinated to be aggressive and pragmatic. He is not trained to be a good policeman and often has to act against his instincts.'[283] Officers from 1st Royal Green Jackets and 19 Field Regiment Royal Artillery asserted that OIRA had a better reputation for delivering projects than central or local government.[284]

Army units knew the four-month tour cycle prevented meaningful partnerships being maintained with local communities.[285] Bruce Davison, a civil representative at Mountpottinger Road, observed: 'Different officers have different characters; some aggressive and impulsive, some thoughtful and receptive to considered views.'[286] Another civil servant noted the army nickname for the short deployments: 'the Paddy-bashing Tour'.[287] Regimental distinctiveness is frequently seen as a hallmark strength of the British Army.[288] To those staying behind as the ferries whisked famous cap-badges back to Britain, the system rather implied having to live with regiments whose behaviour differed markedly. This essentially random experience hampered trust between civilians and soldiers.

From mid 1971 the belief in a vicious, expertly orchestrated republican smear campaign haunted military minds. Generals Tuzo and King subscribed to the idea. NIO ministers backed them up.[289] The VAG passed on General King's disgruntlement in June 1974 at morale being undermined by 'surveillance and frequent criticism' by the media.[290] The official publication *Visor* encouraged soldiers to regard themselves as victims of unfair allegations whenever they lowered the violence level in their area.[291] An analysis for HQNI charged republicans with being 'very keen, very organized and very, very good' at propaganda. Despite improvements in government propaganda through national channels such as the television:

> for news in the local area itself, the IRA have virtually no competition and are winning hands down. Propaganda about the immediate local area is handled by broadsheets, leaflets and word of mouth. This is the vital area for propaganda – for it is evident that people in say the Ardoyne do not regard events in Claudy or even the city centre as any great concern of theirs.[292]

Officers in 2nd Royal Green Jackets doubted the government's powers to convince people 'fed on a diet of propaganda, fantasy and prejudice from the day that they are born'. Unlike the 'mealy-mouthed' government information officers, the IRA pumped out their messages quickly, influencing conversations in the pubs the evening an event happened.[293] In another favoured legend, 'the traditional love of a fight inherent in the Irish' prompted crowds to riot for the entertainment of the waiting television cameras.[294] Hostility towards the media is a recurrent sensibility in military circles quite unrelated to Northern Ireland, and evident to the present day. As an RAF officer writing at the National Defence College in 1975 recognised, the services' demand for obedience stood in opposition to the basic requirement for journalists to question authority.[295] Scorn directed at the media can thus probably be located in the documentary and oral testimony from every unit tour. These sentiments, genuinely felt though they were, must not obscure the army's aptitude for countering propaganda and cultivating the media to the point where hostile voices faded into the background.

HQNI's information policy unit was established in September 1971 to discredit the IRA and protect the army's reputation. The Foreign Office's propaganda office, the information research department, stepped up their output from August 1972 on the prime minister's instructions. Though civilian and military propaganda evidently failed to deprive the IRA of popular support in Northern Ireland, the output designed to justify Britain's actions to an international audience probably proved more effective.[296] At a senior level, the army understood their own limits. General King stated, 'I do not think we can ever win the propaganda war.'[297] Remarkably, information officers ignored a group from Andersonstown who requested leaflets be distributed to explain the grounds for specific house searches.[298] On 19 April 1973, 12-year-old Anthony McDowell was killed during a gun-battle between PIRA and paratroopers in Ardoyne. Army propaganda officers rapidly put out a statement blaming the Provisionals for his death. Forensic tests showed the fatal bullet came from the type of self-loading rifle issued to soldiers, leading to extensive press criticism.[299] By November 1974 the cross-departmental committee on information policy knew they needed a breakthrough, and market research to adequately understand the audiences subjected to official messaging.[300]

On more modest aims the army's propaganda might be adjudged less harshly. In one instance, a former Royal Marine living in Ballymurphy told the *Guardian* his wife had been harassed by paratroopers. Military propaganda officers then shared intelligence with the *Guardian* suggesting that the ex-marine had passed on stolen medical supplies to the IRA. The newspaper published a correction the next day, putting the army's version of events, which successfully cast doubt on the ex-marine's account.[301] Like 1st Royal Green Jackets, many units ran a full-time public relations team to give their version of events on any breaking story.[302] Over the course of the conflict the government managed the news media well enough to prevent any mass opposition in Britain to the army's operations in Northern Ireland developing.[303] Army psychological operations and public relations officers nurtured more sympathetic relationships with journalists from the British national media than with those from Northern Ireland. The Parachute Regiment intended to 'accept the Press and co-operate with it', paying special attention to John Chartres, who reported on Northern Ireland for *The Times*.[304] Chartres described army–media relations as efficient and happy despite the odd disagreement. Major-General Farrar-Hockley was particularly adept at winning friends amongst journalists during his tenure as CLF by granting permission for them to observe military operations.[305]

HQNI denied any co-operation to *Guardian* correspondents Simon Hoggart and Simon Winchester in early 1972 following three stories in the newspaper criticising the army, including over Bloody Sunday. By late 1973 Hoggart noticed a distinct change in officers 'who once ignored, despised or feared the press'. They now appreciated how much power they possessed by virtue of the information at their disposal about violence. Hoggart concluded most media coverage in Britain adopted a generally sympathetic line stemming from a traditional respect for the army.[306] Major T. L. Trotman, writing in March 1976, deemed the majority of television coverage 'reasonably fair and accurate'.[307] Many units prioritised the connection to newspapers in their home region. After 1st Green Howards hosted Tom Leonard from the *Middlesbrough Evening Gazette* in Belfast, he published articles which reassured army families back home that service there was less dangerous than they might fear. In this case, as in others, the battalion sincerely valued the media's role in sustaining morale.[308]

In applying the strategy to decapitate PIRA's leadership the army regularly issued orders for soldiers to treat the civilian population courteously and within the law. The unit rotation policy and the army's regimental structure militated against this imperative. Aggression by soldiers towards civilians was possible because company commanders and below exercised considerable autonomy in deciding what sorts of behaviour to tolerate.[309] Not every unit deployed to Northern Ireland went on the rampage. The strategic implication, however, was that the inherent unpredictability of military conduct made lasting public trust in the army as an institution profoundly fragile. As discussed below, the civil and military justice systems proved incapable of smoothing out these inconsistencies. Screening and searches repeatedly caused problems. During their tour in Belfast in the second half of 1972, 40 Commando noted the need 'not to overdo it [screening] or it can become counter productive. Much local goodwill can be lost.' Despite such a recognition, the unit targeted all 17–30-year-olds in their area for screening.[310] In the Andersonstown and Suffolk areas of Belfast the RUC's community relations officer believed many complaints about soldiers. He asked the army to stop 'lifting 10–15 men for screening and treating them in an uncivilised fashion'.[311] Over the course of four months, 137 Field Battery searched a man 'with a definite touch of the tar brush' every time he passed a check-point, labelling him 'the most unloved man in Derry'. He was never proven to have done anything wrong.[312]

As General King's deputy, Major-General Leng reproduced his dismissive outlook on complaints: 'the Army cannot hope to please everyone'. He did accept house searches 'generate more hostility towards the Army than any other type of operation'. Of 830 houses searched in July 1973, Catholics occupied 82 per cent and Protestants 18 per cent. Only 11 per cent of houses searched produced anything.[313] House searches increased without resulting in a commensurate rise in weapons being discovered. (See Table 7.2.)

Seemingly excessive searches were sometimes carried out on two or three properties near to a house where intelligence indicated arms were

Table 7.2: House searches and weapons finds, 1970–5.[314]

	1970	1971	1972	1973	1974	1975
Houses searched	3,107	17,262	36,617	74,556	71,714	30,092
Weapons found	324	717	1,264	1,595	1,260	825

stored, to prevent anyone working out where the information came from.[315] HQNI tried to mitigate the upset caused by requiring brigade headquarters to authorise planned searches of occupied houses. Immediate reaction searches were permitted close to a violent incident. House searches forced paramilitaries to move weapons around, disrupting their attacks and increasing the chances of interception whilst in transit. The army introduced a 'Docket Scheme' in March 1973. Houses searched without anything incriminating being found were eligible for compensation for any damage.[316] Financial recompense could not undo the sight of soldiers ripping up floorboards. Soldier Steve Corbett remembered 'going to a house one night and the woman who let me in went absolutely hysterical about it all. I suppose she had just had enough.'[317] The *Loyalist News* bridled at the treatment afforded a Mr Scott, 'prominently associated with the Loyalist cause', who suffered 'house wrecking' at the hands of an army and police search team.[318]

For soldiers exposed to republican violence, contempt for the population was perhaps inevitable. In March 1973 the Royal Hampshires experienced a number of serious incidents in County Armagh. On 6 March a booby-trap bomb near Forkhill injured three soldiers, one of whom, Corporal Joseph Leahy, later died as a result. A week later another bomb, this time near Crossmaglen, killed Private John King and wounded several other soldiers. After attending Corporal Leahy's funeral and visiting his wounded men in hospital, Regimental Sergeant Major R. W. Coleman recorded in his diary, 'This is a lawless country.... The whole b ... lot needs exterminating.'[319] Similarly, 45 Commando loathed the average man in south Armagh: 'He is basically dishonest, idle, talks the most unutterable nonsense for much of the time, lies enthusiastically, is scruffy, unhygienic and hates Ulster.'[320] Elsewhere criticism simply bounced off. According to the Royal Anglians, 'the triviality of the majority of complaints gives grounds for some comfort. They've nothing better to rattle on about.'[321] At a more senior level a patrician disdain for the poor, misguided Irish informed the response to complaints. HQNI was willing to concede house searches discriminated by virtue of the army operating mainly in

Catholic districts. The resultant hostility, however, seemed unimportant, or fabricated in some way. Lieutenant-Colonel Tarver saw Catholics as 'outwardly antagonistic towards the Army', implying an inner friendliness. Support for the IRA flowed entirely from intimidation. Most Catholics were 'moderate', just like the British.[322]

Sir Peter Rawlinson and his successor as attorney general, Samuel Silkin, strenuously resisted General King's repeated efforts to shut down criminal prosecutions of soldiers. In January 1974, for example, King worried that the six pending manslaughter and attempted murder charges against soldiers might impede operational efficiency. Soldiers would ask 'Will I get into trouble for doing my duty?'[323] In late May Rawlinson rebutted King's push to transfer service cases to military jurisdiction.[324] Nonetheless, the police, the prosecutors and the courts treated soldiers sympathetically. The political cover against any more vigorous prosecution of military crime survived the 1974 election of a Labour administration, the new Northern Ireland secretary, Merlyn Rees, telling Prime Minister Harold Wilson the security forces were 'a sitting target for irresponsible and totally unconstructive criticism'.[325] According to the NIO, between June 1971 and May 1975, 7,325 complaints were made against the army. From 30 March 1972 to May 1975, 1,496 cases involving alleged assaults or shootings were referred to the DPP. He ordered no further action in 1,330 cases, and prosecutions in 130 (36 cases were still to be decided). By May 1975, eighty-nine soldiers had been convicted and fifty acquitted. Seventy-eight soldiers received convictions for assaults, six for fatal shootings, and five for non-fatal shootings. One conviction for manslaughter was quashed on appeal.[326] The government settled hundreds of civil claims it expected to lose if the case went before a judge. By January 1975, 410 cases had been settled for torts including death, gunshot wounds, assault, battery, wrongful arrest and false imprisonment. In general, doing so kept the cases out of the press. Whilst the MOD guarded the army's good name in Britain and abroad, communities in Northern Ireland could never take military behaviour for granted.[327]

The hands-off approach towards loyalist militancy further accentuated the army's inconsistent protection for wavering Catholics. From cabinet ministers to headquarters and units on the streets in Northern Ireland, the impact of loyalist violence in driving Catholics to seek protection from the IRA was clearly understood. In November 1972 William Whitelaw rebuffed peace feelers from PIRA sources. He doubted whether the Dublin leadership could really enforce a ceasefire.[328] A contact in Andersonstown gave Frank Steele an insight into the Belfast Brigade's thinking about loyalism:

> They were critical of the Army's dual standard as they put it, towards the Catholics and Protestants and said that while the Army continued its dual standard, the IRA had to remain in being as a fighting force to protect the Catholics against both militant Protestants and Army harassment ... their economic warfare (as they describe it – in other words their bombing campaign) was making the Protestants weary and profit conscious Protestant business men were now prepared to consider a united Ireland as one way of ending their troubles. The two IRA representatives agreed that after Operation Motorman there had been a swing against the Provisional IRA in the Catholic areas. However, in recent weeks they claim that this swing had been reversed, due to Army harassment of the Catholics and Catholic fear of militant Protestant organisations.[329]

Whitelaw and Prime Minister Heath heard directly from Catholics in Derry during a visit there in November 1972. The Women's Peace Committee pointed out how unsafe people felt as a result of the UDA being allowed to run wild, unfettered by the security forces. Whitelaw noted several UDA leaders were, in fact, before the courts. Evidently the government's information services were struggling to convey such actions to Catholic audiences. The Alliance Party's Oliver Napier warned Heath 'the successes which had been achieved against the IRA would be wasted as a consequence of failure to deal quickly and effectively with the UDA'.[330] Taoiseach Jack Lynch also raised the issue, in Downing Street. Heath was not listening. He dismissed Lynch's concerns by detailing the four senior UDA and UVF figures recently charged by the police, and the 135 weapons seized in Protestant areas in a four-month period.[331] The inertia came from the top: the army would never switch to a more aggressive posture towards loyalist violence without backing from the prime minister.

The army understood the consequences and refrained from advocating any change. The CGS described the UVF as 'mainly criminal'. He approved of the policy whereby the army arrested a few 'bad men after each Protestant outrage'.[332] Only four days prior to these comments a search in Killinchy, County Down, found 241 3-inch mortars, showing the serious military capability that loyalist groups possessed.[333] Some action was taken. Operation Filter in July 1973 led to the arrests of the commanders of the UVF in Tiger's Bay and the UDA Belfast Brigade.[334] It was not enough. Between January and August 1973 the MOD recorded sixty-five murders, twenty-one by the IRA and forty-four by 'Protestant extremists'.[335] The directorate of military operations admitted what the CGS and cabinet ministers chose to ignore: loyalist violence 'has the effect of driving the Catholics back into the arms of the IRA who can try to justify their existence as a defence against the Protestant threat'.[336] Whitelaw banned the Ulster Freedom Fighters (UFF) and the Red Hand Commandos after seven car bombs went off in Belfast in November.[337] The MOD knew the UFF was nothing more than a cover name for the UDA to disavow their responsibility for despicable acts.[338] Proscribing the UFF meant living under the deliberate fiction that the mainstream UDA was moderate and controllable.

At HQNI, scientific adviser Richard Heagerty wrote: 'The support for the IRA is entrenched in the prot[estant] threat, and this support will never be removed until the locals are convinced that the prot[estant] threat will be dealt with effectively by the government.'[339] Republican propaganda skilfully exploited the security forces' indifference to Catholic victimisation.[340] In November 1972 a church group in south-east Belfast implored 39 Brigade to protect people in the Cregagh estate. Fifty families had been driven out by UDA intimidation despite frequent calls on the army for assistance.[341] A west Belfast man questioned by 1st Queen's Lancashire Regiment described his 'Main bone of contention' as the security forces' 'inability to prevent the sectarian murders'.[342] During their 1973 tour in Andersonstown, 1st Gordon Highlanders tried to protect Catholics on the Ormeau Road from intimidation by Tartan gangs and the UDA. A junior officer spent weeks in the majority-Protestant Belvoir estate making contacts, until he knew sixty-two UDA members living there, and convinced several to 'defect' – implying they left the UDA or acted as informers. Catholic anxieties peaked in the run-up to the border poll in March 1973. A loyalist onslaught was widely expected. The Gordon Highlanders observed, 'The fear in the eyes of these people had to be seen to be believed and plans had already been made by the Catholic community for the evacuation of women and children.'[343] If all registered physical harms are taken into account, rather than deaths alone, the statistics illustrate how, for civilians, the violence continued to be random and unpredictable. (See Figure 7.5.)

CONCLUSION

Whether a more consciously population-centric counter-insurgency plan by the British Army would have made any difference is a moot point. Protecting Catholics from loyalist violence was not the highest priority. Besides being too preoccupied with the campaign to wipe out PIRA's officer corps to pay sufficient attention to Catholic pleas for help, the army lacked the resources

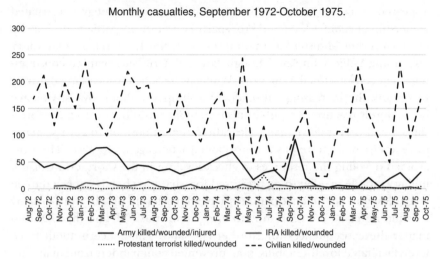

Figure 7.5 Monthly casualties, September 1972–October 1975.[344]

to do enough about the UVF and the UDA. It is important to recognise that moments arose when HQNI and individual units very much pressed for a more aggressive position on loyalism – and they were overruled by their political masters in the NIO and the MOD. PIRA intended to drive the British out of Ireland by killing enough soldiers to make staying unbearable. The nature of the violence applied to these ends only made soldiers more determined to destroy the Provisional movement. To give one example more, on Friday 23 March 1973 two women lured four sergeants to a party in Antrim Road, Belfast, having met and befriended them eleven days earlier. On their arrival, two armed men forced them to lie on a bed before shooting them. Two died instantly, one died later in hospital and the fourth was very seriously injured.[345] Incidents like these help us understand why HQNI put the attrition of PIRA first and foremost, rather than loyalist groups who either killed Catholics or posed a hypothetical threat at some future time. The army could not quite comprehend that measures like mass screening, done in the name of wiping out a terrorist organisation, might have negative side-effects. Nor could HQNI intellectually absorb PIRA's capacity for replacing arrested officers with new candidates perfectly able to carry out the requisite tasks. With few exceptions, the military analysis of PIRA motivation was woefully inadequate, and the social bases for regular recruitment barely considered.

Aggregate violence levels headed downwards from Operation Motorman onwards, so the grounds for overturning the existing strategy might have appeared weak. As in earlier times, adopting a new strategy necessitated leadership at cabinet level and cross-party consensus in parliament. For the most part Prime Minister Heath withdrew from Northern Ireland affairs after appointing Willie Whitelaw. Though extraordinarily successful in constructing a new constitutional framework, Whitelaw refrained from asking the army to rethink the increasingly threadbare assumption about loyalist violence being purely reactive to republicanism. Senior army officers, from the forceful General Carver down, made clear their utter opposition to any rise in the force level, a basic prerequisite for sustained action against loyalists. The army avoided devoting the resources to check loyalism in the short term because military morale needed to be preserved for what was already expected to be an endless war. For defence planners at headquarters in Britain and Germany it would never be the right time to bring down the UVF and the UDA, no matter the consequences for Northern Ireland. The concern about force levels facilitated loyalist mobilisation, prevented commanders from maintaining extended control over the population, and undermined efforts to build trusting connections between soldiers and local people.

8

WE CANNOT ENVISAGE PEACE

... we cannot really envisage a 'peace-time' Northern Ireland.[1]

D. B. Omand, MOD, June 1975

Despondent civil servants in the MOD echoed a widespread exhaustion in Britain by 1975 with the seemingly irresolvable Irish problem. Private Dixon, reflecting a year earlier on his first tour, concluded: 'life will continue to be a misery'.[2] British strategists came to accept permanent conflict in Northern Ireland because they could only imagine things being worse without Britain's presence. Preparing for the long haul meant getting troop numbers down to a sustainable level. Worries about insufficient soldiers sapped the willingness of the army to address the challenge presented by militant loyalism. Matters only became more extreme as the force level dropped. From mid 1973 senior officers expressed anxieties about what the repeated tours to Northern Ireland were doing to their men. Such warnings had been sounded before, but now they tended to be about the effects on military families, and ultimately on soldiers' willingness to re-enlist. Merlyn Rees' committee to establish police primacy first met on 28 January 1976.[3] But the army moved towards a long-war footing well before that. Morale-sustaining measures by regiments and centrally directed by the army played some part in ameliorating the fatigue from repeated deployments. Inserting a longer gap between tours, plus significant pay rises, represented the core initiatives to propagate healthy military morale.

The debate about reductions in the military commitment provides the essential context for understanding the UWC strike in May 1974, which shattered power-sharing and condemned Northern Ireland to a future without any likelihood of constitutional resolution for decades to come. During the strike the MOD determined to save further battalions from being thrown into a situation spiralling out of control. The army's passivity is often deemed as central to the strike's success.[4] Though the army never disobeyed ministerial directions to crush the strike, General Sir Frank King made clear his distaste for receiving such an order.[5] It has been claimed that 'the government's options in using the army during the strike were limited by its numbers and capacity and by the government's desire to avoid a direct armed confrontation with the strikers'.[6] In fact the MOD discouraged the NIO from asking for the reinforcements needed to suppress the strike. By delaying, emphasising police unreliability and presenting a catastrophe as inevitable, the ministry kept the force level down, at a time when the prime minister lacked a majority and was thus predisposed to avoid high-risk political choices. A major arrest operation towards the end of the strike showed armed loyalist insurrection to be a less worrisome prospect than was commonly feared.

Feeling despondent after their public humiliation, ministers in London cast around for ideas about the future. Alternative solutions included a total withdrawal and a deal between loyalists and republicans for an independent state. Several scholars believe Harold Wilson identified withdrawal as his preferred solution to the conflict.[7] The attention devoted to Labour's dalliance with withdrawal as an idea, and PIRA moves towards a negotiated peace, is interesting but irrelevant. An intractable conflict was tolerable to the cabinet as, in 1973–5, the character of the violence turned less 'British' and more 'Northern Irish'. The British refusal to announce an intention to withdraw for fear of provoking a loyalist uprising is sometimes considered to have been based on groundless anxieties.[8] It was not. Senior PIRA and UVF figures met at a fishing lodge in County Cavan in early 1974 for secret talks.[9] These encounters, and others, came to nought. The UDA firmly opposed any weakening of the link between Northern Ireland and Great Britain.[10] Though elements of the UVF and Red Hand Commando leaderships tried to develop a political programme from 1973, they lacked support for the move from their grass-roots members.[11] The majority of loyalists felt they could resist steps towards British withdrawal. Successive London administrations only gave confidence to those who opposed political change by the strategy of limited containment towards violent loyalism.

TROOP NUMBERS FOR THE INDEFINITE FUTURE

Limited military power constrained the British government's ability to confront loyalism, strengthening loyalist self-confidence and indirectly resulting in Catholics seeking protection from the IRA. Labour and Conservative administrations alike aimed to reduce the army's presence in Northern Ireland by building up the local security forces.[12] The army played up the NATO rationale for cutting the deployment to Northern Ireland in part to conceal the more serious concerns about morale among soldiers. In November 1973 NATO's Defence Planning Committee declared the United Kingdom 'met her force commitments' to the alliance, with only 'minor exceptions'. The committee was convinced by the government's promise that troops in Northern Ireland could be returned to Germany within seventy-two hours. Furthermore, the brigades in BAOR were manned at 81 per cent of their full strength. The United Kingdom had actually supplemented NATO's capabilities by introducing new anti-tank weapons, upgrading naval combat readiness and delivering additional ground attack aircraft. Other major equipment improvements, such as the Rapier air defence missile, were planned for 1974 as defence spending rose.[13] As so often since the late nineteenth century, Britain relied on warfighting technology to compensate for manpower shortages.[14]

The need to minimise the number of units derived from calculations about what the army could bear if these rotations continued forever. After his final trip to Belfast before elevation to be CDS, General Carver urged Lord Carrington to prune the deployment from eighteen units to twelve, otherwise 'we may not be able to sustain our effort in following years'.[15] A campaign by military families caused some anxiety in government circles. In May 1973 Peggy and Neville Chaston, whose son served in the army, launched the 'Bring Back the Boys from Ulster' campaign. A month later they handed in a petition with 42,535 signatures to Downing Street. The campaign 'had profound consequences', prompting new measures to placate army wives. This is sometimes read to mean Northern Ireland caused a 'disastrous recruiting' situation, as the intake dropped from 26,484 in 1972–3 to 15,310 in 1973–4. Ministers publicly blamed operations in Northern Ireland for the decline.[16] In reality, the MOD did not take the 'misguided' Chastons seriously. Lance-Corporal Chaston appeared on an ITV television programme to advocate the army's ongoing commitment to Northern Ireland.[17] Furthermore, the recruitment dip proved temporary, rebounding in 1975–6.

The bigger issue confronting the army was declining re-enlistment by experienced soldiers. The twin sources of this problem were the short interval between tours, which disrupted family life, and pay.[18] Military morale can only be partially evaluated on the available sources. Research on the British Army in earlier wars showcases what might be done when fresh material comes to light. Jonathan Fennell examines the relationship between morale and combat performance in the Second World War by mining the extensive censorship reports compiled by officers to monitor how soldiers felt. Quantitative measures such as desertion and psychological casualty rates can be acute indicators for systemic problems in an army.[19] Although such evidence is unavailable for Northern Ireland, we can be quite confident that the army did not suffer a morale crisis, such as arose in North Africa in the summer of 1942. The reasons for military endurance under testing conditions owe much to officer–man relations within small groups.[20] Further work on individual coping strategies, along the lines of that on endurance in the First World War, is clearly desirable, especially as both conflicts lacked any discernible end-point for participants.[21] The armies of 1914–18 and 1969–75 similarly activated complex bureaucracies for fulfilling the material requirements of healthy morale.

At first the MOD largely left units to attend to their own affairs. In early 1970, 1st Royal Scots produced a fortnightly news-sheet to keep families back home informed about their actions in Belfast;[22] 1st Royal Green Jackets arranged weekly briefings for the wives left behind at the barracks in Celle, Germany, during a four-month tour, with tape-recorded messages from riflemen sent over specially from Belfast.[23] Like many units, 1st Royal Regiment of Fusiliers tried to maintain morale by organising a busy sporting schedule, and installed gambling machines and juke boxes to distract from off-duty boredom.[24] Regimental wives' clubs put on keep-fit classes, shopping trips and parties to 'maintain spirits' when soldiers were deployed for a long time away from barracks.[25] As the conflict dragged on, the ministry became more involved in providing comfort to the troops. Subsidised pay phones allowed soldiers to call families in the United Kingdom, and later in Germany.[26] The combined services entertainment organisation put on shows at unit bases;[27] 1st King's Own Scottish Borderers particularly relished 'A gorgeous young blond dolly-bird' entertainer who 'sang to the resounding cheers of the Jocks'.[28]

In a more sombre vein, chaplains accompanying units in Northern Ireland attended to the spiritual needs of soldiers, visited the wounded and liaised with bereaved relatives.[29] Service personnel received subsidised travel to and from Britain for themselves and family members. Soldiers on four-month tours were granted one ninety-six-hour leave period with free air travel. Several hundred television sets were sent to units from schemes run by the government and the *Daily Telegraph* and the *Daily Mirror*.[30] Local newspapers got involved too. An appeal by the *Southern Evening Echo* collected 3,000 books to send to the troops.[31] In May 1974 the ministry rolled out additional entitlements to free telephone calls and travel for service personnel and their families.[32] By November the government had invested in swimming pools at the barracks in Holywood, Ballykelly, Omagh and Ballykinler, 'instant', prefabricated pubs in Omagh, Ballykinler and

Lisburn (adorned with typical pub hunting horns), sauna baths at twelve locations, two bowling alleys and eight squash courts.[33] The army sought to manage expectations about life on duty. A booklet for prospective recruits, with a foreword by General King, profiled a private in the Light Infantry: 'I'm not really keen on Northern Ireland myself. It's soldiering all right, but not the kind I enjoy. It's just one of the jobs soldiers have to do.'[34]

Ministers began picking up on discontent over pay in July 1973. Junior minister Peter Blaker reported: 'the troops and the families with them in Ulster were in good shape'. However, soldiers resented their pay being eaten away by the food and accommodation charges levied on them.[35] From the outset of Edward Heath's administration, wages rose by more than 10 per cent a year. Matters came to a head after Harold Wilson won power in 1974, as inflation hit 19.2 per cent. Wages rose in the second half of the year by 16 per cent.[36] An overseas allowance paid to soldiers in Germany was reduced (if married) or cut entirely (if single) when they went to Northern Ireland. A married private, for example, lost £4.34 a week (c. £38 in current prices); a married captain £7.07 (c. £60). Soldiers deployed from Britain enjoyed a weekly gain – £5.32 (c. £44) for a married private, and £6.86 (c. £58) for a married captain. Single soldiers benefited too.[37] These anomalies caused resentment. After an audience with General King in April 1974, Wilson instructed his defence secretary to immediately improve pay and conditions, due to concern about morale.[38] In May, Wilson announced pay increases for the armed forces ranging from 10 per cent for the lowest paid to 5 per cent for more senior personnel. Soldiers on duty in Northern Ireland received an extra 50 pence a day (c. £4.30 today), and a bonus for the unsocial hours necessarily part of service life was doubled, from 5 to 10 per cent.[39] Another rise dated from 1 April 1975 lifted pay by 29.5 per cent on average.[40] The government had been slow to maintain soldiers' pay sufficiently to track inflation. A relative decline in the purchasing power of the military wage is likely to have affected morale as much as the thought of regular service in Northern Ireland.

Improved conditions and pay could only achieve so much. The frequency with which soldiers found themselves in Northern Ireland had to be addressed. Carver's successor as head of the army was General Sir Peter Hunt, described by his military assistant (MA) as 'a man of natural warmth and avuncular temperament'.[41] Hunt upheld the quest for troop reductions. The implications of the force level for loyalist militancy became apparent long before the UWC strike in May 1974. General King intended to withdraw two units from Protestant areas in Belfast, accepting the risk of being less able to cope with loyalist violence.[42] However, Downing Street intervened to insist the reduction be balanced between Protestant and Catholic districts.[43] King changed his tune to suit the prime minister, now claiming he faced 'more trouble from the Protestant areas than the Catholic ones', and so could 'not afford to reduce the force level'. The CGS was having none of it.[44] In September 1973, Whitelaw and Carrington agreed on a plan to come down to fourteen units by the end of December and twelve by Easter.[45] Troop reductions necessary to preserve the army's long-term stability compelled HQNI to make choices about where to concentrate diminishing resources. The automatic reaction was to target those resources at fighting republicanism.

Amidst turmoil in both Northern Irish and British politics in December 1973 and January 1974 the army pressed again for force reductions. Edward Heath moved Whitelaw to be SoS for employment on 2 December, to handle a miner's strike. His replacement, Francis Pym, struggled to master his brief only days before the Sunningdale conference convened. The agreement signed on 9 December created an assembly and an executive to share power primarily between the Unionists and the SDLP. (See Illustration 8.1.) The Irish and British governments guaranteed

Illustration 8.1 The Sunningdale Agreement is signed, 9 December 1973. Pictured, from left, are Oliver Napier, Liam Cosgrave, Edward Heath, Brian Faulkner and Gerry Fitt. (Courtesy of Express/Hulton Archive/Getty Images.)

stability in Northern Ireland's constitutional status, unless a majority voted for change, and agreed to work more closely on countering terrorism. Within days of the Executive taking office on 1 January 1974 the chief executive, Brian Faulkner, lost a vote in the Ulster Unionist Council over the Council of Ireland, a key component in the Sunningdale Agreement. Mainstream unionist opinion suspected deeper co-operation across the island might pave the way for unification.[46] Meanwhile in London, Heath's inner circle were frantically debating whether to call a general election to head off the growing economic crisis. On 8 January Heath moved Lord Carrington from defence to head a new energy department. Press speculation about the election abounded.[47]

On 1 February General Hunt asked the new defence secretary, Ian Gilmour, to cut the force level to fourteen units. Violence in December had kept the level at sixteen units, despite earlier plans. This gave units from Germany a fourteen-month break between deployments to Northern Ireland (ten months for UK-based troops). The deployment to Northern Ireland interfered with training and had a 'severe' effect on families. Hunt thought fourteen units sufficient, even though a 'Protestant upheaval' seemed inevitable;[48] he made very optimistic assumptions about loyalist violence remaining static in order to justify his agenda for troop withdrawals. The MOD intelligence summary for November 1973 noted the significant impact of the UVF's ceasefire coming into effect on the 18th of the month, following which there were no more loyalist bombings at all. However, the UVF leadership publicly threatened to end the ceasefire if any steps were taken to create a Council of Ireland.[49] General Hunt clearly did not take this threat seriously, and the UVF's announcement in December of an indefinite extension to their ceasefire probably lulled him into a sense of complacency.[50] An obvious turn for the worse in January failed to budge the CGS from his position. A Law Enforcement Commission established by Sunningdale to promote cross-border co-operation convened in Northern Ireland on 16 January. Loyalists blocked 52 roads in Belfast and held a rally of 6,000 people at City Hall addressed by William Craig and Ian Paisley.[51]

General King may have sought to take advantage of ministerial upheaval and pre-occupation with the election to overturn his superior's intention to forge ahead on troop reductions. King met Francis Pym and his permanent secretary, Sir Frank Cooper. Cooper had been a Spitfire fighter pilot in the war and was a long-time defence civil servant. A colleague described him as a 'piratical operator ... both feared and respected'.[52] Over the course of the year Cooper exerted a powerful influence on the NIO's bid to bring the army under tighter control. King expressed 'deep concern' about the proposed troop drawdown. He then attempted to convince Pym to overturn MOD policy, arguing the reductions might produce political uncertainty, an (unspecified) reaction from protestants, succour to the IRA, criticism from the Irish government, depression in the police force and an inability to run detention facilities, and, in the round, be 'unwise'. King suggested that the positive effects of the most recent cut, from seventeen units in October to sixteen in November 1973, had not really been given enough time to bed in throughout the army.[53] Fortunately for HQNI, Heath's decision to hold a general election granted a temporary reprieve. The CGS encouraged King to consider how a sustainable force posture would enable the army to 'bash' the IRA for years to come.[54]

Labour formed a minority government on 4 March 1974. Harold Wilson's second administration has been characterised as 'tired and lack-lustre'. Focused on winning a majority at the next election, Wilson 'had no clear aims, no purpose'.[55] The malaise seeped into all aspects of govern-ance. Merlyn Rees was appointed SoS for Northern Ireland. His mentor, James Callaghan, thought him especially suited to the brief as a 'conciliator' possessed of 'an instinctive politician's flair for detecting shifts in mood and opinion'.[56] He wished to maintain his Conservative predecessor's plan to reduce troop numbers.[57] Rees intended to strengthen the RUC, enact tighter firearms laws, review emergency legislation, run down internment, and bring the UVF and Sinn Féin into electoral politics.[58] The new SoS for defence was Roy Mason, a Yorkshire miner with experience as a junior defence minister in 1967–8. Cecil Blacker, then the AG, described Mason thus: he 'compensated for his total lack of charm by a decisive competence'.[59] Labour fought the election on a pledge to reduce defence spending and announced a review on coming into power.[60] A tightening in the overall resources available is likely to have informed thinking at the top level of the MOD. General Hunt certainly came to believe the Provisionals expected to gain concessions from the Labour government, whom they deemed more pliable than the Conservatives.[61] The UDA was alarmed by Labour parliamentarians openly debating whether the government should leave Northern Ireland forever.[62]

At their inaugural security briefing, Rees and Mason heard that the army assumed they would be in Northern Ireland 'for the indefinite future' and thought about force levels accordingly. The existing sixteen-unit deployment meant a break between tours of eight months for UK-based units and ten months for those stationed in Germany. Getting the level down to twelve to fourteen units would allow those intervals to be extended to eighteen and twenty-four months respectively – a radical improvement. Rees and Mason were told the security situation permitted such a force posture. Achieving it promised to mitigate the harms done to training for war, soldiers' absence from their families, and the 'unacceptably high' rate of serving soldiers who decided against re-enlistment, which sat at 40 per cent.[63] Lance-Corporal Graham Wickes decided whilst in Belfast to leave the army in December 1971: 'if this was what my future in the forces was going to be, perhaps it wasn't for me'.[64]

Quite early on in their relationship General King made clear to Merlyn Rees his desire to pursue a hard line on security. King valued detention as a central tool in his campaign to dismember PIRA's leadership cadre.[65] After a spate of PIRA attacks in mid March 1974 he and the chief constable lobbied Rees for progress with Dublin on border security, and tougher sentences for possessing weapons, car theft and stoning.[66] Despite his personal preference for a more conciliatory approach, Rees listened to King. When Roy Mason formally requested the reduction to thirteen units, Rees only agreed to one unit being withdrawn by the end of April, then one more in late July and the third in September.[67] Mason was advised to object to the delay. The VCGS intimated that unless action to address overstretch was taken straight away, a reduction in a manner likely to be 'highly undesirable' loomed on the horizon.[68] The prospect of having fewer soldiers at his disposal made General King even more determined to retain internment. He contested the view (held by Rees himself) that internment assisted PIRA recruitment by depicting the British as harsh oppressors. Rather, King believed stopping all releases would force PIRA to give up. King observed violence to be on the rise since the Sunningdale Agreement was signed. His broad hostility to force reductions and less use of internment suggests he believed Sunningdale to be too generous to nationalists.[69] Army casualties had been rising since December 1973 (see Figure 7.5).

With the force-level question unresolved, military morale now suffered an unexpected blow, though one bound to fall following the appointment of an independent DPP in 1972. On 15 March 1974 a judge sitting at the Belfast City Commission found Corporal F. W. Foxford guilty of manslaughter for shooting dead 12-year-old Kevin Heatley in February the previous year, in Newry.[70] The case provoked outrage in certain sections of British society. A woman from Halifax whose son was serving in Northern Ireland on his second tour implored Harold Wilson to 'let the Irish people get on with it on their own ... let them kill each other but not our boys'.[71] A retired officer wrote to Conservative MP Sir George Sinclair to express his dismay at the ruling and claimed his contacts still in the army suggested 'a mutiny in Ireland is not beyond the realms of possibility'.[72] Warrant Officer Hawker, from Foxford's battalion, put the position in less hyperbolic terms. Those on a second, third or fourth tour questioned 'whether it will ever end . . . it has now reached such a degree of stagnation that this is beginning to creep back into the Army, and if it does continue it will undoubtedly do much harm to soldiers' morale'.[73] These considerations played into the debate about overstretch.

HQNI hosted Prime Minister Wilson at Lisburn on 18 April. Giving the security briefing, Colonel Mears stated PIRA morale stood at a higher level than for fourteen months. Prison escapes, attacks in the cities, detainee releases and the general election result seemed to be contributory factors. Mears argued Protestants generally accepted power-sharing. It was the UDA who perpetrated most violence aimed at bringing the Executive down. Mears claimed that 'the Army had good intelligence on them'. General King viewed the army's concentration on Belfast and PIRA's leadership as successful until September 1973, when Sunningdale activated the Protestant population in a way not seen before, somewhat contradicting Colonel Mears' assessment. On detention, King advised Wilson to suspend further releases until violence completely stopped. This was a hard-line position: 'If the release of detainees was continued and the strength of the Army reduced, he believed the result would be civil war.' He argued that fifty of the sixty-five prisoners released at Christmas were already involved in terrorism again. Finally, the prime minister was enjoined to pay close attention to the army's morale:

> General King told the Prime Minister that he was becoming a bit worried about the morale of the Army. Some soldiers were now on their fourth or fifth tour of duty in the Province. The soldiers were concerned about the release of detainees whom they had caught with so much difficulty, and by the lenient sentences of the courts. There were also Army matters which caused him concern: soldiers serving in Ulster lost their overseas allowances, which meant financial hardship in many cases. In one battalion currently in Ulster there were no fewer than 100 men receiving public assistance. These were damaging comparisons with the police who earned far more than the soldiers but worked fewer hours and faced fewer dangers. There was also dissatisfaction that soldiers transferred to Ulster from Germany lost their entitlement to duty-free cigarettes. Finally, the case of Corporal Foxford had worried the soldiers a good deal, and there were a number of other similar cases pending.[74]

The MOD worried about General King venturing further and further into political territory that should be off-limits to a serving officer. This happened during Frank Cooper's absence from the scene on sick leave, leaving Merlyn Rees light on official advice in his own department and missing a redoubtable bulwark against military pressure. Roy Mason was told General King therefore found it 'difficult to avoid expressing political judgements', in a rather generous reading of his forceful character. King and the CLF, General Leng, feared a cut in troop numbers would seriously jeopardise Brian Faulkner's ability to retain unionist support for the new executive.[75] King considered Merlyn Rees 'frank and likeable' and 'more robust than Francis Pym'.[76] The two first met at a lunch hosted by Willie Whitelaw at the Culloden Hotel, outside Belfast, in December 1972. Rees confessed his apprehension that a Labour government would face trouble from the Protestants. Even then, King left Rees in no doubt he was 'very stuck on extra troops'.[77] Untangling the reasons for which General King opposed the troop reductions is problematic. He certainly held firm to the conviction that the Provisionals could and should be beaten. Whether the claims about army morale and Faulkner's credibility meant as much to him is less clear. The CGS reprimanded King for contradicting the ministry's position on force reductions, essential for protecting the army's resilience.[78] Mason persuaded Rees to agree to the Queen's Dragoon Guards leaving by the end of May, against General King's advice.[79]

THE UWC STRIKE

The MOD's insistence on force reductions was predicated on loyalist violence continuing at a stable level. The concerted effort to bring units back to barracks in Britain and Germany happened when the UVF was on ceasefire. From late January 1974 this position began to deteriorate, but the MOD refused to adjust its mantra. When the CGS visited HQNI on 25 January, he was briefed that Protestant extremists constituted 'probably now the main potential threat'. They planned assassinations, car-bombings, disruption in rural areas and attacks on the security forces. General King informed the CGS as to his worries about the 'significant number' of Territorial Army and UDR soldiers connected to loyalist groups.[80] General Hunt had already been told about fifty-one RUC officers known to have direct links to 'Protestant extremists'.[81] Yet having fewer soldiers naturally implied a heavier reliance on the police. HQNI's plan for handling widespread loyalist violence, Operation Utmost, envisaged the UVF, assisted by other organisations, trying to wreck the Northern Ireland Executive. Such a campaign was predicted to comprise political assassinations and bombings of Catholic property, supplemented by industrial unrest in Belfast, and might last for three or four months. Operation Utmost tasked the security forces to maintain the offensive against the IRA as the top priority and avoid provoking 'moderate' Protestants – which included the UDA.[82] An updated version of the plan emphasised the reliance upon police support.[83] However, HQNI believed any systematic action against the leadership of the loyalist groups would result in a 'likely breakdown of the RUC will to do anything'.[84]

In February the South East Antrim UDA carried out several sectarian murders. Though the UVF ceasefire held for the most part, loyalists were thought to have planted thirty bombs intended to kill Catholics.[85] The next month intelligence sources disclosed the UDA Inner Council's decision to resume its offensive against Catholics. The MOD noted the emergence of the UWC, intent on opposing the Sunningdale Agreement, and particularly strong in Harland and Wolff, Short Brothers, and the electricity power stations in Belfast and Larne.[86] The organisation formed in January in Cookstown, County Tyrone, and brought together elected politicians Harry West and William Craig with leaders from the UVF, UDA, Orange Volunteers, Ulster Special Constabulary (USC) Association, Ulster Volunteer Service Corps and Down Orange Welfare. The UWC chairman, Glen Barr, represented Vanguard in the Assembly and was also a UDA officer. The recent miners' strike in Britain apparently gave these men confidence in industrial action as a tactic of coercion.[87] Merlyn Rees met representatives from the UWC at Stormont Castle in early April. They asked for fresh elections and argued that the SDLP lacked a mandate to sit in the Assembly because they were 'Republican sympathisers, if not members of the IRA'.[88] The UWC planned a general strike for 8 May but backed down due to opposition from loyalist politicians. This led the MOD to conclude 'Coordinated widespread Protestant activity is not considered likely.'[89]

On 12 May Vanguard leader William Craig publicly excused sectarian murders as 'unfortunate but understandable', and affirmed his party's determination to destroy Sunningdale. Two days later the Northern Ireland Assembly voted down a motion put forward by loyalists for Sunningdale to be renegotiated.[90] The UWC had decided that such a vote would trigger their strike: shipyard union leader Harry Murray announced it that day.[91] Industrial action duly began, on 15 May, but attracted limited backing, some factories in Belfast closing, and an electricity blackout struck from 10.30pm until 3am the following morning. On the second day the UDA put up fifteen pickets in Belfast and intimidated people travelling to work. The MOD expected the strike to run out of steam within a few days.[92] Merlyn Rees shared the optimism: the government was in a strong enough position to think about ratifying Sunningdale.[93] At 39 Infantry Brigade in Belfast, the outlook seemed less bright. Support for the strike had grown, more shops and factories closed and the UDA threat increased, with more than forty roads blocked.[94] Since August 1973 the army had pursued a policy of leaving Protestant roadblocks to the police. Soldiers would only get involved if the police asked for back-up and, even then, be as nonconfrontational as possible.[95]

On 17 May Rees briefed Harold Wilson that the position was deteriorating and complained about the MOD's complacency.[96] That evening, bombs went off in Dublin and Monaghan, killing 33 civilians and an unborn child, and injuring 258. Many people (correctly) believed loyalists to be responsible.[97] London despatched 134 military technicians to be on standby for the power stations, plus 1st Light Infantry.[98] A secret reconnaissance of Ballylumford power station concluded the army could only generate electricity with assistance from the senior management.[99] In the morning of 20 May General King and the chief constable advised Rees to avoid confrontation, to allow public opinion to turn against the strike.[100] Robert Fisk, who covered the strike for *The Times*, argues this advice proved fatal: earlier decisive action by the security forces might have been effective.[101] In fact Rees thought he had secured the prime minister's approval on the telephone for ordering the army to deploy 1,500 soldiers to clear the UDA barricades on the evening of 20 May. Rees said to Wilson: 'All I wanted you to know is that it is not going to be easy. They may well go wrong . . . we must do this.' Wilson replied: 'Yes, I agree. Well, it is a mini motor man really, isn't it?' Rees believed General King supported him 'Very fully', though the police were 'much more wobbly'.[102]

Alerted to these developments, the DMO in the MOD quickly engaged the CGS to thwart Rees' plans. He argued that tackling the UDA would lead to violence on a scale likely to invoke Operation Utmost, with a consequent six-battalion reinforcement, devastating the plan to get the force level under control.[103] General Hunt now lobbied Roy Mason. Whilst acknowledging the Executive's legitimate objection to the barricades, the GOC feared fighting on two fronts. Sending those extra battalions meant 'grave implications for the Army'. The damage 'might prove irretrievable'.[104] In the meantime, on 21 May, the army did the minimum possible, securing the main supply routes into Belfast, but otherwise avoiding confrontation.[105] At the Cabinet Northern Ireland Committee, Rees described the UWC's success in stopping work in factories, shops and service industries. He considered military reinforcements essential;[106] 1st Queen's Regiment arrived in Northern Ireland the next day.[107]

Official attitudes towards the strike did not follow neatly demarcated departmental lines. By 22 May General King believed 80 per cent of

Protestants to be sympathetic – how such an exact statistic was arrived at is unclear.[108] MOD officials hoped the SoS for Northern Ireland would retract his demand for military action.[109] One of Rees' senior officials, Philip Woodfield, thought 'Army intervention will not be successful.' The police were already doing 'the absolute minimum they can get by with in this situation'.[110] Intelligence hinted at pending defections to the strike by policemen and loyalist preparedness to attack the security forces if they tried to clear more roadblocks.[111] These sources confirm Robert Fisk's impression that divided loyalties in the police prevented the strike being decisively squashed in the early days.[112] Military judgements might have been influenced by industrial action by RUC members of the Police Federation between 18 and 20 February, in a dispute about a detective being prosecuted for assaulting a prisoner. The experience 'caused both anxiety and additional tasks for the Army'. Though the dispute only lasted a few days, the prospect of police officers hobbling the entire arrest, questioning and prosecution system cannot have been easily forgotten.[113]

At a private meeting with Stanley Orme, a NIO minister, Brigadier Garrett detected 'exasperation that Army should be holding back now that the Executive wished a strong line'. The brigadier attempted to persuade Orme the situation should be allowed to develop for a few days, as there was no immediate crisis in fuel and food supplies reaching people. The notes of the meeting expressed some disbelief at the minister's portrayal of the strike as political rather than industrial in nature.[114] This was not how HQNI chose to frame events. A later internal account stated of the strikers: 'they were not acting illegally ... the Army was being used more in the strike breaking role than that of maintaining essential services'.[115] General King impressed upon the CGS his reluctance to crush the strike by force. Any attempt to secure the power stations would be met with sabotage and a walkout by managers essential for their functioning. Colonel Mears, the senior intelligence officer at Lisburn, said the UWC 'was now a front for the UDA', with high morale and extensive Protestant support, spreading into the countryside too. If the army tried to stop the strike, there would be a 'full-scale confrontation' with the UDA and a collapse in the police force. RUC Reserve and UDR personnel were being coaxed into joining the strike. General Hunt would only permit reinforcements to be sent for a political purpose he deemed to be correct:

> The CGS stated that the Army was being used as a bludgeon; one which would not be able to solve the situation. MOD could not possibly provide any more reinforcements for a strike-breaking action. Already the supply of

RCT [Royal Corps of Transport] drivers had run out. Obviously if a civil war situation occurred more reinforcements would be found, but for this commitment no more would be forthcoming. If the Government wanted troops to go in, then it must give the Army priorities within the capabilities of the existing force levels.[116]

Flying back to London for the Cabinet Northern Ireland Committee meeting that night, General Hunt echoed King's assertions about popular backing for the strike and probable subversion in the police. The army must avoid being 'sucked into an endless situation' demanding ever more troops.[117] Meeting Harold Wilson at Chequers the next day, Brian Faulkner disputed the army's analysis. Taking control of essential services would damage the strike's popularity. Strikers were likely to avoid fighting the army. Faulkner's answer to a question about police loyalty was hedged with qualifications about how they 'needed encouragement'. Roy Mason remained noncommittal. Faulkner pleaded for action: the 'erosion of support for duly constituted authority could be put right quickly by the assertion of authority on the ground'.[118] Whilst the talks proceeded loyalists bombed four businesses in Belfast that had defied orders to close.[119] General King wrote to Merlyn Rees that moving in on the utilities 'would almost certainly prove to be disastrous' and provoke sabotage. The blame for the ensuing 'near chaos' would tarnish the army.[120] On the streets, the UDA exploited the army's desire to avoid trouble, moving out of the way when soldiers came to clear barricades, only to re-erect them later on.[121]

On the night of 24 May a gang attacked three pubs and a fish and chip shop in Ballymena before going on to murder two Catholic publicans.[122] Police later arrested thirty-five Protestants in connection with these incidents, charging two with murder and thirty-one with more minor offences.[123] Merlyn Rees proposed the army activate Operation Flare – the plan to seize control of oil and petrol supplies and distribution. Recounting the discussion to Roy Mason, General King recalled expressing his 'very grave reservations' about doing so, expecting the army to then be dragged into supporting other essential services. Instead, he suggested arrests in response to the violence in Ballymena;[124] 1st Light Infantry conducted the operation on the night of 25 May, causing 'resentment' in police circles, especially amongst Special Branch officers.[125] The army arrested twenty-eight leaders from the UDA, UVF and Red Hand Commando in north Belfast. There was no violent reaction.[126] Abetted by the NIO, over the preceding two years the army had created an image of the UDA as moderate and unthreatening. For less than a fortnight, HQNI, at the MOD's urging, adopted the contradictory position that the UDA-backed strikers were too dangerous to confront. The arrests by the Light Infantry proved both these perspectives to be fallacious.

The prime minister allowed these inconsistencies to persist, refraining from forcing a follow-up to the Light Infantry arrests. HQNI was dissuaded from pushing for such a move, effectively to support Merlyn Rees, by the stern and consistent instructions from the MOD to avoid a clash with the UDA, and by the CGS's earlier reprimand to King for siding with the wrong ministry over force levels. By this juncture HQNI understood the cabinet's priority to be avoiding blame for the inevitable fall of the Executive.[127] The same night Harold Wilson outraged unionist Northern Ireland by condemning the strikers in a television broadcast as 'sponging on Westminster and British democracy'.[128] Mirroring Edward Heath's decision to go sailing before the fateful march in Derry on 30 January 1972, Harold Wilson went on holiday to the Scilly Isles. Meeting Merlyn Rees at the Royal Navy's Air Station in Penzance, he authorised Rees to launch Operation Flare.[129] At 5am on 27 May soldiers took over two oil depots and twenty-one filling stations without incident.[130] General King declared: 'at all costs we must remain friends with the Protestants'.[131]

The Northern Ireland Executive fell on 28 May. Brian Faulkner tendered his resignation at Stormont Castle, walking round to the back entrance to avoid a farmers' protest addressed by Ian Paisley.[132] At the Cabinet Northern Ireland Committee the next day it was decided to prorogue the Assembly. Rees expressed discontent at the delay between the cabinet decision on 24 May for the army to secure petrol and oil supplies, and this coming into effect three days later.[133] The strike's success was greeted at the time with fatalism or indignation, and has been ever since. Wilson claimed the army lacked the forces to face down several hundred thousand strikers.[134] Staff officers at HQNI maintained majority Protestant opinion demanded the Executive fall.[135] Opposition to Sunningdale manifested itself in people from many social backgrounds accepting the UDA's mobilisation. Excluding the paramilitaries from formal politics encouraged them to destroy the Executive by ramping up the violence.[136]

Critics of the government believe rapid action within the first few days would have been effective and popular.[137] Merlyn Rees is blamed for indecision, thus allowing public support for the strike to gather slowly. Some scholars attribute responsibility in a precise order: to Rees, then Wilson, then 'to a lesser extent' Roy Mason.[138] General King held the NIO's handling of the crisis in almost as much contempt.[139] Neither the pessimists nor the indignant present overwhelming evidence to substantiate their views about what Protestants really wanted. A slim majority had voted against pro-Sunningdale candidates in February, ten weeks before the strike.[140] The ballot paper did not ask them to vote for industrial action backed by systematic intimidation. Whether majority Protestant opinion supported the UWC, as some historians have concluded, cannot be proven.[141] Impressions garnered by journalists, politicians, civil servants and soldiers during the strike were precisely that. The servants of the state most intimately connected to Protestant opinion throughout, and those suspected of wavering loyalty to the crown, were the police. Their archives are shut.

The UWC strike must be put back into the context of army relations with loyalists since mid 1972, and the policy debate over troop numbers since mid 1973. The political shortcomings of the Sunningdale Agreement, especially the provisions on the Council of Ireland and the exclusion of paramilitaries, are not in question. They might have made a breakdown in the Assembly and Executive inevitable at some stage. Above all the UWC strike was enacted through the UDA's military power. Over the previous two years the state, principally the army, had chosen to appease the UDA, signalling weak resolve. Once the MOD had fixed on reductions in the force level, made necessary by PIRA's ability to sustain offensive operations, it was unwilling to be moved no matter what happened to the threat from loyalism. Merlyn Rees acted slowly in pressing for the strike to be suppressed. The MOD exercised a stranglehold on him by making the choices appear catastrophic: the CGS did everything in his power to prevent Operation Utmost from happening. Strategic adaptation only ever kicked in when the Northern Ireland secretary, the defence secretary and the prime minister agreed to change course. Merlyn Rees thought he had achieved that on 20 May. The army, with Roy Mason's blessing, stopped him in his tracks. Harold Wilson failed to mediate between the two ministries, so the default position of placating loyalism prevailed. What is so striking in the official debates is the absence of references, apart from one ill-informed example, to Operation Motorman. For a prime minister without a majority, something on that scale did not even warrant serious consideration. General Hunt got what he wanted. The reinforcements sent during the strike were home by 6 June, leaving fifteen units, one fewer than beforehand.[142]

FROM DESPAIR TO RESIGNATION

In the wake of the strike the government proceeded with the reforms to security policy planned earlier. Before we come on to these, the claims made by some scholars that the British intended to withdraw from Northern

Ireland merit discussion. Niall Ó Dochartaigh believes Harold Wilson deemed withdrawal the 'optimal outcome'.[143] For Thomas Leahy, the Labour administration intended to grant independence or dominion status, by forcing PIRA into a ceasefire and entering negotiations. He calls independence 'a clear policy'.[144] These arguments are mistaken. Bernard Donoughue, a senior adviser to Wilson, recalled the prime minister's determination to keep away from Irish affairs after the strike, 'trying to contain terrorism and just to get through from year to year'.[145] Leahy documents in greater detail than ever before the discussions in official circles about the wisdom of pursuing independence. But a 'clear policy' by the government can only mean a formal decision, reached by the full cabinet or one of its committees. Such a record cannot be cited because the British government never endorsed independence for, or withdrawal from, Northern Ireland.[146] An administration in despair after the strike simply considered many possibilities.[147] Labour and Conservative governments had spent five years attempting to prevent civil war, with varying success. Even if Wilson and other Labour leaders believed in an Ireland without a British presence, they knew parliament would never allow it.

A study on future options by the NIO rejected withdrawal. Removing the army would encourage the IRA to push for total victory and result in widespread communal violence. The Republic of Ireland or the United Nations might then intervene, damaging Britain's reputation. Violence could spread amongst Irish communities in Britain, and nationalism in Scotland and Wales would receive a boost. The potential economic damage to the whole of the UK was bound to be severe.[148] Merlyn Rees rejected both total integration with Britain and withdrawal.[149] Harold Wilson told Liberal leader Jeremy Thorpe that he, and most Labour Party MPs, thought withdrawal a disastrous proposition.[150] In mid July he confided in the taoiseach that leaving Northern Ireland 'was not something which a responsible British Government could do'.[151]

Senior officers tended to agree. In General Hunt's mind, 'this would be a disaster'. Getting the force level down to a sustainable number was essential for him to win the argument against withdrawal in Whitehall.[152] The VCGS, Lieutenant-General Sir David Fraser, thought talk of leaving 'a wretched reneging on what we have, with suffering and casualty, been trying to achieve for five years: and an abandonment of people we have tried to help'.[153] Opinion elsewhere in the armed forces of course varied a great deal. Scout helicopter pilot Michael Booth completed two four-month tours in 1971 and 1972, leaving him 'feeling pretty anti about life, anti about religion in general, very anti about the Irish and what was going on'.[154]

In late 1972 the Duke of Wellington's Regiment responded emotionally to press comments that the time had come for the British to depart: 'there would undoubtedly be serious bloodshed ... If the insurgency was in any other part of the United Kingdom there would be no question of withdrawal and it is merely playing into the hands of the IRA to suggest it.'[155] By March 1976 the thirty experienced NCOs and other ranks surveyed by Major Trotman found attractive the idea of a more limited commitment by the army.[156]

On 4 July 1974 the NIO published a White Paper setting out the government's plans for a constitutional convention. Those elected to the convention would devise some new dispensation for governance, with minimal British interference. The next week Merlyn Rees announced that internment would be phased out.[157] General King was appalled and continued to urge tougher security measures, expecting them to push PIRA towards a more political posture.[158] Rees was not listening. A few weeks later he decided to release about thirty people from detention at intervals.[159] Before the strike the MOD and the NIO commissioned a security review by the GOC and the chief constable. They recommended increasing police numbers to 6,500 and a military force level of sixteen battalions. The review opposed detainee releases, asked for existing powers of arrest to be retained and proposed longer sentences for terrorist offences.[160] Unimpressed, Rees ignored the review by deferring these matters to a commission he had set up under Lord Gardiner to consider counter-terrorism legislation.[161]

These exchanges typified relations between Rees and King after the strike. Beforehand, King managed to bring Rees round to his way of thinking as a buffer against the MOD's demands for units to be returned to normal business. The NIO's permanent secretary, Sir Frank Cooper, emboldened Rees to think critically about the consequences of the army's desire to perpetuate the attritional war on the Provisionals. At an internal seminar Cooper chastised the army for 'fighting a private war with the IRA and bystanders (whether innocent or not) are being hurt'. He argued mass detention constituted a major impediment to peace.[162] With his deep knowledge of the military and contacts throughout the MOD, Cooper probably appreciated how the need to reduce troop numbers might be exploited to effectively curtail HQNI's offensive ambitions. Rees now marched ahead with his agenda to strengthen the police and become less reliant on the army.

At UKLF headquarters Major-General Strawson wished to see the drawdown accelerated, to create a 'tolerable' eight- or nine-month gap between tours.[163] General Hunt advised patience until the dust settled after the strike.[164] As violence receded Hunt asked for the next reductions: 20 Medium Regiment Royal Artillery on 26 August, and 45 Commando Royal Marines on 23 September, without replacement. The deployment of two units to Cyprus in response to the Turkish invasion of the island on 20 July 1974 made this plan all the more desirable.[165] King protested that even if PIRA reined in their operations, thirteen units only allowed him to keep 'running very hard to stand still'.[166] General Hunt reminded King to consider the intolerable overstretch in the army: thirteen units positioned the army for an endless conflict.[167] The MOD compromised, delaying the artillery's departure until 20 September and 45 Commando's until 6 November.[168] HQNI managed, even though General Leng could not now inflict the attritional losses on PIRA he desired. In Derry, new 'technical operations' dramatically improved intelligence collection. Leng planned to expand them to compensate for reduced manpower.[169] The army's leadership in London believed Lisburn perfectly able to live in straitened circumstances. At the end of October the VCGS concluded the security situation looked brighter. For example, 3rd Royal Green Jackets' four-month tour in Ballymurphy was nearly up, and there had only been two shooting incidents the whole time, compared to ten a day in late 1972. The Catholics he met apparently feared a 'blood-bath' if the army left.[170]

On 10 October Harold Wilson won a general election with a small majority.[171] In early November 1974 the force level finally came down to the hallowed thirteen units as 45 Commando went home.[172] The defence review announced by Roy Mason at the end of the year made any upwards revisions even less probable, cutting the army from 166,000 in April 1975 to 165,000 the following year, eventually dropping down to 159,000 in 1979.[173] On 21 November the Provisionals detonated bombs in two Birmingham pubs, killing twenty-one people. This followed other dramatic attacks, such as on a coach carrying soldiers and their families in Yorkshire in February, and in two pubs in Guildford in October. After Birmingham a wave of anti-Irish violence washed over England. Thirty factories in the city closed after fights between Irish and English workers broke out.[174] PIRA declared a temporary ceasefire from midnight on 22 December, after sounding out the British government via a group of Protestant clergymen in Feakle, County Clare.[175] The ceasefire was later extended for much of 1975. On 7 January intelligence officer Michael Oatley told PIRA leader Billy McKee that the British government wanted to discuss withdrawal from Northern Ireland.[176]

Earlier accounts often depicted the PIRA decision as deriving from their military weakness. More recent, extensive research persuasively shows that both sides entered negotiations with a genuine wish to explore whether the conflict could be terminated. As time went on, and especially in the aftermath of those negotiations, some of the British participants sought to portray the whole exercise as an elaborate ploy to deceive the Provisionals.[177] HQNI initially expected PIRA to use the time to stockpile ammunition and explosives.[178] Merlyn Rees, the chief constable and the CGS attributed the ceasefire to successful operations by the security forces.[179] The NIO, grappling with understanding an organisation 'both clandestine and Irish', believed PIRA responded to a 'sharp loss of support in the Republican community'.[180] The MOD's intelligence assessment shows the conflicting evidence available to policymakers and, indeed, the multiple sources of the ceasefire:

> According to a reliable report a meeting took place between Seamus Twomey [PIRA chief of staff] and Seamus Costello [INLA chief of staff] on 19 December when the forthcoming ceasefire was discussed. When pressed by Costello as to the reason for the ceasefire Twomey is reported to have replied that it was purely a tactical suspension of hostilities, and that he needed time to regroup and reorganise. Twomey said he hoped for a release of about 200 detainees as they were needed as 'front-line operators'. Twomey and Costello are reported to have agreed to use the ceasefire period to work together jointly on plans for the New Year.... Earlier intelligence shows that while Provisional morale is low and there is a shortage of explosives and particularly of effective manpower, the supply of weapons and ammunition is adequate, and at least some Provisional leaders appear convinced that victory is in sight.[181]

If accurate, the intelligence suggests that the military wing of the Provisional movement aimed to use the ceasefire to recover capabilities and engineer a pragmatic alliance with a new organisation, the Irish National Liberation Army (INLA), which possessed significant assets in personnel, knowledge and weaponry. From an early stage Merlyn Rees informed his cabinet committee colleagues he aimed to avoid 'conceding anything of substance to the Provisionals' or risking a loyalist backlash. Reaching a meaningful settlement was regarded as an outside chance. Rees recognised PIRA's 'remarkable' cohesion, stating 'they are not beaten'.[182] The British government has been admonished for failing to make the ceasefire stick due to 'strong resistance to compromise within its own security forces'.[183] There is certainly evidence for hostility in the army towards the ceasefire, from General King downwards, but this does not mean the security forces destroyed peace on the ground. The basic reason for King's scepticism was a suspicion that PIRA were exploiting the time afforded them to recover from the attrition inflicted by his forces.[184] And in that view he was entirely correct. The British Army benefited from a period of relative calm too.

Early on in the ceasefire officials in the NIO sensed unease in the army. A number of regimental officers were annoyed at complaints made about the army to the incident centres specially set up to defuse tensions. At a more senior level, staff officers struggled with the NIO dominating policy.[185] HQNI's stance reflected the situation on the ground. During the ceasefire's first 100 days there were 83 explosions, another 41 bombs were defused, and there were 492 shootings (105 involving the security forces); 2 members of the security forces were killed and 57 wounded, and 59 civilians were killed, with another 339 injured.[186] Amidst such violence General Leng perceived 'merely a temporary pause in the PIRA campaign'.[187] The NIO suggested the violence 'has become largely a matter of Ulstermen shooting and blowing one another up'.[188]

HQNI was also frustrated by the decline in both tactical intelligence drawn from street patrols and strategic intelligence from the army council, suggesting a source that may have existed earlier on was no longer productive.[189] Merlyn Rees felt sufficiently anxious about military sentiment to invite three soldiers to Stormont, for an article in *Visor: Weekly Report for Soldiers in Northern Ireland*. Corporal Nash asked him, 'Why did you agree to a ceasefire when we were getting on top?' Rees replied, 'The advantage of a ceasefire is that it gives a chance for people to think more clearly than they do in the wake of bombs and killings every day.'[190] Royal Marine officer Rod Boswell recalled that the men in his commando abhorred the ceasefire. At one point a patrol spotted senior PIRA leader Joe Cahill at a house in Andersonstown and were extremely annoyed to be ordered to leave him well alone. The incident 'caused a fairly major morale blip in the unit's feelings'.[191] Resentful obedience to the constraints on tactical operations better characterises the military reaction to the ceasefire than wilful endangerment.

Rising loyalist violence destabilised the situation, making compromises more difficult.[192] The British negotiators repeatedly explained to PIRA the government's inability to declare an intention to withdraw, either publicly or in private, because they feared provoking a civil war. However, this does not mean the ceasefire collapsed due to republican intransigence.[193] The 1975 ceasefire ended because none of the three central belligerents was willing to abandon its core aims. PIRA demanded unification on their terms; the loyalists of the UDA and UVF wished to remain in the union; and the UK government intended to stop war across the British Isles. All three groups found ways to continue applying deadly violence to further their political aims and believed in their own eventual success. The ceasefire gave Merlyn Rees time to 'think more clearly'. At a meeting at Stormont Castle on 12 May he and Sir Frank Cooper heard from all Lisburn's senior generals their ardent desire to go back to war. The Provisionals enjoyed genuine support from only 1 per cent of Catholics, in General King's estimation, and their political aspirations led only to civil war. Intelligence suggested PIRA intended to renew their campaign; the only question was when. He could see no alternative than 'to defeat the PIRA'. Merlyn Rees rather hoped for a 'really fundamental reappraisal of the Government stance ... to avoid getting snarled up again on the old familiar treadmill of violence'. Military strategy appeared to offer nothing new to change the basic dynamics that made the conflict so intractable. The meeting resulted in Merlyn Rees establishing a working group under civil servant John Bourn to review security policy.[194] The committee formalised the government's agenda to give the police primacy, and to criminalise political violence, leaving the army in a more subordinate role.[195] Some impressions from 40 Commando in 1975 captured the appreciation for some respite, however temporary:

> Our emotions when we left Northern Ireland were mixed. Nobody was sorry to leave but everybody will remember it. Soldiering in Northern Ireland is a fascinating but demanding job. We were delighted to see the ceasefire was holding, and that the politicians, for all their wheeling and dealing, had achieved, albeit possibly only temporarily, peace. The people of the Province and in particular of Belfast are tired. Many have lost their self respect, their pride, but now have a chance to regain it. This is shown in little ways: women washing the pavement in front of their houses and caring about refuse in the area because they know that now if they clean their homes they will not be bombed and turned back into a glass and rubbish strewn slum; teenagers getting hysterical over the Bay City Rollers concert instead of over obscene injuries; or simply being able to go shopping in comparative safety.[196]

CONCLUSION

Michael Carver's perception in 1972 that the conflict must continue for a long time yet proved something of a self-fulfilling prophesy. The CGS exercised a domineering hand over military strategy after direct rule in a way not quite so evident before then. His judgement about PIRA's staying power and the army's vulnerability to sagging morale if not carefully attended to left a lasting impression on the strategic configuration.

Once he was promoted to be CDS it was highly unlikely his successor as CGS would overrule the guiding principle that force levels must be brought down. Indeed, General Hunt understood the strains on the army. These came primarily from pay lagging behind inflation and overly frequent deployments to Northern Ireland, not from poor recruitment or political campaigns to bring the army home. Regiments and the MOD put in place measures designed to hold morale steady. As studies on other wars confirm, soldiers are in any case surprisingly resilient to hardship. Despite the occasional shenanigans by General King to get himself more troops, the cross-government and bipartisan consensus on the necessity to stabilise the army as a whole stuck firm.

The lower force level settled the army into a manageable long-war pattern, but meant a diminished capability to tackle loyalism. The threat was known to be increasing for months before the UWC strike in May 1974. Plans for a Protestant uprising made unrealistic assumptions about the UDA's neutrality and the police force's reliability. Although the army on the streets never refused orders to confront the strikers, the MOD intervened effectively to make sure their SoS prevented his counterpart at the NIO from ever issuing such orders. The arrest of twenty-eight UDA, UVF and Red Hand Commando officers by the Light Infantry seems to imply the government's room for manoeuvre against loyalism was much greater than publicly acknowledged. After the strike, ministers and officials cast around for future policy proposals. A distinction must be drawn between the ideological preference common in many Labour Party circles, including with Prime Minister Wilson, for a united Ireland, and the realities of approved government policy. Labour's public flirtation with independence for Northern Ireland encouraged PIRA to cease fire and negotiate, while also sending loyalist groups into panicked preparations for a coming doomsday. Soldiers of high and lowly rank greeted the ceasefire with outrage; others welcomed the break from the usual, dangerous routine. Their opinions ultimately counted for little. Merlyn Rees ignored HQNI's complaints about Provisional rearmament and repair to press ahead with police primacy and criminalisation. The ceasefire ended amidst rising violence between republicans and loyalists, who decided they would not compromise with each other. True to the credo ingrained in their strategic thinking since 1968, the British government continued to hold that only its army prevented the murderous Irish from descending into a civil war of untold horrors. That nightmare of worse to come made the day-to-day suffering in Northern Ireland feel bearable.

CONCLUSION

Histories of wars normally end in victory or defeat. For nearly two decades after 1998, peace settled on Northern Ireland, and only small-minded hair-splitters devoted much attention to proving who won. The British government only really aimed for victory, in the sense of totally defeating the IRA, for less than a year. In 1975 the government gave up trying for a resolution. This book is a history about how a country and its army became entangled in a war they could not bear to lose but were unwilling to pay the price to win. Ministers, their officials and soldiers fretted over what might happen if they stood aside. The debates in 1969 and 1975 were essentially about the same question: would there be a civil war if Britain left the Irish to their own devices? Writings on civil war often seek to comprehend the intensity of violence, and its variation from one time and place to another.[1] Yet efforts to prevent civil war have also left a lingering mark on many societies.[2]

The temptation is to choose between viewing the government's actions as either effective in stopping civil war or deeply counterproductive. In truth, British strategy was paradoxical in its effects: an all-out civil war across the British Isles was avoided, at the cost of engraining a bitter low-level conflict for decades. The sense of responsibility for Northern Ireland was genuine and motivated by real anguish about the human tragedies beamed into British living-rooms on the television news every day. In contrast to other governments facing an uprising, the British never constructed a compelling political vision for the society they dreamed of creating in Northern Ireland. Even the Sunningdale Agreement was sold nervously. Then, as now, the United Kingdom lacked a meaningful governing ideology. British strategy was always about preventing something negative, not about inventing a shared future.

The persistence of deeply pessimistic beliefs about what the Irish might do to each other without supervision cannot be separated from Britain's coming to terms with its demise as a world power. If this all came down to residual colonialism, then the implication is that colonial thinking endures in British strategic thought to the present day. Twenty years' conducting

271

a fighting retreat from empire had to end somewhere. If one part of the United Kingdom departed, then what happened next? Prior to deployment in August 1969 the army had grappled with what the end of empire meant for itself as an institution. When soldiers arrived off the ferry in Belfast they felt themselves to be at home in a normal British city. These twin influences – intellectually winding up the empire, and cultural rapport with Northern Ireland – hamstrung senior officers and soldiers alike in appreciating just how colonial their conduct might seem to those on the receiving end. Indeed, certain military tactics can be labelled colonial in the superficial sense that they had earlier been practised in the colonies. More importantly, strategists transferred ideas about British society to the dilemmas now confronting them. Why did Wilson and then Heath hesitate for so long in suspending Stormont, despite the abundant evidence the system did not want to be reformed to be inclusive of society as a whole? The practical fears of a Protestant backlash were part of the reason. At a deeper level, British politicians wrestled with the idea that a democratic majority might be the problem.

This book has attempted to interweave loyalist political power more systematically into the analysis of British strategy than is often the case. To be precise, judgements have been reached on British perceptions about loyalism on the available evidence. More research is called for on internal loyalist politics in their own right. Strategists feared the violent potential in loyalist groups like the UVF and the UDA, so adjusted their plans to avoid a direct conflict with them. Extensive intelligence reports from multiple agencies, and the JIC's assessments, are necessary for inquiring into whether these decisions were reasonable. Those records remain closed. Until they open, several preliminary conclusions are possible. Loyalists openly threatened the British state to deter unwelcome concessions to nationalists. A degree of ambiguity over the size of the resistance to come possibly accentuated such deterrence. Threats were occasionally made good, to guarantee their credibility. Soldiers fought on the loyalist Shankill in October 1969 and narrowly averted a major clash with the UDA in the summer of 1972. HQNI decided the UDA was too large an enemy to handle. Limited operations were carried out to suppress loyalist groups, especially as they ramped up their killings of Catholics. The army tried to split away a radical minority from the decent majority in loyalism. Unfortunately, this distinction, which normally accorded to a separation between the UVF and the UDA, ignored the latter group's participation in sectarian violence on a significant scale. Though army intelligence knew about the different groups and often their leaders, the understanding of the popular support base for the UDA in particular was extremely poor. These difficulties derived in part from a practical decision taken in 1969 for the army to concentrate on Catholic areas in cities and the police on Protestants. Consequently, the army depended heavily on the police for intelligence about loyalists, and that information was often either lacking or manipulated for political purposes. There are repeated flashes of light onto British alarm about police reliability in the archival record, which undoubtedly informed the sense of extreme caution in responding to loyalist militancy.

Intelligence on republicanism improved over time. Immense resources came to be devoted to piecing together the order of battle, leadership profiles, operational plans and future intentions of PIRA as the main enemy, and OIRA as a capable potential adversary after their ceasefire in 1972. The disastrous meeting between Seán MacStíofáin and Willie Whitelaw in July 1972 closed down the government's appetite for further negotiation, but did not prevent intelligence assessments from reaching more subtle interpretations about the variety of political opinions in the republican movement. Intelligence on PIRA and its exploitation by the army to make arrests, find supply dumps and technically counter the bombing offensive developed to a formidable degree. Nevertheless, the Provisionals displayed creativity beyond bomb technology alone to maintain their offensive, supplementing organisational reforms and geographical dispersion to pose a serious danger to the security forces and the public. The British Army felt especially wrong-footed by the Provisionals' skill at propaganda, and sometimes frustration about this concealed an inability to contest other strengths – such as the movement's logistics system, which seemed to never run short of weapons or bomb materials. Strategists accurately foresaw PIRA's determination to secure their objectives; for their part, the Provisional army council underestimated the British government's resolve and the British public's willingness to ignore suffering in Ireland. When PIRA escalated by killing more soldiers and then bombing England, they reaped a thirst for harsher anti-terrorism measures, not withdrawal.

It is difficult to tell whether officers running the attritional campaign against the Provisionals did not know about the negative effects of their methods, or did not care. Occasional documents suggest HQNI and the MOD realised that destroying PIRA's leadership cadres by regular screening and arrests caused alienation. These arrests effectively shut down entire PIRA units at times, and placed highly capable leaders in custody where they could not plan or conduct attacks. Arrests became more discriminate over time as intelligence correctly determined who should be picked up.

Suspects were watched for weeks or months in order to prepare detailed dossiers proving their involvement in terrorist acts. In the period studied, however, probably around half of those arrested by the security forces ended up being released without criminal charge or being interned. For soldiers on the streets, the men they repeatedly stopped or brought in for questioning deserved little sympathy because they thought them to be either in the IRA or supporting the movement in some way. As with any decapitation strategy the British version assumed leaders removed from battle could not be replaced. The only problem was that they could. There is hardly any reference in the records available to PIRA recruitment. There are probably two reasons. Firstly, the army lacked any obvious alternative to attrition by arrests. How else could PIRA be stopped short of shooting them down in gun-battles? Secondly, HQNI and the NIO got into a protracted dispute about the efficacy of arrests and detention. Some of those lifted by soldiers ended up back on the streets because the police lacked evidence to prosecute them, ministers refused to intern them, or the SoS for Northern Ireland released them after a certain period in internment. The army's wish to imprison as many republicans as possible could not be reconciled with the NIO's need to run down internment to convince nationalists to engage in constitutional politics. Slowly shifting to more criminal prosecutions was the only solution, and it took time.

After the NIO came into existence in 1972 and, alongside it, keener legal scrutiny by the attorney general, the army felt more constrained in the use of force. The uproar over deep interrogation, and pressure from the Irish government, influenced military strategy too. Judging whether Bloody Sunday changed attitudes within the army is challenging because to admit that the events of that day were a mistake, or a crime, was a taboo within the organisation. Edward Heath's obdurate resistance to anything other than a whitewash compounded the harm inflicted by 1st Parachute Regiment, engrained anger towards the British state and prevented the army from learning why soldiers fired, in order to halt such conduct in the future. This book has avoided generalisations about specific regiments because their behaviour varied so widely. The regiment that shot down unarmed protesters in Derry also produced a soldier who gave his life by using his body to shield civilians from a PIRA bomb. Despite carefully worded rules of engagement, pored over by government lawyers and ministers, the regimental system still exerted a powerful force in determining when and how soldiers chose to shoot, or otherwise apply violence. Units in the same city at the same time behaved differently under similar circumstances. More research is required on how regimental cultures interacted with official policy and local conditions to produce variations in violence. Oral histories can open up further knowledge here.

Operating in an environment where the civil courts had jurisdiction over crimes committed against the population weakened officers' responsibility for their soldiers' conduct. In theory, the justice system applied a searchingly independent spotlight and held wrongdoing to account. In practice, the police lent heavily on the military authorities to investigate themselves, although the DPP imposed a more rigorous regime after direct rule. Controversial killings continued to happen after Bloody Sunday and remain under active investigation. The MOD tried to minimise the political fallout from abuses by soldiers by paying off claimants out of court, which protected the army's reputation in Britain, but hardly changed opinions in Northern Ireland. Such practices exemplified the broader desire at the political leadership level to hold the conflict at a distance, to ensure grubby events over the Irish Sea did not infect ordinary parliamentary life. Strategic adaptation only happened with prime ministerial approval and generally depended upon the relations between the prime minister, the defence secretary and the home secretary (to be replaced by the Northern Ireland secretary). The full cabinet rarely participated in the decision-making process. Parliament heard a great many speeches about Northern Ireland. Few had any impact on policy concerning the army. Major changes came with cross-party support from a small coterie of opposition leaders. Wilson and Callaghan, despite their rhetorical favouritism towards nationalists in public, privately gave the Heath government their blessing for a war on the IRA that would encompass negotiation only after victory. At most, Labour in opposition forced the early abandonment of deep interrogation – to the relief of some in the Conservative Party and the army.

Labour and Conservatives shared too an understanding of the burdens the conflict imposed on the army as a collection of human beings. Apart from Heath's fairly minor decision to reconstitute four company-sized battalions back to full strength, neither governing party contemplated expanding the army to cope with the repeated deployments. This is telling. The lesson drawn from Operation Motorman was that such a large-scale expansion in the force level should not be carried out again – despite the strategic pay-off. When Wilson and Rees discussed what to do about the UWC's bid to destroy power-sharing, they never weighed up whether another Motorman should be launched. The MOD had been sending the message, loud and clear for over a year, that the force level must be reduced to avoid any breakdown in morale. The CGS and those around him knew how to see internal trouble from a distance, and resolved to institute preventative measures before discontent turned to mutiny. Further research on the strains brought about by overstretch is required, but the implication for strategy was manifest: loyalism would be allowed to exercise a whip hand. Beset by domestic crises like the coal miners' strike and inflation, and distracted by international priorities such as entry to the EEC, successive governments put Northern Ireland some way down the list of priorities. Within the governing ideology of majoritarian democracy, the woes of 1.5 million people came after the aspirations of the British. In pursuing a limited military strategy in Northern Ireland, the British government avoided the feared all-out civil war by acquiesing in a less intensive conflict rumbling on into the indefinite future.

A NOTE ON SOURCES

Since the 1998 Good Friday Agreement a more relaxed political atmosphere has encouraged participants in the conflict to talk about their experiences, while archival sources have opened up.[1] This book draws upon an unprecedented array of primary sources, including papers on policy-making in London (cabinet, MOD, NIO and Foreign Office files) and military records created by HQNI, brigade staffs and battalions. Regimental archives were consulted in addition to non-military sources, such as the papers of journalists, politicians, clergymen and lobby groups. Records from NATO's archive were scrutinised to assess whether the army was under pressure to limit the forces sent to Northern Ireland. As with all historical research, there are limits to the available sources. At the time of writing, there were just over 900 files covering the years 1966 to 1975 listed on the National Archives catalogue as closed, or retained by a government department, that had the phrase 'Northern Ireland' in the title. There are many hundreds more unavailable with different file titles yet likely to contain relevant information.

The events examined in this book occurred in living memory. Three problems hindered the recruitment of oral-history interviewees. Firstly, after the Bloody Sunday inquiry reported in June 2010, questions began to be asked about whether surviving military participants should be criminally prosecuted. Secondly, in 2011 the Police Service of Northern Ireland launched legal proceedings to obtain recordings made by a Boston College interview programme with former paramilitaries. These tapes contained information about the 1972 murder of Jean McConville in Belfast by the IRA. Over the following few years several high-profile republicans were arrested and questioned.[2] The attendant media coverage was not missed by army veterans. Consequently, the Cardiff University research ethics policy required potential interviewees for this project to be warned that 'the courts or the police may have the power to demand records'.[3] Thirdly, between 2011 and 2013 the author assisted a group of elderly Kenyans in bringing civil claims against the British government for torture during the 1950s Mau

Mau conflict. The case attracted media attention and was referred to on the author's university web page. Understandably, military veterans proved reluctant to talk.

Fifty army museums were contacted because the units they represented served in Northern Ireland during the early 1970s (including the Royal Marines). Some never replied, some stated they possessed no relevant holdings and others refused to assist owing to the conflict's sensitivity. Records from seven military museums are cited in the book. In conversation during a visit to an army museum in 2018, the curator mentioned that veterans on the regimental association's mailing list had been instructed to avoid contact with academics, journalists or lawyers interested in Northern Ireland. On arrival at another museum, the head curator stated hardly any relevant information survived. When she went home early, her more experienced deputy opened the door to a room lined with boxes full of war diaries, intelligence summaries and tour magazines. Elsewhere a curator, a former regimental officer, claimed the collection contained no intelligence papers. When an enthusiastic volunteer interjected to say they did in fact exist, the curator swiftly told him to shut up. The volunteer later said the intelligence records were deliberately removed before my arrival. In May 2021, I contacted a handful of military museums again because there were grounds for believing they held valuable material. One never replied, another admitted they were too stretched to deal with the request, and a third stated that the relevant personal papers and sound recordings in their possession were closed until their creators died. One museum's chairman, who served in Northern Ireland as a junior officer in the 1970s, invited me to visit the museum and speak with him and other veterans about their experiences. Several days later he wrote to say the trustees had unanimously placed a veto on any co-operation, due to deep distrust and resentment over inquiries into the army's conduct.

I initially explored the possibilities for this study during my time teaching at the Joint Services Command and Staff College (JSCSC). At the outset the MOD's Corporate Memory Branch proved helpful. They invited me for discussions in the Main Building in London, including a tour of the shelves holding the top-secret papers that I would never see, and to Portsmouth to digitally photograph files shortly to be released at the National Archives. At one stage, the Branch offered to upgrade my security clearance to read files without repeatedly bothering them. A year later the idea was shelved. After moving to Aberystwyth University in 2012, and my involvement in the Mau Mau case, the MOD became less obliging. In 2012–13 the Corporate Memory Branch was abolished as part of the government's austerity reforms.[4] Further attempts to find willing military partners failed, proving how 'Of all the potential influences on government, academics are amongst the easiest to ignore as there are no obvious political costs to doing so.'[5]

Freedom of Information Act requests were made from May 2014 for records held by the cabinet office, the Foreign and Commonwealth Office, the Home Office, the MOD, the National Archives, the NIO, and the Public Records Office of Northern Ireland (PRONI). Out of forty-eight files asked for, fifteen were released in full, nine released with sections redacted and twenty-three withheld; one file was lost. As Owen Thomas notes, the Freedom of Information Act is an imperfect instrument, which grants the government considerable latitude to decide what constitutes the 'national interest'.[6] In August 2022 the government decided to replace the cabinet office's 'Clearing House' for co-ordinating Freedom of Information Act responses across Whitehall, following controversy over its efforts to control releases to individuals deemed problematic.[7] One Freedom of Information (FOI) request for this book was rejected on the grounds that the file comprised about thirty chapters plus annexes, and so exceeded the £600 processing limit imposed by the Act.[8] My request for the contents page, to allow a more precise request to be submitted, was met with the response that the document contained none.[9] The file was released to the National Archives several years later without my being informed. It has detailed contents pages. Yet over these same years the ministry has released a large number of Northern Ireland files to the National Archives.

A significant omission is the papers created by the Security Service: MI5 produced assessments on the loyalist threat, and on subversion within the armed forces. These aspects of the conflict are likely to remain hidden for decades to come. The cabinet office declined an FOI request to open the JIC's Northern Ireland assessments written between January 1972 and October 1973.[10] When requesting an internal review of the decision, I asked whether releasing even a single sentence of these reports would endanger national security. The cabinet office turned down the review, stating: 'trying to sanitise these files is not a viable option ... if we were to identify isolated sentences that could be released, this information would be taken out of context and its meaning would be lost'.[11] There are hundreds of MOD documents in the National Archives where words, sentences, paragraphs or pages have been redacted to protect national security. For the cabinet office, such an approach is inconceivable.

After the manuscript's completion, copyright holders were asked for permission to cite their materials in the book. All agreed apart from one – an army museum from whose papers thirty-nine sources were cited. An email to them in July 2022 prompted a panicked response. During one of my research trips the archivist had, by mistake, apparently given me full access to photograph their collections. The regiment sought guidance from the Army Operational Legal Branch, fearing that the excerpts to be printed in the book might lead to veterans being prosecuted. In the United Kingdom only organisations formally designated as 'Places of Deposit' are expected to adhere to the Public Records Act in making their archives available to the public. Out of 144 army museums, only 11 operate under the Places of Deposit rules.[12] The museum in question was not one of them.

In August 2022 the Army Historical Branch warned museum directors that they:

> should not be holding any public records created by the Army or wider Defence after 1958. Any Army/Defence record created at public expense is a 'public record' subject to the Public Records Act, 1958 (PRA). To lawfully hold public records a museum must be a designated place of deposit . . . it is important that no member of the public is allowed access to any public records which are protectively marked . . . particular care should be taken with any material that relates to Northern Ireland.[13]

In September the museum informed me that the thirty-nine sources fell into three categories: those owned by the museum, those now due to be transferred to the MOD for processing and those duplicating documents already held at the National Archives but withheld from public inspection. The museum granted permission for the five excerpts belonging to them to be used in the book. The Army Historical Branch and the MOD Records Transfer Manager declined invitations to meet and discuss the remaining documents. The head of the Army Historical Branch claimed his organisation implemented the Public Records Act in a perfectly reasonable fashion.[14] This assertion was somewhat undermined by the Branch having to survey all army museums in autumn 2022 to find out whether they (illegally) held public records, and to provide special training sessions for curators.[15]

Given the army's unwillingness to discuss what to do about the archival records already in my possession, I submitted Freedom of Information Act requests in early September 2022 to the MOD and the National Archives, setting out precisely which sentences were required from which documents. Attached to the requests were digital photographs of the documents so there could be no confusion. The MOD replied on 11 October (the statutory deadline was on 7 October) to say 'we will have a response with you shortly'.[16] A formal complaint to the ministry finally produced a substantive answer on 17 November. They declined to provide the information because my request paraphrased what the documents said. The FOI team advised the application be resubmitted with reference to specific serial numbers or paragraphs.[17] These details were all listed in the original request. The last FOI request to the MOD before this one, for a report from 1972, elicited a response after nineteen months. The ministry sent a document from 1988.[18] After invoking a ten-day extension to the request for the documents in their possession, the National Archives stated they needed another month to reach a decision because the documents might endanger the safety of an individual. When asked if they would simply redact the four names mentioned in the documents, the National Archives ignored the question, said they had a long backlog and intimated another month's delay might be in the pipeline – which indeed it was.[19]

What is the purpose of such obstruction? The documents being suppressed shed light on one battalion's activities. In May and June 1970 they show the battalion meeting frequently with Catholic and Protestant community groups in Belfast. Officers listened to their concerns and sought to defuse tensions. On several occasions these groups praised the battalion's efforts. As violence spread, the battalion received orders to act with restraint and only open fire at specific targets after issuing warnings, when soldiers faced serious injury or death. The records also discuss the threat posed by loyalist groups, PIRA tactics and how three warnings were issued before a man was shot dead in July 1970 (existing accounts refer to two warnings). In sum the material portrays a battalion seeking to understand the people of Belfast, to get along with them and to protect them where possible. No individual is incriminated. Of the remaining thirty-four excerpts, five have been replaced in the book with information from other sources; twenty-nine have been deleted. These small figures say much about the army's aversion to external scrutiny. Always an insular institution, the army has become less susceptible to researchers' curiosity in recent years. In 2005 the MOD introduced a Research Ethics Committee to approve all projects involving serving personnel. Whether intentional or not, one effect has been to hinder research.[20] Former army officers Mike Martin and Simon Akam fought official opposition to getting their books on the war in Afghanistan published – in Martin's case, even though the army had commissioned the research.[21] While this book has been written in the face of official indifference or hostility, another scholar has composed an in-house volume for the MOD.[22] The British Army recognises that the Northern Ireland conflict remains relevant today; in some circles, the history is judged too raw to be opened up for wider discussion. What such a view ignores is that the army belongs to the British people, who will seek answers about the past, whether the institution likes it or not.

Acknowledgements

This book could not have been written without the generosity of many people. Above all, loving thanks are due to Claudia, Lina and Orla for their inspiration and support. Dianne, Stephen, Carys, John, Debra, Hermann, Maria, Sabine, Heinz, Sarah, Niels, Viktoria, Pia, Amelie, Stephie and Sebastian provided crucial support. Richard English has been a source of advice and encouragement throughout the project, and his warning that it might take rather longer than expected turned out to be entirely accurate. Ed Burke, Thomas Leahy and David Morgan-Owen went beyond the bounds of reasonable assistance in reading the entire manuscript; their comments have improved it in innumerable ways.

I am grateful to the following people for their help in writing the book: David Anderson, Pierre Asselin, Victoria Basham, Matthew Congreve, Rory Cormac, Patricia Coyle, Tony Craig, Pete Dorey, Aaron Edwards, Matthew Ford, Roel Frakking, David French, Robert Gerwarth, Jacqueline Hazelton, R. Gerald Hughes, Matthew Hughes, Branwen Gruffydd Jones, Rachel Kowalski, Nigel de Lee, Brian McAllister Linn, Bart Luttikhuis, Paul MacDonald, Tom Maguire, Ian McBride, Kieran McEvoy, Patrick Porter, Sergey Radchenko, Michael Rainsborough, Peter Romijn, Sibylle Scheipers, Sir Hew Strachan, Martin Thomas, Natalya Vince, Jason Whitelegg and Thijs Brocades Zaalberg. Several former soldiers kindly spoke to me anonymously at a formative stage in the project. Thanks go to my students for indulging my endless digressions on the topic. Michael Watson at Cambridge University Press believed in the project from the outset, has been exceptionally patient with delays and enhanced the final product in many ways. Thanks to Emily Plater, Laura Simmons and Preethika Ramalingam for getting the book into print, and to Christopher Jackson for his heroic efforts in making the text readable.

Ideas for the book were tested out on audiences at the universities of Birmingham, Brunel, Cambridge, Cardiff, Cork, Dublin (UCD), Exeter, Leiden, Northampton, Nottingham, Oxford and St Andrews; at the Institute of Historical Research (London), the JSCSC, the Netherlands

Defence Academy, the Rosscarbery Historical Society, the Royal Military Academy Sandhurst and the United States Naval War College; and to conferences of the Political Studies Association of Ireland, the Political Studies Association (UK) and the Society for Military History. Thanks go to the organisers, and to the audiences for their views.

Funding to undertake the research for this book was generously provided by a British Academy Mid-Career Fellowship, Cardiff University, a Leverhulme Trust Research Fellowship, the Scouloudi Foundation, and during a period spent at the Netherlands Institute for Advanced Study in the Humanities and Social Sciences, in Amsterdam. Thank you to the librarians and archivists at the following institutions, whose assistance has been invaluable: the Airborne Assault Museum, the Bodleian Library, the British Library, Cardiff University Library, the Hobson Library at the JSCSC, the Imperial War Museum, the King's Own Scottish Borderers Regimental Museum, the Labour History Archive and Study Centre at the People's History Museum, the Lancashire Infantry Museum, the Liddell Hart Centre for Military Archives at King's College London, the Linen Hall Library, the London School of Economics and Political Science Library, the National Archives of the United Kingdom, the NATO Archives, the Public Records Office of Northern Ireland, the Royal Electrical and Mechanical Engineers Museum, the Royal Hampshire Regiment Museum, the Royal Marines Museum (now at the National Museum of the Royal Navy), the Royal Regiment of Fusiliers Museum (Royal Warwickshire), the Royal Scots Regimental Museum, Shropshire Archives and the West Sussex Record Office.

An earlier version of some material in Chapter 1 was published as 'Escaping the Empire's Shadow: British Military Thinking about Insurgency on the eve of the Northern Ireland Troubles', in Martin Thomas and Gareth Curless (eds.), *Decolonization and Conflict: Colonial Comparisons and Legacies* (London: Bloomsbury, 2017), 229–46. The following institutions and individuals have kindly given permission to quote from material to which they own the copyright: the Liddell Hart Centre for Military Archives at King's College London, the Bodleian Library, the Conservative Party Archive, the Trustees of The Duke of Lancaster's Regiment – Lancashire Infantry Museum, the Royal Regiment of Fusiliers Museum (Royal Warwickshire), the Museum of The Royal Dragoon Guards, the National Museum of the Royal Navy, the London School of Economics and Political Science Library, the Soldiers of Shropshire Museum, the Labour Party, Mr R. W. Coleman, the Trustees of The Royal Hampshire Regiment Trust, the NATO Archives, the Hobson Library at the JSCSC, the

West Sussex Record Office, the Imperial War Museum, the Royal Scots Regimental Museum and the Trustees of The King's Own Scottish Borderers Association. Thanks to Nick van der Bijl and Peter Wood for permission to reproduce the maps, originally published in Nick van der Bijl, *Operation Banner: The British Army in Northern Ireland 1969–2007* (Barnsley: Pen and Sword, 2009).

Notes

INTRODUCTION

1. British Army, *Operation Banner: An Analysis of Military Operations in Northern Ireland. Army Code 71842* (London: Ministry of Defence, 2006), para 105.
2. The Imperial War Museum opened its first major temporary exhibition on the Troubles in May 2023, entitled 'Northern Ireland: Living with the Troubles'.
3. P. Thane, *Divided Kingdom: A History of Britain, 1900 to the Present* (Cambridge: Cambridge University Press, 2018), 301.
4. M. Conway and R. Gerwarth, 'Europe's Age of Civil Wars? An Introduction', *Journal of Modern European History*, 20/4 (2022), 443; see also: R. Bourke, 'Introduction', in Richard Bourke and Ian McBride (eds.), *The Princeton History of Modern Ireland* (Princeton: Princeton University Press, 2016), 14; N. Sambanis, 'What Is Civil War? Conceptual and Empirical Complexities of an Operational Definition', *Journal of Conflict Resolution*, 48/6 (2004), 814–58.
5. Marine Goulds, '67 Days to Go', *The Globe and Laurel: The Journal of the Royal Marines*, 83/5 (1974), 269.
6. P. Porter, 'Last Charge of the Knights? Iraq, Afghanistan and the Special Relationship', *International Affairs*, 86/2 (2010), 365.
7. C. Mills and D. Torrance, *Investigation of Former Armed Forces Personnel Who Served in Northern Ireland* (London: House of Commons Library, 2020), 6.
8. A. Sanders, '"Attempting to Deal with the Past": Historical Inquiries, Legacy Prosecutions, and Operation Banner', *Small Wars and Insurgencies*, 32/4–5 (2021), 789–811.
9. 'Aidan McAnespie Killing: Ex-soldier Holden Avoids Jail over Troubles Shooting', BBC News, 3 February 2023, accessed 6 February 2023 at: https://www.bbc.co.uk/news/uk-northern-ireland-64499374.
10. A. Jackson, 'Irish History in the Twentieth and Twenty-First Centuries', in A. Jackson (ed.), *The Oxford Handbook of Modern Irish History* (Oxford: Oxford University Press, 2014), 9–10.
11. See further in A Note on Sources.
12. J. Chartres, 'Home Secretary Says IRA May Never Be Totally Eliminated', *The Times*, 16 December 1971, 2.

13. M. Sutton, *An Index of Deaths from the Conflict in Ireland* (1994/2018), electronic version at: https://cain.ulster.ac.uk/sutton/tables/Year.html

14. R. K. Betts, 'Is Strategy an Illusion?', *International Security*, 25/2 (2000), 5.

15. R. Bourke, 'Languages of Conflict and the Northern Ireland Troubles', *Journal of Modern History*, 83/3 (2011), 544–78.

16. L. Freedman, *Strategy: A History* (Oxford: Oxford University Press, 2013), xii.

17. J. Stone, *Military Strategy: The Politics and Technique of War* (London: Continuum, 2011), 4.

18. M. L. R. Smith, *Fighting for Ireland? The Military Strategy of the Irish Republican Movement* (London: Routledge, 1997); R. English, *Armed Struggle: The History of the IRA* (London: Pan, 2012).

19. N. Silove, 'Beyond the Buzzword: The Three Meanings of "Grand Strategy"', *Security Studies*, 27/1 (2018), 27–57.

20. P. Neumann, *Britain's Long War: British Strategy in the Northern Ireland Conflict, 1969–98* (Basingstoke: Palgrave Macmillan, 2003).

21. The National Archives [hereafter TNA] WO 305/4398: Lieutenant A. J. Davies, 'Reflections on Belfast 1972', *Belfast Bulletin. Newsletter of First Battalion the Royal Regiment of Wales in Belfast* (c. July 1972).

22. J. Newsinger, 'From Counter-Insurgency to Internal Security: Northern Ireland 1969–1992', *Small Wars and Insurgencies*, 6/1 (1995), 90; C. Kennedy-Pipe, *The Origins of the Present Troubles in Northern Ireland* (London: Longman, 1997), 54; P. Dixon, '"Hearts and Minds"? British Counter-Insurgency Strategy in Northern Ireland', *Journal of Strategic Studies*, 32/3 (2009), 445; A. Edwards, 'Misapplying Lessons Learned? Analysing the Utility of British Counterinsurgency Strategy in Northern Ireland, 1971–76', *Small Wars and Insurgencies*, 21/2 (2010), 312; A. Alderson, 'Britain', in T. Rid and T. Keaney (eds.), *Understanding Counterinsurgency: Doctrine, Operations, and Challenges* (London: Routledge, 2010), 39; D. Porch, *Counterinsurgency: Exposing the Myths of the New Way of War* (Cambridge: Cambridge University Press, 2013), 282; B. W. Morgan and M. L. R. Smith, 'Northern Ireland and Minimum Force: The Refutation of a Concept?', *Small Wars and Insurgencies*, 27/1 (2016), 100; quotation from: D. Benest, 'Aden to Northern Ireland', in H. Strachan (ed.), *Big Wars and Small Wars: The British Army and the Lessons of War in the Twentieth Century* (London: Routledge, 2006), 137.

23. T. Hennessey, *The Evolution of the Troubles 1970–72* (Dublin: Irish Academic Press, 2007).

24. For a critique: M. Sageman, 'The Stagnation in Terrorism Research', *Terrorism and Political Violence*, 26/4 (2014), 565–80.

25. H. Patterson, 'The British State and the Rise of the IRA, 1969–71: The View from the Conway Hotel', *Irish Political Studies*, 23/4 (2008), 509.

26. S. Prince and G. Warner, 'The IRA and Its Rivals: Political Competition and the Turn to Violence in the Early Troubles', *Contemporary British History* 27/3 (2013), 271–96.

27. A. Sanders and I. S. Wood, *Times of Troubles: Britain's War in Northern Ireland* (Edinburgh: Edinburgh University Press, 2012), 253.

28. W. B. Smith, *The British State and the Northern Ireland Crisis, 1969–73: From Violence to Power Sharing* (Washington, DC: United States Institute of Peace Press, 2011).

29. C. Tuck, 'Northern Ireland and the British Approach to Counter-Insurgency', *Defense and Security Analysis*, 23/2 (2007), 167; R. Thornton, 'Getting It Wrong: The Crucial Mistakes Made in the Early Stages of the British Army's Deployment to Northern Ireland (August 1969 to March 1972)', *Journal of Strategic Studies*, 30/1 (2007), 77; A. Edwards, '"A Whipping Boy If Ever There Was One"? The British Army and the Politics of Civil–Military Relations in Northern Ireland, 1969–79', *Contemporary British History*, 28/2 (2014), 170.

30. D. Richards, *Taking Command* (London: Headline, 2014), 78–9.

31. B. Jackson and D. Bramall, *The Chiefs: The Story of the United Kingdom Chiefs of Staff* (London: Brassey's, 1992), 375.

32. Joint Services Command and Staff College Library [hereafter JSCSC]: Army Staff Course 1971, 'Paraphrase of Brief for Incoming Units for IS Operations in Northern Ireland. Part 3. Operations'.

33. E. Burke, 'Counter-Insurgency against "Kith and Kin"? The British Army in Northern Ireland, 1970–76', *Journal of Imperial and Commonwealth History*, 43/4 (2015), 658–77.

34. R. English, 'The Interplay of Non-violent and Violent Action in Northern Ireland, 1967–72', in A. Roberts and T. Garton Ash (eds.), *Civil Resistance and Power Politics: The Experience of Non-violent Action from Gandhi to the Present* (Oxford: Oxford University Press, 2011), 76.

35. H. Strachan, 'The Lost Meaning of Strategy', *Survival*, 47/3 (2005), 33–54.

36. M. Hobkirk, 'Defence Organisation and Defence Policy Making in the UK and the USA', in L. Martin (ed.), *The Management of Defence* (London: Macmillan, 1976), 10.

37. Pioneering studies by Niall Ó Dochartaigh and Stuart Aveyard underscore how important disputes within government could be; this book applies their insight to a more in-depth examination of the military realm. N. Ó Dochartaigh, 'Bloody Sunday: Error or Design?', *Contemporary British History*, 24/1 (2010), 89–108; S. C. Aveyard, *No Solution: The Labour Government and the Northern Ireland Conflict, 1974–79* (Manchester: Manchester University Press, 2016).

38. B. M. Linn, *The Echo of Battle: The Army's Way of War* (London: Harvard University Press, 2007), 5.

39. J. P. Kiszely, 'The Relevance of History to the Military Profession: A British View', in W. Murray and R. H. Sinnreich (eds.), *The Past as Prologue: The Importance of History to the Military Profession* (Cambridge: Cambridge University Press, 2006), 24.

40. D. A. Charters, *Whose Mission, Whose Orders? British Civil–Military Command and Control in Northern Ireland, 1968–1974* (London: McGill-Queen's University Press, 2017), 7.

41. On contingency, see: R. English, *Does Terrorism Work?* (Oxford: Oxford University Press, 2016), 137; D. Morgan-Owen, 'History and the Perils of Grand Strategy', *Journal of Modern History*, 92 (2020), 352–3.

42. I. McBride, 'The Shadow of the Gunman: Irish Historians and the IRA', *Journal of Contemporary History*, 46/3 (2011), 701.

43. A. J. Echevarria, *Clausewitz and Contemporary War* (Oxford: Oxford University Press, 2007), 6, 86.

44. H. Strachan, 'Strategy in Theory; Strategy in Practice', *Journal of Strategic Studies*, 42/2 (2019), 171–90.

45. M. L. R. Smith and D. M. Jones, *The Political Impossibility of Modern Counterinsurgency: Strategic Problems, Puzzles, and Paradoxes* (New York: Columbia University Press, 2015).

46. T. Leahy, *The Intelligence War against the IRA* (Cambridge: Cambridge University Press, 2020), 8.

47. M. Mulholland, 'Political Violence', in R. Bourke and I. McBride (eds.), *The Princeton History of Modern Ireland* (Princeton: Princeton University Press, 2016), 397.

48. H. Strachan, *The Politics of the British Army* (Oxford: Oxford University Press, 1997).

49. B. Brodie, *War and Politics* (London: Macmillan, 1973).

50. M. Grant and B. Ziemann (eds.), *Understanding the Imaginary War: Culture, Thought and Nuclear Conflict, 1945–90* (Manchester: Manchester University Press, 2016).

51. H. Strachan, 'Operational Art and Britain, 1909–2009', in J. A. Olsen and M. van Creveld (eds.), *The Evolution of Operational Art: From Napoleon to the Present* (Oxford: Oxford University Press, 2010), 117.

52. S. Moody, *Imagining Nuclear War in the British Army, 1945–1989* (Oxford: Oxford University Press, 2020), 1, 5, 22–53.

53. C. von Clausewitz, *On War*. Trans. M. Howard and P. Paret (Princeton: Princeton University Press, 1976).

54. T. C. Schelling, 'Bargaining, Communication, and Limited War', *Journal of Conflict Resolution*, 1/1 (1957), 19.

55. TNA DEFE 24/1919: 'Op Banner. Post Tour Report – 21 Engr Regt', 22 November 1971.

56. T. C. Schelling, *The Strategy of Conflict* (London: Harvard University Press, 1960), 5, 53.

57. E. Burke, *An Army of Tribes: British Army Cohesion, Deviancy and Murder in Northern Ireland* (Liverpool: Liverpool University Press, 2018), 64.

58. M. L. R. Smith and P. Neumann, 'Motorman's Long Journey: Changing the Strategic Setting in Northern Ireland', *Contemporary British History*, 19/4 (2005), 413–35.

59. S. Wall, *The Official History of Britain and the European Community: Volume II, From Rejection to Referendum, 1963–1975* (Abingdon: Routledge, 2013).

60. N. Ó Dochartaigh, 'Northern Ireland since 1920', in R. Bourke and I. McBride (eds.), *The Princeton History of Modern Ireland* (Princeton: Princeton University Press, 2016), 142.

61. No author, 'The 3rd Battalion Letter', *The Royal Green Jackets Chronicle 1974: An Annual Record*, 9 (1974), 78–88.

62. S. Bruce, *The Red Hand: Protestant Paramilitaries in Northern Ireland* (Oxford: Oxford University Press, 1992), 55.

63. S. Nelson, *Ulster's Uncertain Defenders: Protestant Political, Paramilitary and Community Groups and the Northern Ireland Conflict* (Syracuse, NY: Syracuse University Press, 1984), 63, 120.

64. Mulholland, 'Political Violence', 398.

65. LSE Library, Merlyn Rees papers: MERLYN-REES/1/5: Transcripts of tapes on Northern Ireland, 24 November 1974.

66. J. Shy and T. W. Collier, 'Revolutionary War', in P. Paret (ed.), *Makers of Modern Strategy: From Machiavelli to the Nuclear Age* (Oxford: Clarendon Press, 1986), 815–62.

67. J. Bowyer Bell, *IRA Tactics and Targets* (Dublin: Poolbeg Press, 1990), 116; P. Finnegan, 'Professionalization of a Nonstate Actor: A Case Study of the Provisional IRA', *Armed Forces and Society*, 45/2 (2019), 349–67.

68. TNA WO 32/21782: 'Notes on Catholic Communities in Belfast and Londonderry', report by R. J. Heagerty, HQ Northern Ireland, December 1973.

1 BAGGAGE

1. Royal Regiment of Fusiliers Museum (Royal Warwickshire): David Barzilay and Michael Murray, *Four Months in Winter* (Belfast: 2nd Battalion, Royal Regiment of Fusiliers, 1972), 7.

2. Linn, *The Echo of Battle*, 3, 234.

3. B. O'Leary, *A Treatise on Northern Ireland, Volume I: Colonialism* (Oxford: Oxford University Press, 2019), 106–8, 145.

4. L. Freedman, *The Future of War: A History* (London: Allen Lane, 2017), xix.

5. L. Scarman, *Violence and Civil Disturbances in Northern Ireland in 1969: Report of Tribunal of Inquiry*. Cmnd. 566 (Belfast: Her Majesty's Stationery Office, 1972). For views on whether the intervention should be judged as welcome, too late or irrelevant see, respectively: J. Whyte, *Interpreting Northern Ireland* (Oxford: Clarendon Press, 1990), 145; P. Rose, *How the Troubles Came to Northern Ireland* (Basingstoke: Macmillan, 2000), xiv; P. Dorey, 'From Indifference to Intervention: Labour and Northern Ireland', in P. Dorey (ed.), *The Labour Governments 1964–1970* (London: Routledge, 2006), 262. See also the well-documented study: T. Hennessey, *Northern Ireland: The Origins of the Troubles* (Dublin: Gill and Macmillan, 2005).

6. Thornton, 'Getting It Wrong', 73–107; A. Edwards, 'Misapplying Lessons Learned?', 303–30. For a fuller treatment of the themes explored in this section,

see: H. Bennett, 'Escaping the Empire's Shadow: British Military Thinking about Insurgency on the Eve of the Northern Ireland Troubles', in M. Thomas and G. Curless (eds.), *Decolonization and Conflict: Colonial Comparisons and Legacies* (London: Bloomsbury, 2017), 229–46.

7. N. Ó Dochartaigh, *From Civil Rights to Armalites: Derry and the Birth of the Irish Troubles* (Basingstoke: Palgrave Macmillan, 2005), 138.

8. Benest, 'Aden to Northern Ireland', 128.

9. A. Mumford, *The Counter-Insurgency Myth: The British Experience of Irregular Warfare* (London: Routledge, 2012), 95; D. H. Ucko and R. Egnell, *Counterinsurgency in Crisis: Britain and the Challenges of Modern Warfare* (New York: Columbia University Press, 2013), 14.

10. T. R. Mockaitis, *British Counterinsurgency in the Post-Imperial Era* (Manchester: Manchester University Press, 1995), 98, 140.

11. P. Bew and H. Patterson, *The British State and the Ulster Crisis* (London: Verso, 1985), 143.

12. S. Howe, *Ireland and Empire: Colonial Legacies in Irish History and Culture* (Oxford: Oxford University Press, 2002), 7–9, 169–70.

13. T. Rid, 'The Nineteenth-Century Origins of Counterinsurgency Doctrine', *Journal of Strategic Studies*, 33/5 (2010), 727–58.

14. D. French, *The British Way in Counter-Insurgency, 1945–1967* (Oxford: Oxford University Press, 2011), 201–7.

15. A. Sanders, 'Northern Ireland: The Intelligence War 1969–75', *British Journal of Politics and International Relations*, 13/2 (2010), 233; J. Bew, 'Mass, Methods, and Means: The Northern Ireland "Model" of Counter-Insurgency', in C. W. Gventer, D. M. Jones and M. L. R. Smith (eds.), *The New Counter-Insurgency Era in Critical Perspective* (Basingstoke: Palgrave Macmillan, 2014), 160; Mockaitis, *British Counterinsurgency*, 137; G. Bulloch, 'The Development of Doctrine for Counter Insurgency – The British Experience', *British Army Review*, 111 (1995), 23.

16. TNA WO 279/649: *Land Operations. Volume III – Counter Revolutionary Operations. Part 1 – Principles and General Aspects*. Army Code No. 70516 (Part 1), 29 August 1969, 41, 45, 69, 85, 100, 119–30.

17. TNA WO 279/650: *Land Operations. Volume III – Counter Revolutionary Operations. Part 2 – Internal Security*. Army Code No. 70516 (Part 2), 26 November 1969.

18. B. Bond, *The Victorian Army and the Staff College 1854–1914* (London: Methuen, 1972), 3.

19. JSCSC: Army Staff Course 1966, volume 1; Staff College Outline Programme 1966.

20. JSCSC: Army Staff Course 1967, volume 5; 'Overseas Operations 1. An introduction to the series.'

21. JSCSC: Army Staff Course 1969, Provisional Programme Third Term.

22. JSCSC: Army Staff Course 1967, supplementary records; 'Annex B to Geopolitical Studies 3. Recommended books.'

23. R. Drayton, 'Masked Condominia: Pan-European Collaboration in the History of Imperialism, c. 1500 to the Present', *Global History Review*, 5 (2012), 308–31.

24. J. Hyslop, 'The Invention of the Concentration Camp: Cuba, Southern Africa and the Philippines, 1896–1907', *South African Historical Journal* 63/2 (2011), 251–76.

25. P. Paret, *French Revolutionary Warfare from Indochina to Algeria: The Analysis of a Political and Military Doctrine* (London: Pall Mall Press, 1964), 7; M. P. M. Finch, 'A Total War of the Mind: The French Theory of *la guerre révolutionnaire*, 1954–1958', *War in History*, 25/3 (2018), 416–18.

26. É. Tenenbaum, 'Beyond National Styles: Towards a Connected History of Cold War Counterinsurgency', in B. Heuser and E. Shamir (eds.), *Insurgencies and Counterinsurgencies: National Styles and Strategic Cultures* (Cambridge: Cambridge University Press, 2016), 313–31.

27. JSCSC: *Quelling Insurgency*, JSP 1, Supplement (QI), Joint Warfare Committee, 1 January 1965, iv, 3–3, 3–4, 3–5.

28. TNA WO 279/649: *Land Operations. Volume III – Counter Revolutionary Operations. Part 1*, 1–2, 119–30.

29. TNA WO 279/649: *Land Operations. Volume III – Counter Revolutionary Operations. Part 1*, 130.

30. TNA WO 279/649: *Land Operations. Volume III – Counter Revolutionary Operations. Part 1*, 14.

31. JSCSC: Army Staff Course 1966, volume 12; 'DS Notes to Problem 5.b.'

32. TNA WO 279/650: *Land Operations. Volume III – Counter Revolutionary Operations. Part 2*, 1–3, 13, 75–7.

33. S. Stockwell, 'Britain and Decolonization in an Era of Global Change', in M. Thomas and A. Thompson (eds.), *The Oxford Handbook of the Ends of Empire* (Oxford: Oxford University Press, 2017), 35.

34. Alderson, 'Britain', 39; Burke, *An Army of Tribes*, 64.

35. Mockaitis, *British Counterinsurgency*, 7–8; Mumford, *The Counter-Insurgency Myth*, 94.

36. F. Klose, *Human Rights in the Shadow of Colonial Violence: The Wars of Independence in Kenya and Algeria* (Philadelphia: University of Pennsylvania Press, 2013).

37. M. Thomas and A. Thompson, 'Empire and Globalisation: From "High Imperialism" to Decolonisation', *The International History Review*, 36/1 (2014), 158.

38. A. Thompson, 'Humanitarian Principles Put to the Test: Challenges to Humanitarian Action during Decolonization', *International Review of the Red Cross*, 97 (2015), 57–8, 66.

39. D. French, *Fighting EOKA: The British Counter-Insurgency Campaign on Cyprus, 1955–1959* (Oxford: Oxford University Press, 2015), 194–236.

40. B. Drohan, *Brutality in an Age of Human Rights: Activism and Counterinsurgency at the End of the British Empire* (London: Cornell University Press, 2017), 4–5.

41. JSCSC: Army Staff Course 1967, volume 5; 'Overseas Operations 2. Internal Security. DS Notes.'
42. JSCSC: Army Staff Course 1966, volume 12; 'Exercise Snake Bite. DS Notes to Problem 2'; 'DS Notes to Problem 3'; 'DS Notes to Problem 4'.
43. P. de la Billière, 'The Changing Pattern of Guerrilla Warfare', *RUSI Journal*, 114/656 (1969), 42–4.
44. D. Killingray, 'Race and Rank in the British Army in the Twentieth Century', *Ethnic and Racial Studies*, 10/3 (1987), 282–3.
45. J. Beale, 'Racism "Prevalent" in the Armed Forces, Ombudsman Warns', BBC News, 19 December 2019, accessed 22 July 2020 at: www.bbc.com/news/uk-50834217.
46. M. Mulholland, *The Longest War: Northern Ireland's Troubled History* (Oxford: Oxford University Press, 2002), 1–66.
47. Whyte, *Interpreting Northern Ireland*, 23.
48. R. Rose, *Governing without Consensus: An Irish Perspective* (London: Faber and Faber, 1971), 97.
49. K. Bloomfield, *Stormont in Crisis: A Memoir* (Belfast: The Blackstaff Press, 1994), 97.
50. J. Ruane and J. Todd, *The Dynamics of Conflict in Northern Ireland: Power, Conflict and Emancipation* (Cambridge: Cambridge University Press, 1996), 92–3.
51. J. Todd, 'Two Traditions in Unionist Political Culture', *Irish Political Studies*, 2/1 (1987), 11–17.
52. M. Mulholland, *Northern Ireland at the Crossroads: Ulster Unionism in the O'Neill Years 1960–9* (Basingstoke: Macmillan, 2000), 2, 9–11, 26, 34, 57.
53. Rose, *How the Troubles Came to Northern Ireland*, 64.
54. Rose, *Governing without Consensus*, 189, 192–3, 213.
55. Ibid., 101.
56. B. Purdie, *Politics in the Streets: The Origins of the Civil Rights Movement in Northern Ireland* (Belfast: The Blackstaff Press, 1990), 2, 14–15, 82–4, 117, 133.
57. L. K. Donohue, 'Regulating Northern Ireland: The Special Powers Acts, 1922–1972', *The Historical Journal*, 41/4 (1998), 1090–3, 1113–14.
58. G. Walker, *A History of the Ulster Unionist Party* (Manchester: Manchester University Press, 2004), 163.
59. C. Hewitt, 'Catholic Grievances, Catholic Nationalism and Violence in Northern Ireland during the Civil Rights Period: A Reconsideration', *British Journal of Sociology*, 32/3 (1981), 364–5, 367.
60. D. O'Hearn, 'Catholic Grievances, Catholic Nationalism: A Comment', *British Journal of Sociology*, 34/3 (1983), 440–1.
61. Ruane and Todd, *The Dynamics of Conflict in Northern Ireland*, 155.
62. L. Bosi, 'Explaining the Emergence Process of the Civil Rights Protest in Northern Ireland (1945–1968): Insights from a Relational Social Movement Approach', *Journal of Historical Sociology*, 21/2–3 (2008), 258–9.
63. Lord Cameron, *Disturbances in Northern Ireland: Report of the Commission Appointed by the Governor of Northern Ireland*. Cmd. 532 (Belfast: Her Majesty's Stationery Office,

1969), para 14, accessed 21 August 2015 at: http://cain.ulst.ac.uk/hmso/cameron.htm#contentsCameron.

64. Ruane and Todd, *The Dynamics of Conflict in Northern Ireland*, 155.

65. S. Bruce, *The Edge of the Union: The Ulster Loyalist Political Vision* (Oxford: Oxford University Press, 1994), 54.

66. S. Bruce, *Paisley: Religion and Politics in Northern Ireland* (Oxford: Oxford University Press, 2007), 90.

67. Todd, 'Two Traditions in Unionist Political Culture', 3, 10.

68. Bruce, *Paisley*, 5, 44.

69. Walker, *A History of the Ulster Unionist Party*, 150.

70. H. Patterson, 'Unionism, 1921–72', in A. Jackson (ed.), *The Oxford Handbook of Modern Irish History* (Oxford: Oxford University Press, 2014), 704.

71. Hennessey, *Northern Ireland*, 55–6.

72. Bruce, *The Red Hand*, 14.

73. M. O'Callaghan and C. O'Donnell, 'The Northern Ireland Government, the "Paisleyite Movement" and Ulster Unionism in 1966', *Irish Political Studies*, 21/2 (2006), 210–12.

74. Bruce, *Paisley*, 87, 218–20.

75. Nelson, *Ulster's Uncertain Defenders*, 53.

76. P. Dixon, *The British Labour Party and Northern Ireland 1959–74* (PhD thesis, University of Bradford, 1993), 148.

77. Ruane and Todd, *The Dynamics of Conflict in Northern Ireland*, 127.

78. Hennessey, *Northern Ireland*, 153.

79. Purdie, *Politics in the Streets*, 155–8.

80. P. Bishop and E. Mallie, *The Provisional IRA* (London: Corgi, 1989), 84.

81. H. Patterson, *The Politics of Illusion: A Political History of the IRA* (London: Serif, 1997), 107–8, 112.

82. Prince and Warner, *Belfast and Derry in Revolt*, 66, 68, 119, 133.

83. S. Prince, '5 October 1968 and the Beginning of the Troubles: Flashpoints, Riots and Memory', *Irish Political Studies*, 27/3 (2012), 394, 397, 399, 404.

84. Cameron, *Disturbances in Northern Ireland*, para 229.

85. Purdie, *Politics in the Streets*, 145.

86. J. Darby, *Conflict in Northern Ireland: The Development of a Polarised Community* (Dublin: Gill and Macmillan, 1976), 21.

87. Purdie, *Politics in the Streets*, 198, 217.

88. Cameron, *Disturbances in Northern Ireland*, paras 16, 229.

89. R. Bourke, *Peace in Ireland: The War of Ideas* (London: Pimlico, 2012), 94.

90. S. Dockrill, *Britain's Retreat from East of Suez: The Choice between Europe and the World?* (Basingstoke: Palgrave Macmillan, 2002), 122–56.

91. D. French, *Army, Empire and Cold War: The British Army and Military Policy, 1945–1971* (Oxford: Oxford University Press, 2012), 284, 289–90.

92. Public Records Office of Northern Ireland [hereafter PRONI] HA/32/2/14: 'Directive to Commander 39 Infantry Brigade Group', from Lieutenant-General

G. R. D. Fitzpatrick, General Officer Commanding-in-Chief, Northern Ireland Command, 21 June 1965.

93. Dixon, *The British Labour Party and Northern Ireland*, 72.

94. Dorey, 'From indifference to intervention', 251.

95. P. Rose, *Backbencher's Dilemma* (London: Frederick Muller, 1981), 179.

96. Dixon, *The British Labour Party and Northern Ireland*, 55, 87, 113.

97. Dorey, 'From Indifference to Intervention', 252.

98. T. Cradden, 'Labour in Britain and the Northern Ireland Labour Party, 1900–70', in P. Catterall and S. McDougall (eds.), *The Northern Ireland Question in British Politics* (Basingstoke: Macmillan, 1996), 85.

99. C. Blacker, *Monkey Business: The Memoirs of General Sir Cecil Blacker* (London: Quiller Press, 1993), 139.

100. C. Millman, *Stand Easy, or, The Rear Rank Remembers: A Memoir* (Edinburgh: The Pentland Press, 1993), 89, 92.

101. 'The 2nd Battalion', *The Journal of The Queen's Regiment*, 2/3 (September 1968), 24.

102. King's Own Scottish Borderers Regimental Museum [hereafter KOSBRM]: Newsletters: 'Borderer's in Belfast. The Newsletter of the 1st Battalion The King's Own Scottish Borderers in Belfast', 28 July 1970.

103. *The Royal Green Jackets Chronicle 1971: An Annual Record* (Winchester: The Royal Green Jackets, 1971), 46.

104. Museum of The Royal Dragoon Guards, Oral History Project: interview with Ray Binks, available at: www.rdgmuseum.org.uk/history-and-research/oral-history/, accessed 21 February 2019.

105. Imperial War Museum Sound Archive [hereafter IWMSA]: Stephen Robson, catalogue number 31693, reel 23.

106. Millman, *Stand Easy*, 90–1.

107. IWM: Papers of J. E. Parker, catalogue reference 03/51/1.

108. IWMSA: James Alan Comrie Cowan, catalogue number 18802, reel 26.

109. IWMSA: John Napier Cormack, catalogue number 21564, reel 23.

110. JSCSC Library: National Defence College Papers: '2 Course. Exercise thesis. The Use of Violence by Minority Groups to Achieve Their Political Ends', by J. C. Gordon, February 1973.

111. '1st Battalion The Parachute Regiment', *Pegasus: The Journal of Airborne Forces*, 25/1 (January 1970), 22.

112. Blacker, *Monkey Business*, 138.

113. C. Townshend, *Political Violence in Ireland: Government and Resistance since 1848* (Oxford: Clarendon Press, 1983), 1.

114. IWMSA: Paul Garman, catalogue number 24732, reel 14.

115. IWMSA: Michael David Cunningham McBain, catalogue number 11105, reel 25.

116. Burke, *An Army of Tribes*, 29.

117. TNA WO 305/6509: 'Ministry of Defence. Narrative of the Military Operations in Northern Ireland Which Began in August 1969. Vol. 1', preface, I-1, I-5.

118. JSCSC: Army Staff Course 1970; 'Exercise Blue Lamp. DS Notes.'
119. TNA DEFE 25/301: Minute from G. H. Baker, VCGS, to DCDS(I), 8 February 1966.
120. On the border campaign, see: K. Rekawek, '"The Last of the Mohicans?" The IRA's "Operation Harvest" in an International Context', *Terrorism and Political Violence*, 28/3 (2016), 435–51.
121. Rose, *How the Troubles Came to Northern Ireland*, 19.
122. TNA DEFE 25/301: 'COS Committee. Confidential Annex to COS 15th Meeting/66', 17 March 1966.
123. TNA DEFE 25/301: Minute to CGS from G. H. Baker, VCGS, 1 April 1966.
124. TNA DEFE 32/10: COS Committee (informal) meeting minutes, 1 April 1966, COS (I) 1/4/66.
125. PRONI HA/32/2/12: Letter from A. L. Langdon, Home Office, to K. P. Bloomfield, Cabinet Offices, Stormont, 23 November 1966.
126. TNA DEFE 24/882: Letter from Denis Healey to James Callaghan, 14 October 1968.
127. TNA DEFE 24/882: Letter from Lieutenant-General Sir Ian Harris, HQ Northern Ireland, to Lieutenant-General Sir Victor Fitzgeorge-Balfour, VCGS, 20 November 1968.
128. TNA CJ 3/31: Signal from VCGS to GOC Northern Ireland, 21 November 1968.
129. A. Craig, *Crisis of Confidence: Anglo-Irish Relations in the Early Troubles* (Dublin: Irish Academic Press, 2010), 42–3.
130. TNA DEFE 24/1825: Minute from H. F. Ellis-Rees, Head of C2(AD), to AUS(A)(AD), 9 December 1968.
131. TNA DEFE 32/16: Confidential Annex to COS 58th Meeting/68, 10 December 1968.
132. TNA DEFE 25/257: 'Notes by DMO on a visit to Northern Ireland – 11/12 Dec. 68', Director of Military Operations, 16 December 1968.
133. TNA DEFE 25/257: Minute from CDS to Secretary of State for Defence, 12 December 1968.
134. TNA DEFE 13/783: Letter from Attorney General to Secretary of State for Defence, 13 December 1968.
135. TNA DEFE 25/257: Minute from Secretary of State for Defence to Prime Minister, 17 December 1968.
136. Blacker, *Monkey Business*, 155.
137. R. Mead, *'Sam': Marshal of the Royal Air Force the Lord Elworthy* (Barnsley: Pen and Sword, 2018), 18; TNA DEFE 25/257: Minute from Captain P. White, PSO/CDS to MA/CGS, ACDS(Ops) and SCDS(West), 18 December 1968.
138. Charters, *Whose Mission, Whose Orders?*, 44–50.
139. Smith, *The British State and the Northern Ireland Crisis*, 103. This otherwise excellent policy study makes no reference to military records.
140. TNA CJ 3/31: Minute by Neil Cairncross, Home Office, 6 January 1969.

141. S. Prince, '"Do What the Afro-Americans Are Doing": Black Power and the Start of the Northern Ireland Troubles', *Journal of Contemporary History*, 50/3 (2015), 532.
142. TNA HO 325/130: 'Military assistance to the civil power in the United Kingdom. Minutes of a meeting held in the Ministry of Defence on Wednesday 8th January 1969.'
143. TNA DEFE 25/257: 'Northern Ireland. Notes for a meeting of CDS/CGS with PUS Home Office on 30 January 1969.'
144. TNA DEFE 13/1010: Minute from CGS to Secretary of State for Defence, 3 July 1972.
145. Liddell Hart Centre for Military Archives [hereafter LHCMA]: Ministry of Defence, *The Army List, Autumn 1969* (London: HMSO, 1969).
146. LHCMA: Ministry of Defence, *The Army List, Spring 1974, Part I* (London: HMSO, 1974).
147. TNA WO 305/3146: 'Commanders Diary of HQ 24th Infantry Brigade', 21–2 August 1969.
148. IWMSA: Terence Lionel Hubble, catalogue number 33350, reel 25.
149. JSCSC Library: National Defence College Papers: '3 Course. Exercise Thesis. The Modern Guerrilla and His Warfare', by Major R. G. Southerst, 1974.
150. 'The 2nd Battalion', *The Journal of The Queen's Regiment*, 3/2 (June 1969), 24.
151. IWMSA: Frank Brannigan, catalogue number 30295, reel 15.
152. TNA WO 305/5837: 'No 1 (Gds) Indep PARA Coy Report on Operations in Northern Ireland', 12 August 1971.
153. IWMSA: Kenneth Ambrose, catalogue number 32532, reel 13.
154. TNA DEFE 25/257: 'Minute of a meeting held at 1500 on Thursday 30th January 1969 in the Ministry of Defence.'
155. TNA DEFE 25/257: Minute from DMO to CGS, 30 January 1969.
156. The assessment was first uncovered by Anthony Craig in *Crisis of Confidence*, 44. I rely here on a version of the document from a week later. Craig does not discuss the presentation of the document to the prime minister.
157. TNA DEFE 25/257: Minute from CGS to Secretary of State for Defence, 7 February 1969.
158. TNA PREM 13/2842: Letter from Denis Healey to Prime Minister, 14 February 1969.
159. TNA CAB 130/416: MISC 238(69) 2nd Meeting, minutes of the meeting held on 21 April 1969.
160. TNA CJ 4/2996: Letter from Burke Trend, Cabinet Office, to Sir Philip Allen, Home Office, 27 February 1969.
161. TNA CJ 4/2996: Minute from Neil Cairncross to Sir Philip Allen, 13 March 1969.
162. TNA CAB 164/576: Minute from Burke Trend to Prime Minister, 28 April 1969.
163. Smith, *The British State and the Northern Ireland Crisis*, 76.

164. TNA CAB 130/416: MISC 238(69), minutes of the meeting held on 29 April 1969.

165. TNA DEFE 25/302: 'Withdrawal of all RN personnel, facilities and installations from Northern Ireland'; 'The withdrawal of the Army Garrison from Northern Ireland'; 'The implications of redeploying RAF units from Northern Ireland', all under covering minute from D. R. Morris, DS6, 19 May 1969.

166. TNA DEFE 25/302: 'Chiefs of Staff Committee Meeting. Tuesday, 20th May 1969.'

167. TNA CJ 3/2: 'Northern Ireland. Memorandum by the Secretary of State for Defence', 28 May 1969.

168. TNA DEFE 25/272: 'DMO Brief No 37/69. Chiefs of Staff Committee. Meeting to be held on Mon 21 Apr 69.'

169. TNA DEFE 24/882: Minute from Major [name illegible] to Colonel GS, MO3, 21 April 1969.

170. TNA PREM 13/2842: Letter from J. F. Mayne, Ministry of Defence, to P. L. Gregson, 10 Downing Street, 24 April 1969.

171. TNA DEFE 24/882: Signal from Northern Ireland to MoD Army, 24 April 1969; CAB 130/416: MISC 238(69), minutes of the meeting held 25 April 1969.

172. PRONI HA/32/2/35: Letter from Harold Black, Offices of the Cabinet, Northern Ireland, to J. E. Greeves, Ministry of Home Affairs, 7 May 1969.

173. R. Ramsay, *Ringside Seats: An Insider's View of the Crisis in Northern Ireland* (Dublin: Irish Academic Press, 2009), 55.

174. TNA DEFE 24/655: Minute to PS/SoS from AUS(GS), 24 April 1969; DEFE 25/272: 'DMO Brief No 39/69. Briefing for Secretary of State at 0900 hrs Friday 25 April 1969.'

175. TNA DEFE 25/272: 'Northern Ireland. LM to A/BR/20201/MO3', signed for Colonel GS, MO3, 29 April 1969.

176. TNA DEFE 13/903: 'Office Note. Northern Ireland', J. F. Mayne, 7 May 1969.

177. TNA CJ 3/13: Letter from Arthur Hockaday, Ministry of Defence, to N. F. Cairncross, Home Office, 9 May 1969.

178. TNA DEFE 13/903: Minute from CGS to Secretary of State for Defence, 19 May 1969.

179. TNA PREM 13/2843: 'Note of a meeting held at 10 Downing Street, S.W.1., on Wednesday, 21st May 1969.'

180. TNA DEFE 13/903: 'Northern Ireland. Summary of events since sitrep 19 May', 22 May 1969; 'Northern Ireland. Summary of events since sitrep 2 June', 6 June 1969.

181. PRONI HA/32/2/12: Letter from Brigadier A. J. Dyball, Chief of Staff HQNI, to R. W. Porter, Minister of Home Affairs, 24 June 1969; Letter from Brigadier A. J. Dyball, to R. W. Porter, 1 July 1969.

182. TNA DEFE 13/903: Minute by A. P. Hockaday, AUS(GS), to PS/SoS, 8 July 1969.

183. TNA CAB 130/416: MISC 238(69) minutes of the meeting held on 15 July 1969.
184. Airborne Assault Museum, Box 2.33.25: British Army, *Ulster: A Brief* (No place: British Army, June 1970).
185. TNA CJ 3/122: Memorandum for Home Secretary, 'Northern Ireland. 12th to 14th July 1969', signed Neil Cairncross, 14 July 1969.
186. PRONI HA/32/2/35: Letter from Brigadier A. J. Dyball to R. W. Porter, Minister of Home Affairs, 1 August 1969.
187. TNA DEFE 13/903: Letter from B. C. Cubbon to A. N. Halls, 4 August 1969.
188. PRONI HA/32/2/35: 'Discussion on Possible Use of Troops in Aid of the Civil Power Arising out of Disturbances in Belfast on 2nd–3rd August, 1969', initialled by 'HB'.
189. E. O'Halpin, '"A Poor Thing but Our Own": The Joint Intelligence Committee and Ireland, 1965–72', *Intelligence and National Security*, 23/5 (2008), 658–80.
190. E. O'Halpin, 'British Intelligence, PIRA, and the Early Years of the Northern Ireland Crisis: Remembering, Forgetting, and Mythologizing', in P. Maddrell (ed.), *The Image of the Enemy: Intelligence Analysis of Adversaries since 1945* (Washington, DC: Georgetown University Press, 2015), 164, 167.
191. TNA DEFE 25/257: 'Notes by DMO on a visit to Northern Ireland – 11/12 Dec. 68', Director of Military Operations, 16 December 1968.
192. TNA DEFE 4/241: Chiefs of Staff Committee Meeting. 18 August 1969. On MI5's limited early role, see: C. Andrew, *The Defence of the Realm: The Authorized History of MI5* (London: Allen Lane, 2009), 602–4.
193. TNA DEFE 13/903: Minute from CGS to Secretary of State for Defence, 19 May 1969.
194. TNA DEFE 13/903: Letter from Lieutenant-General Sir Ian Freeland to CGS, 15 July 1969.
195. TNA CJ 3/55: Minute from Home Office to Sir Philip Allen, 31 July 1969.
196. PRONI CAB/9/G/49/8A: Letter from James Chichester-Clark to James Callaghan, 6 August 1969.
197. TNA DEFE 13/903: Letter from Private Secretary to the Home Secretary to PS/ Prime Minister, 8 August 1969.
198. TNA DEFE 13/903: Letter from Minister of Defence for Administration to Secretary of State for Defence, 12 August 1969.
199. TNA DEFE 13/903: Letter from Minister of Defence for Administration to Secretary of State for Defence, 14 August 1969.
200. TNA DEFE 24/655: 'Note of a meeting held at R.A.F. St. Mawgan on Thursday, August 14, 1969.'
201. TNA CJ 3/13: Minute by Neil Cairncross, Home Office, 14 August 1969.
202. TNA DEFE 24/882: 'Northern Ireland', summary of events for the night 14/15 August, dated 15 August 1969, signed [name illegible] Colonel GS, MO3.
203. TNA DEFE 4/241: Chiefs of Staff Meeting 32/69, 14 August 1969.

2 THE ARMY'S SHORT-LIVED ULSTER HONEYMOON

1. 'Purely Editorial', *Pegasus: The Journal of Airborne Forces*, 25/2 (1970), 2.
2. TNA WO 305/3808: 'Log Sheet HQ 39 Inf Bde, 18 Aug 69.'
3. C. Douglas-Home, 'British troops may become targets, GOC says', *The Times*, 19 August 1969.
4. Hennessey, *Northern Ireland*, 376.
5. Neumann, *Britain's Long War*, 44–5, 60–1.
6. Ó Dochartaigh, 'Northern Ireland since 1920', 149.
7. Mockaitis, *British Counterinsurgency*, 98.
8. Leahy, *The Intelligence War against the IRA*, 17.
9. English, 'The Interplay of Non-violent and Violent Action in Northern Ireland, 1967–72', 85.
10. Patterson, 'The British State and the Rise of the IRA, 1969–71', 491, 501.
11. O'Halpin, 'British Intelligence, PIRA, and the Early Years of the Northern Ireland Crisis', 167–8.
12. Prince and Warner, *Belfast and Derry in Revolt*, 220.
13. Ó Dochartaigh, 'Northern Ireland since 1920', 150.
14. For police perspectives on the conflict, see: C. Ryder, *The RUC: A Force under Fire* (London: Methuen, 1989); C. Breen, *A Force Like No Other: The Real Stories of the RUC Men and Women Who Policed the Troubles* (Belfast: Blackstaff Press, 2017).
15. TNA WO 305/3808: 'Log Sheet 39 Inf Bde, 14 Aug 69.'
16. TNA DEFE 24/882: 'Northern Ireland', summary of events for the night 14/15 August 1969.
17. TNA WO 305/3808: 'Log Sheet HQ 39 Inf Bde, 15 Aug 69.'
18. TNA DEFE 24/882: 'Northern Ireland. Events day 15/NI 16 Aug 69', minute for VCGS from [illegible] for DMO, 16 August 1969.
19. TNA WO 305/3959: '2nd Battalion The Queens Regiment Historical Record. 1 Apr 68 – 31 Mar 70.'
20. TNA DEFE 13/903: 'Special order of the day by GOC Northern Ireland', 15 August 1969.
21. TNA WO 305/3808: 'Log Sheet HQ 39 Inf Bde, 15 Aug 69.'
22. Prince and Warner, *Belfast and Derry in Revolt*, 211–13; B. Hanley and S. Millar, *The Lost Revolution: The Story of the Official IRA and the Workers Party* (London: Penguin, 2009), 127, 130.
23. TNA DEFE 24/882: 'Northern Ireland. Events day 15/NI 16 Aug 69', minute for VCGS from [illegible] for DMO, 16 August 1969.
24. TNA WO 305/3808: 'Log Sheet HQ 39 Inf Bde, 16 Aug 69'; 'Log Sheet HQ 39 Inf Bde, 17 Aug 69.'
25. PRONI HA/32/3/2: 'Conclusions of a Meeting of the Joint Security Committee', 17 August 1969.
26. TNA WO 305/3808: 'Log Sheet HQ 39 Inf Bde, 18 Aug 69.'
27. '1st Battalion Notes', *The Journal of the Royal Hampshire Regiment*, 59/1 (1970), 17.

28. PRONI HA/32/3/2: 'Instruction from the Prime Minister', 15 August 1969; 'Conclusions of a Meeting of the Joint Security Committee', 16 August 1969.
29. IWM: Papers of Ian Freeland, catalogue reference 79/34/3: 'IS Operations in Northern Ireland since 1969', no date.
30. TNA PREM 13/2844: 'Cabinet. Joint Intelligence Committee (A). Ulster Working Group', 18 August 1969.
31. TNA CJ 3/38: Notes to Mr D. E. R. Faulkner and Mr J. A. McKay, signed 'PA', 15 August 1969; 'Reports of Mr Osmond and Mr Faulkner', 18 August 1969.
32. TNA WO 305/6509: 'Ministry of Defence. Narrative of the Military Operations in Northern Ireland Which Began in August 1969. Vol. 1', III-4.
33. TNA WO 305/3146: 'Op Instr 1. HQ 24 Inf Bde, 18 Aug 69.'
34. Thornton, 'Getting it Wrong', 77; Charters, *Whose Mission, Whose Orders?*, 14, 59.
35. Smith, *The British State and the Northern Ireland Crisis*, 67.
36. J. Callaghan, *A House Divided: The Dilemma of Northern Ireland* (London: Collins, 1973), 102.
37. N. Ó Dochartaigh, *Deniable Contact: Back-Channel Negotiation in Northern Ireland* (Oxford: Oxford University Press, 2021), 28.
38. PRONI HA/32/3/2: 'Conclusions of a Meeting of the Joint Security Committee', 19 August 1969.
39. IWM: Papers of Ian Freeland, catalogue reference 79/34/3: Letter from Lieutenant-General Sir Ian Freeland to General Sir Geoffrey Baker, 18 October 1969, with attached 'Talk at CGS's Conference'.
40. P. C. F. M. Beresford, *The Official IRA and Republican Clubs in Northern Ireland 1968–1974, and Their Relations with Other Political and Paramilitary Groups* (PhD Thesis, University of Exeter, 1979), 124, 126, 130–1, 180.
41. P. Devlin, *Straight Left: An Autobiography* (Belfast: Blackstaff Press, 1993), 85, 110.
42. TNA WO 305/3808: 'Log Sheet HQ 39 Inf Bde, 19 Aug 69.'
43. TNA WO 305/3808: 'Log Sheet HQ 39 Inf Bde, 21 Aug 69.'
44. TNA WO 305/3808: 'Log Sheet HQ 39 Inf Bde, 23 Aug 69.'
45. Millman, *Stand Easy*, 126, 131.
46. M. Reynolds, *Soldier at Heart: From Private to General* (Barnsley: Pen and Sword, 2013), 160.
47. TNA WO 305/3146: 'Log Sheet HQ 24 Inf Bde, 23 Aug 69.'
48. TNA WO 305/3146: 'Log Sheet HQ 24 Inf Bde, 24 Aug 69.'
49. TNA WO 305/3146: Message from HQ 24 Inf Bde to HQ NI, 24 August 1969.
50. TNA WO 305/3146: Telegram from NORIRELAND to 24 Bde, 39 Bde, et al., 24 August 1969.
51. TNA WO 305/3808: 'Log Sheet HQ 39 Inf Bde, 26 Aug 69'; 'Log Sheet HQ 39 Inf Bde, 27 Aug 69.'
52. TNA WO 305/3808: 'Report on a Meeting with the Central Defence Committee in Leeson Street at 2245 hours 27 Aug 69.'

53. TNA WO 305/3808: 'Internal Security Directive. An Assessment of Our Task for the Immediate Future', Brigadier P. Hudson, 39 Infantry Brigade, 25 August 1969.
54. Craig, *Crisis of Confidence*, 58.
55. TNA WO 305/3808: HQ 39 Infantry Brigade, 'Intsum covering period 18–28 Aug 1969', 30 August 1969.
56. TNA WO 305/3146: Message from HQ 24 Inf Bde to 2 Gren Gds, 1 Queens, 1 RGJ, 26 August 1969.
57. TNA WO 305/3146: Message from HQ 24 Inf Bde to HQ NI, 26 August 1969.
58. TNA WO 305/3146: Letter from Brigadier Leng, HQ 24 Inf Bde, to Brigadier E. H. W. Bramall, HQ 5 Infantry Bde, 29 August 1969.
59. TNA WO 305/3146: 'Log Sheet HQ 24 Inf Bde, 30 Aug 69.'
60. TNA WO 305/3146: 'Meeting between DCDA and Comd 24 Bde 31 Aug–1 Sep 69.'
61. Millman, *Stand Easy*, 133.
62. TNA WO 305/3146: Letter from Brigadier Leng, to Major-General A. J. Dyball, HQNI, 1 September 1969. Dyball was promoted to the acting rank of major-general on 29 August 1969.
63. TNA DEFE 24/552: Letter from A. P. Hockaday, AUS(GS), to D. R. E. Hopkins, Home Office, 11 March 1970.
64. Dixon, *The British Labour Party and Northern Ireland*, 216.
65. TNA WO 305/3147: 'Log Sheet HQ 24 Inf Bde, 1 September 1969'; 'Log Sheet HQ 24 Inf Bde, 3 September 1969.'
66. TNA WO 305/3147: Message from HQ 24 Inf Bde to 2 Gren Gds, 1 Queens, 1 RGJ, 4 September 1969.
67. TNA WO 305/3147: Message from HQ 24 Inf Bde to 2 Gren Gds, 1 Queens, 1 RGJ, 6 September 1969.
68. TNA WO 305/3147: 'Log Sheet HQ 24 Inf Bde, 2 September 1969.'
69. TNA WO 305/3808: 'Log Sheet 39 Inf Bde, 30 August 1969.'
70. TNA WO 305/3808: 'Log Sheet HQ 39 Inf Bde, 31 Aug 69.'
71. TNA WO 305/4191: '39 Inf Bde Log, 1 Sep 1969.'
72. TNA WO 305/4191: 'HQ 39 Inf Bde, 3 Sep 69.'
73. TNA WO 305/4191: '39 Inf Bde G (Ops) Log, 2 September 1969.'
74. TNA WO 305/4191: 'HQ 39 Inf Bde, 3 Sep 69.'
75. TNA WO 305/4191: '39 Infantry Brigade. 04 September 1969.'
76. PRONI HA/32/3/2: 'Conclusions of a Meeting of the Joint Security Committee', 5 September 1969.
77. TNA WO 305/4191: '39 Inf Bde. G (Ops) Log, 6 September 1969.'
78. Devlin, *Straight Left*, 111.
79. TNA WO 305/4191: 'HQ 39 Inf Bde. G Log, 7 Sep 69.'
80. TNA DEFE 24/1921: 'Findings of the Board', signed by President: Lt-Col G. L. Weston, 20 September 1969.
81. TNA WO 305/4191: '39 Infantry Brigade. 08 September 1969.'

82. TNA DEFE 4/242: CObrS Committee, Confidential Annex to COS 36th Meeting/69, 9 September 1969.
83. PRONI HA/32/3/2: 'Conclusions of a Meeting of the Joint Security Committee', 9 September 1969.
84. TNA DEFE 24/1213: 'Telephone conversation between CGS and GOC Northern Ireland', 9 September 1969.
85. TNA DEFE 13/904: 'Conclusions of a meeting of the Joint Security Committee', 10 September 1969.
86. TNA WO 305/3147: 'Log Sheet HQ 24 Inf Bde, 9 September 1969.'
87. TNA WO 305/3147: Message from Brigadier P. J. H. Leng, HQ 24 Inf Bde, to Major-General D. A. H. Toler, HQNI, 10 September 1969.
88. TNA WO 305/3147: Message from HQ 24 Inf Bde to 2 Gren Gds, 1 Queens, 1 RGJ, 10 September 1969.
89. TNA WO 305/4191: HQ 39 Inf Bde, 'Intsum No. 3. Covering period 6 Sep – 12 Sep 69'.
90. TNA PREM 13/2845: 'Press notice', 11 September 1969.
91. TNA WO 305/4191: 'HQ 39 Inf Bde. G Ops Log. 12 Sep 69.'
92. TNA WO 305/4191: 'HQ 39 Inf Bde. 13 Sep 69.'
93. TNA WO 305/3147: 'Log sheet HQ 24 Inf Bde, 11 September 1969.'
94. TNA WO 305/3147: Message from HQ 24 Inf Bde to 2 Gren Gds, 1 Queens, 1 RGJ, 12 September 1969.
95. TNA WO 305/3147: Message from HQ 24 Inf Bde to 2 Gren Gds, 1 Queens, 1 RGJ, 13 September 1969.
96. TNA WO 305/4191: 'HQ 39 Inf Bde. 14 Sep 69.'
97. TNA DEFE 13/988: 'Conclusions of a Joint Security Committee meeting', 15 September 1969.
98. TNA DEFE 24/1213: 'Visit by GOC Northern Ireland to MOD 15 Sep 69. Meeting with CGS at 1500 hrs.'
99. TNA PREM 13/2845: 'Northern Ireland. Note of a meeting held at 10 Downing Street', 15 September 1969.
100. TNA WO 305/4191: 'Meeting between Commander 39 Inf Bde and the Central Citizens Defence Committee', 16 September 1969.
101. TNA WO 305/4191: 'HQ 39 Inf Bde. 17 Sep 69.'
102. TNA WO 305/4191: 'Meeting between the CDC, Father Murphy, and Brig P. Hudson', 17 September 1969.
103. TNA WO 305/3147: Message from HQ 24 Inf Bde to 2 Gren Gds, 1 Queens, 1 RGJ, 19 September 1969.
104. TNA WO 305/3958: 'Regimental history – 1 Queens. Period 1 April 1969 – 31 March 1970.'
105. TNA WO 305/4191: 'Meeting between Brig P. Hudson MBE, Fr Murphy, and members of the Citizens' Defence Committee', 23 September 1969.
106. TNA PREM 13/2845: Minute from Denis Healey to Prime Minister, 22 September 1969.

107. TNA WO 305/3147: 'Log Sheet HQ 24 Inf Bde, 24 September 1969.'
108. IWMSA: William Roger Blyth May, catalogue number 18569, reel 7.
109. 'Adept Adaptability', *The Globe and Laurel: The Journal of the Royal Marines*, 77/6 (1969), 341.
110. TNA DEFE 13/988: 'Intelligence sub-committee – 22 September, 1969.'
111. TNA DEFE 24/1213: 'Visit of S of S to Northern Ireland 18–19 Sep (Notes by Colonel GS MO 3)', 22 September 1969.
112. PRONI HA/32/3/2: 'Conclusions of a Meeting of the Joint Security Committee', 20 August 1969.
113. IWM: Papers of Ian Freeland, catalogue reference 79/34/3: 'GOC's Conference, 2 September 1969. Talk to Commanders.'
114. TNA DEFE 24/1213: 'Visit of S of S to Northern Ireland 18–19 Sep (Notes by Colonel GS MO 3)', 22 September 1969.
115. TNA WO 305/3958: 'Regimental history – 1 Queens. Period 1 April 1969–31 March 1970.'
116. TNA WO 305/3147: 'Log Sheet HQ 24 Inf Bde, 25 September 1969.'
117. TNA DEFE 13/988: 'Conclusions of a meeting of the Joint Security Committee', 25 September 1969.
118. TNA WO 305/3147: 'Log Sheet HQ 24 Inf Bde, 26 September 1969'; Message from HQ 24 Inf Bde to 2 Gren Gds, 1 Queens, 60 Sqn RCT, 26 September 1969.
119. TNA WO 305/3147: 'Log Sheet HQ 24 Inf Bde, 27 September 1969.'
120. TNA WO 305/3959: '2nd Battalion The Queens Regiment Historical Record. 1 Apr 68–31 Mar 70.'
121. TNA WO 305/4191: 'HQ 39 Inf Bde. 28 Sep 69'; 'HQ 39 Inf Bde. 29 Sep 69.'
122. TNA DEFE 13/988: 'Report by Chiefs of Staff Duty Office', Defence Operations Centre, 29 September 1969.
123. TNA DEFE 13/988: 'Conclusions of a meeting of the Joint Security Committee', 29 September 1969.
124. TNA DEFE 24/1148: Minute to CGS from J. H. S. Majury, A/DMO, 2 October 1969.
125. A. Sanders, 'Principles of Minimum Force and the Parachute Regiment in Northern Ireland, 1969–1972', *Journal of Strategic Studies*, 41/5 (2018), 668.
126. TNA DEFE 13/988: Minute from D. R. E. Hopkins, AG Secretariat, to PS/Minister(A), 30 September 1969.
127. TNA DEFE 24/1148: 'Directive to Inspector General Royal Ulster Constabulary and to Deputy Commander Army from Director of Operations Northern Ireland, HQ Northern Ireland', 3 October 1969.
128. PRONI HA/32/3/2: 'Conclusions of a Meeting of the Joint Security Committee', 2 October 1969.
129. IWM: Papers of Ian Freeland, catalogue reference 79/34/3: 'Study Period. 5 December 1969.'
130. IWMSA: James Alan Comrie Cowan, catalogue number 18802, reel 23.

131. M. B. Farndale, 'To Belfast as Infantry', *Journal of the Royal Artillery*, 97/2 (1970), 126.

132. Millman, *Stand Easy*, 128–9.

133. IWMSA: Michael Gray, catalogue number 28362, reel 30.

134. Shropshire Archives: Oral history interview, John Kingsford Marsham, reference 6005/SHYKS/2008/2677/9.

135. TNA DEFE 24/1148: Minute to CGS from J. H. S. Majury, A/DMO, 2 October 1969.

136. TNA DEFE 24/1148: Minute from CGS to Secretary of State for Defence, 3 October 1969.

137. TNA DEFE 13/988: Minute from J. F. Mayne to MA/CGS, PS/PUS(A) et al., 3 October 1969.

138. TNA DEFE 24/1148: Minute from MA/VCGS to APS/SoS, 8 October 1969.

139. TNA DEFE 24/1148: Minute from J. F. Mayne, APS/SoS, to MA/VCGS, 8 October 1969.

140. TNA DEFE 24/1148: Signal from NORIRELAND to RBDWC/MOD UK, 5 October 1969.

141. TNA DEFE 24/1921: Letter from Denis Healey to S. McMaster MP, 8 October 1969.

142. TNA DEFE 24/655: Minute to MA/CGS from A. R. M. Jaffray, PS/SoS Defence, 21 August 1969.

143. IWMSA: Christopher Lawton, catalogue number 28698, reel 8.

144. TNA PREM 13/2844: 'Statement to be read by GOC at his press conference at HQ Northern Ireland at 1200 hrs on Friday 22nd August 1969.'

145. TNA DEFE 13/988: Minute from Denis Healey to CGS, 2 October 1969.

146. TNA DEFE 24/1148: Minute to CGS from J. H. S. Majury, A/DMO, 2 October 1969.

147. TNA DEFE 24/1148: Letter from Denis Healey to Jim Callaghan, 3 October 1969.

148. Smith, *The British State and the Northern Ireland Crisis*, 68–71.

149. G. Styles, *Bombs Have No Pity: My War against Terrorism* (London: William Luscombe, 1975), 75.

150. 'Northern Ireland: Text of a Communiqué issued following discussions between the Secretary of State for the Home Department and the Northern Ireland Government in Belfast on 9th and 10th October 1969', accessed 16 June 2019 at: https://cain.ulster.ac.uk/hmso/bni101069.htm.

151. IWM: Papers of Ian Freeland, catalogue reference 79/34/3: Letter from Lieutenant-General Sir Ian Freeland to General Sir Geoffrey Baker, 18 October 1969, with attached 'Report by OC 3 LI of operations on the Shankill Road, Belfast, on night 11/12 Oct 69'.

152. IWM: Papers of Ian Freeland, catalogue reference 79/34/3: Letter from Lieutenant-General Sir Ian Freeland to General Sir Geoffrey Baker, 18 October 1969.

153. TNA DEFE 24/1148: Hansard for 13 October 1969.
154. TNA WO 305/6509: 'Ministry of Defence. Narrative of the Military Operations in Northern Ireland Which Began in August 1969. Vol. 1', III-22.
155. TNA DEFE 13/675: Letter from Oliver Wright, UKREP, to Home Secretary, 17 December 1969.
156. PRONI HA/32/3/2: 'Conclusions of a Meeting of the Joint Security Committee', 14 October 1969.
157. TNA WO 305/3361: Message from HQ 24 Inf Bde to HQ Northern Ireland, 7 October 1969; 'Log Sheet HQ 24 Inf Bde, 8 October 1969.'
158. TNA DEFE 24/655: Minute from J. F. Mayne, APS/SoS, to AUS(GS), 8 October 1969.
159. TNA WO 305/3361: 'Minutes of the Meeting between the General Officer Commanding Northern Ireland, Inspector General of the Royal Ulster Constabulary and Representatives of the Bogside and Creggan Areas', 15 October 1969.
160. TNA WO 305/4306: '1 Para Historical record. 1st April 1969–31st March 1970.'
161. Shropshire Archives: Oral history interview, Timothy David Vaughan Bevan, reference 6005/SHYKS/2008/2677/29.
162. TNA WO 305/3361: HQ 24 Infantry Bde, Intsum No. 43, 19 October 1969.
163. TNA WO 305/3146: 'The Threat to Internal Security in the Western Zone', attached to HQ 24 Inf Bde Intsum No. 12, 29 August 1969.
164. TNA WO 305/3958: 'Regimental history – 1 Queens. Period 1 April 1969–31 March 1970.'
165. TNA WO 305/3362: 'Headquarters 24th Infantry Brigade, Intsum No. 45 (Covering period 25 Oct–1 Nov 69).'
166. TNA WO 305/3361: HQ 24 Infantry Bde, Intsum No. 44, covering period 18 October–24 October 1969.
167. TNA WO 305/3362: 'Headquarters 24th Infantry Brigade, Intsum No. 48 (covering period 17 Nov–23 Nov [1969]).'
168. TNA WO 305/3362: 'Log Sheet HQ 24 Inf Bde, 28 November 1969.'
169. TNA WO 305/3363: 'Log Sheet HQ 24 Inf Bde, 17 December 1969.'
170. TNA DEFE 13/758: 'Intsum No. 15', HQ Northern Ireland, 4 December 1969.
171. TNA DEFE 13/758: 'Intelligence sub-committee assessment for the period ending 4th December, 1969', RUC Headquarters, 4 December 1969.
172. TNA DEFE 13/675: 'Intelligence sub-committee assessment for the period ending 18th December, 1969.'
173. TNA DEFE 13/904: 'An assessment of the threat to military security as at 5th November, 1969', HQ Northern Ireland, 9 November 1969.
174. TNA DEFE 13/758: 'Intelligence sub-committee assessment for the period ending 27th November, 1969', RUC Headquarters, 27 November 1969.
175. E. Moloney, *A Secret History of the IRA* (London: Penguin, 2007), 70.
176. TNA DEFE 13/904: 'Intsum No 11', HQ Northern Ireland, 6 November 1969.

177. TNA DEFE 13/675: 'Director of Operations Intelligence Committee Northern Ireland' [hereafter DOpsINTCOM], 22 December 1969. Assessment for period 9–22 December 1969.

178. TNA DEFE 13/675: HQ Northern Ireland Intsum 19, covering period 24 December 1969–1 January 1970.

179. TNA DEFE 13/675: 'Northern Ireland threat assessment for period 1st January 1970 to 30th June 1970.'

180. TNA DEFE 13/675: DOpsINTCOM, 8 December 1969. Assessment for 22 November–8 December 1969.

181. TNA WO 305/3361: Letter from Brigadier P. J. H. Leng, Commander 24th Infantry Brigade, to Commanding Officers, October 1969.

182. 'The 1st Battalion', *The Journal of The Queen's Regiment*, 3/4 (1969), 12.

183. *The Royal Green Jackets Chronicle 1970: An Annual Record* (Winchester: The Royal Green Jackets, 1970), 24–5.

184. Royal Scots Regimental Museum, Edinburgh [hereafter RSRM]: 'B Company', *The Belfast Thistle*, 1st Battalion The Royal Scots, Edition 4, 11 May 1970, 7.

185. TNA WO 305/4403: Historical Record, 1st Royal Hampshire Regiment, 1 April 1969–31 March 1970, 20–6 October 1969; 27 October–2 November 1969.

186. IWM: Papers of Ian Freeland, catalogue reference 79/34/3: 'Study Period. 5 December 1969.'

187. '1st Battalion The Parachute Regiment', *Pegasus: The Journal of Airborne Forces*, 25/2 (1970), 27–8.

188. TNA WO 305/3814: '1st Regiment Royal Horse Artillery Historical Return', 1 January–31 December 1969.

189. RSRM: 'B Company', *The Belfast Thistle*, 1st Battalion The Royal Scots, Edition 2, 10 April 1970, 12.

190. TNA DEFE 24/560: Letter from Brigadier M. S. Bayley, HQNI, to Head of AG Secretariat, 27 March 1970.

191. TNA DEFE 24/1148: Minute from J. F. Mayne, APS/SoS, to PS/Minister(A), PS/PUS, MA/CGS, AUS/GS, CPR, DPR(A), Home Office (Mr Hockaday), 15 October 1969.

192. IWM: Papers of Ian Freeland, catalogue reference 79/34/3: Letter from Lieutenant-General Sir Ian Freeland to General Sir Geoffrey Baker, 7 November 1969.

193. W. H. Van Voris, *Violence in Ulster: An Oral Documentary* (Amherst: University of Massachussetts Press, 1975), 170.

194. TNA DEFE 24/552: Minute from DMO(3) to VCGS, 15 December 1969.

195. TNA DEFE 24/552: Letter from GOC NI to Sir Arthur Young, [no date] December 1969.

196. TNA DEFE 13/675: Letter from General Freeland to CGS, 9 December 1969.

197. IWM: Papers of Ian Freeland, catalogue reference 79/34/3: Letter from General Sir Geoffrey Baker to Lieutenant-General Sir Ian Freeland, 24 November 1969.

198. IWMSA: James Alan Comrie Cowan, catalogue number 18802, reel 24.
199. TNA DEFE 13/675: HQ Northern Ireland Intsum No. 20, covering the period 1–7 January 1970.
200. TNA DEFE 13/675: Letter from General Freeland to CGS, 7 January 1970; PRONI HA/32/3/3: 'Conclusions of a Meeting of the Joint Security Committee', 15 January 1970.
201. TNA WO 305/4306: '1 Para Historical record. 1st April 1969–31st March 1970.'
202. PRONI HA/32/3/3: 'Conclusions of a Meeting of the Joint Security Committee', 29 January 1970.
203. TNA PREM 13/3386: DOpsINTCOM, 16 February 1970. Assessment for 3–16 February 1970.
204. TNA PREM 13/3386: DOpsINTCOM, 16 March 1970. Assessment for 3–16 March 1970.
205. English, *Armed Struggle*, 106, 109.
206. R. White, 'The Irish Republican Army: An Assessment of Sectarianism', *Terrorism and Political Violence*, 9/1 (1997), 26; R. White, *Ruairí Ó Brádaigh: The Life and Politics of an Irish Revolutionary* (Bloomington: Indiana University Press, 2006), 152.
207. TNA DEFE 13/675: HQ Northern Ireland Intsum No. 20, covering the period 1–7 January 1970.
208. TNA PREM 13/3386: DOpsINTCOM, 2 March 1970. Assessment for 17 February–2 March 1970.
209. Moloney, *Secret History of the IRA*, 85.
210. English, *Does Terrorism Work?*, 138.
211. Bishop and Mallie, *The Provisional IRA*, 156.
212. English, 'The Interplay of Non-violent and Violent Action in Northern Ireland, 1967–72', 83–4.
213. R. Alonso, *The IRA and Armed Struggle* (Abingdon: Routledge, 2003), 17, 26–8, 51–2.
214. P. Gill and J. Horgan, 'Who Were the Volunteers? The Shifting Sociological and Operational Profile of 1,240 Provisional Irish Republican Army Members', *Terrorism and Political Violence* 25/3 (2013), 439–40, 443.
215. L. Bosi, 'Explaining Pathways to Armed Activism in the Provisional Irish Republican Army, 1969–1972', *Social Science History*, 36/3 (2012), 349, 367.
216. TNA DEFE 13/988: Letter from Oliver Wright, UKREP, to James Callaghan, 13 September 1969.
217. TNA DEFE 24/559: 'The future of the Ulster Special Constabulary (USC)', brief by DASD for VCGS, 5 October 1969.
218. TNA DEFE 24/559: Minute from J. F. Mayne, APS/SoS, to PSO/CDS and others, 6 October 1969.
219. TNA DEFE 24/559: 'Short minutes of a meeting of the USC working party with county commandants held on Mon 20 Oct 69.'
220. TNA DEFE 24/559: Minute from A. P. Hockaday, AUS(GS), to DUS(Army), 24 October 1969.

221. G. Ó Faoleán, 'The Ulster Defence Regiment and the Question of Catholic Recruitment, 1970–1972', *Terrorism and Political Violence* 27/5 (2015), 843.

222. TNA DEFE 70/7: Minute from AG Secretariat to VAG, [illegible] October 1969.

223. TNA DEFE 70/7: 'Extract from the minutes of the 82nd meeting of the Army Board held on Monday 27th October 1969.'

224. TNA CAB 148/93: 'Cabinet. Defence and Oversea Policy Committee. The New Defence Force for Northern Ireland. Memorandum by the Secretary of State for Defence', 29 October 1969.

225. TNA DEFE 13/675: DOpsINTCOM, 8 December 1969. Assessment for 22 November–8 December 1969.

226. C. Ryder, *The Ulster Defence Regiment: An Instrument of Peace?* (London: Methuen, 1991), 35–6, 39.

227. J. Potter, *A Testimony to Courage: The Regimental History of the Ulster Defence Regiment* (Barnsley: Leo Cooper, 2001), 21, 24–5.

228. TNA PREM 13/3386: DOpsINTCOM, 13 April 1970. Assessment for period 1–13 April 1970.

229. TNA PREM 13/3386: DOpsINTCOM, 31 March 1970. Assessment for period 17–31 March 1970.

230. M. Farrell, *Northern Ireland: The Orange State* (London: Pluto Press, 1980), 272.

231. TNA PREM 13/3386: DOpsINTCOM, 2 February 1970. Assessment for period 20 January–2 February 1970.

232. TNA PREM 13/3386: DOpsINTCOM, 31 March 1970. Assessment for period 17–31 March 1970.

233. TNA WO 305/4410: 'Historical Record of 2nd Battalion, The Parachute Regiment. 1 April 1969–31 March 1970.'

234. RSRM: 'B Company', *The Belfast Thistle*, 1st Battalion The Royal Scots, Edition 2, 10 April 1970, 8–9.

235. C. de Baróid, *Ballymurphy and the Irish War* (London: Pluto Press, 2000), 3–4.

236. DEFE 25/261: 'Northern Ireland. Briefing for Major-General V. F. Erskine Crum, CIE, MC. GOC (designate) Northern Ireland. 1015–1115 hrs 20 Jan 71.'

237. Prince and Warner, *Belfast and Derry in Revolt*, 233; Neumann, *Britain's Long War*, 53.

238. TNA PREM 13/3386: DOpsINTCOM, 13 April 1970. Assessment for period 1–13 April 1970.

239. JSCSC Library: Pamphlets Collection; Provisional IRA, *Freedom Struggle* (Dublin: Irish Republican Publicity Bureau, 1973), 15.

240. PRONI HA/32/3/3: 'Conclusions of a Meeting of the Joint Security Committee', 9 April 1970.

241. John Chartres, 'Belfast riot injures 28 soldiers', *The Times*, 2 April 1970.

242. TNA DEFE 24/552: Minute from DMO(3) to VCGS, 12 December 1969.

243. TNA PREM 13/3386: DOpsINTCOM, 13 April 1970. Assessment for period 1–13 April 1970.

244. Bowyer Bell, *IRA Tactics and Targets*, 66.
245. IWM: Papers of T. H. Friend, catalogue reference 12/52/1; printed memoirs, 116–17.
246. *The Times*, 8 April 1970.
247. TNA DEFE 24/655: Minute from PS/Minister(A) to PS/US of S(Army) et al., 10 April 1970.
248. TNA DEFE 24/655: Minute from CGS to Minister(A), 20 April 1970.
249. TNA DEFE 24/655: 'The roles of the military and police forces in Northern Ireland', from GOC NI to VCGS, 29 April 1970.
250. G. De Fazio, 'Unpacking Violent Contention: The Troubles in Northern Ireland, 1968–1972', *Terrorism and Political Violence*, 32/8 (2018), 1691–711.

3 ESCALATION AND THE EROSION OF IMPARTIALITY

1. JSCSC: Army Staff Course 1971, 'Urban Operations in Northern Ireland – Notes for DS.'
2. P. J. McLoughlin, *John Hume and the Revision of Irish Nationalism* (Manchester: Manchester University Press, 2010), 23; Kennedy-Pipe, *The Origins of the Present Troubles in Northern Ireland*, 52; Burke, *An Army of Tribes*, 75; Leahy, *The Intelligence War against the IRA*, 19.
3. Smith, *The British State and the Northern Ireland Crisis*, 134; Ó Dochartaigh, *Deniable Contact*, 32.
4. Devlin, *Straight Left*, 126.
5. Ramsay, *Ringside Seats*, 63.
6. J. Smith, '"Walking a Real Tight-Rope of Difficulties": Sir Edward Heath and the Search for Stability in Northern Ireland, June 1970–March 1971', *Twentieth Century British History*, 18/2 (2007), 219–53.
7. Neumann, *Britain's Long War*, 46–7.
8. Mumford, *The Counter-Insurgency Myth*, 97.
9. TNA PREM 13/3386: DOpsINTCOM, 27 April 1970. Assessment for period 14–27 April 1970.
10. 'Conway's attack on RC extremists backed by Falls defence group', *Belfast Telegraph*, 23 May 1970.
11. TNA DEFE 31/28: Minute from A. W. Stephens, APS/SoS, to PS/Minister(A) and MA/CGS, 11 May 1970; PREM 13/3386: DOpsINTCOM, 11 May 1970. Assessment for period 28 April–11 May 1970.
12. Prince and Warner, 'The IRA and Its Rivals', 284; Beresford, *The Official IRA and Republican Clubs*, 288.
13. TNA PREM 13/3386: DOpsINTCOM, 27 May 1970. Assessment for period 12–27 May 1970.
14. TNA WO 305/6509: 'Ministry of Defence. Narrative of the Military Operations in Northern Ireland Which Began in August 1969. Vol. 1', IV-19–20.

15. TNA PREM 15/100: DOpsINTCOM, 23 June 1970. Assessment for period 10–23 June 1970.

16. IWM: Papers of Ian Freeland, catalogue reference 79/34/3, 'IS Operations in Northern Ireland since April 1969', Army report, c. September 1970.

17. TNA DEFE 13/680: Letter from R. Porter to James Callaghan, 8 June 1970.

18. TNA DEFE 13/679: Minute from CGS to Secretary of State for Defence, 11 June 1970.

19. TNA PREM 15/100: 'Cabinet. Northern Ireland. Minutes of a meeting held at 10 Downing Street', 22 June 1970.

20. 'Tried to get march re-routed claim', *Belfast Telegraph*, 29 June 1970.

21. TNA WO 305/3959: '2nd Battalion The Queens Regiment. Historical Record. 1 Apr 70 – 31 Mar 71.'

22. TNA PREM 15/100: DOpsINTCOM, 7 July 1970. Assessment for period 24 June–7 July 1970.

23. TNA PREM 15/100: DOpsINTCOM, 7 July 1970. Assessment for period 24 June–7 July 1970.

24. M. Dewar, *The British Army in Northern Ireland* (London: Guild, 1985), 46.

25. TNA WO 305/3959: '2nd Battalion The Queens Regiment. Historical Record. 1 Apr 70 – 31 Mar 71.'

26. JSCSC: Provisional IRA, *Freedom Struggle* (Dublin: Irish Republican Publicity Bureau, 1973), 16.

27. G. Mulvenna, *Tartan Gangs and Paramilitaries: The Loyalist Backlash* (Liverpool: Liverpool University Press, 2016), 69–70.

28. Moloney, *A Secret History of the IRA*, 90.

29. LHCMA: David Ramsbotham papers, Box 1, 'The Northern Ireland insurgency. Talk to U.S. Army War College – 29 January 1973. Brigadier Frank Kitson.'

30. TNA PREM 15/100: DOpsINTCOM, 7 July 1970. Assessment for period 24 June–7 July 1970.

31. TNA WO 305/3959: '2nd Battalion The Queens Regiment. Historical Record. 1 Apr 70 – 31 Mar 71.'

32. TNA DEFE 32/19: Confidential Annex to COS 18th Meeting/70, 30 June 1970.

33. TNA PREM 15/100: DOpsINTCOM, 7 July 1970. Assessment for period 24 June–7 July 1970.

34. DEFE 25/261: 'Northern Ireland. Briefing for Major-General V. F. Erskine Crum, CIE, MC. GOC (designate) Northern Ireland. 1015–1115 hrs 20 Jan 71.'

35. TNA DEFE 13/730: 'Conclusions of a meeting of the Joint Security Committee', 28 June 1970.

36. TNA DEFE 24/980: Signal from HQNI to MOD UK ARMY, 5 Bde, 8 Bde, 39 Bde, HQ UDR, 29 June 1970.

37. PRONI HA/32/3/3: 'Conclusions of a Meeting of the Joint Security Committee', 29 June 1970.

38. TNA DEFE 24/980: Minute from Head of C2(AD) to Head of DS6, 30 June 1970.

NOTES TO PAGES 70–3

39. TNA DEFE 24/980: Signal from CGS to GOC, Northern Ireland, 30 June 1970.
40. TNA DEFE 24/980: Signal from Norireland to MOD UK, 5 Bde, 8 Bde, 39 Bde, HQ UDR, 30 June 1970.
41. TNA DEFE 24/1611: Minute from Brigadier A. H. Farrar-Hockley, DPR(A), to MA/CGS, 30 June 1970.
42. TNA PREM 15/100: DOpsINTCOM, 7 July 1970. Assessment for period 24 June–7 July 1970.
43. TNA WO 305/6315: 'Summary of Events for the Period 23rd June to 19th October 1970 during 1 RRF Emergency Tour in Belfast.'
44. TNA WO 305/3959: '2nd Battalion The Queens Regiment. Historical Record. 1 Apr 70 – 31 Mar 71.'
45. TNA CAB 164/877: Signal from NORIRELAND, NISEC sitrep 030800A-040800A Jul 70.
46. S. Ó Fearghail, *Law (?) and Orders: The Belfast 'Curfew' of 3–5 July, 1970* (Dundalk: Central Citizens' Defence Committee, 1970), 2, 13.
47. TNA WO 305/3959: '2nd Battalion The Queens Regiment. Historical Record. 1 Apr 70 – 31 Mar 71.'
48. TNA DEFE 13/730: 'Conclusions of a meeting of the Joint Security Committee', 4 July 1970.
49. TNA DEFE 24/730: Minute from Head of C2(AD) to Head of DS6, 8 July 1970.
50. TNA PREM 15/100: Minute from D. H. A. to Prime Minister, 4 July 1970.
51. TNA PREM 15/100: DOpsINTCOM, 7 July 1970. Assessment for period 24 June–7 July 1970.
52. Hanley and Millar, *The Lost Revolution*, 157.
53. G. Warner, 'The Falls Road Curfew Revisited', *Irish Studies Review*, 14/3 (2006), 325–42.
54. KOSBRM: Newsletters: 'Borderer's in Belfast. The Newsletter of the 1st Battalion The King's Own Scottish Borderers in Belfast', 8 July 1970.
55. Ó Fearghail, *Law (?) and Orders*, 13, 16, 34.
56. A. Walsh, *From Hope to Hatred: Voices of the Falls Curfew* (Stroud: The History Press, 2013), 106.
57. Ó Fearghail, *Law (?) and Orders*, 3.
58. TNA DEFE 24/980: 'Meeting between the Minister of Defence, Mr Gerard Fitt, MP, Mr Frank McManus, MP and Mr Paddy Devlin', 6 July 1970.
59. TNA DEFE 25/273: Signal from HQNI to MOD, 6 July 1970.
60. TNA DEFE 25/273: Minute from A. P. Hockaday, AUS(GS), to PS/SoS, 7 July 1970.
61. TNA WO 305/4378: Historical Record, 1st The Royal Scots.
62. '45's Northern Flank', *The Globe and Laurel: The Journal of the Royal Marines*, 78/4 (1970), 216.
63. TNA DEFE 24/1611: Letter from A. P. Cumming-Bruce, HQNI, to D. A. Nicholls, Head of DS6, 9 July 1970.

64. TNA DEFE 24/1611: Minute from D. A. Nicholls, Head of DS6, to Col GS MO3 et al., 16 July 1970.
65. RSRM: *The Belfast Thistle*, 1st Battalion The Royal Scots, Edition 7, 11 July 1970, 11.
66. TNA PREM 15/100: DOpsINTCOM, 7 July 1970. Assessment for period 24 June–7 July 1970; PREM 15/101: DOpsINTCOM, 20 July 1970. Assessment for period 8–20 July 1970.
67. PRONI HA/32/3/3: 'Conclusions of a Meeting of the Joint Security Committee', 6 July 1970.
68. TNA PREM 15/100: DOpsINTCOM, 7 July 1970. Assessment for period 24 June–7 July 1970.
69. J. Peck, *Dublin from Downing Street* (Dublin: Gill and Macmillan, 1978), 52.
70. TNA CAB 134/3011: 'Cabinet. Ministerial Committee on Northern Ireland. Minutes of a Meeting Held at 10 Downing Street', 9 July 1970.
71. PRONI CAB/9/B/312/3A: Letter from James Chichester-Clark to John Mackie, 1 July 1970.
72. TNA PREM 15/101: Letter from James Chichester-Clark to Reginald Maudling, 12 July 1970.
73. TNA CAB 134/3011: 'Cabinet. Ministerial Committee on Northern Ireland. Minutes of a Meeting held at 10 Downing Street', 13 July 1970.
74. PRONI CAB/9/G/98/1: 'Note of a Meeting on 17 July 1970 when the Prime Minister and the Minister of Home Affairs Met the Home Secretary.'
75. TNA PREM 15/101: 'Note of the Prime Minister's meeting with the Prime Minister of Northern Ireland', 17 July 1970.
76. TNA PREM 15/101: DOpsINTCOM, 20 July 1970. Assessment for period 8–20 July 1970.
77. PRONI HA/32/3/3: 'Conclusions of a Meeting of the Joint Security Committee', 21 July 1970.
78. TNA DEFE 25/273: Minute from CGS to SoS Defence, 22 July 1970.
79. TNA CAB 164/877: 'Northern Ireland – situation report for period 9 a.m. 29th July – 9 a.m. 30th July [1970].'
80. 'Youth is shot dead in riot', *Belfast Telegraph*, 31 July 1970; TNA WO 305/7986: 'Historical Record – 1 KOSB. Period 1 March 1970 – 1 April 1971'.
81. TNA WO 305/3959: '2nd Battalion The Queens Regiment. Historical Record. 1 Apr 70 – 31 Mar 71.'
82. TNA PREM 15/101: DOpsINTCOM, 3 August 1970. Assessment for period 21 July–3 August 1970.
83. Bishop and Mallie, *The Provisional IRA*, 168.
84. TNA PREM 15/101: DOpsINTCOM, 17 August 1970. Assessment for period 4–17 August 1970.
85. TNA DEFE 24/730: Letter from Major-General T. H. Acton, HQNI, to Major-General R. E. Coaker, DMO, 11 August 1970, and attached paper, 'The Security Situation in Northern Ireland'.

86. C. King, *Diary, 1970–1974* (London: Jonathan Cape, 1975), 34–5.

87. L. Baston, *Reggie: The Life of Reginald Maudling* (Stroud: Sutton, 2004), 389.

88. TNA DEFE 24/560: 'Community Relations in Northern Ireland', Brigadier M. S. Bayley, 17 August 1970.

89. TNA DEFE 24/560: 'Community Relations Bulletin', 30 September 1970.

90. TNA DEFE 25/274: Minute from D of DOP to VCDS, 1 September 1970.

91. PRONI HA/32/3/4: 'Conclusions of a Meeting of the Joint Security Committee', 27 August 1970.

92. PRONI HA/32/3/4: 'Conclusions of a Meeting of the Joint Security Committee', 1 October 1970.

93. TNA DEFE 24/980: Minute from US of S(Army) to CGS, 3 September 1970.

94. TNA DEFE 24/980: Letter from A. P. Cumming-Bruce, HQNI, to D. A. Nicholls, Head of D 6, 30 September 1970.

95. TNA DEFE 24/980: Minute from Head of DS6 to MA/VCGS, 24 November 1970; Minute from CGS to US of S(Army), 7 December 1970.

96. TNA DEFE 24/980: Letter from Brigadier M. S. Bayley, HQNI, to Army Legal Services, 18 September 1970.

97. TNA DEFE 25/274: Minute from D of DOP to VCDS, 1 September 1970.

98. Airborne Assault Museum: 1st Parachute Regiment, Box 2.33.1: 'Annex A to 1 PARA G 141 dated 18th May 1971. First Battalion the Parachute Regiment. Operations diary for the tour in Northern Ireland starting 24th September 1970.'

99. TNA DEFE 13/676: Minute from Head of DS6 to PS/SoS, 30 November 1970; Record of McCoy Inquiry, 14 November 1970.

100. PRONI CAB/9/B/312/18: Letter from K. P. Bloomfield to I. M. Burns, Home Office, 22 September 1970. Re the price to the taxpayer, see: Bank of England inflation checker, accessed 10 February 2023 at: www.bankofengland.co.uk/monetary-policy/inflation/inflation-calculator.

101. Labour History Archive and Study Centre [hereafter LHASC]: *Report of the sixty-ninth annual conference of the Labour Party. Blackpool, 1970*, 263–7.

102. Thornton, 'Getting it Wrong', 73–107.

103. TNA DEFE 25/274: 'Northern Ireland. Functions of the Army and the Police', brief by Home Office and Ministry of Defence, 11 August 1970.

104. TNA PREM 15/101: 'Note of a meeting held at the Home Office', 17 August 1970.

105. PRONI CAB/9/G/98/1: 'G.O.C.'s Study Day – 8th September, 1970', minute for Chief Constable from A. C. C. 'D' Department, 9 September 1970.

106. PRONI CAB/9/G/98/1: Letter from Sir Arthur Young to General Freeland, 15 September 1970.

107. TNA DEFE 24/730: 'Northern Ireland. Discussion with Secretary of State for Defence', 6 July 1970.

108. M. Carver, *Tightrope Walking: British Defence Policy since 1945* (London: Hutchinson, 1992), 94.

109. TNA DEFE 25/273: Minute from CDS to SoS Defence, 13 July 1970.
110. TNA DEFE 25/274: 'The effect of withdrawing 2–4 battalions from BAOR for Northern Ireland over the period of 18 months or so', Note by Chief of Staff, BAOR, 14 August 1970.
111. TNA DEFE 13/680: 'Ministry of Defence. Chiefs of Staff Committee. Northern Ireland. Note by the Secretary', 11 September 1970.
112. TNA DEFE 13/680: Letter from Air Chief Marshal Sir David Lee, UK Military Representative, NATO, to CDS, 18 November 1970.
113. NATO Archives: CER 1970: Letter from General A. J. Goodpaster to Chairman, North Atlantic Military Council, 29 June 1971, attaching 'SACEUR's Combat Effectiveness Report 1970'.
114. NATO Archives: CER 1969 part 2: 'SACEUR's Combat Effectiveness Report – 1969. Assessment of National Forces by Component in Relation to Assigned Missions', 26 June 1970.
115. F. J. Gavin, 'The Myth of Flexible Response: United States Strategy in Europe during the 1960s', *The International History Review*, 23/4 (2001), 847–75.
116. TNA DEFE 25/261: Minute from CGS to SoS Defence, 12 October 1970.
117. TNA PREM 15/474: Letter from Lord Carrington to Prime Minister, 26 October 1970; Minute from P. L. Gregson, 10 Downing Street, to A. Stephens, Ministry of Defence, 30 October 1970.
118. TNA DEFE 24/1611: Minute from Lt-Col M. R. Johnston, MA/CGS, to PS/US of S(Army), DMO, AUS(GS) and BGS(Int), 29 October 1970, and attached 'Extract of a letter from Comd 8 Inf Bde to CGS dated 26 Oct 70'.
119. TNA CAB 164/877: 'Northern Ireland situation report for period 9 am 29 October to 9 am 30 October [1970]'; 'Northern Ireland report for period from 8 am 30 October to 8 am 2 November [1970].'
120. J. Riley, *Oft in Danger: The Life and Campaigns of General Sir Anthony Farrar-Hockley* (Solihull: Helion, 2015), 317, 324.
121. IWMSA: Paul Garman, catalogue number 24732, reel 6.
122. IWMSA: James Alan Comrie Cowan, catalogue number 18802, reel 24.
123. TNA DEFE 24/1611: Directive NISEC 11, from Maj-Gen A. H. Farrar-Hockley, 'Intensification of operations', 3 November 1970.
124. PRONI DCR/1/82: Letter from Brigadier M. S. Bayley, HQNI, to Mr W. Slinger, Ministry of Community Relations, 3 November 1970; and attached, 'Draft. Security forces liaison with local committees and associations', 12 October 1970.
125. TNA PREM 15/474: Letter from R. Burroughs, UKREP, to Philip Woodfield, Home Office, 8 December 1970.
126. TNA DEFE 13/676: Minute from A. P. Hockaday, AUS(GS), to PS/SoS, 30 November 1970.
127. TNA DEFE 13/676: Minute from Lt-Col M. R. Johnston, MA/CGS, to DMO, 11 January 1971.
128. IWM: Papers of Ian Freeland, catalogue reference 79/34/3: 'Staff College Lecture. 9th December 1970.'

129. Patterson, 'The British State and the Rise of the IRA, 1969–71', 507; C. C. O'Brien, *States of Ireland* (Frogmore: Granada, 1974), 243.

130. Airborne Assault Museum: 1st Parachute Regiment, Box 2.33.1: 'Annex A to 1 PARA G 141 dated 18th May 1971. First Battalion the Parachute Regiment. Operations diary for the tour in Northern Ireland starting 24th September 1970.'

131. PRONI HA/32/3/5: 'Conclusions of a Meeting of the Joint Security Committee', 14 January 1971.

132. PRONI CAB/9/G/98/1: 'Note of a Meeting when the Prime Minister Met the Home Secretary and the Secretary of State for Defence', 18 January 1971.

133. TNA DEFE 13/676: Minute from A. P. Hockaday, AUS(GS), to PS/SoS, 19 January 1971.

134. TNA DEFE 13/676: 'Meeting of Secretary of State for Defence and Minister of State, Home Office, with the Northern Ireland Cabinet', 29 January 1971.

135. PRONI CAB/9/G/49/9: 'Policy for Operations', NISEC 02, signed Lt-Gen I. H. Freeland, 3 February 1971.

136. TNA DEFE 25/303: Minute from Lt-Col M. N. S. McCord, for GOC, to MO3, 7 February 1971.

137. Riley, *Oft in Danger*, 328–9.

138. PRONI HA/32/3/5: 'Conclusions of a Meeting of the Joint Security Committee', 4 February 1971.

139. TNA PREM 15/475: Letter from A. W. Stephens, MoD, to P. L. Gregson, PS/ Prime Minister, 4 February 1971.

140. TNA DEFE 25/303: Minute from Lt-Col M. N. S. McCord, for GOC, to MO3, 7 February 1971.

141. TNA DEFE 25/303: Minute from Lt-Col M. N. S. McCord, for GOC, to MO3, 7 February 1971.

142. Farrell, *Northern Ireland*, 276.

143. Airborne Assault Museum: 1st Parachute Regiment, Box 2.33.1: 'Annex A to 1 PARA G 141 dated 18th May 1971. First Battalion the Parachute Regiment. Operations diary for the tour in Northern Ireland starting 24th September 1970.'

144. TNA DEFE 25/303: Minute from Lt-Col M. N. S. McCord, for GOC, to MO3, 7 February 1971.

145. TNA WO 305/4374: '94th Locating Regiment, Royal Artillery. Battery History Report. 156 (Inkerman) Battery RA. 31 December 1970–31 December 1971. Annexure "A". Report on the incident at New Lodge Road on 6 Feb 71.'

146. TNA DEFE 25/303: Minute from Lt-Col M. N. S. McCord, for GOC, to MO3, 7 February 1971; D. McKittrick, S. Kelters, B. Feeney, C. Thornton and D. McVea, *Lost Lives: The Stories of the Men, Women and Children Who Died as a Result of the Northern Ireland Troubles* (London: Mainstream, 2007), 62–5.

147. Ó Dochartaigh, *Deniable Contact*, 38.

148. IWMSA: Julian Howard Atherden Thompson, catalogue number 28361, reel 22.
149. TNA DEFE 13/683: Minute from A. W. Stephens, APS/SoS, to PS/US of S(Army), 9 February 1971.
150. TNA DEFE 13/731: Minute from US of S(Army) to Secretary of State for Defence, 11 February 1971.
151. S. Campbell, *Gerry Fitt and the SDLP: 'In a Minority of One'* (Manchester: Manchester University Press, 2015), 32–59.
152. TNA DEFE 13/731: 'Note for the Record', Home Office, 12 February 1971.
153. TNA PREM 15/475: Minute from Graham Angel, Private Secretary, Home Office, to Robert Armstrong, 10 Downing Street, 11 February 1971, with attached 'The current security situation'.
154. D. Johnson, *Overconfidence and War: The Havoc and Glory of Positive Illusions* (London: Harvard University Press, 2004), 4.
155. PRONI CAB/9/G/49/9: 'News Release from HQ Northern Ireland Public Relations. Statement by GOC Northern Ireland', 15 February 1971.
156. TNA CAB 134/3012: 'COS 13/71. Ministry of Defence. Chiefs of Staff Committee. Contingency Planning to Cover the Possibility of Direct Rule in Northern Ireland. Note by the Secretary', 9 February 1971.
157. TNA CAB 190/8: 'Cabinet. Joint Intelligence Committee (A). Northern Ireland Intelligence Working Party. Intelligence Arrangements in an Emergency in Northern Ireland', 6 November 1970.
158. Van Voris, *Violence in Ulster*, 184.
159. TNA CAB 164/877: 'Note for the record. Northern Ireland. A meeting was held at Chequers on Saturday 13 February 1971.'
160. TNA PREM 15/475: Minute from Edward Heath to SoS Defence, 15 February 1971; Minute from Edward Heath to Home Secretary, 16 February 1971; DEFE 13/731: Minute from Reginald Maudling to Prime Minister, 26 February 1971.
161. TNA PREM 15/475: Letter from Lord Carrington to Prime Minister, 19 February 1971.
162. TNA WO 305/4374: '57 (Bhurtpore) Battery Royal Artillery Historical Record. 1 January 1971 to 31 December 1971.'
163. PRONI HA/32/3/5: 'Conclusions of a Meeting of the Joint Security Committee', 27 February 1971.
164. PRONI HA/32/3/5: 'Conclusions of a Meeting of the Joint Security Committee', 28 February 1971.
165. PRONI HA/32/3/5: 'Conclusions of a Meeting of the Joint Security Committee', 1 March 1971.
166. PRONI CAB/9/G/49/9: 'Note of a Discussion between the Prime Minister and the Home Secretary', 1 March 1971.
167. TNA DEFE 13/731: Minute from R. Coaker, DMO, to VCGS, 2 March 1971.

168. PRONI HA/32/3/6: 'Note of a Meeting between the Home Secretary and NI Ministers', 4 March 1971.
169. TNA DEFE 25/303: Minute from A. P. Hockaday to PS/SoS, 10 March 1971.
170. TNA PREM 15/475: 'Report on Northern Ireland for period from 9 a.m. 5th March to 8 a.m. 8th March 1971.'
171. TNA CAB 134/3011: 'Cabinet. Ministerial Committee on Northern Ireland. Minutes of a Meeting held at 10 Downing Street', 10 March 1971.
172. R. Maudling, *Memoirs* (London: Sidgwick and Jackson, 1978), 181–2.
173. TNA DEFE 25/303: Minute from A. P. Hockaday to PS/SoS, 10 March 1971.
174. IWMSA: Raymond William Hall, catalogue number 17927, reel 3.
175. '1st Battalion', *Pegasus: Journal of The Parachute Regiment and Airborne Forces*, 26/2 (April 1971), 24.
176. Airborne Assault Museum: 1st Parachute Regiment, Box 2.33.1: 'Annex A to 1 PARA G 141 dated 18th May 1971. First Battalion the Parachute Regiment. Operations diary for the tour in Northern Ireland starting 24th September 1970.'
177. PRONI HA/32/3/6: 'Meeting between the Prime Minister and Ministers and a Deputation of Shop Stewards from Harland and Wolff and International Computers', 12 March 1971.
178. Bloomfield, *Stormont in Crisis*, 133.
179. TNA DEFE 25/303: 'Northern Ireland briefing for Major-General H. C. Tuzo, OBE, MC, BA. GOC (designate) Northern Ireland. 1015–1125 hrs 22 Feb 71.'
180. PRONI CAB/9/G/98/1: 'Meeting between Ministers and the General Officer Commanding', 12 March 1971.
181. TNA DEFE 25/303: Signal from GOC NI to VCGS, 13 March 1971.
182. TNA DEFE 13/731: Signal from Burroughs, UKREP, to Home Office, 14 March 1971.
183. TNA CAB 134/3011: 'Cabinet. Ministerial Committee on Northern Ireland. Minutes of a Meeting held at 10 Downing Street', 15 March 1971.
184. TNA DEFE 25/303: 'Prime Minister's meeting with the Prime Minister of Northern Ireland', 16 March 1971.
185. TNA CAB 134/3011: 'Cabinet. Ministerial Committee on Northern Ireland. Minutes of a Meeting held at 10 Downing Street', 17 March 1971.
186. PRONI HA/32/3/6: 'Note of a Meeting of Ministers, Attended for Part of the Time by the GOC, the United Kingdom Representative and the Chief Constable', 19 March 1971.
187. TNA DEFE 13/915: 'Record of conversation between the Prime Minister and Major Chichester-Clark', 19 March 1971.
188. TNA DEFE 13/731: Minute from A. W. S. to SoS, 19 March 1971, with signal from Acting GOC, CLF and UKREP to Home Office, MoD and FCO.
189. PRONI HA/32/3/6: 'Note of a Meeting between Ministers and the Minister of Defence [sic], the Chief of the General Staff, the GOC and the UK Representative', 20 March 1971.

190. TNA DEFE 24/982: 'Note of a meeting held in the Prime Minister's office at Stormont Castle', 20 March 1971.
191. Smith, *The British State and the Northern Ireland Crisis*, 135.
192. Devlin, *Straight Left*, 153.

4 EDWARD HEATH'S BID FOR VICTORY

1. PRONI HA/32/3/5: 'Conclusions of a Meeting of the Joint Security Committee', 11 August 1971.
2. B. O'Leary, *A Treatise on Northern Ireland, Volume 2: Control* (Oxford: Oxford University Press, 2019), 183.
3. Craig, *Crisis of Confidence*, 104.
4. A. Downes, *Targeting Civilians in War* (Ithaca: Cornell University Press, 2008).
5. Smith, *The British State and the Northern Ireland Crisis*, 125.
6. Hennessey, *The Evolution of The Troubles*, 128.
7. Ó Dochartaigh, 'Bloody Sunday: Error or Design?', 96; Charters, *Whose Mission, Whose Orders?*, 15.
8. TNA CAB 134/3011: 'Cabinet. Ministerial Committee on Northern Ireland. Minutes of a Meeting', 31 March 1971.
9. TNA DEFE 13/676: Letter from A. P. Hockaday, AUS(GS), to Maj-Gen T. H. Acton, HQNI, 8 December 1970.
10. IWMSA: Anonymous, catalogue number 11162, reel 2.
11. PRONI CAB/9/G/49/9: 'Note of a Meeting between Ministers and the GOC', 6 July 1971.
12. Airborne Assault Museum, 1 Para in Belfast, Box 2.33.1: 'Orders Book. Opened 9 Apr 1971. Major [name redacted]. 1 PARA', 2 June 1971.
13. TNA PREM 15/477: 'Northern Ireland. Note of a meeting', 1 April 1971.
14. PRONI HA/32/3/6: 'Conclusions of a Meeting of the Joint Security Committee', 15 April 1971; 'Conclusions of a Meeting of the Joint Security Committee', 20 May 1971.
15. PRONI CAB/9/B/312/12A: 'Duty Officers' [RUC] Report for 24 Hours Ending at 8 a.m. [hereafter "RUC Duty Report"]', 12 April 1971.
16. TNA PREM 15/477: 'Northern Ireland: political summary for the period 2–15 April 1971. Memorandum by the Home Office [hereafter Home Office Summary]', 16 April 1971; PRONI CAB/9/B/312/12A: RUC Duty Report, 14 April 1971; RUC Duty Report, 15 April 1971.
17. IWM: Papers of Ian Freeland, catalogue reference 79/34/3: Letter from Lt-Gen Sir Cecil Blacker to Lt-Gen Sir Ian Freeland, 30 April 1971.
18. TNA DEFE 24/1919: 'Report on operations in Northern Ireland – HQ 16 Para Bde', 14 September 1971.
19. 'Vikings in Derry', *Castle: The Journal of the Royal Anglian Regiment*, 4/1 (May 1971), 12.

20. PRONI CAB/9/B/312/12A: RUC Duty Report, 7 April 1971.
21. PRONI CAB/9/B/312/12A: RUC Duty Report, 24 May 1971.
22. Airborne Assault Museum: Northern Ireland publications. Box 2.33.25: Booklet: 'Some facts about Northern Ireland', 1st Bn. the Parachute Regiment, 22 May 1971, 23, 25.
23. IWMSA: Kenneth Ambrose, catalogue number 32532, reel 10.
24. LHCMA: David Ramsbotham papers, Box 1: 'The Northern Ireland insurgency. Talk to U.S. Army War College – 29 January 1973. Brigadier Frank Kitson.'
25. TNA DEFE 13/918: Minute from PUS, Ministry of Defence, to Secretary of State for Defence, attaching paper, 'The IRA doctrine of counter intelligence and intelligence', 29 November 1971.
26. Moloney, *A Secret History of the IRA*, 100.
27. TNA PREM 15/477: Home Office Summary, 7 May 1971; Letter from R. J. Andrew, MoD, to P. L. Gregson, 18 May 1971.
28. TNA DEFE 24/1919: 'Report on operations in Northern Ireland – HQ 16 Para Bde', 14 September 1971 (incident of 11 May 1971).
29. '1st Battalion', *Castle: The Journal of the Royal Anglian Regiment*, 4/3 (May 1972), 32.
30. TNA WO 305/4394: 1st Royal Highland Fusiliers Historical Diary, April 1971 – March 1972.
31. TNA PREM 15/477: Home Office Summary, 26 May 1971.
32. TNA WO 305/4342: 'Annual Regimental Historical Record. 7th Parachute Regiment, Royal Horse Artillery. 1 January to 31 December 1971.'
33. Airborne Assault Museum, 1 Para in Belfast, Box 2.33.1: 'Orders Book. Opened 9 Apr 1971. Major [name redacted]. 1 PARA', 11 June 1971.
34. TNA PREM 15/477: Home Office Summary, 25 June 1971.
35. TNA CAB 134/3011: 'Cabinet. Ministerial Committee on Northern Ireland. Minutes of a Meeting', 6 July 1971.
36. TNA PREM 15/477: Home Office Summary, 21 May 1971.
37. PRONI HA/32/2/55: Letter from R. J. R. Laverty, Government Security Unit, to H. W. West, 30 April 1971.
38. PRONI CAB/9/B/312/12A: RUC Duty Report, 27 June 1971.
39. Anon, 'The Search', *The Journal of The Queen's Regiment*, 5/2 (June 1971), 27.
40. British Army, *Operation Banner*, para 502.
41. D. Charters, '"Have a Go": British Army/MI5 Agent-Running Operations in Northern Ireland, 1970–72', *Intelligence and National Security*, 28/2 (2013), 218.
42. IWMSA: Clive Marcus Brennan, catalogue number 27190, reel 15.
43. TNA DEFE 25/304: Minute from DCDS(I) to CDS(2), 6 April 1971; Minute from A. P. Hockaday, AUS(GS), to PS/SoS, 26 April 1971.
44. TNA DEFE 24/1919: '3 LI. Report on operations in Northern Ireland', 12 August 1971.
45. TNA WO 305/5838: '3rd Bn The Parachute Regiment. Post-operational Report on Emergency Tour of Duty in Northern Ireland 18 January – 4 June 1971.'

46. TNA DEFE 24/1919: 'Report on Northern Ireland tour', 16 Para Bde, 6 July 1971.
47. TNA WO 305/5621: 'Brigade Commander's General Report', 19 Airportable Brigade, 30 November 1971.
48. Dewar, *The British Army in Northern Ireland*, 55–6.
49. TNA DEFE 13/912: Minute from US of S(Army) to Secretary of State for Defence, 4 December 1972.
50. TNA DEFE 24/1919: '1st Battalion the Royal Green Jackets. End of Northern Ireland tour report May – Sep 1971.'
51. TNA WO 305/5691: 'Report on Operations in Northern Ireland', 42 Commando, 20 January 1972.
52. JSCSC: Army Staff Course 1971, 'Urban Operations in Northern Ireland – Notes for DS.'
53. TNA WO 305/5837: '1 Coldm Gds Report on Operations in Northern Ireland', 12 August 1971.
54. TNA DEFE 24/1908: Minute from J. H. Gibbon, DASD, to CGS, 19 June 1970.
55. TNA DEFE 24/877: Minute from W. G. H. Beach, DASD, to CGS, 8 October 1973.
56. Neumann, *Britain's Long War*, 30.
57. F. Ní Aoláin, *The Politics of Force: Conflict Management and State Violence in Northern Ireland* (Belfast: The Blackstaff Press, 2000), 33–4, 40.
58. Leahy, *The Intelligence War against the IRA*, 21.
59. F. Foley, *Countering Terrorism in Britain and France: Institutions, Norms and the Shadow of the Past* (Cambridge: Cambridge University Press, 2013), 59.
60. Edwards, 'Misapplying Lessons Learned?', 321.
61. Morgan and Smith, 'Northern Ireland and Minimum Force', 81–105; Drohan, *Brutality in an Age of Human Rights*, 152.
62. P. Wilkinson, *Terrorism versus Democracy: The Liberal State Response* (Abingdon: Routledge, 2011), 75, 105, 107.
63. K. McEvoy, 'What Did the Lawyers Do during the "War"? Neutrality, Conflict and the Culture of Quietism', *Modern Law Review*, 74/3 (2011), 350–84.
64. TNA DEFE 13/914: Letter from A. J. Cragg, APS/SoS Defence, to Head of DS10, 6 January 1975.
65. TNA DEFE 24/723: Minute from R. E. Coaker, DMO, to AUS(GS), 25 March 1971.
66. TNA DEFE 24/723: Minute from [illegible], for Head of C2(AD), to Head of DS6, 15 April 1971.
67. PRONI HA/8/1966: Letter from W. Leitch to J. W. B. Kelly, 3 May 1971.
68. Sanders, 'Principles of Minimum Force and the Parachute Regiment', 681.
69. IWM: Papers of T. H. Friend, catalogue reference 12/52/1, Memoirs – 'With a pause of two-three', 120.
70. TNA CAB 164/877: 'Northern Ireland situation report for period 9 am 29 October to 9 am 30 October [1970].'

71. PRONI HA/32/3/4: 'Conclusions of a Meeting of the Joint Security Committee', 5 November 1970.
72. PRONI HA/32/5/5: 'The Queen v. Norbert Jan Bek. Malicious Wounding. Transcript of the Official Shorthand Note Relating to the Trial', 30 March 1971.
73. R. Fisk, 'Jury acquit marine who fired in Belfast clash', *The Times*, 31 March 1971.
74. Ó Dochartaigh, *From Civil Rights to Armalites*, 232.
75. PRONI HA/32/3/6: 'Conclusions of a Meeting of the Joint Security Committee', 8 July 1971.
76. TNA WO 305/6509: 'Ministry of Defence. Narrative of the Military Operations in Northern Ireland Which Began in August 1969. Vol. 1', VI-15.
77. TNA DEFE 24/723: 'Royal Military Police. Statement Form (Military). Lt "A"', 8 July 1971.
78. 'Ulster rioters who carry rifles, nail bombs and petrol bombs asking for trouble – minister', *The Times*, 13 July 1971.
79. TNA DEFE 24/723: Letter from PS/Minister of State for Defence, to Mr Johnson and Mr Ekins-Daukes, 14 July 1971.
80. TNA PREM 15/488: Letter from A. W. Stephens, Ministry of Defence, to P. L. Gregson, 10 November 1971, attaching Gifford report.
81. G. Murray and J. Tonge, *Sinn Féin and the SDLP: From Alienation to Participation* (London: Hurst, 2005), 26.
82. B. O'Duffy, 'The Price of Containment: Deaths and Debate on Northern Ireland in the House of Commons, 1968–94', in P. Catterall and S. McDougall (eds.), *The Northern Ireland Question in British Politics* (Basingstoke: Macmillan, 1996), 106.
83. PRONI CAB/9/B/312/12A: RUC Duty Report, 11 July 1971.
84. TNA DEFE 24/731: Minute from A. P. Hockaday, AUS(GS), to PS/SoS, 5 July 1971.
85. TNA DEFE 24/731: Letter from A. W. Stephens, Ministry of Defence, to PS/US of S (Army), 19 July 1971.
86. TNA PREM 15/478: Minute from P. L. Gregson to A. W. Stephens, 22 July 1971.
87. TNA DEFE 13/915: Minute from CGS to Secretary of State for Defence, 22 July 1971.
88. TNA DEFE 24/742: 'Annex B to MO minute of 23 July giving a first [illegible word] on the disruptive operation.'
89. TNA DEFE 24/742: Signal from HQNI to MO 3, 25 July 1971.
90. TNA DEFE 24/742: Signal from FCO to Dublin, 24 July 1971.
91. TNA DEFE 24/742: Signal from GOC NI to DMO, 25 July 1971.
92. TNA DEFE 24/742: Minute from A. P. Hockaday, AUS(GS), to PS/SoS, 28 July 1971.
93. PRONI: CAB/9/B/312/12A: RUC Duty Report, 24 July 1971.
94. PRONI: CAB/9/B/312/14A: RUC Duty Report, 1 August 1971.
95. TNA DEFE 13/915: Minute from CGS to Secretary of State for Defence, 28 July 1971.

96. TNA DEFE 13/915: Minute from A. P. Hockaday, AUS(GS), to PS/SoS, 26 July 1971; TNA DEFE 24/742: Minute from Major R. I. C. Macpherson, Duty GSO 2, to GSO 1 Ops, 27 July 1971.

97. TNA CAB 134/3011: 'Cabinet. Ministerial Committee on Northern Ireland. Minutes of a Meeting', 29 July 1971.

98. TNA DEFE 13/915: Minute from VCGS to PS/SoS, 4 August 1971.

99. PRONI HA/32/3/6: 'Conclusions of a Meeting of the Joint Security Committee', 5 August 1971.

100. PRONI CAB/9/B/312/14A: RUC Duty Report, 7 August 1971; RUC Duty Report, 8 August 1971.

101. '1st Battalion', *The Green Howards' Gazette: A monthly chronicle of The Green Howards*, 79/930 (September 1971), 916.

102. PRONI CAB/9/B/312/14A: RUC Duty Report, 9 August 1971.

103. Hennessey, *The Evolution of The Troubles*, 85–117.

104. L. K. Donohue, *The Cost of Counterterrorism: Power, Politics, and Liberty* (Cambridge: Cambridge University Press, 2008), 36–7.

105. Smith, *The British State and the Northern Ireland Crisis*, 128; Charters, *Whose Mission, Whose Orders?*, 15.

106. M. McCleery, *Operation Demetrius and Its Aftermath: A New History of the Use of Internment without Trial in Northern Ireland, 1971–75* (Manchester: Manchester University Press, 2015), 33, 46.

107. TNA CAB 134/3012: 'Cabinet Official Committee on Northern Ireland. Minutes of a meeting', 15 March 1971.

108. TNA CJ 4/101: Internal Security Instruction 2/71, HQ Northern Ireland, 6 August 1971.

109. Tuck, 'Northern Ireland and the British Approach to Counter-Insurgency', 175.

110. McCleery, *Operation Demetrius and Its Aftermath*, 38–40.

111. TNA CAB 165/951: Minute from Burke Trend to Prime Minister, 16 March 1971.

112. TNA WO 305/6509: 'Narrative of the Military Operations in Northern Ireland', VIII-1, VIII-2.

113. IWMSA: James Alan Comrie Cowan, catalogue number 18802, reel 25.

114. TNA PREM 15/480: 'Northern Ireland. Note of a meeting at the Home Office', 13 September 1971.

115. TNA DEFE 13/683: Note from A. W. Stephens to Secretary of State for Defence, 22 September 1971.

116. Charters, *Whose Mission, Whose Orders?*, 117.

117. TNA PREM 15/478: 'Northern Ireland. Note of a meeting held at 10 Downing Street', 5 August 1971.

118. McCleery, *Operation Demetrius and Its Aftermath*, 40.

119. Donohue, *The Cost of Counterterrorism*, 51.

120. B. Faulkner, *Memoirs of a Statesman* (London: Weidenfeld and Nicolson, 1978), 124.

121. M. Carver, *Out of Step: Memoirs of a Field Marshal* (London: Hutchinson, 1989), 410.

122. H. Bennett, 'Detention and interrogation in Northern Ireland, 1969–75', in S. Scheipers (ed.), *Prisoners in War* (Oxford: Oxford University Press, 2010), 191–2.

123. TNA DEFE 24/744: Letter from J. M. H. Lewis, BGS(Int), to H. D. Eastwood, HQNI, 6 August 1971.

124. TNA PREM 15/478: 'Northern Ireland. Note of a meeting held at 10 Downing Street', 5 August 1971.

125. P. Ziegler, *Edward Heath: The Authorised Biography* (London: HarperPress, 2010), 300.

126. Craig, *Crisis of Confidence*, 97–8.

127. IWMSA: Clive Marcus Brennan, catalogue number 27190, reel 15.

128. LHCMA: David Ramsbotham papers, Box 1: Lecture Notes and Northern Ireland; O'Leary, *A Treatise on Northern Ireland, Volume II*, 183.

129. Ardoyne Commemoration Project, *Ardoyne: The Untold Truth* (Belfast: Beyond the Pale, 2002), 52.

130. IWMSA: Kenneth Ambrose, catalogue number 32532, reel 11.

131. McCleery, *Operation Demetrius and Its Aftermath*, 2.

132. Donohue, *The Cost of Counterterrorism*, 38.

133. TNA WO 305/6509: 'Narrative of the Military Operations in Northern Ireland', VIII-7.

134. PRONI CAB/9/B/312/14A: RUC Duty Report, 10 August 1971.

135. TNA WO 305/6509: 'Narrative of the Military Operations in Northern Ireland', VIII-6, VIII-7.

136. TNA CAB 164/879: Minute from Col GS, MO3, to PS/SoS, 10 August 1971.

137. PRONI CAB/9/B/312/14A: RUC Duty Report, 11 August 1971.

138. TNA WO 305/6509: 'Narrative of the Military Operations in Northern Ireland', VIII-6, VIII-7.

139. PRONI CAB/9/B/312/14A: RUC Duty Report, 11 August 1971.

140. TNA WO 305/6509: 'Narrative of the Military Operations in Northern Ireland', VIII-6, VIII-7.

141. The judgements, delivered on 11 May 2021, are available at: www.judiciaryni.uk/judicial-decisions/2021-nicoroner-6.

142. 'Ballymurphy Inquest: Residents Asked Army for "Protection"', BBC News, 25 February 2019, accessed 5 November 2020 at: www.bbc.co.uk/news/uk-northern-ireland-47365296.

143. J. Keegan, *In the Matter of the Coroners Act (Northern Ireland) 1959. In the Matter of a Series of Deaths That Occurred in August 1971 at Ballymurphy, West Belfast. Summary of Coroner's Verdicts and Findings* (Belfast: Judicial Communications Office, 2021), 21–2.

144. 'Ballymurphy Inquest: Ex-soldier Says What He Saw Was "Murder"', 3 April 2019, accessed 5 November 2020 at: www.bbc.co.uk/news/uk-northern-ireland-47797514.

145. Keegan, *Summary of Coroner's Verdicts and Findings*, 22–6.
146. 'Ballymurphy inquest: "Most If Not All" Victims "Were Not IRA"', 11 March 2019, accessed 5 November 2020 at: www.bbc.co.uk/news/uk-northern-ireland-47527495.
147. Airborne Assault Museum, 1 Para in Belfast, Box 2.33.1: 'Orders Book. Opened 9 Apr 1971. Major [name redacted]. 1 PARA', 16 August 1971.
148. PRONI CAB/9/B/312/14A: RUC Duty Report, 24 August 1971; RUC Duty Report, 30 August 1971.
149. PRONI HA/32/3/5: 'Conclusions of a Meeting of the Joint Security Committee', 11 August 1971.
150. '2nd Battalion', *Pegasus: Journal of The Parachute Regiment and Airborne Forces*, 26/4 (October 1971), 9.
151. TNA PREM 15/478: 'Home Secretary's meeting with Mr Fitt and Mr Hume', 11 August 1971.
152. TNA CAB 130/522: 'Minutes of a Meeting held at 10 Downing Street', 12 August 1971.
153. King, *Diary, 1970–1974*, 129–30.
154. IWM, Papers of Ian Freeland, catalogue number 79/34/4: Letter from Anthony Farrar-Hockley to Ian Freeland, 11 August 1971.
155. Beresford, *The Official IRA and Republican Clubs*, 357, 361–2.
156. Bennett, 'Detention and Interrogation in Northern Ireland', 192; for an extensive account, see: S. Newbery, *Interrogation, Intelligence and Security: Controversial British Techniques* (Manchester: Manchester University Press, 2015), 62–84.
157. TNA CAB 163/173: 'Report on Operation Calaba – August 1971', Lt-Col J. R. Nicholson.
158. 'The Torture Files', *RTÉ Investigations Unit*, broadcast 4 June 2014, accessed 5 November 2020 at: www.rte.ie/news/player/2014/0604/10289849-rte-investigations-unit-the-torture-files.
159. TNA FCO 33/1461: Home Office Summary, 13 August 1971.
160. Donohue, *The Cost of Counterterrorism*, 38.
161. 'This Week', *Thames Television Archive*, broadcast 30 September 1971, accessed 6 November 2020 at: www.youtube.com/watch?v=n_azaxf3GCQ&list=PL7WD0g9dS3jlc2vaHrWhAhB9xq74fi0MR&index=16.
162. 'This Week', *Thames Television Archive*, transmitted 26 August 1971, accessed 6 November 2020 at: www.youtube.com/watch?v=wmMIswNQixc&list=PL7WD0g9dS3jlc2vaHrWhAhB9xq74fi0MR&index=6.
163. PRONI CAB/9/B/312/14A: RUC Duty Report, 17 August 1971.
164. 'Government rejects Labour plea to recall Parliament', *The Times*, 17 August 1971.
165. TNA PREM 15/479: Minute from Edward Heath, to R. Andrew, Ministry of Defence, 17 August 1971.
166. PRONI CAB/9/B/312/14A: RUC Duty Report, 19 August 1971.

167. PRONI HA/32/3/6: 'Conclusions of a Meeting of the Joint Security Committee', 19 August 1971.

168. TNA DEFE 24/731: Signal from UKREP Belfast to Home Office, 17 August 1971.

169. PRONI CAB/9/B/312/14A: RUC Duty Report, 24 August 1971; RUC Duty Report, 27 August 1971.

170. PRONI CAB/9/B/312/14A: RUC Duty Report, 3 September 1971.

171. PRONI CAB/9/B/312/14A: RUC Duty Report, 7 September 1971.

172. 'Company Notes', *The Iron Duke: The Regimental Journal of the Duke of Wellington's Regiment*, 47/157 (December 1971), 92–3.

173. TNA CAB 164/879: Minute from R. T. Armstrong, 10 Downing Street, to G. L. Angel, Home Office, 19 August 1971.

174. TNA DEFE 13/954: Minute from P. J. Woodfield to P. Gregson, 20 August 1971.

175. TNA DEFE 13/954: Signal from GOC Northern Ireland to VCGS, 23 August 1971.

176. TNA DEFE 13/954: Signal from VCGS to GOC Northern Ireland, 24 August 1971.

177. TNA CJ 4/95: Letter to Sir Edmund Compton from G. L. Angel, Home Office, 31 August 1971.

178. TNA DEFE 13/954: Minute from C. H. Henn, PS/Minister of State, to MA/VCGS, 25 August 1971.

179. TNA DEFE 13/954: Minute from A. P. Hockaday, AUS(GS), to PS/Minister of State, 27 August 1971.

180. PRONI HA/32/5/8: 'Emergency Committee Meeting', 3 September 1971.

181. TNA DEFE 13/683: Letter from CGS to Lt-Gen Tuzo, 7 September 1971.

182. TNA DEFE 13/683: 'Report on information work: Northern Ireland', by Clifford Hill, 16 September 1971.

183. TNA DEFE 13/683: Minute from Donald Maitland, 10 Downing Street, to K. McDowall, Home Office, 15 October 1971.

184. TNA PREM 15/483: Minute from Burke Trend to Prime Minister, 29 October 1971; on propaganda, see: R. Cormac, 'The Information Research Department, Unattributable Propaganda, and Northern Ireland, 1971–1973: Promising Salvation but Ending in Failure?', *English Historical Review*, 131/552 (2016), 1074–104.

185. TNA CAB 164/879: Minute from P. L. Gregson, 10 Downing Street, to N. J. Barrington, FCO, 24 August 1971, with attached 'British Policy in Northern Ireland. Note by the Central Policy Review Staff.'

186. TNA PREM 15/479: Home Office Summary, 27 August 1971.

187. TNA PREM 15/480: Home Office Summary, 3 September 1971.

188. TNA PREM 15/480: Minute from Burke Trend to Prime Minister, 3 September 1971.

189. TNA PREM 15/480: 'Text of a telephone conversation between Mr Faulkner and the Prime Minister', 10 September 1971.

190. PRONI HA/32/3/6: 'Conclusions of a Meeting of the Joint Security Committee', 16 September 1971.

191. TNA CAB 164/881: 'Record of a discussion with the Prime Minister of Northern Ireland', 26 September 1971; TNA CAB 164/880: 'Telephone conversation between the Prime Minister and Mr Faulkner', 11 September 1971.

192. PRONI CAB/9/G/49/9: Letter from Lt-Gen Sir Harry Tuzo to Brian Faulkner, 27 September 1971.

193. A. MacLeod, *The United Kingdom, Republic of Ireland, United States and the Conflict in Northern Ireland, August 1971–September 1974* (PhD thesis, University of Glasgow, 2011), 22, 26–8, 50.

194. TNA PREM 15/482: Letter from A. W. Stephens, Ministry of Defence, to R. T. Armstrong, 4 October 1971, and attached 'Military appreciation of the security situation in Northern Ireland as at 4th October 1971'.

195. TNA DEFE 24/742: Minute from R. E. Coaker, DMO, to CGS et al., 5 October 1971, with attached 'Future military policy for Londonderry', 4 October 1971.

196. TNA PREM 15/482: Signal from UKREP to Woodfield, Home Office, 5 October 1971.

197. TNA DEFE 32/21: 'Ministry of Defence. Chiefs of Staff Committee. Confidential Annex to COS 32nd Meeting/71', 5 October 1971.

198. TNA CAB 130/522: 'Minutes of a Meeting held at 10 Downing Street', 6 October 1971.

199. TNA PREM 15/482: 'Record of a discussion with the Prime Minister of Northern Ireland', 7 October 1971.

200. PRONI HA/32/5/8: 'Emergency Committee Meeting', 3 September 1971.

201. PRONI HA/32/5/8: 'Emergency Committee Meeting', 1 October 1971.

202. TNA PREM 15/483: Signal from UKREP Belfast to Home Office, 25 October 1971, citing telegram from HQ Northern Ireland to 8, 19 and 39 Bdes and HQ UDR, 15 October.

203. TNA DEFE 13/732: Signal from UKREP Belfast to Home Office, 26 October 1971.

204. TNA DEFE 13/954: Minute from VCGS to Minister of State, 25 August 1971; Minute from Lord Balniel to VCGS, 1 September 1971.

205. TNA CJ 4/1744: Letter from J. M. Parkin, Ministry of Defence, to J. T. Williams, Northern Ireland Office, 8 February 1973.

206. TNA CJ 4/95: Letter from Lt-Gen Tuzo to CGS, 12 October 1971.

207. TNA DEFE 13/917: 'Note for the record', 18 October 1971.

208. TNA CAB 130/522: 'Minutes of a Meeting held at 10 Downing Street', 18 October 1971.

209. TNA DEFE 13/685: Minute from A. W. Stephens, APS/SoS, to PS/Minister of State, 20 October 1971.

210. TNA CAB 163/173: 'Report on Interrogation Methods used in Northern Ireland', from B. T. W. Stewart to Intelligence Co-ordinator, 22 October 1971.
211. TNA DEFE 13/954: Minute from H. J. Maguire, DGI, to AUS(GS), 20 October 1971; 'Air Marshal Sir Harold Maguire', *The Daily Telegraph*, 12 February 2001.
212. TNA PREM 15/485: Minute from P. L. G. to Prime Minister, 25 October 1971.
213. TNA CAB 130/522: 'Minutes of a Meeting held at 10 Downing Street', 29 October 1971.
214. TNA DEFE 13/732: Minute from A. W. Stephens, APS/SoS, to PS/Minister of State, 20 October 1971.
215. TNA DEFE 23/108: Minute from GOC Northern Ireland to CPR, 18 October 1971.
216. TNA DEFE 13/685: 'Ministry of Defence Northern Ireland Policy Committee', 25 October 1971.
217. TNA DEFE 13/685: Minute from L. J. Dunnett, PUS MoD, to Sir Burke Trend, 27 October 1971.
218. TNA DEFE 13/685: 'Northern Ireland – current situation: 28 October 1971'; PRONI HA/32/3/5: 'Conclusions of a Meeting of the Joint Security Committee', 28 October 1971.
219. PRONI HA/32/3/5: 'Conclusions of a Meeting of the Joint Security Committee', 4 November 1971.
220. TNA DEFE 13/685: Minute from L. J. Dunnett, PUS MoD, to Sir Burke Trend, with attached memo, 'Northern Ireland: current situation', 27 October 1971.
221. TNA DEFE 13/732: 'Note of Meeting. Northern Ireland – The Newry Incident', K. P. Jeffs, PS/Minister of State, 27 October 1971.
222. TNA DEFE 13/685: 'Northern Ireland: current situation report No 3 – 29 October 1971.'
223. TNA DEFE 13/732: Minute from MA/CGS, 'Telephone conversation with CLF', 29 October 1971.
224. TNA DEFE 24/724: Minute from J. M. Parkin, Head of C2(AD), to AUS(GS), 2 November 1971.
225. McKittrick et al., *Lost Lives*, 108.
226. TNA DEFE 13/684: 'Public opinion and the Northern Ireland situation. A note by the Colonel GS (Information Policy). HQ Northern Ireland', 9 November 1971.
227. '1st Battalion', *The Green Howards' Gazette: A monthly chronicle of The Green Howards*, 79/932 (November 1971), 963.
228. TNA DEFE 13/685: 'Northern Ireland: current situation report No 7 – 4 November 1971.'
229. TNA DEFE 13/685: 'Ministry of Defence Northern Ireland Policy Committee', 8 November 1971.
230. TNA CAB 130/522: 'Minutes of a Meeting held at 10 Downing Street', 4 November 1971.

231. TNA PREM 15/483: Signal from CWR, Chequers, to Robert Armstrong, No 10, 5 November 1971.
232. TNA DEFE 24/1919: 'CLF's appreciation of the situation given to CGS on Wednesday 10th November 1971.'
233. Dixon, *The British Labour Party and Northern Ireland*, 268, 279.
234. T. McKearney, *The Provisional IRA: From Insurrection to Parliament* (London: Pluto Press, 2011), 108.

5 THE ROAD TO BLOODY SUNDAY

1. TNA DEFE 13/1539: 'Ministry of Defence Northern Ireland Policy Group', 22 December 1971 (quoting Lord Carrington).
2. P. Arthur, 'The Heath Government and Northern Ireland', in S. Ball and A. Seldon (eds.), *The Heath Government 1970–74: A Reappraisal* (London: Routledge, 1996), 240–1.
3. Strachan, *The Politics of the British Army*, 182.
4. E. Heath, *The Course of My Life: My Autobiography* (London: Coronet, 1999), 423.
5. Lord Saville, *Report of the Bloody Sunday Inquiry, Volume I* (London: The Stationery Office, 2010), 91–2.
6. Neumann, *Britain's Long War*, 68; Craig, *Crisis of Confidence*, 114; Leahy, *The Intelligence War against the IRA*, 23–4; Ó Dochartaigh, *Deniable Contact*, 40.
7. Smith, *The British State and the Northern Ireland Crisis*, 195; Charters, *Whose Mission, Whose Orders?*, 144–5.
8. English, *Armed Struggle*, 151.
9. Hennessey, *The Evolution of the Troubles*, 313.
10. Ó Dochartaigh, 'Bloody Sunday: Error or Design?', 89–108; O'Leary, *A Treatise on Northern Ireland: Volume II*, 190.
11. A. Mack, 'Why Big Nations Lose Small Wars: The Politics of Asymmetric Conflict', *World Politics*, 27/2 (1975), 175–200; G. Merom, *How Democracies Lose Small Wars: State, Society, and the Failures of France in Algeria, Israel in Lebanon, and the United States in Vietnam* (Cambridge: Cambridge University Press, 2003); J. D. Caverley, 'The Myth of Military Myopia: Democracy, Small Wars, and Vietnam', *International Security*, 34/3 (2010), 119–57; J. R. Goodman, '"In the Wider View": The Geostrategic Determinants of Counterinsurgency Strategy and Adaptation, Evidence from the Arab and Jewish Rebellions in the Palestine Mandate', *Security Studies*, 29/1 (2020), 162–98.
12. J. R. Goodman, *Negotiating Counterinsurgency: The Politics of Strategic Adaptation* (PhD dissertation, Yale University, 2018), 86.
13. Smith, *The British State and the Northern Ireland Crisis*, 195–6.
14. S. McDaid and C. McGlynn, 'Northern Ireland', in A. S. Roe-Crines and T. Heppell (eds.), *Policies and Politics under Prime Minister Edward Heath* (Basingstoke: Palgrave Macmillan, 2021), 191.

15. Ziegler, *Edward Heath*, 236.
16. TNA DEFE 13/1539: 'Ministry of Defence Northern Ireland Policy Group', 13 December 1971.
17. Lord Carrington, *Reflect on Things Past* (London: Collins, 1988), 249, 250.
18. C. Lee, *Carrington: An Honourable Man* (London: Viking, 2018), 62–120, 277, 302, 334.
19. TNA CAB 130/522: 'Minutes of a Meeting held at 10 Downing Street', 11 November 1971.
20. P. Dixon, '"A House Divided Cannot Stand": Britain, Bipartisanship and Northern Ireland', *Contemporary Record*, 9/1 (1995), 165.
21. Smith, *The British State and the Northern Ireland Crisis*, 202–3.
22. LHASC: Shadow Cabinet meetings, 1330-SC-1971–72: 'Research Department. Labour Party. Northern Ireland – Brief for N.E.C. delegation to Commission Meeting on 11 November 1971.'
23. LHASC: LP/RD/43/3: 'Commission on Northern Ireland. Meeting in Dunardry Hotel, Belfast', 11 November 1971.
24. Callaghan, *A House Divided*, 174–5.
25. T. Benn, *Office without Power: Diaries 1968–72* (London: Hutchinson, 1988), 384–5.
26. Drohan, *Brutality in an Age of Human Rights*, 151, 161–2.
27. Newbery, *Interrogation, Intelligence and Security*, 87–91.
28. TNA DEFE 13/685: 'Northern Ireland: current situation report', 17 November 1971.
29. LHASC: Shadow Cabinet meetings, 1330-SC-1971–72: 'Minutes of a Parliamentary Committee Meeting', 18 November 1971.
30. TNA DEFE 13/918: Minute from M. Gainsborough, PS/PUS, to PS/Minister of State, 23 November 1971, and attached 'Note of a telephone conversation between PUS and Mr Roy Hattersley MP'.
31. TNA DEFE 13/917: 'Note for action', signed PS/Minister of State, 25 October 1971.
32. TNA CAB 164/1175: 'Visit by the Leader of the Opposition to Northern Ireland 15–18 November 1971. Introduction to the Record' [hereafter 'Visit by the Leader of the Opposition'].
33. J. Haines, *The Politics of Power* (London: Jonathan Cape, 1977), 122.
34. TNA CAB 164/1175: 'Visit by the Leader of the Opposition. Meeting with the GOC Northern Ireland, Lieutenant-General Sir Harry Tuzo 9.30 am 16 November 1971. Confidential Annex.'
35. TNA CAB 164/1175: 'Visit by the Leader of the Opposition. Meeting with members of the Northern Ireland Cabinet', 16 November 1971.
36. TNA CAB 164/1175: 'Visit by the Leader of the Opposition. Meeting with the Roman Catholic Archbishop of Armagh (Cardinal Conway)', no date.
37. TNA CAB 164/1175: 'Visit by the Leader of the Opposition. Meeting with Canon Murphy and Mr Conaty', 17 November 1971.

38. TNA CAB 164/1175: 'Visit by the Leader of the Opposition. Meeting with the Social Democratic and Labour Party (SDLP)', 17 November 1971.
39. Campbell, *Gerry Fitt and the SDLP*, 80.
40. TNA PREM 15/484: 'Note for the Record', 22 November 1971.
41. Dixon, *The British Labour Party and Northern Ireland*, 288.
42. C. McGlynn and S. McDaid, 'Northern Ireland', in A. S. Crines and K. Hickson, *Harold Wilson: The Unprincipled Prime Minister? Reappraising Harold Wilson* (London: Biteback, 2016), 128.
43. Benn, *Office without Power*, 387.
44. LHASC: Shadow Cabinet meetings, 1330-SC-1971–72: 'Minutes of a Parliamentary Committee Meeting', 6 December 1971.
45. TNA CAB 164/1175: 'Note for the record. Northern Ireland', 15 December 1971.
46. TNA CAB 164/1175: 'Note of the Home Secretary's meeting with Mr Callaghan', 17 December 1971.
47. Benn, *Office without Power*, 389.
48. TNA DEFE 23/109: Minute from P. L. Gregson, 10 Downing Street, to G. Angel, Home Office, 18 November 1971.
49. TNA DEFE 13/905: 'Visit of Mr Parkin (Head of C2(AD)), Mr Morris (Chief Claims Officer) and Mr Gowan (C2(AD)) to Belfast', 30 November – 1 December 1971.
50. TNA DEFE 23/160: Letter from Secretary of the Parker Committee, to C. A. Whitmore, Ministry of Defence, 4 January 1972.
51. P. Rawlinson, *A Price Too High: An Autobiography* (London: Weidenfeld and Nicolson, 1989), 218.
52. G. Howe, 'Rawlinson, Peter Anthony Grayson, Baron Rawlinson of Ewell', *Oxford Dictionary of National Biography*, accessed 9 December 2020 at: www .oxforddnb.com/view/10.1093/ref:odnb/9780198614128.001.0001/odnb-978 0198614128-e-97248?rskey=Kehh1O&result=11; TNA CJ 4/118: Letter from Tony Hetherington, Legal Secretary to the Attorney General, to Sir Kenneth Jones, 7 January 1972.
53. TNA WO 296/25: 'Note of a Meeting of the Northern Ireland Policy Group', 7 January 1972.
54. Hennessey, *The Evolution of the Troubles*, 217–19.
55. Newbery, *Interrogation, Intelligence and Security*, 124–5.
56. Bennett, 'Detention and Interrogation in Northern Ireland, 1969–75', 191.
57. TNA DEFE 24/745: 'Interrogation in Northern Ireland: An assessment of local factors affecting its operation, and a record of its value in security force activities', by GOC Northern Ireland, 24 November 1971.
58. TNA DEFE 70/1067: 'Monthly report on Northern Ireland for December 1971. Annex C. Statistical summary' [hereafter 'Ministry of Defence Monthly Statistical Summary'], Maj-Gen R. E. Coaker, 10 January 1972.
59. TNA DEFE 13/685: 'Northern Ireland: current situation report', 26 November 1971.

60. TNA PREM 15/1001: 'Northern Ireland: current situation report', 13 January 1972.
61. TNA WO 305/5715: 'Report on Northern Ireland Tour', 5 Airptbl Bde, 6 April 1972.
62. TNA DEFE 24/731: Letter from Sir James Dunnett to Sir Philip Allen, 19 May 1971.
63. G. A. Daddis, *No Sure Victory: Measuring U.S. Army Effectiveness and Progress in the Vietnam War* (Oxford: Oxford University Press, 2011), 8–10, 223.
64. S. S. Gartner, *Strategic Assessment in War* (London: Yale University Press, 1997), 26, 44, 55.
65. TNA PREM 15/483: Minute from Burke Trend to Prime Minister, 26 October 1971.
66. TNA DEFE 13/954: Minute from Chief of the Defence Staff to DCDS(I), 29 October 1971.
67. Available in: TNA DEFE 70/1067.
68. Available in: TNA DEFE 70/1548.
69. Compiled from reports in TNA DEFE 70/1067. Figures are weekly aggregates of military, police, terrorist and civilian categories. Those for 'Terrorist killed/ wounded (unconfirmed)' are excluded. Data for the week ending 3 December 1971 covers nine days. Data for 29 and 30 January, and 26 February– 3 March, 1972 is missing.
70. 'McGurk's bar-bombing victims launch legal action against PSNI chief', *Belfast Telegraph*, 21 June 2019.
71. M. Handel, 'Intelligence and Military Operations', in M. Handel (ed.), *Intelligence and Military Operations* (London: Routledge, 1990), 22.
72. TNA DEFE 70/1548: HQ Northern Ireland operational summary, 17 December 1971.
73. TNA DEFE 70/1548: HQ Northern Ireland operational summary, 7 January 1972.
74. TNA DEFE 70/1548: HQ Northern Ireland operational summary, 21 January 1972.
75. TNA DEFE 70/1067: 'Monthly report on Northern Ireland for November 1971. Annex A. Intelligence summary' [hereafter 'Ministry of Defence Monthly Intelligence Summary'], Maj-Gen R. E. Coaker, 9 December 1971.
76. TNA DEFE 70/1067: Ministry of Defence Monthly Intelligence Summary, 10 January 1972.
77. TNA DEFE 13/685: 'Northern Ireland: current situation report', 15 November 1971.
78. TNA DEFE 13/685: 'Northern Ireland: current situation report', 16 November 1971.
79. TNA DEFE 13/685: 'Northern Ireland: current situation report', 24 November 1971.
80. RSRM: *Pilate's Post*, 1st Battalion The Royal Scots, Edition 8, 1 December 1971.

81. T. Farrell, 'Improving in War: Military Adaptation and the British in Helmand Province, Afghanistan, 2006–2009', *Journal of Strategic Studies*, 33/4 (2010), 569–73.

82. B. Cochrane, *The Development of the British Approach to Improvised Explosive Device Disposal in Northern Ireland* (MPhil thesis, Cranfield University, 2012), 2, 105–7, 114, 121.

83. PRONI CAB/9/G/45/10A: Minute from Major S. G. Styles, Senior Ammunition Technical Officer, HQ Northern Ireland, to Chief of Staff, 1 October 1971.

84. S. Smith, *3–2–1 Bomb Gone: Fighting Terrorist Bombers in Northern Ireland* (Stroud: Sutton, 2006), 49–50.

85. Styles, *Bombs Have No Pity*, 143.

86. Explosives Act (Northern Ireland) 1970, accessed 14 May 2021 at: www.legislation.gov.uk/apni/1970/10/data.pdf.

87. '2nd Battalion', *The Fusilier: The Journal of the Royal Regiment of Fusiliers*, 1/8 (June 1972), 676.

88. TNA WO 305/4361: '25 Light Regiment RA. Jan–Dec 1971.'

89. TNA WO 305/4400: Record of Events, 1st Gloucestershire Regiment, 22 December 1971, 6–11 January 1972.

90. P. Taylor, *Brits: The War against the IRA* (London: Bloomsbury, 2001), 128.

91. TNA DEFE 24/210: Minute from BGS(Int) to DGI and VCGS, 22 December 1971.

92. 'Wanted arrests' were of a person on a wanted list (compiled by Special Branch), an arrest operation planning list, or a local list compiled by a formation or unit.

93. Royal Marines Museum: 2/18/5, '42 Commando Royal Marines Unit Newsletter', 1/72 (October 1971–January 1972).

94. IWMSA: David Milner Woodford, catalogue number 19896, reel 3.

95. TNA DEFE 24/542: Minute from Brigadier J. M. H. Lewis, BGS(Int), to AUS(GS), 10 March 1972.

96. TNA DEFE 13/732: Minute from A. P. Hockaday, AUS(GS), to PS/SoS Defence, 5 November 1971; PREM 15/483: Letter from A. W. Stephens to P. L. Gregson, 10 November 1971.

97. K. A. Harkness and M. A. Hunzeker, 'Military Maladaptation: Counterinsurgency and the Politics of Failure', *Journal of Strategic Studies*, 38/6 (2015), 778.

98. D. Hurd, *Memoirs* (London: Little, Brown, 2003), 193.

99. TNA DEFE 13/685: 'Ministry of Defence Northern Ireland Policy Committee', 15 November 1971.

100. TNA PREM 15/484: Signal from UKREP Belfast to Home Office, 22 November 1971.

101. TNA PREM 15/484: Minute from Burke Trend to Prime Minister, 25 November 1971.

102. TNA DEFE 13/685: 'Ministry of Defence Northern Ireland Policy Group', 26 November 1971.
103. TNA DEFE 13/1539: 'Ministry of Defence Northern Ireland Policy Group', 1 December 1971.
104. Bloomfield, *Stormont in Crisis*, 157.
105. S. McDaid, *Template for Peace: Northern Ireland 1972–75* (Manchester: Manchester University Press, 2013), 14–15.
106. TNA DEFE 13/905: Signal from UKREP Belfast to Home Office, 20 December 1971.
107. TNA DEFE 13/905: Minute from CGS to SoS Defence, 'Report on visit to Northern Ireland 15–17 December 1971', 20 December 1971.
108. TNA DEFE 13/905: Minute from R. J. Andrew, PS/SoS Defence, to MA/CGS, 20 December 1971.
109. TNA DEFE 13/905: Letter from Lord Carrington to Major Derek Cooper, 20 December 1971.
110. TNA DEFE 13/1539: 'Ministry of Defence Northern Ireland Policy Group', 22 December 1971.
111. TNA DEFE 13/1539: 'Ministry of Defence Northern Ireland Policy Group', 7 January 1972, 18 January 1972.
112. Ó Dochartaigh, *From Civil Rights to Armalites*, 287.
113. K. Kenny and N. Ó Dochartaigh, 'Power and Politics in Public Inquiries: Bloody Sunday 1972', *Journal of Political Power*, 14/3 (2021), 394–6, 403.
114. TNA DEFE 13/905: 'Statement by Lt Gen Sir Harry Tuzo at press conference 20 Dec 1971.'
115. TNA DEFE 24/2581: 'Record of meeting between GOC and Cardinal Conway [11 January]', 18 January 1972.
116. TNA DEFE 25/308: 'Report of a visit to Northern Ireland. January, 12–14, 1972. By Norman St. John-Stevas, MP.'
117. TNA DEFE 13/1672: Letter from David James MP to Lord Carrington, 1 February 1972, with attached 'Report on Northern Ireland visit January 10–14th, 1972'.
118. TNA CAB 134/3536: 'Official Committee on Northern Ireland. Minutes of a Meeting', 5 January 1972.
119. TNA CAB 134/3536: 'The probable reactions to the introduction of direct rule in Northern Ireland. Report by the Joint Intelligence Committee (A)', 6 January 1972.
120. TNA PREM 15/998: 'Visit by Secretary JIC to Northern Ireland (10–12 January, 1972).'
121. TNA WO 305/6509: 'Ministry of Defence. Narrative of the Military Operations in Northern Ireland Which Began in August 1969. Vol. 1', IX-10; TNA CAB 130/522: 'Minutes of a Meeting held at 10 Downing Street', 11 January 1972.
122. Moloney, *A Secret History of the IRA*, 107.

123. Ó Dochartaigh, *Deniable Contact*, 38.
124. M. A. Hunzeker and K. A. Harkness, 'Detecting the Need for Change: How the British Army Adapted to Warfare on the Western Front and in the Southern Cameroons', *European Journal of International Security*, 6/1 (2021), 70.
125. Lancashire Infantry Museum: 1st Queen's Lancashire Regiment end of tour report, 21 March 1972.
126. TNA WO 305/4617: HQ Northern Ireland Intelligence Summary, 9 December 1971.
127. TNA WO 305/4617: HQ Northern Ireland Intelligence Summary, 16 December 1971.
128. TNA DEFE 24/724: Letter from Tom Sergeant, HQ Northern Ireland, to J. M. Parkin, Ministry of Defence, 23 December 1971.
129. TNA DEFE 24/724: Minute from Brigadier Lewis, BGS(Int), to Head of DS10, 11 January 1972.
130. LSE Library, Merlyn Rees papers: MERLYN-REES/7/3: Letter from Dr Paul Moxon to Merlyn Rees, 12 December 1971; Letter from Richard Sharples, Home Office, to Merlyn Rees, 1 February 1972.
131. P. Gill, 'Tactical Innovation and the Provisional Irish Republican Army', *Studies in Conflict and Terrorism*, 40/7 (2017), 580–1.
132. TNA WO 32/21784: Minute from DCS(A) to CSA, 16 November 1972, attaching 'Annex to A/BR/523/1 (SA/NI) Dated 16 November 1972. The IRA and Their Use of Explosives' [hereafter 'The IRA and Their Use of Explosives'].
133. Smith, *3–2–1 Bomb Gone*, 38, 41, 43, 47.
134. G. Ó Faoleán, 'Ireland's Ho Chi Minh trail? The Republic of Ireland's Role in the Provisional IRA's Bombing Campaign, 1970–1976', *Small Wars and Insurgencies*, 25/5–6 (2014), 980.
135. TNA WO 32/21784: 'The IRA and Their Use of Explosives.'
136. TNA DEFE 70/1067: 'Monthly report on Northern Ireland for January 1972. Annex B. Operational summary' [hereafter 'Ministry of Defence Monthly Operational Summary'], Maj-Gen R. E. Coaker, 10 February 1972.
137. TNA DEFE 70/1067: Ministry of Defence Monthly Operational Summary, 9 December 1971.
138. S. MacStiofáin, *Memoirs of a Revolutionary* (Edinburgh: Gordon Cremonesi, 1975), 207.
139. TNA WO 32/21784: 'The IRA and Their Use of Explosives.'
140. MacStíofáin, *Memoirs of a Revolutionary*, 208.
141. H. Patterson, 'Sectarianism Revisited: The Provisional IRA Campaign in a Border Region of Northern Ireland', *Terrorism and Political Violence*, 22/3 (2010), 342–5.
142. TNA DEFE 70/1067: Ministry of Defence Monthly Operational Summary, 10 January 1972.
143. TNA DEFE 70/1067: Ministry of Defence Monthly Operational Summary, 10 February 1972.

144. TNA DEFE 70/1548: HQ Northern Ireland operational summary, 7 January 1972.
145. TNA DEFE 70/1548: HQ Northern Ireland operational summary, 14 January 1972.
146. TNA DEFE 70/1548: HQ Northern Ireland operational summary, 21 January 1972.
147. TNA PREM 15/1001: Northern Ireland: current situation report, 21 January 1972.
148. TNA PREM 15/1001: HQ Northern Ireland operational summary, 21 January 1972.
149. TNA DEFE 70/1067: Ministry of Defence Monthly Intelligence Summary, 10 February 1972.
150. TNA CAB 130/522: 'Minutes of a Meeting held at 10 Downing Street', 20 January 1972.
151. TNA CAB 164/1175: Note of a meeting between the Prime Minister and the Irish Ambassador, 18 January 1972.
152. TNA PREM 15/1001: 'Note for the record', 23 January 1972.
153. TNA CAB 164/1175: 'Note for the record', 27 January 1972.
154. Goodman, *Negotiating Counterinsurgency*, 93.
155. Lord Saville, *Principal Conclusions and Overall Assessment of the Bloody Sunday Inquiry* (London: The Stationery Office, 2010), 8.
156. PRONI HA/32/3/7: 'Conclusions of a Meeting of the Joint Security Committee', 13 January 1972.
157. Statement of Lord Carver to the Bloody Sunday Inquiry, 24 July 1999, accessed 9 May 2021 at: https://webarchive.nationalarchives.gov.uk/20101017074940/http://report.bloody-sunday-inquiry.org/evidence/K/KC_0008.pdf.
158. Statement of General Sir Robert Ford to the Bloody Sunday Inquiry, 23 March 2000, accessed 10 May 2021 at: https://webarchive.nationalarchives.gov.uk/20101017071251/http://report.bloody-sunday-inquiry.org/evidence/B/B1123.pdf.
159. TNA DEFE 24/1919: 'Report on Northern Ireland tour', HQ 16 Para Bde, 6 July 1971.
160. TNA DEFE 70/1548: HQ Northern Ireland operational summary, 7 January 1972, 14 January 1972, 21 January 1972.
161. IWMSA: James Alan Comrie Cowan, catalogue number 18802, reel 24.
162. Saville, *Report of the Bloody Sunday Inquiry, Volume I*, 201.
163. Ó Dochartaigh, 'Bloody Sunday: Error or Design?', 89–108.
164. TNA DEFE 13/1539: 'Ministry of Defence Northern Ireland Policy Group', 18 January 1972.
165. TNA DEFE 70/1067: Ministry of Defence Monthly Operational Summary, 10 February 1972.
166. Saville, *Report of the Bloody Sunday Inquiry, Volume I*, 257.

167. LHCMA: David Ramsbotham papers, Box 1: Notes for the Official History of the Northern Ireland operations.

168. PRONI CAB/9/B/320/11: Letter from Lieutenant-General Sir Harry Tuzo to Brian Faulkner, 25 January 1972.

169. Saville, *Report of the Bloody Sunday Inquiry, Volume I*, 325–6.

170. PRONI PM/5/81/4: Letter from [names redacted], Palace Barracks Detention Centre, to Brian Faulkner, 8 February 1972.

171. S. Corbett, *Belfast Diaries: A Gunner in Northern Ireland, 1971–74* (Solihull: Helion, 2013), 28.

172. TNA WO 305/4400: Record of Events, 1st Gloucestershire Regiment, 16–17 December 1971.

173. PRONI HA/32/3/7: 'Conclusions of a Meeting of the Joint Security Committee', 27 January 1972.

174. Proceedings of the Bloody Sunday Inquiry: Day 280, 19 December 2002. Lord Carrington, accessed 25 April 2021 at: https://webarchive.nationalarchives .gov.uk/20101017062313/http://report.bloody-sunday-inquiry.org/transcripts/ Archive/Ts280.htm.

175. Saville, *Report of the Bloody Sunday Inquiry, Volume I*, 51, 310.

176. TNA DEFE 70/1067: Ministry of Defence Monthly Operational Summary, 10 February 1972.

177. P. Taylor, *Provos: The IRA and Sinn Fein* (London: Bloomsbury, 1997), 118.

178. John Hume, in: 'As the smoke clears in Derry the question is: who fired first?', *The Times*, 1 February 1972.

179. Saville, *Report of the Bloody Sunday Inquiry, Volume I*, 56–9.

180. 'Remember Bloody Sunday', *Inside Story*, broadcast on BBC1, 28 January 1992, accessed 14 September 2021 at: www.youtube.com/watch?v=j3FCPe6vgS8.

181. Saville, *Report of the Bloody Sunday Inquiry, Volume I*, 60, 63–4, 66.

182. Saville, *Report of the Bloody Sunday Inquiry, Volume I*, 68, 70.

183. Lord Saville, *Report of the Bloody Sunday Inquiry, Volume VI* (London: The Stationery Office, 2010), 408.

184. Saville, *Report of the Bloody Sunday Inquiry, Volume I*, 72–3, 78–9.

185. Statement of Brian Rainey to the Bloody Sunday Inquiry, 15 June 1999, accessed 18 May 2021 at: https://webarchive.nationalarchives.gov.uk/201010 17074745/http://report.bloody-sunday-inquiry.org/evidence/AR/AR_0003 .pdf.

186. Statement of Maura Duffy to the Bloody Sunday Inquiry, 19 June 1999, accessed 18 May 2021 at: https://webarchive.nationalarchives.gov.uk/201010 17073204/http://report.bloody-sunday-inquiry.org/evidence/AD/AD_0162 .pdf.

187. G. Dawson, 'Trauma, Place and the Politics of Memory: Bloody Sunday, Derry, 1972–2004', *History Workshop Journal*, 59/1 (2005), 151.

188. Charters, *Whose Mission, Whose Orders?*, 119, 134.

189. Gartner, *Strategic Assessment in War*, 10.

190. E. McCann with M. Shiels and B. Hannigan, *Bloody Sunday in Derry: What Really Happened* (Dingle: Brandon, 1992), 182.

191. N. J. Mitchell, *Democracy's Blameless Leaders: From Dresden to Abu Ghraib, How Leaders Evade Accountability for Abuse, Atrocity, and Killing* (London: New York University Press, 2012), 98, 106–8.

192. TNA DEFE 25/308: Minute from Lt-Col D. J. Ramsbotham to PSO/CDS, 31 January 1972, with attached, 'Events in Londonderry on 30 January 1972', by Brigadier M. E. Tickell, HQ Northern Ireland.

193. Statement of Lord Carver to the Bloody Sunday Inquiry, 24 July 1999.

194. TNA PREM 15/1001: 'Telephone conversation between the Prime Minister and the Prime Minister of the Republic of Ireland', 30 January 1972.

195. TNA CAB 130/522: 'Minutes of a Meeting held at 10 Downing Street', 31 January 1972.

196. Proceedings of the Bloody Sunday Inquiry: Day 287, 22 January 2003. Sir Edward Heath, accessed 24 April 2021 at: https://webarchive.nationalarchives.gov.uk/20101017062434/http://report.bloody-sunday-inquiry.org/transcripts/Archive/Ts287.htm.

197. *Hansard* HC Deb. vol. 830 cols. 32–43, 31 January 1972.

198. *Hansard* HC Deb. vol. 830 cols. 264–331, 1 February 1972.

199. TNA CAB 130/560: 'Cabinet. Northern Ireland. GEN 79(72) 1st Meeting', 9 February 1972.

200. LHASC: Shadow Cabinet meetings, 1330-SC-1971–72: 'Minutes of a Parliamentary Committee Meeting', 9 February 1972, 16 February 1972.

201. C. Chapman, *Notes from a Small Military* (London: John Blake, 2015), 78.

202. LHCMA: David Ramsbotham papers, Box 1: Notes for the Official History of the Northern Ireland operations.

203. M. Carver, 'Morale in Battle – the Medical and the Military', *Journal of the Royal Army Medical Corps*, 139 (1989), 9.

204. Carver, *Out of Step*, 261–3.

205. K. Hearty, 'Misrecognising the Victim of State Violence: Denial, "Deep" Imperialism and Defending "Our Boys"', *Crime, Law and Social Change*, 73/2 (2020), 218–19.

206. TNA DEFE 13/684: Minute from PS/US of S (Army) to APS/SoS Defence, 11 November 1971, and attached 'The Army in Northern Ireland: Publicity and the Communications Media'.

207. '1st Battalion', *The Iron Duke: The Regimental Journal of The Duke of Wellington's Regiment*, 47/157 (December 1971), 91.

208. TNA DEFE 13/905: 'Visit of Mr Parkin (Head of C2(AD)), Mr Morris (Chief Claims Officer) and Mr Gowan (C2(AD)) to Belfast', 30 November – 1 December 1971.

209. TNA PREM 15/1002: HQ Northern Ireland operational summary, 4 February 1972.

210. '1st Battalion', *Pegasus: Journal of The Parachute Regiment and Airborne Forces*, 27/3 (July 1972), 20–1.

211. '1st Battalion', *Castle: The Journal of The Royal Anglian Regiment*, 4/4 (1973), 19.

212. TNA WO 305/5715: 'Report on Northern Ireland Tour', 5 Airptbl Bde, 6 April 1972.

213. TNA DEFE 70/1067: 'Monthly report on Northern Ireland for February 1972. Annex E. Training matters', Maj-Gen R. E. Coaker, 7 March 1972.

214. KOSBRM: KOSB C2/9: Letter from Lt-Col R. W. Riddle to Lt-Col Simon Bland, 5 February 1972.

215. Interview with Liam Wray, by Joanne O'Brien, 17 April 1997, accessed 18 May 2021 at: https://webarchive.nationalarchives.gov.uk/20101017072044/http://report.bloody-sunday-inquiry.org/evidence/AW/AW_0029.pdf.

216. Museum of The Royal Dragoon Guards, Oral History Project: interview with General Sir Robert Ford, available at: www.rdgmuseum.org.uk/history-and-research/oral-history/.

217. TNA DEFE 24/2525: 'Note of a meeting attended by PUS at Headquarters Northern Ireland', 3 February 1972.

218. TNA PREM 15/1002: HQ Northern Ireland operational summary, 4 February 1972.

219. TNA WO 305/4359: '22nd Light Air Defence Regiment Royal Artillery. Historical Report. Operations in Northern Ireland November 1971– March 1972.'

220. TNA PREM 15/1002: Minute from Maj-Gen R. E. Coaker to CGS, 4 February 1972.

221. TNA PREM 15/1002: 'Northern Ireland: current situation report', 7 February 1972.

222. Hennessey, *The Evolution of the Troubles*, 312–41; Smith, *The British State and the Northern Ireland Crisis*, 165–247; Charters, *Whose Mission, Whose Orders?*, 138–54.

223. Smith, *The British State and the Northern Ireland Crisis*, 198, 206.

224. TNA PREM 15/1002: Letter from Brian Faulkner to Edward Heath, 16 February 1972.

225. TNA PREM 15/1003: Letter from Brian Faulkner to Edward Heath, 1 March 1972.

226. TNA CAB 130/560: 'Cabinet. Northern Ireland. GEN 79(72) 6th Meeting', 2 March 1972.

227. 'Report of meeting held in Council Chamber', 11 February 1972. National Archives, Ireland, accessed 20 May 2021 at: https://cain.ulster.ac.uk/nai/1972/nai_TSCH-2003-16-462_1972-02-11.pdf.

228. Craig, *Crisis of Confidence*, 106.

229. TNA DEFE 13/920: Memorandum from CLF to GOC Northern Ireland, 'The campaign against the IRA. An assessment of the current operational situation', 20 March 1972.

230. TNA DEFE 70/1067: Ministry of Defence Monthly Operational Summary, 7 March 1972.
231. TNA CAB 130/522: 'Minutes of a Meeting held at 10 Downing Street', 28 February 1972.
232. TNA PREM 15/1002: 'Note for the record', 16 February 1972.
233. J. W. Young, 'The Heath Government and British Entry into the European Community', in S. Ball and A. Seldon (eds.), *The Heath Government 1970–74: A Reappraisal* (London: Routledge, 1996), 275.
234. P. Norton, 'Divided Loyalties: The European Communities Act 1972', *Parliamentary History*, 30/1 (2011), 56–7.
235. H. Patterson, *Ireland's Violent Frontier: The Border and Anglo-Irish Relations during the Troubles* (Basingstoke: Palgrave Macmillan, 2013), 35.
236. P. Mulroe, *Bombs, Bullets and the Border. Policing Ireland's Frontier: Irish Security Policy, 1969–1978* (Dublin: Irish Academic Press, 2017), 68–9.
237. Hennessey, *The Evolution of the Troubles*, 316.
238. 'Mr Lynch suggests "Irish institution" in province', *The Times*, 21 February 1972.
239. D. Taylor, 'IRA men freed by "inexplicable" rulings are to be retried', *The Times*, 21 February 1972.
240. TNA DEFE 70/1548: HQ Northern Ireland Operational Summary, 18 February 1972.
241. TNA PREM 15/1003: HQ Northern Ireland Operational Summary, 25 February 1972.
242. D. Taylor, 'Official IRA's Chief of Staff is held in Dublin raids', *The Times*, 24 February 1972.
243. D. Taylor, 'Nine more republicans held as Eire leader attacks IRA', *The Times*, 25 February 1972.
244. TNA DEFE 70/1067: Ministry of Defence Monthly Intelligence Summary, 7 March 1972.
245. TNA DEFE 25/295: Minute from CDS to Secretary of State for Defence, with attached report 'The Defence Implications to Great Britain of a United Ireland', 16 February 1972.
246. TNA DEFE 23/112: Minute from CGS to Secretary of State for Defence, 23 February 1972.
247. TNA DEFE 25/308: Minute from D. R. J. Stephen, AUS(GS), to PS/Secretary of State for Defence, 14 February 1972.
248. TNA PREM 15/1003: Letter from P. L. Gregson, 10 Downing Street, to R. J. Andrew, Ministry of Defence, 28 February 1972.
249. TNA DEFE 13/989: Signal from GOC Northern Ireland to CGS, 15 March 1972; Signal from CGS to GOC Northern Ireland, 15 March 1972.
250. TNA CAB 130/561: 'Cabinet. Northern Ireland. Memorandum by Home Secretary', 29 February 1972.

251. TNA DEFE 70/1548: HQ Northern Ireland Operational Summary, 10 March 1972.
252. TNA DEFE 70/1067: Ministry of Defence Monthly Intelligence Summary, 12 April 1972.
253. TNA DEFE 70/1067: Ministry of Defence Monthly Statistical Summary, 7 March 1972, 12 April 1972.
254. TNA DEFE 70/1548: HQ Northern Ireland Operational Summary, 24 March 1972.
255. TNA DEFE 70/1548: HQ Northern Ireland Operational Summary, 10 March 1972.
256. J. Chartres, 'Ulster signs of backlash from private armies', *The Times*, 14 February 1972.
257. TNA DEFE 70/1548: HQ Northern Ireland Operational Summary, 10 March 1972.
258. TNA PREM 15/1004: HQ Northern Ireland Operational Summary, 17 March 1972.
259. TNA DEFE 70/1548: HQ Northern Ireland Operational Summary, 24 March 1972.
260. TNA DEFE 13/989: Signal from UKREP Belfast to Home Office, 13 March 1972.
261. PRONI HA/32/3/7: 'Conclusions of a Meeting of the Joint Security Committee', 16 March 1972.
262. TNA DEFE 70/1548: HQ Northern Ireland Operational Summary, 24 March 1972.
263. R. Fisk, '60,000 Protestants hear Craig call for "positive action"', *The Times*, 20 March 1972.
264. Ó Dochartaigh, *Deniable Contact*, 39–40.
265. Taylor, *Provos*, 131–3.
266. Bodleian Library: Harold Wilson papers, MS. Wilson c.908: 'Talks with the Provisional Wing', 11 March 1972.
267. TNA DEFE 13/989: Minute from R. T. Armstrong, 10 Downing Street, to G. L. Angel, Home Office, 10 March 1972.
268. Bodleian Library: Harold Wilson papers, MS. Wilson c.908: 'Talks with the Provisional Wing', 11 March 1972.
269. Bodleian Library: Harold Wilson papers, MS. Wilson c.908: Typed notes, 'Dublin, March 13, 1972'.
270. TNA PREM 15/1004: HQ Northern Ireland Operational Summary, 17 March 1972.
271. B. Gingell, 'Catholics, Anglicans, Free Churchmen pray for Ulster', *The Times*, 15 March 1972.
272. TNA DEFE 13/989: Minute from P. L. Gregson, 10 Downing Street, to G. L. Angel, Home Office, 15 March 1972.

273. TNA DEFE 13/920: 'Notes on discussion between CGS and GOC Northern Ireland', 13 March 1972.
274. Bodleian Library: Harold Wilson papers, MS. Wilson c.908: 'Talks with Tom MacGuila [sic], President (Official) Sinn Fein', 18 March 1972.
275. TNA DEFE 70/1548: HQ Northern Ireland Operational Summary, 24 March 1972.
276. Beattie Smith, *The British State and the Northern Ireland Crisis*, 206.
277. TNA CAB 130/560: 'Cabinet. Northern Ireland. GEN 79(72) 10th Meeting', 21 March 1972.
278. TNA CAB 130/560: 'Cabinet. Northern Ireland. GEN 79(72) 12th Meeting', 23 March 1972.
279. TNA DEFE 70/1067: Ministry of Defence Monthly Intelligence Summary, 12 April 1972.
280. Neumann, *Britain's Long War*, 68.
281. TNA WO 305/6509: 'Ministry of Defence. Narrative of the Military Operations in Northern Ireland Which Began in August 1969. Vol. 1', X-13.
282. Carrington, *Reflect on Things Past*, 248.

6 THE MOST DEADLY YEAR

1. TNA WO 305/4398: Major M. T. O. Lloyd, 'A View of the Irish Situation and Its Possible Solution', *Belfast Bulletin. Newsletter of First Battalion the Royal Regiment of Wales in Belfast* (c. July 1972).
2. Rawlinson, *A Price Too High*, 131; LSE Library, Merlyn Rees papers: MERLYN-REES/1/1: Transcripts of tapes on Northern Ireland, 1972; W. Whitelaw, *The Whitelaw Memoirs* (London: Aurum Press, 1989), 77–90.
3. Burke, *An Army of Tribes*, 98.
4. M. J. Cunningham, *British Government Policy in Northern Ireland, 1969–89: Its Nature and Execution* (Manchester: Manchester University Press, 1991), 243; P. Dixon, 'British Policy towards Northern Ireland 1969–2000: Continuity, Tactical Adjustment and Consistent "Inconsistencies"', *British Journal of Politics and International Relations*, 3/3 (2001), 340–68.
5. Neumann, *Britain's Long War*, 77.
6. Beattie Smith, *The British State and the Northern Ireland Crisis*, 251.
7. McKittrick et al., *Lost Lives*, 1552–3.
8. Bishop and Mallie, *The Provisional IRA*, 231; Charters, *Whose Mission, Whose Orders?*, 158.
9. Smith, *Fighting for Ireland?*, 115.
10. T. Hennessey, *The First Northern Ireland Peace Process: Power-Sharing, Sunningdale and the IRA Ceasefires, 1972–76* (Basingstoke: Palgrave Macmillan, 2015), 8.
11. M. Mulholland, 'Irish Republican Politics and Violence before the Peace Process, 1968–1994', *European Review of History*, 14/3 (2007), 404.

12. Moloney, *Secret History of the IRA*, 115, 117.
13. Ó Dochartaigh, *Deniable Contact*, 46, 58, 62.
14. Smith and Neumann, 'Motorman's Long Journey', 414.
15. Craig, *Crisis of Confidence*, 125, 143–4.
16. Patterson, *Ireland's Violent Frontier*, 38.
17. J. Coakley and J. Todd, *Negotiating a Settlement in Northern Ireland, 1969–2019: From Sunningdale to St Andrews* (Oxford: Oxford University Press, 2020), 48–106.
18. McDaid, *Template for Peace*, 4.
19. See the essays in: D. McCann and C. McGrattan (eds.), *Sunningdale, the Ulster Workers' Council Strike and the Struggle for Democracy in Northern Ireland* (Manchester: Manchester University Press, 2017).
20. M. Kerr, *The Destructors: The Story of Northern Ireland's Lost Peace Process* (Dublin: Irish Academic Press, 2011), 13.
21. A. Guelke, *Northern Ireland: The International Perspective* (Dublin: Gill and Macmillan, 1988), 66; English, *Armed Struggle*, 160.
22. B. O'Leary, *A Treatise on Northern Ireland, Volume III: Consociation and Confederation* (Oxford: Oxford University Press, 2019), 57.
23. Charters, *Whose Mission, Whose Orders?*, 177.
24. Burke, *An Army of Tribes*, 223.
25. D. Walsh, *Bloody Sunday and the Rule of Law in Northern Ireland* (Basingstoke: Macmillan, 2000), 237.
26. B. Dickson, 'Counter-Insurgency and Human Rights in Northern Ireland', *Journal of Strategic Studies*, 32/3 (2009), 489.
27. TNA DEFE 23/112: 'Directive for the General Officer Commanding Northern Ireland as Director of Operations', signed Chief of the Defence Staff, 23 March 1972.
28. TNA DEFE 24/2525: Minute from Col GS, MO4, to MA/CGS, with attached 'Draft. Notes for operational briefing of Secretary of State for Northern Ireland Monday 27 March 1972'.
29. TNA DEFE 24/2525: Minute from Col GS, MO4, to MA/CGS, with attached 'Intelligence brief. S of S for Northern Ireland. 27 Mar 72'.
30. Lord Windlesham, *Politics in Practice* (London: Jonathan Cape, 1975), 108.
31. Bloomfield, *Stormont in Crisis*, 169–70.
32. W. F. Deedes, *Dear Bill: W. F. Deedes Reports* (London: Macmillan, 1997), 251.
33. Linen Hall Library: 'Direct rule means Outlaw Whitelaw', *Loyalist News*, 11/3, 1 April 1972.
34. TNA DEFE 24/544: Letter from VCGS to Maj-Gen R. C. Ford, 28 April 1972.
35. TNA DEFE 24/543: Minute from R. E. Coaker, DMO, to PUS, DUS(Army), Head of DS10 et al., 23 March 1972.
36. Charters, *Whose Mission, Whose Orders?*, 160.
37. IWMSA: Terence Lionel Hubble, catalogue number 33350, reel 26.
38. '1st Battalion', *The Men of Harlech: The Journal of The Royal Regiment of Wales*, 6 (May 1972), 17, 20.

39. '1st Battalion News', *Firm and Forester. The Journal of The Worcestershire and Sherwood Foresters Regiment*, 2/2 (November 1972), 53, 56–7.
40. JSCSC Library: National Defence College Papers: '1 Course. Exercise thesis. The Role of the Army in Northern Ireland', by Lt-Col J. st C. Simmons, 1972, 14.
41. TNA PREM 15/1005: 'Northern Ireland: current situation report', 27 March 1972.
42. TNA PREM 15/1006: 'Northern Ireland: Political Summary for the period 24 March 1972 – 28 March 1972. Memorandum by the Home Office', 29 March 1972.
43. TNA PREM 15/1006: HQ Northern Ireland Operational Summary, 31 March 1972.
44. TNA PREM 15/1006: Minute from Douglas Hurd, 10 Downing Street, to Mr Gregson, 29 March 1972.
45. TNA DEFE 70/1548: HQ Northern Ireland Operational Summary, 7 April 1972.
46. TNA DEFE 70/1548: HQ Northern Ireland Operational Summary, 14 April 1972.
47. TNA PREM 15/1006: 'Northern Ireland Office. Note of a meeting held at 11 a.m. on 11 April 1972.'
48. TNA DEFE 70/1548: HQ Northern Ireland Operational Summary, 26 April 1972.
49. Beresford, *The Official IRA and Republican Clubs*, 588.
50. TNA DEFE 24/543: Minute from CGS to Secretary of State for Defence, 'CGS visit to Northern Ireland 5–7 April', 10 April 1972.
51. TNA DEFE 24/543: Minute from Lt-Col D. J. Ramsbotham, MA to CGS, to MA/VCGS, DMO, DASD et al., 11 April 1972.
52. TNA PREM 15/1006: 'Northern Ireland Office. Note of a meeting at 10 a.m. on 7 April [1972].'
53. TNA PREM 15/1005: 'Northern Ireland: current situation report', 28 March 1972.
54. TNA DEFE 70/1548: HQ Northern Ireland Operational Summary, 7 April 1972.
55. TNA CAB 130/561: 'Northern Ireland situation and prospects. Memorandum by the Secretary of State for Northern Ireland', 28 April 1972.
56. TNA DEFE 70/1067: Ministry of Defence Monthly Operational Summary, 8 May 1972.
57. TNA PREM 15/1007: Signal from Dublin to FCO, 28 April 1972.
58. Compiled from monthly reports in TNA DEFE 70/1067. Data for the following dates is missing: 26 February–2 March 1972, 29 April–2 May 1972, 27 July–2 August 1972, 28 September–3 October 1972.
59. TNA WO 305/6510: 'Ministry of Defence. Narrative of the Military Operations in Northern Ireland Which Began in August 1969. Vol. 2 [hereafter 'Narrative of Military Operations Vol. 2']', XI-6.
60. Mulroe, *Bombs, Bullets and the Border*, 73.
61. TNA PREM 15/1008: Signal from Dublin (Peck) to FCO, 2 June 1972.

62. Beresford, *The Official IRA and Republican Clubs in Northern Ireland*, 578.
63. TNA DEFE 70/1548: 'HQ Northern Ireland Operational Summary', 24 May 1972.
64. TNA PREM 15/1008: 'Northern Ireland situation report 230700hrs – 240700hrs MAY 1972.'
65. TNA PREM 15/1008: 'Northern Ireland: Political summary for the period 19 May – 24 May, 1972. Memorandum by the Northern Ireland Office [hereafter 'Northern Ireland Office Political Summary'].'
66. TNA PREM 15/1008: 'Northern Ireland situation report from 250800 to 300800 May 72.'
67. TNA PREM 15/1008: 'Note of a meeting held on 30th May [1972].'
68. TNA WO 305/6510: 'Narrative of Military Operations Vol. 2', XI-13.
69. TNA DEFE 70/1067: Ministry of Defence Monthly Intelligence Summary, 6 June 1972.
70. TNA CAB 130/560: 'Cabinet. Northern Ireland. GEN 79(72) 19th Meeting', 25 May 1972.
71. TNA PREM 15/1008: 'Northern Ireland Office: Political summary', 2 June 1972.
72. TNA PREM 15/1007: 'Record of Meeting', Secretary of State for Defence's Office, 14 April 1972.
73. TNA WO 305/6510: 'Narrative of Military Operations Vol. 2', XI-16.
74. TNA DEFE 24/543: Minute from Lt-Col D. J. Ramsbotham, MA to CGS, to PS/Secretary of State for Defence et al., 21 April 1972.
75. TNA DEFE 24/543: 'Record of telephone conversation between VCGS and CLF', 26 April 1972.
76. Compiled from monthly reports in TNA DEFE 70/1067. Data for the following dates is missing: 26 February–2 March 1972, 29 April–2 May 1972, 27 July–2 August 1972, 28 September–3 October 1972.
77. TNA DEFE 24/544: 'An assessment of the low-profile strategy', Major-General R. C. Ford, 28 April 1972.
78. TNA PREM 15/1007: 'Note of a meeting held on 21 April [1972].'
79. TNA PREM 15/1007: Minute from Burke Trend to Prime Minister, 1 May 1972.
80. TNA DEFE 24/544: 'Northern Ireland Policy Group', 1 May 1972.
81. TNA CAB 130/560: 'Cabinet. Northern Ireland. GEN 79(72) 16th Meeting', 5 May 1972.
82. TNA CAB 130/560: 'Cabinet. Northern Ireland. GEN 79(72) 17th Meeting', 12 May 1972.
83. TNA CAB 130/560: 'Cabinet. Northern Ireland. GEN 79(72) 18th Meeting', 18 May 1972.
84. TNA WO 305/4346: 2nd Field Regiment, Royal Artillery. Regimental History 1972; entry for 18 May 1972.
85. Burke, *An Army of Tribes*, 5, 11, 64.
86. H. Bennett, '"Smoke without Fire"? Allegations against the British Army in Northern Ireland, 1972–5', *Twentieth Century British History*, 24/2 (2013), 279.

87. IWMSA: Kenneth Ambrose, catalogue number 32532, reel 15.

88. Dawson, 'Trauma, Place and the Politics of Memory', 153.

89. McCann with Shiels and Hannigan, *Bloody Sunday in Derry*, 225.

90. The Rt. Hon. Lord Widgery, *Report of the Tribunal Appointed to Inquire into the Events of Sunday, 30ᵗʰ January 1972, Which Led to Loss of Life in Connection with the Procession in Londonderry on That Day*. H.C. 220 (London: Her Majesty's Stationery Office, 1972), 8, 12, 21, 26, 29, 33, 35, 36, 38.

91. Walsh, *Bloody Sunday and the Rule of Law in Northern Ireland*, 66, 72, 77, 80, 114–15, 154–5.

92. N. T. Aiken, 'The Bloody Sunday Inquiry: Transitional Justice and Postconflict Reconciliation in Northern Ireland', *Journal of Human Rights*, 14/1 (2015), 114.

93. G. McLaughlin and S. Baker, '"Every Man an Emperor": The British Press, Bloody Sunday and the Image of the British Army', in G. Dawson, J. Dover and S. Hopkins (eds.), *The Northern Ireland Troubles in Britain: Impacts, Engagements, Legacies and Memories* (Manchester: Manchester University Press, 2017), 188, 195.

94. TNA PREM 15/1007: 'Record of Meeting', Secretary of State for Defence's Office, 14 April 1972.

95. Proceedings of the Bloody Sunday Inquiry: Day 289, 27 January 2003. Sir Edward Heath, accessed 24 April 2021 at: https://webarchive.nationalarchives.gov.uk/20101017062456/http://report.bloody-sunday-inquiry.org/transcripts/Archive/Ts289.htm.

96. Mitchell, *Democracy's Blameless Leaders*, 26.

97. J. G. T. Dewar, 'How Television Has Affected the Army', *The Journal of the Royal Hampshire Regiment*, 62/1 (May 1973), 40.

98. IWMSA: George Styles, catalogue number 12375, reel 3.

99. Reynolds, *Soldier at Heart*, 195.

100. Rawlinson, *A Price Too High*, 87, 221.

101. TNA DEFE 24/545: Letter from Attorney General to Barry Shaw QC, 15 June 1972.

102. TNA PREM 15/1007: 'Northern Ireland: current situation report', 17 April 1972.

103. TNA WO 296/74: Minute from D. R. J. Stephen, AUS(GS), to VCGS, 18 April 1972, and attached 'Preliminary Report. Death of Joseph McCann', HQNI, 17 April 1972.

104. TNA WO 296/74: Minute from VCGS to Secretary of State for Defence, 28 April 1972.

105. 'Joe McCann: Trial of Two Soldiers Collapses', BBC News, 4 May 2021, accessed 15 July 2021 at: www.bbc.co.uk/news/uk-northern-ireland-56942056.

106. TNA DEFE 24/545: 'The legal picture in Northern Ireland. A note by the Attorney General', 2 June 1972.

107. For further discussion of civil litigation, see Chapter 7.

108. TNA DEFE 24/543: Minute from R. C. Kent, DUS(Army), to PUS, 27 March 1972.

109. TNA DEFE 24/543: Minute from D. R. J. Stephen, AUS(GS), to Head of C2 (AD), 21 March 1972, attaching Minute for AUS(GS) and MA/CGS.

110. TNA DEFE 24/543: Letter from Vice Adjutant General to Lt-Gen Sir Harry Tuzo, 20 April 1972.

111. TNA DEFE 24/725: Minute from D. R. Fisher, DS10, to A. Ekins-Daukes, C2 (AD), 26 April 1972.

112. TNA DEFE 24/544: Minute from Lord Balniel to VCGS, 10 May 1972.

113. TNA CJ 4/203/2: 'Application of the Government of Ireland', 29 May 1972, with attached statements.

114. '3 security men are cleared', *Belfast Telegraph*, 17 March 1973.

115. TNA DEFE 24/545: 'The legal picture in Northern Ireland. A note by the Attorney General', 2 June 1972.

116. TNA DEFE 24/725: Letter from J. M. Parkin, Head of C2(AD), to Brigadier M. E. Tickell, Chief of Staff, HQNI, 5 June 1972.

117. TNA DEFE 24/545: 'Arrest policy', signed Lt-Col C. D. Piggins, for Commander Land Forces, 28 June 1972.

118. TNA DEFE 24/544: Letter from A. W. Stephens, DS10, to Brigadier M. E. Tickell, HQNI, 9 May 1972, with attached 'Extract from a letter sent by a soldier serving in Northern Ireland to his brother in prison in England'.

119. TNA PREM 15/1008: 'Note of a meeting held on 23rd May [1972].'

120. TNA DEFE 24/545: Minute from A. W. Stephens, Head of DS10, to DUS(Army), 8 June 1972, with attached 'Draft minute from DUS(Army) to CGS'.

121. Hennessey, *The First Northern Ireland Peace Process*, 21; Leahy, *The Intelligence War against the IRA*, 58; Ó Dochartaigh, *Deniable Contact*, 68, 71.

122. F. Cowper-Coles, '"Anxious for Peace": The Provisional IRA in Dialogue with the British Government, 1972–75', *Irish Studies Review*, 20/3 (2012), 223–42; J. Bew, M. Frampton and I. Gurruchaga, *Talking to Terrorists: Making Peace in Northern Ireland and the Basque Country* (London: Hurst, 2009), 42–3.

123. Mulvenna, *Tartan Gangs and Paramilitaries*, 120.

124. C. Crawford, *Inside the UDA: Volunteers and Violence* (London: Pluto Press, 2003), 34.

125. Bruce, *The Red Hand*, 55.

126. McKittrick et al., *Lost Lives*, 1553.

127. L. Harris, 'Implications of a Strategic Analysis: The Operational Strategy of Loyalist Paramilitaries', *Behavioral Sciences of Terrorism and Political Aggression*, 4/1 (2012), 4–25.

128. A. Aughey and C. McIlheney, 'The Ulster Defence Association: Paramilitaries and Politics', *Journal of Conflict Studies*, 2/2 (1981), 35.

129. TNA DEFE 70/1548: HQ Northern Ireland Operational Summary, 7 April 1972.

130. TNA DEFE 70/1548: HQ Northern Ireland Operational Summary, 14 April 1972.

131. TNA DEFE 70/1548: HQ Northern Ireland Operational Summary, 21 April 1972.
132. TNA DEFE 70/1548: HQ Northern Ireland Operational Summary, 26 April 1972.
133. TNA DEFE 70/1548: HQ Northern Ireland Operational Summary, 3 May 1972.
134. PRONI DCR/1/17: Minute from D. E. K. Boyd to Secretary, 5 May 1972.
135. Compiled from monthly reports in TNA DEFE 70/1067. Data for the following dates is missing: 29 April–2 May 1972, 27 July–2 August 1972, 28 September–3 October 1972.
136. TNA DEFE 70/1548: HQ Northern Ireland Operational Summary, 10 May 1972.
137. TNA PREM 15/1008: 'Northern Ireland situation report from 160700 to 170700 May [1972].'
138. M. Urwin, *A State in Denial: British Collaboration with Loyalist Paramilitaries* (Cork: Mercier Press, 2016), 169–70.
139. TNA DEFE 70/1548: HQ Northern Ireland Operational Summary, 17 May 1972.
140. M. McGuire, *To Take Arms: A Year in the Provisional IRA* (London: Quartet Books, 1973), 6, 109–11.
141. R. White, 'The Irish Republican Army and Sectarianism: Moving beyond the Anecdote', *Terrorism and Political Violence*, 9/2 (1997), 122.
142. Ibid., 32, 42–3.
143. M. McCleery, 'Sectarianism and the Provisional Irish Republican Army', *Small Wars and Insurgencies*, 32/4–5 (2021), 665–86.
144. S. Bruce, 'Victim Selection in Ethnic Conflict: Motives and Attitudes in Irish Republicanism', *Terrorism and Political Violence*, 9/1 (1997), 56, 67.
145. Patterson, 'Sectarianism Revisited', 352–3.
146. TNA DEFE 70/1548: HQ Northern Ireland Operational Summary, 21 April 1972.
147. TNA DEFE 70/1548: HQ Northern Ireland Operational Summary, 17 May 1972.
148. TNA PREM 15/1008: 'Northern Ireland situation report 170700hrs to 180700hrs MAY 72.'
149. TNA DEFE 70/1548: HQ Northern Ireland Operational Summary, 24 May 1972.
150. TNA PREM 15/1008: 'Northern Ireland situation report from 190800 to 220800 May [1972]' and Annex A.
151. TNA CAB 130/560: 'Cabinet. Northern Ireland. GEN 79(72) 19th Meeting', 25 May 1972.
152. TNA PREM 15/1008: '0800 hrs Sat 27 May – 0800 hrs Sun 28 May 1972.'
153. TNA DEFE 70/1067: Ministry of Defence Monthly Intelligence Summary, 6 June 1972.

154. LHCMA: David Ramsbotham papers, Box 1: Letter from CGS to Secretary of State for Defence, 30 May 1972.
155. TNA DEFE 24/545: 'Note for the Record. Northern Ireland Policy Group', 1 June 1972.
156. TNA WO 305/4287: 'Historical record. 2nd Battalion The Parachute Regiment for the period 1 April 1972 to 31 March 1973.'
157. TNA WO 305/4384: 'Historical record. 1st Battalion The King's Own Royal Border Regiment. Annex A, Operational Diary 1 Apr 72 – 31 Mar 73.'
158. TNA DEFE 70/1548: HQ Northern Ireland Operational Summary, 7 June 1972.
159. PRONI CAB/9/G/27/6/2: 'Meeting between the Secretary of State, GOC and Chief Constable', 5 June 1972.
160. PRONI CAB/9/G/27/6/2: 'Conclusions of the Secretary of State's Daily Meeting', 5 June 1972.
161. TNA DEFE 24/746: Minute from Brigadier M. S. Bayley, BGS(Int), to MA/CGS, 6 June 1972.
162. TNA DEFE 70/1548: HQ Northern Ireland Operational Summary, 14 June 1972.
163. LSE: H. A. Hetherington papers, Box 19: 'Points from a meeting with Lt-Gen Sir Henry Tuzo', 9 June 1972.
164. LSE: H. A. Hetherington papers, Box 19: 'Notes of a meeting with Sir Graham Shillington', 9 June 1972.
165. TNA CAB 130/560: 'Cabinet. Northern Ireland. GEN 79(72) 20th Meeting', 12 June 1972.
166. LSE: H. A. Hetherington papers, Box 19: 'Notes of a meeting with Mr William Whitelaw', 12 June 1972.
167. TNA PREM 15/1009: 'Note of a meeting between the Secretary of State and representatives of the UDA and Mr Billy Hull', 13 June 1972.
168. TNA PREM 15/1009: 'Note of a meeting. Meeting between the Secretary of State and the Security Council of the UDA', 14 June 1972.
169. LSE: H. A. Hetherington papers, Box 19: 'Note of a meeting with John Hume', 8 June 1972.
170. Hennessey, *The First Northern Ireland Peace Process*, 14.
171. TNA PREM 15/1009: 'Note of a meeting between the Secretary of State and Mr Hume and Mr Devlin', 15 June 1972.
172. TNA PREM 15/1009: 'Note of a meeting on 16 June [1972].'
173. TNA CAB 130/560: 'Cabinet. Northern Ireland. GEN 79(72) 21st Meeting', 16 June 1972.
174. TNA DEFE 70/1548: HQ Northern Ireland Operational Summary, 28 June 1972.
175. 'Panorama', BBC Television, 26 June 1972, accessed 10 August 2021 at: www.britishpathe.com/video/VLVA7R72M5H42FDP2FKLC2CEPK8X6-UK-PROVISIONAL-IRA-POLITICAL-LEADER-DAVID-OCONNELL-CONFIDENT/query/northern+ireland.

176. TNA PREM 15/1009: 'Note of a meeting between the Secretary of State and SDLP representatives (Mr Hume and Mr Devlin)', 18 June 1972.

177. TNA PREM 15/1009: 'Note of a meeting with representatives of the Provisional IRA', P. J. Woodfield, 1 June 1972.

178. TNA CAB 130/560: 'Cabinet. Northern Ireland. GEN 79(72) 22nd Meeting', 22 June 1972.

179. TNA WO 305/4398: '*Belfast Bulletin. Newsletter of First Battalion the Royal Regiment of Wales in Belfast.* Operational round up III. By Lt-Col C. J. Lee', c. July 1972.

180. T. Craig, 'From Backdoors and Back Lanes to Backchannels: Reappraising British Talks with the Provisional IRA, 1970–1974', *Contemporary British History*, 26/1 (2012), 108.

181. TNA DEFE 24/545: 'Commander Land Forces Directive for Future Internal Security Operations', signed Major-General R. C. Ford, 24 June 1972.

182. TNA DEFE 70/1548: HQ Northern Ireland Operational Summary, 5 July 1972.

183. TNA CAB 130/560: 'Cabinet. Northern Ireland. GEN 79(72) 24th Meeting', 7 July 1972.

184. PRONI CAB/9/G/27/6/3: 'Conclusions of Morning Meeting Held at Stormont Castle', 5 July 1972.

185. TNA DEFE 70/1548: 'HQ Northern Ireland Operational Summary', 5 July 1972.

186. TNA PREM 15/1010: 'Northern Ireland situation report 050700 to 060700 hrs July 72.'

187. TNA DEFE 70/1548: 'HQ Northern Ireland Operational Summary', 12 July 1972.

188. TNA PREM 15/1010: Minute from RJA to Prime Minister, 7 July 1972.

189. Hennessey, *The First Northern Ireland Peace Process*, 21; Leahy, *The Intelligence War against the IRA*, 58; Ó Dochartaigh, *Deniable Contact*, 68.

190. TNA CAB 130/560: 'Cabinet. Northern Ireland. GEN 79(72) 25th Meeting', 10 July 1972.

191. Taylor, *Provos*, 146.

192. LSE: H. A. Hetherington papers, Box 19: 'Meeting with Harold Wilson in London', 19 July 1972.

193. TNA PREM 15/1010: 'Note for the record', by CWR, 21 July 1972.

194. TNA WO 305/6510: 'Narrative of Military Operations Vol. 2', Appendix XII.1.

195. TNA DEFE 70/1548: HQ Northern Ireland Operational Summary, 12 July 1972.

196. TNA PREM 15/1010: 'Northern Ireland situation report 130700 hrs to 140700 hrs July 1972.'

197. '1st Battalion', *Pegasus: Journal of the Parachute Regiment and Airborne Forces*, 28/1 (January 1973), 13.

198. TNA DEFE 13/1010: Minute from R. A. Custis, Ministry of Defence, to C. W. Roberts, 18 July 1972.

199. TNA DEFE 70/1548: HQ Northern Ireland Operational Summary, 25 July 1972.
200. TNA PREM 15/1011: 'Northern Ireland situation report for the period 210700 to 240700 July 1972.'
201. Charters, *Whose Mission, Whose Orders?*, 162–5.
202. TNA PREM 15/1010: Minute from Burke Trend to Prime Minister, 23 July 1972.
203. TNA DEFE 13/910: Minute from R. E. Coaker, Director of Military Operations, to CGS, 23 July 1972.
204. PRONI CAB/9/G/27/6/3: 'Conclusions of Morning Meeting Held at Stormont Castle', 23 July 1972.
205. TNA DEFE 24/726: 'Note for the record. Northern Ireland: legal powers of Army', 24 July 1972.
206. TNA PREM 15/1011: Minute from Burke Trend to Prime Minister, 26 July 1972.
207. PRONI CAB/9/G/27/6/3: 'Conclusions of Morning Meeting Held at Stormont Castle', 26 July 1972.
208. TNA CAB 130/560: 'Cabinet. Northern Ireland. GEN 79(72) 30th Meeting', 27 July 1972.
209. TNA DEFE 13/910: 'Commander Land Forces' Directive for Operation Motorman', 27 July 1972.
210. TNA DEFE 13/910: Minute from R. A. Custis to Secretary of State for Defence, 28 July 1972.
211. Charters, *Whose Mission, Whose Orders?*, 175.
212. TNA WO 305/6510: 'Narrative of Military Operations Vol. 2', Appendix XII.7.
213. TNA WO 305/6510: 'Narrative of Military Operations Vol. 2', XIII-2, XIII-3.
214. TNA PREM 15/1011: Minute from Burke Trend to Prime Minister, 31 July 1972; 'Sitrep on Operation Motorman as at 310700A Jul'.
215. TNA PREM 15/1012: HQ Northern Ireland Operational Summary, 4 August 1972.
216. Airborne Assault Museum, 2 Para in Belfast, Box 2.33.15: 'Intsum One for the week ending 6 August 1972, INT(NI)10, 2nd Battalion The Parachute Regiment. Annex D to INT(NI)10 dated 6 Aug 72.'
217. Smith and Neumann, 'Motorman's Long Journey', 426–30.
218. H. Bennett, 'From Direct Rule to Motorman: Adjusting British Military Strategy for Northern Ireland in 1972', *Studies in Conflict and Terrorism*, 33/6 (2010), 511–32.
219. TNA DEFE 70/1067: Ministry of Defence Monthly Intelligence Summary, 8 August 1972.
220. PRONI CAB/9/G/27/6/4A: 'Conclusions of Morning Meeting Held at Stormont Castle', 1 August 1972.
221. Bodleian Library, Conservative Party Archive, CRD 3/18/1: 'Northern Ireland Committee. 3rd August 1972.'

222. PRONI CAB/9/G/27/6/4A: 'Conclusions of Morning Meeting Held at Stormont Castle', 7 August 1972.
223. PRONI CAB/9/G/27/6/4A: 'Conclusions of Morning Meeting Held at Stormont Castle', 9 August 1972.
224. IWMSA: David Storrie, catalogue number 11139, reel 3.
225. TNA WO 305/6510: 'Narrative of Military Operations Vol. 2', XIII-6.
226. TNA PREM 15/1012: 'Note of meetings between the Secretary of State and the Social Democratic and Labour Party beginning at 7 20 pm on Monday, 7 August 1972.'
227. TNA CJ 4/209: Minute from F. F. Steele to Mr Woodfield, 9 August 1972.
228. TNA PREM 15/1012: HQ Northern Ireland Operational Summary, 9 August 1972.
229. TNA CJ 4/436: Letter from Sir Graham Shillington, RUC, to P. J. Woodfield, NIO, 8 June 1972.
230. TNA DEFE 13/910: Minute from General Sir Michael Carver to Secretary of State for Defence, 31 July 1972.
231. TNA DEFE 24/726: Letter from Lieut.-Gen. Sir Harry Tuzo to General Sir Michael Carver, 31 July 1972.
232. TNA DEFE 13/910: Minute from Lt-Col D. J. Ramsbotham, MA to CGS, to PS/ Secretary of State for Defence, 26 July 1972.
233. TNA CJ 4/436: 'Note of a meeting between the Secretary of State and the CGS', 3 August 1972.
234. TNA CJ 4/436: Minute by W. J. Smith, NIO, 3 August 1972.
235. TNA PREM 15/1012: Letter from R. J. Andrew, Ministry of Defence, to T. C. Platt, NIO, 7 August 1972.
236. TNA CJ 4/436: Minute by W. J. Smith, NIO, 15 August 1972.
237. TNA CAB 130/560: 'Cabinet. Northern Ireland. GEN 79(72) 32nd Meeting', 10 August 1972.
238. TNA PREM 15/1012: 'Note of a meeting between the Secretary of State and the Social Democratic and Labour Party beginning at 2.45 pm on Friday 11 August 1972.'
239. TNA CJ 4/436: Minute by W. J. Smith, NIO, 15 August 1972.
240. TNA CJ 4/436: Minute by W. J. Smith, NIO, 21 August 1972.
241. PRONI CAB/9/G/27/6/4A: 'Conclusions of Morning Meeting Held at Stormont Castle', 23 August 1972.
242. TNA DEFE 24/726: 'Minutes of a meeting on arrest and detention policy held at HQ Northern Ireland', 24 August 1972.
243. TNA DEFE 24/726: Minute from Chief of Staff, HQ Northern Ireland, to GOC, 26 August 1972.
244. West Sussex Record Office: Papers of Lance-Corporal W. E. Kempton. Catalogue number RSR/C/1332/2/6; Transcript of 1972/3 diaries, entry for 10 August 1972.

245. TNA DEFE 24/726: Instruction from Lt-Col A. T. P. Millen for CLF, HQNI, to Commanders 3, 8, 24 and 39 Brigades, Ulster Defence Regiment and 1st King's Own Scottish Borderers, 31 August 1972.
246. IWMSA: Robin Evelegh, catalogue number 11148, reel 3.
247. TNA DEFE 13/1358: HQ Northern Ireland Operational Summary, 30 August 1972.
248. PRONI CAB/9/G/27/6/4A: 'Conclusions of Morning Meeting Held at Stormont Castle', 29 August 1972.
249. Burke, *An Army of Tribes*, 96–7.
250. TNA DEFE 24/824: Letter from William Whitelaw to Lieutenant-General Sir Harry Tuzo, 1 September 1972.
251. McCleery, *Operation Demetrius and Its Aftermath*, 41.
252. PRONI CAB/9/G/27/6/4A: 'Conclusions of Morning Meeting Held at Stormont Castle', 14 August 1972.
253. TNA WO 305/6510: 'Narrative of Military Operations Vol. 2', XIV-7, XIV-8.
254. PRONI CAB/9/G/27/6/4A: 'Conclusions of Morning Meeting Held at Stormont Castle', 21 August 1972.
255. TNA DEFE 13/1358: HQ Northern Ireland Operational Summary, 6 September 1972.
256. TNA CAB 130/560: 'Cabinet. Northern Ireland. GEN 79(72) 33rd Meeting', 11 September 1972.
257. TNA PREM 15/1013: 'UDA activity in Belfast – Shankill area 7/8 Sep 72.'
258. TNA WO 305/6510: 'Narrative of Military Operations Vol. 2', XIV-3.
259. TNA DEFE 13/1358: HQ Northern Ireland Operational Summary, 13 September 1972.
260. Airborne Assault Museum, 2 Para in Belfast, Box 2.33.15: 'Intsum Six for week ending 10 September 1972, INT(NI)10, 2nd Battalion The Parachute Regiment'; 'Annex E to INT(NI) 10 dated 11 Sep 72'.
261. TNA DEFE 13/1358: HQ Northern Ireland Operational Summary, 20 September 1972. The UDA battalion to which C Company belonged is unclear.
262. TNA PREM 15/1013: 'Northern Ireland situation report for the period 150700 to 180700 hours September 1972.'
263. TNA DEFE 25/307: Minute from CGS to Secretary of State for Defence, 11 August 1972.
264. TNA CAB 164/882: Letter from Lord Carrington to Prime Minister, 11 October 1971; Carver, *Tightrope Walking*, 96.
265. TNA DEFE 13/1010: Minute from CDS to Secretary of State for Defence, 11 November 1971.
266. NATO Archives: IMSM-0272–72_ENG_PDP, Memorandum from Lieut.-Gen. J. H. S. Read, British Army, to Assistant Director, INT Division and Assistant Director, P&P Division, 19 May 1972.

267. NATO Archives: CER 1971 Supplement to 1970, 'Supreme Headquarters Allied Powers Europe. 1971 Annual Supplement to SACEUR's 1970 Combat Effectiveness Report', 29 June 1972.
268. TNA DEFE 25/307: Signal from UKDEL NATO to FCO, 4 August 1972.
269. NATO Archives: PO(72)392, Memorandum from Lieut.-Gen. E. Rowny, US Army, to the Secretary General, 12 September 1972, with attached signal from SACEUR, 23 August 1972. This document was first uncovered in: J. aan de Wiel, *East German Intelligence and Ireland, 1949–90: Espionage, Terrorism and Diplomacy* (Manchester: Manchester University Press, 2014), 205.
270. W. Mulligan and B. Simms, 'Introduction', in W. Mulligan and B. Simms (eds.), *The Primacy of Foreign Policy in British History* (Basingstoke: Palgrave Macmillan, 2010), 3–4.
271. B. Heuser, *NATO, Britain, France and the FRG: Nuclear Strategies and Forces for Europe, 1949–2000* (Basingstoke: Palgrave, 1997), 3, 7–8, 12–13, 52–3, 60.
272. I. H. Daalder, *The Nature and Practice of Flexible Response: NATO Strategy and Theatre Nuclear Forces since 1967* (New York: Columbia University Press, 1991), 108.
273. J. S. Duffield, *Power Rules: The Evolution of NATO's Conventional Force Posture* (Stanford: Stanford University Press, 1995), 194–9.
274. V. M. Zubok, *A Failed Empire: The Soviet Union in the Cold War from Stalin to Gorbachev* (London: University of North Carolina Press, 2007), 222.
275. TNA DEFE 24/545: 'Military Information Policy Working Party. Review No 12', signed Colonel M. A. J. Tugwell, 8 June 1972.
276. TNA DEFE 24/545: 'Northern Ireland: Secretary of State's visit 19–20 June', 23 June 1972.
277. TNA WO 305/6510: 'Narrative of Military Operations Vol. 2', XI-17.
278. TNA DEFE 70/1067: 'Ministry of Defence Monthly Operational Summary', 5 October 1972. These figures include the Ulster Defence Regiment.
279. Airborne Assault Museum, 16 Para Bde in Northern Ireland, Box 2.33.24: 'AG's conference 1972', paper by Colonel K. C. Came, Regimental Colonel, 18 September 1972.
280. Airborne Assault Museum, 16 Para Bde in Northern Ireland, Box 2.33.24: Letter from Brigadier Ward-Booth, 16 Parachute Brigade, to HQ UK Land Forces, 3 October 1972.
281. TNA DEFE 70/600: 'Record of service. Peter Gabriel John McMullen. Army number 24075221.'
282. TNA DEFE 70/600: Minute from Lt-Col K. D. Jago, OC 9 Sy Coy, Int & Sy Gp (UK), Old Sarum, to Lt-Col D. D. Vigors, HQ UKLF, 16 January 1973.
283. TNA DEFE 70/600: Minute by SSgt A. N. McClenaghan, Aldershot Detachment, 90 Security Section, 7 June 1974.
284. TNA DEFE 70/600: Minute by SSgt A. N. McClenaghan, Aldershot Detachment, 90 Security Section, 7 June 1974.

285. O. Boycott, 'Paratrooper who joined IRA freed after sentence', *The Irish Times*, 8 November 1996, accessed 8 April 2022 at: www.irishtimes.com/news/para troooper-who-joined-ira-freed-after-sentence-1.103816.

286. TNA DEFE 25/307: Minute dictated by CGS to Secretary of State for Defence, 8 September 1972.

287. TNA DEFE 25/307: 'Note of a meeting on Northern Ireland force levels', 12 September 1972.

288. TNA DEFE 70/1067: 'Monthly report on Northern Ireland for September 1972. Annex D. Current business as at 1 Oct 72', Brigadier P. D. F. Thursby, Acting DMO, 5 October 1972.

289. TNA CAB 130/560: 'Cabinet. Northern Ireland. GEN 79(72) 34th Meeting', 21 September 1972.

290. LSE Library, Merlyn Rees papers, MERLYN-REES/7/3: Letter from [redacted] to William Whitelaw, 28 August 1972.

291. Airborne Assault Museum, 2 Para in Belfast, Box 2.33.15: 'Intsum Eight for week ending 24 September 1972, INT(NI)10, 2nd Battalion The Parachute Regiment.'

292. Lieutenant-Colonel I. D. B. Mennell, 'Ulster – Low Profile', *The Men of Harlech: The Journal of The Royal Regiment of Wales*, 7 (November 1972), 22.

7 STRATEGY IN THE SHADOW OF LOYALIST POWER

1. TNA DEFE 24/211: 'Note for the Record. Northern Ireland. Note of a meeting held in the Defence Secretary's room at the House of Lords', 9 November 1972.

2. Coakley and Todd, *Negotiating a Settlement in Northern Ireland*.

3. Aveyard, *No Solution*, 37.

4. J. Blaxland, 'Thinking outside the (Temporal) Box to Explain Protracted Intrastate Conflict', *Journal of Peace Research*, 58/6 (2021), 1271–83.

5. J. McGarry and B. O'Leary, *The Northern Ireland Conflict: Consociational Engagements* (Oxford: Oxford University Press, 2004), 194–216; Kerr, *The Destructors*, xv.

6. M. McGovern, *Counterinsurgency and Collusion in Northern Ireland* (London: Pluto Press, 2019), 4.

7. E. Burke, 'Loyalist Mobilization and Cross-Border Violence in Rural Ulster, 1972–1974', *Terrorism and Political Violence* (published online 14 April 2020), 3; accessed 6 March 2023 at: https://www.tandfonline.com/doi/full/10.1080/0 9546553.2020.1745777.

8. Urwin, *A State in Denial*, 63.

9. Neumann, *Britain's Long War*, 77.

10. Faulkner, *Memoirs of a Statesman*, 173.

11. Bruce, *The Red Hand*, 115.

12. English, *Armed Struggle*, 160.

13. McDaid, *Template for Peace*, 136.
14. Mulholland, 'Political Violence', 398.
15. Leahy, *The Intelligence War against the IRA*, 5.
16. Ibid., 5, 81, 90.
17. McDaid, *Template for Peace*, 16–28.
18. Linen Hall Library: 'Victory goes to the bold', *The Ulster Militant*, 2, September 1972.
19. J. Groser, 'Mr Craig warns MPs that Ulster is set on course to civil war', *The Times*, 20 October 1972.
20. TNA DEFE 13/1358: HQ Northern Ireland Operational Summary, 27 September 1972.
21. TNA CAB 130/560: 'Cabinet. Northern Ireland. GEN 79(72) 35th Meeting', 6 October 1972.
22. TNA DEFE 13/1358: HQ Northern Ireland Operational Summary, 11 October 1972.
23. TNA DEFE 24/211: Minute from Col H. S. L. Dalzell-Payne, MO4, to A/DMO, 12 October 1972; TNA PREM 15/1014: 'Northern Ireland situation report 110700 to 120700 hrs October 1972.'
24. '1st Battalion', *Pegasus: Journal of The Parachute Regiment and Airborne Forces*, 28/1 (January 1973), 15.
25. TNA DEFE 24/211: Minute from Col H. S. L. Dalzell-Payne, MO4, to A/DMO, 12 October 1972; TNA PREM 15/1014: 'Northern Ireland situation report 110700 to 120700 hrs October 1972.'
26. TNA DEFE 13/1358: HQ Northern Ireland Operational Summary, 18 October 1972.
27. TNA DEFE 13/1358: HQ Northern Ireland Operational Summary, 25 October 1972.
28. TNA DEFE 70/1067: Ministry of Defence Monthly Intelligence Summary, 8 November 1972.
29. TNA WO 305/6510: 'Narrative of Military Operations Vol. 2', XIV-9, XIV-10.
30. Bruce, *The Red Hand*, 214.
31. TNA CJ 4/838: Letter from HQ Northern Ireland to 3 Inf Bde, 8 Inf Bde, 39 Inf Bde et al., 6 November 1972.
32. TNA DEFE 24/824: Letter from William Whitelaw to General Tuzo, 6 November 1972.
33. TNA WO 305/4414: '2 RGJ Historical Diary. 1 April 1972 – 31 March 1973', entry for 6 November 1972.
34. PRONI HA/32/2/55: Minute from Major-General Ford to GOC, 7 November 1972.
35. Linen Hall Library: '999 Calls for Micks Only!', *The Ulster Militant*, 10, November 1972.
36. TNA CAB 130/560: 'Cabinet. Northern Ireland. GEN 79(72) 36th Meeting', 9 November 1972.

37. TNA DEFE 13/1525: 'Notes of a MOD internal meeting on Northern Ireland', 16 November 1972.
38. TNA WO 305/6510: 'Narrative of Military Operations Vol. 2', XVI-4.
39. TNA CAB 130/560: 'Cabinet. Northern Ireland. GEN 79(72) 37th Meeting', 22 November 1972.
40. PRONI CAB/9/G/27/6/5: 'Conclusions of Meeting Held at Stormont Castle', 4 December 1972.
41. TNA DEFE 24/824: Minute from J. T. Howe, Civil Adviser to the GOC, to GOC Northern Ireland, 27 November 1972.
42. TNA PREM 15/1689: Ministry of Defence Monthly Operational Summary, 5 January 1973, and 'Annex D. Current business as at 1 January 1973'; PRONI CAB/9/G/27/6/6A: 'Conclusions of Meeting Held at Stormont Castle', 3 January 1973.
43. TNA CJ 4/458: 'Commander Land Forces Directive for Future Operations', 7 December 1972.
44. TNA CJ 4/458: Paper by GOC Northern Ireland, 'Arrest Policy for Protestants', 9 December 1972.
45. TNA DEFE 13/1525: 'Notes of a MOD internal meeting on Northern Ireland', 14 December 1972.
46. TNA CAB 130/560: 'Cabinet. Northern Ireland. GEN 79(72) 39th Meeting', 14 December 1972.
47. TNA DEFE 13/912: Letter from CGS to General Tuzo, with attached directive, 15 December 1972.
48. Bodleian Library, Conservative Party Archive, CRD 3/18/1: 'Northern Ireland Committee', 20 December 1972.
49. TNA DEFE 70/1549: Headquarters Northern Ireland Operational Summary, 29 December 1972.
50. A. Cadwallader, *Lethal Allies: British Collusion in Ireland* (Cork: Mercier Press, 2013), 216.
51. TNA PREM 15/1689: 'Northern Ireland situation report from 020700 to 030700 hrs January 1973.'
52. PRONI CAB/9/G/27/6/6A: 'Conclusions of Meeting Held at Stormont Castle', 2 January 1973.
53. TNA PREM 15/1689: 'Note of a meeting between the Secretary of State and representatives of the Grand Orange Lodge of Ireland', 2 January 1973.
54. TNA CJ 4/458: Record of the Secretary of State for Northern Ireland's morning meeting, 3 January 1973.
55. PRONI CAB/9/G/27/6/6A: 'Conclusions of Meeting Held at Stormont Castle', 8 January 1973.
56. PRONI CAB/9/G/27/6/6A: 'Conclusions of Meeting Held at Stormont Castle', 10 January 1973.
57. TNA DEFE 24/876: Minute from Col C. R. Huxtable, MO4, to MA/CGS et al., attaching 'The White Paper threat study', 5 January 1973.

58. LSE: H. A. Hetherington papers, Box 20: 'Points from a discussion with Sir Robert Mark', 2–3 March 1973.
59. TNA DEFE 70/1068: Ministry of Defence Monthly Operational Summary, 8 March 1973; McKittrick et al., *Lost Lives*, 320–7.
60. TNA DEFE 70/1549: HQ Northern Ireland Operational Summary, 7 February 1973.
61. TNA DEFE 13/1525: 'Notes of a MOD internal meeting on Northern Ireland', 8 February 1973.
62. TNA PREM 15/1689: 'Note for the record', 8 February 1973.
63. TNA PREM 15/1689: Minute from Brigadier M. S. Bayley, BGS(Int), to VCGS, 'Northern Ireland. Weekly intelligence report: 9 February 1973.'
64. TNA PREM 15/1689: 'Note of a meeting in Stormont Castle', 9 February 1973.
65. TNA DEFE 24/876: Minute from Brigadier H. E. M. L. Garrett, for GOC, HQ Northern Ireland, to Ministry of Defence, 6 February 1973, and attached, 'Military Planning for the publication of the White Paper'.
66. TNA CAB 190/55: 'Cabinet. Joint Intelligence Committee (A). Border Plebiscite and White Paper: Threat Assessment', 15 February 1973.
67. TNA DEFE 13/1525: 'Notes of a MOD internal meeting on Northern Ireland', 15 February 1973.
68. TNA PREM 15/1690: Ministry of Defence Monthly Operational Summary, 8 March 1973.
69. TNA CJ 4/6116: Minute from William Nield to Secretary of State for Northern Ireland, 1 March 1973.
70. TNA CJ 4/6116: 'Note of a meeting to discuss arrest policy held at Stormont Castle', 7 March 1973.
71. TNA DEFE 70/1549: HQ Northern Ireland Operational Summary, 14 March 1973.
72. See the monthly reports in: TNA DEFE 70/1068, DEFE 70/1069 and DEFE 70/1070.
73. TNA PREM 15/1691: 'Note of a meeting', 14 March 1973.
74. TNA DEFE 70/1549: HQ Northern Ireland Operational Summary, 21 March 1973.
75. McDaid, *Template for Peace*, 17.
76. TNA CJ 4/668: Letter from P. J. H. Leng, HQ Northern Ireland, to 'Frank' [probably Cooper], 10 September 1973, with attached, 'The Army's method of operations'.
77. Craig, *Crisis of Confidence*, 130.
78. McDaid, *Template for Peace*, 41; Patterson, *Ireland's Violent Frontier*, 43.
79. Mulroe, *Bombs, Bullets and the Border*, 99, 119.
80. TNA DEFE 70/1069: 'Monthly report on Northern Ireland for November 1973. Annex C. Northern Ireland monthly statistics for the month of November 1973', Maj-Gen W. N. R. Scotter, DMO, 5 December 1973.

81. Patterson, *Ireland's Violent Frontier*, 50, 60; Mulroe, *Bombs, Bullets and the Border*, 116.
82. TNA DEFE 24/747: 'Notes of an internal meeting on Northern Ireland', 15 November 1973.
83. TNA PREM 15/482: Letter from A. W. Stephens, Ministry of Defence, to R. T. Armstrong, 4 October 1971, and attached 'Military appreciation of the security situation in Northern Ireland as at 4th October 1971'.
84. A. E. Grubb, 'Microlevel Dynamics of Violence: Explaining Variance in Violence amongst Rural Districts during Northern Ireland's Troubles', *Security Studies*, 25/3 (2016), 460–87; Burke, 'Loyalist Mobilization and Cross-Border Violence in Rural Ulster'; P. Mulroe, '"The Most Notorious Trouble Spot along the Entire Border": Exploring the Dynamics of Political Violence in an Irish Border Town, 1971–1974', *Irish Political Studies*, 35/4 (2020), 566–84.
85. Compiled from monthly reports in: TNA DEFE 70/1067; DEFE 70/1068; DEFE 70/1069; and DEFE 70/1070.
86. TNA DEFE 70/1068: Ministry of Defence Monthly Intelligence Summary, 3 October 1973.
87. Leahy, *The Intelligence War against the IRA*, 98–9.
88. TNA WO 305/5694: 'Post Tour Report Part 1', 1st Royal Hampshire Regiment, 2 January 1974.
89. Neumann, *Britain's Long War*, 80.
90. A. King, *Urban Warfare in the Twenty-First Century* (Cambridge: Polity Press, 2021), 50.
91. Compiled from monthly reports in: TNA DEFE 70/1067; DEFE 70/1068; DEFE 70/1069; and DEFE 70/1070.
92. Compiled from monthly reports in: TNA DEFE 70/1067; DEFE 70/1068; DEFE 70/1069; and DEFE 70/1070.
93. R. Brooks, 'Tying the Hands of Militants: Civilian Targeting and Societal Pressures in the Provisional IRA and Palestinian Hamas', *Journal of Global Security Studies*, 7/1 (2022), 11.
94. TNA DEFE 70/1069: 'Monthly report on Northern Ireland for December 1973. Appendix 1 to Annex C. Northern Ireland statistics for 1973', Maj-Gen W. N. R. Scotter, DMO, 4 January 1974.
95. T. Farrell, 'Military Adaptation and Organisational Convergence in War: Insurgents and International Forces in Afghanistan', *Journal of Strategic Studies*, 45/5 (2022), 719.
96. P. Gill, J. Horgan, S. T. Hunter and L. D. Cushenbery, 'Malevolent Creativity in Terrorist Organizations', *The Journal of Creative Behavior*, 47/2 (2013), 126, 130, 133.
97. M. C. Horowitz, E. Perkoski and P. B. K. Potter, 'Tactical Diversity in Militant Violence', *International Organization*, 72/1 (2018), 139, 146.
98. J. Horgan and M. Taylor, 'The Provisional Irish Republican Army: Command and Functional Structure', *Terrorism and Political Violence*, 9/3 (1997), 9–10, 14.

99. J. Bowyer Bell, *The IRA, 1968–2000: An Analysis of a Secret Army* (London: Frank Cass, 2000), 180.

100. McKearney, *The Provisional IRA*, 76.

101. TNA WO 32/21782: 'IRA Gunmen in Belfast', report by R. J. Heagerty, HQ Northern Ireland, 25 August 1972.

102. K. Conway, *Southside Provisional: From Freedom Fighter to the Four Courts* (Rathcoole: Orpen Press, 2014), 46–7, 50.

103. TNA DEFE 70/1067: Ministry of Defence Monthly Intelligence Summary, 5 October 1972.

104. TNA DEFE 70/1067: Ministry of Defence Monthly Intelligence Summary, 8 November 1972.

105. TNA DEFE 70/1068: Ministry of Defence Monthly Intelligence Summary, 5 June 1973.

106. TNA DEFE 70/1069: Ministry of Defence Monthly Intelligence Summary, 5 March 1974.

107. Airborne Assault Museum, 2 Para in Belfast, Box 2.33.15: 'Intsum Four for week ending 27 August 1972, INT(NI)10, 2nd Battalion The Parachute Regiment. Annex H to INT(NI)10 dated 28 Aug 72.'

108. TNA DEFE 70/1068: Ministry of Defence Monthly Operational Summary, 8 December 1972, and 'Appendix 1 to Annex E, Methods and tactics of IRA gunmen'.

109. TNA DEFE 70/1549: HQ Northern Ireland Operational Summary, 4 April 1973.

110. TNA DEFE 70/1068: Ministry of Defence Monthly Operational Summary, 8 December 1972, and 'Appendix 2 to Annex E'.

111. TNA DEFE 70/1068: Ministry of Defence Monthly Operational Summary, 4 May 1973.

112. TNA DEFE 70/1069: Ministry of Defence Monthly Operational Summary, 5 March 1974, and 'Appendix 2 to Annex E. Defeating the IRA sniper. Evolving tactics.'

113. Leahy, *The Intelligence War against the IRA*, 97.

114. Ó Faoleán, 'Ireland's Ho Chi Minh trail?', 983.

115. Gill, 'Tactical Innovation and the Provisional Irish Republican Army', 573–85.

116. Gill et al., 'Malevolent Creativity in Terrorist Organizations', 143.

117. G. McGladdery, *The Provisional IRA in England: The Bombing Campaign, 1973–1997* (Dublin: Irish Academic Press, 2006), 57–8, 61, 63–5.

118. Moloney, *A Secret History of the IRA*, 10.

119. TNA DEFE 70/1068: Ministry of Defence Monthly Intelligence Summary, 5 June 1973.

120. TNA DEFE 70/1069: Ministry of Defence Monthly Operational Summary, 3 April 1974.

121. TNA DEFE 70/1067: Ministry of Defence Monthly Intelligence Summary, 8 November 1972, and 'Appendix 4 to Annex E. Terrorists bombing activity.'

122. TNA DEFE 70/1068: Ministry of Defence Monthly Operational Summary, 5 April 1973, and 'Appendix 3 to Annex E. Terrorist bomb activity – March 1973.'
123. TNA DEFE 70/1068: Ministry of Defence Monthly Operational Summary, 4 May 1973.
124. TNA DEFE 70/1068: Ministry of Defence Monthly Intelligence Summary, 6 November 1973, and 'Annex E. Training matters.'
125. TNA DEFE 70/1068: Ministry of Defence Monthly Operational Summary, 5 June 1973, and 'Appendix 2 to Annex B. Significant bomb incidents.'
126. TNA DEFE 70/1068: Ministry of Defence Monthly Operational Summary, 4 July 1973.
127. TNA DEFE 70/1069: Ministry of Defence Monthly Intelligence Summary, 3 April 1974, and 'Appendix 1 to Annex B. Terrorist and security forces activity.'
128. PRONI CENT/1/3/39: 'Note of a Meeting Held at Stormont Castle', 6 February 1974.
129. TNA DEFE 70/1068: Ministry of Defence Monthly Intelligence Summary, 3 October 1973.
130. TNA DEFE 70/1069: Ministry of Defence Monthly Operational Summary, 4 January 1974.
131. TNA WO 305/4218: 'Headquarters 3 Infantry Brigade Intelligence Summary', 30 October 1973.
132. TNA DEFE 70/1069: Ministry of Defence Monthly Operational Summary, 3 April 1974, and 'Appendix 1 to Annex B. Terrorist and security forces activity.'
133. TNA DEFE 70/1069: Ministry of Defence Monthly Operational Summary, 3 May 1974.
134. TNA WO 305/5685: 'Report on Operations in Northern Ireland. 1 Glosters', 25 November 1974.
135. 'From the Companies', *The Iron Duke: The Regimental Journal of The Duke of Wellington's Regiment*, 49/163 (December 1973), 97.
136. TNA PREM 15/1690: HQ Northern Ireland Operational Summary, 7 March 1973.
137. TNA DEFE 70/1069: Ministry of Defence Monthly Operational Summary, 3 May 1974.
138. TNA WO 305/5694: 'Post Tour Report Part 1', 1st Royal Hampshire Regiment, 2 January 1974.
139. Smith, *3–2–1 Bomb Gone*, 123–4.
140. Cochrane, *The Development of the British Approach to Improvised Explosive Device Disposal*, 221–4, 237, 263–5.
141. TNA DEFE 70/1068: Ministry of Defence Monthly Operational Summary, 5 June 1973.
142. IWMSA: David Greenaway, catalogue number 33208, reel 3.
143. Compiled from monthly reports in: TNA DEFE 70/1067; DEFE 70/1068; DEFE 70/1069; and DEFE 70/1070.

144. TNA DEFE 70/1068: Ministry of Defence Monthly Operational Summary, 8 December 1972, and 'Appendix 2 to Annex E'.

145. Lancashire Infantry Museum: 1st Queen's Lancashire Regiment Commanding Officer's Brigade Conference Notes, December 1972–January 1973, entry for 6 December 1972.

146. TNA DEFE 70/1068: Ministry of Defence Monthly Operational Summary, 6 September 1973.

147. TNA DEFE 70/1068: Ministry of Defence Monthly Operational Summary, 3 October 1973.

148. TNA WO 305/4219: 'Headquarters 3 Infantry Brigade Intelligence Summary', 20 November 1973.

149. TNA WO 305/4219: 'Headquarters 3 Infantry Brigade Intelligence Summary', 27 November 1973.

150. TNA DEFE 70/1069: Ministry of Defence Monthly Operational Summary, 6 February 1974.

151. TNA DEFE 70/1068: Ministry of Defence Monthly Operational Summary, 6 November 1973.

152. TNA DEFE 70/1069: Ministry of Defence Monthly Operational Summary, 5 December 1973.

153. TNA DEFE 70/1069: Ministry of Defence Monthly Operational Summary, 4 January 1974.

154. TNA DEFE 70/1069: Ministry of Defence Monthly Operational Summary, 5 March 1974.

155. TNA DEFE 70/1069: Ministry of Defence Monthly Operational Summary, 3 April 1974.

156. TNA DEFE 70/1069: Ministry of Defence Monthly Operational Summary, 3 May 1974.

157. TNA DEFE 70/1069: Ministry of Defence Monthly Intelligence Summary, 4 January 1974.

158. TNA DEFE 70/1069: Ministry of Defence Monthly Intelligence Summary, 5 February 1974.

159. TNA DEFE 70/1069: Ministry of Defence Monthly Intelligence Summary, 3 May 1974.

160. TNA DEFE 24/969: 'Commander Land Forces' Directive for Future Operations', signed Maj-Gen P. J. H. Leng, 13 July 1973.

161. B. Bamford, 'The Role and Effectiveness of Intelligence in Northern Ireland', *Intelligence and National Security*, 20/4 (2005), 581–607; M. Kirk-Smith and J. Dingley, 'Countering Terrorism in Northern Ireland: The Role of Intelligence', *Small Wars and Insurgencies*, 20/3–4 (2009), 551–73; J. Moran, 'Evaluating Special Branch and the Use of Informant Intelligence in Northern Ireland', *Intelligence and National Security*, 25/1 (2010), 1–23.

162. J. Ferris (ed.), *The British Army and Signals Intelligence during the First World War* (Stroud: Alan Sutton for the Army Records Society, 1992), 1.

163. TNA WO 305/5704: 'Post Tour Report – Part I. 2 PARA', 12 September 1975.
164. TNA DEFE 70/1522: 'CLF Northern Ireland Study Period 8 Oct 74. Intelligence gathering, storing and retrieval', and attached: 'The Future Intelligence System by Dr P. E. Haskell RARDE'.
165. LHCMA: David Ramsbotham papers, Box 1: Notes for the Official History of the Northern Ireland operations.
166. IWMSA: Angus Southwood, catalogue number 33979, reel 10.
167. TNA DEFE 13/914: 'Progress report on Operation Vengeful', 10 January 1975.
168. T. Craig, '"You will be responsible to the GOC": Stovepiping and the Problem of Divergent Intelligence-Gathering Networks in Northern Ireland, 1969–1975', *Intelligence and National Security*, 33/2 (2018), 220.
169. Bennett, 'From Direct Rule to Motorman', 523.
170. Royal Marines Museum: 2/18/3, 'Newsletter. 40 Commando RM', June–October 1972.
171. TNA DEFE 70/1522: 'CLF Northern Ireland Study Period 8 Oct 74. Intelligence gathering, storing and retrieval', and attached: 'The Present Intelligence System by Col P. J. Goss Col GS Int HQ Northern Ireland'.
172. A. Alderson, *The Validity of British Army Counterinsurgency Doctrine after the War in Iraq 2003–2009* (PhD thesis, Cranfield University, 2009), 122–3.
173. A. King, *The Combat Soldier: Infantry Tactics and Cohesion in the Twentieth and Twenty-First Centuries* (Oxford: Oxford University Press, 2013), 224, 337.
174. TNA WO 305/5750: 'Report on Tour in Northern Ireland', 2nd Parachute Regiment, 28 September 1971.
175. TNA WO 32/21733: Letter from Colonel D. E. Blum, UKLF, to Ministry of Defence, 29 September 1972.
176. Bennett, 'From Direct Rule to Motorman', 518–19.
177. TNA DEFE 70/1069: 'Monthly report on Northern Ireland for November 1973. Annex E. Training notes', 5 December 1973; 'Monthly report on Northern Ireland for February 1974. Annex E. Training matters', 5 March 1974.
178. TNA WO 305/4403: Historical Record of 1st Royal Hampshire Regiment, 1 April 1972–31 March 1973.
179. '1st Battalion', *Castle: The Journal of The Royal Anglian Regiment*, 6 (January 1975), 36.
180. TNA WO 32/21782: Minute from T. H. Sergeant, DS10, to AT1, 5 December 1972.
181. TNA WO 32/21782: Letter from Colonel P. I. Chiswell, Ministry of Defence, to Brigadier F. E. Kitson, School of Infantry, 8 September 1972.
182. TNA DEFE 70/1067: 'Monthly report on Northern Ireland for April 1972. Annex E. Training matters', 8 May 1972.
183. TNA WO 305/5703: 'Reports on Operations in Northern Ireland', 2nd Parachute Regiment, 30 June 1972.

184. TNA WO 32/21784: 'Op Banner Post Tour Report – 1 Green Howards', 27 April 1973.

185. McKearney, *The Provisional IRA*, 77–8.

186. W. C. Moffat, 'British Forces Casualties Northern Ireland', *Journal of the Royal Army Medical Corps*, 122/1 (1976), 4–6.

187. TNA WO 32/21782: 'A Study of the IRA Gunman: Their Effectiveness and Our Counter-Measures', by Bayly Pike, Scientific Adviser, HQ Northern Ireland, 31 August 1972.

188. TNA WO 305/5703: 'Reports on Operations in Northern Ireland', Capt. D. R. Chaundler, for Lt-Col Commanding 2nd Parachute Regiment, 30 June 1972.

189. TNA WO 32/21784: 'End of Tour Report. 1st Bn The Green Howards', 27 April 1973.

190. TNA WO 305/5806: 'End of Tour Report', 1st Gordon Highlanders, 21 June 1973.

191. TNA WO 305/4404: '1 Staffords Historical Record 1 Apr 72–31 Mar 73.'

192. TNA WO 305/5958: 'End of Tour Report', 42 Commando, Royal Marines, 12 June 1973.

193. TNA WO 305/5670: 'Report on Operations in Northern Ireland', 2 Royal Anglians, 22 November 1973.

194. Royal Marines Museum: 2/18/3, 'Newsletter. 40 Commando RM. 1973.'

195. TNA WO 305/5679: 'Post Tour Report – Part 1. 1 Green Howards', 14 August 1975.

196. Lt P. L. Bancroft, 'Combatting Terrorism from the Air', *The Globe and Laurel: The Journal of the Royal Marines*, 81/6 (December 1972), 363.

197. TNA WO 305/5831: 'Northern Ireland Emergency Tour – Post Tour Report', 1 Cheshire Regiment, 24 June 1973.

198. TNA WO 305/5807: '1 Gordons – End of Tour Report', 24 October 1972.

199. TNA DEFE 70/1068: Ministry of Defence Monthly Operational Summary, 4 July 1973, and 'Annex D. Current business as at 2 July 1973.'

200. TNA WO 32/21784: 'End of Tour Report. 1st Bn The Green Howards', 27 April 1973.

201. TNA WO 305/5672: 'Post Tour Report Part 1 – 3 R Anglian', 19 March 1975.

202. TNA DEFE 70/1068: Ministry of Defence Monthly Operational Summary, 6 August 1973.

203. 'Intelligence Section', *The Lancashire Lad: The Journal of The Queen's Lancashire Regiment*, 1/2 (September 1970), 53.

204. Charters, '"Have a Go"', 202–29.

205. TNA WO 305/4277: 2nd Royal Regiment of Fusiliers, Historical Record, April 1968 – March 1973, entry for 6 October 1972.

206. TNA WO 305/4351: Historical Record Return for 1973, 40th Field Regiment Royal Artillery, '137 (Java) Field Battery in Northern Ireland', February–June 1973.

207. TNA WO 305/6510: 'Narrative of Military Operations Vol. 2', XIX-10, XIX-11.
208. IWMSA: Kenneth Ambrose, catalogue number 32532, reel 16.
209. PRONI CAB/9/G/27/6/6A: 'The Peace Box', memorandum by K. D. McDowall, Director of Information Services, 27 February 1973; 'Conclusions of Meeting Held at Stormont Castle', 28 February 1973.
210. TNA PREM 15/1689: 'Annex B to A/BR/30/8/MO4 Dated 5 February 1973.'
211. TNA DEFE 70/1068: Ministry of Defence Monthly Operational Summary, 5 June 1973.
212. Lancashire Infantry Museum: 1st Queen's Lancashire Regiment Commanding Officer's Brigade Conference Notes, January–March 1973, entry for 19 March 1973.
213. TNA DEFE 70/690: Letter from Lieut.-Gen. Sir Frank King to CGS, 16 August 1974.
214. TNA WO 305/5690: 'Report on Operations in Northern Ireland Part One – Operations and Training', 1st The Duke of Wellington's Regiment, 26 September 1974.
215. TNA DEFE 24/544: Minute from VCGS to Secretary of State for Defence, 11 May 1972; TNA WO 305/6510: 'Narrative of Military Operations Vol. 2', XV-11.
216. D. A. Charters, 'Professionalizing Clandestine Military Intelligence in Northern Ireland: Creating the Special Reconnaissance Unit', *Intelligence and National Security*, 33/1 (2018), 132.
217. R. Cormac, *Disrupt and Deny: Spies, Special Forces, and the Secret Pursuit of British Foreign Policy* (Oxford: Oxford University Press, 2018), 204.
218. TNA PREM 15/1008: 'Note of a meeting held on 19th May [1972].'
219. C. Young, 'Files on seven former British soldiers linked to MRF killings in west Belfast sent to Public Prosecution Service', *The Irish News*, 6 June 2020.
220. Leahy, *The Intelligence War against the IRA*, 32–3.
221. TNA DEFE 13/1358: Headquarters Northern Ireland operational summary, 4 October 1972.
222. Bennett, 'From Direct Rule to Motorman', 523.
223. TNA DEFE 68/838: Minute from Brigadier M. S. Bayley, to VCGS (2), 20 July 1973.
224. TNA DEFE 13/990: 'Telephone conversation CGS/GOC Northern Ireland 17 October 1973'; DEFE 13/1525: 'Notes of a MOD internal meeting on Northern Ireland', 18 October 1973.
225. TNA DEFE 70/690: Minute from Brigadier M. S. Bayley, to MA/CGS, 7 August 1974.
226. O'Leary, *A Treatise on Northern Ireland, Volume I*, 79.
227. Ibid., *Volume III*, 56.
228. T. Craig and M. McCleery, 'Political Bargaining Chips: Republican Internees in Northern Ireland 1972–1975', *Small Wars and Insurgencies*, 31/3 (2020), 645–6.

229. R. J. Spjut, 'Internment and Detention without Trial in Northern Ireland 1971–1975: Ministerial Policy and Practice', *The Modern Law Review*, 49/6 (1986), 728–31.

230. TNA CJ 4/6071: Minute from J. T. A. Howard-Drake to Mr Cooper, 28 December 1973.

231. TNA CJ 4/6077: Minute from N. K. Finlayson, PS/Mr van Straubenzee, to Mr Howard-Drake, 22 January 1974.

232. TNA DEFE 13/1210: 'Visit of CGS to Northern Ireland – 25th January 1974', 29 January 1974.

233. K. Boyle, T. Hadden and P. Hillyard, *Law and State: The Case of Northern Ireland* (London: Martin Robertson, 1975), 40, 42.

234. Leahy, *The Intelligence War against the IRA*, 86.

235. TNA DEFE 13/1849: Minute from CGS to Secretary of State for Defence, 14 May 1974.

236. TNA DEFE 70/1549: Headquarters Northern Ireland Operational Summary, 27 September 1972.

237. TNA DEFE 24/969: 'Record of a meeting between VCGS and GOC Northern Ireland', 24 May 1973.

238. TNA DEFE 70/1068: Ministry of Defence Monthly Operational Summary, 6 August 1973.

239. TNA DEFE 70/1069: Ministry of Defence Monthly Operational Summary, 5 March 1974.

240. TNA WO 305/5703: 'Reports on Operations in Northern Ireland', Capt. D. R. Chaundler, for Lt-Col Commanding 2nd Parachute Regiment, 30 June 1972.

241. Lancashire Infantry Museum: 1st Queen's Lancashire Regiment Commanding Officer's Brigade Conference Notes, December 1972–January 1973, entry for 14 December 1972.

242. Lancashire Infantry Museum: 1st Queen's Lancashire Regiment Commanding Officer's Brigade Conference Notes, January–March 1973, entry for 20 January 1973.

243. TNA WO 32/21784: HQ Northern Ireland Operational Summary, 30 May 1973.

244. Moloney, *A Secret History of the IRA*, 129.

245. TNA DEFE 70/1069: Ministry of Defence Monthly Operational Summary, 4 January 1974.

246. TNA DEFE 70/1070: Ministry of Defence Monthly Operational Summary, and 'Annex D. Current Business and Political Affairs', 3 July 1975.

247. TNA DEFE 70/1549: HQ Northern Ireland Operational Summary, 27 September 1972, and 'Annex C. Statistical Progress Report on Operation Motorman.'

248. TNA DEFE 70/1550: HQ Northern Ireland Operational Summary, 8 August 1973, 15 August 1973, 22 August 1973, 29 August 1973 [data for 1–29 August

only]; DEFE 70/1068: Ministry of Defence Monthly Operational Summary, 6 September 1973.

249. Compiled from monthly reports in: TNA DEFE 70/1068, DEFE 70/1069; and, for internments: Spjut, 'Internment and Detention without Trial', 740.

250. TNA DEFE 70/1068: Ministry of Defence Monthly Operational Summary, 6 August 1973.

251. D. Byman, 'Counterterrorism Strategies', in E. Chenoweth, R. English, A. Gofas and S. N. Kalyvas (eds.), *The Oxford Handbook of Terrorism* (Oxford: Oxford University Press, 2019), 626.

252. Lt-Col J. C. M. Baynes, *The Soldier in Modern Society* (London: Eyre Methuen, 1972), 106.

253. R. J. Heuer, Jr., *Psychology of Intelligence Analysis* (Langley: Central Intelligence Agency, 1999), 70.

254. J. Jordan, 'Attacking the Leader, Missing the Mark: Why Terrorist Groups Survive Decapitation Strikes', *International Security*, 38/4 (2014), 7–38.

255. TNA WO 305/5670: 'Report on Operations in Northern Ireland', 2 R. Anglian, 22 November 1973.

256. McDaid, *Template for Peace*, 51.

257. For a study of civilian community relations, see: J. T. Morgan, *Counter-Terror Ideology: The Community Relations Commission and the Provisional Irish Republican Army, 1969–1979* (PhD dissertation, Carnegie Mellon University, 2011).

258. E. Moxon-Browne, 'The Water and the Fish: Public Opinion and the Provisional IRA in Northern Ireland', *Terrorism*, 5/1–2 (1981), 50, 68.

259. F. Burton, *The Politics of Legitimacy: Struggles in a Belfast Community* (London: Routledge, 1978), 83, 85.

260. PRONI DCR/1/83: 'Housing Intimidation in Belfast', Community Relations Commission report, 1973, 102.

261. A. King, 'Urban Insurgency in the Twenty-First Century: Smaller Militaries and Increased Conflict in Cities', *International Affairs*, 98/2 (2022), 620.

262. 'An Ever-Changing Scene', *The Globe and Laurel: The Journal of the Royal Marines*, 81/5 (October 1972), 267.

263. PRONI CREL/4/2/8: Letter from Major J. H. C. James, HQ Northern Ireland, to Unit HQ Folders, 21 January 1972.

264. PRONI DCR/1/15: 'Ministry of Community Relations. Circular to All Staff', 24 March 1972.

265. PRONI CREL/4/2/8: Minute by Major C. J. Smith, 40 Cdo RM, 11 September 1972.

266. TNA WO 305/5707: 'Report on Operations in Northern Ireland. Part I – Operations and Training', 2 Royal Green Jackets, 13 February 1975.

267. TNA WO 305/5670: 'Community Relations. Appx 3 to Annex A to 2 R Anglian 5101 G', 22 November 1973.

268. KOSBRM, Newsletters: 'Borderers in Belfast. The Newsletter of the 1st Battalion The King's Own Scottish Borderers in Belfast', 19 December 1972.

269. PRONI DCR/1/18: 'Report on Meeting at Holy Cross with Fr Aquinas', 31 March 1973.
270. PRONI DCR/1/18: 'Meeting with Fr Aquinas at Tennent Street HQ', 16 April 1973.
271. PRONI DCR/1/18: 'Report from the Civil Representative', E. Cadden, 9 May 1973.
272. PRONI DCR/1/18: '3 Para Community Relations Report', 6 June 1973.
273. PRONI DCR/1/18: 'Report on Situation in Ardoyne', E. Cadden, 30 June 1973.
274. 'Major Gordon Burt obituary', *The Times*, 2 April 2021.
275. Burton, *The Politics of Legitimacy*, 107.
276. LSE Library, Merlyn Rees papers: MERLYN-REES/7/6: Letter from Paddy Devlin to William Whitelaw, 31 March 1973.
277. Ardoyne Commemoration Project, *Ardoyne: The Untold Truth*, 180.
278. LSE Library, Merlyn Rees papers: MERLYN-REES/7/6: Letter from David Howell to Paddy Devlin, 8 May 1973.
279. TNA DEFE 70/1550: HQ Northern Ireland Operational Summary, 10 October 1973.
280. IWMSA: Steve Kirvan, catalogue number 32370, reel 3.
281. PRONI CREL/2/5: 'Report of a Meeting at Bedford House on Wednesday 28 July 1971 between Representatives of Army Community Relations Personnel and the Community Relations Commission staff.'
282. '1st Battalion Notes', *The Journal of the Royal Hampshire Regiment*, 62/1 (May 1973), 19.
283. TNA WO 32/21784: 'End of Tour Report', 1st Green Howards, 27 April 1973.
284. PRONI CREL/4/2/8: 'Outline Record of a Community Relations Meeting Held at HQ Northern Ireland', 23 October 1972.
285. '1st Battalion', *Pegasus: Journal of The Parachute Regiment and Airborne Forces*, 26/1 (January 1971), 21.
286. PRONI DCR/1/17: Minute from Bruce Davison to Secretary, 15 June 1973.
287. PRONI CENT/1/4/16: Minute from L. S. Duncan to Mr Ramsay, 7 February 1975.
288. On the regimental system, see: D. French, *Military Identities: The Regimental System, the British Army, and the British People c. 1870–2000* (Oxford: Oxford University Press, 2005).
289. Bennett, '"Smoke without Fire"?', 280–2.
290. TNA DEFE 70/204: Minute from Vice Adjutant General to Minister of State, 18 June 1974.
291. Linen Hall Library: 'Double edged', *Visor: Weekly Report for Soldiers in Northern Ireland* (HQ Northern Ireland: Army Information Services), Serial 25, 15 August 1974.
292. TNA WO 32/21782: 'IRA Gunmen in Belfast', by Richard Heagerty, HQ Northern Ireland, 25 August 1972.

293. TNA WO 305/5707: 'Report on Operations in Northern Ireland. Part I – Operations and Training', 2 Royal Green Jackets, 13 February 1975.

294. JSCSC Library: National Defence College Papers: '3 Course. Exercise thesis. The Services and the Media', by Commander J. L. Palmer, RN, 1974, 11.

295. JSCSC Library: National Defence College Papers: 'No. 4 Course. The Military and the Media', by Wing Commander K. R. Edmonds, 1975, 6.

296. Cormac, 'The Information Research Department, Unattributable Propaganda, and Northern Ireland', 1084–6, 1098–9.

297. TNA CJ 4/876: Evidence of Lt-Gen Sir Frank King to the Gardiner Committee, 7 November 1974.

298. TNA CJ 4/523: Joint Information Policy Committee minutes, 31 January 1973.

299. TNA PREM 15/1692: 'Northern Ireland situation report from Thursday 190700 to Tuesday 240700 hrs April 1973.'

300. TNA DEFE 68/87: Minute from M. Cudlip to PS/Secretary of State for Northern Ireland, 1 November 1974.

301. TNA PREM 15/1690: 'Military information policy working party. Review No 15', 13 February 1973, and attached 'Annex A to 240 G dated 13 Feb 73. Campaign to discredit the Army.'

302. TNA DEFE 24/1919: 'Op Banner – end of tour report. 1 RGJ, May–Sep 71', 18 November 1971.

303. D. Miller, *Don't Mention the War: Northern Ireland, Propaganda and the Media* (London: Pluto Press, 1994).

304. 'Purely Editorial', *Pegasus: Journal of The Parachute Regiment and Airborne Forces*, 26/3 (July 1971), 2.

305. J. Chartres, 'Reporting the Northern Ireland Scene', *Pegasus: Journal of The Parachute Regiment and Airborne Forces*, 26/3 (July 1971), 8.

306. S. Hoggart, 'The army PR men of Northern Ireland', *New Society*, 11 October 1973.

307. JSCSC Library: National Defence College Papers: '5 Course. The Constabulary Role of the British Soldier in Urban Areas of Ulster', by Major T. L. Trotman, 1976, 21.

308. 'From the Céilide', *The Green Howards' Gazette: A monthly chronicle of The Green Howards*, 79/931 (October 1971), 941.

309. Burke, *An Army of Tribes*, 120.

310. Royal Marines Museum: 2/18/3, 'Newsletter. 40 Commando RM', June–October 1972.

311. PRONI CREL/4/2/8: 'Minutes of the Andersonstown and Suffolk Co-ordination Committee', 28 November 1972.

312. TNA WO 305/4351: Historical Record Return for 1973, 40th Field Regiment, Royal Artillery; 137 (Java) Field Battery in Northern Ireland February to June 1973.

313. TNA CJ 4/668: Letter from P. J. H. Leng, HQ Northern Ireland, to 'Frank' [probably Cooper], 10 September 1973, with attached, 'The Army's method of operations'.
314. PRONI CENT/1/5/3: 'Secretary of State's quarterly bulletin – Oct–Dec 1975. Statistics on Security.' Figures are for occupied and unoccupied houses.
315. TNA WO 305/5685: 'Report on Operations in Northern Ireland. 1 Glosters', 25 November 1974.
316. TNA CJ 4/836: Letter from Major P. J. C. Moore for GOC, HQ Northern Ireland, to B. Webster, Northern Ireland Office, 17 April 1975, and attached 'Appendix 1 to Annex A to HQ Norireland 1112 G dated 17 Apr 75. Search damage claim scheme.'
317. Corbett, *Belfast Diaries*, 204.
318. Linen Hall Library: 'Special powers, special deeds', *Loyalist News*, 24 February 1973.
319. Royal Hampshire Regiment Museum: Northern Ireland Box 1-D4, File M4619: R. W. Coleman, 'A Northern Ireland Diary', 6 and 15 March 1973.
320. Royal Marines Museum: 2/18/8, '45 Commando Royal Marines Unit Newsletter', April–November 1974.
321. 'The Poachers', *Castle: The Journal of The Royal Anglian Regiment* 5/5 (January 1974), 20.
322. TNA CJ 4/836: Letter from Lt-Col C. L. Tarver, HQ Northern Ireland, to B. Webster, NIO, 23 June 1975, and attached 'Discrimination in security forces' activity'.
323. TNA CJ 4/668: 'Attorney-General's visit – 8th January 1974. GOC's briefing notes on soldier prosecutions.'
324. TNA DEFE 70/204: Letter from Attorney General to Lieutenant-General Sir Frank King, 23 May 1974.
325. TNA PREM 16/150: Letter from Merlyn Rees to Prime Minister, 29 July 1974.
326. LSE Library, Merlyn Rees papers: MERLYN-REES/12/1: Letter from Roland Moyle MP, Northern Ireland Office, to P. Whitehead MP, 14 May 1975.
327. Bennett, '"Smoke without Fire"?', 290–7.
328. Hennessey, *The First Northern Ireland Peace Process*, 25.
329. TNA DEFE 24/1933: Signal from UKREP Belfast to Dublin, 4 December 1972.
330. TNA PREM 15/1015: 'Record of a meeting between the Prime Minister and the Londonderry Women's Peace Committee', 17 November 1972; 'Record of a meeting between the Prime Minister and a delegation from the Alliance Party', 17 November 1972.
331. TNA PREM 15/1015: 'Note for the record', 25 November 1972.
332. TNA DEFE 13/990: Minute by D. J. Ramsbotham, 'CGS visit to Northern Ireland 28 September 1973'.
333. TNA WO 305/4218: 'Headquarters 3 Infantry Brigade Intelligence Summary', 2 October 1973.

334. TNA DEFE 13/1525: 'Notes of a MOD internal meeting on Northern Ireland', 2 August 1973.

335. TNA DEFE 13/1525: 'Notes of a MOD internal meeting on Northern Ireland', 30 August 1973.

336. TNA DEFE 70/1068: Ministry of Defence Monthly Operational Summary, 6 August 1973.

337. TNA PREM 15/1696: Minute from F. E. R. B. to Prime Minister, 12 November 1973.

338. TNA DEFE 13/1525: 'Notes of a MOD internal meeting on Northern Ireland', 21 June 1973.

339. TNA WO 32/21782: 'IRA Gunmen in Belfast', by Richard Heagerty, HQ Northern Ireland, 25 August 1972.

340. TNA PREM 15/1689: Ministry of Defence Monthly Operational Summary, 5 January 1973, and 'Annex D. Current business as at 1 January 1973.'

341. LSE Library, Merlyn Rees papers: MERLYN-REES/7/3: Letters from [redacted], St Bernadette's Church, Belfast, to Brigadier S. Boswell, 7 November 1972, 16 November 1972.

342. Lancashire Infantry Museum: 1st Queen's Lancashire Regiment Commanding Officer's Brigade Conference Notes, January–March 1973, entry for 2 February 1973.

343. '1st Battalion Notes', *The Tiger and Sphinx: Journal of The Gordon Highlanders* (August/September 1973), 28–9.

344. Compiled from monthly reports in: TNA DEFE 70/1067; DEFE 70/1068; DEFE 70/1069; and DEFE 70/1070.

345. TNA DEFE 70/1068: Ministry of Defence Monthly Operational Summary, 5 April 1973.

8 WE CANNOT ENVISAGE PEACE

1. TNA DEFE 24/1859: Minute by D. B. Omand, DS10, Ministry of Defence, 20 June 1975.

2. Pte. Dixon, 'Thoughts of a Newcomer', *The Iron Duke: The Regimental Journal of The Duke of Wellington's Regiment*, 50/164 (April 1974), 18.

3. Aveyard, *No Solution*, 135.

4. O'Leary, *A Treatise on Northern Ireland: Volume III*, 62; Kerr, *The Destructors*, 13.

5. Charters, *Whose Mission, Whose Orders?*, 195; Edwards, '"A Whipping Boy If Ever There Was One"?', 174.

6. Charters, *Whose Mission, Whose Orders?*, 204.

7. Ó Dochartaigh, 'Northern Ireland since 1920', 158; Leahy, *The Intelligence War against the IRA*, 63, 66, 68.

8. Leahy, *The Intelligence War against the IRA*, 108; Ó Dochartaigh, *Deniable Contact*, 123, 146–7.

9. P. Taylor, *Loyalists* (London: Bloomsbury, 1999), 124.

10. R. J. Reed, 'Blood, Thunder and Rosettes: The Multiple Personalities of Paramilitary Loyalism between 1971 and 1988', *Irish Political Studies*, 26/1 (2011), 52.

11. T. Novosel, *Northern Ireland's Lost Opportunity: The Frustrated Promise of Political Loyalism* (London: Pluto Press, 2013), 90–1, 119.

12. P. Neumann, 'The Myth of Ulsterization in British Security Policy in Northern Ireland', *Studies in Conflict and Terrorism*, 26/5 (2003), 369–70.

13. NATO Archives: DPC-D(73)23, 'North Atlantic Council. Defence Planning Committee. NATO Defence Planning 1974–1978. United Kingdom', 23 November 1973.

14. D. Edgerton, 'Liberal Militarism and the British State', *New Left Review*, 185/1 (1991), 139. See further: D. Edgerton, *Warfare State: Britain, 1920–1970* (Cambridge: Cambridge University Press, 2005).

15. TNA DEFE 13/1425: Minute from CGS to Secretary of State for Defence, 9 July 1973.

16. P. Dixon, 'Britain's "Vietnam Syndrome"? Public Opinion and British Military Intervention from Palestine to Yugoslavia', *Review of International Studies*, 26/1 (2000), 110–12.

17. TNA DEFE 70/1068: Ministry of Defence Monthly Operational Summary, 4 July 1973, Annex D.

18. TNA CAB 130/633: 'GEN 79(73) 8th Meeting. Cabinet. Northern Ireland. Minutes of a Meeting', 12 July 1973.

19. J. Fennell, *Combat and Morale in the North African Campaign: The Eighth Army and the Path to El Alamein* (Cambridge: Cambridge University Press, 2011), 2, 7, 27, 189.

20. Burke, *An Army of Tribes*, 123–5.

21. A. Watson, *Enduring the Great War: Combat, Morale and Collapse in the German and British Armies, 1914–1918* (Cambridge: Cambridge University Press, 2008).

22. RSRM: *The Belfast Thistle*, 1st Battalion The Royal Scots, Edition 1, 28 March 1970.

23. *The Royal Green Jackets Chronicle 1971: An Annual Record* (Winchester: The Royal Green Jackets, 1971), 31–2.

24. '1st Battalion', *The Fusilier. The Journal of the Royal Regiment of Fusiliers*, 1/5 (December 1970), 391.

25. Linen Hall Library: 'Unit feature: 1st Battalion The Royal Regiment of Fusiliers', *Visor: Weekly Report for Soldiers in Northern Ireland* (HQ Northern Ireland: Army Information Services), Serial 52, 20 February 1975.

26. TNA DEFE 70/1262: Letter from B. J. Hordle, for Commander, 2 Signal Group, Aldershot, to External Telecommunications Executive, London, 11 August 1972; Letter from Colonel D. A. Gilchrist, for Director of Personal Services (Army), to HQ Northern Ireland, 5 September 1972.

27. TNA DEFE 70/1262: Letter from Lt-Gen Harry Tuzo to Maj-Gen de C. Martin, Director of Personal Services (Army), 4 September 1972.

28. KOSBRM, Newsletters: 'Borderers in Belfast. The Newsletter of the 1st Battalion The King's Own Scottish Borderers in Belfast', 18 February 1973.

29. TNA DEFE 70/1262: Letter from Chaplain General, Ministry of Defence, to HQ Northern Ireland, 24 August 1972.

30. TNA DEFE 70/1262: Memo from AG Sec to PS4(A), 15 March 1974.

31. Royal Hampshire Regiment Museum: 'The Royal Hampshires Tiger Rag', Edition 20, February 1973.

32. TNA DEFE 70/1262: Letter from Roy Mason to Prime Minister, 9 May 1974.

33. TNA DEFE 70/1262: Letter from William Rodgers, Minister of State for Defence, to Ted Leadbitter MP, 20 November 1974.

34. Airborne Assault Museum, Northern Ireland Publications, Box 2.33.25: *Northern Ireland: What Is It Like for Soldiers?* (London: Ministry of Defence, no date).

35. TNA DEFE 13/1425: Minute from USofS(Army) to Secretary of State for Defence, 16 July 1973.

36. A. Cairncross, *The British Economy since 1945: Economic Policy and Performance* (Oxford: Blackwell, 1995), 188, 202.

37. TNA PREM 16/327: Letter from Roy Mason to Prime Minister, 30 April 1974. Prices in parentheses are estimated present-day equivalents taken from the Bank of England's online inflation calculator, at www.bankofengland.co.uk/monet ary-policy/inflation/inflation-calculator.

38. TNA PREM 16/327: Minute from Harold Wilson to Roy Mason, 30 April 1974.

39. H. Stanhope, '50p a day Northern Ireland bonus in Forces' £100m deal', *The Times*, 17 May 1974. For the currency conversion, see note 37 above.

40. Linen Hall Library: 'Pay review', *Visor: Weekly Report for Soldiers in Northern Ireland* (HQ Northern Ireland: Army Information Services), Serial 65, 22 May 1975.

41. C. Guthrie, *Peace, War and Whitehall: A Memoir* (Oxford: Osprey, 2021), 93.

42. TNA DEFE 24/877: Minute from W. G. H. Beach, DASD, to CGS, 29 August 1973.

43. TNA DEFE 24/877: Letter from Tom Bridges, 10 Downing Street, to W. F. Mumford, Ministry of Defence, 20 September 1973; Minute from N. H. Nicholls, Ministry of Defence, to Lord Bridges, 25 September 1973.

44. TNA DEFE 13/990: 'Telephone conversation CGS/GOC Northern Ireland', 20 September 1973.

45. TNA DEFE 24/877: Letter from Lord Carrington to William Whitelaw, 10 September 1973; Letter from William Whitelaw to Lord Carrington, 14 September 1973.

46. McDaid, *Template for Peace*, 25, 28.

47. D. Kavanagh, 'The Fatal Choice: The Calling of the February 1974 Election', in S. Ball and A. Seldon (eds.), *The Heath Government 1970–74: A Reappraisal* (London: Routledge, 1996), 360.

48. TNA DEFE 70/588: Minute from CGS to Secretary of State for Defence, 1 February 1974.
49. TNA DEFE 70/1069: Ministry of Defence Monthly Intelligence Summary, 5 December 1973.
50. TNA DEFE 70/1069: Ministry of Defence Monthly Intelligence Summary, 4 January 1974.
51. TNA DEFE 24/747: 'Notes of an internal meeting on Northern Ireland', 17 January 1974.
52. Ramsay, *Ringside Seats*, 131.
53. TNA CJ 4/839: 'Note for the record', F. Cooper, 6 February 1974.
54. TNA DEFE 70/588: Letter from CGS to Lieutenant-General Sir Frank King, 7 February 1974.
55. C. Ballinger and A. Seldon, 'Prime Ministers and Cabinet', in K. Hickson and A. Seldon (eds.), *New Labour, Old Labour: The Wilson and Callaghan Governments 1974–1979* (London: Routledge, 2004), 173.
56. J. Callaghan, *Time and Chance* (London: Fontana, 1988), 234.
57. Rees, *Northern Ireland*, 51.
58. Aveyard, *No Solution*, 23.
59. Blacker, *Monkey Business*, 176–7.
60. D. Greenwood, 'The 1974 Defence Review in Perspective', *Survival*, 17/5 (1975), 224.
61. TNA DEFE 32/22: 'Chiefs of Staff Committee. Confidential Annex to COS 7th Meeting/74', 30 April 1974.
62. Linen Hall Library: 'On the way out', *Mid-Ulster U.D.A. News*, 2/2, 20 April 1974.
63. TNA CJ 4/839: 'Note for the record. Ministry of Defence security briefing', 8 March 1974.
64. IWMSA: Graham Wickes, catalogue number 26933, reel 2.
65. TNA DEFE 24/824: Letter from Lt-Gen Sir Frank King to Merlyn Rees, 18 March 1974.
66. PRONI CENT/1/3/39: 'Note of a Meeting Held at Stormont Castle', 19 March 1974.
67. TNA DEFE 70/588: Letter from Roy Mason to Merlyn Rees, 22 March 1974; Letter from Merlyn Rees to Roy Mason, 25 March 1974.
68. TNA DEFE 13/836: Minute from VCGS to Secretary of State for Defence, 26 March 1974.
69. TNA CJ 4/2819: Letter from Lt-Gen Sir Frank King to Merlyn Rees, 28 March 1974.
70. TNA DEFE 13/1185: Minute by AAG, PS2(Army), 21 March 1974.
71. TNA DEFE 13/1186: Letter from [name redacted], Halifax, to Harold Wilson, 25 March 1974.
72. TNA DEFE 13/1186: Letter from [name redacted], Ockley, to Sir George Sinclair, 21 March 1974.
73. '1st Battalion', *The Journal of the Royal Hampshire Regiment*, 63/1 (May 1974), 8.

74. TNA PREM 16/145: 'Record of a meeting held at Headquarters, Northern Ireland', 18 April 1974.
75. TNA DEFE 13/836: Minute from N. H. Nicholls to Secretary of State for Defence, 18 April 1974.
76. TNA DEFE 70/692: Letter from Lt-Gen Sir Frank King to CGS, 19 April 1974.
77. LSE Library, Merlyn Rees papers: MERLYN-REES/1/2: Transcripts of tapes on Northern Ireland, 1972–73, 10–11.
78. TNA DEFE 70/695: Letter from CGS to Lt-Gen Sir Frank King, 23 April 1974.
79. TNA PREM 16/145: Letter from Roy Mason to Prime Minister, 25 April 1974.
80. TNA DEFE 13/991: Minute from Lt-Col J. C. V. Biles, MA/CGS, to PS/Secretary of State for Defence, 29 January 1974.
81. TNA DEFE 13/990: Minute by D. J. Ramsbotham, 'CGS visit to Northern Ireland 28 September 1973'.
82. TNA DEFE 24/877: 'Op Instr 11/73 – Op Utmost', HQ Northern Ireland, 30 November 1973, and attached Annex A, 'Protestant extremists – the threat'.
83. TNA WO 305/4642: 'Op Instr 2/74 – Op Utmost', HQ Northern Ireland, 22 March 1974.
84. TNA DEFE 70/692: Minute from Lt-Col J. C. V. Biles, MA/CGS, to PS/Secretary of State for Defence, 15 March 1974.
85. TNA DEFE 70/1069: Ministry of Defence Monthly Intelligence Summary and Monthly Operational Summary, 5 March 1974.
86. TNA DEFE 70/1069: Ministry of Defence Monthly Intelligence Summary, 3 April 1974.
87. R. Fisk, *The Point of No Return: The Strike Which Broke the British in Ulster* (London: Times Books/André Deutsch, 1975), 44–5.
88. TNA CJ 4/2038: 'Notes of a meeting between the Secretary of State and representatives of the United Ulster Workers' Council', 8 April 1974.
89. TNA DEFE 70/1069: Ministry of Defence Monthly Intelligence Summary, 3 May 1974.
90. TNA PREM 16/146: 'Summary of political events in Northern Ireland for the period 9–16 May 1974.'
91. G. Gillespie, 'The Ulster Workers' Council Strike: The Perfect Storm', in D. McCann and C. McGrattan (eds.), *Sunningdale, the Ulster Workers' Council Strike and the Struggle for Democracy in Northern Ireland* (Manchester: Manchester University Press, 2017), 27–8.
92. TNA DEFE 13/1994: 'Notes of an internal meeting on Northern Ireland held on 16 May 1974.'
93. TNA PREM 16/146: Minute from F. E. R. B. to Lord Bridges, 16 May 1974.
94. TNA WO 305/5779: 39 Infantry Brigade. Diary of Events 1974: entry for 16 May.
95. PRONI CENT/1/3/39: 'Note of a Meeting Held at Stormont Castle', 16 January 1974.
96. TNA PREM 16/146: 'Record of a conversation between the Prime Minister and the Secretary of State for Northern Ireland at 1.00 p.m. on Friday, 17 May 1974.'

97. TNA PREM 16/146: Signal from Dublin (Galsworthy) to FCO, 20 May 1974.

98. TNA PREM 16/146: Letter from N. H. Nicholls to Lord Bridges, 20 May 1974.

99. McDaid, *Template for Peace*, 138.

100. TNA CJ 4/2038: 'Note of a meeting between the Secretary of State, the GOC and the Chief Constable', 20 May 1974.

101. Fisk, *The Point of No Return*, 72.

102. TNA PREM 16/146: 'Record of a telephone conversation between the Prime Minister and the Secretary of State for Northern Ireland', 20 May 1974.

103. TNA DEFE 70/589: Minute from DMO to CGS, 20 May 1974.

104. TNA DEFE 70/589: Minute from CGS to Secretary of State for Defence, 21 May 1974.

105. TNA PREM 16/147: 'Northern Ireland: summary of security events for period 9–22 May 1974.'

106. TNA CAB 134/3778: Cabinet. Ministerial Committee on Northern Ireland. Minutes of a Meeting, 21 May 1974.

107. TNA DEFE 70/1069: Ministry of Defence Monthly Operational Summary, 5 June 1974.

108. TNA DEFE 70/204: 'Office Note. Record of a conversation between CGS and GOC Northern Ireland – AM 22 May 1974.'

109. TNA DEFE 13/1994: 'Notes of an internal meeting on Northern Ireland held on 23 May 1974.'

110. TNA CJ 4/2038: Minute from P. J. Woodfield to Mr Cooper, 23 May 1974.

111. TNA PREM 16/147: Signal from Northern Ireland Office Belfast, to PUSD, FCO, 'Daily intelligence summary No 341', 23 May 1974.

112. Fisk, *The Point of No Return*, 96.

113. TNA DEFE 70/1069: Ministry of Defence Monthly Operational Summary, 5 March 1974.

114. TNA DEFE 70/1104: 'Notes on COS's debrief', Lt-Col P. L. Newth, 23 May 1974.

115. TNA DEFE 70/1104: 'The Ulster Workers' Council (UWC) disruption and strike, May 1974', HQ Northern Ireland, 10 August 1974.

116. TNA DEFE 70/1104: 'Note for the record – briefing/discussions with CGS held at HQNI on Thursday 23 May at 1515 hrs', Lt-Col W. R. W. Pike, 24 May 1974.

117. TNA CAB 134/3778: 'Cabinet. Ministerial Committee on Northern Ireland. Minutes of a Meeting', 23 May 1974.

118. TNA PREM 16/147: 'Record of conversation between the Prime Minister and the Chief Executive of Northern Ireland at Chequers at 12.30 p.m. on Friday 24 May 1974.'

119. TNA WO 305/5779: '39 Infantry Brigade. Diary of Events 1974', entry for 24 May.

120. TNA CJ 4/2038: Letter from General Sir Frank King to Merlyn Rees, 24 May 1974.

121. Taylor, *Loyalists*, 131.
122. TNA CJ 4/2038: 'Note of a meeting between Secretary of State, GOC and Chief Constable', 25 May 1974.
123. TNA DEFE 70/1550: HQ Northern Ireland Operational Summary, 5 June 1974.
124. TNA DEFE 70/1104: 'Note for the record – Briefing of the Secretary of State for Defence at HQNI on Tuesday 28 May [1974].'
125. TNA DEFE 13/1994: 'Notes of an internal meeting on Northern Ireland', 30 May 1974.
126. TNA DEFE 70/1069: Ministry of Defence Monthly Operational Summary, 5 June 1974.
127. TNA DEFE 70/1104: 'Notes on Chief of Staffs Meeting 251545', Lt-Col P. L. Newth, 26 May 1974.
128. Gillespie, 'The Ulster Workers' Council Strike', 34.
129. TNA PREM 16/148: 'Record of a conversation between the Prime Minister and the Secretary of State for. Northern Ireland at RNAS Caldrose Penzance between 4.15 pm and 5.45 pm on Sunday 26 May 1974.'
130. TNA PREM 16/148: 'Summary of political events in Northern Ireland for the period 23–30 May 1974.'
131. TNA DEFE 70/204: 'Office Note. Record of CGS' visit to HQ Northern Ireland Monday 27 May 1974.'
132. TNA PREM 16/148: 'Record of a meeting between the Secretary of State [Rees] and Mr Brian Faulkner at Stormont Castle at 12 30 pm on Tuesday 28 May 1974.'
133. TNA CAB 134/3778: 'Cabinet. Ministerial Committee on Northern Ireland. Minutes of a Meeting', 29 May 1974.
134. TNA PREM 16/148: Minute from Harold Wilson to Mr Armstrong, 30 May 1974.
135. TNA DEFE 70/1104: 'Note for the record – Briefing of the Secretary of State for Defence at HQNI on Tuesday 28 May [1974].'
136. McDaid, *Template for Peace*, 4, 66, 126, 128–9, 148.
137. Kerr, *The Destructors*, 13.
138. B. O'Leary, 'Northern Ireland', in K. Hickson and A. Seldon (eds.), *New Labour, Old Labour: The Wilson and Callaghan Governments 1974–1979* (London: Routledge, 2004), 244, 256.
139. TNA DEFE 70/204: Letter from Lieutenant-General Sir Frank King to General Sir Peter Hunt, 30 May 1974.
140. Aveyard, *No Solution*, 17, 37.
141. Charters, *Whose Mission, Whose Orders?*, 180.
142. TNA DEFE 13/1994: 'Notes of an internal meeting on Northern Ireland held on 6 June 1974.'
143. Ó Dochartaigh, 'Northern Ireland since 1920', 158; Ó Dochartaigh, *Deniable Contact.*

144. Leahy, *The Intelligence War against the IRA*, 63, 66, 68.
145. B. Donoughue, *Prime Minister: The Conduct of Policy under Harold Wilson and James Callaghan* (London: Jonathan Cape, 1987), 132.
146. Leahy, *The Intelligence War against the IRA*, 63–80.
147. McDaid, *Template for Peace*, 147.
148. TNA PREM 16/147: Letter from Frank Cooper, Northern Ireland Office, to R. T. Armstrong, 10 Downing Street, 22 May 1974, with attached 'Constitutional options in Northern Ireland. Report by Group of Officials.'
149. TNA CAB 134/3778: Cabinet. Ministerial Committee on Northern Ireland. Minutes of a Meeting, 12 June 1974.
150. TNA PREM 16/148: 'Note for the Record', 29 May 1974.
151. TNA PREM 16/149: 'Record of a conversation between the Prime Minister and Mr Jack Lynch at 10 Downing Street at 5.30 p.m. on Monday 15 July 1974.'
152. TNA DEFE 70/589: Letter from Chief of the General Staff to Lt-Gen Sir Frank King, 30 May 1974.
153. TNA DEFE 70/204: Letter from Lt-Gen Sir David Fraser, VCGS, to Lt-Gen Sir Frank King, 3 June 1974.
154. IWMSA: Michael Booth, catalogue number 33200, reel 3.
155. '1st Battalion', *The Iron Duke: The Regimental Journal of The Duke of Wellington's Regiment*, 48/160 (December 1972), 91.
156. JSCSC Library: National Defence College Papers: '5 Course. The Constabulary Role of the British Soldier in Urban Areas of Ulster', by Major T. L. Trotman, 1976, 4, 25.
157. Aveyard, *No Solution*, 45.
158. TNA DEFE 70/204: Letter from Lt-Gen Sir Frank King to Merlyn Rees, 11 June 1974.
159. TNA CJ 4/6077: Letter from Frank Cooper, Northern Ireland Office, to Lt Gen Sir Frank King, 8 July 1974.
160. TNA CJ 4/648: 'The Joint Security Review Northern Ireland', by the Chief Constable and the General Officer Commanding, 17 May 1974.
161. Aveyard, *No Solution*, 46–7.
162. TNA CJ 4/524: Minute from N. C. Abbott to Sir Frank Cooper et al., 16 September 1974, with attached paper.
163. TNA DEFE 70/695: Letter from Maj-Gen J. M. Strawson, HQ UK Land Forces, to Maj-Gen A. J. Archer, Director of Army Staff Duties, 20 June 1974.
164. TNA CJ 4/826: Minute from CGS to Secretary of State for Defence, 28 June 1974.
165. TNA DEFE 13/836: Minute from CGS to Secretary of State for Defence, 22 July 1974.
166. TNA DEFE 70/589: Letter from Lt-Gen Sir Frank King to CGS, 5 August 1974.
167. TNA DEFE 70/696: Letter from CGS to Lt-Gen Sir Frank King, 7 August 1974.
168. TNA PREM 16/150: Minute from William Rodgers, Ministry of Defence, to Prime Minister, 12 August 1974.

169. TNA DEFE 70/696: Letter from Maj-Gen P. J. H. Leng to Maj-Gen W. N. R. Scotter, 24 October 1974.
170. TNA DEFE 70/696: Minute from VCGS to CGS et al., 1 November 1974.
171. Aveyard, *No Solution*, 46.
172. TNA DEFE 68/87: 'Notes of a meeting on Northern Ireland on 7 November 1974.'
173. Greenwood, 'The 1974 Defence Review in Perspective', 225.
174. McGladdery, *The Provisional IRA in England*, 88–93.
175. Cowper-Coles, '"Anxious for Peace"', 228.
176. Taylor, *Provos*, 179.
177. Ó Dochartaigh, *Deniable Contact*, 117–49. Although other scholars cover the ceasefire, Ó Dochartaigh was, from 2011 onwards, the first to discover and publish on new source material that is central to the entire period.
178. TNA DEFE 13/914: Minute from A. J. Cragg, APS/Secretary of State for Defence, to MA/CGS, 23 December 1974.
179. TNA CJ 4/860: 'Note of a meeting held at 6.45 pm on Monday 6 January 1975'; CAB 134/3921: Cabinet. Ministerial Committee on Northern Ireland, 8 January 1975; DEFE 32/22: 'Chiefs of Staff Committee. Confidential Annex to COS 1st Meeting/75', 14 January 1975.
180. LSE Library, Merlyn Rees papers: MERLYN-REES/5/6: Northern Ireland Political Review, 12 January 1975.
181. TNA DEFE 70/1070: Ministry of Defence Monthly Intelligence Summary, 7 January 1975. The Irish National Liberation Army (INLA) was formed in December 1974 as a breakaway group from OIRA.
182. TNA CAB 134/3921: 'Cabinet. Ministerial Committee on Northern Ireland. The IRA ceasefire. Memorandum by the Secretary of State for Northern Ireland', 18 February 1975.
183. Ó Dochartaigh, *Deniable Contact*, 138–9.
184. Aveyard, *No Solution*, 93.
185. TNA CJ 4/865: Minute from B. M. Webster to Mr England, 19 February 1975.
186. TNA DEFE 68/87: 'Notes of a meeting on Northern Ireland on 29 May 1975.'
187. TNA CJ 4/832: 'Commander Land Forces' directive for future operations', signed Maj-Gen Leng, HQ Northern Ireland, 14 April 1975.
188. LSE Library, Merlyn Rees papers: MERLYN-REES/5/6: Northern Ireland Political Review, 7 April 1975.
189. TNA DEFE 68/87: 'Notes of a meeting on Northern Ireland on 15 May 1975.'
190. Linen Hall Library: 'Soldiers at the Castle', *Visor: Weekly Report for Soldiers in Northern Ireland* (HQ Northern Ireland: Army Information Services), Serial 54, 6 March 1975.
191. IWMSA: Rod Boswell, catalogue number 11134, reel 2.
192. Ó Dochartaigh, *Deniable Contact*, 146–7.
193. Hennessey, *The First Northern Ireland Peace Process*, 194, 237.
194. TNA CJ 4/839: 'Force levels and the ceasefire. Note of a meeting', 12 May 1975.

195. For a thorough analysis, see: Aveyard, *No Solution*, 134–72.
196. 'Between Belfast and Autumn Manoeuvres', *The Globe and Laurel: The Journal of the Royal Marines*, 84/5 (September–October 1975), 270.

CONCLUSION

1. The most important recent study remains: S. N. Kalyvas, *The Logic of Violence in Civil War* (Cambridge: Cambridge University Press, 2006).
2. D. Armitage, *Civil Wars: A History in Ideas* (London: Yale University Press, 2017), 12.

A NOTE ON SOURCES

1. Jackson, 'Irish History in the Twentieth and Twenty-First Centuries', 9.
2. Leahy, *The Intelligence War against the IRA*, 12–13.
3. Cardiff University School of Law and Politics, Participant Information Sheet, reference SREC/070616–00, 17 May 2016.
4. A. Hoskins and M. Ford, 'Flawed, yet Authoritative? Organisational Memory and the Future of Official Military History after Chilcot', *British Journal for Military History*, 3/2 (2017), 121.
5. L. Freedman, 'Academics and Policy-Making: Rules of Engagement', *Journal of Strategic Studies*, 40/1–2 (2017), 264.
6. O. Thomas, 'Paradoxical Secrecy in British Freedom of Information Law', in D. Mokrosinska (ed.), *Transparency and Secrecy in European Democracies: Contested Trade-offs* (London: Routledge, 2020), 135–56.
7. H. Siddique, '"Orwellian" government unit accused of blocking FoI requests to be replaced', *Guardian*, 25 August 2022: www.theguardian.com/politics/2022/aug/25/cabinet-office-clearing-house-orwellian-government-unit-accused-of-blocking-foi-requests-to-be-replaced.
8. Letter from DBS KI FOI Team, Ministry of Defence, to Huw Bennett, 13 July 2016.
9. Email from Huw Bennett to DBS KI FOI Team, Ministry of Defence, 14 July 2016; email from DBS KI FOI Team, Ministry of Defence, to Huw Bennett, 1 November 2016.
10. Email from Huw Bennett to cabinet office, 26 May 2021, requesting files CAB 190/31, CAB 190/32, CAB 190/33; email from FOI Team, cabinet office, 19 October 2021.
11. Letter from cabinet office to Huw Bennett, 24 February 2022.
12. Army Museums Ogilby Trust, *Annual Review 2020–21* (Salisbury: Army Museums Ogilby Trust, 2021), 5; available at: www.armymuseums.org.uk/annual-review-news. The museums listed as a Place of Deposit are: Airborne Assault – The Museum of the Parachute Regiment and Airborne Forces, the Museum of Army

Chaplaincy, Cheshire Military Museum, Regimental Headquarters The Coldstream Guards, the Grenadier Guards Regimental Archives, the Museum and Archive of The Irish Guards, the National Army Museum, the Royal Military Academy Sandhurst Archives, Regimental Headquarters The Scots Guards, the Tank Museum, The Welsh Guards. See: www.nationalarchives.gov.uk/archives-sector/legislation/approved-places-of-deposit/places-of-deposit. In fact, several of these collections, such as those of the Grenadier, Coldstream, Irish and Welsh Guards, have been transferred to the Ministry of Defence. This highlights the inadequacy of the Places of Deposit scheme.

13. Email from Army Museums Ogilby Trust to Huw Bennett, 4 August 2022.
14. Email from head of Army Historical Branch to Huw Bennett, 7 September 2022.
15. Email from Army Museums Ogilby Trust to Huw Bennett, 14 October 2022.
16. Email from DBS KI-RR FOI team, Ministry of Defence, to Huw Bennett, 11 October 2022.
17. Email from DBS KI-RR FOI team, Ministry of Defence, to Huw Bennett, 18 November 2022.
18. Email from DBS KI-RR FOI team, Ministry of Defence, to Huw Bennett, 20 May 2022.
19. Email from FOI assessor, the National Archives, to Huw Bennett, 20 October 2022; email from Huw Bennett to FOI team, the National Archives, 20 October 2022; email from FOI assessor, the National Archives, to Huw Bennett, 21 October 2022; email from FOI Centre service adviser, the National Archives, to Huw Bennett, 21 November 2022.
20. S. Catignani and V. Basham. 'The Gendered Politics of Researching Military Policy in the Age of the "Knowledge Economy"', *Review of International Studies*, 47/2 (2021), 211–30.
21. S. Cain, '"A terrifying precedent": Author describes struggle to publish British army history', *Guardian*, 23 July 2021, available at: www.theguardian.com/books/2021/jul/23/author-describes-struggle-to-publish-army-history-simon-akam-the-changing-of-the-guard.
22. Confidential information.

Bibliography

PRIMARY SOURCES

UNPUBLISHED

AIRBORNE ASSAULT MUSEUM, DUXFORD

Box 2.33.1: 1st Parachute Regiment in Belfast, 1969–1971.
Box 2.33.15: 2nd Parachute Regiment in Belfast, 1972–1977.
Box 2.33.24: 16 Parachute Brigade in Northern Ireland, 1972.
Box 2.33.25: Northern Ireland publications.

BODLEIAN LIBRARY, UNIVERSITY OF OXFORD

CONSERVATIVE PARTY ARCHIVE

CRD 3/18/1: Northern Ireland Backbench Committee, 1971–1973.

DEPARTMENT OF SPECIAL COLLECTIONS AND WESTERN MANUSCRIPTS

MS. Wilson c.908: Harold Wilson papers, confidential filing: Opposition years, 1970–1974.

HOBSON LIBRARY, JOINT SERVICES COMMAND AND STAFF COLLEGE (JSCSC), SHRIVENHAM

ARMY STAFF COLLEGE, CAMBERLEY

Army Staff College Course papers, 1966–1975.

NATIONAL DEFENCE COLLEGE, LATIMER

Alexander, P. D. *Morale in Modern War.* Exercise thesis, 1972.
Atkinson, D. J. *Moral Approaches to Maintaining the Balance in a Developing Democratic Society.* Exercise thesis, 1972.

Blackwell, B. A. *Are Industrial Democracies Governable? A Case Study of the Ulster Workers' Council Strike in Northern Ireland in May 1974.* Exercise thesis, 1976.

Dixon, A. K. *Some Historical Background to the Irish Problem: The Men that God Made Mad.* Exercise thesis, 1972.

Edmonds, K. R. *The Military and the Media.* Exercise thesis, 1975.

Gordon, J. C. *The Use of Violence by Minority Groups to Achieve Their Political Ends.* Exercise thesis, 1973.

Jeapes, A. S. *Defeating the Urban Guerilla.* Exercise thesis, 1972.

Lucas, J. N. D. *The Army and Urban Violence.* Exercise thesis, 1973.

Palmer, J. L. *The Services and the Media.* Exercise thesis, 1974.

Pipe, D. G. *An Examination of Future Terrorism and Violence in Britain and Its Impact on Defence.* Exercise thesis, 1976.

Pothecary, I. J. W. *Defence and the Media.* Exercise thesis, 1972.

Roberts, N. O. *The Status of the Serviceman in the Nation Today.* Exercise thesis, 1972.

Sewell, Wg Cdr. *An Analysis of the Constitutional Arrangements and Problems of Northern Ireland.* Exercise thesis, 1972.

Simmons, J. st C. *The Role of the Army in Northern Ireland.* Exercise thesis, 1972.

Southerst, R. G. *The Modern Guerrilla and His Warfare.* Exercise thesis, 1974.

Trotman, T. L. *The Constabulary Role of the British Soldier in Urban Areas of Ulster.* Exercise thesis, 1976.

Winchcombe, P. *The Armed Forces and Society in the United Kingdom: A Consideration of the Role, Image and Manpower Problems.* Exercise thesis, 1972.

ROYAL COLLEGE OF DEFENCE STUDIES, LONDON

Dalzell-Payne, H. S. L. 'The People, the Police and the Army', *Seaford House Papers*, 1973.

IMPERIAL WAR MUSEUM (IWM), LONDON

DEPARTMENT OF DOCUMENTS

Freeland, Lieutenant-General Sir I., catalogue references 79/34/3 and 79/34/4.
Friend, T. H., catalogue reference 12/52/1.
Parker, J. E., catalogue reference 03/51/1.

SOUND ARCHIVE (IWMSA)

Anonymous, catalogue number 11162.
Ambrose, K., catalogue number 32532.
Booth, M., catalogue number 33200.

Boswell, R., catalogue number 11134.
Brannigan, F., catalogue number 30295.
Brennan, C. M., catalogue number 27190.
Cormack, J. N., catalogue number 21564.
Cowan, J. A. C., catalogue number 18802.
Evelegh, R., catalogue number 11148.
Garman, P., catalogue number 24732.
Gray, M., catalogue number 28362.
Greenaway, D., catalogue number 33208.
Hall, R. W., catalogue number 17927.
Hubble, T. L., catalogue number 33350.
Kirvan, S., catalogue number 32370.
Lawton, C., catalogue number 28698.
May, W. R. B., catalogue number 18569.
McBain, M. D. C., catalogue number 11105.
Robson, S., catalogue number 31693.
Southwood, A., catalogue number 33979.
Storrie, D., catalogue number 11139.
Styles, G., catalogue number 12375.
Thompson, J. H. A., catalogue number 28361.
Wickes, G., catalogue number 26933.
Woodford, D. M., catalogue number 19896.

KING'S OWN SCOTTISH BORDERERS REGIMENTAL MUSEUM (KOSBRM), BERWICK-UPON-TWEED

KOSB C2/9: Correspondence and papers, 1st King's Own Scottish Borderers, 1972.
Newsletters: 'Borderer's in Belfast. The Newsletter of the 1st Battalion King's Own Scottish Borderers in Belfast', 1970–1973.

LABOUR HISTORY ARCHIVE AND STUDY CENTRE (LHASC), PEOPLE'S HISTORY MUSEUM, MANCHESTER

1330-SC-1971–72: Shadow Cabinet meetings. 'Research Department. Labour Party. Northern Ireland – Brief for N.E.C. delegation to Commission Meeting on 11 November 1971.'
1330-SC-1971–72: Shadow Cabinet meetings. Minutes of Parliamentary Committee Meetings, 1971.
LP/RD/43/3: 'Commission on Northern Ireland. Meeting in Dunardry Hotel, Belfast', 11 November 1971.
Report of the sixty-ninth annual conference of the Labour Party. Blackpool, 1970.

LANCASHIRE INFANTRY MUSEUM, PRESTON

1st Queen's Lancashire Regiment Commanding Officer's Brigade Conference Notes, 1972–1973.

1st Queen's Lancashire Regiment end-of-tour report, 1972.

LIDDELL HART CENTRE FOR MILITARY ARCHIVES (LHCMA), KING'S COLLEGE LONDON

Ramsbotham, General Sir D. J., reference code GB 0099 KCLMA Ramsbotham. Box 1: Lecture Notes and Northern Ireland.

LINEN HALL LIBRARY, BELFAST

Loyalist News, 1972–1973.

Mid-Ulster U.D.A. News, 1974.

The Ulster Militant, 1972.

Visor: Weekly Report for Soldiers in Northern Ireland (HQ Northern Ireland: Army Information Services), 1974–1975.

LONDON SCHOOL OF ECONOMICS AND POLITICAL SCIENCE (LSE) LIBRARY

Hetherington, H. A., Box 19: Interviews, 1971–1972.

Hetherington, H. A., Box 20: Interviews, 1972–1973.

Rees, M., reference MERLYN-REES/1: Transcripts of tapes on Northern Ireland, 1972–1976.

Rees, M., reference MERLYN-REES/5: Northern Ireland: official papers, 1974–1983.

Rees, M., reference MERLYN-REES/7: Northern Ireland correspondence, 1971–1997.

Rees, M., reference MERLYN-REES/12: Northern Ireland subject files: security, 1969–2002.

THE NATIONAL ARCHIVES OF THE UNITED KINGDOM, KEW (TNA)

FILE SERIES

CAB 130: Cabinet. Miscellaneous Committees.

CAB 134: Cabinet. Miscellaneous Committees.

CAB 148: Cabinet Office. Defence and Oversea Policy Committees and Sub-Committees.

CAB 163: Joint Intelligence Sub-Committee.

CAB 164: Cabinet Office. Subject (Theme Series) Files.

CAB 165: Cabinet Office. Committees (C Series) Files.

CAB 190: Joint Intelligence Committee: Working Groups and Working Parties.

CJ 3: Home Office and Northern Ireland Office.
CJ 4: Home Office and Northern Ireland Office.
DEFE 4: Ministry of Defence. Chiefs of Staff Committee.
DEFE 13: Ministry of Defence. Private Office.
DEFE 23: Ministry of Defence. Permanent Under-Secretary of State for Defence.
DEFE 24: Ministry of Defence. Defence Secretariat Branches.
DEFE 25: Ministry of Defence. Chief of Defence Staff.
DEFE 31: Ministry of Defence. Defence Intelligence Staff.
DEFE 32: Ministry of Defence. Chiefs of Staff Committee.
DEFE 68: Ministry of Defence. Central Staffs.
DEFE 70: Ministry of Defence (Army). Registered Files and Branch Folders.
FCO 33: Foreign Office. Western Department and Western European Department.
HO 325: Home Office. Queen's Peace (QPE Symbol Series).
PREM 13: Prime Minister's Office: Correspondence and Papers, 1964–1970.
PREM 15: Prime Minister's Office: Correspondence and Papers, 1970–1974.
PREM 16: Prime Minister's Office: Correspondence and Papers, 1974–1979.
WO 32: War Office and successors.
WO 279: War Office and Ministry of Defence. Confidential Print.
WO 296: War Office and Ministry of Defence. Central Department C2 Branch.
WO 305: War Office and Ministry of Defence. Army Unit Historical Records and
   Reports.

NATO ARCHIVES, BRUSSELS

FILE SERIES

CER: Supreme Allied Commander Europe's Combat Effectiveness Reports and
   supplements.
DPC: Defence Planning Committee.
IMSM: International Military Staff Memoranda.
PO: Private Office of the Secretary General papers.

PUBLIC RECORDS OFFICE OF NORTHERN IRELAND (PRONI), BELFAST

FILE SERIES

CAB/9/B: Ministry of Home Affairs.
CAB/9/G: Military and Police 'G' files.
CENT/1: Central Secretariat, Numerical Series.
CREL/2: Community Relations Commission, Research Files.
CREL/4: Community Relations Commission, Director's Files.
DCR/1: Department of Community Relations.
HA/8: Ministry of Home Affairs, Miscellaneous.

HA/32/2: Ministry of Home Affairs, 'SM' files.
HA/32/3: Cabinet Security Committee and Joint Security Committee.
HA/32/5: Home Affairs. Secret Series Miscellaneous files.
PM/5/81: British Army regiments.

ROYAL HAMPSHIRE REGIMENT MUSEUM, WINCHESTER

Coleman, R. W., 'A Northern Ireland Diary', 1972–1973. Northern Ireland Box 1-D4, File M4619.
'Tiger Rag: The magazine of the 1st Bn The Royal Hampshire Regiment', 1972.
'The Royal Hampshires Tiger Rag', 1973.

ROYAL MARINES MUSEUM, PORTSMOUTH

2/18/3: 40 Commando Royal Marines Unit Newsletters.
2/18/5: 42 Commando Royal Marines Unit Newsletters.
2/18/8: 45 Commando Royal Marines Unit Newsletters.

ROYAL REGIMENT OF FUSILIERS MUSEUM (ROYAL WARWICKSHIRE)

Barzilay, D. and M. Murray, *Four Months in Winter* (Belfast: 2nd Battalion, Royal Regiment of Fusiliers, 1972).

ROYAL SCOTS REGIMENTAL MUSEUM (RSRM), EDINBURGH

NORTHERN IRELAND TOUR MAGAZINES

The Belfast Thistle, 1st Battalion The Royal Scots, 1970.
Pilate's Post, 1st Battalion The Royal Scots, 1971.

SHROPSHIRE ARCHIVES, SHREWSBURY

SOLDIERS OF SHROPSHIRE MUSEUM ORAL HISTORY RECORDINGS

Bevan, T. D. V., reference 6005/SHYKS/2008/2677/29.
Marsham, J. K., reference 6005/SHYKS/2008/2677/9.

WEST SUSSEX RECORD OFFICE, CHICHESTER

Kempton, W. E., catalogue number RSR/C/1332/2/6: Transcript of 1972/3 diaries.

PUBLISHED

BALLYMURPHY INQUEST

Keegan, J. *In the Matter of the Coroners Act (Northern Ireland) 1959. In the Matter of a Series of Deaths That Occurred in August 1971 at Ballymurphy, West Belfast. Summary of Coroner's Verdicts and Findings* (Belfast: Judicial Communications Office, 2021).

BLOODY SUNDAY INQUIRY

THE REPORT

Lord Saville. *Report of the Bloody Sunday Inquiry, Volume I* (London: The Stationery Office, 2010).

Lord Saville. *Report of the Bloody Sunday Inquiry, Volume VI* (London: The Stationery Office, 2010).

Lord Saville. *Principal Conclusions and Overall Assessment of the Bloody Sunday Inquiry* (London: The Stationery Office, 2010).

WITNESS EVIDENCE

Interview with Liam Wray, by Joanne O'Brien, 17 April 1997, accessed 18 May 2021 at: https://webarchive.nationalarchives.gov.uk/20101017072044/http://report.bloody-sunday-inquiry.org/evidence/AW/AW_0029.pdf

Statement of Lord Carver, 24 July 1999, accessed 9 May 2021 at: https://webarchive.nationalarchives.gov.uk/20101017074940/http://report.bloody-sunday-inquiry.org/evidence/K/KC_0008.pdf

Statement of Maura Duffy, 19 June 1999, accessed 18 May 2021 at: https://webarchive.nationalarchives.gov.uk/20101017073204/http://report.bloody-sunday-inquiry.org/evidence/AD/AD_0162.pdf

Statement of General Sir Robert Ford, 23 March 2000, accessed 10 May 2021 at: https://webarchive.nationalarchives.gov.uk/20101017071251/http://report.bloody-sunday-inquiry.org/evidence/B/B1123.pdf

Statement of Brian Rainey, 15 June 1999, accessed 18 May 2021 at: https://webarchive.nationalarchives.gov.uk/20101017074745/http://report.bloody-sunday-inquiry.org/evidence/AR/AR_0003.pdf

PROCEEDINGS

Day 280, 19 December 2002. Lord Carrington, accessed 25 April 2021 at: https://webarchive.nationalarchives.gov.uk/20101017062313/http://report.bloody-sunday-inquiry.org/transcripts/Archive/Ts280.htm

Day 287, 22 January 2003. Sir Edward Heath, accessed 24 April 2021 at: https://we barchive.nationalarchives.gov.uk/20101017062434/http://report.bloody-sunday-inquiry.org/transcripts/Archive/Ts287.htm

Day 289, 27 January 2003. Sir Edward Heath, accessed 24 April 2021 at: https://we barchive.nationalarchives.gov.uk/20101017062456/http://report.bloody-sunday-inquiry.org/transcripts/Archive/Ts289.htm

INTERNET SOURCES

Explosives Act (Northern Ireland) 1970, accessed 14 May 2021 at: www .legislation.gov.uk/apni/1970/10/data.pdf

Howe, G. 'Rawlinson, Peter Anthony Grayson, Baron Rawlinson of Ewell', *Oxford Dictionary of National Biography*, accessed 9 December 2020: www .oxforddnb.com/view/10.1093/ref:odnb/9780198614128.001.0001/odnb-9 780198614128-e-97248?rskey=Kehh1O&result=11

Museum of The Royal Dragoon Guards, Oral History Project: interview with Ray Binks, available at: www.rdgmuseum.org.uk/history-and-research/oral-history/, accessed 21 February 2019.

Museum of The Royal Dragoon Guards, Oral History Project: interview with General Sir Robert Ford, available at: www.rdgmuseum.org.uk/history-and-research/ oral-history/

Northern Ireland: Text of a Communiqué Issued Following Discussions between the Secretary of State for the Home Department and the Northern Ireland Government, 10 October 1969, accessed 16 June 2019 at: https://cain .ulster.ac.uk/hmso/bni101069.htm

'Report of Meeting Held in Council Chamber', 11 February 1972. National Archives, Ireland, accessed 20 May 2021 at: https://cain.ulster.ac.uk/nai/1972/nai_ TSCH-2003-16-462_1972-02-11.pdf

Sutton, M. *An Index of Deaths from the Conflict in Ireland* (1994/2018), electronic version at: https://cain.ulster.ac.uk/sutton/tables/Year.html

MEMOIRS

Benn, T. *Office without Power: Diaries 1968–72* (London: Hutchinson, 1988).

Blacker, C. *Monkey Business: The Memoirs of General Sir Cecil Blacker* (London: Quiller Press, 1993).

Bloomfield, K. *Stormont in Crisis: A Memoir* (Belfast: The Blackstaff Press, 1994).

Callaghan, J. *A House Divided: The Dilemma of Northern Ireland* (London: Collins, 1973).

   Time and Chance (London: Fontana, 1988).

Carrington, C. *Reflect on Things Past* (London: Collins, 1988).

Carver, M. *Out of Step: Memoirs of a Field Marshal* (London: Hutchinson, 1989).

Chapman, C. *Notes from a Small Military* (London: John Blake, 2015).

Corbett, S. *Belfast Diaries: A Gunner in Northern Ireland, 1971–74* (Solihull: Helion, 2013).

Deedes, W. F. *Dear Bill: W. F. Deedes Reports* (London: Macmillan, 1997).

Devlin, P. *Straight Left: An Autobiography* (Belfast: Blackstaff Press, 1993).

Donoughue, B. *Prime Minister: The Conduct of Policy under Harold Wilson and James Callaghan* (London: Jonathan Cape, 1987).

Faulkner, B. *Memoirs of a Statesman* (London: Weidenfeld and Nicolson, 1978).

Guthrie, C. *Peace, War and Whitehall: A Memoir* (Oxford: Osprey, 2021).

Haines, J. *The Politics of Power* (London: Jonathan Cape, 1977).

Heath, E. *The Course of My Life: My Autobiography* (London: Coronet, 1999).

Hurd, D. *Memoirs* (London: Little, Brown, 2003).

King, C. *Diary, 1970–1974* (London: Jonathan Cape, 1975).

MacStíofáin, S. *Memoirs of a Revolutionary* (Edinburgh: Gordon Cremonesi, 1975).

Maudling, R. *Memoirs* (London: Sidgwick and Jackson, 1978).

McGuire, M. *To Take Arms: A Year in the Provisional IRA* (London: Quartet Books, 1973).

Millman, C. *Stand Easy, or, The Rear Rank Remembers: A Memoir* (Edinburgh: The Pentland Press, 1993).

Peck, J. *Dublin from Downing Street* (Dublin: Gill and Macmillan, 1978).

Rees, M. *Northern Ireland: A Personal Perspective* (London: Methuen, 1985).

Ramsay, R. *Ringside Seats: An Insider's View of the Crisis in Northern Ireland* (Dublin: Irish Academic Press, 2009).

Rawlinson, P. *A Price Too High: An Autobiography* (London: Weidenfeld and Nicolson, 1989).

Reynolds, M. *Soldier at Heart: From Private to General* (Barnsley: Pen and Sword, 2013).

Richards, D. *Taking Command* (London: Headline, 2014).

Styles, G. *Bombs Have No Pity: My War against Terrorism* (London: William Luscombe, 1975).

Whitelaw, W. *The Whitelaw Memoirs* (London: Aurum Press, 1989).

Windlesham, D. *Politics in Practice* (London: Jonathan Cape, 1975).

MILITARY JOURNALS

Army Quarterly and Defence Journal.

British Army Review.

Castle: The Journal of The Royal Anglian Regiment.

Firm and Forester: The Journal of The Worcestershire and Sherwood Foresters Regiment.

Journal of the Royal Army Medical Corps.

Journal of the Royal Artillery.

Journal of the Royal Electrical and Mechanical Engineers.

Pegasus: Journal of the Parachute Regiment and Airborne Forces.

RUSI Journal.

The Fusilier: The Journal of the Royal Regiment of Fusiliers.

The Globe and Laurel: The Journal of the Royal Marines.

The Green Howards' Gazette: A monthly chronicle of The Green Howards (Alexandra, Princess of Wales's Own Yorkshire Regiment).

The Iron Duke: The Regimental Journal of The Duke of Wellington's Regiment.

The Journal of The Queen's Regiment.

The Journal of the Royal Hampshire Regiment.

The Lancashire Lad: The Journal of The Queen's Lancashire Regiment.

The Men of Harlech: The Journal of The Royal Regiment of Wales.

The Royal Green Jackets Chronicle.

The Silver Bugle: Journal of The Light Infantry.

The Tiger and Sphinx: Journal of The Gordon Highlanders.

NEWS SOURCES

BBC News Online.

Belfast Telegraph.

New Society.

The Daily Telegraph.

The Guardian.

The Irish News.

The Irish Times.

The Times.

OFFICIAL PUBLICATIONS

British Army. *Operation Banner: An Analysis of Military Operations in Northern Ireland. Army Code 71842* (London: Ministry of Defence, 2006).

Hansard. *House of Commons Debates: Volume 830,* 1972.

Lord Cameron. *Disturbances in Northern Ireland: Report of the Commission Appointed by the Governor of Northern Ireland.* Cmnd. 532 (Belfast: Her Majesty's Stationery Office, 1969).

Lord Scarman. *Violence and Civil Disturbances in Northern Ireland in 1969: Report of Tribunal of Inquiry.* Cmnd. 566 (Belfast: Her Majesty's Stationery Office, 1972).

Lord Widgery. *Report of the Tribunal Appointed to Inquire into the Events of Sunday, 30th January 1972, Which Led to Loss of Life in Connection with the Procession in Londonderry on That Day.* H.C. 220 (London: Her Majesty's Stationery Office, 1972).

Mills, C. and D. Torrance. *Investigation of Former Armed Forces Personnel Who Served in Northern Ireland* (London: House of Commons Library, 2020).

Ministry of Defence. *The Army List, Autumn 1969* (London: Her Majesty's Stationery Office, 1969).

Ministry of Defence. *The Army List, Spring 1974, Part I* (London: Her Majesty's Stationery Office, 1974).

TELEVISION DOCUMENTARIES

Panorama, BBC Television, broadcast 26 June 1972, accessed 10 August 2021 at: www.britishpathe.com/video/VLVA7R72M5H42FDP2FKLC2CEPK8X6-UK-PROVISIONAL-IRA-POLITICAL-LEADER-DAVID-OCONNELL-CONFIDENT/ query/northern+ireland

'Remember Bloody Sunday', *Inside Story*, broadcast on BBC1, 28 January 1992, accessed 14 September 2021 at: www.youtube.com/watch?v=j3FCPe6vgS8

'The Torture Files', *RTÉ Investigations Unit*, broadcast 4 June 2014, accessed 5 November 2020 at: www.rte.ie/news/player/2014/0604/10289849-rte-investigations-unit-the-torture-files/

'This Week', *Thames Television Archive*, broadcast 26 August 1971, accessed 6 November 2020 at: www.youtube.com/watch?v=wmMIswNQixc&list=PL7WD0g9dS3jlc2vaHrWhAhB9xq74fi0MR&index=6

'This Week', *Thames Television Archive*, broadcast 30 September 1971, accessed 6 November 2020 at: www.youtube.com/watch?v=n_azaxf3GCQ&list=PL7WD0g9dS3jlc2vaHrWhAhB9xq74fi0MR&index=16

SECONDARY SOURCES

BOOKS AND ARTICLES

aan de Wiel, Jérôme. *East German Intelligence and Ireland, 1949–90: Espionage, Terrorism and Diplomacy* (Manchester: Manchester University Press, 2014).

Aiken, N. T. 'The Bloody Sunday Inquiry: Transitional Justice and Postconflict Reconciliation in Northern Ireland', *Journal of Human Rights*, 14/1 (2015), 101–23.

Alderson, A. 'Britain', in Thomas Rid and Thomas Keaney (eds.), *Understanding Counterinsurgency: Doctrine, Operations, and Challenges* (London: Routledge, 2010), 28–45.

Alonso, R. *The IRA and Armed Struggle* (Abingdon: Routledge, 2003).

Andrew, C. *The Defence of the Realm: The Authorized History of MI5* (London: Allen Lane, 2009).

Ardoyne Commemoration Project, *Ardoyne: The Untold Truth* (Belfast: Beyond the Pale, 2002).

Armitage, D. *Civil Wars: A History in Ideas* (London: Yale University Press, 2017).

Arthur, P. 'The Heath Government and Northern Ireland', in S. Ball and A. Seldon (eds.), *The Heath Government 1970–74: A Reappraisal* (London: Routledge, 1996), 235–58.

Aughey, A. and C. McIlheney. 'The Ulster Defence Association: Paramilitaries and Politics', *Journal of Conflict Studies*, 2/2 (1981), 32–45.

Aveyard, S. C. *No Solution: The Labour Government and the Northern Ireland Conflict, 1974–79* (Manchester: Manchester University Press, 2016).

Ballinger, C. and A. Seldon. 'Prime Ministers and Cabinet', in K. Hickson and
A. Seldon (eds.), *New Labour, Old Labour: The Wilson and Callaghan
Governments 1974–1979* (London: Routledge, 2004), 173–89.

Bamford, B. 'The Role and Effectiveness of Intelligence in Northern Ireland',
Intelligence and National Security, 20/4 (2005), 581–607.

de Baróid, C. *Ballymurphy and the Irish War* (London: Pluto Press, 2000).

Baston, L. *Reggie: The Life of Reginald Maudling* (Stroud: Sutton, 2004).

Baynes, Lt-Col J. C. M. *The Soldier in Modern Society* (London: Eyre Methuen, 1972).

Benest, D. 'Aden to Northern Ireland', in H. Strachan (ed.), *Big Wars and Small Wars:
The British Army and the Lessons of War in the Twentieth Century* (London:
Routledge, 2006), 115–44.

Bennett, H. 'Detention and Interrogation in Northern Ireland, 1969–75', in
S. Scheipers (ed.), *Prisoners in War* (Oxford: Oxford University Press, 2010),
187–204.

'Escaping the Empire's Shadow: British Military Thinking about Insurgency on
the Eve of the Northern Ireland Troubles', in M. Thomas and G. Curless
(eds.), *Decolonization and Conflict: Colonial Comparisons and Legacies* (London:
Bloomsbury, 2017), 229–46.

'From Direct Rule to Motorman: Adjusting British Military Strategy for Northern
Ireland in 1972', *Studies in Conflict and Terrorism*, 33/6 (2010), 511–32.

'"Smoke without Fire"? Allegations against the British Army in Northern Ireland,
1972–5', *Twentieth Century British History*, 24/2 (2013), 275–304.

Betts, R. K. 'Is Strategy an Illusion?', *International Security*, 25/2 (2000), 5–50.

Bew, J. 'Mass, Methods, and Means: The Northern Ireland "Model" of Counter-
Insurgency', in C. W. Gventer, D. M. Jones and M. L. R. Smith (eds.), *The New
Counter-Insurgency Era in Critical Perspective* (Basingstoke: Palgrave Macmillan,
2014), 156–72.

Bew, J., M. Frampton and I. Gurruchaga. *Talking to Terrorists: Making Peace in Northern
Ireland and the Basque Country* (London: Hurst, 2009).

Bew, P. and H. Patterson. *The British State and the Ulster Crisis* (London: Verso, 1985).

Bishop, P. and E. Mallie. *The Provisional IRA* (London: Corgi, 1989).

Blaxland, J. 'Thinking outside the (Temporal) Box to Explain Protracted Intrastate
Conflict', *Journal of Peace Research*, 58/6 (2021), 1271–83.

Bond, B. *The Victorian Army and the Staff College 1854–1914* (London: Methuen, 1972).

Bosi, L. 'Explaining the Emergence Process of the Civil Rights Protest in Northern
Ireland (1945–1968): Insights from a Relational Social Movement Approach',
Journal of Historical Sociology, 21/2–3 (2008), 242–71.

'Explaining Pathways to Armed Activism in the Provisional Irish Republican
Army, 1969–1972', *Social Science History*, 36/3 (2012), 347–90.

Bourke, R. 'Introduction', in Richard Bourke and Ian McBride (eds.), *The Princeton
History of Modern Ireland* (Princeton: Princeton University Press, 2016), 1–18.

'Languages of Conflict and the Northern Ireland Troubles', *Journal of Modern
History*, 83/3 (2011), 544–78.

Peace in Ireland: The War of Ideas (London: Pimlico, 2012).

Bowyer Bell, J. *IRA Tactics and Targets* (Dublin: Poolbeg Press, 1990).

The IRA, 1968–2000: An Analysis of a Secret Army (London: Frank Cass, 2000).

Boyle, K., T. Hadden and P. Hillyard. *Law and State: The Case of Northern Ireland* (London: Martin Robertson, 1975).

Breen, C. *A Force Like No Other: The Real Stories of the RUC Men and Women Who Policed the Troubles* (Belfast: Blackstaff Press, 2017).

Brodie, B. *War and Politics* (London: Macmillan, 1973).

Brooks, R. 'Tying the Hands of Militants: Civilian Targeting and Societal Pressures in the Provisional IRA and Palestinian Hamas', *Journal of Global Security Studies*, 7/1 (2022).

Bruce, S. *The Edge of the Union: The Ulster Loyalist Political Vision* (Oxford: Oxford University Press, 1994).

Paisley: Religion and Politics in Northern Ireland (Oxford: Oxford University Press, 2007).

The Red Hand: Protestant Paramilitaries in Northern Ireland (Oxford: Oxford University Press, 1992).

'Victim Selection in Ethnic Conflict: Motives and Attitudes in Irish Republicanism', *Terrorism and Political Violence*, 9/1 (1997), 56–71.

Burke, E. *An Army of Tribes: British Army Cohesion, Deviancy and Murder in Northern Ireland* (Liverpool: Liverpool University Press, 2018).

'Counter-Insurgency against "Kith and Kin"? The British Army in Northern Ireland, 1970–76', *Journal of Imperial and Commonwealth History*, 43/4 (2015), 658–77.

'Loyalist Mobilization and Cross-Border Violence in Rural Ulster, 1972–1974', *Terrorism and Political Violence*, published online 14 April 2020: www.tandfonline.com/doi/abs/10.1080/09546553.2020.1745777

Burton, F. *The Politics of Legitimacy: Struggles in a Belfast Community* (London: Routledge, 1978).

Byman, D. 'Counterterrorism Strategies', in E. Chenoweth, R. English, A. Gofas and S. N. Kalyvas (eds.), *The Oxford Handbook of Terrorism* (Oxford: Oxford University Press, 2019), 623–39.

Cadwallader, A. *Lethal Allies: British Collusion in Ireland* (Cork: Mercier Press, 2013).

Cairncross, A. *The British Economy since 1945: Economic Policy and Performance* (Oxford: Blackwell, 1995).

Campbell, S. *Gerry Fitt and the SDLP: 'In a Minority of One'* (Manchester: Manchester University Press, 2015).

Carver, M. 'Morale in Battle – the Medical and the Military', *Journal of the Royal Army Medical Corps*, 139 (1989), 5–9.

Tightrope Walking: British Defence Policy since 1945 (London: Hutchinson, 1992).

Catignani, S. and V. Basham. 'The Gendered Politics of Researching Military Policy in the Age of the "Knowledge Economy"', *Review of International Studies*, 47/2 (2021), 211–30.

Caverley, J. D. 'The Myth of Military Myopia: Democracy, Small Wars, and Vietnam', *International Security*, 34/3 (2010), 119–57.

Charters, D. A. '"Have a Go": British Army/MI5 Agent-Running Operations in Northern Ireland, 1970–72', *Intelligence and National Security*, 28/2 (2013), 202–29.

'Professionalizing Clandestine Military Intelligence in Northern Ireland: Creating the Special Reconnaissance Unit', *Intelligence and National Security*, 33/1 (2018), 130–8.

Whose Mission, Whose Orders? British Civil–Military Command and Control in Northern Ireland, 1968–1974 (London: McGill-Queen's University Press, 2017).

von Clausewitz, C. *On War*. Trans. Michael Howard and Peter Paret (Princeton: Princeton University Press, 1976).

Coakley, J. and J. Todd. *Negotiating a Settlement in Northern Ireland, 1969–2019: From Sunningdale to St Andrews* (Oxford: Oxford University Press, 2020).

Conway, K. *Southside Provisional: From Freedom Fighter to the Four Courts* (Rathcoole: Orpen Press, 2014).

Conway, M. and R. Gerwarth. 'Europe's Age of Civil Wars? An Introduction', *Journal of Modern European History*, 20/4 (2022), 442–51.

Cormac, R. *Disrupt and Deny: Spies, Special Forces, and the Secret Pursuit of British Foreign Policy* (Oxford: Oxford University Press, 2018).

'The Information Research Department, Unattributable Propaganda, and Northern Ireland, 1971–1973: Promising Salvation but Ending in Failure?', *English Historical Review*, 131/552 (2016), 1074–104.

Cowper-Coles, F. '"Anxious for Peace": The Provisional IRA in Dialogue with the British Government, 1972–75', *Irish Studies Review*, 20/3 (2012), 223–42.

Cradden, T. 'Labour in Britain and the Northern Ireland Labour Party, 1900–70', in P. Catterall and S. McDougall (eds.), *The Northern Ireland Question in British Politics* (Basingstoke: Macmillan, 1996), 71–87.

Craig, A. *Crisis of Confidence: Anglo-Irish Relations in the Early Troubles* (Dublin: Irish Academic Press, 2010).

Craig, T. 'From Backdoors and Back Lanes to Backchannels: Reappraising British Talks with the Provisional IRA, 1970–1974', *Contemporary British History*, 26/1 (2012), 97–117.

'"You Will Be Responsible to the GOC": Stovepiping and the Problem of Divergent Intelligence-Gathering Networks in Northern Ireland, 1969–1975', *Intelligence and National Security*, 33/2 (2018), 211–26.

Craig, T. and M. McCleery, 'Political Bargaining Chips: Republican Internees in Northern Ireland 1972–1975', *Small Wars and Insurgencies*, 31/3 (2020), 639–60.

Crawford, C. *Inside the UDA: Volunteers and Violence* (London: Pluto Press, 2003).

Cunningham, M. J. *British Government Policy in Northern Ireland, 1969–89: Its Nature and Execution* (Manchester: Manchester University Press, 1991).

Daalder, I. H. *The Nature and Practice of Flexible Response: NATO Strategy and Theatre Nuclear Forces since 1967* (New York: Columbia University Press, 1991).

Daddis, G. A. *No Sure Victory: Measuring U.S. Army Effectiveness and Progress in the Vietnam War* (Oxford: Oxford University Press, 2011).

Darby, J. *Conflict in Northern Ireland: The Development of a Polarised Community* (Dublin: Gill and Macmillan, 1976).

Dawson, G. 'Trauma, Place and the Politics of Memory: Bloody Sunday, Derry, 1972–2004', *History Workshop Journal*, 59/1 (2005), 151–78.

De Fazio, G. 'Unpacking Violent Contention: The Troubles in Northern Ireland, 1968–1972', *Terrorism and Political Violence*, 32/8 (2018), 1691–711.

Dewar, M. *The British Army in Northern Ireland* (London: Guild, 1985).

Dickson, B. 'Counter-Insurgency and Human Rights in Northern Ireland', *Journal of Strategic Studies*, 32/3 (2009), 475–93.

Dixon, P. '"A House Divided Cannot Stand": Britain, Bipartisanship and Northern Ireland', *Contemporary Record*, 9/1 (1995), 147–87.

'Britain's "Vietnam Syndrome"? Public Opinion and British Military Intervention from Palestine to Yugoslavia', *Review of International Studies*, 26/1 (2000), 99–121.

'British Policy towards Northern Ireland 1969–2000: Continuity, Tactical Adjustment and Consistent "Inconsistencies"', *British Journal of Politics and International Relations*, 3/3 (2001), 340–68.

'"Hearts and Minds"? British Counter-Insurgency Strategy in Northern Ireland', *Journal of Strategic Studies*, 32/3 (2009), 445–74.

Dockrill, S. *Britain's Retreat from East of Suez: The Choice between Europe and the World?* (Basingstoke: Palgrave Macmillan, 2002).

Donohue, L. K. *The Cost of Counterterrorism: Power, Politics, and Liberty* (Cambridge: Cambridge University Press, 2008).

'Regulating Northern Ireland: The Special Powers Acts, 1922–1972', *The Historical Journal*, 41/4 (1998), 1089–120.

Dorey, P. 'From Indifference to Intervention: Labour and Northern Ireland', in P. Dorey (ed.), *The Labour Governments 1964–1970* (London: Routledge, 2006), 247–64.

Downes, A. *Targeting Civilians in War* (Ithaca: Cornell University Press, 2008).

Drayton, R. 'Masked Condominia: Pan-European Collaboration in the History of Imperialism, c. 1500 to the Present', *Global History Review*, 5 (2012), 308–31.

Drohan, B. *Brutality in an Age of Human Rights: Activism and Counterinsurgency at the End of the British Empire* (London: Cornell University Press, 2017).

Duffield, J. S. *Power Rules: The Evolution of NATO's Conventional Force Posture* (Stanford: Stanford University Press, 1995).

Echevarria, A. J. *Clausewitz and Contemporary War* (Oxford: Oxford University Press, 2007).

Edgerton, D. 'Liberal Militarism and the British State', *New Left Review*, 185/1 (1991), 138–69.

Warfare State: Britain, 1920–1970 (Cambridge: Cambridge University Press, 2005).

Edwards, A. 'Misapplying Lessons Learned? Analysing the Utility of British Counterinsurgency Strategy in Northern Ireland, 1971–76', *Small Wars and Insurgencies*, 21/2 (2010), 303–30.

'"A Whipping Boy If Ever There Was One"? The British Army and the Politics of Civil–Military Relations in Northern Ireland, 1969–79', *Contemporary British History*, 28/2 (2014), 166–89.

English, R. *Armed Struggle: The History of the IRA* (London: Pan, 2012).

Does Terrorism Work? (Oxford: Oxford University Press, 2016).

'The Interplay of Non-violent and Violent Action in Northern Ireland, 1967–72', in A. Roberts and T. Garton Ash (eds.), *Civil Resistance and Power Politics: The Experience of Non-violent Action from Gandhi to the Present* (Oxford: Oxford University Press, 2011), 75–90.

Farrell, M. *Northern Ireland: The Orange State* (London: Pluto Press, 1980).

Farrell, T. 'Improving in War: Military Adaptation and the British in Helmand Province, Afghanistan, 2006–2009', *Journal of Strategic Studies*, 33/4 (2010), 567–94.

'Military Adaptation and Organisational Convergence in War: Insurgents and International Forces in Afghanistan', *Journal of Strategic Studies*, 45/5 (2022), 718–42.

Fennell, J. *Combat and Morale in the North African Campaign: The Eighth Army and the Path to El Alamein* (Cambridge: Cambridge University Press, 2011).

Ferris, J. (ed.). *The British Army and Signals Intelligence during the First World War* (Stroud: Alan Sutton for the Army Records Society, 1992).

Finch, M. P. M. 'A Total War of the Mind: The French Theory of *la guerre révolutionnaire*, 1954–1958', *War in History*, 25/3 (2018), 410–34.

Finnegan, P. 'Professionalization of a Nonstate Actor: A Case Study of the Provisional IRA', *Armed Forces and Society*, 45/2 (2019), 349–67.

Fisk, R. *The Point of No Return: The Strike Which Broke the British in Ulster* (London: Times Books/André Deutsch, 1975).

Foley, F. *Countering Terrorism in Britain and France: Institutions, Norms and the Shadow of the Past* (Cambridge: Cambridge University Press, 2013).

Freedman, L. 'Academics and Policy-Making: Rules of Engagement', *Journal of Strategic Studies*, 40/1–2 (2017), 263–8.

The Future of War: A History (London: Allen Lane, 2017).

Strategy: A History (Oxford: Oxford University Press, 2013).

French, D. *Army, Empire and Cold War: The British Army and Military Policy, 1945–1971* (Oxford: Oxford University Press, 2012).

The British Way in Counter-Insurgency, 1945–1967 (Oxford: Oxford University Press, 2011).

Fighting EOKA: The British Counter-Insurgency Campaign on Cyprus, 1955–1959 (Oxford: Oxford University Press, 2015).

Military Identities: The Regimental System, the British Army, and the British People c. 1870–2000 (Oxford: Oxford University Press, 2005).

Gartner, S. S. *Strategic Assessment in War* (London: Yale University Press, 1997).

Gavin, F. J. 'The Myth of Flexible Response: United States Strategy in Europe during the 1960s', *The International History Review*, 23/4 (2001), 847–75.

Gill, P. 'Tactical Innovation and the Provisional Irish Republican Army', *Studies in Conflict and Terrorism*, 40/7 (2017), 573–85.

Gill, P. and J. Horgan. 'Who Were the Volunteers? The Shifting Sociological and Operational Profile of 1240 Provisional Irish Republican Army Members', *Terrorism and Political Violence*, 25/3 (2013), 435–56.

Gill, P., J. Horgan, S. T. Hunter and L. D. Cushenbery. 'Malevolent Creativity in Terrorist Organizations', *The Journal of Creative Behavior*, 47/2 (2013), 125–51.

Gillespie, G. 'The Ulster Workers' Council Strike: The Perfect Storm', in D. McCann and C. McGrattan (eds.), *Sunningdale, the Ulster Workers' Council Strike and the Struggle for Democracy in Northern Ireland* (Manchester: Manchester University Press, 2017), 22–37.

Goodman, J. R. '"In the Wider View": The Geostrategic Determinants of Counterinsurgency Strategy and Adaptation, Evidence from the Arab and Jewish Rebellions in the Palestine Mandate', *Security Studies*, 29/1 (2020), 162–98.

Grant, M. and B. Ziemann (eds.). *Understanding the Imaginary War: Culture, Thought and Nuclear Conflict, 1945–90* (Manchester: Manchester University Press, 2016).

Greenwood, D. 'The 1974 Defence Review in Perspective', *Survival*, 17/5 (1975), 223–9.

Grubb, A. E. 'Microlevel Dynamics of Violence: Explaining Variance in Violence amongst Rural Districts during Northern Ireland's Troubles', *Security Studies*, 25/3 (2016), 460–87.

Guelke, A. *Northern Ireland: The International Perspective* (Dublin: Gill and Macmillan, 1988).

Hamill, D. *Pig in the Middle: The Army in Northern Ireland 1969–1985* (London: Methuen, 1985).

Handel, M. 'Intelligence and Military Operations', in M. Handel (ed.), *Intelligence and Military Operations* (London: Routledge, 1990), 1–95.

Hanley, B. and S. Millar. *The Lost Revolution: The Story of the Official IRA and the Workers Party* (London: Penguin, 2009).

Harkness, K. A. and M. A. Hunzeker. 'Military Maladaptation: Counterinsurgency and the Politics of Failure', *Journal of Strategic Studies*, 38/6 (2015), 777–800.

Harris, L. 'Implications of a Strategic Analysis: The Operational Strategy of Loyalist Paramilitaries', *Behavioral Sciences of Terrorism and Political Aggression*, 4/1 (2012), 4–25.

Hearty, K. 'Misrecognising the Victim of State Violence: Denial, "Deep" Imperialism and Defending "Our Boys"', *Crime, Law and Social Change*, 73/2 (2020), 217–35.

Hennessey, T. *The Evolution of the Troubles 1970–72* (Dublin: Irish Academic Press, 2007).

The First Northern Ireland Peace Process: Power-Sharing, Sunningdale and the IRA Ceasefires, 1972–76 (Basingstoke: Palgrave Macmillan, 2015).

Northern Ireland: The Origins of the Troubles (Dublin: Gill and Macmillan, 2005).

Heuer, Jr., R. J. *Psychology of Intelligence Analysis* (Langley: Central Intelligence Agency, 1999).

Heuser, B. *NATO, Britain, France and the FRG: Nuclear Strategies and Forces for Europe, 1949–2000* (Basingstoke: Palgrave, 1997).

Hewitt, C. 'Catholic Grievances, Catholic Nationalism and Violence in Northern Ireland during the Civil Rights Period: A Reconsideration', *British Journal of Sociology*, 32/3 (1981), 362–80.

Hobkirk, M. 'Defence Organisation and Defence Policy Making in the UK and the USA', in L. Martin (ed.), *The Management of Defence* (London: Macmillan, 1976), 1–28.

Horgan, J. and M. Taylor. 'The Provisional Irish Republican Army: Command and Functional Structure', *Terrorism and Political Violence*, 9/3 (1997), 1–32.

Horowitz, M. C., E. Perkoski and P. B. K. Potter. 'Tactical Diversity in Militant Violence', *International Organization*, 72/1 (2018), 139–71.

Howe, S. *Ireland and Empire: Colonial Legacies in Irish History and Culture* (Oxford: Oxford University Press, 2002).

Hunzeker, M. A. and K. A. Harkness. 'Detecting the Need for Change: How the British Army Adapted to Warfare on the Western Front and in the Southern Cameroons', *European Journal of International Security*, 6/1 (2021), 66–85.

Hyslop, J. 'The Invention of the Concentration Camp: Cuba, Southern Africa and the Philippines, 1896–1907', *South African Historical Journal* 63/2 (2011), 251–76.

Jackson, A. 'Irish History in the Twentieth and Twenty-First Centuries', in A. Jackson (ed.), *The Oxford Handbook of Modern Irish History* (Oxford: Oxford University Press, 2014), 3–26.

Jackson, B. and D. Bramall. *The Chiefs: The Story of the United Kingdom Chiefs of Staff* (London: Brassey's, 1992).

Johnson, D. *Overconfidence and War: The Havoc and Glory of Positive Illusions* (London: Harvard University Press, 2004).

Jordan, J. 'Attacking the Leader, Missing the Mark: Why Terrorist Groups Survive Decapitation Strikes', *International Security*, 38/4 (2014), 7–38.

Kalyvas, S. N. *The Logic of Violence in Civil War* (Cambridge: Cambridge University Press, 2006).

Kavanagh, D. 'The Fatal Choice: The Calling of the February 1974 Election', in S. Ball and A. Seldon (eds.), *The Heath Government 1970–74: A Reappraisal* (London: Routledge, 1996), 351–70.

Kennedy-Pipe, C. *The Origins of the Present Troubles in Northern Ireland* (London: Longman, 1997).

Kenny, K. and N. Ó Dochartaigh. 'Power and Politics in Public Inquiries: Bloody Sunday 1972', *Journal of Political Power*, 14/3 (2021), 383–408.

Kerr, M. *The Destructors: The Story of Northern Ireland's Lost Peace Process* (Dublin: Irish Academic Press, 2011).

Killingray, D. 'Race and Rank in the British Army in the Twentieth Century', *Ethnic and Racial Studies*, 10/3 (1987), 276–90.

King, A. *The Combat Soldier: Infantry Tactics and Cohesion in the Twentieth and Twenty-First Centuries* (Oxford: Oxford University Press, 2013).

'Urban Insurgency in the Twenty-First Century: Smaller Militaries and Increased Conflict in Cities', *International Affairs*, 98/2 (2022), 609–29.

Urban Warfare in the Twenty-First Century (Cambridge: Polity Press, 2021).

Kirk-Smith, M. and J. Dingley. 'Countering Terrorism in Northern Ireland: The Role of Intelligence', *Small Wars and Insurgencies*, 20/3–4 (2009), 551–73.

Kiszely, J. P. 'The Relevance of History to the Military Profession: A British View', in W. Murray and R. H. Sinnreich (eds.), *The Past as Prologue: The Importance of History to the Military Profession* (Cambridge: Cambridge University Press, 2006), 23–33.

Klose, F. *Human Rights in the Shadow of Colonial Violence: The Wars of Independence in Kenya and Algeria* (Philadelphia: University of Pennsylvania Press, 2013).

Leahy, T. *The Intelligence War against the IRA* (Cambridge: Cambridge University Press, 2020).

Lee, C. *Carrington: An Honourable Man* (London: Viking, 2018).

Linn, B. M. *The Echo of Battle: The Army's Way of War* (London: Harvard University Press, 2007).

Mack, A. 'Why Big Nations Lose Small Wars: The Politics of Asymmetric Conflict', *World Politics*, 27/2 (1975), 175–200.

McBride, I. 'The Shadow of the Gunman: Irish Historians and the IRA', *Journal of Contemporary History*, 46/3 (2011), 686–710.

McCann, D. and C. McGrattan (eds.). *Sunningdale, the Ulster Workers' Council Strike and the Struggle for Democracy in Northern Ireland* (Manchester: Manchester University Press, 2017).

McCann, E. with M. Shiels and B. Hannigan. *Bloody Sunday in Derry: What Really Happened* (Dingle: Brandon, 1992).

McCleery, M. *Operation Demetrius and Its Aftermath: A New History of the Use of Internment without Trial in Northern Ireland, 1971–75* (Manchester: Manchester University Press, 2015).

'Sectarianism and the Provisional Irish Republican Army', *Small Wars and Insurgencies*, 32/4–5 (2021), 665–86.

McDaid, S. *Template for Peace: Northern Ireland 1972–75* (Manchester: Manchester University Press, 2013).

McDaid, S. and C. McGlynn. 'Northern Ireland', in A. S. Roe-Crines and T. Heppell (eds.), *Policies and Politics under Prime Minister Edward Heath* (Basingstoke: Palgrave Macmillan, 2021), 189–209.

McEvoy, K. 'What Did the Lawyers Do during the "War"? Neutrality, Conflict and the Culture of Quietism', *Modern Law Review*, 74/3 (2011), 350–84.

McGarry, J. and B. O'Leary. *The Northern Ireland Conflict: Consociational Engagements* (Oxford: Oxford University Press, 2004).

McGladdery, G. *The Provisional IRA in England: The Bombing Campaign, 1973–1997* (Dublin: Irish Academic Press, 2006).

McGlynn, C. and S. McDaid. 'Northern Ireland', in A. S. Crines and K. Hickson, *Harold Wilson: The Unprincipled Prime Minister? Reappraising Harold Wilson* (London: Biteback, 2016), 128–35.

McGovern, M. *Counterinsurgency and Collusion in Northern Ireland* (London: Pluto Press, 2019).

McKearney, T. *The Provisional IRA: From Insurrection to Parliament* (London: Pluto Press, 2011).

McKittrick, D., S. Kelters, B. Feeney, C. Thornton and D. McVea. *Lost Lives: The Stories of the Men, Women and Children Who Died as a Result of the Northern Ireland Troubles* (London: Mainstream, 2007).

McLaughlin, G. and S. Baker. '"Every Man an Emperor": The British Press, Bloody Sunday and the Image of the British Army', in G. Dawson, J. Dover and S. Hopkins (eds.), *The Northern Ireland Troubles in Britain: Impacts, Engagements, Legacies and Memories* (Manchester: Manchester University Press, 2017), 183–98.

McLoughlin, P. J. *John Hume and the Revision of Irish Nationalism* (Manchester: Manchester University Press, 2010).

Mead, R. *'Sam': Marshal of the Royal Air Force the Lord Elworthy* (Barnsley: Pen and Sword, 2018).

Merom, G. *How Democracies Lose Small Wars: State, Society, and the Failures of France in Algeria, Israel in Lebanon, and the United States in Vietnam* (Cambridge: Cambridge University Press, 2003).

Miller, D. *Don't Mention the War: Northern Ireland, Propaganda and the Media* (London: Pluto Press, 1994).

Mitchell, N. J. *Democracy's Blameless Leaders: From Dresden to Abu Ghraib, How Leaders Evade Accountability for Abuse, Atrocity, and Killing* (London: New York University Press, 2012).

Mockaitis, T. R. *British Counterinsurgency in the Post-Imperial Era* (Manchester: Manchester University Press, 1995).

Moloney, E. *A Secret History of the IRA* (London: Penguin, 2007).

Moody, S. *Imagining Nuclear War in the British Army, 1945–1989* (Oxford: Oxford University Press, 2020).

Moran, J. 'Evaluating Special Branch and the Use of Informant Intelligence in Northern Ireland', *Intelligence and National Security*, 25/1 (2010), 1–23.

Morgan, B. W. and M. L. R. Smith. 'Northern Ireland and Minimum Force: The Refutation of a Concept?', *Small Wars and Insurgencies*, 27/1 (2016), 81–105.

Morgan-Owen, D. 'History and the Perils of Grand Strategy', *Journal of Modern History*, 92 (2020), 351–85.

Moxon-Browne, E. 'The Water and the Fish: Public Opinion and the Provisional IRA in Northern Ireland', *Terrorism*, 5/1–2 (1981), 41–72.

Mulholland, M. 'Irish Republican Politics and Violence before the Peace Process, 1968–1994', *European Review of History*, 14/3 (2007), 397–421.

The Longest War: Northern Ireland's Troubled History (Oxford: Oxford University Press, 2002).

Northern Ireland at the Crossroads: Ulster Unionism in the O'Neill Years 1960–9 (Basingstoke: Macmillan, 2000).

'Political Violence', in R. Bourke and I. McBride (eds.), *The Princeton History of Modern Ireland* (Princeton: Princeton University Press, 2016), 382–402.

Mulligan, W. and B. Simms. 'Introduction', in W. Mulligan and B. Simms (eds.), *The Primacy of Foreign Policy in British History* (Basingstoke: Palgrave Macmillan, 2010), 1–14.

Mulroe, P. *Bombs, Bullets and the Border. Policing Ireland's Frontier: Irish Security Policy, 1969–1978* (Dublin: Irish Academic Press, 2017).

'"The Most Notorious Trouble Spot along the Entire Border": Exploring the Dynamics of Political Violence in an Irish Border Town, 1971–1974', *Irish Political Studies*, 35/4 (2020), 566–84.

Mulvenna, G. *Tartan Gangs and Paramilitaries: The Loyalist Backlash* (Liverpool: Liverpool University Press, 2016).

Mumford, A. *The Counter-Insurgency Myth: The British Experience of Irregular Warfare* (London: Routledge, 2012).

Murray, G. and J. Tonge. *Sinn Féin and the SDLP: From Alienation to Participation* (London: Hurst, 2005).

Nelson, S. *Ulster's Uncertain Defenders: Protestant Political, Paramilitary and Community Groups and the Northern Ireland Conflict* (Syracuse, NY: Syracuse University Press, 1984).

Neumann, P. *Britain's Long War: British Strategy in the Northern Ireland Conflict, 1969–98* (Basingstoke: Palgrave Macmillan, 2003).

'The Myth of Ulsterization in British Security Policy in Northern Ireland', *Studies in Conflict and Terrorism* 26/5 (2003), 365–77.

Newbery, S. *Interrogation, Intelligence and Security: Controversial British Techniques* (Manchester: Manchester University Press, 2015).

Newsinger, J. 'From Counter-Insurgency to Internal Security: Northern Ireland 1969–1992', *Small Wars and Insurgencies*, 6/1 (1995), 88–111.

Ní Aoláin, F. *The Politics of Force: Conflict Management and State Violence in Northern Ireland* (Belfast: The Blackstaff Press, 2000).

Norton, P. 'Divided Loyalties: The European Communities Act 1972', *Parliamentary History*, 30/1 (2011), 53–64.

Novosel, T. *Northern Ireland's Lost Opportunity: The Frustrated Promise of Political Loyalism* (London: Pluto Press, 2013).

O'Brien, C. C. *States of Ireland* (Frogmore: Granada, 1974).

O'Callaghan, M. and C. O'Donnell. 'The Northern Ireland Government, the "Paisleyite Movement" and Ulster Unionism in 1966', *Irish Political Studies*, 21/2 (2006), 203–22.

Ó Dochartaigh, N. 'Bloody Sunday: Error or Design?', *Contemporary British History*, 24/1 (2010), 89–108.

    Deniable Contact: Back-Channel Negotiation in Northern Ireland (Oxford: Oxford University Press, 2021).

    From Civil Rights to Armalites: Derry and the Birth of the Irish Troubles (Basingstoke: Palgrave Macmillan, 2005).

    'Northern Ireland since 1920', in Richard Bourke and Ian McBride (eds.), *The Princeton History of Modern Ireland* (Princeton: Princeton University Press, 2016), 141–67.

O'Duffy, B. 'The Price of Containment: Deaths and Debate on Northern Ireland in the House of Commons, 1968–94', in P. Catterall and S. McDougall (eds.), *The Northern Ireland Question in British Politics* (Basingstoke: Macmillan, 1996), 102–28.

Ó Faoleán, G. 'Ireland's Ho Chi Minh Trail? The Republic of Ireland's Role in the Provisional IRA's Bombing Campaign, 1970–1976', *Small Wars and Insurgencies*, 25/5–6 (2014), 976–91.

    'The Ulster Defence Regiment and the Question of Catholic Recruitment, 1970–1972', *Terrorism and Political Violence*, 27/5 (2015), 838–56.

Ó Fearghail, S. *Law (?) and Orders: The Belfast 'Curfew' of 3–5 July, 1970* (Dundalk: Central Citizens' Defence Committee, 1970).

O'Halpin, E. 'British Intelligence, PIRA, and the Early Years of the Northern Ireland Crisis: Remembering, Forgetting, and Mythologizing', in P. Maddrell (ed.), *The Image of the Enemy: Intelligence Analysis of Adversaries since 1945* (Washington, DC: Georgetown University Press, 2015), 162–91.

    '"A Poor Thing but Our Own": The Joint Intelligence Committee and Ireland, 1965–72', *Intelligence and National Security*, 23/5 (2008), 658–80.

O'Hearn, D. 'Catholic Grievances, Catholic Nationalism: A Comment', *British Journal of Sociology*, 34/3 (1983), 438–45.

O'Leary, B. 'Northern Ireland', in K. Hickson and A. Seldon (eds.), *New Labour, Old Labour: The Wilson and Callaghan Governments 1974–1979* (London: Routledge, 2004), 240–59.

    A Treatise on Northern Ireland, Volume I: Colonialism (Oxford: Oxford University Press, 2019).

    A Treatise on Northern Ireland, Volume II: Control (Oxford: Oxford University Press, 2019).

A Treatise on Northern Ireland, Volume III: Consociation and Confederation (Oxford: Oxford University Press, 2019).

Paret, P. *French Revolutionary Warfare from Indochina to Algeria: The Analysis of a Political and Military Doctrine* (London: Pall Mall Press, 1964).

The Politics of Illusion: A Political History of the IRA (London: Serif, 1997).

Patterson, H. 'The British State and the Rise of the IRA, 1969–71: The View from the Conway Hotel', *Irish Political Studies*, 23/4 (2008), 491–511.

Ireland's Violent Frontier: The Border and Anglo-Irish Relations during the Troubles (Basingstoke: Palgrave Macmillan, 2013).

'Sectarianism Revisited: The Provisional IRA Campaign in a Border Region of Northern Ireland', *Terrorism and Political Violence*, 22/3 (2010), 337–56.

'Unionism, 1921–72', in A. Jackson (ed.), *The Oxford Handbook of Modern Irish History* (Oxford: Oxford University Press, 2014), 692–710.

Porch, D. *Counterinsurgency: Exposing the Myths of the New Way of War* (Cambridge: Cambridge University Press, 2013).

Porter, P. 'Last Charge of the Knights? Iraq, Afghanistan and the Special Relationship', *International Affairs*, 86/2 (2010), 355–75.

Potter, J. *A Testimony to Courage: The Regimental History of the Ulster Defence Regiment* (Barnsley: Leo Cooper, 2001).

Prince, S. '"Do What the Afro-Americans Are Doing": Black Power and the Start of the Northern Ireland Troubles', *Journal of Contemporary History*, 50/3 (2015), 516–35.

'5 October 1968 and the Beginning of the Troubles: Flashpoints, Riots and Memory', *Irish Political Studies*, 27/3 (2012), 394–410.

Prince, S. and G. Warner, *Belfast and Derry in Revolt: A New History of the Start of the Troubles* (Dublin: Irish Academic Press, 2012).

'The IRA and Its Rivals: Political Competition and the Turn to Violence in the Early Troubles', *Contemporary British History* 27/3 (2013), 271–96.

Purdie, B. *Politics in the Streets: The Origins of the Civil Rights Movement in Northern Ireland* (Belfast: The Blackstaff Press, 1990).

Reed, R. J. 'Blood, Thunder and Rosettes: The Multiple Personalities of Paramilitary Loyalism between 1971 and 1988', *Irish Political Studies*, 26/1 (2011), 45–71.

Rekawek, K. '"The Last of the Mohicans?" The IRA's "Operation Harvest" in an International Context', *Terrorism and Political Violence*, 28/3 (2016), 435–51.

Rid, T. 'The Nineteenth-Century Origins of Counterinsurgency Doctrine', *Journal of Strategic Studies*, 33/5 (2010), 727–58.

Riley, J. *Oft in Danger: The Life and Campaigns of General Sir Anthony Farrar-Hockley* (Solihull: Helion, 2015).

Rose, P. *How the Troubles Came to Northern Ireland* (Basingstoke: Macmillan, 2000).

Rose, R. *Governing without Consensus: An Irish Perspective* (London: Faber and Faber, 1971).

Ruane, J. and J. Todd. *The Dynamics of Conflict in Northern Ireland: Power, Conflict and Emancipation* (Cambridge: Cambridge University Press, 1996).

Ryder, C. *The Ulster Defence Regiment: An Instrument of Peace?* (London: Methuen, 1991).

The RUC: A Force under Fire (London: Methuen, 1989).

Sageman, M. 'The Stagnation in Terrorism Research', *Terrorism and Political Violence*, 26/4 (2014), 565–80.

Sambanis, N. 'What Is Civil War? Conceptual and Empirical Complexities of an Operational Definition', *Journal of Conflict Resolution*, 48/6 (2004), 814–58.

Sanders, A. '"Attempting to Deal with the Past": Historical Inquiries, Legacy Prosecutions, and Operation Banner', *Small Wars and Insurgencies*, 32/4–5 (2021), 789–811.

'Northern Ireland: The Intelligence War 1969–75', *British Journal of Politics and International Relations*, 13/2 (2010), 230–48.

'Principles of Minimum Force and the Parachute Regiment in Northern Ireland, 1969–1972', *Journal of Strategic Studies*, 41/5 (2018), 659–83.

Sanders, A. and I. S. Wood. *Times of Troubles: Britain's War in Northern Ireland* (Edinburgh: Edinburgh University Press, 2012).

Schelling, T. C. 'Bargaining, Communication, and Limited War', *Journal of Conflict Resolution*, 1/1 (1957), 19–36.

The Strategy of Conflict (London: Harvard University Press, 1960).

Shy, J. and T. W. Collier. 'Revolutionary War', in P. Paret (ed.), *Makers of Modern Strategy: From Machiavelli to the Nuclear Age* (Oxford: Clarendon Press, 1986), 815–62.

Silove, N. 'Beyond the Buzzword: The Three Meanings of "Grand Strategy"', *Security Studies*, 27/1 (2018), 27–57.

Smith, J. '"Walking a Real Tight-Rope of Difficulties": Sir Edward Heath and the Search for Stability in Northern Ireland, June 1970–March 1971', *Twentieth Century British History*, 18/2 (2007), 219–53.

Smith, M. L. R. *Fighting for Ireland? The Military Strategy of the Irish Republican Movement* (London: Routledge, 1997).

Smith, M. L. R. and D. M. Jones. *The Political Impossibility of Modern Counterinsurgency: Strategic Problems, Puzzles, and Paradoxes* (New York: Columbia University Press, 2015).

Smith, M. L. R. and P. Neumann. 'Motorman's Long Journey: Changing the Strategic Setting in Northern Ireland', *Contemporary British History*, 19/4 (2005), 413–35.

Smith, S. *3–2–1 Bomb Gone: Fighting Terrorist Bombers in Northern Ireland* (Stroud: Sutton, 2006).

Smith, W. B. *The British State and the Northern Ireland Crisis, 1969–73: From Violence to Power Sharing* (Washington, DC: United States Institute of Peace Press, 2011).

Spjut, R. J. 'Internment and Detention without Trial in Northern Ireland 1971–1975: Ministerial Policy and Practice', *The Modern Law Review*, 49/6 (1986), 712–39.

Stockwell, S. 'Britain and Decolonization in an Era of Global Change', in M. Thomas and A. Thompson (eds.), *The Oxford Handbook of the Ends of Empire* (Oxford: Oxford University Press, 2017), 65–84.

Stone, J. *Military Strategy: The Politics and Technique of War* (London: Continuum, 2011).

Strachan, H. 'The Lost Meaning of Strategy', *Survival*, 47/3 (2005), 33–54.

'Operational Art and Britain, 1909–2009', in J. A. Olsen and M. van Creveld (eds.), *The Evolution of Operational Art: From Napoleon to the Present* (Oxford: Oxford University Press, 2010), 96–136.

The Politics of the British Army (Oxford: Oxford University Press, 1997).

'Strategy in Theory; Strategy in Practice', *Journal of Strategic Studies*, 42/2 (2019), 171–90.

Taylor, P. *Brits: The War against the IRA* (London: Bloomsbury, 2001).

Loyalists (London: Bloomsbury, 1999).

Provos: The IRA and Sinn Fein (London: Bloomsbury, 1997).

Tenenbaum, É. 'Beyond National Styles: Towards a Connected History of Cold War Counterinsurgency', in B. Heuser and E. Shamir (eds.), *Insurgencies and Counterinsurgencies: National Styles and Strategic Cultures* (Cambridge: Cambridge University Press, 2016), 313–31.

Thane, P. *Divided Kingdom: A History of Britain, 1900 to the Present* (Cambridge: Cambridge University Press, 2018).

Thomas, M. and A. Thompson. 'Empire and Globalisation: From "High Imperialism" to Decolonisation', *The International History Review*, 36/1 (2014), 142–70.

Thomas, O. 'Paradoxical Secrecy in British Freedom of Information Law', in D. Mokrosinska (ed.), *Transparency and Secrecy in European Democracies: Contested Trade-Offs* (London: Routledge, 2020), 135–56.

Thompson, A. 'Humanitarian Principles Put to the Test: Challenges to Humanitarian Action during Decolonization', *International Review of the Red Cross*, 97 (2015), 45–76.

Thornton, R. 'Getting It Wrong: The Crucial Mistakes Made in the Early Stages of the British Army's Deployment to Northern Ireland (August 1969 to March 1972)', *Journal of Strategic Studies*, 30/1 (2007), 73–107.

Todd, J. 'Two Traditions in Unionist Political Culture', *Irish Political Studies*, 2/1 (1987), 1–26.

Townshend, C. *Political Violence in Ireland: Government and Resistance since 1848* (Oxford: Clarendon Press, 1983).

Tuck, C. 'Northern Ireland and the British Approach to Counter-Insurgency', *Defense and Security Analysis*, 23/2 (2007), 165–83.

Ucko, D. H. and R. Egnell. *Counterinsurgency in Crisis: Britain and the Challenges of Modern Warfare* (New York: Columbia University Press, 2013).

Urwin, M. *A State in Denial: British Collaboration with Loyalist Paramilitaries* (Cork: Mercier Press, 2016).

van der Bijl, N. *Operation Banner: The British Army in Northern Ireland 1969–2007* (Barnsley: Pen and Sword, 2009).

Van Voris, W. H. *Violence in Ulster: An Oral Documentary* (Amherst: University of Massachussetts Press, 1975).

Walker, G. *A History of the Ulster Unionist Party* (Manchester: Manchester University Press, 2004).

Wall, S. *The Official History of Britain and the European Community: Volume II, From Rejection to Referendum, 1963–1975* (Abingdon: Routledge, 2013).

Walsh, A. *From Hope to Hatred: Voices of the Falls Curfew* (Stroud: The History Press, 2013).

Walsh, D. *Bloody Sunday and the Rule of Law in Northern Ireland* (Basingstoke: Macmillan, 2000).

Warner, G. 'The Falls Road Curfew Revisited', *Irish Studies Review*, 14/3 (2006), 325–42.

Watson, A. *Enduring the Great War: Combat, Morale and Collapse in the German and British Armies, 1914–1918* (Cambridge: Cambridge University Press, 2008).

White, R. 'The Irish Republican Army: An Assessment of Sectarianisms', *Terrorism and Political Violence*, 9/1 (1997), 20–55.

   'The Irish Republican Army and Sectarianism: Moving beyond the Anecdote', *Terrorism and Political Violence*, 9/2 (1997), 120–31.

   Ruairí Ó Brádaigh: The Life and Politics of an Irish Revolutionary (Bloomington: Indiana University Press, 2006).

Whyte, J. *Interpreting Northern Ireland* (Oxford: Clarendon Press, 1990).

Wilkinson, P. *Terrorism versus Democracy: The Liberal State Response* (Abingdon: Routledge, 2011).

Young, J. W. 'The Heath Government and British Entry into the European Community', in S. Ball and A. Seldon (eds.), *The Heath Government 1970–74: A Reappraisal* (London: Routledge, 1996), 259–84.

Ziegler, P. *Edward Heath: The Authorised Biography* (London: HarperPress, 2010).

Zubok, V. M. *A Failed Empire: The Soviet Union in the Cold War from Stalin to Gorbachev* (London: University of North Carolina Press, 2007).

THESES

Alderson, A. *The Validity of British Army Counterinsurgency Doctrine after the War in Iraq 2003–2009* (PhD thesis, Cranfield University, 2009).

Beresford, P. C. F. M. *The Official IRA and Republican Clubs in Northern Ireland 1968–1974, and Their Relations with Other Political and Paramilitary Groups* (PhD thesis, University of Exeter, 1979).

Cochrane, B. *The Development of the British Approach to Improvised Explosive Device Disposal in Northern Ireland* (MPhil thesis, Cranfield University 2012).

Dixon, P. *The British Labour Party and Northern Ireland 1959–74* (PhD thesis, University of Bradford, 1993).

Goodman, J. R. *Negotiating Counterinsurgency: The Politics of Strategic Adaptation* (PhD thesis, Yale University, 2018).

MacLeod, A. *The United Kingdom, Republic of Ireland, United States and the Conflict in Northern Ireland, August 1971–September 1974* (PhD thesis, University of Glasgow, 2011).

Morgan, J. T. *Counter-Terror Ideology: The Community Relations Commission and the Provisional Irish Republican Army, 1969–1979* (PhD thesis, Carnegie Mellon University, 2011).

Index